THE PAPERS OF
Andrew Johnson

Sponsored by
The University of Tennessee
The National Historical Publications and Records Commission
The National Endowment for the Humanities
The Tennessee Historical Commission

President Andrew Johnson, 1865
By Mathew B. Brady
Courtesy National Archives

THE PAPERS OF
Andrew Johnson

Volume 9, September 1865-January 1866

PAUL H. BERGERON
EDITOR

PATRICIA J. ANTHONY

LeROY P. GRAF

RICHARD B. McCASLIN

R. B. ROSENBURG

MARION O. SMITH

THE EDITING STAFF

1991
THE UNIVERSITY OF TENNESSEE PRESS
KNOXVILLE

Library of Congress Cataloging in Publication Data
(Revised for vol. 9)

Johnson, Andrew, 1808–1875.
   The papers of Andrew Johnson.

   Vol. 8–9 edited by Paul H. Bergeron.
   Includes bibliographical references and indexes.
   Contents: v. 1. 1822–1851—[etc.]—v. 8. May–
August 1865—v. 9. September 1865–January 1866.
   1. United States—Politics and government, 1849–
1877—Sources. 2. Johnson, Andrew, 1808–1875—
Manuscripts. 3. Presidents—United States—Manuscripts.
I. Graf, LeRoy P., ed.   II. Haskins, Ralph W., ed.
III. Bergeron, Paul H., 1938–   IV. Title.

E415.6.J65   1967   973.8′1′0924 [B]

                                      67-25733

ISBN 0-87049-098-2 (v. 2)
[ISBN 0-87049-689-1 (v. 9)]

TO
LeRoy P. Graf
Patriarch of the Johnson Project for more
than three decades. His past and present
editing labors, devotion, and good cheer
have been, and remain, indispensable.

Contents

Illustrations

Introduction

By December 1865 the proverbial clock had begun ticking away its last moments of Andrew Johnson's "finest hour"; the day of reckoning had at last arrived. The members of Congress who streamed into Washington presented a new and significant challenge to Johnson, who in his brief presidency had not yet had to deal with the legislative branch. This is not to suggest, however, that the Johnson administration was doomed once Congress convened, for indeed there is ample evidence that the President remained in control of circumstances for several more weeks. But one senses in the documentary record that the period of "executive hegemony" was fading or receding and that legislative parity, if not hegemony, was on the immediate horizon.[1]

Johnson had had seven-and-a-half months of presidential experience by the time of the convening of Congress. During that apprenticeship period great strides toward the "restoration" of the Union had been taken. In the late spring and the summer months, for example, Johnson had appointed provisional governors in seven of the former Confederate states, had accepted the governments in the other four (Virginia, Tennessee, Arkansas, and Louisiana), had dealt with the Lincoln assassins, had provided procedures for presidential pardon of ex-Rebels, and had formulated, however imprecisely, his notions about the relationship between the triumphant North and the defeated South.

Foremost on Johnson's agenda in the fall months of 1865 was the satisfactory movement of his seven provisional states toward the establishment of their own governments. By the beginning of September, only one of them, Mississippi, had already held a convention; but in the next three months the remaining states, with the exception of Texas which delayed until early 1866, met in convention and afterwards proceeded to the election of governors and legislators. As presidential policy evolved, Johnson stipulated three requirements of the conventions: they must nullify the secession ordinances, abolish slavery, and repudiate all Confederate debts. Unfortunately and somewhat typically, Johnson did not lay down these demands clearly and consistently enough. Had he done so, the assumption is, he might have had less

---

1. My essay is based upon documents published in this volume and also upon several secondary works: Hans L. Trefousse, *Andrew Johnson: A Biography* (New York, 1989); LaWanda Cox and John H. Cox, *Politics, Principle, and Prejudice, 1865–1866* (New York, 1963); Dan T. Carter, *When the War Was Over: The Failure of Self-Reconstruction in the South, 1865–1867* (Baton Rouge, 1985); Eric L. McKitrick, *Andrew Johnson and Reconstruction* (Chicago, 1960); James E. Sefton, *Andrew Johnson and the Uses of Constitutional Power* (Boston, 1980); and Albert Castel, *The Presidency of Andrew Johnson* (Lawrence, Kan., 1979).

difficulties with the southern conventions than he did. Eventually, but
not without a somewhat defiant attitude on the part of the conventions,
most of them endorsed Johnson's requirements. Nevertheless, it should
be noted that, as indicative of the sometimes strained relations between
the President and the southern political leaders, neither Mississippi nor
South Carolina repudiated its debt; and North Carolina did so only
after direct intervention (in the form of a telegram) by Johnson.[2]

Progress was evident, yet so were problems. In October and November, for instance, gubernatorial and legislative elections were held in all
of the seven provisional states, except Texas which waited until the
summer of 1866. While this was certainly what Johnson desired, he
was not prepared for the widespread election of ex-Rebels, including
unpardoned ones, to the legislatures and also to the governor's chair.
Admittedly there was a shortage of bona fide unionists in the southern
states, but there was something of a taunting attitude apparent in the
actions of the voters. Mississippi's election of former Confederate general Benjamin G. Humphreys as governor, for example, was irritating
and troubling to Johnson, as were the elections of many other officials
throughout all of the South. Nevertheless, the President did not attempt to block these persons from assuming office, although in some
instances he did delay their formal elevation to power. Generally he
busied himself with extending the necessary presidential pardons in a
rather shameless caving in to southern demands. While there was cause
for worry on the part of the President over the state elections, there was
even more so with regard to the Congressional elections.[3] Voters in the
southern states decided to send to Washington a formidable collection
of former Confederate leaders—including generals and other high-
ranking officers, as well as Vice President Alexander H. Stephens—to
take seats in the U.S. Congress. No one outside of the South, not even
Johnson, believed that the Congressional leaders would welcome such
men into the halls of national power.

Meanwhile the legislative bodies in the South had given Johnson
additional reason to fret over the "restoration" process. The President
was not without blame, if one believes that his lack of forthright dealings with the states caused or enabled them to plot their own course.

2. See, for example, Johnson to William W. Holden, Oct. 18, 1865; Holden to Johnson, Oct. 17, 20, Nov. 4, 1865. For South Carolina and repudiation, see James B. Campbell to Johnson, Dec. 31, 1865. Mississippi's convention met in August, prior to debt
repudiation becoming a requirement; subsequently, in the fall months its legislature
simply ignored the issue.
3. The following documents are representative of the ones that deal with elections in
the South: Benjamin F. Perry to Johnson, Oct. 5, 27, Nov. 27, 29, 1865; Johnson to
Perry, Nov. 27, 1865; Benjamin G. Humphreys to Johnson, Oct. 26, Nov. 1, 1865;
William W. Holden to Johnson, Nov. 2, 4, 27, Dec. 1, 6, 1865; Johnson to Holden, Nov.
5, 1865; Joseph S. Cannon to Johnson, Nov. 13, 1865; Joseph C. Bradley to Johnson,
Nov. 15, 27, 1865; Joshua Hill to Johnson, Nov. 23, 1865; Alexander N. Wilson to
Johnson, Nov. 25, 1865; Johnson to James Johnson, Nov. 26, Dec. 11, 1865; Johnson
to James B. Steedman, Nov. 26, 1865; Robert Powell to Johnson, Dec. 2, 1865.

Johnson's desire that the states ratify the Thirteenth Amendment met some resistance throughout the South (much as had the requirement that the conventions abolish slavery) but eventually Mississippi was the only one to reject the amendment.[4] A second persistent issue, though not much evident in the fall months, was the matter of black suffrage. Johnson had moved in that direction in mid-August when he suggested to Governor William L. Sharkey of Mississippi that the convention, then in session, should consider a limited suffrage for blacks. That was the only overt or direct action taken by the President, although he indicated elsewhere his inclination toward black suffrage. There was some sentiment scattered through the southern states that endorsed a qualified suffrage, but it soon evaporated under the pressure of the prevailing views in the region and in the absence of presidential leadership on the issue.[5] Not surprisingly, black suffrage became a paramount concern in Congress, certainly among the Radicals.

A third disturbing matter for Johnson and eventually the Congress was the enactment of Black Codes by southern legislatures in the fall months. That these laws had some worthy goals—to afford certain protections to newly-freed blacks—should not obscure the reality that they were "unequivocally discriminatory and designed to keep blacks in a subordinate economic and social relationship to whites." They were in essence "a melange of paternalism and repression, a fitful attempt to accommodate the wishes of northerners and the prejudices and fears of southern whites."[6] Whatever else one might say about the Black Codes, it is obvious that their passage, prior to the convening of Congress, presented political complications for Johnson.[7] The fact that Freedmen's Bureau commissioners disavowed parts or all of some of the Codes and that Johnson did not contravene his commissioners did little to lessen the bitterness and anger felt by many northerners.[8]

4. Among the documents that deal with ratification of the Thirteenth Amendment are: Johnson to William L. Sharkey, Nov. 1, 17, 1865; Johnson to William Marvin, Nov. 20, 1865; Marvin to Johnson, Dec. 29, 1865; Lewis E. Parsons to Johnson, Dec. 2, 1865; Johnson to James Johnson, Dec. 8, 1865.

5. The President and various southerners discussed the black suffrage issue in the following sample documents: Christopher G. Memminger to Johnson, Sept. 14, 1865; Sterling R. Cockrill to Johnson, Sept. 18, 1865; Joseph C. Bradley to Johnson, Nov. 15, 1865; Jesse J. Finley to Johnson, Nov. 18, 1865; Aaron A. Bradley to Johnson, Dec. 7, 1865; Interview with George L. Stearns, Oct. 3, 1865.

6. Carter, *The War Was Over*, 217, 218.

7. The following are some of the documents which discuss the Black Codes: Lewis Parsons to Johnson, Sept. 13, 28, Oct. 2, Dec. 2, 1865; Benjamin F. Perry to Johnson, Sept. 23, Oct. 27, Nov. 1, Dec. 9, 1865; Johnson to Perry, Nov. 27, 1865; Joseph C. Bradley to Johnson, Sept. 28, 1865; James L. Orr to Johnson, Oct. 2, Dec. 23, 1865; Benjamin H. Hill to Johnson, Nov. 1, 1865; Andrew J. Hamilton to Johnson, Nov. 27, 1865; Taliaferro P. Shaffner to Johnson, Jan. 2, 1866.

8. The matter of permitting blacks to testify in the courts of the South was also a controversial topic throughout the fall months. Some of the documents which treat this are: Lewis E. Parsons to Johnson, Oct. 2, 1865; John P. Pryor to Johnson, Oct. 10, 1865; Henderson Crawford to Johnson, Nov. 5, 1865; Alvan C. Gillem to Johnson, Nov. 11, 1865; Joseph C. Bradley to Johnson, Nov. 15, 1865; Benjamin G. Humphreys

Although Johnson did not visit the defeated Confederacy during the period under review, he did not lack information about the attitudes and actions of southerners. Salmon P. Chase and Harvey M. Watterson, for instance, had already sent letters and reports in the late spring and early summer. Carl Schurz left in late summer for his grand tour of the South and continued sending reports through the month of September. In addition, Watterson made a second tour, beginning in late September and lasting through October. Concurrently, Benjamin C. Truman commenced his visit in October but did not conclude until the early months of 1866. And finally none other than Ulysses S. Grant made a limited tour of the South and issued his much anticipated report in mid-December 1865.[9] These five men were not, of course, the only prominent individuals who toured the Confederacy in 1865, for one should note that Generals George G. Meade, O. O. Howard, and George H. Thomas made similar trips and sent back reports to Washington. Indeed one might claim that in the summer and fall months southern tours became something of a growth industry. Just as there was a notable mixture of motives that actuated the visitors, so there was a variety of information and interpretation that they relayed to the nation's capital. The President was, so it appears, free to choose whatever fitted his beliefs; likewise were the persons who favored a harsher policy toward the South.

Shrewdly anticipating the critical importance of his first Annual Message to Congress, Johnson in late October began recruiting George Bancroft to lend his literary skills and historical knowledge. Bancroft readily agreed to assist the President and with subsequent personal visitations to the White House and exchange of communications, he devoted himself to the task.[10] Submitted to Congress on December 4, the Message stated Johnson's position with felicitous phrasing, if not with complete accuracy. Later critics and historians have not viewed the Message in a very favorable light, but that should not diminish the reality that upon its publication and receipt it was highly acclaimed in most circles. Indeed Johnson's office was flooded by letters and well-wishers praising the document.[11] Its vagueness or

to Johnson, Nov. 16, 1865; Jesse J. Finley to Johnson, Nov. 18, 1865; William Marvin to Johnson, Nov. 18, 1865; Andrew J. Fletcher to Johnson, Nov. 20, 1865; John M. Lea to Johnson, Dec. 8, 1865; James L. Orr to Johnson, Dec. 23, 1865.

9. A convenient source for the letters and reports of the five men who visited the South is: Brooks D. Simpson, LeRoy P. Graf, and John Muldowny, eds., *Advice After Appomattox: Letters to Andrew Johnson, 1865–1866* (Knoxville, 1987).

10. See, for example, Johnson to George Bancroft, Oct. 24, 29, 1865; Bancroft to Johnson, Nov. 9, Dec. 6, 1865.

11. Among the early letters praising the Annual Message are the following: Bancroft to Johnson, Dec. 6, 1865; William W. Holden to Johnson, Dec. 6, 1865; Oliver P. Morton to Johnson, Dec. 7, 1865; Henry Watterson to Johnson, Dec. 7, 1865; John M. Lea to Johnson, Dec. 8, 1865; James Thompson to Johnson, Dec. 8, 1865; Benjamin F. Perry to Johnson, Dec. 9, 1865.

ambiguity at key points did nothing to erase lingering suspicions on the part of some, to be sure; but generally Johnson's Annual Message seemed to augur well for good relations between the two branches of the national government.

Yet within a few weeks troubles began to swirl around the presidency. On the very day that Johnson sent over his Message, two things happened to cloud the President's optimism. It probably surprised no one in Washington that the clerk of the House, Edward McPherson, refused to read the names of the newly-elected Representatives from the former Confederacy and thereby denied them seats in that chamber. Although the strategy had been planned long in advance, it was nonetheless galling to Johnson, particularly the refusal to permit Horace Maynard of Tennessee a place in the House. Second, at the urging of Thaddeus Stevens, the House passed a resolution setting up a Joint Committee on Reconstruction. Viewed subsequently in some quarters, especially the White House, as an anti-Johnson measure, the establishment of the committee was actually treated as a routine matter at the time, so much so that it stimulated virtually no discussion or opposition. In any event, Congress flashed signals to the President that it intended to have a voice in the reconstruction process.

A recess for the holidays gave everyone some breathing room; but when Congress reconvened in early January, it was ready to assert its role. Senator Lyman Trumbull introduced two bills: one would extend and expand the original Freedmen's Bureau bill; and the other, in response to the Black Codes of the South, would protect all persons in their civil rights. The Senator had no deliberate intention of challenging Johnson's leadership of reconstruction; in fact he had conferred with the President prior to submitting the two proposals. Similarly, leaders of the Joint Committee also attempted to effect some sort of accommodation with Johnson. But as the days slipped by, the likelihood of executive-legislative compromise seemed to fade. Near the end of the month, the Senate passed the Freedmen's Bureau bill and the House approved a proposal that would permit black suffrage in the District of Columbia.[12] By then the President and certain Congressional leaders realized that conflict between them was inevitable and the events of February would confirm their apprehensions.

In the meantime, Johnson could look back over the past several

12. At the end of December, voters in the District of Columbia had defeated black suffrage by astronomical numbers: 7369 against and 36 for. Castel, *The Presidency*, 63. Foner's report of the vote evidently does not take into account the Georgetown vote. Eric Foner, *Reconstruction: America's Unfinished Revolution, 1863–1877* (New York, 1988), 240. The District vote and the suffrage bill are discussed in several documents; for example: Henry Addison to Johnson, Jan. 12, 1866; Lewis D. Campbell to Johnson, Jan. 19, 1866; Benjamin Rush to Johnson, Jan. 20, 1866; John Cochrane to Johnson, Jan. 23, 1866; Miami Valley Citizens to Johnson, Jan. 23, 1866; William Patton to Johnson, Jan. 30, 1866.

months and derive general satisfaction from progress on restoration. To be sure, he had been plagued by the continuing dilemma of presidential pardon. Thousands more applied for and received individual pardons during the fall months.

The President also dealt with perennial concerns over patronage. He had gratified himself and some Republicans with the appointment of his friend, Preston King, as collector of the port of New York. But King's suicide in November compounded Johnson's frustrations and difficulties with the dispersal of the presidential loaves and fishes.[13] Seldom was he without advice or special pleadings from members of Congress, other political leaders, and plain folk as well concerning government jobs.

While Johnson derived solace and pleasure from having his family with him at the White House, there were complications, not the least of which was Eliza's apparently incapacitating illness. Fortunately, his two daughters ably handled the social and ceremonial functions at the White House. The President's son, Robert, however, continued to be more of an embarrassment, thanks to his drinking and carousing habits, than an aide to Johnson. In October out in Texas the President's brother William, holder of a minor federal appointment, died as a result of a somewhat bizarre hunting accident. Johnson dutifully notified his nephews in Tennessee and enabled one of them to travel to Texas. Several months later he provided for the family by giving a Galveston appointment to one of his brother's sons.[14]

So there was more to being president than the monumental matters of restoring the Union. But it was this latter challenge that consumed Johnson's energy and effort throughout the months of September 1865-January 1866. And these concerns gradually took their toll upon his leadership capabilities and found him wanting. By the end of January, his "finest hour" was over, although he was not without resources and determination.

ACKNOWLEDGMENTS

Once again it is my pleasure to recognize those individuals and institutions that have been directly and significantly helpful to the Johnson Project and to the publication of this volume.

At the seat of the federal government are two agencies that have been and continue to be indispensable to the life and progress of our work.

13. See Moses F. Odell to Johnson, Nov. 14, 1865; John A. Dix to Johnson, Nov. 15, 1865; Thomas J. Sizer to Johnson, Dec. 18, 1865.
14. John Adriance to Johnson, Oct. 26, 1865; Harris T. Garnett to Johnson, Oct. 31, 1865; Johnson to James Johnson, Nov. 17, 1865; Andrew Johnson, Jr., to Johnson, Dec. 23, 1865; James Johnson to Johnson, Jan. 10, 1866.

I am referring naturally to the National Historical Publications and Records Commission and to the National Endowment for the Humanities. Both have provided vital financial support and other forms of assistance. Agency personnel who have been most directly involved with us on a regular basis include: Mary Giunta and Sara Dunlap Jackson of the NHPRC, and David Nichols and Gordon B. McKinney of the NEH.

The Tennessee Historical Commission, led by Executive Director Herbert L. Harper, continues to make annual financial contributions to the Johnson Project, for which we are grateful.

The University of Tennessee has made it possible in a variety of ways for our work to go forward. First, we have enjoyed the constant support of Dean Lorman A. Ratner and Associate Dean Charles O. Jackson of the College of Liberal Arts. In addition, we have been quite dependent upon the assistance of the leaders and staffs of the John C. Hodges Library and of the Special Collections Department. Finally, the production and publication of this volume have been aided by the University's Development Office and by the University of Tennessee Press.

Needless to say, numerous libraries, archives, and historical societies have assisted us with copies of documents and with responses to our various research inquiries. We have placed ourselves in notable debt, for example, to the Library of Congress, the National Archives, and to the Lawson McGhee Library (Knox County Public Library). We certainly could not function without the help afforded us by these and many other repositories.

In addition to the above-named, there have been several other individuals and groups that have offered financial assistance to us. Our longtime benefactors and friends, Margaret Johnson Patterson Bartlett and Ralph M. Phinney, both of Greeneville, have continued their generosity. Moreover, we have reaped some direct monetary benefits from the Tennessee Presidents Trust, a new organization of Tennesseans committed to the support of the three presidential editing projects headquartered at the University of Tennessee.

I gratefully acknowledge my indebtedness to the staff here at the Johnson Project. I have depended heavily upon them throughout the preparation of this volume and they have not disappointed me. Their names appear on the title page as *partial* recognition of their invaluable and highly competent work (and also their ability to tolerate the demands and whims of the Editor). All of us have been aided by the tasks so ably performed by our volunteer staff person, Ruth P. Graf, whose commitment is now of many years' duration. Together we all have functioned as an efficient and effective team, for which I am profoundly appreciative.

Finally, I add a personal note. Whatever accomplishments I have enjoyed in my three years at the Johnson Project are traceable in large measure to the encouragement and affection I have received from my family: Mary Lee and our sons, Pierre, Andre, and Louis Paul. Words cannot adequately convey my deep gratitude to them.

Paul H. Bergeron

Knoxville, Tennessee
July 1990

Editorial Method

This volume, like Volume 8, deals exclusively with the time of the Johnson presidency. Not surprisingly therefore, the amount of available documents is almost overwhelming. As announced in the immediately preceding volume, we are following a selections policy that enables us to handle the challenge of choosing certain documents for inclusion while excluding hundreds more. In Volume 9 we have documents from more than fifty different public and private collections, the most numerous of which are from the various National Archives collections and the Johnson Papers at the Library of Congress. We refer the reader to the statements made in Volume 8 about the types of documents published, because those observations hold true for this new volume as well. We continue to adhere to the view that the main focus and function of the Johnson presidency was politics; the decision to include documents for publication has been governed by that belief.

Letters previously published in our special volume, *Advice After Appomattox: Letters to Andrew Johnson, 1865–1866*, which fall within the chronological confines of Volume 9 are not included but instead are listed in Appendix IV of this volume.

Compared with previous volumes, Volume 9 contains considerably fewer summarized documents. This situation reflects our deliberate attempt to reduce the overall percentage of documents rendered in such a manner. This has been done primarily for the purpose of providing more space for documents which are published in full.

Concerning the transcription and rendering of documents for publication, we remind the reader of guidelines stated in earlier volumes, particularly Volume 8. Our decision to omit inside addresses and complimentary closings from the documents published in Volume 9 is the only significant departure from previous practices. With regard to documents that incorporate the complimentary closing as a part of the concluding sentence, we have published most of the sentence but then have provided elipses to indicate the omission of the complimentary closing.

Once again we have striven diligently to identify all persons and to explain all references to specific events, developments, or circumstances in the various documents. Persons identified in earlier volumes (consult the Index) are provided with brief mention in Volume 9 or else are passed over silently. And from time to time we have had to admit, however reluctantly, that we have been unable to explain a reference or to identify a specific person.

Readers who compare this present volume with earlier ones will note the absence of a listing in the Table of Contents of all the documents published herein. This drastic curtailment has been done to conserve valuable space and to eliminate the duplication of information provided in the Index. That is to say, a reader may simply consult the Index to ascertain whether a particular individual sent or received a document.

In all our involvement with the nineteenth century Johnson documents we have attempted to render them in published form with as much faithfulness to the original as possible, recognizing the complexities and difficulties of moving from handwritten to published format.

SYMBOLS AND ABBREVIATIONS

REPOSITORY SYMBOLS

A-Ar   Alabama Department of Archives and History, Montgomery

DLC   Library of Congress, Washington, D.C.

DNA   National Archives, Washington, D.C.

RECORD GROUPS USED*

RG15   Records of the Veterans Administration

RG24   Records of the Bureau of Naval Personnel

RG45   Naval Records Collection of the Office of Naval Records and Library

RG48   Records of the Office of the Secretary of the Interior

RG56   General Records of the Department of the Treasury

RG58   Records of the Internal Revenue Service

RG59   General Records of the Department of State

RG60   General Records of the Department of Justice

RG75   Records of the Bureau of Indian Affairs

RG92   Records of the Office of the Quartermaster General

RG94   Records of the Adjutant General's Office, 1780s– 1917

RG105   Records of the Bureau of Refugees, Freedmen, and Abandoned Lands

RG107   Records of the Office of the Secretary of War

RG108   Records of the Headquarters of the Army

RG109   War Department Collection of Confederate Records

RG153   Records of the Office of the Judge Advocate General (Army)

RG204   Records of the Office of the Pardon Attorney

RG366   Records of Civil War Special Agencies of the Treasury Department
RG393   Records of United States Army Continental Commands, 1821–1920

*We have also used a number of microfilm collections from the National Archives, all of which are parts of the various Record Groups listed here.

GU   University of Georgia, Athens
ICU   University of Chicago, Illinois
MHi   Massachusetts Historical Society, Boston
Ms-Ar   Mississippi Department of Archives and History, Jackson
NHi   New-York Historical Society, New York
NN   New York Public Library, New York
Nc-Ar   North Carolina Division of Archives and History, Raleigh
NcD   Duke University, Durham, North Carolina
NjMoHP Morristown National Historical Park, Morristown, New Jersey
OFH   Rutherford B. Hayes Library, Fremont, Ohio
ScU   University of South Carolina, Columbia
TxU-A   Barker Texas History Center, University of Texas at Austin
TSLA   Tennessee State Library and Archives, Nashville

Manuscripts

AL   Autograph Letter
ALcopy   Autograph Letter, copy by writer
ALS   Autograph Letter Signed
ALScopy Autograph Letter Signed, copy by writer
ALSdraft Autograph Letter Signed, draft
Copy   Copy, not by writer
CopyS   Copy Signed
D   Document
DS   Document Signed
Draft   Draft Signed
ES   Endorsement Signed
L   Letter
LBcopy   Letter Book copy
LBcopyS Letter Book copy, Signed
LS   Letter Signed
LS(X)   Letter Signed "X"
Mem   Memorial
PD   Printed Document
Pet   Petition
PL   Printed Letter

PLS   Printed Letter Signed
Tel   Telegram

ABBREVIATIONS

ACP   Appointment, Commission, and Personal Branch
Appl(s).   Application(s)
Appt(s).   Appointment(s)
Appt. Bk. Appointment Book
Arty.   Artillery
Atty. Gen. Attorney General
Bde.   Brigade
Brig.   Brigadier
Bty.   Battery
Bvt.   Brevet
Cav.   Cavalry
Cld.   Colored
Co.   Company
Commr.   Commissioner
Corres.   Correspondence
CSR   Compiled Service Records
Enum.   Enumeration
fl.   flourishing
Inf.   Infantry
JP   Andrew Johnson Papers
Let. Bk.   Letter Book
Lgt.   Light
Pt(s).   Part(s)
Recd.   Received
Recomm.   Recommendation
Rgt.   Regiment
Ser.   Serial, Series
Supp(s).   Supplement(s)
USCT   United States Colored Troops
Vols.   Volunteers

SHORT TITLES

BOOKS

Advice   Brooks D. Simpson, LeRoy P. Graf,
                                  and John Muldowny, eds., *Ad-*
                                  vice After Appomattox: Letters to
                                  Andrew Johnson, 1865–1866
                                  (Knoxville, 1987).
American Annual Cyclopaedia   *American Annual Cyclopaedia and*
                                  Register of Important Events (42

	vols. in 3 series, New York, 1862–1903).
Appleton's Cyclopaedia	James G. Wilson and John Fiske, eds., *Appleton's Cyclopaedia of American Biography* (6 vols., New York, 1887–89).
Baker, *Secret Service*	Lafayette C. Baker, *History of the United States Secret Service* (Philadelphia, 1867).
BDAC	*Biographical Directory of the American Congress, 1774–1961* (Washington, D.C., 1961).
BDTA	Robert M. McBride et al., comps., *Biographical Directory of the Tennessee General Assembly* (5 vols., Nashville, 1975–).
Boatner, *CWD*	Mark M. Boatner, III, *The Civil War Dictionary* (New York, 1959).
Brewer, *Alabama*	Willis Brewer, *Alabama: Her History, Resources, War Record, and Public Men* (Tuscaloosa, 1964[1872]).
Brown, *Am. Biographies*	John H. Brown, ed., *Cyclopaedia of American Biographies* (7 vols., Boston, 1897–1903).
Cyclopedia of the Carolinas	*Cyclopedia of Eminent and Representative Men of the Carolinas of the Nineteenth Century* (2 vols., Madison, Wis., 1892).
DAB	Allen Johnson and Dumas Malone, eds., *Dictionary of American Biography* (20 vols., supps., and index, New York, 1928-).
DNB	Leslie Stephen and Sidney Lee, eds., *The Dictionary of National Biography* (22 vols. and supps., London, 1938- [1885–1901]).
Dorris, *Pardon and Amnesty*	Jonathan T. Dorris, *Pardon and Amnesty Under Lincoln and Johnson* (Chapel Hill, 1953).
Durkin, *Stephen R. Mallory*	Joseph T. Durkin, *Stephen R. Mallory: Confederate Navy Chief* (Chapel Hill, 1954).

Fairman, *Reconstruction and Reunion* — Charles Fairman, *Reconstruction and Reunion, 1864–88, Part One* (New York, 1971) [Vol. 6 of *History of the Supreme Court of the United States*].

Fleming, *Alabama* — Walter L. Fleming, *Civil War and Reconstruction in Alabama* (New York, 1905).

Gandrud, *Alabama Records* — Pauline J. Gandrud, comp., *Alabama Records* (Easley, S.C., 1981).

Goodspeed's *Tennessee, East Tennessee, Fayette* [and other counties] — Goodspeed Publishing Company, *History of Tennessee, from the Earliest Time to the Present . . .* (Chicago, 1886–87).

Harris, *Presidential Reconstruction* — William C. Harris, *Presidential Reconstruction in Mississippi* (Baton Rouge, 1967).

Heitman, *Register* — Francis B. Heitman, *Historical Register and Dictionary of the United States Army, from Its Organization, September 29, 1789 to March 2, 1903* (2 vols., Washington, D.C., 1903).

Hermann, *Pursuit of a Dream* — Janet S. Hermann, *The Pursuit of A Dream* (New York, 1981).

Howard, *Black Liberation* — Victor B. Howard, *Black Liberation in Kentucky* (Lexington, Ky., 1983).

Johnson Papers — LeRoy P. Graf, Ralph W. Haskins, and Paul H. Bergeron, eds., *The Papers of Andrew Johnson* (8 vols., Knoxville, 1967-).

Johnston, *Vance Papers* — Frontis W. Johnston, ed., *The Papers of Zebulon Baird Vance, 1843–1862* (Raleigh, 1963).

McFeely, *Yankee Stepfather* — William S. McFeely, *Yankee Stepfather: General O. O Howard and the Freedmen* (New York, 1968).

NCAB — *National Cyclopaedia of American Biography . . .* (63 vols. and index, New York, 1893–1984 [I-XVIII, Ann Arbor, 1967]).

NUC

Nuermberger, *Clays*

OR

Owen, *History of Ala.*

Powell, *Army List*

Raper, *Holden*

Richardson, *Messages*

Simon, *Grant Papers*

Sobel and Raimo, *Governors*

Taylor, *La. Reconstructed*

TICW

U.S. Off. Reg.

Library of Congress, *The National Union Catalog: Pre-1956 Imprints* (754 vols., London, 1968-).

Ruth K. Nuermberger, *The Clays of Alabama* (Lexington, Ky., 1958).

War of the Rebellion: A Compilation of the Official Records of the Union and Confederate Armies (70 vols. in 128, Washington, D.C., 1880–1901).

Thomas M. Owen, *History of Alabama and Dictionary of Alabama Biography* (4 vols., Chicago, 1921).

William H. Powell, *List of Officers of the Army of the United States from 1779 to 1900* (Detroit, 1967 [1900]).

Howard W. Raper, *William W. Holden: North Carolina's Political Enigma* (Chapel Hill, 1985).

James D. Richardson, comp., *A Compilation of the Messages and Papers of the Presidents, 1789–1897* (10 vols., Washington, D.C., 1896–99).

John Y. Simon, ed., *The Papers of Ulysses S. Grant* (16 vols., Carbondale, Ill., 1967-).

Robert Sobel and John Raimo, eds., *Biographical Directory of the Governors of the United States, 1789–1978* (4 vols., Westport, Conn., 1978).

Joe Gray Taylor, *Louisiana Reconstructed, 1863–1877* (Baton Rouge, 1974).

Civil War Centennial Commission, *Tennesseans in the Civil War: A Military History of Confederate and Union Units with Available Rosters of Personnel* (2 pts., Nashville, 1964–65).

Register of the Officers and Agents,

	Civil, Military and Naval in the Service of the United States . . . (Washington, D.C., 1851-).
Wakelyn, *BDC*	Jon L. Wakelyn, *Biographical Dictionary of the Confederacy* (Westport, Conn., 1977).
Warner, *Blue*	Ezra J. Warner, *Generals in Blue* (Baton Rouge, 1964).
Warner, *Gray*	Ezra J. Warner, *Generals in Gray* (Baton Rouge, 1959).
Warner and Yearns, *BRCC*	Ezra J. Warner and Wilfred Buck Yearns, *Biographical Register of the Confederate Congress* (Baton Rouge, 1975).
Webb et al., *Handbook of Texas*	Walter Prescott Webb and H. Bailey Carroll, eds., *The Handbook of Texas* (2 vols., Austin, 1952).

JOURNALS

AR	*Alabama Review*
ArHQ	*Arkansas Historical Quarterly*
At Mon	*Atlantic Monthly*
Con Vet	*Confederate Veteran*
ETHS *Pubs.*	East Tennessee Historical Society's *Publications*
GHQ	*Georgia Historical Quarterly*
IaHR	*Iowa Historical Record*
IaJHP	*Iowa Journal of History and Politics*
JAzH	*The Journal of Arizona History*
JSH	*Journal of Southern History*
KHSR	*The Register of the Kentucky Historical Society*
LHQ	*Louisiana Historical Quarterly*
MdHM	*Maryland Historical Magazine*
NCHR	*North Carolina Historical Review*
RCHS *Pubs.*	Rutherford County Historical Society *Publications*
SCHM	*South Carolina Historical Magazine*
SWHQ	*Southwestern Historical Quarterly*
THQ	*Tennessee Historical Quarterly*
VMHB	*Virginia Magazine of History and Biography*

THE PAPERS OF
Andrew Johnson

September 1865

From Cherokee County, Alabama, Citizens[1]

[ca. September 1865][2]

The undersigned who are citizens of Cherokee County Alabama respectfully show, that on the 24th August last an unfortunate encounter occurred in this County between Josiah M. Daniel[3] the Sheriff of this county with his Posse and a squad of U.S. Troops under command of Lt Thompson.[4] During the latter part of the Rebellion this was a border County, between the Federal and Confederate Forces, subject to marauding raids; which were kept up after the surrender and up to the date above, by citizens and by soldiers, seizing and carrying off cattle, horses and mules under pretended Military orders. This squad of Troops were supposed to be another gang of marauders. They were reputed, not without some foundation there for, as lawless marauders, robbing citizens and plundering houses. A universal panic was produced where they went, and the masses believed they were what they had been represented to be. The citizens appealed to the Legal Authorities for relief and protection and the Sheriff was called upon to assemble his posse and arrest them. Under the full conviction of the truth of their reputed character, believing it to be his duty under the laws of the State and of the Proclamation of the Provisional Governor, he with promptness responded to the demands of public sentiment summoned his posse and went to the arrest; when a rencounter took place, under circumstances which should excuse the Sheriff. These Troops had the day before made Prisoners of the Sheriff's Deputy and several citizens,[5] had refused to show any authority, and the officer in command swore he would show no authority until his squad was whipped out, and gave his men orders never to surrender. They were advised of the panic they had produced and were expecting the sheriff and his Posse and when they did meet instead of obeying the demands of the Sheriff to surrender the Troops fired into the Sheriff's Posse and a fight ensued in which one soldier was killed and one wounded. Such are the received statements of the County and are believed to be true. The Military Authorities have issued orders for the arrest of the Sheriff and heavy threats have been made against him. He has become alarmed and has concealed himself,[6] hopeing that time will dethrone passion; and reason and justice will assume control, when his motives and conduct will receive calm consideration.

We do not wish to be understood as prejudging his case, but we do believe that he acted in good faith and not from any desire to violate law or to put at defiance, the Military authority, but as he believed in the discharge of duty.

The Grand Jury of our county is now in session. We expect they will take cognizance of the case. We respectfully ask Your Excellency to grant to said J. M. Daniel a pardon for any violation of the laws of the U.S. If you cannot do this we would respectfully urge upon you to issue an order to the Military authorities not to take jurisdiction of the case but to turn it over to the civil Authorities to be disposed of, and for said Military to act only subordinate to and in aid of the civil authorities in the premises.[7]

Pet, DNA-RG393, Dept. of Tennessee, Lets. Recd.
   1. There were 141 signatures.
   2. The late August date of the within incident and the probable time needed to gather the petitioners' signatures lead to the conclusion that this document could not be dated earlier than September 1865.
   3. Daniel (1827–*fl*1896), a grocer, served as sheriff several times between 1863 and 1874. Mrs. Frank R. Stewart, *Cherokee County History, 1836–1856* (2 vols., Birmingham, 1958–59), 2: 255, 258; 1860 Census, Ala., Cherokee, 2nd Dist., 80.
   4. Archibald H. Thomson (1835–1920), a Scottish-born hotel clerk, served as a private in the 19th Ohio Inf. and 2nd Ohio Cav. before becoming a lieutenant and captain in the 12th Ohio Cav. After the war he settled in Coshocton, Ohio, where he conducted a seed, grain, and building supply business. Pension Records, Maria R. Thomson, RG15, NA.
   5. The deputy sheriff has not been identified. At least sixteen men captured by Thomson, who had been sent to recover stolen government livestock, were turned over to the provost marshal at Chattanooga, where they were released in late September. *Montgomery Advertiser*, Sept. 5, 1865; *Nashville Union*, Sept. 27, 1865.
   6. Despite the assertions of two historians that Daniel was arrested soon after his clash with Thomson, he was still at large as late as September 19, 1865. Stewart, *Cherokee County*, 2: 258; Fleming, *Alabama*, 268; *Philadelphia Bulletin*, Sept. 20, 1865.
   7. By late February 1866 Daniel was "under military arrest at Talledaga, charged with the killing of a soldier named Tatson." The Alabama legislature sent a memorial to the President requesting that Daniel either be pardoned or released to civil authorities. *Acts of the Session of 1865–6 of the General Assembly of Alabama . . .* (Montgomery, 1866), 598–600.

From Irish-American Soldiers [1]

[ca. September 1865][2]

We, whose names are undersigned, Soldiers and Officers of various Regiments, composed of citizens of the United States, of Irish birth or descent, respectfully pray the attention of your Excellency to the facts herein after mentioned, which have been to us subject of deep and painful interest:

On the 13th day of June last, a citizen of the United States, like most of us, of Irish birth, was arrested in the City of New York, by officers of the United States Army, professing to act under orders from your Excellency, and immediately transported in a Government ship to Fortress Monroe, where he has since then been incarcerated.

The name of the person, in whose behalf we appeal to your Excellency, is John Mitchel[3]—a name dear to his countrymen in Ireland and in the United States. His devotion to the cause of that unhappy Island, and his sufferings in her behalf, form part of her History.

If, however, he has in aught, offended against the laws of the United States, we ask no immunity for him on that account.

But as far as we are able to learn, no charge has as yet been preferred against him—no intimation has been given to him of the nature of the crime for which he is punished—no opportunity has been afforded him to prove, if he can, his innocence—all communication between him and his family, or friends, has been rigidly cut off—and he lies a solitary prisoner—condemned without accusation—deprived of his liberty without any apparent cause, or any definite prospect of release.

If, as we are ready to believe, it seemed to your Excellency proper and for the public good, that Mr. Mitchel should have been thus summarily arrested, the condition of the United States has since then undergone, as we respectfully submit, a beneficent change.

The War is at an end; armed resistance to the National authority has ceased.

The terrible crisis which may have rendered such vigorous measures necessary has happily passed away.

Thousands of the soldiers and officers, who, but a few months' ago, opposed in arms the National forces, have returned to their allegiance, and are now quietly pursuing the paths of industry, pardoned by the Government whose complete triumph they freely acknowledge, and to whose generous indulgence they owe the liberty they enjoy.

We pray your Excellency that this generosity and mercy be not denied to this man, to whose unhappy condition, we entreat your merciful consideration.

For the sake of the thousands of his countrymen who love him for his devotion to Ireland long ago, and who have testified their devotion to the United States, by the liberal effusion of their blood on many a hard fought field—in the name of Humanity and Justice, we ask you that, if Mr. Mitchel have offended against the Law, the charge against him be publicly made and speedily and fairly investigated; and if, as we hope and trust, no crime can be proved against him; if, as we believe, the crisis which may have seemed to your Excellency to warrant his arrest, has passed away, that your Excellency will order his release and restore him to his family, who need his help, and to whom his imprisonment is the bitterest calamity.[4]

Pet, DLC-JP.

1. Eleven copies of this printed petition were signed by eighty-two persons.

2. A "Congress" of the Fenian Brotherhood met at Philadelphia in September 1865 and forwarded petitions for the release of John Mitchel. *American Annual Cyclopedia* (1865), 334.

3. Mitchel (1815–1875), an Irish nationalist, had been exiled from his homeland for publishing incendiary articles. A Knoxville resident and newspaperman in the 1850s, he

edited the *Richmond Enquirer* and wrote for the *Richmond Examiner* during the Civil War. He was arrested for "his articles in defence of the southern cause." *DNB*; Samuel C. Williams, "John Mitchel, the Irish Patriot, Resident of Tennessee," ETHS *Pubs.*, 10 (1938): 44–56.

4. Johnson ordered Mitchel's release on October 28, 1865. At his own suggestion, the Irish journalist was exiled, but, after a year in France, he returned to the United States, where he again published a political newspaper for a time. *OR*, Ser. 1, Vol. 8: 725, 775, 782; *DNB*.

From Clinton B. Fisk

Personal

Office Ass't Com. for Ky., Tenn., and North. Ala.,
Nashville, Tenn., Sept 1st 1865.

Dear Sir—

I trust you will pardon me for trespassing upon your time with a brief report of my action touching the restoration of "Abandoned Property" to Mrs Margaret Donelson of Sumner County Tenn.

The following telegram from yourself was this day shown me.[1]

I have the honor to state that when on the 1st of July I entered upon duty as Assistant Comr. of the Bureau for this District, the Donelson plantation was, and had been for a long time—occupied as a Freedmen's Camp. There were at that date Four hundred and forty eight (448) colored persons in the Camp and Two hundred and fifty (250) acres of Corn—besides other crops—in Cultivation on the farm. On the 8th of July last Mrs Donelson arrived in Nashville from Florida, and called upon me with an application for the restoration of the Estate. I kindly advised her of the difficulties in the way of immediately complying with her request: but assured her that as my energies would be devoted to the closing out of *all Freedmen's Camps* in the District in the earliest possible time consistent with humanity, I should be able to place her in possession of the property within a very few weeks. I called her attention to Circular No 3 of this Bureau, copy of which is herewith enclosed,[2] and told her that while I would do all in my power to place her in early possession of her home, I must protect the interests of the Freedmen and the Government. It has not been an easy task to break up the Camp, and distribute the people in localities where they would be self-supporting, especially as among them were thirty five (35) families who were the widows and orphans of deceased colored soldiers.

I found in Middle Tenn alone, upon my arrival here, Four thousand nine hundred and one (4901) in Camps, subsisted by the Government. I have succeeded in reducing that number to seven hundred and sixty nine (769) at *this* date. And only twenty three (23) of that number are remaining in the Camp on the Donelson place.

I had given Mrs Donelson an order for her dwelling house. She has been in possession of it many days. She claimed all the products of the plantation as *hers*, without payment therefor and because I could not justly give her what belonged to the Government and the Freedmen the complaining telegram was sent you. I really think Mrs Donelson has cause to be grateful rather than censorious.

It has been my constant and earnest effort, to adjust the vexed question of restoration of "abandoned property" to claimants entitled to it with as little delay and friction as possible—and quite generally to the entire satisfaction of all parties interested.

Clinton B. Fisk   Brig Genl Asst. Commr

ALS, DLC-JP.

1. Johnson to Andrew J. Martin, Aug. 29, 1865, appears at this point in the text. For this document see *Johnson Papers*, 8: 669.

2. Although not enclosed, Circular No. 3 required that abandoned lands were to remain in the possession of the freedmen until the growing season had ended or until they had been compensated for their labor, products, and expenditures. *House Ex. Docs.*, 39 Cong., 1 Sess., No. 11, "Freedmen's Bureau," p. 44 (Ser. 1255).

From James Johnson

Milledgeville Ga   Sept 1st 1865

Dr Sir

I declined for some time after my return from Washington to make any judicial appointments for the state.[1] This I did for two reasons 1st because you advised me to appoint as few officers as possible & 2nd because Mr Speed[2] was of opinion that I did not have the power. The Provisional Governors of the other States proceeded to make such appointments and their course was cited as evidence of the power & duty on my part to do as they did. I refused still for some time but at length the pressure became so great that I yielded on that point to the general clamor for the restoration of civil law, by passing a general order[3] directing all the civil officers of the state to proceed with the discharge of the functions of their several offices under they laws as they existed prior to the year 1861, not inconsistent with our present condition. Many of these officers had participated in the Rebellion and some of them no doubt had rendered themselves very obnoxious to Union citizens. But notwithstanding I thought such an order was the better course and when complaint should be made of any officer upon any good ground to remove him and then to make an appointment. I am still of that opinion. This is all the means that I have used to promote the Rebels at the expense of Union men and it was done not to benefit them but to quiet the state if possible & to secure to the Union men a permanent ascendency.

In my recommendations for office I may have in some few instances been imposed upon by representations of those in whom I have had confidence. It has been & is my desire to give no man a recommendation who has been a Rebel if I can find a proper Union man to supply the place. At this time it does not occur to me that I have recommended any but Union men.

I presume that you are well *posted* on the condition of the State. I have succeeded beyond my expectations and the public mind is daily accomodating itself to the policy of the Administration. I trust by our election[4] we shall all be of one mind on all material points and that all obstacles in the way of our delegates being received into Congress will on our part be removed.

To this point I direct my efforts.

Give me advice freely—it shall be well received & appreciated.

J. Johnson

ALS, DLC-JP.

1. The governor is responding to the Circular to Provisional Governors, Aug. 22, 1865, *Johnson Papers*, 8: 639. See also his telegram to the President, Sept. 2, 1865, Johnson Papers, LC.

2. Attorney General James Speed.

3. See the governor's proclamation of August 7, 1865. Allen D. Candler, ed., *The Confederate Records of the State of Georgia* (6 vols., Atlanta, 1909–11), 4: 19–20.

4. Probably an allusion to the state election scheduled for mid-November.

From Hugh Kennedy

[New Orleans] City Hall   1st day of Septbr: 1865.

Sir,

A week ago, as I am informed by Gov. Wells,[1] the correspondence which passed between Genl. Canby[2] and myself, and between the Governor and me in regard to the leasing of the wharves of this port, was transmitted to you by the Govr., with his views fully given in reference to the same.[3]

I have President, upon every occasion studiously avoided acceptance of provocation to angry controversies with federal officials, whether civil or military; and I am determined to avoid in the future all such involutions; but if the real interests of government and people are to be promoted, I am clearly of opinion it can only be accomplished by every department cordially cooperating to that end.

At present it is almost an absolute certainty that whatever measures I may devise for the good of this City will be discountenanced or forbidden by the military; and this exercise of authority by the latter has in every instance been in direct conflict with your wishes as expressed to Govr. Wells and myself in Washington. In no respect, upon any matter, have I deviated from what I understood to be your views; nor will I whether my official career be more or less brief; but it is clear to my mind, and becomes more so every day, that unless the municipal concerns of this place are intelligently and firmly administered, great trouble will spring from it.

In previous letters I have invited your attention President, to the spread of Know Nothing and other secret political associations here.[4] Many of the leaders in these are desperate men, fellows of no political principles, and whose only aim is to secure the election of men to high office who will connive at their crimes, or divide with them their products. At this time I hold them in check with a strong grasp; and if let alone do not doubt my capacity to deal with them. They certainly, however, meditate mischief.

Two newspapers, the True Delta & N.O. Times, conducted by former attaches[5] of a Know Nothing journal called the Crescent (confiscated by Butler),[6] now lead off in opposition to my administration, and as the Times has a sort of *quasi*-military recognition, the multitude attach some significance to its abuse. So soon as "The Southern Star"[7] gets fairly started, which will be in a day or two, the State & City authorities will have a hearing & defence of their policy and conduct.

I challenge the continent to produce a better policed City in every respect than New Orleans is now; and were I permitted to carry out my financial plans by Genl. Canby, in a few months it would be free from financial embarrassment. I hope, however, the Genl. is actuated in his opposition by the same motives which govern me in my conduct. I shall ascribe nothing to him or others uncharitably.[8]

Govr. Wells is now absent from the City, on a short visit to Northern Louisiana. He will return about the 10th inst.

I have written you very fully President, since my resumption of Mayoralty duties, and have explained affairs just as they exist. I shall with your permission continue to do so, and hold myself in constant readiness to give an account of, or surrender my stewardship on your requisition.

Hu. Kennedy   Mayor

ALS, DLC-JP.
1. J. Madison Wells.
2. Edward R.S. Canby.
3. See Wells to Johnson, Aug. 25, 1865, *Johnson Papers*, 8: 655–56.
4. See, for example, Kennedy to Johnson, July 21, 1865, ibid., 443–44. See also Kennedy to Johnson, Nov. 23, 1865.
5. Editor William R. Adams (c1823-fl1868) of the *True Delta* purchased an interest in the *Crescent* in 1855, which he retained until his election to the Louisiana legislature on the Know-Nothing ticket in 1859. He served periodically as editor of the *Crescent* for seven years, until its suspension in 1862. William H.C. King, editor of the *Times*, had been the foreman of the *Crescent* office for eight years, beginning in 1854. 1860 Census, La., Orleans, 3rd Rep. Ward, New Orleans, 215; Fayette Copeland, "The New Orleans Press and the Reconstruction," *LHQ*, 30 (1947): 271–73, 281–82, 303, 307; New Orleans directories (1857–68).
6. Begun in 1848 and suspended by Gen. Benjamin F. Butler in 1862, the *Crescent* resumed publication in October 1865. Winifred G. Gerould, comp., *American Newspapers, 1821–1936: A Union List of Newspapers* (New York, 1936), 240.
7. Kennedy joined Thomas Cottman and Gov. J. Madison Wells in establishing this pro-administration daily. Ibid., 243; Walter M. Lowrey, "The Political Career of James Madison Wells," *LHQ*, 31 (1948): 1041.
8. See Kennedy to Johnson, Sept. 6, 1865.

From Sam Milligan
Private

Greeneville Ten   Sept. 1. 1865

Dear Sir:

I must be allowed to say your order turning over the Rail Roads so promptly obeyed by Gen Thomas,[1] has done you much good in this and other portions of the State. Mr Branner and Tate[2] are, I believe, doing all in their power to sustain your administration. They have a commanding influence over & through their roads; and they both together with Mr Calaway[3] assured me they would employ no man on their roads unless they fully sustained the Government and its present administration.

In the Rail Road Department every thing is going on well, except the infernal Quarter Masters, who are attempting to swindle the Government on a large scale.[4] They manifested a good deal of reluctance to turn over the roads, and affirm they can not render the accounts required by your Order. Gen Thomas says, they ought to be able to do it without difficulty. The matter is, they have been smuggling, and that order exposes them. Why I have been told—and this for the present must be regarded strictly confidential—they now have on hands, thirty six Engines, which are in no way credited to the Government, besides vast amounts of other materials, and which, as I have been informed, they are proposing to dispose of at private sale. I have laid a plan to learn more certainly these facts, and if they are as I have been informed, I will advise you of it. One thing is certain, you can not be to stringent with them, as they are, I mean some of them, prepared to do any thing.

I believe it would be a good plain to send a competent & disinterested man or two down South, not heretofore connected with the Army, to take Inventories of Rail Road property, and to investigate on the ground, the true State of things. It would in my opinion devellop some astounding frauds.[5]

I do not like the aspect of things in Ten. Governor Brownlow is in evey way in his power attempting to secure the future control of the State. He has appointed, as Judge Patterson[6] can tell you, many of the Sheriffs and other officers of the State, and now is using his influence to have all the troops removed from E. Ten., so that his Sheriffs, and Adjutant General can under the late acts of the assembly supply the necessary military force at the expense of the people, and thereby perpetuate his power.

I do not think the U.S. troops ought all to be withdrawn. No part of the Country is in worse disorder than parts of E. Ten. Not to be sure, from a spirit of rebellion but from the lawless conduct of the returned soldiers. Not a day passes but some man or family is either beaten almost to death, or driven from the county, and all as it would seem, from the Governor's organ under his sanction.[7] I do not think this is right, and as soon as the troops are removed, it will produce bloody contests all over the County. Besides in Sullivan county, there is a band of discharged soldiers, running all the negros out of the county.[8] Such is the state of things evey where, which, as I believe require the presence of a small military forc for some time to come.

I see Shackleford has been appointed in Houston's place.[9] It will make a hot Supreme court. I will try it week after next at Knoxville, and do the best I can, but as things now stand, I have no idea I can or ought to continue to hold the position.[10] Houston, I think, did wrong in resigning when he did. His services were needed in the State more than else where.[11]

I will in a day or so write you my views on the negro.[12] I have been studying him.

God bless you.

Sam Milligan

ALS, DLC-JP.

1. On August 8, 1865, Stanton, by order of the President, had directed Thomas to return all Tennessee railroads to their owners. *House Reports*, 39 Cong., 2 Sess., No. 34, pp. 459–60 (Ser. 1306).

2. John R. Branner and Samuel Tate, presidents of the East Tennessee and Virginia, and the Memphis and Charleston, respectively.

3. The president of the East Tennessee and Georgia, Thomas H. Callaway.

4. The 1862 Railroad Act stipulated that captured lines were to be under the supervision of Quartermaster General M. C. Meigs. In the Tennessee theatre superintendent Daniel C. McCallum operated independently of Meigs while quartermasters and various army commanders decided what the roads would carry. Russell F. Weigley, *Quartermaster General of the Union Army: A Biography of M. C. Meigs* (New York, 1959), 239–40.

5. Johnson apparently did not do this, but Congress did later undertake an investigation of southern railroad management. See *House Reports*, 39 Cong., 2 Sess., No. 34, passim (Ser. 1306), and *House Reports*, 40 Cong., 2 Sess., No. 15, passim (Ser. 1357).

6. David T. Patterson.

7. Issuing unofficial proclamations in his *Knoxville Whig and Rebel Ventilator* throughout the summer of 1865, Governor Brownlow repeatedly urged East Tennessee unionists to seek vengeance for "atrocities" committed by former Confederates. E. Merton Coulter, *William G. Brownlow: Fighting Parson of the Southern Highlands* (Chapel Hill, 1937), 272–73.

8. The Freedmen's Bureau reported that similar incidents had occurred in Knox, Blount, and Sevier counties by the fall of 1865. Charles F. Bryan, Jr., "The Civil War in East Tennessee: A Social, Political, and Economic Study" (Ph.D. diss., University of Tennessee, Knoxville, 1978), 332–33.

9. James O. Shackleford replaced Russell Houston as a state supreme court justice on August 24, 1865. Charles A. Miller, comp., *The Official and Political Manual of the State of Tennessee* (Nashville, 1890), 181.

10. In spite of his reservations, Milligan continued serving on the state supreme court until January 1867.

11. Houston had relocated to Louisville, Ky.

12. Not found.

To Lewis E. Parsons

Washington, D.C.   September 1st 1865.

Referring to your dispatch[1] relative to the stationing of Troops in Alabama I would suggest for your consideration the propriety of raising in each county an armed mounted *posse comitatus* organized under your Militia Law and under such provisos as you need to secure their loyalty and obedience to your authority and that of the Military Authorities to repress crime and arrest criminals.

A similar organization by me in Tennessee when Military Governor worked well.[2] Governor Sharkey has begun to raise such a force in Mississippi.

It seems to me that in some such way your citizens would be committed to the cause of Law and Order and their loyalty to the Union would become not merely passive but active. In any Event while Society is reorganizing the people would themselves by Vigilance Committees or by like unauthorized, spontaneous and quasi illegal manner Endeavor to repress lawlessness and punish marauding. And it seems preferable to give this natural impulse a proper legal shape and control than to have it illegal and uncontrolled.

I should like to know your views of this proposition.[3]

Andrew Johnson   Prest U.S.

Tel copy, DLC-JP.

1. See Parsons to Johnson, Aug. 30, 1865, *Johnson Papers*, 8: 682.
2. Johnson had authorized the recruitment of mounted "Union Guards" in September 1863. Provision for such forces had been granted under the congressional act Johnson himself had introduced in the Senate on July 20, 1861. *TICW*, 1: 410–11; *Johnson Papers*, 4: 592–93; 6: 368–69.
3. See Parsons to Johnson, Oct. 2, 1865.

From Anderson R. Edmonds

washington Co va   Glade Springs Depot   Sept 2 1865

Dear Sir

May I presume to write you a Line? The time has bin when I cold write you freely and Expect to Git a kind and pleasant answer from you but now the Gulf between us appears to me to be all most as Great as that of Divers and the Rich Mans friends.[1] You *and I am Glad of it,* are at the very top most Round of the Ladder and I at the bottom or Eavin Lower if possible but being a Subject of your Murcy or parden I will Make the attempt. You know that until this unfortunate Rebellian came up I was all ways your frind. I only had to know How you was on any polittical Subject to be the same way My Self. I never had an opportunity in my Life to say or do any thing for you or to advance your Causes but what I done it anchusly & freely up to that time but O

I Maid the fatal Error like thousands others that was better Informed
than I was. I was onst in the belief that I was rite and I Maid the Error
and O God the Concequence to me is offul to think of. Before that Error
I was in Comfortble circumstances and ought to have bin Satisfide and
happy. Now I am Redut to absolute Poverty and want a Reffuge from
My Good old State of Ten. God Bless here. My Children all did [died]
but one and I am now old as you Know and My wife[2] very feeble and
2 Little Grand Children Depending on us for a Living. My property
all Gone for you Know it consisted in negroes. Indited at Knoxville I
am told for treson and dont Know what day I May be Marcht off to
Jail or prison to abide my fait or trial. If you are the Same Man you ust
to be or have the Same Hart you onst had if you Knew My condition
you cold not help feeling for Me whether you Grant My pardon or not.[3]
I am Living on a Little pore place 8 miles from Glade Spring Depot
washington co va. I have walked and traveld for the Last 5 weeks to
try to Git aplace that I cold make a Living on but can Git none. All the
Good Land in this Cuntry is ownd by Rich men that is now asking
pardons from you and a pore man it Seems can not Git an acre to tend
of it. If I cold only go back to Tennessee and Live in peace the Remainder of My days and be pardon for my Past Error I wood be very Glad.
You Know How I onct Lived. Now Sir Meet is allmost a stringer to
My Mouth. I have workd Harder for the 2 Last years than Ever I did
in My Life and am now porrer than I Ever was in my Life and have no
one to blame for it but My Self but enough of that. I took the amnsty
oth the 21 august at Marion va the first opportunity I had with out
Going to withville or Lynchburg and I had not the mony to have my
Expences and it wood have bin a Long walk for me. I took it in Good
faith and intend to Live a peacible Life if permited to Live at all. My
Son william went to rogersville and got A. A. Kyle to draw up a petition to you for a parden and I have Sent a certificate of My othe to him
to Go on with My petition.[4] Mr Kyle Says that the inditment Rest on
me in Relation to the Post office. I oneley Resignd the Post office of the
united States after the so cald [illegible] held the cuntry and was talking about appointg or Having appointed a nother Post Master. I was
then appointed by Mr Davis at Richmond and I Sent on all the assets
of the P.O. of the U.S. via Nashvill after communications had Stopt via
Richmond, but Some Say that I can not be Pardend until I pay over all
the dues to the united States that I collected for the So Calld Confederate States. If that Shood be So My Parden wood be a ded Letter for
I cold not Pay it if it wood Save me from Perdition. That was all collected in confederate mony and Paid over and infact I have nothing to
Pay with nor no frinds to helpe me. I paid over or Sent on to P.O. of
U.S. all dues Except the postage from 1 of June to the 8 of June which
P.O. Dept at Richmond collected off of me $8.04 Eight dollars and 4
cents. I do not Know why I cold not be permitted to Live in Tenn. I

never was a combatten in the war. I never had a man arrested or Hurt in any way. I was not [illegible] and tride to Live friendly with all but I have bin thretend of being whipt and Hung and all that sort of thing. It is true I was Desided in My vews as I allwas was when I took a Stand as you Know. I think there is some old Political Enamays there that wood Like to See me Suffer and if the Knowd what I have all Ready Suffered I do think it wood Satisfy any Reasonable Man. Well My Earley frind I Most Hartaly thank you for what you have done for me in days that is Gone and Hope and trust to God that you may Live Long to Enjoy your High Position. I did not Help to put you in that position but Had I bin permmited I wood. For think of it as you pleas So Help me God I never Had any thing but a Kind feeling for you for if I have any trate in My composition stronger than a nother it is Grattitude and I tell it now as I all way have that you have bin the Best frind to me that I Ever Had in my Life. My Dear Sir there is from all Riliable acconts there is a terrable State of things Going on in East Tennessee. It seams that no Man will be permited to Live there that Has any property. This Country is crowded with Reffugees from Ten and they are coming Dayly. They Git orders to Leave in So many days or take the concequances. Some union men Have bin whipt and Some Run out. Will Sturm was here a few days a go from Rogersville. They had him Hung him to Kill Him. Many Express the opinion that if you Knew how bad it was that you wood try to have a *Stop put to it*. The thought cums up to me will Andrew Jonston the President of the u.s. of Amera condisend to Read this pore old mans Letter. I think you will for the Sake of bygone years for you Know that no man ever possest a nother mans confidence more than you have Mine, *but I Erd and sind. Will you for give?* Peter Sind and our savour forgive Him. My Dear past frind My case is before you. Do what you think best in the premises. I am old and worn down with affictions in My family and other wise. I dont no whether you wood Recognise me if you was to see me. I do not Expect an answer to this for I have forfited all Claims to you notice. I Expect if permited to Live to Live in Poverty and obscurity the Balance of My Life. It Seams Hard but I must bar it. May God prosper you and inable you to carry on the Govement in Such a way as will make a Great and Happy nation agin the South fields Runed. Some Say had Mr. Lincon of Livd it wood Have bin better for us. I all was Say no. If you cant do for us and better for us than any man North of Mason & Dixon Line I am very much mistaken. You have My umble prays. I dont Know that they are worth Much. You May never here from me a gain. I am as ever your frind at Hart.

A. R. Edmonds

ALS, DNA-RG94, Amnesty Papers (M1003, Roll 60), Va., A. R. Edmonds.
    1. Luke 16: 19–31.
    2. Elizabeth S. Edmonds (1810–1874). Ada Grace Catron et al., comps., *Tombstone Inscriptions of Lee County, Virginia* (Pennington Gap, Va., 1966), 47; Hawkins

County Genealogical Society, *Cemeteries of Hawkins County* (2 vols., Rogersville, Tenn., 1985–86), 2: 213.

3. A September 30 memo requesting that a warrant for the pardon of Edmonds be forwarded from the Attorney General's office bears Andrew Johnson's signature. Edmonds was apparently pardoned on the same date. Johnson to James Speed, Sept. 30, 1865, Amnesty Papers (M1003, Roll 49), Tenn., Anderson R. Edmonds, RG94, NA.

4. See Edmonds to Johnson, July 10, 1865, and Absalom A. Kyle et al. to Johnson, July 5, 1865, ibid.

From Fanny M. Jackson[1]

Pulaski Tenn.   Sept 2nd 1865

My Dear President

After reaching my home I feel that I cannot rest, until I thank you *cordially*, for your kind reception of me, and the interest you took in my mission to Washington. The commutation of young Herron's[2] sentence has had a most salutary effect upon the community, and they bless you for your clemency, and graciousness, to a subdued and suffering people. I most solemnly beleive, my dear President, that God in his wise providence has selected *you* in mercy to reign over us, to heal the evils brought about by political and social confusion, and that you will be sustained and blessed in your efforts to administer the goverment for the benefit of the whole people. Our *Southern* brothers are begining to know that you are their friend, their protector, and to *feel* that "In thy hands a nation's fate lies circled," its danger great and its peril imminent! To you they look and pray for pardon, beleiving great misfortunes would be theirs if the rains of goverment should unfortunately fall into the hands of the radicals! That the guillotine would be erected, and the spirit that animated the French Revolutionist's would soon ensanguine our country with the blood of our good citizens. Their earthly Salvation, they beleive, is in your hands. And my dear President, when I look upon these poor repentant people, crushed, heart-broken, with desolated homes, seeking pardon for the past, with a determination to do right in the future, I can but pray, that you will in your great heart, remember them with mercy.

The Freedman's Bureau. Since my return I have—as I promised you—made every inquiry in regard to the Officer Barnes,[3] intermarry with a negro-woman, and have no *proof* of anything of the kind occurring. Gen'l Fisk has visited here recently to look into matters, and I am inclined to beleive the department will be managed so as to insure better satisfaction in future.

I regret seeing so little of you while in Washington, but your great cares prevented me from intruding. I hope I shall see you again soon.

If I can serve you, or my country, may I hope to hear from you, whenever my services are required.

Mrs. John A Jackson

ALS, DLC-JP.

1. Jackson (b. *c*1824) was the wife of the soon-to-be-appointed local agent of the Freedmen's Bureau. 1860 Census, Tenn., Giles, Southern Subdiv., 36; *Nashville Union,* Sept. 17, 1865.

2. William F. Herron (b. *c*1848), a farmer and a private in Gilbert's Ala. Battalion, CSA, had recently been convicted by the army for the December 1864 murder of Clark White in Giles County and sentenced to be hanged on August 11. General Thomas respited him for two weeks, and on August 17 Johnson commuted his sentence to life imprisonment. *Tenn. House Journal, Nov. 1866-Mar. 1867: Appendix,* 105–6; Lets. Recd. (Main Ser.), File J-187-1865 (M619, Roll 368), RG94, NA; *Nashville Press and Times,* Aug. 15, 16, 1865; Johnson to George H. Thomas, Aug. 17, 1865, Tels. Sent, President, Vol. 2 (1865), RG107, NA.

3. Lorenzo D. Barnes (1840-*fl*1906), formerly a member of the 7th Ill. Inf., and later lt. and capt., 111th Inf., USCT, had been detailed at the Pulaski contraband camp since late 1863. After leaving the army he superintended the construction of Stones River National Cemetery and remained a Tennessee resident. Pension File, Lorenzo D. Barnes, RG15, NA.

From James Speed

Attorney General's Office,
Washington, Sept 2nd 1865

Sir

I have the honor to acknowledge the receipt of your note of the 17th refering to me the petition of sundry citizens of Vicksburg[1] for the restoration of their property in possession of Military and Treasury departments.

I would most respectfully recommend that the petitioners prefer their respective complaints to the Military or Treasury as the case may require. No doubt those departments will act justly and promptly.[2]

Upon the facts as now presented no intellegent order or opinion could be made or given.

James Speed   Attorney General.

LS, DNA-RG94, Amnesty Papers (M1003, Roll 35), Miss., Misc.

1. The petition of twenty-six Mississippians, who in fact resided in fifteen different counties, had been endorsed by Governor Sharkey and sent to the President, who forwarded it to the Attorney General. Amnesty Papers (M1003, Roll 35), Miss., Misc., RG94, NA.

2. To facilitate the return of their property, those petitioners who had not received pardons—twenty-four of the twenty-six—were pardoned "by order of the President" on either August 19 or September 4, 1865. *House Ex. Docs.,* 40 Cong., 2 Sess., No. 32, pp. 63–83 (Ser. 1311); Amnesty Papers (M1003, Rolls 32 and 35), Miss., Frank Hawkins and Misc., RG94, NA. See Order *re* Freedmen's Bureau, Sept. 7, 1865.

From Orville Eastland[1]

Carrollton, Pickens County Ala.
Sept. 3rd. 1865

Dear sir

Believing that your exelency would be pleased to understand the true state of feeling now in the asendency in the lately conquared regions of the South, I take the liberty, though a total stranger to your Exelncy, to state a few facts, from which you can draw correct conclusions of the ruling spirit of susession, in this section, and which I believe predominates throughout the richer portions of the whole South.

1st *All influential susessionist, feel the same malignant spirit* towards those who have entertained union sentiments throughout the rebelion that they did before the armies of the South were forced to surender. As evidence of this, in the canvass for members of the convention, which has just closed called by governor Parsons there was first a county meeting gotten up and called by the rankest susessionist in the County, for the purpose of nominating candidates; and two of the original susessionist, both officers in the southern army, one a Colonel and the other a Lutenant[2] were nominated, and though opposed by two good & true Union men with equal ability, were elected, by a majorty from 50 to 100 votes. And in the canvas one of them questioned the legality of the abolition of slavery in a maner to induc the people to believe that if he and his coleage should be elected, that there was still a chance to save the institution.

2ndly, *There are a large majority of large slaveholders*, who in my opinion, would willingly and gladly *murder* their slaves if they dared to do so, rather than to see them set free. In fact there are many instances as I am informed of this spirit being carried into affect. In truth it seem imposible for this class of men to realize the fact, that by their own action they have made the negro as free as they are themselves; and they seem to glory in the great crime they have commited in bringing about this monstrous rebelion. They never can be convinced of their folly and crime by religious or morral teaching, nothing but the power of the law, inforced by armed men will ever cure them of their insanity, and induce them to repent of their most awful crime, in bringing on the wicked rebelion. Aall such, and they are in the majority in all the southern part of Ala, in my opinion, judging from the spirit that prevails here in Pickens County, would rejoice to see the Country again immersed in blood and carnage.

3rdly. *I regret to say I am convinced that if the fedral* forces *were removed* from amongst us the negro would stand but little chance for the protection of his life from lawless mobs, and as little for the maintainance of his rights before courts and juries, and if right minded men should open their mouth in behalf of law & justice of this great question upon principles of strict justice, without regard to the predjudice engendered by past teachings. It is a great question, and if left to selfish hands directed by bad hearts, great and fearfull will be the consequences both social & political.

In view of the whole subject from "prcipitation" to the present moment, I am fearfull that the great clemency the government has extended to the most wicked set of trators that ever disgraced the name of civilization, liberty, and christianaty, was a mistaken policy. Was there ever in the whole history of the world, a more fiendish spirrit exhibited than that which controled secession in its whole history; even in the days of the full sway of the helish inqusition of the Roman church? And, in four fifths, of these blood thirsty trators the same spirit still raneles with, supressed, but unabated fury. And there is no hope for them in the exercize of clemency. Nothing but the infliction of the punishment their crimes so justly merrit will ever urge them.

It seems to me it would be well for your Exelency to issue an address to the people, making known the true state of the questions above mentioned.

O. Eastland

ALS, DNA-RG105, Records of the Commr., Lets. Recd. from Executive Mansion.

1. A native North Carolinian, Eastland (b. c1807) was a planter, lawyer, merchant, and former co-proprietor of the *Carrollton Republican*. Nelson F. Smith, *History of Pickens County, Alabama* (Spartanburg, S.C., 1980 [1856]), 196–97.

2. Martin L. Stansel (1822–1903), a lawyer and state legislator who had commanded the 41st Ala. Inf., and probably Robert J. Henry (b. c1827), a Pickens County planter who had served as 2nd lt., 12th Miss. Cav. Henry S. Marks, comp., *Who Was Who in Alabama* (Huntsville, 1972), 168; *Montgomery Advertiser*, Sept. 12, 1865; 1860 Census, Ala., Pickens, Henrys Beat, 103; CSR, RG109, NA.

From "Kentucky"

Louisville   Sep 3rd 1865

Mr President Sir

I pen you a few lines to let you know how things are going on in kentucky which i suppose you are not aware of at the present time. Sir there are a great many strong Sesesh in this state, and since Jeff Davis has been caught there are secret sesesh Meetings held throughout this state nearly every day and night,[1] and if i understand the thing right, Kentucky is going to brake out in a short time worse than South Carolinia did, and they are determined to raise men enough here very soon to go and release Jeff Davis out of prison. Mr President Sir i think you can not be too fast in sending some thing of an Army to prevent any men from leaving this state for that purpose. Mr President i have been a Soldier in the Union Army ever since the 2nd Union Kentucky Infantry[2] were gotten up, until a few weeks ago and i live 23 miles from louisville in this state and i dare not go home for fear of being killed by my neighbors which still live out there (simply because i volunteered in a Yankee Rigiment[)]. I think some steps should be taken to save our lives who have fought & bled so manfully for our Union. President Johnson if you were to know how horribly we Union Soldiers were treated in Andersonville Prison & in Libby Prison in Richmond, i am sure you would have Jeff Davis & all of his Cabinet hung before 2 weeks. If i were to write to you in this letter and tell you how we were treated you would not believe me even if i were to be your own brother. Mr President we were offered our choice in them prisons either to enlist in the Confederate Army or starve, the majority of us choose the latter. President Johnson Jeff Davis ought to have as good a prison to stay in as we had at Andersonville and no better. Every bit as dirty and as lousy & as stinking as the Sesesh Prisons were for us poor Union soldiers.[3]

Mr President i will not detain you any longer with this letter, but i simply write now that i could write enough to you about how horribly we were treated in them prisons to fill a Newspaper full, too horrible to mention. Too hard. Too hard for human nature to bear. I will now come to a close.

An Ever Union Soldier   Kentucky.

ALS, DNA-RG94, Amnesty Papers, Jefferson Davis, Pets. to A. Johnson.

1. Although the returning Kentucky Confederate veterans were variously received, there was a general tendency to welcome them back. In some instances picnics were held which were attended only by former southern soldiers. E. Merton Coulter, *The Civil War and Readjustment in Kentucky* (Chapel Hill, 1926), 274, 275.

2. The 2nd Kentucky Inf., USA, was organized in May and June 1861 and was mustered out on June 19, 1864. Dyer, *Compendium*, 1198.

3. Many petitions *re* Davis were sent to President Johnson in 1865, some from anti-Davis quarters such as this one, and some from a pro-Davis stance.

From Helena W. Knox[1]

Nashville Tenn   4 Sept 1865

Most Respected President

I am in trouble. If you were here I would call and see you; but as you are not; I am forced to adopt the next best means of communication which is to address you by letter.

I know your time is very much occupied, & the only apology I shall offer for trespassing on a few minutes of it, is the kind & considerate reception I met with from you last summer, when I came to ask your assistance in procuring a School room, & afterwards in regard to a house we were then occupying on Summer St. I showed you all the receipts for rent punctually paid & told you how the land lady wished to force us to vacate immediately, simply because she had been offered a higher rent for her house. You were so kind then—that now in the midst of a greater trouble I am induced to call on you once more.

We were forced to leave that house & in moving had to take one which had been abandoned by the owner (Mrs. L C Brown at that time now Mrs Gen Ewell) & taken possession of by the United States Commissioners. At the time we got the house it was filled with refugess, & contrabands who had burnd the fence & at that time were burning the banisters from around the porch, & even tearing out the door facings & in fact all the wood work that could be taken & burned leaving the walls & the roof to shelter them from the weather.

Recently the place has been restored to Mrs Ewell. She has placed it in the hands of Messrs Nelson & Murfree[2] who wish to sell it immediately for cash. Now the trouble is this. When we first took the place we went to work at a very great expense. We could not buy lumber here but had to sent down to Clarksville buy a raft of logs & have them sawed [(]then the freight was more than the first cost of the logs) & put a good fence round the lot built a Store, & Stable fixed the porch, roof, pavement & infact repaired it—generally spending about half what they ask for the place which is $3500.00. We wish to get the place so as not to lose what we have already spent on it, but the fact of having spent so much on it cramps us for ready means. We could pay for it easily, if they would let us pay $200.00 monthly with interest, but they are not willing to do that.

Pa (Mr Knox the Bell Hanger[3] you remember him I doubt not) mentioned to Mr Murfree (when he was asking him to wait on us a little while) that Mrs Ewell was well enough off to give a poor man such a small place as this was & never miss it. He said yes she was rich in property but had no funds & that her future plans were such she needed a great deal of ready cash.

Would you through some Agent buy the place & let us pay you say $200.00 monthly with interest. We could pay your Agent or remit the amount to you. We could pay monthly, quarterly, semi-annally or annually any way to suit. If you could do so you would confer a great & lasting favor on one who is & has been an acquaintance & *warm* friend of yours ever since you were first elected Governor of Tennessee. Oh! do help us if you can.

Have pity on your poor friend.

Generosity is one of your characteristics I have always heard.

I have a situation at $70.00 per mo. in the Public School where I taugh before & since the war when they were open. One of my brothers[4] has a situation in the Rail Road Department at $90.00 per mo. Pa & my crippled brother[5] are keeping a retail Produce Store & the younger ones[6] are willing to add their mite if we can get the place. We can pay for it. All we want is a little time. Oh! do please help us & accept our unbounded thanks. The thoughts of loseing the place has laid Pa up sick. His health is very poor now at best. Grant my request, & May God bless you & yours is my prayer.

Rest assured, dear Sir, that your kindness will not be forgotten, but will ever command the gratitude & service of. . . .

Helena W. Knox

P.S. Since writing the above I have heard that in case of some one else buying the place we will not be allowed to remove any of the improvements, when we have a written contract from the U.S. Commissioners to remove the improvements. Will not the United States Government see that justice is done? Are not contracts made by said Commissioners legal & binding?

Please answer immediately, & oblige. . . . [7]

H.W K

ALS, DLC-JP.
  1. Knox (c1841–1873) taught at several public schools in Nashville. Nashville directories (1867–70); 1870 Census, Tenn., Davidson, 9th Dist., Nashville, 332; *Nashville Union and American*, Sept. 25, 1873.
  2. Anson Nelson (1821–1892), former editor and city revenue collector, and William L. Murfree were real estate agents. Nashville directories (1865–66); *Nashville Banner*, Aug. 5, 1892; W. Woodford Clayton, *History of Davidson County, Tennessee* (Philadelphia, 1880), 303.
  3. Scottish-born William W. Knox, Sr. (1815–1879) also listed his occupation as mechanic and blacksmith. 1850 Census, Ky., Boyle, 2nd Dist., 792; 1870 Census, Tenn., Davidson, 9th Dist., Nashville, 332; *Nashville American*, Mar. 8, 1879.
  4. A yard conductor for the Nashville, Chattanooga and St. Louis, William W. Knox, Jr. (c1847–fl1933) advanced to clerk, ticket agent, and eventually assistant paymaster. Nashville directories (1866–1933); 1860 Census, Tenn., Davidson, 6th Ward, Nashville, 116.
  5. George R. Knox (c1845–fl1913) later worked with his older brother as general freight agent. Nashville directories (1866–1913); 1870 Census, Tenn., Davidson, 9th Dist., Nashville, 332.
  6. Miss Knox's siblings consisted of three other brothers and a sister, ranging from fifteen to four years of age. 1860 Census, Tenn., Davidson, 6th Ward, Nashville, 116; (1870), 9th Dist., Nashville, 332.
  7. On September 28 the President referred Helena Knox's letter to Lizinka C. Ewell, who replied that her agent had deeded the property to Mr. Knox. A few days later she informed the President that her agent and Mr. Knox had reached an agreement and therefore the latter had gained possession of the house. Johnson to L. C. Ewell, Sept. 28, 1865, and L. C. Ewell to Johnson, Sept. 30, Oct. 2, 1865, Johnson Papers, LC.

From Maria Louisa Longstreet[1]

Lynchburg   Sept 4th 1865

The petition of Maria Louisa Longstreet respectfully represents that she is the daughter of the late Gen John Garland[2] of the United States who died in that service, and is the wife of Gen James Longstreet recently a Lieut Gen in the Confederate States Army and on the 24 day of June took the oath of allegiance to the United States government in due form of law, the certificate of which is herewith enclosed filed marked A. as a part of this petition.

She further represents that by the decease of her Father, she is the joint owner with Bessie Deas, David S. Garland, and John Spotswood Garland[3] of a tract of land on Flint River in the county of Genesee, in the state of Michigan, worth less than twenty thousand dollars to each divisee, which remains undivided, and in which her husband as she is advised has no interest.

She further represents that she is now a resident of the city of Lynchburg and did not as far as she has any knowledge do any act during the late war in violation of the laws & constitution of the United States.

She further represents that proceedings have been taken against her in the District or Circuit Court of the United States in the State of Michigan for the confiscation of her one undivided part of said tract of land, which she prays may be discontinued and she fully pardoned. She therefore respectfully asks that the benefit of a pardon may be granted her.[4]

Maria Louisa Longstreet.

ALS, DNA-RG94, Amnesty Papers (M1003, Roll 64), Va., Maria Louisa Longstreet.
    1. Longstreet (1827–1889), born at Fort Snelling, Minn., had married the future Confederate general in 1848. *Atlanta Constitution*, Dec. 31, 1889.
    2. Garland (1792–1861), a career army officer, was brevetted a brigadier general for his service during the Mexican War. Powell, *Army List*, 324.
    3. Mary E. Deas (b. c1827), Maria Longstreet's sister who resided in Flint, Mich., had also married a career soldier who became a Confederate officer. John S. Garland (c1824–1897) had been a regular army officer from 1847 until 1861 when he retired to Washington, D.C. David S. Garland is not further identified. Deas to Johnson, ca. Sept. 7, 1865, Amnesty Papers (M1003, Roll 17), Ga., Mary E. Deas, RG94, NA; 1870 Census, Mich., Genessee, Flint, 1st Ward, 39; D.C., Washington, 1st Ward, 260; Heitman, *Register*, 1: 363, 447; Washington, D.C., directories (1862–71).
    4. Within a few weeks Longstreet wrote a second pardon request on which Johnson pencilled: "Atty Genl will examine this case and issue pardon if his Judgement approve." The pardon was granted on September 21, 1865. Longstreet to Johnson, ca. Sept. 20, 1865, Amnesty Papers (M1003, Roll 64), Va., Maria Louisa Longstreet, RG94, NA; *House Ex. Docs.*, 40 Cong., 2 Sess., No. 16, p. 73 (Ser. 1330).

From Christopher G. Memminger[1]

Flat Rock [N.C.], Sep. 4, 1865.

Every Southern man is so deeply interested in the great questions of public policy which are now under your consideration, that it will scarcely be deemed officious in one of them to offer you some suggestions, if made solely with a view to the public good. Although I am not personally known to your Excellency, and at present am under the Ban of the Government, yet I feel assured that your judgment can easily discern the ring of truth, and will justly appreciate any effort to relieve the immense responsibilities which are now pressing upon you.

I take it for granted that the whole Southern Country accepts emancipation from Slavery as the condition of the African race; but neither the North nor the South have yet defined what is included in that emancipation. The boundaries are widely apart which mark on the one side, political equality with the white races, and on the other, a simple recognition of personal liberty. With our own race, ages have intervened between the advance from one of these boundaries to the other. No other people have been able to make equal progress, and many have not yet lost sight of the original point of starting. Great Britain has made the nearest approach; Russia has just started; and the other nations of Europe, after ages of struggle, are yet on the way from the one point to the other, none of them having yet advanced even to the position attained by England. The question now pending is, as to the station in this wide interval which shall be assigned to the African race. Does that race possess qualities, or does it exhibit any peculiar fitness which will dispense with the training which our own race has undergone, and authorize us at once to advance them to equal rights? It seems to me that this point has been decided already by the Laws of the free States. None of them have yet permitted equality, and the greater part assert this unfitness of the African by denying him any participation in political power.[2]

The Country then seems prepared to assign to this race an inferior condition; but the precise nature of that condition is yet to be defined, and also the Government which shall regulate it. I observe that you have already decided (and I think wisely) that the adjustment of the right of suffrage belongs to the State Governments, and should be left there. But this, as well as most of the other questions on this subject, rest upon the decision which shall be made upon the mode of organizing the labor of the African race. The Northern people seem generally to suppose that the simple emancipation from slavery will elevate the African to the condition of the white laboring classes; and that contracts and competition will secure the proper distribution of labor. They see, on the one hand, the owner of land wanting laborers, and on the other, a multitude of landless laborers without employment; and they naturally conclude that the law of demand and supply will adjust the exchange in the same manner as it would do at the North. But they are not aware of the attending circumstances which will disappoint these calculations.

The laborer in the Southern States, with his whole family, occupies the houses of his employer, built upon plantations widely separate. The employment of a laborer involves the employment and support of his whole family. Should the employer be discontent with any laborers and desire to substitute others in their place, before he can effect that object, he must proceed to turn out the first with their entire families into the woods, so as to have houses for their successors. Then he must encounter the uncertainty and delay in procuring other laborers; and also the hostility of the laborers on his own plantation, which would probably exhibit itself in sympathy with the ejected families and combinations against himself. Should this occur at any critical period of the crop, its entire loss would ensue. Nor would his prospect of relief from other plantations be hopeful. On them arrangements will have been made for the year, and the abstraction of laborers from them would result in new disorganization. The employer would thus be wholly at the mercy of the laborer.

It may be asked why the laborer is more likely to fail in the performance of his contract than his employer. The reasons are obvious. The employer by the possession of property affords a guarantee by which the law can compel his performance. The laborer can offer no such guarantee, and nothing is left to control him but a sense of the obligation of the contract.

The force of this remedy depends upon the degree of conscientiousness and intelligence attained by the bulk of a people. It is well known that one of the latest and most important fruits of civilization is a perception of the obligation of contracts. Even in cultivated nations, the Law must be sharpened at all points to meet the efforts to escape from a contract which has become onerous; and nothing short of a high sense of commercial honor and integrity will secure its strict performance. It would be vain, under any circumstances, to count upon such performance from an ignorant and uneducated population. But where that population is from constitution or habit peculiarly subject to the vices of an inferior race, nothing short of years of education and training can bring about that state of moral rectitude and habitual self-constraint which would secure the regular performance of contracts. In the present case, to these general causes must be added the natural indolence of the African race, and the belief now universal among them that they are released from any obligation to labor. Under these circumstances the employer would have so little inducement to risk his Capital in the hands of the laborer, or to advance money for food and working animals in cultivating a Crop which, when reaped, would be at the mercy of the laborers, that he will certainly endeavor to make other arrangements. The effect will be the abandonment of the negro to his indolent habits, and the probable relapse of large portions of the Country into its original forest condition. The two races, instead of exchanging mutual good offices, will inflict mutual evil on each other; and the final result must be the destruction or removal of the inferior race.

The appropriate remedy for these evils evidently points to the necessity of training the inferior race; and we are naturally led to look to the means which would be employed by our own race for the same purpose. The African is virtually in the condition of the youth, whose inexperience and want of skill unfit him for the privileges of manhood. He is subjected to the guidance and control of one better informed. He is bound as an apprentice to be trained and directed; and is under restraint until he is capable of discharging the duties of manhood.

Such, it seems to me, is the proper instrumentality which should now be applied to the African race. The vast body are substantially in a state of minority. They have been all their lives subject to the control and direction of another; and at present are wholly incapable of self-government. Alongside of them are their former masters, fully capable of guiding and instructing them, needing their labor, and not yet alienated from them in feeling. The great point to be attained is the generous application by the one of his superior skill and resources, and their kindly reception by the other. This can be effected only by some relation of acknowledged dependence. Let the untrained and incapable African be placed under indentures of apprenticeship to his former master, under such regulations as will secure both parties from wrong; and whenever the apprentice shall have obtained the habits and knowledge requisite for discharging the duties of a citizen, let him then be advanced from youth to manhood and be placed in the exercise of a citizen's rights, and the enjoyment of the privileges attending such a change.

I have no means of procuring here a Copy of the Laws passed by the British Parliament on this subject, for the West India Colonies.[3] They are founded upon this idea of apprenticeship. Such an adjustment of the relations of the two races would overcome many difficulties, and enable the emancipation experiment to be made under the most favorable circumstances. The experience of the British colonies would afford valuable means for improving the original plans; and no doubt the practical common sense of our people can, by amending their errors, devise the best possible solution of the problems and afford the largest amount of good to the African race.

The only question which would remain would be as to the Government which should enact and administer these Laws. Unquestionably the jurisdiction under the Constitution of the United States belongs to the States. This fact will most probably disincline the Congress to an early recognition of the Southern States upon their original footing under the Constitution, from the apprehension of harsh measures towards the former slaves. The difficulty would be obviated, if a satisfactory adjustment could be previously made of the footing upon which the two races are to stand. If by general agreement an apprentice system could be adopted in some form which would be satisfactory as well as obligatory, it seems to me that most of the evils now existing, or soon to arise, would be remedied; and that a fair start would be made in the proper direction. The details of the plan could be adjusted from the experience of the British Colonies; and if it should result in proving the capacity of the African race to stand upon the same platform with the white man, I doubt not but that the South will receive that conclusion with satisfaction fully equal to that of any other section.

C G Memminger.

LS, DLC-JP.
1. Memminger (1803–1888), a German-born Charleston attorney and antebellum state legislator, had served as Confederate secretary of the treasury (1861–64). Wakelyn, *BDC*.
2. On the eve of the war most northern states had restrictions on black suffrage and civil rights, and some had exclusion laws on black immigration as well. The latter were repealed between 1863 and 1866. James M. McPherson, *Ordeal by Fire: The Civil War and Reconstruction* (New York, 1982), 80–81, 467.
3. The Abolition of Slavery Act of 1833 allowed for an apprenticeship period of four

to six years during which blacks would work for their former masters for housing, clothing, and food, with a supplementary wage to be paid for over forty-five hours work in a week. In addition, the owners were to be compensated for the loss of the slaves. Cyril Hamshere, *The British in the Caribbean* (Cambridge, 1972), 147.

To George H. Thomas

Washington, D.C., Sept 4 1865.

I have information of the most reliable character[1] that the negro troops stationed at Greenville, Tenn,[2] are under little or no restraint and are committing depredations throughout the country, domineering over and in fact running the white people out of the neighborhood. Much of this is said to be attributable to the officers who countenance and rather encourage the negroes in their insolence, & in their disorderly conduct. The negro soldiery take possession of, and occupy property in the town at discretion, and have even gone so far as to have taken my own house and converted it into a rendezvous for male and female negroes who have been congregated there, in fact making it a common negro brothel.[3] It was bad enough to be taken by traitors and converted into a rebel hospital, but a negro whore house is infinitely worse. As to the value of the property I care nothing for that, *but* the reflection that it has been converted into a sink of pollution, and that by our own forces, is, I confess, humiliating in the extreme.

The people of East Tennessee above all others are the last who should be afflicted with the outrages of the negro soldiery. It is a poor reward for their long and continued devotion to the country through all its perils. It would be far better to remove every negro soldier from East Tennessee and leave the people to protect themselves as best they may. I hope you will at once give instructions to every officer in command of negro troops to put them under strict discipline and reduce them to order. I also hope as suggested in a former dispatch[4] that you will relieve that part of the state from negro troops as soon as practicable. If they are not needed for the public service in your Department let them be sent where they are, or if not needed at all it would be better that they be taken to the proper points and mustered out of service and thereby reduce the enormous expense of the Government.

Can't instructions be given Gen Gillam[5] to attend to and see that proper discipline and order are without delay restored and enforced.[6]

Andrew Johnson

Tel, DNA-RG107, Tels. Sent, President, Vol. 2 (1865).

1. The informant may have been James W. Harold, an old acquaintance who had earlier written David T. Patterson "in reference to the conduct of colored troops stationed in East Tennessee." The President assured Harold that "steps have been taken to correct the evil you complain of." Johnson to Harold, Sept. 6, 1865, Tels. Sent, President, Vol. 2 (1865), RG107, NA.

2. Both the 14th and the 40th Inf., USCT, had been garrisoned in Greeneville

throughout the summer of 1865. Dyer, *Compendium*, 472; *Greeneville New Era*, July 8, 1865.

3. Thomas denied this rumor, stating that "the house is now occupied by a white family" placed there by Patterson. See Thomas to Johnson, Sept. 18, 1865, Johnson Papers, LC.

4. Two days earlier the President had asked about the removal of "the colored troops now at Greeneville either to Bristol or down the Mississippi, where their services are more needed." Thomas responded that he would "order them either to Georgia or Alabama" as soon as he had heard from Generals Steedman and Wood. Johnson to Thomas, Sept. 2, 1865, Tels. Sent, President, Vol. 2 (1865); Thomas to Johnson, Sept. 4, 1865, Tels. Recd., President, Vol. 4 (1865–66), RG107, NA.

5. Alvan C. Gillem, commander of the district of East Tennessee.

6. See Thomas to Johnson, Sept. 7, 1865, and Johnson to Thomas, Sept. 8, 1865.

From Lizinka C. Ewell

Warrenton [Va.]   Tuesday [Sept.] 5th [1865][1]

My dear Friend

On reaching here today with a terrible headache I found Hattie[2] had sent to Washington a letter from my Agent in St. Louis saying the District-Attorney Mr Glover[3] declared the order of the Attorney-General *too vague* & said he would not relinquish my property without a special order or an explicit order from the *President himself*. I know I am not presuming on your friendship in asking for such an order & would return at once to Washington for the purpose but am really sick. Remember our old friendship & for its sake pardon the trouble I am constrained to give you—& *please* let some one write me what further steps I must take (if any) in this matter.[4]

Lizinka C. Ewell

ALS, DNA-RG60, Office of Atty. Gen., Lets. Recd., President.

1. The month and year are supplied, based upon the endorsement found on the cover sheet of the letter.

2. Her daughter, Harriot C. Brown.

3. William N. Grover (b. *c*1818), U.S. District Attorney for the eastern district of Missouri, had been directed by his Washington superiors "to discontinue the proceeding" against Mrs. Ewell. 1860 Census, Mo., St. Louis, 5th Ward, 208; *U.S. Off. Reg.* (1865); J. Hubley Ashton to Ewell, Sept. 2, 1865, Office of Atty. Gen., Lets. Sent, Vol. E (M699, Roll 10), RG60, NA.

4. Lizinka's letter was referred to Attorney General Speed, who the next day wrote Grover that proceedings against Mrs. Ewell were dismissed "upon her paying *all* the costs." Speed to Grover, Sept. 6, 1865, ibid. See Ewell to Johnson, Dec. 4, 1865.

From Edwin W. Hickman[1]

Nashville Tenn.   Sept. 5th, 1865.

Dear Sir:

I know you must be worried by the numerous complaints made by the *people* of this section of Tennessee, but respectfully beg your attention a moment.

The *people* are setling down and trying to become good and loyal Citizens, by conforming as best they can to the new order of things, *but they are not permitted to do it*. There is in Nashville an Institution known as the "Freedman's Bureau" that is giving more trouble than all other things together. Allmost every household is living in terror on account of the dictatorial and tyranical acts of Genl. Fisk and his subordinates. *I write knowingly*. My house has been entered as often as four different times within a short period, by armed soldiers invariably accompanied by Contrabands, the soldiers in every instance acting under orders from the "Bureau" upon silly and false charges made by contraband negroes. Now I respectfully ask what can be done in the premises. Resistance by the people would be wrong. You, and you alone, are competent to save the people from the oppression practiced upon them. This it strikes me, can be done by the prompt removal of "Genl Fisk," or by a Proclamation from you defining and regulating the power of those who manage the "Freedman's Bureau." By doing this you will draw to your support your old Democratic friends in this State, and relieve the great suffering of the people.[2]

Edwin W. Hickman

ALS, DNA-RG105, Records of the Commr., Lets. Recd. (M752, Roll 16).

1. Hickman (c1821-fl1880) was a lawyer whose combined estate before the war amounted to $43,350. 1860 Census, Tenn., Davidson, 18th Dist., 50; (1880), 77th Enum. Dist., 28.

2. On September 13 the President's secretary referred Hickman's letter to General Howard, who in turn forwarded it to Gen. Clinton B. Fisk. Ten days afterward Fisk sent the original letter back to Howard, along with a retraction reportedly written and signed by Hickman. In the latter document Hickman stated that he had misunderstood the facts and that actually Fisk had never authorized the entering of Hickman's house, but it had been done by another official whom Fisk had just removed from duty. All of the documents relative to the case were returned to the President's office on September 27.

From William P. Johnson

Columbia, Texas, September 5th 1865

Dear Brother:

I now sit myself down to ask the favor of you to look into the case of my friend and Neighbor Mr. John Adriance[1] in his application for a pardon. He never was a Secessionist at heart, and never has persecuted a Union man since the beginning of the war, or said any one ought to be hung or shot because they were Union Men, or refused to aid or assist a man because he was a Union man, and he has always been a good Citizen and as Loyal as he dared to be and save his life, and as a Gentleman no man fills the measure better, and as a true friend he is unsurpassed by any man in the Country, and the best test of it is his readiness to comply with the terms of the law. As a neighbor he is kind and obliging, and he commands the respect of all who know him. As a Merchant and Factor he is considered strictly honest, and I hope such a man may find favor with you. Brother, I ask you to grant Mr. Adriance a free pardon he being my true friend and benefactor in my time of greatest need under the most, trying circumstances, and your most favorable and earliest consideration will very much oblige your friend and Brother.

Sir I have the honor to say that I remain your friend and brother until death.

William P. Johnson

P.S.—This leaves myself and family in good health at this time, and I hope this may find you and family in Good health. Give my Love to sister and all of your children. I remain as above stated.

W. P. Johnson

I would be glad if you could send Mr. Adriance's pardon by Adams Express addressed to me at Columbia to the care of Mr. Adriance as we have no mails and may not have one very soon. Your compliance will much oblige.

W.P.J.

P.S.—Sept. 21st—Since writing the above, my friend A. Underwood[2] has received the Governor's recommendation for a pardon, and he wishes me to have his petition favorably considered by you, and I should be glad if you would be pleased to send his and Adriances together as they are both business men, and they are at a dead stand, untill they are pardoned and we the people are in great need of their services as business men in our neighborhood, and having to [do] without their services puts us to a great nonplus in our daily dealings in our ordinary business, and brother your compliance will ⟨not only⟩ much oblige me, but the neighborhood almost to a single man, and I know if you knew them that you would not hesitate a moment to extend your pardon, and that without delay, and if you may please to send a pardon you can send them together by the same Express to me in care of Mr. J. Adriance.[3]

William P. Johnson

CopyS, TxU-A, John Adriance Papers.

1. Born in New York, Adriance (1818–1903) owned a Columbia mercantile firm and cotton warehouse used by the Confederate commissary department. Amnesty Papers (M1003, Roll 52), Tex., John Adriance, RG94, NA; Webb et al., *Handbook of Texas*, 1: 10. See Adriance to Johnson, Oct. 26, 1865.

2. Boston native Ammon Underwood (1810–1887) was a Columbia merchant and cotton planter who had served as postmaster (1836–45). Amnesty Papers (M1003, Roll 55), Tex., A. Underwood, RG94, NA; Webb et al., *Handbook of Texas*, 2: 817–18.

3. Both men received their pardon under the 13th exception to Johnson's Amnesty Proclamation on December 8, 1865. *House Ex. Docs.*, 39 Cong., 2 Sess., No. 116, pp. 54, 72 (Ser. 1293).

From John Livingston[1]

Washington   Sept 5 1865

Mr President.

I very respectfully lay before you my case in as few words as possible. I was paroled at Greensboro N.C April 26 & on my arrival in Richmond, took the amnesty oath. My rank was that of Major & I do not come within any of the exceptions of the proclamation of May the 29th.

I am on my way to New Orleans, the place of my residence, to resume the practice of the law, my sole dependency now, for the support of myself & family. But I find that by act of Congress I cannot resume my profession in the Federal Courts. This act requires me to take an oath that I have not aided or assisted the late rebellion.[2] In every other walk of life individuals can pursue their vocations. In my judgment it was not the intention of Congress, nor is the policy of the administration to make any distinctions between pursuits in life.

The pardoning power is conferred by the Constitution upon the President. It is the prerogative of mercy established by the organic law. Whenever exercised it remits all penalties for the violation of laws & restores the recipient to all his rights. It is a power which cannot be interferred with by Congress. A pardon, or the amnesty oath places the individual in his status before the war. I did practice law in the Federal Courts before the war. That was a right I enjoyed—that was the profession I had adopted. This right, now important to me is withheld. Property in the possession of the United States is restored to the recipient of a pardon by virtue of the organic law. The right of suffrage forfeited by rebellion is restored by the amnesty proclamation.

His Honor Judge Durell of La refuses to permit attys to practice unless the test oath is taken. In an interview with the Attorney General he informed me that His Honor Judge Triggs of Tennessee had permitted them to practice without the oath, but the Judges generally have refused. The Attorney General considers the right to practice law a mere privilege which Congress may take away or not. I consider it a natural right of which I cannot be deprived. He was disposed to let the Courts decide. In Louisiana the Court has decided adversely & I am excluded. In Leigh's[3] case Munford, Va page 486[4] the Court held that an atty could not be compelled to take the anti-duelling oath, as he was not an officer in any sense of the word—that practising law was a simple pursuit & that the oath could not be exacted. Now as all other classes are permitted to follow their calling it seems hard that attys should be prevented.

I regret very much that I cannot remain to have personal interview with the President. At the suggestion of the Hon The Secretary of the

Treasury I send in this communication, and most respectfully ask for relief if it can consistently be granted.[5]

J. Livingston

ALS, DNA-RG60, Office of Atty. Gen., Lets. Recd., President.

1. Livingston (c1820-fl1886) served in several posts as a quartermaster during the Civil War. New Orleans directories (1861–86); CSR, RG109, NA.

2. Congress on January 24, 1865, had prohibited attorneys from practicing in Federal courts unless they took an oath affirming that they had never taken part in or supported the rebellion. Fairman, *Reconstruction and Reunion*, 58.

3. Benjamin W. Leigh (1781–1849) was a Virginia legislator and U.S. Senator (1835–36). *DAB*.

4. William Munford (1775–1825), a Virginia legislator and poet, produced ten volumes as reporter for the Virginia supreme court of appeals. The opinion delivered in Leigh's case appears in *Virginia Reports*, 1 Munford 468. *DAB*.

5. Johnson forwarded this letter to Speed, who responded that "the President is not able to give any further relief than he has already extended to you by his pardon," and that only the courts could decide whether an attorney would be allowed to practice "without taking the oath referred to." He added that if Johnson did decide in Livingston's favor, "the Courts would be under no obligation to follow his opinion." Speed to Livingston, Sept. 14, 1865, Office of Atty. Gen., Lets. Sent, Vol. E (M699, Roll 10), RG60, NA. See Samuel B. Maxey to Johnson, Oct. 24, 1865.

From Isaac E. Morse[1]

New Orleans   Sept 5 1865

Dear Sir

I perceive that many gentlemen have gone from the south with a view of aiding in the reconstruction of the Union &c.

Perhaps the idea I have may not have occurred to you & if favorably received would facilitate this consummation most devoutly to be wished for.

You no doubt recollect a spirited debate between Rhett & John Q Adams in which the great statesman of the north in reply to a question from Rhett said that the only way slavery could be legally abolished (without the consent of the States) was by the war making power.[2] That is, the right which either of the belligerent parties have to destroy, take & dispose of the property captured as a means of successful warfare, ought to settle forever this question.

In regard to Louisiana, there was a popular majority before the war opposed to secession & I think there can be no doubt that if submitted to the people there would be a large majority of the people who would recognize the end of slavery as a fixed fact & who would be glad to see La resume her position in the union under the new order of things—without reference to the action of the late convention in this state which was only composed of a few parishes. The President might safely assume that the war making power had abolished slavery & that the states disposed to recognize that fact might elect their members of congress & other officers.

Besides the enormous expense the army of the U.S in this state particularly are not only useless but are absolutely injurious. Constant collisions are of frequent occurrence & numbers of persons have been shot (among others an officer of the U S navy) by the negro sentinels who seem disposed to exercise their authority without that discretion which belongs to the white race.[3]

I think the black population with their freedom acknowledged may be safely left to themselves, & the kindly influence of the white population.

The idea that freedmen's bureaus & all the concomitant paraphernalia should be necessary to protect them by the same persons who think that tho' unable to manage their own concerns, they ought to have a voice in the state is simply ridiculous.

As a lover of the union a democrat from instinct & princple and one perhaps as well acquainted with the sentiment of my native state, I assure you that your announcement that slavery no longer existing, the people of Louisiana were restored to all their constitutional rights, would be hailed with joy by a large majority of the people & La would resume her position & association particularly with the people of the *west* with whom her fate is indissolubly connected.

Whatever you may think of these views, I know that our association on the same committees, will enable you to do justice to the motives which have inspired.

Isaac. E. Morse

ALS, DNA-RG105, Records of the Commr., Lets. Recd. from Executive Mansion.

1. Former congressman from Louisiana.

2. On April 15, 1842, during Robert Barnwell Rhett's tenure in Congress, Adams asserted that either the President or the commander of the army could free slaves when a state of war existed. *Congressional Globe*, 27 Cong., 2 Sess., 429.

3. Subsequent research does not substantiate this allegation. Taylor, *La. Reconstructed*, 67–68.

From Francis P. Blair, Sr.

Silver Spring [Md.]   6 Sep '65

My Dear Sir:

I called to see you on Saturday, but sunk under the heat before my turn came. It was to say that one of the counsel of Jeff Davis[1] desired me to communicate a wish that the question of law, arising in a state's secession, as affecting the action of one of its citizens making war on the United States should be adjudged by the Chief Justice on the Supreme Court—the question being brought up on habeas corpus served on behalf of Jeff Davis. I presume there is no doubt the Supreme Court would decide against the right of secession—and if so, it would have a salutary effect as having that Dept. of the Govt coinciding with the Executive on that question which has so agitated the nation. Chase might decide otherwise, as he holds the states out of the union & so mere belligerents.[2]

F. P. Blair

ALS, DLC-F. P. Blair Family Papers.
    1. Presumably George Shea (1826–1895), corporation attorney for New York and co-counsel for Davis, who visited the Blairs in early September 1865. *Appleton's Cyclopaedia*; W. Stewart Wallace, comp., *A Dictionary of North American Authors Deceased Before 1950* (Detroit, 1968[1951]), 410; William E. Smith, *The Francis Preston Blair Family in Politics* (2 vols., New York, 1933), 2: 325.
    2. Blair errs in his analysis of Chief Justice Salmon P. Chase's position on Reconstruction. In *Texas v. White*, Chase declared that the Constitution provided for an "indestructible Union, composed of indestructible States." Although Congress had a duty to reorganize their governments, no state had ever ceased to be a part of the Union. Frederick J. Blue, *Salmon P. Chase: A Life in Politics* (Kent, Ohio, 1987), 272–73.

From Hugh Kennedy

City Hall [New Orleans]   6th day of Septber 1865

Sir,

The day following that on which I last had the honor of addressing you,[1] we managed to get out the first number of "The Southern Star," copies of which were that day, the 2nd inst., duly mailed for the Executive and the different departments.

I now beg leave to enclose you the number for last Sunday, and one or two editorials which I have furnished among others during the week.[2] I have promised Jewell[3] the publisher, to give him all the literary & official aid in my power, and so far as I am able to judge at this remote point, I will endeavor to keep the paper in strong supporting line of your policy, state and national.

You will see already it is surpassed by no Southern, and by but few Northern journals in substantial patronage or handsome appearance; and as the first out & out, uncompromising Johnson democratic organ in the country, so far as I am aware, I think it does no discredit to the cause.

I had hoped President, that I should not again have been compelled to complain of the course Genl. Canby seems to have determined upon persistently following, either by orders from the War department, or else, as I cannot help believing, in conjunction with others, and as part of a plan of reducing Louisiana into a species of satrapy wherein the friends for your person & policy shall have neither voice nor influence.

I enclose you copy of a strange letter which I received from him on the 5th ins[4] in reply to one of mine of the 24th ult which Govr. Wells informed me he had transmitted for your consideration.[5]

I mentioned before President that I was resolved not to be drawn into unprofitable controversies by such men and notwithstanding the provocation in this, I shall adhere to my resolution. My answers to Genl. Canby I send you copy of also herewith.[6]

The opponents of Govr. Wells and the civil government are represented as acting on the principle that if they can break me down or
intrigue me out of office they can then extort their own terms from the
Governor, forgetting or not dreaming of such a thing as proper as my
perfect willingness to surrender my most responsible & important place
at any moment President you deem it necessary for the public interests,
or when one better qualified than myself presents for preferment.

No combination, however homogeneous or incongruous, it may be
under the manipulation of Genl. Canby & Hahn[7] and their associates,
or others shall *force* resignation upon me; and as my administration of
New Orleans has the approval of every upright and impartial citizen, I
feel I can rely, when I leave office, upon the justice of the Executive to
sustain me for my official conduct.

Govr. Wells writes most encouragingly from North Louisiana, and
assures me that the best feelings are every where manifested for the
national & state administrations. I expect him back about the end of
this week or beginning of next.

Our City is orderly & healthy in a remarkable degree.

Hu. Kennedy   Mayor

ALS, DLC-JP.

1. See Kennedy to Johnson, Sept. 1, 1865.
2. Not found.
3. Edwin L. Jewell.
4. Gen. Edward R.S. Canby had asserted that the federal government should not
formally surrender its rights to confiscated property until a state had been fully restored
to the Union. However, in consideration of the "commercial and financial" significance
of New Orleans' wharves and levees, he would recommend "to the War Department"
that it relinquish control of all but its permanent reservations "at the earliest practicable
moment." Canby to Kennedy, Sept. 4, 1865, Johnson Papers, LC.
5. See J. Madison Wells to Johnson, Aug. 25, 1865, *Johnson Papers*, 8: 655–56.
6. Kennedy had replied that, as mayor, he had "faithfully and undeviatingly adhered
to the verbal instructions" of the President, and was therefore "entitled to at least respectful consideration," rather than "rude or contumelious nullification." Kennedy to Canby,
Sept. 6, 1865, Johnson Papers, LC.
7. Michael Hahn.

From Henrietta Lee[1]

Shepherds Town [W. Va.]   Sept: 6th 65

It is with the utmost timidity that I address a few lines to President
Johnson in behalf of my son, Brig: Gen: Edwin G. Lee of the late
Confederate Army, who is now in Canada, where in November last he
went by the advice of his Physician's for the *sole* purpose of trying a
cold dry climate to restore his broken health.[2] He is very anxious to
return to Virginia and yield his allegience in *good faith*, to the United
States Gov: I have been informed that some weeks ago his application
for pardon had been sent on to the Att: General. My son is a Democrat;

has always been one, as was his Grand-father, my father,[3] and his Uncle, the late Henry Bedinger[4] formerly Minister to Denmark under the Administration of Mr. Buchanan, and once a member of Congress from this District. Perhaps President Johnson may have known him, and have been his friend, and that kindly feelings towards my brother, may influence him to grant the boon I ask. Most earnestly I appeal for his return, and supplicate President Johnson to favour the appeal of One, who now has nothing left to comefort her, but the society of her children. My home, the house which my Father built, as a retreat, after the Independance of our Country had been achieved, and which his good and true sword aided to win; That dear, revered old pile, which Time and the elements spared, was destroyed by order of General Hunter,[5] and what was once so fair, now stands a frightful mass of blackened ruins, "Silent unroofed and desolate, all its loved tenants gone." My children are scattered, and now, my earnest desire is to have the mournful pleasure of attending and ministering to my first-born, in his feeble and uncertain health. Hoping for an early and favourable response, I shall enclose this to my husband's relative Admiral S. P. Lee[6] and request him to deliver it.[7]

Henrietta Lee

ALS, DNA-RG94, Amnesty Papers (M1003, Roll 64), Va., Edwin G. Lee.

1. Lee (1810-*fl*1895) was the wife of Edmund Jennings Lee, first cousin of Robert E. Lee. Edmund Jennings Lee, M.D., *Lee of Virginia, 1642–1892* (Philadelphia, 1895), 468–69; "Notes and Queries," *VMHB*, 27 (1918): 406.

2. Edwin Gray Lee (*c*1835–1870), whose nomination as brigadier the Confederate Senate never confirmed, suffered from a chronic respiratory ailment and had taken a leave of absence from the army. His younger brother later asserted, however, that the Virginia colonel had actually been sent to Canada on a secret mission, a charge that Lee himself denied. Warner, *Gray*; Lee, *Lee of Virginia*, 510; Edwin G. Lee to Johnson, July 1, 1865, Amnesty Papers (M1003, Roll 64), Va., Edwin G. Lee, RG94, NA.

3. Daniel Bedinger. Not otherwise identified.

4. Bedinger (1812–1858) had served in the House with Johnson before Pierce appointed him minister resident to Denmark. *BDAC*.

5. David Hunter had ordered "Bedford," the Bedinger homestead, to be burned in July 1864. Millard K. Bushong, *A History of Jefferson County, West Virginia* (Charles Town, 1941), 174–76.

6. Francis P. Blair's son-in-law, Samuel Phillips Lee (1812–1897), retired from the U.S. Navy in 1873, after nearly fifty years of continuous service. *DAB*.

7. Johnson pardoned Lee on July 26, 1866. Amnesty Papers (M1003, Roll 64), Va., Edwin G. Lee, RG94, NA.

From Rolfe S. Saunders

Oakland, Md.   Sept. 6 1865

To the President:

My newspaper project I think is *complete* and we will give you the aid you need from West Tennessee.[1]

If you can, grant the Pardons of Robt L. Caruthers[2] & R. C. Brinkley.[3] My reward is that I *know* them both to be your earnest friends & will lend all their influence to sustain you. They regard it as *our only hope. This I know.*

I would not have you depart from your designs & the path of duty to serve any friend of mine. *I know their* feeling. I know that when Sam Tate spoke to Brinkley to raise money to start an Administration paper in Memphis, he at once responded that he would "Cheerfully contribute as much as any body else." I know they are both honest & earnest.

When I commenced my canvass for Congress Caruthers advised me to sustain you fully & without reserve. He said all depended on your being sustained & to make no half-way work of it.

Rolfe S Saunders.

ALS, DLC-JP.

1. Probably the acquisition of the *Memphis Commercial* by Saunders, John Heart, and Leonidas Trousdale. *Nashville Press and Times*, Oct. 23, 1865; *Memphis Directory* (1866), 125, 135.

2. See Caruthers to Johnson, Sept. 28, 1865.

3. Memphis banker and railroad speculator Robert C. Brinkley (1816–1878) received his pardon within two weeks, on September 14, 1865. O. F. Vedder, *History of the City of Memphis and Shelby County Tennessee* (Syracuse, N.Y., 1888), 2: 191–94; Stanley J. Folmsbee et al., *History of Tennessee* (4 vols., New York, 1960), 3: 109; Amnesty Papers (M1003, Roll 48), Tenn., R. C. Brinkley, RG94, NA.

From Hugh Kennedy

City Hall [New Orleans]   7th day of Septber 1865

President,

General Canby is determined that there shall be no quiet in his department. Last evening on the meeting of the new school Board, for the reorganization of the Public Schools for the next scholastic year, the order as published in the slip herewith annexed,[1] was handed in by one of his Staff, and all proceedings of the Board suspended until he had satisfied himself of "some allegations touching the loyalty of members of the Board."

How long this suspension will last, or what inconvenience meantime may be caused to the Schools, is of course with the General alone to determine.

That you may President, understand this whole school matter,—altho' I do not think the schools underlie the motive for the General's *coup d'etat*—I will place before you the following statement.

When I acceded to the Mayoralty in May last, I found I became thereby *ex officio* president of the School Board. On its first meeting—the meetings—were monthly—I found that the Board consisted of fifteen persons, exclusive of the presiding officer. Of these eight were then in public office, four others were so recently, and three were citizens unconnected with office. Teachers were removable at pleasure, without assignment of any cause and this led to perpetual & indecent electioneering, in which decent, modest and obscure persons, however deserving, had little encouragement.

I abolished the Board and the system, substituting twenty four respectable and well known citizens, unconnected with politics, for fifteen, on the Board, leaving them to elect a president from among their number, and excluding the Mayor, to give whom any direct connection with the Board was to expose him to the imputation of acting from interested motives. I also attach hereto copy of the school ordinance[2] which I approved for the future government of an primary educational establishment.

In selecting men to constitute the New Board, the considerations which weighed with me were character, moral standing, intellectual culture and loyalty, and I sought to obtain from the diversified walks of life the required number, wholly irrespective of the personal relations they have to myself in any other consideration than their fitness by the above standard.

Classified, the new Board stands thus:

4 Physicians
1 Apothecary
3 Presidents of Insurance companies
1 Notary Public
4 Lawyers
2 Mechanics
1 Factor
1 Spirit & Wine Importer
1 Editor of the Southern Star
4 Wholesale Grocers
1 Ship Agent
1 Capitalist

I tried to embrace in this list persons who represented, and measurably, in accepting, guaranteed the good behavior of influential classes; and if one or two of them participated in the rebellion, of which I have no knowledge, my reasons for their appointment I am prepared to vindicate.[3]

They are universally admitted to be, all things considered, the best Board of School directors ever chosen here.

Hu. Kennedy   Mayor

ALS, DLC-JP.

1. Kennedy enclosed an article that contained the text of an order from Gen. Edward R.S. Canby postponing the school board's election of a superintendent of public schools. After receiving the communication the board immediately adjourned. *New Orleans Picayune*, Sept. 6, 1865.

2. Ibid. Kennedy had endorsed the ordinance on August 26, 1865.

3. On September 16 Kennedy angrily reported that Canby had two days earlier rescinded his order postponing the election of a school superintendent. William O. Rogers
was subsequently elected to that position. Kennedy to Johnson, Sept. 16, 1865, Johnson
Papers, LC. See Carl Schurz to Johnson, Sept. 15, 23, 1865., *Advice*, 135–49.

From Wallace S. McElwain[1]

Washington D.C.   Sept 7th 65.

I beg leave to call your attention to the following facts.

The Cahawba Iron Works of which I am proprietor consists of about
one thousand (1,000) acres of land, situated in Jefferson Co. State of
Alabama, and on the same one Furnace for the manufacture of Pig Iron.

The Buildings and most of the machinery and Tools were destroyed
by the forces under Genl Wilson[2] on the 29th of March last during his
march through that State.

I am a practical mechanic and worked for and made my property. I
moved South in 1859 and my property being there at the commencement of the rebelion I remained there to take care of it.

I have never held any office, nor have I ever been a candidate for one.
I was opposed to secession, and during the existance of the rebelion I
endeavoured to conduct myself as became a citizen. I was exempt from
the Army as a skilled mechanic, and afterwards detailed as such. I sold
to the socalled Confederate States Goverment about one half of the Iron
made in order to secure the detail of such employees as would enable
me to carry on the business to support my family. The socalled Confederate States Goverment never had any claim upon my property nor do
I owe it anything.

The property is probably over Twenty thousand dollars in value but
I have liabilities, to pay, which would reduce my resources below that
amount. But I am anxious to resume business without risk of being
interfered with by Goverment Agents, some of whom claim the right
to take possession of property so situated.

I have taken the Amnesty Oath, and am willing to take any further
obligation of fidelity to the National Goverment, and to comport myself
in all respects as a loyal citizen. I respectfully request from your Excellency the necessary documents to protect me in the possession of my
property and the prosecution of business for the support of myself and
family.[3]

W. S. McElwain

ALS, DNA-RG94, Amnesty Papers (M1003, Roll 7), Ala., Wallace S. McElwain.
    1. Before the war McElwain (c1832-fl1882) was an iron manufacturer at Holly
Springs, Miss. From 1866 to 1872 he supervised the rebuilt Cahaba Iron Works and
afterwards was a clerk in Chattanooga. 1870 Census, Ala., Jefferson, T17R2W, 1; *Chattanooga Directory* (1882), 234; Ethel Armes, *The Story of Coal and Iron in Alabama*
(Birmingham, 1910), 164–67, 196–99.
    2. James H. Wilson.

3. McElwain was pardoned on September 11, 1865. *House Ex. Docs.*, 40 Cong., 2 Sess., No. 16, p. 25 (Ser. 1330).

Order re *Freedmen's Bureau*[1]

Executive Office, September 7, 1865

It is hereby ORDERED, that so much of the Executive Order bearing date the 7th day of June, 1865,[2] as made it the duty of all officers of the Treasury Department, military officers, and all others in the service of the United States, to turn over to the authorized officers of the Bureau of Refugees, Freedmen, and Abandoned Lands all funds collected by tax or otherwise for the benefit of refugees or freedmen, or accruing from abandoned lands or property set apart for their use, be, and the same is hereby suspended.[3]

Andrew Johnson, Pres.

CopyS, DNA-RG56, Misc. Div., Claims for Cotton and Captured and Abandoned Property.

1. Johnson approved this order against the advice of McCulloch, who provided the text but recommended that "Perhaps under the circumstances, instead of signing the order, it might be as well for you to address me a letter requesting me to instruct our agents not to pay over the money in their hands to the Freedmen's Bureau." McCulloch to Johnson, Sept. 7, 1865, Johnson Papers, LC.

2. The Executive Order was actually dated June 2 but was promulgated from the War Department five days later as General Orders Number 110. Richardson, *Messages*, 6: 340, 349; *House Ex. Docs.*, 39 Cong., 2 Sess., No. 11, pp. 41–42 (Ser. 1255).

3. This order, forwarded by McCulloch to his agents on September 14, was issued in response to Gen. O. O. Howard's Circular Number 13 (dated July 28) for land redistribution, which was rescinded by order of Johnson on September 12. McFeely, *Yankee Stepfather*, 103–35 passim.

From Thomas Shankland[1]

Washington   Sept. 7, 1865—

The President is aware that I have been actively his friend, that I came on from New York, expressly to have a talk, which on the 6th of March he expressed a wish to have with me. I have been here ten days, and as a Northern Man, I have learned that I had no business at the White House. A good Southern President has no time for Northern Men or interests. His Son in Law, appears to be doing a good business,[2] but it does not profit the North. The Administration seems to be perpetuating the Sectional and Geographical, limits and feelings of the people, and the great battle of Freedom, is still to be fought out. When the President remarked to me, on the 6th of March "that things were going wrong here" I agreed with him, in sentiment, and find no reason to change my views.

Thos Shankland

President Andrew Johnson Pardoning Rebels at the White House
Harper's Weekly, October 14, 1865

ALS, DLC-JP.
  1. New York attorney.
  2. Probably an allusion to David T. Patterson's unofficial role as presidential advisor. See Johnson to James W. Harold, Sept. 6, 1865, and Johnson to Edward H. East, Sept. 7, 1865, Tels. Sent, President, Vol. 2 (1865), RG107, NA.

From George H. Thomas

Nashville   Sept 7th 1865

Your telegram of the 4th instant just received, directing the withdrawal of the negro troops from East Tennessee. I have given the necessary orders but have to report that I have no white troops to send to East Tennessee to preserve the peace. Complaints reach me almost daily of difficulty between the returned Rebels and loyal citizens either in defiance of the civil authorities or that the civil authority is inefficient and does not act. The Negro troops in Tennessee can be reduced still more by sending them to Georgia & Alabama to replace a like number of white troops who are clamorous to be mustered out of service.

Geo H Thomas   Maj Genl

Tel, DLC-JP.

From George A. Trenholm

Fort Pulaski Georgia   September 7 1865

Sir,

After transmitting my petition[1] for pardon to your Excellency, I studiously refrained from further efforts to excite a special interest in my behalf, being entirely willing to repose upon your clemency. I am now constrained by circumstances to depart from this resolution, and respectfully ask your indulgence in explaining the reasons.

When arrested at Columbia So:Ca: I was just recovering from a severe illness of several months duration, which had left me greatly reduced in health and strength. The Commanding officer[2] on that station was of opinion that the condition of my health justified an appeal to be put on parole, instead of being actually imprisoned. But I then believed that my health was sufficiently restored to bear without injury the hardships to which I might be exposed, and that an application for indulgence on that ground, could not be conscientiously made by me. I find however that I overrated my strength, and a recent attack of fever, accompanied by returning symptoms of my former malady of neuralgia admonishes me of the danger to be incurred in such circumstances on the approach of winter. I venture therefore with great respect to renew my appeal for the exercise of the Executive clemency in my behalf. Left by adverse fortune at the early age of twelve years to commence the battle of life, with little education, less fortune, and no friends, my whole life since that period, has been laboriously devoted to the unob-trusive pursuits of industry, and the imperfect effort to discharge the duties and fulfil the obligations of a man and a christian. I have re-pressed the promptings of ambition, and refused the distinctions and honors of public station. It is well known however that in a country like ours, there are occasions when the demands of our fellow citizens upon us, cannot be refused without forfeiting their respect & confi-dence. My public services have been limited to such occasions as these, and my ardent desire now is to return to the quiet and obscurity of private life.[3] Animated by these sentiments and urged by the motive I have stated, and by the claims of a numerous family and large body of dependants,[4] I am induced once more to appeal to your Excellency and solicit an early and favorable decision on my petition.[5]

G A Trenholm

ALS, DNA-RG94, Amnesty Papers (M1003, Roll 47), S.C., George A. Trenholm.

1. See Trenholm to Johnson, June 6, 1865, *Johnson Papers*, 8: 193–94.

2. As of May 27, 1865, Nathaniel Haughton (c1834–1899), a Toledo resident and lt. col. of the 25th Ohio Inf., commanded the U.S. forces at Columbia. *Charleston Courier*, June 2, 1865; CSR, RG94, NA; Pension Records, Frances C. Haughton, RG15, NA.

3. Trenholm returned to public office after his election in 1874 as a Democrat to the South Carolina House. Wakelyn, *BDC*.

4. His household after the war consisted of his wife and as many as a dozen children and grandchildren. 1870 Census, S.C., Charleston, 6th Ward, Charleston, 168.

5. About five weeks later Trenholm was granted a limited parole. Johnson did not pardon Trenholm, however, until two months after receiving his third petition, written from Charleston on August 10, 1866. Amnesty Papers (M1003, Roll 47), S.C., George A. Trenholm, RG94, NA. See Order *re* Release of Prominent Confederate Prisoners, Oct. 11, 1865.

From Joseph A. Wright[1]

Private

Berlin, Prussia Sept 7th 1865

My Dear President,

I am just in receipt of a letter from our mutual friend Geo. W. Jones of Tennessee.

I have written him fully, giving him my advice, & hope he will confer freely with you on the same subject.

Where is your son Robert, and what is he doing? Can I serve you or in any way carry out any suggestions you may wish in relation to Roberts studying or travel abroad? You know how happy both Mrs Wright[2] & I will be to give you, not only any information, but to ad-vance his interests. I trust friend Jones will send you my letter, and that you will follow my advice. While writing you privately, permit me to say to you frankly, that both Mr Judd & Krieman[3] (now returning home) are opposed to you, and your policy. I have had several conver-sations with them. Judd denounces your appointment of Odell[4] at New

York. You will find Senator Trumbull of Illinois, to whom they look for counsel in the same Category. They associate here with those Americans who are opposed to your policy. They go with the Ultras, and both are opposed to Secretary Seward. I know the path they run in. Do not for one moment think of doing any thing for either of them. If you *do*, you will regret it.[5]

I have just taken possession of my office, and to day send my first dispatch.

Mrs Wright sends her kind regards to you & yours, and be pleased to accept assurances of your friend

Joseph A Wright

ALS, DLC-JP.

1. Minister to Prussia.

2. Wright married his third wife, Caroline Rockwill, in 1863. Sobel and Raimo, *Governors*, 1: 402.

3. Lincoln appointees Norman B. Judd, retiring minister at Berlin, and Herman Kreismann (c1830–1911), who resigned as secretary to the American legation, but returned as consul to Berlin (1867-c80). *U.S. Off. Reg.* (1863–79); Bessie L. Pierce, *A History of Chicago* (3 vols., New York, 1937–57), 2: 228, 252; *New York Times*, Sept. 23, 1911.

4. Democratic congressman Moses F. Odell (1818–1866) had been appointed naval officer of the customs bureau. *BDAC*; *U.S. Off. Reg.* (1865), 106.

5. Some three months later Wright again warned Johnson that Judd and Kriesmann "will do all they can to injure you or your friends." Wright to Johnson, Dec. 13, 1865, Misc. Lets., 1789–1906 (M179, Roll 231), RG59, NA.

From Nathaniel P. Banks

New Orleans   8. Sept. 1865

Sir.

I concur in the opinion entertained by the Union men of Louisiana that the officers of the present civil governmt. are pursuing a policy disadvantageous to the best interests of the country and to your administration, and that a change in the offices of Governor, and Mayor of New Orleans[1] is advisable, for these reasons.

1st Their appointments are in a great measure from the ranks of returned Rebel officers and soldiers (who are excluded from civil rights by the terms of your Amnesty proclamation of the 29." May.) and tend to depress the spirits and efforts of Union men, and to encourage those who are still avowedly hostile to the people and governmnt of the United States, and who were ready and willing upon their return from the Rebel army, to accept terms of amnesty that could in no wise endanger the govermt. on any important public interest.

2d. That it appears that these officers do not intend to appeal to the people for support at any general election but hope to perpetuate their power by disregarding the general wishes of all classes of people, who seek an election.

3d. The violent removal from responsible officers by the Governor, of men who were elected on the same ticket with himself by the same voters, encourages a belief that any election to office may be disregarded and that it is therefore useless to register or to vote.

The appointment of wise just and patriotic men, who will dispense political favors for the advantage of the cause of the Union and your administration—who will not seek to perpetuate their own power by indefinite postponemt of general elections: and who will impart to the public mind a belief that an expression of opinion by the people at the ballot box, if it be just and loyal, will be [recaptioned?] and sustained by the acting governor, and his subordinates, will greatly benefit all public interests and satisfy the best and most numerous portions of the people of Louisiana.[2]

N. P Banks

ALS, DLC-JP.
    1. J. Madison Wells and Hugh Kennedy.
    2. This letter was among twelve enclosures forwarded with Carl Schurz's September 4, 1865, report to the President. See *Advice*, 124, 131, 132.

From Joseph C. Bradley
Private

Huntsville Alabama   Sept 8 1865

As a mark of respect for and the confidence our Union or loyal people have in General R S Granger, lately Commanding in North Alabama, I send you this letter without any intimation or wish on his part. Genl Granger has been the most acceptable Commander (Military) to all the people since the Federal Army took possession of our country in 1862. He has tried to do full justice to all of our Citizens be they unionist or Secessionist. And I Can assure your Excellency that we union administration men sincerly regret the departure of Genl Granger from the Command of North Alabama.[1] I want Genl Granger to talk with you, for he knows the Secret or hiden political sentiments of men among us who yet retain feelings of hostility against the United States Government. When I was with you I surely beleived that our people had felt so sorely the Calamities of the rebellion that they would now settle down into quiet & peace towards the Federal Government,—but I am sorry to have it to say to you, that the wholesale appointments of State officers—made by my friend Govr Parsons, has not worked well. There are many bitter secessionist left in office, and by their influence, our State will be Contrould & you will see that a strong effort will be made to prevent our State from Voteing for the Amendment to the Constitution of the United States forever abolishing Slavery. In the election for Delegates to our State Convention 31st ulto. the strong Union candidate Hon D C Humphreys was defeated by a man,[2] who took decided grounds against amending the Constitution of the United States abolishing Slavery. Govr Parsons done what he thought would be best for the State in makeing his wholesale appointments but he Commited a great mistake, and I remonstrated with him about the Course,—which was also disapproved of by the ["]Advocate" the Administration paper of this place, and also by J Q Smith the United States District Atty for Ala. The Govr. is trying to correct the mistake he made—but it will not be complete until he removes every secessionist from office in the State. The people of Ala must be taught to Consider that it is a magnanimous act on the part of the Federal Government to restore the state to her proper place in the Union, instead of *demanding* terms of restoration by a people lately in rebellion. You ought to make every rebel feel when you bestow on him a pardon, that he must keep it strictly or it will be recalled, and in granting pardons that the Government is bestowing favors which the recipient had no right to demand. It may surprise you, when I state to you that we have many among us who really beleive that if a sufficient number of states thro their Legislatures do not ratify the amendment to the Constitution of the United States abolishing slavery that this Institution will be restored in full sway in 18 months. I want to see this disturbeing question settled and therefore I entirely abandon any objections I may have had heretofore in regard to the Constitutional amendment. If Alabama is received again into her proper place in the union, by the State Convention abolishing slavery, and the Convention or Legislature refusing to ratify the Constitutional amendment the secessionist will become so intolerant and proscriptive towards union men that nearly every one of them will have to leave the State. I will here say to you, that it is now my honest opinion, that if the Federal Troops were taken from this place that no union man could remain with safety to himself. I ask that you notice the action of our Convention, and I am afraid that you will see a strong effort made to pass by the War debt of Fifteen to Twenty millions of Dollars, & allow our Legislature, to fix it up by imposeing a heavy debt on our people—made while in rebellion to carry it on this *Monstrocity* ought not to be allowed. The secessionist in the Convention will oppose its action being Submited to the people for their ratification—or rejection—because they do not want the amendment to the Constitution of the U States agitated, which will surely be done & the Legislature instructed to vote for it, if the labouring classes have a chance to act.

I feel a great hesitancy in writeing you, because I know how much you are harrassed by others, but allow me to say, that for many years I have been your political friend, which is well known in this State, & I feel an interest in every thing that Concerns you, and for this reason you will make due allowance for me when you receive my letter. I want no office myself—but feel a deep & abideing interest for union men being placed in Federal offices in our State. I want men who will sustain the policy of your administration. This letter is for you individually &

not as President. Genl Granger does not know the Contents of this letter. I have talked with him on some of its subjects.

Joseph C Bradley

ALS, DLC-JP.
1. Having been mustered out of volunteer service in late August 1865, Robert S. Granger was apparently allowed to return home on leave before resuming his duties in the regular army. Powell, *Army List*, 338; *Senate Ex. Docs.*, 39 Cong., 1 Sess., No. 12, p. 27 (Ser. 1237).
2. John N. Drake (*c*1809-*fl*1870), a prosperous Madison County farmer, not only defeated Republican rival David C. Humphreys in the August 31 contest, but beat him again in the subsequent election for the state senate. 1860 Census, Ala., Madison, NW Div., 6; (1870), TGR2E, 50th Dist., 10; *Huntsville Advocate*, Nov. 9, 16, 1865.

From Ulysses S. Grant

September 8, 1865, Galena, Ill.; ALS, DLC-JP.

On the basis of his conversations with "all classes of people" during his seven weeks away from Washington, Grant reports that "all agree" that the United States should intervene in Mexico against "the usurpers in that Country." In "previous communications" he had given his "views on our duty in the matter," and conversations with Johnson had convinced him "that you think about it as I do." Grant recommends "that notice be given the French that foreign troops must be withdrawn from the Continent and the people left free to govern themselves in their own way." He urges selling "on credit, to the Government of Mexico all the arms, munitions, and clothing they want," as well as aiding them "with officers to Command troops." Grant concludes that "a terrible strife in this Country is only to be averted by prompt action in this matter with Mexico."

From Frank L. James[1]

Mobile   [September 8, 1865][2]

Andrew Johnson

Have any military authorities the right to suppress a loyal & true paper because it does not happen to suit them?[3]

L.[F.] L James   associate   Mobile Daily News

Tel, DLC-JP.
1. James (1842–1907), a former private in the 21st Ala. Inf., CSA, later removed to St. Louis, where he practiced medicine and edited several medical journals. *Who Was Who in America, 1607–1896* (Chicago, 1963), 190; *NCAB*, 12: 226; 1860 Census, Ala., Mobile, 6th Ward, 9; CSR, RG109, NA.
2. The Library of Congress has assigned September 10, 1865, as the date of this document, but Johnson's telegram of September 11, as well as the copy of James's initial dispatch found in Tels. Recd., President, Vol. 4 (1865–66), RG107, NA, confirm that September 8 was the actual date.
3. Johnson asked: "What reason is assigned for the suppression of your paper?" James replied: "The order for suppression was not given, the threat being never carried into Execution." Johnson to James, Sept. 11, 1865, Tels. Sent, President, Vol. 2 (1865), RG107, NA; James to Johnson, Sept. 14, 1865, Tels. Recd., President, Vol. 4 (1865–66), RG107, NA.

From Davidson M. Leatherman[1]

Memphis Tenn   8th Sept 1865

In obedience with your suggestion and desire I have the honor and pleasure of saying to you,

Since my return home I have made it my business to carefully and frequently examine into the workings of the freedmans Beareau in this City and the surrounding District of Country, and am gratified to inform you, That nothing ever was being inaugarated that had no precedent, that so much met the approbation of all here as the course that has been pursued here upon this subject by Genl. Tilson[2] in connection with this new order of things.

There is not an opposing element here to the system or to any measure or Policy of your administration. There is a fredom and fulness of acquiesence in this new order of things that surpass all expectation of the true Patriot and *real* Union man.

All regret the removal of Genl. Tilson, and the comming in of a new man,[3] that they know not of. I hope it may be that he can be returned permanently to this point, increasing his jurisdiction if you please, to New Orleans including Eastern Ark, West Tennessee and North Miss—with the power of adding to Genl. Howards present policy, the apointing of a Superintendent upon each plantation whose services are to be agreed upon and paid by the Planter and to be selected equally by the Planter and the Commanding Officer of the freedmans Bearreau in the several Departments. They would soon make it a self sustaining institution. By this system, the vast number of young would be fed and provided for. This is a meer suggestion in connection with my views upon this *great question*, presenting so much interest least it usurps the *rights* of *the state*.

I had the opportunity of seeing in the City since returning Col Bailey[4] Provost Marshal of the freedmans Bureau for Bolivar County Miss. He informed me that some trouble had existed before he received his Commission from Judge sharkey[5]—but promised that every thing would move smoothly on in that County. He is a good appointment.

I will keep you truthfully posted as well as I can from time to time. All important that the enclosed order or Policy of General Smith[6] and Genl. Tilson be *sustained and rigidly* carried out.

Be assured that no President ever had such full cooperation, and all are looking to you with more anxious interest than to any and all since the days of Washington. This comes to me from so many sources reliable it is more than beyond all question to my mind, earnest and deep without a dissenting voice.

I hope your public duties has allowed you to look over the Elm Wood

Cemetery papers. *We feel this* case has great *merit* and it is our only chance for compensation for the ground occupied. There are fifty (50) stock holders in this institution having no other object or motive in the association than to beautify and embelish the resting place of the dead, and a large majority [of] the same never took any part in the rebellion & have never abandoned their homes or their institutions.[7]

D. M. Leatherman

ALS, DLC-JP.

1. Leatherman (1813–1873) was a prominent attorney and real estate developer. Joseph Lenow et al., *Elmwood: Charter, Rules, Regulations and By-laws of Elmwood Cemetery Association of Memphis* (Memphis, 1874), 131.

2. Davis Tillson had served as subassistant commissioner in Memphis since July 1865 before being transferred in late September to head the Freedmen's Bureau, District of Georgia. McFeely, *Yankee Stepfather*, 121–22; Paul A. Cimbala, "The Freedmen's Bureau, the Freedmen, and Sherman's Grant in Reconstruction Georgia, 1865–1867," *JSH*, 55 (1989): 607–27; Preliminary Inventory of the Records of the Field Officers of the [Freedmen's Bureau], Part 3, p. 440, RG105, NA.

3. Massachusetts native Nathan A.M. Dudley (1825–1910), a professional soldier, had been brevetted a brigadier general. Jack D.L. Holmes, "The Underlying Causes of the Memphis Race Riot of 1866," *THQ*, 17 (1958): 209–10; *Who Was Who in America, 1897–1942* (New York, 1943), 343.

4. William E. Bayley (b. c1838), an Australian native, Chicago bank teller, and former lieutenant in the 9th Ill. Cav., had been appointed provost marshal and commander of the Bolivar County militia on June 22. CSR, RG94, NA; Bayley to Morgan L. Smith, June 28, 1865, Asst. Commr., Miss., Unregistered Lets. Recd., RG105, NA.

5. Mississippi provisional governor, William L. Sharkey.

6. John E. Smith, commander of the District of Western Tennessee.

7. We have not been able to identify the matter to which Leatherman refers.

To George H. Thomas

Washington, D.C., Sept 8th 1865.

Your dispatch has been received. In withdrawing the colored troops from Eastern Tennessee I would send them where they are needed and no where else. If there are too many of them in the service, it would be better to have them mustered out. In the event of an insurrection it is feared that the colored troops, so great in number, could not be controlled. It is believed that there are mischievous persons, acting as Emissaries, inciting the Negro population to acts of violence, revenge, and insurrection. This should be carefully looked to and all conflict between the whites and blacks should be avoided as far as practicable. There would be no danger of this kind if this description of persons could be expelled from the country—whose business it is to excite and originate discontent between the races. If there were a sufficient number of white troops instead of colored to protect the country, it would exert a much better influence upon the people. I think I shall have Miss. added to your Department.[1] If the Southern States can be encouraged, I have no doubt in my own mind, that they will proceed and restore their Governments within the next six or seven months and renew their former relations with the Federal Gov't. You can do much in the consummation of this great end. The whole South has confidence in you, & any move you make in that direction, will inspire confidence & encourage them in the work they have undertaken.

Andrew Johnson

Tel, DNA-RG107, Tels. Sent, President, Vol. 2 (1865).
1. Thomas's original postwar command apparently included Mississippi but a June 27, 1865, order gave that state to Gen. Philip H. Sheridan. Mississippi was restored to Thomas in the succeeding fall. Freeman Cleaves, *Rock of Chickamauga: The Life of General George H. Thomas* (Norman, Okla., 1948), 286; Francis F. McKinney, *Education in Violence: The Life of George H. Thomas and the History of the Army of the Cumberland* (Detroit, 1961), 454.

From Alfred R. Wynne[1]

Castalian Springs Sumner County Tenn.
Sept 8th 1865

Thinking it would not be obtrusive, after a silence of some three or four years—for an old friend to drop you a line, in a quiet hour, from a "moral district" inviting, most respecfully your attention, to some of the embarrassments now surrounding our unfortunate country I take the liberty of writing this.

The many unhappy incidents, connected with the revolutionary struggle, of the last four years has separated many friends of former days & made sad havoc, socially pecuniarily and politically, amind all, (though honestly), difering with you on some points, I never forget the old democratic "landmarks" by which we used to steer, & have never been without hope that they would again be visible even, amid, the *debris*, of rebellious times. There has been no time, since your accession, to presidential power, I have not looked to you with hope, & confidence, for the salvation, of this country. I know, it is impossible for a man of your ardent, temperament and, *strong will* to forget the ties, and devotion of "better" days, and, believeing, that, I feel assured, that, evry, thing which possibly can be done, to alleviate a suffuring, people, will be, most earnestly, & I trust efficiently done, by your, excellency! In my judgement, it is much easier to reunite elements, the congeniality of which has been temporarily disturbed, than unite those, which were always antagonistic. Our people, properly treated, would, I think unhesitatingly sustain you, above any other man. Its natural that, many of them should be full of complaint, on account of their great loss of estate, and, various, other causes. Yet there, is evidently a tone of liberality even among those, especially as they see indications of a liberal polacy towards the south. I tell them, that they have tried you, long & seen you, personally and, officially, under all the phases of good and evil fortune, and that you will not exact more than, the exigencies,

of the times require, and, will relieve, intolerable oppression, of "Freedman's Bureau["]—and negro soldiers—as soon as it can be done, with
safety to your administration. You, have been in public life too long, as
the "darling of the people"—not to know the most reliable information,
touching their rights, is obtained from the plain spoken, farmer, who
sees things as they are; and, is given to call them by, their, right names.
I am that sort of man, and, other days have written you letters as un-
varnished, and, ingenuous as I knew how.[2] This people, (Sumner
County) you know, were always democratic, & ever gave you, the largest, majority in the state, save, the county of Lincoln. They had been
taught and honestly believed in the right of secession, and appealed in
good faith, however inconsiderate, to the arbitriment, of the sword; the
result was, and is to them, disastrous. They admit it with all the frankness of brave, and generous, manhood, and, with much, alacrity. I am
glad to see that they are seeking to mend their broken, fortunes, by
useful occupations; & especially, is this so, with returned paroled, soldiers. If the Freedman's Bureau could be done away with, I see no
reason, why our thrifty and energetic people, should not soon recuper-
ate their exhausted means—angain make the country blossom, under
genial influence. I am, perhaps, too frank, I hope, however not, pres-
umtive—when I say to you that this Bureau—as it is now conducted,
is the greatest disturber of the peace & quietude & prosperity of our
people. I cannot think, that if you were, aware, of its practical operations, that it would not be kept amongst, us. It is not only in direct
conflict with our, "civil authorities" but superceds their operations, to
a great extent. The terror which it holds over our people—by listening
to and sustaining the negro in evy frivolous & malicious complaint—amounts to a practical denial of the rights of the white man.
The negro can now, in this neighbourhood, steal and commit other &
more violent depredations, without the fear of apprehension—because,
if prosecuted—he threatens, to commit, arson, murder, and other lawless acts; by way of vengeance—and, if tried by the "*Beaureau*" is put
on a par as a witness with the white man & owing in part to the former
existence of the institution of slavery, a respectable whiteman has such
a repugnance to that kind of Contact (especially with no show of justice
to himself) that he daily suffers, injustice, & insult, rather than seek
redress. For many months, prior to the establishment of this "Bureau"
we were quiet and, felt secure. Col Gilfillen[3] was in command at Gallatin & the restoration of Courts was in progress, but since the Bureau,
has been in operation, it neutralizes, the promised good results of restoring courts & law. I might give you numerous instances of outrages
commited but will not tresspass on your time. The negro troops, too,
at Gallatin—are permitted to pass through the country, without the
attenddance of white officers; and are, constantly encroaching most in-
delicately, upon the rights, of the citizen. They thrust themselves, un-

invited upon the privacy of our families—demand their meals, and, in one instance, where, my neighbour, Esq Payne,[4] refused, them—[assaulted?] him. Rapes have been committed upon respectable white women, and murders upon innocent men; traceable, to the negro, soldiers. Independent of this, there are now fifty mounted men—(troops) in this county who report to the *Sheriff*—for what purpose, the good citizens cannot divine—but understand, as guard, for him, in the, service of writs &c. This is not needed allow me to say, for there, never, was a time, in the history of this country, when process could be more easily served—& resistence to law would be so cautiously, resorted to. The presence of the bayonet acts more as an irritant than a paliative to a peaceful and submissive people. If you can consistently have these oppressive, and, irritating causes, removed it would *enure* not a little, I assure you to the quiet, & comfort of this people, and to the esteem, in which they hold you. In conclusion, permit me my dear Sir, to say, that, the faith I have in your ability, justice & liberality, has induced me to write this. Hopeing that you will be able to stand firm, on the *constitution* and maintain yourself, in sustaining the rights of the people, against the assaults of *Radicalism*, and trusting you may find time to let me hear from you, touching upon these important points.

A. R. Wynne

P.S. As, to the "Freed men" whom I omitted to mention—I find that there are—but a very few—who, are doing well. Those are such as remain with their former masters, from the memory of their long kindness, and protection, and their attachment, to the old home steads, where perhaps, they have spent the greater part of their lives. This class give their service to their former masters; for, which they receive, a reasonable compensation. But, the large, majority of the "Freed men" I am sorry, to say, are doing badly in this vicinity. They assemble, around the Towns, vilages, and Camps—spending their time in idleness, and disipation, without any visible means of support. And, from the complaint of the people, I am forced to the belief, that they subsist alone by theft & pilage. It is due, the Officers & Citizens, at Gallatin, to say—they have used evry, pursuasive, argument, to induce them, to go to the country and find employment.

However the Citizens show no disposition to, thwart, the real, purpose of the Government, and evince, a perfect wilingness to employ the negro—and amply compensate him for his labor, yet they naturally want some guarantee a contract made with them, will be kept in good faith.

Hopeing Sir, that you will pardon me, for further tresspassing. . . .

A. R. Wynne

ALS, DLC-JP.

1. Wynne (1800–1893) was a prominent Sumner County merchant, land speculator, resort operator, and former Castalian Springs postmaster. Walter T. Durham, "Wynnewood," *THQ*, 33 (1974): 129, 147, 150, 152–53.

2. See, for example, Alfred R. Wynne to Johnson, Jan. 23, 1861, Johnson Papers, LC.
3. James Gilfillan.
4. Not identified.

To Robert M. Brown[1]

Washington, Sept. 9, 1865.

My Dear Sir:

I have received and read your letter of the 1st instant,[2] and thank you for its kind tone, and for the interest you still have in one of your "old boyhood associates."

I regret as much as any can regret, the sad devastation and havoc occasioned by the war, and I trust that now all our people will devote themselves to the pursuits of Peace, and to cherishing a love for the government which our fathers founded. If they do so, our nation cannot fail to have a growth and grandeur greater than that of any nation that has preceded it in history.

Andrew Johnson

Raleigh Standard, Jan. 14, 1866.
1. Postmaster of New Hill, N.C., since 1850, Brown (*c*1814-*fl*1872) was the nephew of James J. Selby, for whom Johnson had worked in Raleigh. 1850 Census, N.C., Wake, Western Div., 391; Elizabeth R. Murray, *Wake: Capital County of North Carolina* (Raleigh, 1983), 427, 659; Brown to Johnson, July 8, 1865, Amnesty Papers (M1003, Roll 37), N.C., R. M. Brown, RG94, NA; Brown to Johnson, Sept. 1, 1865, Johnson Papers, LC.
2. Brown related his "trobles and sufferings" during the past "unholy war." Following Lee's surrender some Federal troops pillaged Brown's farm, leaving his large family of fourteen with "nothing to eat" and "no money." Nevertheless, he professed hope in the future of "our blessed country" under the direction of Johnson, "the right man, and in the right place." Ibid.

From Rebecca A. Butler[1]

Geoa. Macon   Sepr. 9th 1865

Dear Sir

Your present petitioner is the sister of John A Campbell, late Judge of the Supreme Court, of the United States, and now confined as a prisoner, in Fort Pulaski. She feels confident, that an earnest application to You, for his release, will not be in vain. Your past magnanimity, and forbearance, leads her to hope, for the exercise of Executive clemensy, in the case now under consideration. Your firm, and yet conciliatory course, has commanded, the confidence, and admiration of the whole Southern people. My Brother was strenuously, opposed to the war, and did not resign his seat, or return to Alabama, his adopted state, for some months after she formally declared herself out of the Union. He held no official connexion, with the socalled Confederate Government, except he acted for a short time as Assistant Secretary of

War. Will not the President, release this *peace loving* Brother, who has been a ministering angel to the destitute, and afflicted, in his *misfortune*, the *poor* and *needy* will rise and call him *blessed*. If it will comport with your high sense of duty, to grant the above request, it will challenge the warmest gratitude, of the numerous friends of my Brother, in *this*, his *native* state. That great peace and prosperity, may attend you both, in public and in private, is the fervent prayer of your humble petitioner. This Brother has been the staff, and support of a widowed Mother, sisters[2] &c for near forty years, united with their efforts. My Brothers family require his assistance. *All all* have suffered in this terrible conflict. Widows and orphans are pennyless. Receive from *your* petitioner, unfeigned thanks, for kindness to my *Brother* while a prisoner. Humanity is represented, the pedominat element of *your* character.[3]

Rebecca A. Butler   Macon Georgia

ALS, NHi-Andrew Johnson Papers.

1. Since her husband's untimely death in 1842, Butler (b. *c*1815) had reared two sons. Jean S. Willingham and Berthenia C. Smith, comps., *Bibb County, Georgia Early Wills and Cemetery Records* (Macon, *c*1961), n.p.; 1860 Census, Ga., Bibb, Macon, 93.

2. Campbell's mother, possibly the Mary L. Campbell (*c*1793–1862) buried in Mobile, and his other sister Sarah G. Chandler (1809–1887), whose husband was for several years Judge Campbell's law partner in Mobile. *DAB*; Owen, *History of Ala.*, 3: 315; Helen A. Thompson, ed., *Magnolia Cemetery* (New Orleans, 1974), 126.

3. Gov. Lewis E. Parsons later forwarded a petition from the Alabama constitutional convention, with his own endorsement, for the release of Campbell, which was effected on October 12, 1865. Parsons to Johnson, Sept. 20, 1865; Campbell to Johnson, Oct. 13, 1865, Lets. Recd. (Main Ser.), Files C-1481-1865 and W-2276-1865 (M619, Rolls 345 and 442), RG94, NA. See Order *re* Release of Prominent Confederate Prisoners, Oct. 11, 1865.

From Thomas Cottman

New Orleans   Sept 9th 1865

Sir

A reasonable impression prevails that you have sent Genl. Carl Schurz down here to lend his aid in establishing *Civil* Government. If such be the case expectations are not likely to be realized. For the natural instincts of an Austrian would be to exercise his influence through Lager Beer Saloons, but common sense would suggest other than the enemies of State & Federal Government for associates. No civil officer of this State has seen him elsewhere than at a Restaurat with Generals Banks & Hahn who are as inimical to you & your policy as men can well be: and since my return here I am induced to think Genl Canby not only cooperates but agrees with them. My frankness may appear to you rude, but whatever I think, affects you; affects me, personally. I act as though it were an individual affront or injury; and you must excuse my ardor. When I entertain friendship those who know me are ready to concede that it knows no limits & insiduous enemies are my peculiar aversion. The garb of friendship frequently covers the worst enemies which I have reason to believe is the case with many clad with Federal authority in this Department. The State officials are true to you & the Government. You may say they are aware it is their only safety. Let the reason be what it may the fact remains the same. Your time is too precious for me to occupy it with my comments, hence I only submit facts for your consideration.

Thos Cottman

ALS, DLC-JP.

From Andrew Jackson, III[1]

Hermitage near Nashville Ten
Sept. 9th 1865

Sir

I have the honor to state, that being a graduate of West Point and in the United States Army when the late war commenced, I come under the fifth and eighth exceptions of the Presidents Amnesty Proclamation and am therefore excluded from its benefits. I now ask the Presidents clemency and that my disabilities be removed, that in being and intending to remain a quiet, peaceable, and law abiding, citizen, I may enjoy the privileges usually extended to such.[2]

The Government has never taken possession of any of my property. There are no proceedings pending against me in a United States Court, and the resignation of my commission in the United States Army was accepted before I joined the Confederate Army.

A. Jackson

ALS, DNA-RG94, Amnesty Papers (M1003, Roll 49), Tenn., Andrew Jackson.

1. Jackson (1834–1906), offspring of President Jackson's adopted son, had been colonel of a heavy artillery regiment. Manager of the Hermitage estate until 1894, he then served as an internal revenue collector. Knoxville Journal and Tribune, Dec. 19, 1906.

2. Jackson's amnesty oath and letter were received at the White House on October 3, 1865. Johnson endorsed the letter, asked the Attorney General to issue a pardon, and it was done on the same day. Amnesty Papers (M1003, Roll 49), Tenn., Andrew Jackson, RG94, NA.

To James Johnson

Washington D.C., Sept 9 1865.

The mere fact of an applicant for pardon taking the Amnesty oath to accompany such application does not entitle the party to vote under the proclamation.[1] The Amnesty oath furnished with the petition for Pardon was required by the Attorney General as evidence of loyalty and a reason why special pardon should be granted. We will try and pardon all who deserve it by the time their votes are needed. I hope all is working well. Your efforts all seem to succeed. We are looking to your ultimate success with confidence and anxiety.[2]

Andrew Johnson

Tel, DNA-RG107, Tels. Sent, President, Vol. 2 (1865).
1. The Georgia governor had wired the previous day from Atlanta: "Will an individual who has taken the oath of amnesty made application for pardon & who has been recommended by me for pardon be entitled to vote or seat in the Convention?" James Johnson to Johnson, Sept. 8, 1865, Johnson Papers, LC.
2. Apparently the President's dispatch, sent to Atlanta, failed to reach the governor. This same telegram was transmitted to Macon on September 29, following Governor Johnson's second query of the 26th. James Johnson to Johnson, Sept. 26, 1865, Johnson Papers, LC; Johnson to James Johnson, Sept. 29, 1865, Tels. Sent, President, Vol. 2 (1865), RG107, NA.

From George W. Jones

Private

Fayetteville, Tennessee   September 9 1865

Dear Sir

With many doubts and misgivings as to the propriety of the step, I venture to address you upon a subject and in behalf of an old and zealous friend of yours and mine in times that have past and gone, trusting to the kindness of your heart to look with charity upon this effort to relieve a friend, if you do not approve the course.

Robt. Mathews of Shelbyville Tennessee well known to you in former times as an ardent and zealous—trust worthy and reliable friend and supporter of yours and the principles you advocated involved himself in the late rebellion and war, as consequence of which he has been a sufferer to an extent that few have endured. He has already lost a large amount in money and debts due him prior to and at the commencement of the war and now his remaining property is advertised by the marshal to be sold under the confiscation laws, and if carried out will complete his ruin pecuniarily, and that of his interesting family of daughters, who will be made suffer for the acts of their father. Is it the policy of the government to enforce the confiscation laws in Tennessee, in those portions of Tennessee and other States in rebellion, which were held by the military power of the government, and had legal proceedings instituted before the suppression of the rebellion and the publication of your Amnesty Proclamation of the 29th of May last, in which you offer full pardon and Amnesty to all persons as therein specified, to person and property, except cases in which legal proceedings shall have been instituted, against the property under the confiscation laws? Should the confiscation law be enforced against persons in Tennessee, when the government had the power to institute legal proceedings before the suppression of the rebellion and those persons within the rebel lines, when the government had no courts and consequently could not commence legal proceedings against the property of rebels prior to the suppression of the rebellion, be entirely relieved from the operations of that law merely from the fact that the government could not execute the law? I know you possess clear and well settled convictions of right and wrong and you are an advocate of the equal and uniform operation of the laws of the land and the power of the government and I cannot believe that you will rigidly enforce the confiscation law against persons in Tennessee that will have no force of effect in other portions of the rebellious states. Your sense of justice and equality will I feel confident incline you to the exercise of those noble attributes of perfection, justice and Mercy. I appeal to you in behalf of Robt. Mathews and his daughters to grant him a full pardon for his person and a restoration of the remnant of his property now advertised for sale. The small sum it would bring can be no object to the government and will be disastrous to him and those dependent upon him if taken from them. I doubt not but, that you have granted full relief to many rebels, both as to person and property, less meritorious than Mr Mathews. May I venture to recall to your mind your answer in the memorable canvass of 1855 to the charge against you of a too full exercise of the pardoning power as Governor "that it was better to err on the side of Mercy, than on the other side." We all thought so then and vindicated your action by your reelection. May I hope for your favorable action in behalf of Robt. Mathews?[1]

G. W. Jones

ALS, DLC-JP.

1. Mathews, a Democratic supporter of Johnson, had written on his own behalf on two previous occasions. Johnson pardoned Mathews on September 13, 1865. In response to the President's endorsement, proceedings against Mathews's property were suspended two weeks later. Mathews to Johnson, July 11, Sept. 6, 1865, Amnesty Papers (M1003, Roll 50), Tenn., Robert Mathews, RG94, NA.

From David L. Swain

ca. September 9, 1865, Raleigh, N.C.; ALS, DNA-RG94, Amnesty Papers (M1003, Roll 42), N.C., David L. Swain.

The longtime president of the University of North Carolina, former governor and political rival of William W. Holden, exempted from the Amnesty Proclamation because of owning taxable property in excess of twenty thousand dollars, requests a pardon. In December 1860 Swain had "protested most earnestly against" the proposed North Carolina secession ordinance at two separate political meetings and, two months later, had traveled to Confederate Montgomery as a peace commissioner. After his state seceded he chose not to "array himself against her public authorities," believing that was "the only way to prevent an internecine war among ourselves." Throughout the conflict he "availed . . . himself of every fair opportunity to encourage harmony and secure fidelity to the Union." For this reason he declined serving in the Confederate

Senate, though he "contributed his fair proportion . . . to feed and clothe our hungry and naked soldiers . . . and their families." For these "errors" committed "in the performance of his public duties," Swain petitions the President to grant him amnesty. [Johnson did so, on September 28, 1865.]

From George H. Thomas

Nashville   Sept 9, 1865

Have just received your telegram of the 8th inst. I do not believe that there is the least foundation for fearing an insurrection among the negros, nor that in the event of any disturbances the negro troops in this Military Division would attempt to commit violence.[1] As a general rule the negro Soldiers are under good discipline. I have required all commanding officers to keep their commands under good discipline and as a general rule I believe they have. I believe in the majority of cases of collision between whites and negro Soldiers that the white man has attempted to bully the negro, for it is exceedingly repugnant to the Southerners to have negro Soldiers in their midst & some are so foolish as to vent their anger upon the negro because he is a Soldier. It was my desire to have retained in Service all the one year white troops to garrison the different important points in each State until the States were reorganized and resumed their proper Status & functions in the Union. All these Regts have now been ordered to be mustered out in Kentucky & Tennessee which compels me to use negro troops to garrison the important points in those States. If Genl Palmer thinks it safe to withdraw the troops from Kentucky all the negro troops in that State can be mustered out of Service. It is necessary to have a few regiments at the depots in this state to guard public property, the balance I contemplate sending to Alabama & Georgia to enable the Commanding General of those two Depts to discharge an equal number of white troops who are clamorous for their discharge & in reality are doing but little good in most places. The white troops are particularly hostile to the negro & with the utmost care it is difficult to prevent collision between them. I have always endeavored to observe a just & conciliatory course towards the people of the States within my command & believe they are as a mass Satisfied, but there are always, in every community evilminded persons to whom nothing seems right except when they can have all their whims & caprices Satisfied. These I find are always ready to misrepresent and exaggerate every event however trifling that does not in some manner benefit them. From what I observe of the Sentiments & acts of the people of Georgia & Alabama I am convinced that after the organization of these States it will only be necessary to hold the fortifications on the Sea coast and concentrate a force of five or six thousand well disciplined troops either white or black at some central points as Atlanta and Chattanooga to ensure the supremacy of the Government.

Geo H Thomas   Maj General

Tel, DLC-JP.

1. In a telegram to Johnson nine days later, Thomas repeated his beliefs that there was no likelihood of black revolts in Tennessee and Kentucky or in Alabama and Georgia. Thomas to Johnson, Sept. 18, 1865, Johnson Papers, LC.

From James E. Bell[1]

West Point N.Y.   Sept. 10th 1865.
Sir.

While in Washington lately, I did not have an opportunity of calling upon you again, because of my return to the Military Academy.

I wrote Father[2] the substance of the conversation I had with you, from the first day you saw me in Washington. I do not desire to engage your attention long. I told you nearly all I had to say when I last saw you.

I hope that you will deem it proper to confer upon Father the Mission I asked for him.[3] The salary is small—being only $7,500—but, of course money can be made. A person who is not a friend of yours, has held the position for several years, and is now in *Europe*.[4] Father desires it for only two years, as he intends to take an active part in the next Presidential Campaign.

I do not desire to urge the appointment to too great an extent—for, it is not absolutely necessary to his success, but *very desirable*; besides the more successful *he* is, the better able will he be to serve *his friend* when the time comes. When I last saw you, you thought it "too early to talk about that time."

Mr. Chase's friends have already commenced in the West. I also learn, from personal friends of the following, that Stanton, Butler, Seward, Grant and Sherman, all have high hopes, and, that some have commenced their work.

I will not trouble you longer. Mr. Stanton has been here for the past few days.

Should you leave Washington, you could not find a more pleasant spot, in which to pass away a few days, than this—and, before I graduate, I hope to have the honor of being one of those who shall welcome you to this lovely home, given us by the Government.

Jas. Edw. Bell   Cadet U.S.M.A.

ALS, DNA-RG59, Lets. of Appl. and Recomm., 1861–69 (M650, Roll 4), J. Warren Bell.

1. Bell (c1844–1873), a Tennessee appointee to West Point on Johnson's recommendation, graduated in 1867. An artillery officer, he died while stationed at Fort Jefferson, Fla. The West Point Alumni Foundation, Inc., *Register of Graduates and Former Cadets of the United States Military Academy: Cullum Memorial Edition* (West Point, 1970), 262.

2. Joseph Warren Bell, formerly colonel of the 13th Ill. Cav.

3. Probably minister to Japan. See William Thorpe to Johnson, July 25, 1865, *Johnson Papers*, 8: 475–76.

4. Robert H. Pruyn (1815–1882), a Seward Republican and Lincoln appointee, had resigned his Japanese post in the spring of 1865. *DAB*.

From Andrew G. Boyd[1]

Hancock, Md., Sept 10, 1865.

Sir:

I am in a quandary as to the position I occupy otherwise I would not add this communication to your Excellencys many other annoyances.

In March 1863, I resided at Hagerstown in this state—was the editor and publisher of the "Maryland Free Press," a Democratic Journal, when, falling under the displeasure of Maj Gen Schenk,[2] I was *sent* under guard into the Confederate lines, where I attached myself to the Army in the capacity of a Private and there done duty until the surrender of Lee, when I took a parole and afterwards the Amnesty Oath.

The question is: Was I or not entitled to the benefit of your amnesty proclamation, it having only excluded those who voluntarily *left* loyal states to join the Rebel Army, and not those who were *sent* out and afterwards joined it.

The matter was submitted to Gen Hancock,[3] commanding this Department, who, although answering kindly, gave no decided opinion.

I have stated facts as briefly as possible, and shall be gratified to receive from you such a reply as will allay all doubts on the subject.[4]

Andrew G Boyd

ALS, DNA-RG60, Office of Atty. Gen., Lets. Recd., President.

1. Boyd (*c*1825-*fl*1870), a veteran of the 1st Md. Cav., CSA, returned to Hagerstown. CSR, RG109, NA; 1870 Census, Md., Washington, Hagerstown, 65.

2. Robert C. Schenk commanded the Middle Department and VIII Corps at Baltimore at this time.

3. Gen. Winfield S. Hancock currently headed the Military Middle Division headquartered at Baltimore. See Boyd to Hancock, Aug. 8, 1865, CSR, RG109, NA.

4. Eight days later the assistant attorney general replied: "The [Amnesty] Proclamation, like the Statutes of the Country must be construed by each citizen for himself. The President cannot undertake to be the expounder of his own words. The citizen in the first instance, and the Courts in the last instance, must interpret them." No record of an individual pardon for Boyd has been found. J. Hubley Ashton to Boyd, Sept. 18, 1865, Office of Atty. Gen., Lets. Sent, Vol. E (M699, Roll 10), RG60, NA.

From Hugh Kennedy

City hall [New Orleans]   10th day of Septbr 1865

President,

In my previous correspondence I have endeavored to place before you in as succinct and impartial shape as possible, the various grounds of difference which Genl Canby has produced between the military &

civil power. He early after my resumption of the Mayoralty began his vexatious encroachments on my civil power and to strike at my private interests. In the latter instance by forcing me from the Bank of which by the unanimous choice of its five hundred stock-holders, I was the president. The reason of his proceedings in this case can be found in the fact that the Bank was the claimant as rightful owner of sixteen thousand bales of cotton in Alabama, which the General alleged was captured by the United States and consequently forfeited by the Bank. This, of course, I did not and could not admit; but I proposed to him to appoint an agent to act in conjunction with one to be appointed by the Bank, who together would go to Alabama, collect the cotton, put it in marketable condition, bring it & dispose of it, paying from the proceeds the charges, and depositing the balance in the state treasury here until the government could determine the question of ownership.

This proposition, so unobjectionable as I thought, the Genl. declined, and as I was not malleable for his purposes, I was superseded in the Bank, and three liquidators were appointed by him, not one of whom owns a dollar in the stock of the institution, or has a known claim as creditor; while two of the three have been conspicuous in their malignant hostility to the Union.

I have heretofore President, sent you printed copy of correspondence between Genl. Canby & myself on this subject, and I take the liberty to do so again herewith.[1]

This case was the commencement on the part of Genl. Canby of that system of disrespectful interference with my administration of City affairs to which the accompanying correspondence has reference. Genl. Banks first set the example which Genl. Canby is now imitating; and between them the loss for the coming year would be, in my opinion over seven hundred & fifty thousand dollars, if uninterrupted.

I am not sure, that I do not transcend the requirements of my official position in mentioning what is common conversation in political circles here, namely the coalition of Canby, with Hahn, Banks, Dostie,[2] the late auditor of the State, and accomplice of Hahn, the ex govr. Fish & Shaw[3] in the Convention printing frauds; so fully exposed in the records of the Special Commission of which Genl. W. F. Smith is the President.[4]

As most of the persons who come hitherward from Washington, as real or pseudo commissioners or representatives of the government to spy out the land, are of the radical & anti-State reorganizing class; the parties above named immediately fraternize with them, full charge them with every species of misrepresentation, feast & drink them ostentatiously, & finally, it is said, make a joint stock concoction in the form of a report to the Secretary at War, and another, of a different type for the President's information.

Recently Mr. Cavode[5] of Penn. was so used, and now Major Genl.

Carl Shurz, who is said to be charged with important duties, is monopolized by them, is taken to places of high Flown resort, in company of Hahn, Banks & similar personages, to be manipulated, if possible, to advance their schemes. It is said the parties named have already despatched the notorious radical seditionist Dostie, with a full equipment of charges of high crimes & misdemeanors against Govr. Wells & myself, and also with their programme of cooperation for submission to leaders who are supposed to be managing in the interests of the head of the War department, in accordance with the Harrisburg resolutions of old Thad Stevens.[6]

What is very strange in all this, that neither Genl. Shurz nor any other of the government officials charged with special missions, ever disclose themselves to Govr. Wells or me; or honor us even with a call; but give their days & nights to the society of men notoriously, aye, vauntingly, the declared enemies of your person, your principles & your humane & enlightened policy.

I attach very little importance however, to all such combinations here if they were stripped of official influence; but with all the civil servants of the government, with the exception of Bullitt, Marshal, and Wells,[7] Surveyors of the Port, the Freedmens Bureau, and its drum head power of taxation & collection at short notice, as you will see from the enclosed orders, to the extent of hundreds of thousands of dollars, and the military power in the hands of your enemies, in opposition, I cannot answer even for Louisiana; for these men are capable of any crime, and I have no doubt will hesitate at nothing that can serve their purposes at the polls.

I am no alarmist, and I am not much troubled with fear, but I have my solicitude, unless God spares you, for our institutions and our liberties. As to myself or my concerns President, they are of no earthly importance in connection with the consideration of public affairs; for I am at any moment ready to surrender my commission if one more capable, worthy, & deserving your confidence presents himself to you.

No charge can be made against my personal integrity, my zeal to carry out your policy, my efforts to conciliate, or, I believe, my capacity.

If I can serve you better out of office than in, I am ready to make way for my successor.

I have administered the amnesty oath free of charge to twenty five hundred poor citizens, who could not afford two dollars and a half each, the price charged by U.S. commissioners and the clerk of the U.S. Court. The provost marshals and other attaches of the military power refuse to recognize, it is reported to me, evidences of loyalty so furnished, thus adding to the number of interferences with the most necessary exercise of civil power.

I renew my expressions of regret that I should be obliged to trouble you with complaints, but I feel that any attempt to carry out your policy here, with your enemies in possession of both the civil patronage & military power of the government, must ignobly fail, & I deem it my duty to state the cause and leave the remedy in your hands.

Govr. Wells has not yet returned to the City but writes cheerfully of the feeling in North Louisiana. The country will be a unit in the support of your policy.

Hu. Kennedy   Mayor

ALS, DLC-JP.

1. See Kennedy to Johnson, July 29, 1865, *Johnson Papers*, 8: 499.
2. Anthony P. Dostie.
3. William R. Fish and Alfred Shaw.
4. See J. Madison Wells to Johnson, July 3, 1865, *Johnson Papers*, 8: 341.
5. John Covode.
6. The Union party convention at Harrisburg, Pa., in August 1865 had adopted a "Stevens-inspired" resolution that called for the continued subjugation of the former Confederate states under the direction of Congress, not the President. Erwin S. Bradley, *The Triumph of Militant Republicanism: A Study of Pennsylvania and Presidential Politics,1860–1872* (Philadelphia, 1964), 230–31, 252–53.
7. Marshal Cuthbert Bullitt and Thomas M. Wells, the naval officer.

From William M. Daily[1]

Washington, D.C.   Sept. 11th, 1865

Sir:

There is *one favor*, you can grant *your importuning friend*—and for which, I would forever be grateful. And that is, you could *order* and *direct*, that I be *at once* appointed a *Chaplain in the Regular U.S. Army*. My recommendations for this Office are on file in the Presidents Office where I placed them ten days ago. They are certainly as flatter as any man could ask—even if any thing of the kind were necessary.

If appointed, I would like to be assigned to duty at the *Arsenal* at *St. Louis*, but will be satisfied with any *post*, or *duty*.

As I leave the City this evening it is proper I should say that my Post Office Address is St. Louis, Missouri—(Benton Barracks) where my appointment can be sent.[2]

Wm. M. Daily   Late Hospital Chaplain U.S.A.

ALS, DNA-RG94, ACP Branch, File D-475-CB-1865, William M. Daily.

1. Daily (1812–1877), former congressional chaplain and president of Indiana University, had served as a military chaplain until he was mustered out in August 1865. He subsequently submitted several dozen applications for a variety of federal posts during Johnson's presidency. *NCAB*, 13: 101; Powell, *Army List*, 784.
2. Johnson endorsed this application to Stanton, asking "whether there is any vacancy, to which Dr Daily could be appointed." Assistant adjutant general Samuel F. Chalfin reported there was not, and responded negatively as well to a later Johnson endorsement on Daily's request to be appointed chaplain of the 13th Inf., USA. By the end of September 1865, Daily had been appointed special agent for the Post Office in Louisiana and Texas, a position he held at least until August 1868. Daily to Johnson, Sept. 23, 1865, ACP Branch, File D-507-CB-1865, William M. Daily, RG94, NA; Daily to Johnson, Aug. 15, 1868, Appts., Customs Service, Collector, New Orleans, William M. Daily, RG56, NA; *U.S. Off. Reg.* (1865).

From Robert Mills

September 11, 1865, Boston, Mass.; ALS, DNA-RG94, Amnesty Papers (M1003, Roll 55), Tex., Two or More Name Files.

A Kentucky native, resident in Texas for thirty-five years, applies for pardon for himself and his brother. Although he was a commission merchant in Galveston before the war, he had joined with his brother, David G. Mills, in developing a plantation with over five hundred slaves. He had never been "actively connected with politics," but adhered to the "Old Whig, National, and Union School," believing the "doctrine of the so called States Rights party" to be "heresy to the Constitution." After secession became a "consummated fact," he confesses that he did hope for "Southern success," but he did not hold office or join the military. In June 1863 he went abroad "for the recovery of my health" and remained there until he arrived in Boston on September 9, 1865. Having heard that his business "would be subject to very great embarrassments for the want of the Pardon of the President," he applies for executive clemency for himself and his brother under the thirteenth exception to the Amnesty Proclamation. [Both brothers were pardoned on October 6, 1865.]

From Lewis E. Parsons

MONTGOMERY, ALA., *September* 11, 1865.

Sir:

My request to suspend action on applications for pardons recommended by me[1] is respectfully withdrawn as to all except Theo. Nunn and W. D. Smiths,[2] both of Autauga county. The following were candidates for the convention, which meets on the 12th instant, and if elected[3] will be good members: Jno. A. Weinston and J. R. Dillard, Sumter county;[4] Thos. Mathews, Wm. Byrd, and John S. Hunter, Dallas county;[5] and C. P. Gage, Mobile county.[6] I respectfully ask your excellency to advise me by telegraph, at the earliest moment possible, if they are or will be pardoned.[7] Will write at length. The election returns so far are highly favorable.

L. E. PARSONS, *Provisional Governor.*

Senate Ex. Docs., 39 Cong., 1 Sess., No. 26, p. 245 (Ser. 1237).

    1. Parsons had requested suspension of the pardoning process after allegations involving his secretary of state, William Garrett, surfaced. An investigating committee found that officer guilty of accepting payments from pardon applicants, forcing Garrett's resignation in early September. Majorie H. Cook, "Restoration and Innovation: Alabamians Adjust to Defeat, 1865–1867" (Ph.D. diss., University of Alabama, 1968), 23–24; *Montgomery Advertiser*, Sept. 5, 1865. See Parsons' dispatch of August 18, 1865, and Johnson's notification of compliance two days later. Tels. Recd., President, Vol. 4 (1865–66); Tels. Sent, President, Vol. 2 (1865), RG107, NA.

    2. Planters Theodore Nunn (b. c1822) and William D. Smith (b. c1809) had been pardoned on September 8, 1865. Amnesty Papers (M1003, Rolls 8, 10), Ala., Theodore Nunn, William D. Smith, RG94, NA.

    3. The election had taken place on August 31, 1865.

    4. Here Parsons must have intended Anthony W. Dillard, a self-proclaimed unionist whom ex-Governor John A. Winston defeated in the Sumpter County delegate race.

James R. Dillard (1818-*fl*1881), a former Whig planter and Confederate colonel, lost his election bid for Montgomery County delegate. See Anthony W. Dillard to Johnson, Aug. 14, 1865, *Johnson Papers*, 8: 582–83; Owen, *History of Ala.*, 3: 492; *Huntsville Advocate*, Aug. 17, 1865; William M. Cash, "Alabama Republicans During Reconstruction: Personal Characteristics, Motivations, and Political Activity of Party Activists, 1867–1880" (Ph.D. diss., University of Alabama, 1973), 152.

5. Thomas M. Mathews (b. *c*1814), a wealthy Cahaba planter; Judge William M. Byrd; and Hunter (*c*1799–1866), prominent attorney, legislator, planter, and erstwhile Kentucky stockraiser. Mathews and Hunter served as convention delegates. 1860 Census, Ala., Dallas, River Beat, Cahaba, 792; Brewer, *Alabama*, 219–20; Amnesty Papers (M1003, Roll 6), Ala., John S. Hunter, RG94, NA; *Montgomery Advertiser*, Sept. 22, 1865.

6. Charles P. Gage (1814–1868), merchant and Confederate artillery officer, served in the convention and Alabama senate (1865–67). Owen, *History of Ala.*, 3: 624; Thompson, *Magnolia Cemetery*, 95; Amnesty Papers (M1003, Roll 4), Ala., Charles P. Gage, RG94, NA.

7. Both Byrd and James R. Dillard had already been pardoned on August 11, 1865. Winston, Mathews, Hunter and Gage received their pardons on September 12, 1865. Neither an amnesty application nor a pardon date for Anthony W. Dillard has been found. Amnesty Papers (M1003, Roll 3), Ala., James R. Dillard, RG94, NA; *House Ex. Docs.*, 40 Cong., 2 Sess., No. 15, pp. 5, 9, 14, 17, 25 (Ser. 1330).

Speech to Southern Delegation [1]

September 11, 1865

GENTLEMEN:

I can only say, in reply to the remarks of your chairman,[2] that I am highly gratified to receive the assurances he has given me. They are more than I could have expected under the circumstances. I must say I was unprepared to receive so numerous a delegation on this occasion; it was unexpected. I had no idea it was to be so large, or represent so many States. When I expressed as I did my willingness to see at any time so many of you as chose to do me the honor to call upon me and stated that I should be gratified at receiving any manifestations of regard you might think proper to make, I was totally unprepared for anything equal to the present demonstration. I am free to say it excites in my mind feelings and emotions that language is totally inadequate to express. When I look back upon my past actions and recall a period scarcely more than four short years ago, when I stood battling for principles which many of you opposed and thought were wrong, I was battling for the same principles that actuate me today, and which principles I thank my God you have come forward on this occasion to manifest a disposition to support. I say now, as I have said on many former occasions, that I entertain no personal resentments, enmities or animosities to any living soul south of Mason and Dixon's line, however much he may have differed from me in principle. The stand I then took I claim to have been the only true one. I remember how I stood pleading with my Southern brethren when they stood with their hats in their hands ready to turn their backs upon the United States; how I implored them to stand with me there and maintain our rights and fight our battles under the laws and Constitution of the United States. I think now, as I thought then, and endeavored to induce them to believe, that our true position was under the law and under the Constitution of the Union with the institution of slavery in it; but if that principle made an issue that rendered a disintegration possible—if that made an issue which should prevent us from transmitting to our children a country as bequeathed to us by our fathers—I had nothing else to do but stand by the Government, be the consequences what they might; I said then, what you all know, that I was for the institutions of the country as guaranteed by the constitution, but above all things I was for the Union of the States. I remember the taunts, the jeers, the scowls with which I was treated. I remember the circle that stood around me, and remember the threats and intimidations that were freely uttered by the men who opposed me, and whom I wanted to befriend and guide by the light that led me; but feeling conscious in my own integrity, and that I was right, I heeded not what they might say or do to me, and was inspired and encouraged to do my duty regardless of aught else, and have lived to see the realization of my predictions and the fatal error of those whom I vainly essayed to save from the results I could not but foresee. Gentlemen, we have passed through this rebellion. I say we, for it was we who are responsible for it. Yes, the South made the issue, and I know the nature of the Southern people well enough to know that when they have become convinced of an error they frankly acknowledge it, in a manly, open, direct manner; and now, in the performance of that duty, or, indeed, in any act they undertake to perform, they do it heartily and frankly; and now that they come to me I understand them as saying that: "We made the issue. We set up the union of the States against the institution of slavery; we selected as arbitrator the God of battles; the arbitrament was the sword. The issue was fairly and honorably met. Both the questions presented have been settled against us, and we are prepared to accept the issue." I find on all sides this spirit of candor and honor prevailing. It is said by all: The issue was ours, and the judgment has been given against us, and the decision having been made against us, we feel bound in honor to abide by the arbitrament. In doing this we are doing ourselves no dishonor, and should not feel humiliated or degraded, but rather that we are ennobling ourselves by our action; and we should feel that the government has treated us magnanimously, and meet the government upon the terms it has so magnanimously proffered us. So far as I am concerned, personally, I am uninfluenced by any question, whether it affects the North or the South, the East or the West. I stand where I did of old, battling for the constitution and the union of these United States. In doing so, I know I opposed some of you gentlemen of the South when this doctrine of secession was being urged upon the country, and the declaration of your right to break up the Government and disentegrate the Union was made. I stand to-

day, as I have ever stood, firmly in the opinion that if a monopoly con-
tends against this country the monopoly must go down, and the country must go up. Yes, the issue was made by the South against the
government, and the government has triumphed; and the South, true
to her ancient instincts of frankness and manly honor, comes forth and
expresses her willingness to abide the result of the decision in good
faith.[3] While I think that the rebellion has been arrested and subdued,
and am happy in the consciousness of a duty well performed, I want
not only you, but the people of the world to know that while I dreaded
and feared disintegration of the States, I am equally opposed to consolidation or concentration of power here, under whatever guise or
name; and if the issue is forced upon us, I shall still endeavor to pursue
the same efforts to dissuade from this doctrine of running to extremes;
but I say let the same rules be applied. Let the constitution be our
guide. Let the preservation of that and the union of the States be our
principal aim. Let it be our hope that the government may be perpetual, and that the principles of the government founded as they are
on right and justice, may be handed down without spot or blemish to
our posterity. As I have before remarked to you, I am gratified to see
so many of you here to-day. It manifests a spirit I am pleased to observe.
I know it has been said of me that my asperities are sharp, that I had
vindictive feelings to gratify, and that I should not fail to avail myself of
the opportunities that would present themselves to gratify such despi-
cable feelings. Gentlemen, if my acts will not speak for me and for
themselves then any professions I might now make would be equally
useless. But, gentlemen, if I know myself, as I think I do, I know that
I am of the Southern people, and I love them and will do all in my
power to restore them to that state of happiness and prosperity which
they enjoyed before the madness of misguided men in whom they had
reposed their confidence led them astray to their own undoing. If there
is anything that can be done on my part, on correct principles, on the
principles of the constitution, to promote these ends, be assured it shall
be done. Let me assure you, also, that there is no disposition on the
part of the government to deal harshly with the Southern people. There
may be speeches published from various quarters that may breathe a
different spirit. Do not let them trouble or excite you, but believe that
it is, as it is, the great object of the government to make the union of
these United States more complete and perfect than ever, and to maintain it on constitutional principles, if possible, more firm than it has
ever before been. Then why cannot we all come up to the work in a
proper spirit? In other words, let us look to the constitution. The issue
has been made and decided; then, as wise men—as men who see right
and are determined to follow it as fathers and brothers, and as men who
love their country in this hour of trial and suffering—why cannot we
come up and help to settle the questions of the hour and adjust them

according to the principles of honor and justice? The institution of slavery is gone. The former status of the negro had to be changed, and we, as wise men, must recognize so patent a fact and adapt ourselves to circumstances as they surround us. (Voices— We are willing to do so. Yes, sir, we are willing to do so.) I believe you are. I believe when your faith is pledged, when your consent has been given, as I have already said, I believe it will be maintained in good faith, and every pledge or promise fully carried out. (Cries— It will.) All I ask or desire of the South or the North, the East or the West, is to be sustained in carrying out the principles of the constitution. It is not to be denied that we have been great sufferers on both sides. Good men have fallen on both sides, and much misery is being endured as the necessary result of so gigantic a contest. Why, then, cannot we come together, and around the common altar of our country heal the wounds that have been made? Deep wounds have been inflicted. Our country has been scarred all over. Then why cannot we approach each other upon principles which are right in themselves and which will be productive of good to all? The day is not distant when we shall feel like some family that have had a deep and desperate feud, the various members of which have come together and compared the evils and sufferings they had inflicted upon each other. They had seen the influence of their error and its result, and governed by a generous spirit of conciliation, they had become mutually forbearing and forgiving, and returned to their old habits of fraternal kindness, and become better friends than ever. Then let us consider that the feud which alienated us has been settled and adjusted to our mutual satisfaction, and that we come together to be bound by firmer bonds of love, respect and confidence than ever. The North cannot get along without the South, nor the South from the North, the East from the West, nor the West from the East; and I say it is our duty to do all that in our power lies to perpetuate and make stronger the bonds of our Union, seeing that it is for the common good of all that we should be united. I feel that this Union, though but the creation of a century, is to be perpetuated for All time, and that it cannot be destroyed except by the all-wise God who created it. Gentlemen, I repeat I sincerely thank you for the respect manifested on this occasion; and for the expressions of approbation and confidence please accept my sincere thanks.[4]

New York Herald, Sept. 12, 1865.

1. Some fifty representatives of the former Confederate states, except North Carolina and Louisiana, assembled in the East Room of the White House to pay their respects to the President, "to express their sincere determination to cooperate" in promoting the interests of the country, and to state that they were faithful in their allegiance. *Washington Morning Chronicle*, Sept. 12, 1865; *National Intelligencer*, Sept. 13, 1865.

2. Prominent Richmond banker William H. MacFarland (1799–1872), Virginia secessionist delegate and provisional Confederate congressman, obtained his pardon this same date. Warner and Yearns, *BRCC*; *House Ex. Docs.*, 39 Cong., 2 Sess., No. 31, p. 14 (Ser. 1289).

3. According to the *Chronicle*'s September 12 abbreviated version of the speech, Johnson intimated that he "did not believe the *sensation* letter-writers and editors who were endeavoring to create the impression that there existed in the South disaffection and dissatisfaction" because the presence of so many men "representing such a large constituency" disproved that contention.

4. MacFarland, on behalf of the delegation, returned "sincere thanks for your kind, generous, aye, magnanimous expressions of kindly feeling towards the people of the South." *National Intelligencer*, Sept. 13, 1865.

From William B. Thomas

Custom House, Philadelphia.
Collector's Office, Sept. 11th 1865

Dr Sir

I have the honour to acknowledge the receipt of your letter of the 4th inst[1] which only reached me this morning.

I have been waiting since our interview, to weeks ago, for a call from Dr Batton & Mr Burr[2] and it was only late in last week that I learned their residence.

Mr. Burr called upon me this morning; and I hope to be able to assign him to some position that will be acceptable to him in a few days.

I have sent for Dr Batton for the purpose of ascertaining the place he desires to occupy—and if I can gratify him, shall be pleased to do so.

I was informed by Mr. Burr that he the Dr felt offended at some enquiries that were made as to his political views.

When you named these gentlemen to me you remarked, that, "I could, perhaps, learn more about them" or something to that effect. Having found the name of the Dr. in the directory I requested a gentleman of the Custom house from the same ward, to ascertain wither he was the man I was in search for, and if so, to gently inquire as to his qualifications and political standing. He returned for answer that he was a *gentleman* of *ability*, but a violent "*Copperhead*."

This induced further enquiry which resulted in my conviction of his Loyalty and entire devotion to your administration.

He (like many more of us) has heretofore been identified with the *old* democracy but as I am informed his politicks are now of the New or Jeffersonian school, (if this can be called new) and therefore entirely satisfactory.

Wm B Thomas   *Collector*

ALS, DLC-JP.

1. In his letter Johnson had noted that A. Nelson Batten "has been long and favorably known by me" and "I should be personally, much gratified, if some good and suitable appointment, within your gift, could be conferred upon him." Johnson to Thomas, Sept. 4, 1865, Andrew Johnson National Historic Site, Greeneville.

2. Joshua E. Burr, another Philadelphia patronage seeker. See Rae Burr Batten to Johnson, May 26, 1865, *Johnson Papers*, 8: 109–10.

From Maria S. Wofford[1]

Bulls Gap   Greene County   East Tennessee
Sept. 11th 1865

Dear Sir.

I hope you will excuse my addressing you a few lines. It is about four weeks since I arrived here from New York City, came on to visit a Dear Sister.[2] I heard the Country had become quiet—but I found it any thing else. Men were driven from their homes, some severely beat[3]—& why; just because they were what they term here Southern men, the returned Confederate Soldiers many of them beaten severely & ordered to leave in five days. The People have taken the Oath of Allegiance the Soldiers also to our Goverment. When the latter surrendered to our Generals—protection was promised to all who came home & were Peaceable. I have not heard of one who was not so. I cant for a moment beleive you know the state of affairs here. I have always been for the Union and feel it my duty to write you these few lines hopeing for the sake of humanity, you will do something. How can these People pay their Taxes when they are driven from their homes—and how can there be a reunion of feeling between the North & South? Governor Brownlow in his last Proclamation[4] invites Emigration because the Southern men are leaving. I assure you they are driven off, all more or less have to fly in the night. A Union gentleman told me to-day he was with a Federal Officer, who said to him they were determined to drive off every Southern man. He said to this Officer how could there be Peace, or a reunion of feeling, if that was done. Those who had to fly on account of their opinions, dare not come home. Is it not a sad state of things? I would not live in East Tennessee if they were to give me the whole of it, unless there is a change. Haveing had the Pleasure some years ago meeting with Mrs. Patterson[5] at Mr. Humphreys Wells,[6] please give my love to her. Please excuse me I write to you beleiveing something will be done, to bring order out of Chaos, and restore Peace. I trust your health has been entirely restored, and you will be spared to see all the States back again in the Union—& Peace & plenty be again in our once Beautiful & happy Country.[7]

Maria S Wofford

P.S. I forgot to say by whom all this sad work is done. The discharged Tennessee Soldiers & the low class of Citizens. The Union Men are all for puting it down. Please excuse bad writing as I am very old.

M S W

For our erring Brethern of the South I would say with the Poet—[8]

"Teach me to feel anothers woe,
To hide the fault I see,

That mercy I to others show,
That mercy show to me."

ALS, DNA-RG94, Misc. Correspondence [Enclosed in Johnson to George H. Thomas, Oct. 4, 1865].

1. Wofford (1803–1883) married Benjamin Wofford in 1836; she is not otherwise identified. Buford Reynolds, *Greene County Cemeteries* (Greeneville, Tenn., 1971), 16; Goldene F. Burgner, comp., *Greene County, Tennessee, Marriages, 1783–1863* (Easley, S.C., 1981), 107.

2. Ann C. Wells (1807–1883) lived with her husband Felix W. Wells on a farm near Bulls Gap, about fourteen miles northwest of Greeneville. Reynolds, *Greene County Cemeteries*, 17; Mildred Archer, "A Southern Part of East Tennessee," *Tennessee Ancestors*, 3 (December 1987): 199.

3. As a matter of fact, Wofford's brother-in-law, Felix Wells, had fled recently to North Carolina, and Wells's son-in-law, Thomas J. Lee, had been "driven away" from his Hawkins County home. See Ann C. Wells to Johnson, Sept. 26, 1865, Union Provost Marshal's File of Papers Relating to Two or More Civilians (M416, Roll 65), RG109, NA.

4. Brownlow's most recent "advice" to "leading Rebels" in the region had been to "sell out and go to a new country." *Knoxville Whig and Rebel Ventilator*, Aug. 30, 1865.

5. Johnson's daughter, Martha.

6. Wells (1803–1871) was a Greene County farmer and brother of Felix. Reynolds, *Greene County Cemeteries*, 473; 1860 Census, Tenn., Greene, 9th Dist., Greeneville, 17.

7. Forwarding this letter to Gen. George H. Thomas, Johnson ordered him to "confer with Govr. Brownlow upon this subject and take the proper steps to stop these outrages." Johnson to Thomas, Oct. 4, 1865, Misc. Correspondence, RG94, NA.

8. From Alexander Pope's "The Universal Prayer." John Bartlett, comp., *Familiar Quotations* (Boston, 1948), 216.

From Charles Clark

September 12, 1865, Ft. Pulaski, Ga.; ALS, DNA-RG94, Amnesty Papers (M1003, Roll 31), Miss., Charles Clark.

The wartime governor of Mississippi, crippled while serving as a brigadier general at Baton Rouge in August 1862, applies for pardon. Imprisoned since June 1865, he delayed his application awaiting the outcome of the convention in his state. Having taken the oath of loyalty, he asks amnesty while urging "no appeal to sympathy on account of my wounds, physical disability, & loss of fortune, although they may well be deemed a severe expiation of any error of judgement or action on my part in the late unhappy convulsions." He points out that, after the surrender of Confederate forces in Mississippi, he had convened the legislature and recommended that a convention be held to abolish slavery and to renew his state's ties to the Union. Recounting his activities during the war, he asserts that he is no more guilty than "thousands of others who have been made, even without petition the grateful recipients of Executive Clemency." However, should "it be deemed that my country needs my death, I ask that I may have the privilege of a trial by my peers before a civil tribunal." [Johnson paroled Clark on September 28, 1865, but issued no individual pardon for him.]

From Andrew J. Hamilton

Executive Office
Austin Texas   12th Septr. 1865

I have known the petitioner Saml. A Maverick[1] personally for many years, and I also know his reputation throughout Texas—for he is known either personally or by reputation all over the State.

No man has enjoyed a higher or more deserved reputation for integrity of character—honour and probity—in this State than he.

His crime against the Government is fully and fairly stated in his petition;[2] and if there is any man who feels deeply sorrowful for his participation in the rebellion I believe that he can claim to be such. He brings to me testimonials from the best Union men in the City of San Antonio where he resides, among whom I may mention the Hon Thomas H Stribbling[3] who was in Exile with me. If it be the policy of the Govt to forgive the truly repentant and honest who desire to help repair the injuries inflicted upon the Country then do I most cheerfully recommend the pardon of this old and almost heartbroken man.[4]

A J Hamilton   Provl. Govr. of Texas.

ALS, DNA-RG94, Amnesty Papers (M1003, Roll 54), Tex., Samuel A. Maverick.

1. Maverick (1803–1870) emigrated in 1835 from his native South Carolina to Texas, signed the Texas Declaration of Independence, was elected to the Congress of the Republic, and served in the legislature. Webb et al., *Handbook of Texas*, 2: 161.

2. Although Maverick applied for amnesty under the 13th exception, he confessed that he had accepted an appointment in 1861 as one of three commissioners who negotiated the surrender of United States troops and property in Texas. Maverick to Johnson, n.d., Amnesty Papers (M1003, Roll 54), Tex., Samuel A. Maverick, RG94, NA. See Thomas J. Devine to Johnson, Nov. 16, 1865.

3. Stribling (c1830–1873), a San Antonio attorney who moved to Texas from his native Alabama in 1837, was elected judge of the fourth district in 1866. The legislature subsequently abolished his post but General Sheridan reinstated him in 1867. Ellis A. Davis and Edwin H. Grobe, *The New Encyclopedia of Texas* (4 vols., Dallas, 1929), 2: 1677; *Senate Ex. Docs.*, 40 Cong., 1 Sess., No. 14, pp. 218–19 (Ser. 1308).

4. Johnson pardoned Maverick under the 13th exception on November 18, 1865. *House Ex. Docs.*, 39 Cong., 2 Sess., No. 116, p. 66 (Ser. 1293).

From Hugh Kennedy

City Hall [New Orleans]   12th day of Sept. 1865

President,

I have the honor to inform you that Maj. Genr'l Carl Schurz did me the honor to call upon me this day, and we had a long, and to me, a very interesting conversation. I hope I succeeded in disabusing the Genr'ls mind of some, and in my opinion, very erroneous impressions made on it, and to convince him that outside of a small pestilential circle in this city, which has a momentary importance from its supposed connection or dependence on the military power, there is no sentiment in opposition to the plans of the President ever heard.

He thinks the public opinion in favor of negro education is not quite demonstrative enough, forgetting that a country lately in the throes of revolution is not exactly in the mood for academical discussions.

The General seems much indoctrinated with New England fancies, and not to be indisposed to putting the South in pupillage for Eastern experimenting.

I beg leave to invite your attention to the accompanying letter from our City Surveyor[1] with a front view of our river wharves for one section, which I also send.

Annually in the subsidence of the flood in the Mississipi river, these wharves, composed of heavy wooden frame work, give way and entail heavy expenses for reparation or reconstruction. This year our Surveyor estimates it at two hundred and fifty thousand dollars.

Heretofore this has been a fruitful source of corporation jobbery and electoral corruption, and with the double object of preventing these and making a large annual profit anstead of a heavy annual loss, I proposed the plan of leasing them which as I have explained in accompanying letters, General Canby has forbidden.[2]

                                                 Hu Kennedy   Mayor

LS, DLC-JP.
    1. Civil engineer George W.R. Bayley (c1812–1876) briefly served as city surveyor before becoming chief engineer and general superintendent of the New Orleans, Opelousas and Great Western Railroad. His letter and accompanying material have not been found. Glenn R. Conrad, ed., *A Dictionary of Louisiana Biography* (2 vols., New Orleans, 1988), 1: 49.
    2. See Wells to Johnson, Aug. 25, 1865, *Johnson Papers*, 8: 655–56, and Kennedy to Johnson, Sept. 6, 1865.

From Bartholomew F. Moore[1]

                                              Raleigh   Sep. 12/65
Sir:
    You will pardon me if there be any want of proper etiquette in introducing to you, upon our slight acquaintance, William T. Dortch Esqr.[2] of the town of Goldsboro N C. He visits Washington upon matters of deep personal interest to himself and family—namely, to obtain his pardon, and the restoration of his farm near Goldsboro.

    Mr. Dortch was a student at law of mine about twenty one years ago, and was both in his preparation for the study and on his entrance upon practice destitute of funds. His application & industry, however, soon placed him beyond the reach of need, and he continued to illustrate the bar until he was called into public life. In our practice we often met, and I know that he was much opposed to the attempted secession of the State, and never gave way till all hope of reconcilement seemed at an end. Afterwards he filled important offices under the Confederate government, and was a senator for several years. In his public career, I have every reason to believe, that he prevented the arbitrary proscription of several distinguished union men by the government.

Mr. Dortch has suffered very severely. By his industry & ability he had accumulated a handsome estate, consisting of a valuable tract of land and about fifty slaves. The latter are all emancipated—his lands have been wasted; and not a house now stands on them, except a lot in this town. His provisions and teams were all destroyed in the beginning of the year and he was compelled (for there was not a fence on his lands) to remove to his mothers, a very elderly widowed woman,[3] about forty miles from Goldsboro, where he now lives. Several of the family are dependant on his industry besides his wife and six children. His lands are claimed by the Freedmans bureau, but they are of no advantage to them, for they are unfenced, & will remain so unless they be turned over to him.

I am very sure that he has suffered more than any other public man in the State. Indeed nearly all is gone save his land and some doubtful bonds. In this condition he has lived since the surrender of Gen. Johnson, and is likely so to live, unless he can have his lands restored to him and be pardoned of his participation in the rebellion.

I am very certain, & I think I can be his pledge, that he will, if pardoned, abstain from all intermeddling in the affairs of government & demean himself as a quiet and loyal citizen of the U. States.

It gives me pleasure to make this appeal to your generosity on behalf of öne of my students, and especially one who is so well entitled to your clemency.[4]

B. F. Moore

ALS, DNA-RG94, Amnesty Papers (M1003, Roll 39), N.C., William T. Dortch.

1. A staunch unionist who was among several North Carolinians to preview Johnson's May 1865 proclamation establishing a provisional government in their state, Moore (1801–1878) played a prominent role during the subsequent constitutional convention. *DAB*; Raper, *Holden*, 60–61, 74–75.

2. Prior to his tenure in the Confederate Senate, Dortch (1824–1889) served in the General Assembly and was speaker of that body when North Carolina seceded. Warner and Yearns, *BRCC*.

3. Drucilla Dortch (b. c1785), whose husband, William, had died in 1830. 1860 Census, N.C., Nash, Arrington Dist., 129; Joseph W. Watson, *Abstract of Early Records of Nash County, North Carolina, 1777–1859* (Rocky Mount, N.C., 1963), 11, 31.

4. The words scrawled on Moore's envelope read: "Mr Dortch's application for pardon—B. Moores letter in reference—Referred to the Atty Genl. A. J. Pres." Dortch was finally pardoned on June 18, 1866. Amnesty Papers (M1003, Roll 39), N.C., William T. Dortch, RG94, NA.

From Benjamin F. Perry

Greenville S.C.   Sept 12th 1865

My Dear Sir

Nicholas W. Woodfin[1] of Asheville North Carolina has requested me to write you in reference to his application for a Pardon.

I have known Mr Woodfin for many years, & have always understood that he was a union man till his state seceded.[2] He is now very penitent of his errors, & sincerely disposed to return to his allegiance & act the part of a loyal citizen in all things. I have great confidence in his honor & good faith. He is only excepted from your Proclamation by his worth. He never bore arms, I think, against the U States, or held office under the so called Confederate States. He is a very worthy & excellent man & will exercise a wholesome influence in the Western part of North Carolina.[3]

Bn. F. Perry

ALS, DNA-RG94, Amnesty Papers (M1003, Roll 43), N.C., Nicholas W. Woodfin.

1. A successful jury lawyer, farmer, and Whig state senator (1844–52), Woodfin (1819–1875) had applied for pardon on September 4. Johnston, *Vance Papers*, 92; William J. Battle, ed., *Memories of an Old-Time Tar Heel* (Chapel Hill, 1945), 90; Amnesty Papers (M1003, Roll 43), N.C., Nicholas W. Woodfin, RG94, NA.

2. Despite this and his own claims to the contrary, Woodfin had publicly advocated secession as early as December 1860, several months before his May 1861 vote in favor of disunion. Ibid; Johnston, *Vance Papers*, 92.

3. Woodfin was pardoned on February 1, 1866. Amnesty Papers (M1003, Roll 43), N.C., Nicholas W. Woodfin, RG94, NA.

From Thomas J. Rawls[1]

Columbia, S C.   Sep. 12 '65

My Dear Sir:

I have frequently been present when conversations were going on in relation to your clemency towards the South and particularly S. Ca. and the conclusion generally was that you would get the entire support of the Southern States for next president; and especially if you continue to use that forgiveness as all seem to agree is in your nature.

I have heard this frequently in the most respectable and influential assemblies; although there may be a great outside pressure against your Clemency towards the South among the Northern fanatics; yet it is hoped that your determined character may dispel all such.

One great move which seems to please all here is the removal from the interior of the State the Colored troops.[2] I merely write you this note to advise you of what is going on in your favor.

Thos: Jeff. Rawls, M.D.

ALS, DLC-JP.
1. Rawls (b. c1816) was a prosperous planter before the war. 1860 Census, S.C., Richland, Columbia, 61; 1860 Census, Slave Schedules, S.C., Richland, Columbia, 97.
2. See Perry to Johnson, Aug. 25, 1865, *Johnson Papers*, 8: 651.

From William Conner[1]

Memphis   Sept 13 1865

Dear Sir

I take the liberty as one of your old political friends & supporters to say that I thank you for your support of Judge Sharkey against the miserable military that savages this country.[2]

I live as you know in Lauderdale County Tenn. and I had to suggest to our friends that by calling a meeting endorsing your conduct they would possibly injure you—that they were premature, but I can assure you that all parties here are ready to sustain you just as soon as we think we can do so without injury to the cause of State rights which you have stood up to. I mean of course as to the people of Tennessee & other Southern States fixing themselves the right of sufrage.

"The People must be trusted with the Government" will go down to future generations as one of our great political landmarks.

This will be handed you by our friend Mr. Galloway[3] formerly of the Avalanche than whom there is not a more honest man living as to any thing he promises to do. I will endorse him for the due performance of any thing he undertakes & can do.

Whenever you think we can move properly in the matter write me or some other friend, and without distinction of party we will give you our support in a public meeting.

William Conner

ALS, DLC-JP.
1. Conner (1803-*fl*1884) was a planter and merchant. Kate J. Peters, ed., *Lauderdale County From Earliest Times* (Ripley, Tenn., 1957), 279–82.
2. For an exchange regarding the question of Mississippi militia and Governor Sharkey's proclamation, see Johnson to Carl Schurz, Aug. 30, 1865, *Johnson Papers*, 8: 683, and Sharkey to Johnson, Aug. 30, 1865, ibid., 685.
3. Matthew C. Gallaway, Memphis editor.

From Lewis E. Parsons
(*Private & Confidential*)

Montgomery   Septr. 13th 1865.

Sir:

I have the honor to inform you that the Convention met on yesterday. Ninety two members were present & five more took their seats to day. This leaves only three vacant seats which probably [will] be filled during the week.[1]

We shall have no difficulty in adopting the amendment prohibiting slavery, as far as I can see now, but there is a considerable difference of opinion in relation to the manner in which the question touching the right of the negro to testify shall be disposed of.

Some of the members think it should be inserted in the Constitution itself, & with these I agree,[2] while others think, it should be made obligatory on the Legislature to pass all laws necessary to secure to freedmen the protection of law to life, liberty & property.

The special object of this communication is to request your Excellency to inform me by telegraph immediately, if you regard it indispensible to the interests of the people of Alabama that such a clause should be inserted.[3]

Lewis E Parsons   Provl. Gov. Ala.

ALS, DLC-JP.
1. The actual number of delegates in attendance fell one short of the governor's projection. Fleming, *Alabama*, 358.
2. Ten days later Parsons reiterated: "I am satisfied we cannot govern the 440,000 people of color in this state, without allowing them the right to testify in the Courts." Parsons to Johnson, Sept. 23, 1865, Johnson Papers, LC. For more on this issue, see John B. Myers, "The Freedman and the Law in Post-Bellum Alabama, 1865–1867," *AR*, 23 (1970): 56–57.
3. Apparently the President thought otherwise, since there is no record of an immediate response. For further developments related to this issue, see Parsons to Johnson, Sept. 28, Oct. 2, and Dec. 2, 1865.

From Benjamin F. Perry

Columbia S C   Sept 13th 1865.

President Johnson

The State Convention assembled today one hundred (100) members present. The ablest body ever convened in the State. Resolutions of discontent were offered,[1] and received only five (5) votes, laid on the table and refused to be printed. I send in my message tomorrow, which is a strong one; sustaining your reconstruction policy. All is going on well.[2]

B. F Perry

Tel, DLC-JP.
1. Perhaps resolutions such as those proposed by delegate Alfred P. Aldrich. *Senate Ex. Docs.*, 39 Cong., 1 Sess., No. 26, p. 121 (Ser. 1237); Lillian A. Kibler, *Benjamin F. Perry: South Carolina Unionist* (Durham, N.C., 1946), 406.
2. See Perry to Johnson, Sept. 23, 1865.

From Benjamin H. Bigham[1]

Washington D.C.   Sept 14, 1865

In regard to the petition[2] which I had the honor to send to you a few days since asking a temporary *parole* for Alexander H. Stephens, unless you should meanwhile find that the same may be granted in accordance with your views and without apprehended detriment to the public service I have the honor to petition that you suspend decision a few days, because I have reason to expect that other representations will be made to you on the subject.[3]

I believe I understand that the reasons that stand between Mr. Stephens and this great favor are reasons of state. These I would most gladly see removed and hope they will be removed in a short time. The friends of Mr. Stephens are amongst your staunchest & most reliable friends. I feel that I (humble as I am) am amongst that number. I came here fully & cheerfully committed before our people to the support of your administration & go away confirmed, by the noble speech I heard you make a few days since, in my determination to support you vigorously & faithfully.

In the resistance he rendered to this lamentable war the courage of Mr Stephens was sublime. No man risked so much or done so much against it in Geo. Yet he is now the only man who is held, from Geo, as a political prisoner. I do not think this is reproach to my Government. Whatever you do I know you are wiser than I and I submit therefore confidently. Mere reference to this fact will furnish excuse however for the anxiety Mr. S. friends feel. We resisted this tide and after it has smothered us into silence for four long years of tyranny shall those who succeeded over us, contrasting their situation to that of Mr Stephens feel that after all he is to be the only sufferer. I advocate a general amnesty at heart but we would not have a sentiment of exultation, however quietly indulged, to find a place. We would not be considered importunate. We would not needlessly consume your valuable time but the interests of orphans & they for whom he has exercised fiduciary duties the interest of the freedmen on his place, his own health many many reasons appeal in behalf of Mr Stephens, and no consideration I know is of greater importance in the eye of your Excellency than the brilliant services national aye continental in their character which he so long and so faithfully rendered to the country.[4]

B. H. Bigham

ALS, DLC-JP.

1. Bigham (c1828-fl1870) was an attorney, a three-time member of the Georgia Assembly, and a state judge. 1870 Census, Ga., Troup, LaGrange, 45; Isaac W. Avery, *The History of the State of Georgia from 1850 to 1881* (New York, 1881), 52, 212, 262.

2. This petition, assigned an incorrect date of July 4, 1865, is found in Johnson Papers, LC.

3. See Stephens to Johnson, Sept. 16, 1865.

4. Bigham had recently obtained two interviews with the President. During the second, Johnson had reportedly said that, while he "did not forget the sacrifices of any public servant," he "must have a due regard to the general tranquility and the good of the whole country." *Augusta Constitutionalist*, Sept. 30, 1865.

From Bushrod R. Johnson

September 14, 1865, Nashville, Tenn.; ALS, DNA-RG94, Amnesty Papers (M1003, Roll 49), Tenn., Bushrod R. Johnson.

Falling under the third and eighth exceptions, Johnson, an 1840 West Point graduate who resigned from the army in 1847, seeks amnesty and pardon. He is currently under an indictment in the U.S. circuit court, issued in 1863, for treason, "but no arrest has been made." "From a conception of duty" he entered the southern service as a major of engineers in 1861 and served until paroled as a major general under the terms of Lee's surrender at Appomattox Court House; yet he served "in a strictly subordinate capacity . . . neither planned campaigns or counciled the policies pursued." Johnson protests that he fairly and honorably has discharged his obligations, both military and civil; thus, "if the same character of mercy which I have shown to others . . . be meted out to me I shall have nothing further to solicit." Having never owned a slave and regarding slavery "as the prolific cause of angry discussions, embittered feelings and constant prejudices and dissensions between the two sections of the Union," he "cheerfully accepts its overthrow" and is "implicitly obedient . . . to the reestablished authority of the United States Government." [Johnson never received an individual pardon but benefitted from the general amnesty promulgated on Christmas Day, 1868.]

From Hugh McCulloch

[Washington]   September 14th 1865.

Dear Sir:

Will you do me the favor to examine the accompanying application of Duff C. Green[1] of Alabama, son of General Duff Green, formerly of this city?

You will notice that his pardon is recommended by Governor Parsons and other influential gentlemen.[2] It seems that he has been performing some duties (very acceptably), for the Treasury Department; and I am clearly of the opinion that a compliance with his wishes would not be detrimental to the public interests. Mr. Green, it is true, was a graduate at West Point, but had no connection with the United States service for a number of years before the Rebellion broke out. He has held office in the State of Alabama, but I understand has had no position in the Confederate service.

I should be personally obliged to you will give Mr. Green's application a favorable consideration.[3]

H McCulloch

Have you come to any conclusion as to Governor Fenton's[4] matter?

LS, DNA-RG94, Amnesty Papers (M1003, Roll 4), Ala., Duff C. Green.

1. During the war Green (1828–1865) served as quartermaster general of Alabama. Owen, *History of Ala.*, 3: 696.

2. Green's amnesty application bore the endorsements of Treasury agents Thomas C.A. Dexter, John H. Collins and Mobile customs collector R. V. Montague. A petition

from twenty Pickens County residents, including John A. Winston and Anthony W. Dillard, accompanied the application. Amnesty Papers (M1003, Roll 4), Ala., Duff C. Green, RG94, NA.

3. The President pardoned Green on September 14, the very day that McCulloch wrote this letter. Less than two months later, Green died. Ibid.

4. Reuben E. Fenton (1819–1885), currently governor of New York, later served in the Senate. The "matter" McCulloch alludes to here is unknown. *DAB.*

From Joseph McJames [1]

Danville Ky   September 14th 1865

Sir

Allow me to call your attention to the enclosed letter to me from Col Jas. F Jaquess, of the Freedmans Beaurou, Commanding at Lexington in this State.[2] The letter was elicited by the complaint of a Colored man prefered against me, as I think without right. The case stands thus. To the services of the negro man in question I am entitled, as my slave: he is freed by no Proclamation of the Executive hitherto issued, nor by any law passed by Congress, but remains mine by all the law of which I am informed. I had from time to time paid him wages, out of kindness, but when, under proviking circumstances, he left me, and found employment with another, I notified that other, not to pay to him the price of his services. On this the complaint was based—And from this protection was given him.

Having supported most heartily the Govrnmet in its recent struggle, and being a friend to your administration, I will render to the laws of my country the most exact obedience; but do not think the order relied upon in the enclosed letter is here applicable, and it is in relation to this, I wish information. I do not think such a case is reached by the order, but not desiring to come in conflict with the "Powers that be", on the one hand, and on the other, not wishing to suffer any wrong myself, I have written to you to ascertain what are my rights under the circumstances.

If your Excellency can find time to answer this, you will subserve very much the interests of the public. . . . [3]

Joseph McJames

ALS, DNA-RG105, Records of the Commr., Lets. Recd. from Executive Mansion.

1. On the eve of the war McJames (b. c1819) was a farmer whose personal property included three slaves. 1860 Census, Ky., Boyle, Danville, 4; 1860 Census, Slave Schedule, Ky., Boyle, 17.

2. Jaquess had reminded McJames that his agency, under "Genl Order No 32," sought to protect the rights of blacks to seek employment for fair wages. Jaquess to McJames, Sept. 8, 1865, Records of the Commr., Lets. Recd. from Executive Mansion, RG105, NA.

3. We have not found a response from Johnson.

From George W. Morgan[1]

Cleveland O   Sept. 14th 1865

Dear Sir,

It having been decided that the declaration of the cessation of war is a political, and not a judicial act, it is claimed by the Ohio republicans that war still exists, inasmuch as the President has not proclaimed Peace.

By a law of Ohio, soldiers absent from the State during war, are entitled to vote, and republican agents have been sent to the Ohio troops. This opens the door to fraud and imposition upon the soldiers, which should not be allowed. I will get *full* one half of the soldier vote at home.

If not inconsistent with the public good, I would be glad if you would proclaim the cessation of war, as peace does in fact exist.[2]

Genl. Cox[3] has gone over to the Schenck[4] platform of excluding the Southern States from Congress.

To me it is evident that in the coming congress, your most earnest support will be from the democracy and the conservative element of the republican party. I have the honor to enclose you my speech of yesterday.[5] I leave here at once.

George W. Morgan

ALS, DLC-JP.

1. The former brigadier general currently was campaigning as the Democratic gubernatorial candidate.

2. Johnson declared the war officially over, in all states except Texas, on April 2, 1866.

3. Jacob D. Cox, Morgan's Republican opponent, won the election.

4. Ohio congressman Robert C. Schenck.

5. Not found, though it was probably Morgan's address delivered at Elyria on September 12, in which he warned that Republican policies would invariably lead to black immigration and school integration. Felice A. Bonadio, *North of Reconstruction: Ohio Politics, 1865–1870* (New York, 1970), 90.

From Elisha M. Pease[1]

Austin Texas   14 Sept 1865

Sir

Although I have not the pleasure of a personal acquaintance with you, I take the liberty of addressing you in regard to the course pursued by Gov Hamilton since his arrival here, because I have learned that rumors are being circulated at Washington that his course has not been satisfactory to the original union men of the state.[2]

I am an old resident, of Texas and for twenty years previous to the Rebellion was much engaged in Public affairs. I took an active part against it at the commencement and never ceased to express my opinion freely in regard to it during its progress. Being at the capital, I had opportunities for communication with the union men from all parts of the state, and believe that I know their wishes as well as any other man in the state. In making so many appointments as have been necessary to put the government in operation, it was impossible to give satisfaction in every case where there were rival applicants, but I say without fear of contradiction, that he has made the best selections that could have been made under the circumstances, and I have yet to hear the first complaint from any loyal citizen in regard to the policy that has been pursued by the Governor in reorganizing the government.

It is my belief that Texas is now in a better condition to resume her position in the union than any other of the late confederate states, and that the policy pursued by Gov Hamilton has contributed greatly to produce this state of affairs. I trust that he will continue to receive the confidence and support of the administration, as he has of all the disinterested supporters of the union in this state.

E M Pease

ALS, DLC-JP.
1. Pease (1812–1883), a native of Connecticut, had served as governor of Texas (1853–57). Although defeated as the Union party candidate for governor in 1866, he was appointed provisional governor the following year. Webb et al., *Handbook of Texas*, 2: 351–52.
2. See Andrew J. Hamilton to Johnson, Sept. 23, 1865.

From Charles T. Quintard[1]

Steamer United States.   14 Sept 1865.

Dear Sir—

A paragraph which I find in an evening paper,[2] expressing your views touching the approaching Genl Convention of the Episcopal Church induces me to address you this note.

I have recently been elected Bishop of the Diocese of Tenn. As such I desire most cordially to respond to the sentiments attributed to your Excellency, in the paragraph referred to—& I unite with you in expressing the hope that the Convention will be characterized by a cordial conservatism such as will heal the seams & scars of war & operate with power in restoring to our land peace & good will towards all men.

I have taken the oath to support the Government of the United States. I have kept back no part of the price. I desire now to renew my pledge & to assure you Sir that you will find in the length & breadth of the land none more sincere none more faithful—or more true in sustaining your administration—& so restoring law & order.

As my friend Mr White[3] has consented to deliver this note—I venture to say that it would afford me great gratification to have a personal interview. My address will be for the next two weeks "Stamford Conn."

C. T. Quintard

LS, DLC-JP.
1. Quintard (1824–1898), a trained physician, held rectorships in Memphis and Nashville before serving as Confederate chaplain, 1st Tenn. Inf., CSA. Consecrated bishop at the church's General Convention held at Philadelphia in October 1865, Quintard subsequently committed himself to reopening the University of the South at Sewanee, Tennessee. *DAB*.
2. Not found.
3. Not identified.

From Joseph Medill[1]

Chicago   Sept 15, 65

Sir

It is truly to be hoped that you do not judge of the political opinions of the 20. millions of Northern people from the colums of the N Y World or Herald.[2] It is further to be hoped that you are *aware of the fact* that the late civil war emancipated the *minds* of the Northern people from the dominion of the Oligarchy as well as the bodies of the Slaves. No scheme of reconstruction will ever again include the vassalage of the North to the southern aristocracy. The day is passed forever of the rule of the chivalry. In the future they will stand before the country as whipped rebels, and not haughty dictators and swaggering task masters.

You may affect to despise the Radicals: but their votes made you President, their bayonets and principles put down the southern rebels and held their allies the Northern copperheads by the throats. They number two millions of brave, earnest, men pressing will, nerve, conscience and power.

They Control 20 states and both branches of Congress. Four fifths of the soldiers sympathise with them. Can you afford to quarrel with these two millions of voters? Can you afford to *Tylerize*[3] your party? True, you can inflict great injury on the union cause, but you can not break up the great Republican anti slavery party, which will follow in the footsteps of the martyr Lincoln and in the end triumph over treachery within and treason without.

For God sake move cautiously and carefully. Don't show so much eagerness to rush into the embrace of the "$20,000 rebels." They will suck you like an orange and when done with you throw the peel away. Better stick close to old friends who carried you into the White House than to exchange them for Copperheads & rebels who will garrote you after using you.

The great doctrine of *equal rights* is bound to prevail. It is your high privilege to lead the colum.

J. Medill

ALS, DLC-JP.
1. Medill (1823–1899) owned and edited the *Chicago Tribune*, a staunch Republican organ. *DAB*.

2. Medill's Democratic rivals.

3. To forsake the party to which a person owes office or allegiance as President John Tyler had done. Mitford M. Mathews, ed., *A Dictionary of Americanisms on Historic Principles* (2 vols., Chicago, 1951), 2: 1790.

From Pierre G.T. Beauregard

"Copy"

New Orleans La., Sepber. 16th, 1865.

Sir,

I have the honor to apply for the benefits of the Amnesty proclamation of May 29th, 1865—from which I am excluded by exceptions third—eight & thirteenth.

In taking up arms during the late struggle (after my native state, Louisiana, had seceded) I believed, in good faith, that I was defending the constitutional rights of the South against the encroachments of the North. Having appealed to the arbitration of the Sword, which has gone against us, I accept the decision as settling finally the questions of secession & slavery—& I offer now my allegiance to the Govt. of the United States, which I promise, truly & faithfully, to serve & uphold hereafter, against all external or internal foes.

Enclosed please find my oath of allegiance taken before the Mayor of this city.[1]

(Signed) G. T. Beauregard[2]   late Genl. C.S.A.

CopyS, DNA-RG94, Amnesty Papers (M1003, Roll 27), La., Pierre Gustave Toutant Beauregard.

1. Beauregard's oath is dated September 16. Although a recipient of a parole from Johnson, he was not granted an individual pardon, despite the recommendations of Hugh Kennedy, Governor Wells, and Thomas Cottman. Beauregard was eventually included in the general amnesty on Christmas Day 1868. Amnesty Papers (M1003, Roll 27), La., Pierre Gustave Toutant Beauregard, RG94, NA; Johnson to Beauregard, May 5, 1866, Johnson Papers, LC. See John Van Buren to Johnson, Oct. 9, 1865.

2. Beauregard endorsed this document as "A true copy."

From Thomas H. Benton, Jr.[1]

Confidential

McGregor, Iowa, Sep. 16th 1865

Dear Sir

The enclosed printed letter will explain itself.[2] I am a native of Williamson County, Tennessee, nephew of the late Senator Benton of Missouri & for the last twenty five years a citizen of Iowa. I write to advise you of the exact state of things here. A threat is now *secretly* made by leading Republicans that all Federal officers in this State who refuse to support my opponent[3] & endorse the resolution in the Republican platform on the subject of negro suffrage, of which I enclose a copy,[4] shall be removed. I am satisfied that this resolution is incorporated in the platform to be used as a lever against you in your reconstruction policy, & for that reason I am giving it my open & unequivocal opposition. I believe that your policy is the true one & shall oppose any measure designed to throw obstructions in your way & defeat your plans. I trust therefore that you will consider the matter maturely before you take any action in making removals in Iowa. I wish the influence of this threat could be counteracted before the election. You are endorsed in the Republican platform, but I am fully convinced that the design is to oppose you whenever opportunity offers & the Republican paper at this place[5] has already declared against you. Notwithstanding the strong influences against me, I shall get the cordial support of a large body of Republicans & would carry the State had I two weeks more time & may possibly do so as it is. I send this through a friend that it may be sure to reach you direct. My address at present is Desmoines, Iowa.

Thomas H Benton Jr.

ALS, DLC-JP.

1. Former educator, state senator and brevet brigadier general, Benton (1816–1879) currently headed a "Soldiers' Ticket" opposing black suffrage. Losing the election for governor in 1865, he was appointed an assessor of internal revenue the following year. T. S. Parvin, "Thomas Hart Benton, Jr.," *IaHR*, 16 (1900): 4–13; Benton to Hugh McCulloch, Oct. 23, 1866, Appts., Internal Revenue Service, Assessor, Iowa, 6th Dist., Thomas H. Benton, Jr., RG56, NA; *U.S. Off. Reg.* (1867), 75.

2. Not found, though the secretary's note on the document indicates that Benton forwarded a copy of his "letter of acceptance" as gubernatorial nominee, perhaps like the one published in the *Iowa State Press* (Iowa City) on September 13, 1865. See Clarence R. Aurner, "Some Early Educational Leaders in Iowa," *IaJHP*, 22 (1924): 543n.

3. The incumbent, William M. Stone (1827–1893), a former newspaperman, district judge, and brevet brigadier general, who, after his second term as governor, served in the state legislature, and later as land office commissioner. Sobel and Raimo, *Governors*, 2: 433.

4. The resolution favored removing the word "white" from the article on suffrage, thereby "recognizing & affirming the equality of all men before the law." Johnson Papers, LC.

5. Frank W. Palmer's *Iowa State Register*. Will Porter, *Annals of Polk County, Iowa, and the City of Des Moines* (Des Moines, 1898), 607–9.

From Charles J. Biddle[1]

Philadelphia, Pa   September 16." 65

Sir

I beg leave to address a few words to you in regard to the approaching election in this state. It is firmly believed by the Democrats of Pennsylvania that the state elections, for the past three years, have been carried against them through the influence and authority of the civil and military officers of the Federal Government. We now hope, under your administration, to enjoy free and fair elections. No ground exists on which to base a pretext that the interests of the country can be prejudiced by the prevalence of the will of the majority of the people of Pennsylvania at the polls. The Democratic party here sustains your wise and patriotic policy for the restoration of tranquillity to the whole country. Being myself a candidate on the Democratic ticket for a local office in this city,[2] I can truly say that always, and especially when a member of the 37th Congress, the principles on which I acted were those anounced by you, at its first session, on the 29th July "61,[3] though I was not in my seat during that session, being then in Military service. My associates on the Democratic ticket are many of them men who have served their country in the field for more than I have, and all are governed by the same conservative principles. We look now for a triumph of those principles if "fair play" is accorded. If the Federal authority is not abused by the subordinate agents who exercise it, we think the result in this state will be such as should occasion no regret to you, or to any patriot who looks to the good of the whole country. It is believed that the abuses which have existed heretofore would be corrected by an intimation of your disapproval of them. Hoping that the matter may be deemed worthy of your consideration, and that you will excuse the liberty I take in addressing you upon it. . . .

Charles J. Biddle

ALS, DLC-JP.
  1. Newspaper editor and chairman of the state Democratic central committee.
  2. He lost his bid for city solicitor the next month. *Philadelphia Evening Bulletin*, Oct. 11, 1865.
  3. See Speech in Support of Presidential War Program, July 27, 1861, *Johnson Papers*, 4: 606–42.

From Virginia C. Clay[1]

Huntsville, Ala.   Sept. 16th 1865.

My dear Sir,

Hon. Duff Green, of your city, was kind enough, some weeks since, to apply to you for a permit for me to visit Washington.[2] I have this day only, received it, with the endorsement of your Secretary[3] in the following language: "I am directed by the President to say, that an application for permit to visit W. made by Mrs. C. C. Clay Jr., over her own name will be considered by him." May I trespass for a moment Sir, on your valuable time, to explain my position, wh. however you may already fully comprehend. When I requested Mr. Green, & other friends to apply for a permit, it was deemed indispensable, but, I thought the necessity had now passed by. At all events, Sir, I, unhappily, cannot visit W. unless I can thereby accomplish an important object.

Months ago, Mr. President, *I* would have presented myself to you, to ask permission to visit my husband, and sue for his release. But wiser heads & riper judgments than mine, assured me that *no appeal* in behalf of Mr. Clay wd. be considered by you, until *after* some disposition of Mr. Davis's case. I have waited for nearly four long months, (to me years,) for that event, but in vain!

My patience & fortitude being exhausted, I take counsel of my own head & heart, & will test the right & power of appeal to you, the Chief Ex. of this nation. I write to ask of you, the precious privilege of *seeing my husband*. Gen. Miles[4] & he, both write me of his sickness, & "I die daily," fearing to hear the saddest intelligence that can ever come to my stricken heart. I have no objection to Gen. Miles being present at our interview.

It is needless for me, Mr. President, to remind you of the high ground upon wh. my husband stands, as a *self-surrendered* prisoner to the Gov'mt., nor to Eulogise him to one, who, once his confrere in the Senate, cd. not fail to know & appreciate his qualities of mind & heart in every relation & position of life.

My confidence in your Judgment assures me, that, this day you esteem him, as entirely innocent of the heinous crime imputed to him, as I, his wife, *Know him to be*! Incapable of *any* baseness, with a stainless record, life-long, private & public (awarded him by even his enemies), how cd. he descend to participation in a cold-blooded murder plot? But I fear to weary you.

I would hurry to Washington instantly, to prefer this request in *person*, but for lack of means to expend in what might prove a useless journey. I wd. gladly bankrupt myself for a visit to Mr. Clay, but it wd. be sad to do so for only a refusal, & I know not what *clemency*, (tho' I hope mine/*Clement-C.*), you feel disposed to show me.

In Washington, I might be an object of persecution, and without the friends of yore, & I dare not go, without some assurance of your protecting aegis. As a daughter of the South & the wife of your noble prisoner, I implore you to grant this appeal of an agonized woman! Say that I can see my husband, (Mrs. Mallory[5] & others have visited theirs) or give me one hope of his release, & I will fly to you with words & tears of grateful thanks for your Justice, magnanimity & clemency.[6]

Hoping you are enjoying the health of body & mind necessary for the duties of your high & responsible position. . . .

V. C. Clay

ALS, DLC-JP.

1. Clay (1825–1915) was the wife of the Alabama Confederate senator who had been implicated in the plot to assassinate Lincoln and confined at Fortress Monroe since May 1865. See Jeremiah S. Black to Johnson, July 3, 1865, *Johnson Papers*, 8: 339–40.

2. After having written Johnson "a note on the subject, to which I have as yet received no reply," Green personally delivered his endorsement of Mrs. Clay's request. Green to Johnson, Sept. 5, 1865, Clement C. Clay Papers, NcD.

3. Robert Morrow.

4. Fortress Monroe jailer Nelson A. Miles (1838–1925) had dutifully kept Mrs. Clay informed of her husband's condition throughout the summer. Warner, *Blue*; Nuermberger, *Clays*, 274–75. For a decidedly different appraisal of the officer's role as jailer, see Bennett H. Young, "Review of Gen. Miles's Cruelty to Mr. Davis," *Con Vet*, 13 (1905): 217–19.

5. Angela Moreno Mallory (c1822-*fl*1873) visited her husband in late July 1865, at Fort Lafayette, New York harbor. Durkin, *Stephen R. Mallory*, 16, 354, 414; 1870 Census, Fla., Escambia, Pensacola, 37. See Stephen R. Mallory to Johnson, Sept. 27, 1865.

6. After a series of interviews with the President, Mrs. Clay traveled to Fortress Monroe in late December 1865 and was authorized by Johnson to visit her husband the following month. Nuermberger, *Clays*, 279–82; Virginia C. Clopton, *A Belle of the Fifties* (New York, 1904), 331; Nelson A. Miles to Edwin D. Townsend, Dec. 28, 1865, Lets. Recd. (Main Ser.), File M-2528-1865 (M619, Roll 387), RG94, NA; Johnson to Miles, Jan. 12, 1866, Johnson Papers, LC.

From Francis H. Peirpoint

Richmond, Sept 16 1865.

Sir

This will introduce to you Gen Joseph R Anderson[1] of this city. He visits you to procure his pardon. He will explain. You know him by character. I know him personally. He happened to own the Tredegar Iron works, in part, at the commence of the rebellion. He made cannon while thousands of others made wheat corn and pork. Others fought in the field. Anderson is not a politician. I believe never aspired to anythig in that line beyond a seat in the house of delegates in Va., then to forward some work of improvement. But he is a man of great energy and has done much to develope the mechanical and manufacturing interst of the state. He had the force of character to engage in manufacturey pursuits in the state when labor among the first circles was not very honorable. He has lost from his mills perhaps what was worth to him or his firm one hundred thousand dollars most of it siezed by the government and carred away.[2] I have thought much about this case, and it strikes me under all the circumstances, it is not policy to strike down men of great energy like Anderson where his skill and talents are engaged in developing the country. It is such we now want. The petty amt of his property is of no consideration in a national point of view when compared with the great benefit he may render the state. Perhaps I have a false estimate of this class of men, if I have it is because they are scarce. I would not give one of them for as many politicians as will fill an acre field. It is on this ground I ask for his pardon.[3]

F. H. Peirpoint

P.S. Gen Anderson has thrown his whole influence since I arrived here in favor of state and federal government and has I have no doubt acted sincerely and his influence has been potent for good.

F. H. P.

ALS, DNA-RG94, Amnesty Papers (M1003, Roll 56), Va., Joseph R. Anderson.

1. Anderson (1813–1892) had been excluded from Johnson's May 29 amnesty because he had been a Confederate brigadier general, a West Point graduate, and owner of substantial property. Charles B. Dew, *Ironmaker to the Confederacy: Joseph R. Anderson and the Tredegar Iron Works* (New Haven, 1966), 295; Warner, *Gray*.

2. At the close of the war the most vital forge in the Confederate arsenal had been closed, placed under military guard and libelled for confiscation. Dew, *Ironmaker*, 297–98.

3. With the Virginia governor's endorsement in hand, Anderson immediately traveled to Washington and, after several interviews with the Chief Executive, received his pardon on September 21. Ibid., 300.

From Alexander H. Stephens

Fort Warren B.H. Mass   16" Sept. 1865

Dear Sir—

You will I trust excuse me for again earnestly soliciting your attention to my case. More than four weeks ago I addressed you[1] asking for a personal interview. I was informed by the officer here[2] under whose charge I then was a few days afterwards that a telegram[3] had been received by the Commandant at the Post authorizing and directing him to make me as comfortable as he could in the Post, and to say to me that my letter to you had been received and would be replied to. This is the substance of the telegram as given to me. Since then I have been made as comfortable as I can be here. The very uncomfortable quarters occupied by me before were immediately changed—for which I felt and do feel greatly obliged. Had I been kept where I was my opinion is I should have died. Hence you can form a proper idea of my sense of obligation for this change. But the object of this letter is to say to you that I have been *patiently* and *anxiously* waiting to hear from you upon the subject of the personal interview. If my great anxiety upon the subject causes me now to begin to grow impatient on this point I submit to your consideration these current reasons—time is rapidly passing by. If I am to have a parole at all it is of the utmost importance in every point of view in which it is most desirable to use that it should be at an early day. My affairs at home—the settlement of estates in my hands and my plan for the future arrangement with and settlement of those who have heretofore stood in the relation of slaves to me by our laws as set forth in my first letter to you require my presence at least by the middle or latter part of October. Again if I am not paroled before cold weather sets in I fear the State of my health will not permit me without risk to undertake the travel home. If I am to be paroled at all it is of the utmost importance to me personally as well as to my affairs at home that the parole be granted soon. I am induced to make this statement to you and to call your *special* attention again to the matter from an announcement this day seen by telegram from Washington[4] that I was not to be paroled until after the delegations from the southern states should be admitted into Congress. This may not be true; but it awakens my apprehensions. Again you will allow me to state that I have been told by a number of friends that my confinement is simply a matter of state policy. How this is I do not know. But it is upon this point mainly I wished to confer with you, and I therefore again earnestly solicit the interview. It does seem to me that this might be granted as it has been granted to great numbers certainly infinitely more responsible for all our late trouble than I am. I am as earnestly desirous to be for a speedy restoration of harmony and prosperity to our united country upon permanent principles as any man living can be—and if it can be shown to me upon rational principles that my confinement for a day or a year or for life or that even the sacrifice of my life itself will contribute essentially in any degree to that great result I wish you to thoroughly understand that I will cheerfully submit. I can say with the utmost truth that there has not been a day since I left the old Congress that I would not have willingly offered up my life for the permanent peace and happiness of this country. All my present sufferings & privations & trials I would cheerfully bear if it can be made to appear to me that the public good founded upon any reasons of state can be subserved thereby. I can not see how my release on parole or bail, if it be thought best, can in any way thwart any just policy of state in regard to me. All these matters however I am desirous to talk over with you and if the views I entertain upon them do not meet your approval I will as stated again return to this place. Hoping that you will at least excuse this letter for the reasons assigned even if you do not grant this request I remain yours.[5]

Alexander H. Stephens

ALS, DLC-JP.

1. See Stephens to Johnson, Aug. 16, 1865, *Johnson Papers*, 8: 606.

2. Lt. William H. Woodman (b. *c*1834), 1st Btn. Mass. Heavy Arty., who worked as a bootmaker before the war. CSR, RG94, NA; Myrta L. Avary, ed., *Recollections of Alexander H. Stephens: His Diary Kept When a Prisoner at Fort Warren, Boston Harbour, 1865 . . .* (New York, 1910), 474.

3. See Johnson to Commanding Officer, Fort Warren, Mass., Aug. 18, 1865, *Johnson Papers*, 8: 608.

4. We have not been able to locate the announcement to which Stephens refers.

5. Johnson directed the Attorney General to "please have the letter filed with the others of Mr A.H.S." On October 11, 1865, the President granted Stephens a special parole and nine days later the two men talked for nearly two hours in Johnson's office. Richardson, *Messages*, 6: 352; Avary, *Recollections*, 536–37.

From Anna Bunting Powell[1]

Montgomery Ala.   Sept. 17th [1865][2]

Dear Sir,

In the ruinous condition of the Southern states the negroes are threatening us with midnight assassination and massacre. So abundant are the proofs[3] that conviction forces itself upon us the evil day is *not far of* when their wicked purpose is to be put in execution. As you are the only person possessing the power and *will* to save us from the fury of the fiends we earnestly entreat you will *speedily* provide for us. I but speak the sentiments of every lady and gentleman in our State in this *our appeal* to *you*.

I feel convinced that my application will meet with assistance—and protection from one of my own native state and county. Will you be pleased to honor me with a reply?[4]

Mrs Anna Bunting Powell

ALS, DNA-RG105, Asst. Commr., Ala., Registered Lets. Recd., File E-9-1865.

1. Powell (b. c1832) was the wife of James W. Powell, delegate to the Alabama seces-
sion convention, Confederate captain, and Montgomery alderman. Joel C. DuBose, ed.,
Notable Men of Alabama (2 vols., Spartanburg, S.C., 1976[1904]), 1: 85–87; 1860
Census, Ala., Montgomery, 1st Dist., Montgomery, 169; *Con Vet*, 31 (1923): 104.

2. We have supplied the year, based upon the endorsements by clerks which accompany the letter.

3. Three newspaper clippings, which had appeared originally in the *Mobile News, New
York News*, and *Jackson Mississippian*, accompanied Powell's letter. The excerpts warned
of an imminent rebellion by Alabama's blacks.

4. Received by the President's office, Powell's letter was referred to General Howard
of the Freedmen's Bureau later in the month for investigation.

To Thadden C. Bolling[1]

Washington, D.C., Sept 18 1865.

Your dispatch received.[2] The admission of members into the present
Congress is a question to be determined by the respective houses. I
think the members from Tennessee will be permitted to take their
seats—provided the other Southern States elect members who are un-
mistakeably union in practice and sentiment and so amend their con-
stitutions and pass laws in regard to emancipation and freedmen which
will give them proper protection. This being done the basis for opposition will be substantially removed.

Please inform me as to the amendments made to your Constitution
and Laws. I hope all will work harmonious and right.

Andrew Johnson   Prest U.S.

Tel, DNA-RG107, Tels. Sent, President, Vol. 2 (1865).

1. A unionist delegate to the secession convention, Bolling (1816–1866) currently
represented Greenville, S.C., at the state constitutional convention. Bolling to Johnson,
Sept. 23, 1865, Office of Atty. Gen., Lets. Recd., President, RG60, NA; *Senate Ex.
Docs.*, 39 Cong., 1 Sess., No. 26, p. 174 (Ser. 1237); Greenville Chapter of South Caro-
lina Genealogical Society, *Greenville County, SC Cemetery Survey* (5 vols., Greenville,
S.C., 1977–83), 2: 155.

2. From Columbia on September 17 Bolling had wired the President: "Have the
members of Congress in Tennessee been elected on the free basis? If so will they be
entitled to their seats?" Bolling to Johnson, Sept. 17, 1865, Johnson Papers, LC.

From James G. Bourland[1]

Lamar Co., Texas, Sept. [18] 1865[2]

The petition of James Bourland, a resident citizen of Cook County,
Texas, who, being within the exceptions specified in the President's
proclamation of General Amnesty of the 29th of May 1865, applies for
special pardon, respectfully represents:

Petitioner represents that he was born in Pendleton District, South
Carolina on the 11th of August A.D. 1801—was carried by his Father
to Kentucky in 1805, where he remained until Twenty-one years of
age, then moved to Tennessee and from thence to Mississippi, and from

thence to Texas in the year A.D. 1837 and settled in the County of Lamar where he engaged in Farming, which had been his occupation previously. In 1842 he was appointed, by Gen. Sam Houston, then President of the Republic of Texas, Collector of Customs for the Red River District of Texas, and re-appointed by President Miller[3] just prior to the annexation of Texas to the United States. He was a member of the State Senate during the 1st and 2nd Sessions of the Legislature of Texas after her annexation to the United States. In 1846 the petitioner raised a regiment of Volunteers for service in the Mexican War, declined to run for Col. but accepted the office of Lt. Col. and served until discharged. His authority for raising the regiment was from Gov. Henderson,[4] and sent to him, without application for the same by him, at the time he was a member of the State Senate.

He moved from Lamar County to Cook County in 1851 where he has since resided and still resides, engaged in farming, and occasionally in merchandizing.

Petitioner was absent from home attending to business in New Orleans at the time (in 1861) when Major Emory[5] the U.S. officer in command at Fort Washita I.T. was forced by the volunteers from Texas to abandon said post and move towards Kansas. Petitioner joined Gen Cooper[6] in the Winter of 1861–2 for a few days only, in an expedition against the Indians, and after the retreat of the Indians from the vicinity of the frontier where he resides, he remained at home until the Summer of A.D. 1863, when at the earnest solicitation of Gen. J. Bankhead Magruder,[7] he took command of a Regiment raised for the protection of the frontier of Texas against the Indians. He continued in command of the frontier, as Col, until the surrender of the Trans Miss. Department.

Immediately after the surrender he was appointed by Gen. E. Kirby Smith to collect the men together to be paroled at Bonham; and to collect government property. Petitioner immediately issued a circular requiring the men to come forward to be paroled. He also required all citizens to turn over government property to the proper authorities, and from that time to the present he has exerted himself to his utmost to induce his neighbors and fellow citizens, to not only submit quietly but to support and sustain cheerfully the authorities of the United States Government. To establish this fact he might bring forward scores of witnesses.

He further states that the exception in the Amnesty Proclamation which applies to him, if any does apply to him, is the clause with reference to the amount of property owned, his property having been assessed at over $20,000 towit at about $30,000.00 in A.D. 1861.[8]

He further states that he has taken the Amnesty Oath in good faith, a copy of which is hereto annexed.

He further states that during the war he has not been engaged in any kind of speculation; that his property at the present time does not exceed in value fifteen thousand dollars: That he is not now under arrest, nor is any of his property in the possession of the United States, or any of its agents, nor have any proceedings been instituted for the confiscation of his property or any part thereof.

Wherefore he asks for amnesty and pardon for all past offences or supposed offences charged against him growing out of said rebellion[9] &c, and for general relief; and he pledges himself to be a peaceable and loyal citizen in the future.

Petitioner further states that there is no Chief Justice in Cook County before whom to make affidavit—hence his application to an officer of another county.

Jas Bourland

LS, DNA-RG94, Amnesty Papers (M1003, Roll 52), Tex., James Bourland.

1. Bourland (1801–1879) had been a horse and slave trader in Tennessee until the Panic of 1837 prompted him to relocate in Texas. In addition to the public services outlined in this petition, he also commanded several volunteer units in campaigns against Indians. Richard B. McCaslin, "Tainted Breeze: The Great Hanging at Gainesville, Texas, October 1862" (Ph.D. diss., University of Texas, Austin, 1988), 56–57, 499, 566–68.

2. William Bramlette, chief justice of Lamar County, certified Bourland's petition on this date.

3. Probably James B. Miller (d. 1854), who served as secretary of the treasury in Houston's second administration. Webb et al., *Handbook of Texas*, 2: 195.

4. James P. Henderson (1808–1858) served in several offices for the Republic of Texas, including brigadier general. He was elected the first governor after annexation, but spent much of his term with the United States Army in Mexico, rising to the rank of major general. He was a United States senator at the time of his death. Ibid., 1: 795–96.

5. William H. Emory.

6. Douglas H. Cooper (1815–1879) was a United States agent in the Indian Territory when the Civil War began. Although he commanded Indian units as large as a brigade and was belatedly appointed commander of the Indian Territory for the Confederacy, his appointment as brigadier general was never confirmed. Warner, *Gray*. See Douglas H. Cooper to Johnson, Dec. 1865.

7. Magruder (1807–1871), after a poor performance in the Peninsula Campaign, was assigned to command the District of Texas (1862–65), which later included New Mexico and Arizona. Warner, *Gray*; Boatner, *CWD*.

8. In 1860 Bourland was the second largest slaveholder in Cooke County, with twenty-three bondsmen. McCaslin, "Tainted Breeze," 41.

9. As Confederate provost marshal for Cooke County, Bourland condoned the hanging of several men, and at least one woman, as dissidents against the South. The climax to these activities came in October 1862, when a vigilance committee under his direction initiated the lynching of at least forty suspected unionists. Several of his subordinates in the Border Regiment later tried to have him court-martialled for continuing to execute prisoners without trial, but their petition was quashed. Governor Hamilton refused to endorse Bourland's application, but Johnson pardoned him on November 30, 1866. Ibid., 171–78, 199–278 passim, 313–75 passim, 427, 444–45, 498–99.

From Edmund Burke[1]

Newport, N.H.   Sept. 18, 1865.

Sir.

I write, briefly, to express to you my unqualified thanks and gratitude, for the patriotic and noble stand which you have taken in favor of the restoration of the Union upon the principles of the Constitution.

I knew you had been nurtured in the School of Jefferson and Jackson, the principles of which you most faithfully and ably advocated when I was in Congress with you. But, in these perilous and changing times, I had some fears that the powerful influences by which you are surrounded, might swerve you from your early political faith and principles. But, thank God, you are proving true to them, and to the principles upon which our glorious Republic was founded.

As you well know, I have always been a supporter of the just rights of the South under the Constitution. But, when they unfortunately made the issue of disunion, I was forced to go with a party whom I hated, for the preservation of the Union. Although, not liable to military duty, I had my substitute in the Army pledged to fight for the Constitution and the Union, and not for the abolition of Slavery, although that might be a result of the war. The question of Secession has been decided by the arbitrament of the Sword. Slavery has fallen as an incident of the war, but, under your policy the Union is to be preserved under the Constitution, and upon the principles upon which it was founded by Washington and the Fathers.

I can foresee that you will encounter from the Radicals a fierce and vindictive opposition. But, "be just and fear not," God and the people will sustain you. In your great and patriotic work I think I may assure you, that you will have the undivided support of the Democratic Party of the North. Large numbers of the conservative Republicans will also support you, and the South must be a unit in your favor. The result, therefore, cannot be doubtful. Your policy will triumph, and you will rise a name in history second only to that of Washington.

I have presumed to write to you because words of encouragement, even from a humble man and private citizen, will be cheering to you in the great struggle which you are destined to go through.

There are other matters which in due time will demand your attention. They are 1. the reduction of the Tariff to a standard which will produce the most revenue; and 2. the restoration of Specie payments.

The present Tariff is prohibatory in respect to many kinds of merchandise—such as cotton goods; woollens, [many?] &c, paper; leather; Boots & shoes; India Rubber fabrics &c. The high rate of exchange, growing out of paper money, gives an additional protection of at least

50 per cent. By the operation of these two causes, the manufacturers are coining fortunes yearly, at the expense of the poor consumers. The Paper makers cleard 100 per cent on their capital. The cotton and woolen manufacturers nearly the same. The Manchester Print Works in this State clear between 60 and 100 per cent on their great capital. The mass of these immense profits comes out of the laboring classes. With the exorbitant loses which they are now compelled to pay, they should not be burthened with these enormous profits of the manufacturing capitalists.

I *respectfully* direct your attention to these matters, because I know you, like myself, have always sympathised with the toiling millions. But, the great work to be first accomplished, is re-construction. That attained, I trust your attention will be turned to the relief of the people from the burthens of unequal taxation and monopoly.

Edmund Burke

ALS, DLC-JP.
1. Burke (1809–1882), currently a lawyer, had been a newspaper editor, Democratic congressman (1839–45), and commissioner of patents (1846–50). *BDAC*.

From James B. Campbell[1]

Columbia So Ca   Septr 18/65

Dear Sir/
I have been here for several days. Have mingled freely with the members of the Convention most of whom are personally known to me. There is no doubt of their disposition to do what is proper but there is a remarkable ignorance or forgetfulness of our strange position. This arises in a great measure from the want of mail facilities and means of intercommunication. It can hardly be said that newspapers have been circulated in this state for the last six months or more. Hence members advance crude and inconsiderate suggestions. They have not only to rely upon you for their salvation, but to consider it already secure, forgetful that they must do their full share to aid and strengthen your efforts to maintain the government in their behalf and as a part of the great whole against those who would consign us to hopeless ruin and degradation.

But I do not doubt every thing will in the main go right. I have not hesitated to remind my friends that our restoration to the Union and to participation in the Govt. does not mean a restoration of old politicians who have served with equal complacency in Rebel and in Loyal Congresses. That to attempt to restore such persons is to put additional embarrassments upon you.

There is one proposition, in amendment of the Constitution which is urged by a powerful party at the head of which is Mr Orr. It is to make the basis of Representation *White* population excluding the negro altogether from representation and of course I suppose from Taxation. This I think wrong in itself and besides, it is very impolitic.[2] It gives a much stronger point to the New England party to make their stand upon than the suffrage question. It certainly makes the hope of progress for the negro very hopeless indeed, and if seized upon would I think increase your burden in our behalf. I said this to Col Orr but he insists that his views are just such as you would approve if submit[ted] to you. It may be Sir and that I take an improper view. I am disposed to advocate entire acquiesence in whatever you wish. Indeed would be content that you should write the state Constitution for us for in fact it is your battle and without you I become satisfied we would have no hope. You are the Breakwater between us and the overwhelming [surge?] of hopeless ruin that would other wise sweep over us. I have stated this point so that you may be informed and if you should consider it of any consequence that in the state Constitution, the freed men shall be enumerated as population and represented, you may express your views to Govr. Perry.

Jas B Campbell

ALS, DLC-JP.

1. A delegate to the constitutional convention, Campbell (1808–1883) was an affluent Charleston attorney, businessman, and state legislator (1850–56, 1862–66, 1876–78). Kibler, *Perry*, 356, 391, 427, 469; N. Louise Bailey et al., eds., *Biographical Directory of the South Carolina Senate, 1776–1985* (3 vols., Columbia, 1986), 1: 261–63.

2. The record reveals otherwise; on September 21, when another delegate offered a substitute amendment striking out the word "white," Cambell joined James L. Orr's faction in narrowly defeating the measure. *Senate Ex. Docs.*, 39 Cong., 1 Sess., No. 26, pp. 144–45 (Ser. 1237).

From Sterling R. Cockrill[1]

Courtland [Ala.]   Septr. 18th 1865.

Mr President,

I have just read your Speech to the "Delegates of the Southern States,"[2] and being highly pleased with its manly tone, and a fixed resolution, to do all in your power, to restore prosperity and happiness to the South, you will accept my *thanks*, for this public avowal of those generous Sentiments.

We have much to say in vindication of our conduct, but *this* we must leave to history. The bloody conflict between brothers, is *closed*, and we "come to bury Caesar, not to praise him." The *South* had $2,000,000,000 invested in Slaves. It was very natural, that they should desire to protect, and not lose this amount of property. Their action in this effort, resulted in War. There was no desire to dissolve the *Union*, but to protect this property. The issue was made and it is decided. The fife, and drum, and canon's roar are no longer heard, and the agitated land has vibrated to rest, and the South is ready to abide by the issue, in *good faith*. She was Chivalric in War, and will be faithful in peace. This fidelity, when once promised, can only be disturbed, by an attempt to rule her with a rod of iron. Hence the quieting effects, of such expressions as, "I am, of the Southern people, and I love them." Let me assure you also "that there is no disposition on the part of the Government, to deal harshly with them."

These sentiments, are *soothing*, to a people who have lost *so much* in property and the best blood of the land. We of the *south* who know you personally can pledge you to the maintainance of any declaration which you may make.

I have been among the Agriculturists of the South for 35 years. I had $250,000 invested in Slaves; and I think I understand *them*, and what they as a *body intended* in 1860; and the points bearing most heavily at *present*.

The gallant *dead* are *gone*, and they can only revere their memories and Commemorate their deeds of valor. The *living* are to be provided for, and how far, and what manner the Government can aid in doing that, are the questions. The class excepted in your proclamation 29th May 65, are restless and unsettled, and fearing that the Govt is still intending to take more of their property. They are the class who own much of the lands which have been heretofore cultivated by the slave labor. They are the persons to make permanent arrangements with the emancipated Negroes. They hesitate to do so, as they think the *Government* may disturb their possession by confiscation.

Then there is much property, holden as *abandoned* and tho not abandoned, according to the Act of Congress, everything is in doubt, till possession be restored, either by special pardon, or an Order from the Comr. of the Freedmen's Bureau. The late Circular of 15th,[3] of Genl Howard, is some relief but a generous, speedy policy, on the part of the Govt secures possession of their lands, and then they begin to give homes, and employment to the emancipated Negroes, which is very important to them; whilst it gives quiet, and a prospect of support to the *living* whites.

The Govt has changed the Status of the Negro. That is, he is no longer a *Slave*, and the South will make *no effort* to change that status. You may rely upon that *with absolute certainty*; and may withdraw your garrisons as fast as you wish. The "*State Militia*," can be substituted whenever needed. The Negroes are docile, peaceful, and indolent. There is no danger from them whatever. They will be indolent, and thriftless, and they have the deepest sympathy of the intelligent portion of the south who will have to take care of many thousands of them, and the policy of the Government is, to trust *that* to the Legislatures of the States, which will be composed of men, who understand the questions, and will finally devise the most practical and humane plans of releif.

The intelligent men of the South dont blame the Negroes, and hence there is no ill feeling among them. The poor white men, who are the majority are not in favor of "*negro suffrage.*" They say, they fought for the "*flag and the Union*"; not to make the Negro their *equal.*

As a native of Tennessee, and long a citizen of Alabama, and a Cotton grower of Arkansas, I think I know something of the true sentiments of the South.[4]

S. R. Cockrill

ALS, DLC-JP.
1. The previous month Cockrill had applied for executive amnesty, admitting his Confederate sympathies and brief service as receiver, Mid. Dist., Tenn., until the fall of Nashville. Amnesty Papers (M1003, Roll 48), Tenn., Sterling R. Cockrill, RG94, NA.
2. See Speech to Southern Delegation, Sept. 11, 1865.
3. Howard's Circular Number 15, issued on September 12, 1865, had redefined confiscated property as only that sold under court decree, and ordered the return of all other real estate to prior owners who had received pardons. The Freedmen's Bureau currently possessed Cockrill's plantation in Jefferson County, Arkansas. McFeely, *Yankee Stepfather*, 134; Amnesty Papers (M1003, Roll 48), Tenn., Sterling R. Cockrill, RG94, NA.
4. Johnson granted Cockrill a pardon on October 24, 1865. *House Ex. Docs.*, 40 Cong., 2 Sess., No. 16, p. 9 (Ser. 1330).

From James Lyons [1]

Washington City   Sept. 18 1865

My dear Mr. President

On Thursday last, when I had the honor to present to you my application for a pardon, you were so kind as to say that you would do me the honor to see me again on Saturday. On Saturday I presented myself at your door, but the usher declined to take in my card to you, saying that [you] would neither see any person, or receive any more cards on that day, and I retired, and was not therefore present when your door was opened to visitors.

I now therefore most respectfully request, that you will be so good as to grant me an interview, this morning, or at such other hour, as will best suit your convenience. My situation is a very painful one. Since my petition was filed with the Atty Genl., my property has been libelled and a portion of my revenue taken by the Marshall, and I am under bond to account for the residue to the Court which will sit on the 12th of October next, to decide whether my property (and that of others) shall be confiscated or not. If that question should be decided against me, I shall, at the age of Sixty three, be left pennyless, with a large family.

By my petition you have been informed who I am, and my opinions and feelings have been truthfully expressed, in the invitation to you from the people of Richmond, to visit this City, which I had the honor to prepare.[2]

I trust that under these circumstances you will grant me the interview which I request, and generously extend to me the clemency which you have, so justly, extended to many of my colleagues.[3]

James Lyons

ALS, DNA-RG94, Amnesty Papers (M1003, Roll 64), Va., James Lyons.

1. Lyons (1801–1882), Virginia secessionist and Confederate representative, later served as defense counsel for Jefferson Davis, his close friend. Warner and Yearns, *BRCC*.

2. See Richmond Citizens to Johnson, Aug. 25, 1865, *Johnson Papers*, 8: 652.

3. Having read this, Johnson directed Lyons to "confer with" Attorney General Speed. A pardon date of September 18, 1865, appears on Lyons's file, but a different date—March 4, 1866—was reported to Congress. Amnesty Papers (M1003, Roll 64), Va., James Lyons, RG94, NA; *House Ex. Docs.*, 39 Cong., 2 Sess., No. 31, p. 14 (Ser. 1289).

To J. Madison Wells

Washington, D.C.   Sept 18 1865.

Your telegram and letter have been received[1]—also a letter from Senator Hahn taking decided ground against the appointment of a Provisional Governor.[2]

I have been much inclined to appoint one but still hold it in suspense. I hope you are progressing successfully and with the prospect of restoring the authority of the State.

I hope that General Canby will afford every facility in his power to aid you in the accomplishment of the work you have undertaken.

It is expected of him to do so.

If there are any conflicts between the Military and any measure you may have adopted for the restoration of the State you will without delay communicate with the Government and steps will be at once taken to reconcile all disagrements.

I hope that you will act with promptness and decision and cause the work of reorganization to go forward without delay or hindrance.

Andrew Johnson   Prest U.S.

Tel, DNA-RG107, Tels. Sent, President, Vol. 2 (1865).

1. On August 12, 1865, Johnson had telegraphed Wells asking his opinion on the appointment of a provisional governor for Louisiana. In a telegram on August 16 and a letter on August 25, Wells had recommended the appointment of himself to the position. This wire was in response to Wells's query on the previous day as to whether his previous communications had been received. Wells to Johnson, Sept. 17, 1865, Johnson Papers, LC. See Wells to Johnson, Aug. 25, 1865, *Johnson Papers*, 8: 654–55.

2. Seward had forwarded to Johnson a letter from Michael Hahn that declared there was no "good and valid reason" to repeal the "good and liberal constitution of 1864" by appointing a provisional governor. Another letter from Hahn, outlining Wells's abuses of power as governor, was forwarded by Schurz along with his report of September 4, 1865. Hahn to Seward, Aug. 31, 1865, Hahn to Schurz, Sept. 6, 1865, Johnson Papers, LC; *Advice*, 124, 130, 131n.

To James P. Boyce[1]

Washington, D.C., Sept 19th 1865.

Your pardon has been granted,[2] and will be forwarded to you by mail. The proceedings of your convention so far is giving great satisfaction here. I hope that all will terminate right and that in less than the next twelve months, the Union of the States will be complete & restored.

Andrew Johnson   President

Tel, DNA-RG107, Tels. Sent, President, Vol. 2 (1865).

1. The South Carolina Baptist minister was one of several convention delegates who appealed for executive clemency at this time. Boyce to Johnson, Sept. 19, 1865, Johnson Papers, LC. See, for example, W. R. Robertson to Johnson, Sept. 20, 1865, and John Britton to Johnson, Sept. 22, 1865, Johnson Papers, LC.

2. Boyce was actually pardoned on July 22, 1865, though the pardon document itself obviously had not been forwarded. *House Ex. Docs.*, 40 Cong., 1 Sess., No. 32, p. 46 (Ser. 1311).

To William G. Brownlow

Washington, D.C., Sept. 19th 1865.

In reference to Vincent,[1] to be handed over to be tried by Civil authority, you will please confer with General Thomas, who no doubt will do whatever the circumstances in the case requires.[2] I hope there will be no conflict between the Civil and Military Authorities, and if you and Genl. Thomas have a conference upon this subject I feel well assured there will be none.

Andrew Johnson   President

Tel, DNA-RG107, Tels. Sent, President, Vol. 2 (1865).

1. Mustered out of the Union army in late June 1865, Bartlett C. Vinson (b. c1840) had been charged with the September 5 murder of Pvt. Jesse David, 1st Hvy. Arty., USCT. 1860 Census, Tenn., Hamilton, 7th Dist., Harrison, 160; CSR, RG94, NA.

2. Tennessee's secretary of state, Andrew J. Fletcher, assured Johnson that Brownlow and Thomas would confer. Almost a month later, Thomas, temporarily in Washington, stated that the President fully understood the Vinson case and that he, Thomas, had no authority to delay the trial nor was he disposed to do so. On the following day, October 17, Thomas ordered Vinson, who had already been indicted by a Chattanooga grand jury, to stand trial by military commission. Before his trial took place, however, Vinson "escaped" from military prison on December 6. Brownlow to Johnson, Sept. 19, 1865, Johnson Papers, LC; Johnson to Thomas, Sept. 19, 1865, Tels. Sent, President, Vol. 2 (1865), RG107, NA; Fletcher to Johnson, Sept. 22, 1865, Johnson Papers, LC; Thomas to Ramsay, Oct. 16, 1865, Tels. Sent, Sec. of War (M473, Roll 90), RG107, NA; CSR, RG94, NA.

From Edward Donnelly[1]

Philadelphia   Sept. 19th 1865.

Your Excellency:

I have the honor to inform you, as a reason, why *Rodger A Pryor*,[2] should not be pardoned, that he committed murder at the second battle of Bull Run, by killing a Union soldier, and mortally wounding another, after having surrendered and whilst being conducted as a prisoner of war, thereby making his escape and afterwards boasting in my presence of his dexterity in killing his victims and the wiles used to throw his escort off their guard till he had an opportunity to assassinate them.[3]

     E. Donnelly M.D. Late Surgeon 1st Provl Pa. Cavalry
N.B. At the above mentioned time I was Surgeon of the 2d Regt. Pa. Reserves.

ALS, DNA-RG94, Amnesty Papers (M1003, Roll 67), Va., Roger A. Pryor.

 1. Donnelly (1822–1891) served as a surgeon in various Pennsylvania units during the war. He settled after the war in Pittsburgh then relocated in 1879 to the San Francisco Bay area, where he continued to practice medicine. Pension File, Florence Donnelly, RG15, NA.

 2. The Confederate congressman and brigadier general was pardoned, by "special request" of the Attorney General, on September 20, the same date Donnelly's letter was received by the President. Amnesty Papers (M1003, Roll 67), Va., Roger A. Pryor, RG94, NA.

 3. Johnson forwarded Donnelly's complaint to the Attorney General. Donnelly later informed the Secretary of War of his charges against Pryor, and that letter was likewise referred to Speed. Donnelly to E. M. Stanton, Nov. 15, 1865, ibid.

From Lovell H. Rousseau [1]

           Louisville Ky. Sept. 19th 1865.
My Dear Sir.

 I returned from Nashville on yesterday, after a stay of eleven days at that place. On my return from Washington, I went directly to Nashville and Saw most of the leading men of Tennessee. They are very heartily & cordially for your policy and your Self. Tennessee will be a unit for you and for your Administration. The feeling in Tennessee towards your Administration, and yourself personally is all you could wish.

 The correspondence between Messrs Cooper, Campbell, & Thomas & myself[2] was to be published in the Nashville Papers this morning. On its reception I will send you a copy. I have it in contemplation to go for a few days into Illinois & Indiana, and See Some of the leading men there.

               Lovell H Rousseau

ALS, DLC-JP.

 1. Commander, District of Middle Tennessee.

 2. Six days earlier Rousseau had requested Edmund Cooper, William B. Campbell, and Dorsey B. Thomas, Tennessee congressmen-elect, to define their positions toward the Johnson government. On September 16 the trio issued a joint statement affirming their loyalty to and uniform support of the administration. *Nashville Union*, Sept. 20, 1865.

From Albemarle County Citizens [1]

Charlottesville, Va., Sept. [20][2] 1865

Dear Sir:

We, the undersigned, citizens of the County of Albemarle and State of Virginia and friends of your administration, are prompted by the difficulties which surround us in relation to the approaching Congressional elections to appeal to you for counsel and advice as to our proper course of action. In this Congressional District for example, three gentlemen are soliciting the suffrages of the people.[3] They were all conservative men before the war and opposed to secession. Two of them admit that they countenanced the Southern cause during the war to an extent which prohibits them from taking the oath which was prescribed by the Congress of the U.S. in 1862.[4] The third says that he can conscienciously take it: and the question presents itself—how shall we vote?

Some of us prefer one candidate and some another; but being wholly uninformed as to whether the test oath will probably be repealed or modified so as to admit Southern members, we have thought it possible that you might enlighten us on the subject. Our first wish is to send men to Congress who will give the most efficient support to your administration, whether they be of the one class or the other. Should it be your opinion that the oath will most probably be insisted on, and that our object will most likely be attained by voting only for those who can stand the test, then we are disposed to relinquish our individual preferences and cast our suffrages for those who are qualified to take the oath. If on the other hand, you should entertain the opinion that men whose antecedents have been conservative will be admitted, notwithstanding their inability to take the oath, then we may vote otherwise than we would do under a difficult state of things. We truly & sincerely desire information on the subject, & should you be able to spare the time from your other duties and see no impropriety in complying with our request, we would be greatly obliged to you to furnish the information asked for. Our main purpose is to pursue that course which [will] be most likely to sustain you and your policy in the administration of the Government.[5]

Pet, DNA-RG60, Office of Atty. Gen., Lets. Recd., President.

1. The names of eleven signatories appear at the end of this petition.

2. Various printed versions of this document provide no exact date. We have chosen September 20, since this was when the petition was received and referred to the Attorney General's office. See *Philadelphia Evening Bulletin*, Sept. 28, 1865; *New York Times*, Oct. 1, 1865; *New Orleans Picayune*, Oct. 20, 1865.

3. Candidates for the Sixth Congressional District of Virginia were Alexander H.H. Stuart (1807–1891), a Whig congressman (1841–43) and secretary of interior under Fillmore; John F. Lewis (1818–1895), who eventually served in the Senate (1870–75); and unionist John R. Woods, who withdrew early in the race. Stuart prevailed in the October election. *Charlottesville Chronicle*, Sept. 6, 19, 21, Oct. 11, 1865; *BDAC*.

4. Subscribers to this "ironclad oath" had to swear that they had never been disloyal, that is, had never borne arms against the United States or held office under the Confederate government, either local or national. *U.S. Statutes*, 12: 502–3. See Thomas Grasty to Johnson, Sept. 16, 1865, Office of Atty. Gen., Lets. Recd., President, RG60, NA. See also John Letcher to Johnson, Nov. 3, 1865.

5. The Attorney General, responding on behalf of Johnson, stated that, while the President desired only "loyal and true men" be elected, he would not speculate as to what Congress would do about the oath. *Philadelphia Evening Bulletin*, Sept. 28, 1865.

From Simon Cameron

Harrisburg   Sept 20. 1865.

My dear Sir:

A certain General Knipe,[1] who claims a very intimate personal acquaintance with you, makes himself ridiculous by running about our streets with a petition for his own appointment as Post mater here, saying that you have promised him the office. Mr Knipe is also very busy trying to defeat our county ticket, by a coalition with the Copperheads, of which however there is no great danger. He can exert no influence.

Our Post-master[2] is the Editor of the only Union Newspaper in this city—a warm upholder of your Policy, and was reappointed on the recommendation of the entire representatives of the Union party of the state. He is now a member of our state central Committee, and a most excellent officer, and no respectable persons here desire his removal, unless it may be a small clique, who in conjunction with Knipe are trying without much success to get control of the county.[3]

We are now in the midst of our fall campaign, and will carry the state.[4] And when this is done we will sustain Your Policy, be it what it may.

Simon Cameron.

ALS, DLC-JP.

1. Joseph F. Knipe.

2. George W. Bergner (1818–1874), editor and co-proprietor of the *Pennsylvania Telegraph*, a Cameron mouthpiece, had been appointed by Lincoln in 1861. William H. Egle, *History of Dauphin and Lebanon Counties* (Philadelphia, 1883), 465–66; Erwin S. Bradley, *Simon Cameron, Lincoln's Secretary of War: A Political Biography* (Philadelphia, 1966), 138, 152, 180, 353–54; *U.S. Off. Reg.* (1865), 307.

3. In May 1866 Johnson replaced Bergner with Knipe, a development that undoubtedly contributed to Cameron's break with the President. Bergner regained his position after Grant took office. Ser. 6B, Vol. 2: 63, Johnson Papers, LC; *U.S. Off. Reg.* (1867–69); Bradley, *Cameron*, 265–69.

4. When Cameron's "Unionist Republicans" won a decisive majority in the October election, he congratulated Johnson "on having carried Pennsylvania." Cameron to Johnson, Oct. 10, 1865, Johnson Papers, LC.

From Robert H. Glass

'Republican office'   Lynchburg, Virginia
Sept 20th 1865.

Dear Sir:

When in Washington a few days ago, I was shown by Mr. Pleasants,[1] a newspaper paragraph said to have been clipped from my paper in 1862, in which your name is coupled with those of Messrs Botts & Brownlow[2] in very uncourtly & harsh terms. I further understand that said paragraph was filed among my papers for pardon by Mr. Botts, in order to visit upon me the vengeance of a great goverment for the personal affront & wrong offered him in said article.

While I have no sort of fear that you can be influenced against so humble an individual as myself at a time like the present, by any such vindictive feelings as these which seam to influence Mr. Botts, yet, I nevertheless deem it due to me as well as to your Excellency, that I should frankly explain, & apologize for the character of the said article.

At the time it appeared I was Post Master in this city, as I had been for years, & wrote very little & paid little attention to my paper, other parties writing for me. I really cannot say, therefore, whether I wrote it or not. But I am responsible for it, & supposing that I was the author of it also, I am free to say that its language is coarse, its sentiments wrong & the article improper. It was written however, in the midst of a bloody war, when our passions & prejudices & hates on both sides, were intense, & when I am free to say that I, in common with our people in the south, looked upon you & others opposed to us, as our [direiists?] enemies & when any calamity upon them would have been a source of gratification. The same feeling, no doubt, was held by the people of the north towards our leading men, Davis, Yancey & others, & it was a perfectly natural feeling with enemies of equal honesty of purpose, & when killing each other was the whole occupation of the people. But the war is over & the passions & hates which it occasioned are also ended, or ought to be. We no longer regard you as our enemy, but our best friend—our only refuge from our enemies in this terrible hour of distress. There is not a man or woman amongst us who would not look upon any disaster to you as a disaster to us & the country, although we might have "hung" you during the war. And we are just as honest now as we were then, whatever may be said to the contrary. Nor have we any doubt that your feelings toward us are as much changed & as kindly as ours toward you. "*Wise men change—fools never.*"

I feel no more hesitency, therefore, in asking you for a pardon now than I did when I did not suppose that the slighest objection would be filed against me. I do not ask for it because I have any fortune to save. I am as poor as you were when you left No. Carolina for Tennessee, having lost everything by the war save my office. I simply want it to reinstate myself to all the rights of citizenship, & relieve my family from unnecessary fears. And while I make no promises or professions, I can safely say that you will find in me a much better friend & supporter than your excellency will ever find in Mr Botts & some others who have been & *are* now your life long enemies.[3]

R. H. Glass

ALS, DNA-RG94, Amnesty Papers (M1003, Roll 61), Va., Robert H. Glass.

1. Matthew F. Pleasants, pardon clerk.
2. John Minor Botts and William G. Brownlow. The newspaper clipping has not been found.
3. Glass's pardon application had earlier been approved but immediately suspended. There is no evidence that the suspension was ever revoked. See Glass to Johnson, Aug. 12, 1865, *Johnson Papers*, 8: 570–71, 572n.

From Joseph Holt

September 20, 1865, Washington, D.C.; CopyS, DNA-RG94, USCT Div., Lets. Recd., File P-1419-1865.

Holt recommends the pardon of Samuel Smith, a black sergeant in the 5th Cav., USCT. A court-martial on July 31, 1865, had convicted Smith of involuntary manslaughter for shooting Alf Goins, a livery stable attendant in Hopkinsville, Kentucky. Witnesses for the prosecution testified that Smith had entered the stable searching for a halter he had lost. He found one that he thought was his and ordered Goins to surrender it or a suitable replacement, but the latter refused. When Smith left and returned with his gun to take the halter, Goins "faced the prisoner, leaning on his dung-fork as if to argue with him, and was at once and without a word, shot down." Four of Smith's fellow troopers spoke in his defense, recalling that he "quietly . . . requested" the return of his halter, and that Goins had responded by telling him "that if he didn't clear out, 'he would knock his God damned son of a bitch's black head off,' or words similar." Smith used his gun only after Goins attacked him with the dung-fork. Holt admits Smith was "clearly wrong" to have used his gun rather than report Goins to a superior officer, but asserts that the prisoner "has been sufficiently, if not more than sufficiently, punished" by being imprisoned for over seven months "for an act for which he is thought to have had quite sufficient justification." [On October 2, 1865, Johnson "remitted" the "unexecuted portion" of Smith's sentence of five years at hard labor in the Kentucky State Penitentiary.]

From George W. Paschal

Washington, 20th Sept. 1865.

To the President:

I this morning filed a request with the Attorney General, requesting that the warrant of pardon of E. B. Nicholls[1] of Galveston Texas, should be suspended, until I could be heard in behalf of the Provisional Governor of Texas. I now state, as reasons, that Gov. Hamilton refused to indorse the application of Mr. Nichols: 1. Because, at his own expense, he had furnished a Steamer & wood—gone to Brownsville, and aided in Capturing the U.S. troops, in March or February, 1861; and had acted as Commissioner in receiving the public property there; all this under the orders of the Revolutionary Convention, which deposed Genl. Sam Houston, Governor of Texas, of which Convention Nichols was a member.[2]

2. Gov Hamilton informed Genl. Nichols, that he would never recommend his pardon, until his accounts with Texas should be Settled. Nichols had been the agent of the "Military Board of Texas,"[3] for exporting cotton. His accounts had not been settled. Gov. Pease and others had been appointed to investigate the affairs of this board;[4] and nefarious swindling was being daily developed. He believed Nichols was liable to the State for large amounts, and he regarded the suspension of pardon as of the utmost consequence.

3. As to Geo. W. White.[5] Evidence exists that he is a defaulter to Texas for over $156,000 U.S. indemnity bonds. I see evidences in the Treasury which convinces me that he has smuggled ten thousand dollars of these bonds through the Treasury, through the agency of his brother John P. White. His violation of Trust is felonious by the laws of Texas. Gov. Hamilton has asked the President that he may be arrested, as he left under a *gross* violation of his parole. Surely he ought to be arrested and his pardon withheld until he accounts for so large an amount of funds placed in his hands, by the rebel government of Texas, as late, as March last past.[6]

Geo. W. Paschal

ALS, DNA-RG94, Amnesty Papers (M1003, Roll 55), Tex., Misc.

1. Ebenezar B. Nichols (d. 1872) prospered before the war as a Galveston cotton factor and commission merchant and in 1866 organized the National Bank of Texas. There is no evidence that his pardon, which was issued on September 2, 1865, was suspended. *House Ex. Docs.*, 39 Cong., 2 Sess., No. 116, p. 67 (Ser. 1293); Webb et al., *Handbook of Texas*, 2: 278–79.

2. Nichols was appointed by the Texas secession convention as a commissioner "to raise and disburse funds for the public safety." His steamboat, the *General Rusk*, assisted in the capture of Federal garrisons on Brazos Island and at Fort Brown. Ibid., 2: 279; Dudley G. Wooten, *Comprehensive History of Texas* (2 vols., Dallas, 1898), 2: 520–21.

3. The Texas State Military Board was created in January 1862 to raise funds for the Confederate war effort by disposing of United States bonds held by the state and by selling cotton. Webb et al., *Handbook of Texas*, 2: 763.

4. Elisha M. Pease and Swante Palm were appointed by Hamilton to investigate the financial condition of Texas. William W. Pierson, Jr., "Texas *Versus* White," *SWHQ*, 18 (1915): 349.

5. White (c1822-fl1900) was an attorney who served as a beef contractor for the Confederacy in Texas. He returned to Tennessee after the war and later became president of the Tennessee Fair Association. 1850 Census, Tenn., Franklin, Dist. No. 1, p. 13; Nashville directories (1867–1900); Hamilton to Johnson, Aug. 30, 1865, Johnson Papers, LC.

6. George W. White had been given United States bonds by the Military Board to

purchase supplies in England, which he failed to do. He was not arrested, and Johnson on Hamilton's recommendation pardoned him on March 13, 1866, but Texas officials filed suit against him and other bondholders. A landmark decision by the Supreme Court in April 1869 brought the recovery of only a small fraction of the writs. John L. Waller, *Colossal Hamilton of Texas* (El Paso, 1968), 69–71; Amnesty Papers (M1003, Roll 55), Tex., George W. White, RG94, NA. See Levin R. Marshall to Johnson, June 26, 1865, *Johnson Papers*, 8: 295–97.

From Charles T. Quintard

New York   20th Sept/65.

Sir—

My friend, Dr Sam Bard,[1] a journalist of well-established reputation & experience, proposes to revive his paper, the Memphis Avalanche in support of your administration.

Accepting the issues of the past as dead, & laboring for the restoration of order—& the re-establishment of the industry of the South, Dr Bard will bring to his work the resources of a well stored mind—& the energy of a firmly constituted character.

Intimately acquainted [with] the institutions, social & political of the South—& identified with its educational interests, he possesses peculiar qualifications to render efficient assistance to your Excellency, in your efforts to restore order & promote harmony & goodwill among all sorts & conditions of men.

C. T. Quintard   Bishop-elect of Tenn—

ALS, DLC-JP.

1. Bard (1825–1878) was a man of many talents and activities before, during, and after the war. New York-born, Bard moved to the South in the mid-1840s; at one time or another in the antebellum years he was commissioner of public education in Louisiana and then part-owner of the *Memphis Avalanche*. He served in the Confederate army with the rank of captain; he evidently did not return to the *Avalanche* in Memphis upon the conclusion of the war. Instead, after a stay in New Orleans, Bard moved to Atlanta where he became involved with several different newspapers, including the *New Era*. He served as Atlanta postmaster and was also appointed governor of the Idaho territory but never actually took office. He died in Baton Rouge of yellow fever. *New York Times*, Sept. 20, 1878; *Atlanta Constitution*, Sept. 20, 24, 1878; *Nashville Union and American*, Mar. 5, 1874; *OR*, Ser. 1, Vol. 15: 82, 805; Vedder, *History of Memphis*, 2: 218; Thomas A. McMullin and David Walker, eds., *Biographical Directory of American Territorial Governors* (Westport, Conn., 1984), 130; Thomas C. MacDowell to Johnson, Feb. 25, 1866, Johnson Papers, LC.

From Dixon C. Topp

September 20, 1865, Grenada, Miss.; ALS, DNA-RG105, Records of the Commr., Lets. Recd. (M752, Roll 16).

Convinced that his and other families are marked for murder by a conspiracy of blacks under the leadership of one of his former slaves and that military officials in the vicinity "do not intend to punish a negro immaterial what crime he might be guilty of," Topp appeals to the President, asking him "to interpose your authority for our protection." He denounces General Slocum's recent order depriving white citizens of their private arms "whilst negro soldiers are busy in arming the Negroes." The agents of the Freedmen's Bureau "have thus far proved a curse to the blacks and whites," attempting to "sunder all the ties of friendship and good feeling which heretofore existed between the owners and their former slaves." These agents, together with "a host of Officers and Speculators from the North," intend to get possession of the most valuable plantations all over the South "then work the negroes on their own account." Topp urges Johnson "to remove from this State if not from the entire South all the troops both white & black—especially the latter and disband them." In conclusion, he paints a dismal picture of the South. [The October 30, 1865, endorsement of Samuel Thomas, assistant commissioner of the Freedmen's Bureau in Mississippi, indicates that following an investigation, he does "not believe there is any truth in the reports circulated by the citizens of this State, that there is danger of an insurrection among the Freedmen."]

To Edward H. East
Private

Washington, D.C.　Sept 21th 1865

Will you do me the favor to examine the files of the "Nashville Union" of 1855, in the month of April or May I think, and have that portion of my speech made at Murfreesboro reproduced, which reviews the power of the Federal Government in reference to the elective franchise of citizens in the States.[1] Have it published in Nashville or send me a copy of that portion of it, so that I can have it published here.[2]

Andrew Johnson

Tel, DNA-RG107, Tels. Sent, President, Vol. 2 (1865).

　1. See *Johnson Papers*, 2: 288–91 for the excerpt in question.

　2. See East to Johnson, Sept. 23, 1865.

To William W. Holden

Washington, D.C.　Sept 21 1865

Your decision[1] is correct that under the proclamation they cannot vote for members or sit in convention as members without first being pardoned or taking the Amnesty Oath. If the party comes within any one of the exceptions they must obtain a pardon before voting or sitting as a member. All those who are aspirants to seats in the Convention and are elected will be pardoned upon your recommendation and a submission of their names by telegraph.[2]

Andrew Johnson　President U.S

Tel, DNA-RG107, Tels. Sent, President, Vol. 2 (1865).

　1. A few hours earlier Holden had wired the President that unpardoned persons were, in his opinion, ineligible to serve as delegates to the state constitutional convention. Holden to Johnson, Sept. 21, 1865, Johnson Papers, LC.

　2. Of the 120 delegates elected on September 21, eleven lacked presidential pardons, which Holden promptly recommended and Johnson granted in time for the men to take

their seats on opening day, October 2. Holden to Johnson, Sept. 23, 25, 29, 30; Robert J. Powell to Johnson, Sept. 24, 1865, Johnson Papers, LC; Johnson to Holden, Sept. 30, 1865, Tels. Sent, President, Vol. 2 (1865), RG107, NA; Raper, *Holden*, 73, 278; William C. Harris, *William Woods Holden: Firebrand of North Carolina Politics* (Baton Rouge, 1987), 186–87.

From Oliver O. Howard

Richmond Va.   Sept. 21 1865.

Sir

I have had a conference with the Governor, Dept. Commander and the Assistant Commissioner.[1] The utmost harmony exists between them.

The Governor declines the recognition of his courts as Freedmen's courts for the present, because it is against the constitution of Virginia for a man to hold office under the State and the U.S. at the same time. He wishes to postpone this matter until the Legislature of Va. meets in December.

He and Gen. Terry earnestly advise the retention of the Military force for the present.

Through the convention of clergymen[2] I have been able to get the views of men from different sections of the state.

They seem cordially to endorse your policy in every quarter, and believe the Freedmen's Bureau, with some modifications and changes in the local agents, to be necessary, and as much for the interest of the white man as the black.

There is considerable social coldness and prejudice, but I find things much better than when I was here before.

What troubles me most is the difficulty of making proper provision for the Freed men in the vicinity of Norfolk and Fortress Monroe, who will soon be disposed of their land by the last circular,[3] and that of providing for the indigent.

The Governor declares the State and counties too much impoverished to meet the wants of the poor, black and white. In the Norfolk section parties are bringing suits against U.S. officers, holding them responsible for all the acts of Government officials during the last two years.[4] Gen. Terry promises to correct this.

O. O. Howard   Major General.

LS, DNA-RG105, Records of the Commr., Lets. Recd from Executive Mansion.

1. Francis Peirpoint, Gen. Alfred H. Terry, and Col. Orlando Brown. The latter (b. *c*1827), a former medical officer of the 18th and 29th Mass. Inf., remained with the Freedmen's Bureau until 1868. CSR, RG94, NA.

2. The Virginia diocesan convention of the Protestant Episcopal Church. *Washington Morning Chronicle*, Sept. 25, 1865.

3. Circular No. 15. See Sterling R. Cockrill to Johnson, Sept. 18, 1865.

4. See, for example, the complaints made by the Taylor brothers of Norfolk against

two Freedmen's Bureau agents, as investigated and reported by H. B. Scott to Orlando Brown, Oct. 29, 1865, Records of the Commr., Lets. Recd. (M752, Roll 25), RG105, NA.

From West H. Humphreys

September 21, 1865, Nashville, Tenn.; ALS, DNA-RG94, Amnesty Papers (M1003, Roll 49), Tenn., West H. Humphreys.

The judge of the district courts of Tennessee under the Confederacy, who has been "indicted for conspiracy against the government of the United States," offers an extended statement concerning his course in "the late troubles." In January 1861 Humphreys had expressed a desire to preserve the Union, "if the rights of the states can be protected." He sought an "adjustment" of the slavery issue and did not favor withdrawal of states, yet did not think the Constitution permitted the federal government to "hold the states by military power." He thus later supported Tennessee's separation and regarded his state's action "as terminating my official relations with the government of the United States without other act on my part." As judge of the district courts during the war, he felt that those who stayed in Tennessee should obey the laws of the de facto government; those who adhered to the United States and who were captured in acts of hostility to the Confederacy "could not be tried condemned and executed as a traitor but must be held as a prisoner of war," to be tried not in his civil court, but rather in a military court. Humphreys interpreted the laws affecting the "property of aliens" as "temporary sequestrations, not confiscations." He concludes his plea for pardon by declaring: "I took this course because it was sustained by the leading writers on public law; because it was most consistent with humanity; because the opposite course would have produced retaliation and weakened the Confederate government; and because permanent harmony would more likely be restored thereby, whether the Confederate government was maintained or that of the united states reestablished." [Humphreys's petition was enclosed in his September 22 letter to David T. Patterson. Referred to the President, it was then forwarded to the Attorney General's office. We have been unable to find any record of a pardon for Humphreys.]

From Emily H. Barnwell

[Augusta, Ga.][1]   September 22nd, 1865

Sir,

Having understood that the Confiscation Act, passed by Government in 1862, exempted the property of Widows, Unmarried Females, Orphans & Trust Estates, as irresponsible parties, I beg leave to present the claims of my Sisters & Self,[2] to property in the Town of Beaufort, So. Carolina, & of lands on Port Royal Island, & as we were non combatants in the later movements, of attempted Separation from this Union, & did not *abandon* our property, but left it in charge of persons we considered responsible, & only removed from *necessity*, orders having been issued to that effect, we trust to your justice & clemency, to be re-instated in our former rights of property, *slave* property *excepted.*

The property consisted of a Tract of Land, adjoining Port Royal Ferry, ten miles from the Town of Beaufort belonging to Mrs Middleton Stuart, Widow—also a Residence & out buildings, in the Town of Beaufort, 3 vacant Lots south of the residences, & Pigeon Point Tract to the north of this Town, the property of Misses Sarah, & Emily H. Barnwell.

We made application to Genl Gillmore[3] in June, but it was not in his power to give the desired information. We were about to apply to the "Freedmen's Bureau," but understood that all operations of the Bureau had been suspended for the present. This must be our apology, for intruding upon your valued time, but as we have been left destitute, by the sudden emancipation of our Negroes, we are compelled to apply to you in our distress, & most respectfully beg your attention to our petition.[4]

Should you direct a communication to be made us, on the subject, please direct to. Miss Emily H. Barnwell. Care of Messrs Carmichael & Bean[5]—Augusta—Georgia.

Emily H. Barnwell.

ALS, DNA-RG105, Records of the Commr., Lets. Recd. from Executive Mansion.

1. The letter's cover sheet, endorsed by a White House secretary, indicates that the Barnwell letter came from Augusta, Georgia.

2. Emily H. (1820–1894) and Sarah B. Barnwell (1814–1881), both spinsters, and their sister Mary H. (1812–1876), the widow of planter Middleton Stuart (1806–1840), all lived in Beaufort District before the war. "Barnwells of South Carolina," *SCHM*, 2 (January 1901): 56; 1860 Census, S.C., Beaufort, St. Helena Parish, 4, 23.

3. Quincy A. Gillmore.

4. Barnwell's letter was referred by order of the President to the Freedmen's Bureau head, General Howard. The day after it had been sent to him, Howard returned the letter with the notation that the property had been sold for taxes and the title vested in the U.S.; it had been used as a general hospital and was now in use as a post hospital.

5. William P. Carmichael (b. c1826) and Joseph S. Bean (b. c1820) were hardware merchants. 1860 Census, Ga., Richmond, Augusta, 3rd Ward, 102; *Directory for the City of Augusta* (1859), 49.

From Joseph E. Davis

Tuscaloosa Alabama   Sep't 22nd 1865

Sir,

I am advised that to have my home and property restored it will be necessary to apply to the President of the United States, and to get some persons of influence at Washington to present my claim; now I have no friends in Washington to whom I could apply, nor the means of making such. I must, therefore, rely upon the *justice* of my claim; and I feel assured, if your Excellency can spare the time to examine the annexed statement of facts and circumstances, you will make such order in the premises as the nature of the case requires. In the year 1818 I purchased of the United States some land on the Mississippi river about thirty miles below the Walnut Hills, now Vicksburg; upon this land I fixed my residence and occupied it for forty years. In the Spring of 1862 an unprecedented flood made it necessary to remove my white family, stock of cattle, and some other property. About this time a clamor was raised against me, on account of opposition to the burning of my cotton, by such persons as had no cotton to burn and a portion of the press, particularly the Hinds County Gazette; to such an extent did the excitement go as to influence a mob, as I am informed, to burn a few hundred bales of cotton that I had removed to a distance from the river, and the ballance was burned by the military authorities of the Confederate States, amounting in all, according to the statement of the overseer, to 841 bales.[1] I left on the plantation the overseer[2] & most of the negroes, and after the fall of the river I had the stock, or so much of it as could be found, driven back to the river, but soon after it was occupied by the Military Authorities of the United States, and, as I am informed, made a depot for captured or fugitive negroes, and has been so held ever since under a garrison of negroe soldiers.[3] It may be out of place here to state the devastation and destruction of property. Some white persons are in occupation of the place & cultivating, also some of my negroes, something over one hundred left on the place with women and children. The young men I learn have mostly been taken into the army; those remaining are said to have a promising crop. I have about forty that accompanied me and are very desirous of getting home and I hope to take them back if I am allowed to do so. Finding my return to the river obstructed I procured a place in Hinds County between Vicksburg and Jackson, and on this place I intended to remain under the assurance that those who *remained quietly at home should not* be disturbed. In this situation I remained until sometime in June sixty three when a party under the command of Capt. Hanna,[4] of *Ohio*, visited my place, carried off most of the negroes, stock of horses, mules, oxen, waggons, carriages, other property, but offered no indignity to myself or family. By Capt. Hanna I wrote to Gen McClernand,[5] the only Federal officer that I knew in the department, and for whom I entertained a high regard. I informed him of the fact that I was "non combatant," in my 79th year, that my family consisted of myself and four ladies,[6] three of whom were invalids, and asked his interference in my case; to this I received no reply. The day following another party entered, and passed through, every part of the house, not spareing the sick rooms, *broke* open the store rooms and carried off the provisions and family supplies. The night following a party of soldiers under Major Hawkins[7] came some time in the night, broke open the desks in search of valuables; the Maj apologized by stating that he was acting under orders and regreted the necessity. Some weeks after a party under command of Lieutenant Miller[8] came with orders, as he said, from Gen. Osterhaus[9] to *burn* the house, that he would give me *half* an *hour* to remove the furniture. Dr. M. Emanuel[10] of Vicksburg, President of the Rail Road, happened to be there at the time and remonstrated with the officer; stated that he had known me for thirty years, that I had never been engaged in politics, had always been a private citizen, and never had any connection with the Goverment. To this remonstrance he replied that he was acting under orders. By Lieut' Miller I again wrote to Gen McClernand hastily, but of the same purport as the former letter, to neither of which did I receive any answer; I think it probable he never received them. They left after burning the corn house and some other buildings without burning the dwelling house, but such was the shock that the sick had received that it became necessary to remove them father into the interior. I remained until about the sixth of July. After the surrender of Vicksburg the army came on and took possession and occupied the house a few days, as I understand, but on leaving burnt the house, gin, and an estimated amount of cotton of 80 bales. My means of transportation was so limited that I could carry very little. After a time I reached this place in the Spring of '64, where I have remained ever since. Your Excellency will perceive that I could have given no aid to the rebellion, and I gave none; I contributed nothing, subscribed nothing; attended no convention or other public meeting, and now at the age of over *four score* myself and family are left almost destitute. My opinion of the right of a State to secede was the same as that of most democrats, that it might be done peaceably, but had been always opposed to a disolution of the Union from the belief that it would destroy the *grandure* and *power* of the *great Republic*, until 1848 when the strife became such as to create the belief that it was better to seperate. I believe that much of the wrong that I have suffered was caused by my relationship to Jefferson Davis, who is my brother, twenty odd years my junior, whose sufferings & misfortunes you are familiar with, and whatever may be thought of his judgement, he must be regarded as one of the purest of men. Your Excellency will have the goodness to direct such orders in the premises to Governor Sharkey, or, through him, to the proper military authorities of the district, or to make such order therein as the wisdom of your Excellency shall deem proper.[11]

J. E. Davis

ALS, DNA-RG105, Land Div., Lets. Recd.

1. After Confederate authorities ordered the destruction of cotton that might fall into enemy hands, Davis had cached about 200 bales. An angry mob, incited by editorials in local newspapers, burned this hoard, while the remainder of his crop was destroyed by Confederate soldiers. Hermann, *Pursuit of a Dream*, 39.

2. James Magill (b. c1826), a native Kentuckian. Davis to Johnson, Aug. 2, 1866, TxU-A; 1860 Census, Miss., Warren, Vicksburg, 175.

3. Federal troops took possession of the two Davis Bend plantations, "Hurricane" and

"Brierfield," in December 1863 and, under the direction of Samuel Thomas, established a model farm for former slaves. Hermann, *Pursuit of a Dream*, 46–106 passim.

    4. Lt. William H. Hannah (1840–1919), 4th Ohio Indpt. Cav., whose regiment participated in the siege of Vicksburg in 1863. Pension File, Agnes D. Hannah, RG15, NA; Dyer, *Compendium*, 1481.

    5. John A. McClernand.

    6. His wife Eliza (c1800–1863), who died enroute to Alabama; Lise Mitchell, his granddaughter; Martha Harris, his chronically-ill adopted daughter; and either Martha's daughter, Margaret, or "Cousin Nannie," Anna Bradford Miles. Haskell M. Monroe, Jr. et al., *The Papers of Jefferson Davis* (6 vols. to date, Baton Rouge, 1971-), 1: 528; Hermann, *Pursuit of a Dream*, 40, 73; Janet S. Hermann to Patricia P. Clark, Jan. 14, 1987, Andrew Johnson Project Files.

    7. Henry P. Hawkins commanded the 6th Mo. Cav. during the Vicksburg campaign of 1863. *Off. Army Reg.* (1863–67), 7: 24; CSR, RG94, NA; *OR*, Ser. 1, Vol. 24, Pt. 3: 336.

    8. Joseph W. Miller (c1839-fl1868) of the 45th Ill. Inf. served as a staff officer for generals Henry W. Slocum, Mortimer D. Leggett, and John E. Smith. Pension File, Joseph W. Miller, RG15, NA; CSR, RG94, NA; *OR*, Ser. 1, Vol. 24, Pt. 2: 149, 294.

    9. Peter J. Osterhaus.

    10. Morris Emanuel (b. c1804), a Vicksburg druggist, served as president of the Southern Mississippi Railroad during the last year of the war. James T. Currie, *Enclave: Vicksburg and Her Plantations, 1863–1870* (Jackson, Miss., 1980), 7, 221; *OR*, Ser. 1, Vol. 48, Pt. 2: 792; 1860 Census, Miss., Warren, Vicksburg, 41.

    11. This letter was forwarded to Samuel Thomas, who reported that the Davis plantations had been retained for use by freedmen. Thomas to Howard, Oct. 19, 1865, Land Div., Lets. Recd., RG105, NA. See Davis to Johnson, Oct. 30, 1865.

From John Grant[1]

Mobile   Sept 22ond/65

    The undersigned would most respectfully represent to your Excellency that: he is owner of Grant's Pass; an artificial channel which connects Mobile Bay with Mississippi Sound, forming an inland passage between Mobile and New Orleans; he having constructed that work under a charter from, or act of, the Legislature of Alabama passed in 1839.[2] He also built an artificial island at the Pass, on which he had constructed houses, Shops, and other buildings which were deemed necessary in the management of the pass. And shortly after the beginning of the war, the island was taken possession of by the Confederate forces and the houses and other buildings which had been erected at great cost to the undersigned, were pulled down and destroyed and what was was called Fort Powell, was constructed in their place. About the time of the capitulation of Fort Gaines, Fort Powell was blown up and the island evacuated by the Confederates, and it was shortly after occupied by the U.S. forces under Genl. Canby; to whom the undersigned applied to have it restored to him. This application was by Genl Canby referred to the Secretary of War with a recommendation that it be restored with certain reservations and restrictions. This recommendation was not approved by the Secretary of War,[3] and the property still remains in the possession of the millitary Authorities of the United States, as captured property, and the undersigned is deprived of the tolls or fees for it's use, which were the only remuneration he was to receive for the large outlay and risk he incurred in it's construction. The tolls which would have been collected for the time the pass has been in the occupancy of the U.S., under the great increase of intercourse between Mobile and New Orleans would not have been less than $20000 to $25000, all of which has been lost in consequence of this millitary interference. The undersigned cannot see the justice of making his work an exception to all other works of internal improvement in the State of Alabama, as nearly all the others have long since been turned over to the respective companies, while his is still held by the Millitary authorities under a claim as captured property, which claim he thinks unfounded, as he is now, and always has been a loyal citizen of the U.S. and had a right to expect the protection of his Government. He was *always* opposed to the dissolution of the Union, voted against that Act, never voted for any officer in the So-called Confederacy either general, State, or municipal; never took the oath of alegiance to them; never held any office, place, or employment under them, or either of them; never contributed voluntarily one dollar to any organized forces in rebellion against the United States; but he did take the amnesty oath under Mr Lincoln's proclamation, and also the oath required under the proclamation of your Excellency of May 29th 1865.

The truth of all the above statements can be proved by affidavits and other papers which the undersigned has with him, and which will be produced if required.[4]

With this state of facts, the undersigned would most respectfully ask of your Excellency to cause such order to issue to the proper Department as will secure the return to the undersigned of the Pass and Island, with the least possible delay and that he be allowed to proceed to the collection of the tolls now due, or that may become due as fully as he would have been entitled to have done if there had been no Millitary interference.[5]

John Grant

ALS, DNA-RG107, Lets. Recd., EB12 President 2549 (1865).

1. Grant (*c*1810-*fl*1876) listed as his occupation "Gentleman" and "Capt." 1860 Census, Ala., Mobile, 1st Ward, Mobile, 680; Mobile directories (1861–77).

2. According to the provisions of the act, Grant's twenty-five-year charter had expired on February 2, 1864. "Exhibit 'A'" attached to Charles R. Woods to William D. Whipple, Aug. 16, 1865, Lets. Recd., EB12 President 2549 (1865), RG107, NA.

3. In an endorsement dated June 9, 1865, and directed to Lorenzo Thomas, Gen. Edward R.S. Canby had stipulated that the U.S. government would reserve its right to use Grant's Pass free of charge and that the charter could not be extended without previous consent of the U.S. government. Stanton had rejected Grant's application on June 29. "Exhibit 'B,'" ibid.; E. D. Townsend to Canby, June 29, 1865, ibid.

4. Endorsements by all four Mobile County convention delegates and Governor Parsons accompanied Grant's petition. Ibid.

5. On October 3, 1865, Stanton submitted Grant's petition to Johnson with the recommendation that Gen. George Thomas decide the matter. The President endorsed
Stanton's recommendation as "Approved." Within a few weeks Thomas ordered the
property fully reinstated, provided that Grant adhered to Canby's stipulations. In early
December 1865 Grant, then a state legislator, introduced a bill renewing his charter, but
his fellow members overwhelmingly defeated the measure. See "Special Orders No. 83,"
Oct. 23, 1865, ibid.; *Mobile Register and Advertiser*, Dec. 3, 1865, Jan. 21, 24, Feb. 6,
1866.

From Ladies of Greenbrier County, West Virginia[1]

Lewisburg. West Virginia.   Sept 22nd. 1865.

Sir:

We, the ladies of Greenbrier County respectfully and earnestly appeal to you for pardon and amnesty for Mr Jefferson Davis.

The course which you have pursued since you have been elevated to
the high position which you now occupy, justifies us in the belief that
it is your sincere desire to restore peace, harmony and prosperity to the
whole country and to secure the complete establishment of civil government; that you entertain no feelings of vindictiveness; that you desire
no gratification from either the anxiety, punishment or impoverishment
of the people of the Southern States who have been in rebellion against
the Federal government; and that when the restoration of "the Union
as it was," and the establishment of the supremacy of "the Constitution
as it is" as the supreme law of the land have been effected, your great
object will have been attained.

Our plain view of the war is simply this. For a long series of years
the people of the North differed with those of the South upon the questions of slavery and the relations between the states and the Federal
government. All peaceable means of adjustment were resorted to and
failed to reconcile us. At last the controversy was reffered to that tribunal from whose decision there is no appeal—to the tribunal of
war,—the arbitrament of the sword. After four years of war waged with
a gallantry and earnestness almost unparralled, the decision was rendered—and in favour of the Federal Authority. The people of the South
accept it and intend in good faith to abide by it. Slavery no longer exists
and the doctrine of secession can not be maintained. There will never
again be an attempt to revive the one nor to establish the other.

Mr Davis, it is true, held the highest office in the Confederacy; but
he was called to that position by the almost unanimous voice of his
countrymen,—and we are unable to understand how that position
should increase his guilt. If guilt consists in the intention, he is not
more guilty than the masses in the South. His life, both public and
private, before and during the war, has been characterized by integrity,
moderation and manliness. Thousands of others not less devoted to the

Cause of the South, and not less hostile to the Federal government, have received pardon and amnesty. We only appeal for like clemency for him.

You, Sir, are clothed with the Authority to grant repreives and pardons for offences against the United States, and when you consider that the trial and punishment of Mr Davis can not possibly add anything to the stability of the government nor render more odious rebellion and insurrection against its laws, we confidently believe that you will exercise your prerogative in a manner which will show to the world that in victory you are magnanimous; that you will relieve the anxiety of thousands as to the fate of one whose life has been endangered by *their* act, and attach them to you by ties of gratitude and affection,—and that you will remove from prison and restore to a family already heart-broken and over whelmed with sadness, the husband and father.

Pet, DNA-RG94, Amnesty Papers, Jefferson Davis, Pets. to A. Johnson.

1. This document—signed by Mrs. R. McElhenney, Mrs. E. A. Fry, Susan E. McElhenney, Virginia W. Spotts, and Mary E. Weatt—is among the scores of petitions from ladies' groups on behalf of the Confederate President which are in Amnesty Papers, Jefferson Davis, Pets. to A. Johnson, RG94, NA.

From Silas D. Wood[1]

Marshall Texas   Sept 22nd. 1865

Through the kindness of a friend I have the opportunity of address you. Doubtless in the laps of time and the many thousands that you have had to recollect you have entirely forgotton one so humble as myself.

From 1840 to 1846 I was well acquainted with you. I lived in Leesburg just 20 miles from Greenville, where you then lived. You used frequently to stop in our town at Old man Davaul's,[2] dutch as crout though a very clever man. I have still a vivid recolliction of how Brooks Campbell[3] used to hate you because you beat him for Congress.

But I had forgotten that I was writing to President, not Andrew, Johnson and howeve much the one might be delighted to recur to the occurances of by gone days the other has not the time to spare to even read hastily what an old friend might wish to write. But I must tell you how badly I was whiped by you proclimation freeing the nigroes and I must send you the peace I wrote and published just after we had learned that you were the President. You sent me your speach which you made in the Senate in 1860[4] and I must say, it is one of the ablest speaches that was made during that memorable session. I had calculated on keeping my negroes[5]—when I found you were president and had been boasting considerably to some of my neighbors, and in order that I might encourage the desponding I published the peace alluded to and which I have cut out and enclosed;[6] please read it and as sure as there is a God in Heaven to day so sure would your have been President of the United State twelve years and all history would have pronounced you the greatest man of the age. Oh if I could but influence you I know you would be President longer than any man ever has been or than any other ever can be. I know you are much smarter in politics than I am but this is one of the times when destiny marked you out just for the time that I have named. What was it that influenced you in the course you have pursued?

I have been a Union man all the time though the secessionists imprisoned and came very near hanging me. I told them that they could not succeed. I told them they would have to go back into the Union; but they said it was imposible and I was a fool. But you see how things have terminated. I have suffered in the flish by this rebellion. The rebals took ever thing I had except our Negroes and they took their labour without any pay. The Federals came a long and set all my negroes free so I am poor indeed. So poor that I could not get to Washington to ask a little office.

The Secessionists are still very insubordinate but very anxious for some office. Gov. Hamilton is giving satisfaction to all who are loyal or intend to be. The Secessionists do not intend to be satisfied. That 13 exception was a good measure and should be administered with a good deal of caution. The wealthy lead the poorer classes a stray. I have read you orations about this rebellion; its causes and the influence of its Leaders and I have found you wright generally. If you would let me advise you about five minutes I could place every thing upon the right track.[7]

S. D. Wood

ALS, DLC-JP.

1. Wood (c1823–1893), a Virginia-born merchant, planter, and editor, was a Whig who joined the Texas Republican Party. Although he held several federal appointments, including collector of internal revenue (1866–c73) and commissioner of the 5th Circuit Court (c1885–c89), he failed in his attempts to be elected to a state office. James Smallwood, "Mr. Republican: Silas D. Wood," *Chronicles of Smith County, Texas*, 9 (1970): 1–7; Randolph B. Campbell, "The Whig Party of Texas in the Elections of 1848 and 1852," *SWHQ*, (1969): 31, 33; *U.S. Off. Reg.* (1867–73, 1885–89).

2. Frederick Davault (1778–1847), a planter, was originally from Pennsylvania. 1840 Census, Tenn., Washington, 213; Charles M. Bennett and Loraine Bennett Rae, eds., *Washington County, Tennessee, Tombstone Inscriptions Plus Genealogical Notes* (3 vols., Nashville, 1977–79), 3: 227.

3. Brookins Campbell, whom Johnson defeated for the Democratic nomination to Congress in 1845.

4. Johnson had forwarded a copy of his speech against secession in response to Wood's request of January 20, 1861. Johnson Papers, LC. For the address itself, see *Johnson Papers*, 4: 3–46.

5. Wood "managed" twenty slaves for his widowed mother-in-law. Smallwood, "Mr. Republican," 3.

6. Not found.

7. There is no record of a response from Johnson.

From James R. Doolittle
Private

Racine   Sept 23, 1865

My dear Sir;

You are right in your policy of reconciliation. Your speech[1] was the
voice of a magnanimous nation to her own rebellious children, seeking
to lead them through repentence to forgiveness and restoration to its
confidence and affection. The friends of humanity, and of the American
Republic abroad will shout in triumph as they read it.

Of course it will be denounced by those who desire to hold them as
conquered alien territories and to make them our vassals. Hardly had
your speech died away upon our ears when from Sumner of Massachusetts and Stevens of Pa. the voice of unforgiving hate, avarice and lust
of unlimited despotic power comes upon the nation like the voices of
fiends from the Infernal world. Please read the enclosed copy of a letter
just received from an intimate friend[2] one of the ablest men in Wisconsin. He has been and is one of our leaders, is now our Collector at
Milwaukee, and has been heretofore leading Editor of the Milwaukee
sentinel.

The howling against me of which he speaks is the howling of some
of our press because I attended our late Union Convention was chairman of the Committee on resolutions which sustain your course and
policy, and especially because I opposed resolutions of the minority
condemning your policy of reconciliation.[3]

I am going into the fight. The great mass of our people will sustain
you. The democratic party in their resolutions endorse your policy. I
speak not of the Copperhead portion, but of the mass of their patriotic
men. I am also of opinion that about 2/3 of all our republican or Union
party are in favor of your policy about 1/3 will follow the lead of Sumner & Stevens, and strange to say my Colleague[4] who all his life has
been a Conservative old whig has been made to yeild to their position.
This portion of our party are noisy & clamorous. They have got control
of many newspapers, who follow the lead of the Chicago Tribune. That
eternal trial of Wirz[5] continually adding fuel to the fire by publishing
its lurid details of testimony ought to be finished. The matter of Davis
trial postponed until Congress meets to see if Congress will pass the
necessary law as to jurors so that intelligent and loyal men can sit upon
the jury. If Congress will not pass such a law the responsibility of his
trial will rest with Congress. My Conviction is clear that he ought not
to be tried in a Military Court unless the evidence of his complicity in
the Andersonville starvation of our prisoners is made Certain, then I
would Consent. But I am equally clear that Congress should pass such

Senator James R. Doolittle
of Wisconsin
*Courtesy Johnson-Bartlett
Collection, Greeneville*

Dr. A. Nelson Batten
of Philadelphia
*Courtesy Johnson-Bartlett
Collection, Greeneville*

a law as to qualification of Jurors, and then have him tried with all the forms of law, and Condemned. I know the south will appeal for his release. But they will never realize the crime of treason, nor how great is the clemency of the nation until some one or two of the most wicked have been tried in Courts of law, and have suffered the penalty.[6]

J. R. Doolittle

ALS, DLC-JP.

1. See Speech to Southern Delegation, Sept. 11, 1865.

2. Christopher L. Sholes (1819–1890), a former state legislator and Lincoln appointee, had asked Doolittle to advise Johnson to "stand firm," adding that "If the programme of Stevens and Sumner prevails, the North will be brutalized, the South crushed, and the nation ruined." *DAB*; Sholes to Doolittle, Sept. 20, 1865, Johnson Papers, LC.

3. Doolittle had already forwarded resolutions endorsing Johnson's Reconstruction policy, which had been adopted in place of others that embodied the "crazy idea" that the former Confederate states were "mere conquered *territories.*" Doolittle to Johnson, Sept. 9, 1865, Johnson Papers, LC.

4. Timothy O. Howe (1816–1883) served in the U.S. Senate (1861–79) and as postmaster general under President Arthur (1882–83). *BDAC*.

5. Swiss native Henry Wirz (1822–1865), superintendent of the Confederate prison camp at Andersonville, Ga., was convicted of war crimes by a military commission on October 25, 1865. David C. Roller and Robert W. Twyman, eds., *The Encyclopedia of Southern History* (Baton Rouge, 1979), 1351; *House Ex. Docs.*, 40 Cong., 2 Sess., No. 23, p. 809 (Ser. 1331). See Louis Schade to Johnson, Oct. 26, 1865.

6. On the same day Doolittle wrote Johnson another letter, recommending patronage for a pair of Wisconsin judges and urging the removal of the chief justice of New Mexico and all three federal judges in Colorado. The President assured him "Anything that can consistently be done to comply with" his recommendations would "be done," and subsequently did replace the justices as Doolittle requested. Doolittle to Johnson, Sept. 23, 1865, Office of Atty. Gen., Lets. Recd., President, RG60, NA; Johnson to Doolittle, Sept. 26, 1865, Johnson Papers, LC; *U.S. Off. Reg.* (1865–67). See David Davis to Johnson, Jan. 10, 1866.

From Edward H. East

Nashville   Sept 23/65.

Dr Sir

I herewith enclose to you, the Extract of your speech of 1855, as requested. I had it published together with an Editorial notice of it.[1] I also enclose some resolutions, passed at a public meeting which meeting was composed of a number of leading men.[2] You will see several speeches were made. Several resolutions, of different kinds were sent to the committee after they had retired, and while they differed about minor matters and details, &c all concured, in the support of your administration. I regret that the notice of the meeting, could not have been more extended and that the committee on resolutions had no notice of their appointment so as to have prepared resolutions, probably better. The meeting was a success, any how, and each resolution was cheered, when read—The first enthusiastically.[3] Foote Brown, Frank Cheatham,[4] and in fact all the men of this place with either state or local prominence were present and committed themselves fully and I think cheerfully. I think resolutions would have passed—to the effect, "That the people of Tennessee were *glad* that slavery had been abolished." Some of our people throw *cold water* on these promiscuous meetings composed of all political complexions. I think they are to be desired, at present at least. I think it to the interest of the country and your administration. These men are our fellow citizens and I think if [they] can be won, with whatever of talents, social and political influence they have, it will be an advantage, while the contrary course,—that of exclusive isolation—socially and politically—will force them to the opposition. I would be glad to know your opinion on this subject, and will also, be glad to assist in any views or policy—you may desire to effect in Tennessee, either before the people or Legislature. I think, any views you may have in regard to Tennessee, as effecting her as state, or as relating to national affairs, would be gladly acquiesced in, and supported by the people, of this state. I am not more certain of any undetermined question, than I am of this. I also enclose Circular of the Brokers in regard to Union & Planters Banks. They are givin 55, for the one today—and 52 for the other.[5]

I have made enquiry, in a quiet way of many persons, and all demand these prices or more. The Banks have commenced suing, and their debtors are buying up their money to pay them. This makes a demand. I think they will be up to 60 in a few days. I learn several Brokers have large orders at 55 & even as high as 58.

Edward H East

ALS, DLC-JP.

1. Although the extract referred to is no longer attached to the East letter, it is presumably the one published in the *Nashville Dispatch*, Sept. 24, 1865.

2. Although accounts of the Nashville meeting of September 23 appeared in the *Nashville Press and Times*, Sept. 25, the enclosed resolutions mentioned by East could not be located.

3. The first of several resolutions read: "That the flag of the Union is our flag, and we pledge ourselves to protect and defend the same, when and wherever assailed." Ibid.

4. Henry S. Foote, Neill S. Brown, and Benjamin F. Cheatham.

5. On September 21 Johnson had asked East to purchase for him $20,000 in Union Bank notes and the same amount in Planter's Bank notes. Nashville newspapers carried reports of quotations from brokers regarding various bank notes. Thomas S. Marr offered 52 cents for Planters Bank notes and 54 cents for Union Bank notes. Johnson to East, Sept. 21, 1865, Tels. Sent, President, Vol. 2 (1865), RG107, NA; *Nashville Dispatch*, Sept. 23; *Nashville Press and Times*, Sept. 25, 1865.

From Andrew J. Hamilton

Austin Texas   23rd Septr 1865

Mr President

Herewith I have the honour to enclose several copies of an address[1] which I have lately issued to the people of Texas, and which I am informed and believe is producing a healthy tone in the public mind. Your labours are so great and unremiting that I can scarcely hope that you will find time to read it; yet I would be pleased if your Excellency could do so and favour me with your candid opinion of it.

My labours are very arduous and sometimes, as you can well conceive, unpleasant, but I entered upon the work with a full sense of its importance to the Country and of my own responsibilities, and have devoted myself wholly to the accomplishment of the great object of brining Texas back to her proper position in the Union by the free voluntary act of her people, upon the policy of the General Gov't. This could only be done by opposing facts to prejudices—truth to falsehood, in such manner as to make them realize that in their action duty and interest are inseparable. I am, myself, astonished at the great change which has been wrought in the two months of my adminstration. Much yet remains to be done—but certainly I may claim that it is much to have brought the minds of the thoughtful men of the State all to the conclusion and admission that what I announced to them in two or three public speeches when I first arrived in the State, was true, although distasteful to them then.[2]

Having done this it only requires a little time to diffuse through the minds of the masses a recognition of the truth. And this will be comparatively easy of accomplishment, for to them, being for the most part men who never owned Negroes, the truth will not be unwelcome as it was to the more intelligent late Slaveowners. I know, not only, how much the public interest depends upon the success of my efforts but also how much I have at stake personally in the way of reputation. I am willing to rest my future upon the result if I am sustained in my course. I did not at once call a Convention for many and good reasons. The public mind was wholy unprepared for prudent and wise Counsels. It had been poisoned by the argument that Slavery was not dead—that the Presidents Proclamation of emancipation was but a military order which only took effect during the existence of the War and where the presence of our Armies had given effect to it.

It required time for the appointment of Officers to administer the oath of Amnesty & for the people to avail themselves of your pardon to prepare themselves for voting. We have no mail facilities and but few Presses of the better sort. All these things considered I was not disposed to precipitate action which might be detrimental to the interests of Texas and to the policy of the Gov't.[3]

As it is I feel sure of a steady approach to such conclusions in the public mind as will insure acceptable action by the Convention when called. I hazzard the prediction that the action of Texas will meet the public expectation if not forced too soon.

But I must again say to Your Excellency that I feel sadly the want of the influence of the Federal Courts. I would most respectfully urge the appointment of Marshals, and Attorneys for the two Districts in

Texas.[4] Nothing that I have any knowledge of would so certainly secure obediance to the laws of the Gov't and support of its policy.

I have through want of proper information and misrepresentation recommended two or three Petitions for Amnesty which I am now satisfied should not receive your favourable action.[5] In a day or two I will forward to you a list of those which I have recommended, noting those, the recommendations of which I withdraw, asking you in the mean time not to take action on any from Texas until it reaches you.[6]

In regard to the reports which you advised me by telegram, were being circulated to the effect, that in my appointments & recommendations to office I had studiously ignored Union Men and prefered rebels, I repeat that it is *shamelessly false*.[7] If I could have been so *base* I could not have been so great a *fool*. The whole State will attest, friend & foe, that I have sought to appoint Union men alone. This I publicly announced when I first entered the State and so I have announced in my enclosed published addressed.

In some instances I have been deceived by false representations but have promptly corrected the error as soon as ascertained.

Hopeing to have a word of encouragement from you soon.

A J Hamilton

ALS, DLC-JP.

1. Not found enclosed. A lengthy autobiographical and historical treatise written by Hamilton on September 11, 1865, denounced secession and states' rights, and advised Texans to accept the consequences of the war, particularly the end of slavery and the extension of judicial and civil rights to freedmen. *San Antonio Herald*, Sept. 21, 23, 1865.

2. After his return to Texas, Hamilton bitterly denounced the state's Confederate leaders and repudiated those who advocated a plan of gradual emancipation. Waller, *Hamilton of Texas*, 61–64.

3. Despite repeated requests from Johnson, the Texas constitutional convention did not meet until February 1866. Carl H. Moneyhon, *Republicanism in Reconstruction Texas* (Austin, 1980), 31–33. See Hamilton to Johnson, Oct. 21 and Nov. 27, 1865. See also Johnson to Hamilton, Dec. 1, 1865, Johnson Papers, LC, and Oct. 30, 1865, Tels. Sent, President, Vol. 2 (1865), RG107, NA.

4. All four positions were filled by mid-April 1866. Ser. 6B, Vol. 4: 211, Johnson Papers, LC.

5. See David J. Baldwin to Johnson, Aug. 19, 1865, *Johnson Papers*, 8: 612–13; and George W. Paschal to Johnson, Sept. 20, 1865.

6. Not found, but for Hamilton's amnesty policy, see Hamilton to Johnson, Oct. 21, 1865.

7. Johnson had telegraphed the seven provisional governors in August 1865, inquiring about reports that former Confederates were favored over Union men in their appointments. In his initial response, Hamilton had dismissed any such statement as a "most unmitigated and malignant falsehood." See Circular to Provisional Governors, Aug. 22, 1865, *Johnson Papers*, 8: 639; and Hamilton to Johnson, Sept. 20, 1865, Johnson Papers, LC.

From Benjamin F. Perry

Columbia, S.C.   Sept 23d 1865

My dear Sir

I have sent you despatches almost daily of the action of the Convention,[1] but have not heard whether they have been received.

The Convention have repealed the ordinance of secession, abolished slavery in the terms of the proposed amendment to the Federal Constitution, repealed the Parish system, & equalized the basis of representation in the Senate, giving each Federal district one Senator.

The Convention have like wise instructed the Legislature to give the election of Electors of President & Vice President to the people. A Committee has reported in favor of giving the election of Governor to the people which will be adopted by a large vote of the Convention.[2] Several other changes have been & will be made to popularize our Constitution.

I can assure your Excellency that the members are loyal & disposed to do their duty in good faith. I have sent you my Message to the Convention, and almost all of my recommendations will be adopted. I hope the members, who have thus acted with loyalty & magnanimity, will all be pardoned by Your Excellency. After their adjournment I will give you their names.[3]

I have made the acquaintance of General Ames[4] who is in Command of this portion of the State, & was formerly in Command in North Carolina. He has by his wise & judicious course here gained great favor with the members of the Convention from every portion of the State. They all wish him retained here in his present Command. I heartily concur in making this request of your Excellency. Under his directions I am organizing a police force in each District & the loss of General Ames here would disconcert the plan perhaps. A police force has become absolutely necessary for safety.

I had an interesting interview with General Meade & General Gilmore[5] two or three weeks since & arranged to open the Courts & restore civil law in South Carolina.

The members of our Legislature will be elected under the new Constitution on the 18th day October & I will convene them the next week, so as to provide for the election of Senators & members of Congress, & make provision for the protection of the "freed men" by law.[6]

I have written the Secretary of State giving an account of the attrocious conduct of the negro or colored troops in South Carolina. We do not object to them on account of their *color*, but on account of their horrible conduct.

In order to open our courts I ask that Chancellor B F Dunkin Chancellor C P Carroll & Judge D. L. Wardlaw may have their pardons sent to me as soon as possible.[7]

The speech of Your Excellency to the Southern gentlemen ten or twelve days since has won you, most assuredly, golden opinions in South Carolina. It is full of noble sentiments beautifully expressed.

May your administration continue, as it has commenced, till we are all once more a free, united and happy [nation] is the earnest prayer of your friend & admirer.

Bn. F. Perry

ALS, DLC-JP.

1. See Perry's two telegrams of September 19, another pair sent on the 20th, and one on the 23rd, as well as the President's September 22 acknowledgement of Perry's second dispatch of the 20th, all in Johnson Papers, LC.

2. Perry's wire of September 29 confirmed this prediction. Johnson Papers, LC.

3. Perry actually did so two days before adjournment. See Perry to Johnson, Sept. 25, Johnson Papers, LC.

4. Adelbert Ames (1835–1933) retained his command until he was mustered out in the spring of 1866. Later he served as a United States senator (1870–74) and governor of Mississippi (1874–75). Warner, *Blue*; Powell, *Army List*, 161; Richard N. Current, *Those Terrible Carpetbaggers* (New York, 1988), 113, 435.

5. George G. Meade and Quincy A. Gillmore.

6. See Perry to Johnson, Oct. 27, 1865.

7. Benjamin F. Dunkin (1792–1874), presiding judge of the state court of appeals, James P. Carroll (c1809–1883), a former chancellor, and David L. Wardlaw (1799–1873), circuit court judge and president of the state constitutional convention, all had been *ab initio* secessionists. The former and latter had already been pardoned on September 6, while Carroll was granted executive clemency on September 29. John A. May and Joan R. Faunt, *South Carolina Secedes* (Columbia, 1960), 137; 1860 Census, S.C., Edgefield, Edgefield C. H., 89; John A. Chapman, *History of Edgefield County From the Earliest Settlements to 1897* (Newberry, S.C., 1897), 263–64; *Cyclopedia of the Carolinas*, 1: 207–8; *House Ex. Docs.*, 40 Cong., 1 Sess., No. 32, pp. 47–48, 62 (Ser. 1311).

From J. Madison Wells

New Orleans, September 23d 1865

President,

Yesterday your telegram of 18th instant reached me.[1]

It is perhaps unfortunate that my telegram and letter which I had the honor to address you last month,[2] have remained unanswered so long, inasmuch as I was thereby measurably precluded from taking such steps as in my judgment might be most expedient and wise to secure a healthy and safe reorganization of the State in accordance with your policy and what I believed to be the true interests of the nation.

That any representations of Mr Michael Hahn or other unscrupulous and tainted opponents of your policy and avowed purposes, should have caused a doubt in the Executive mind as to the line of political conduct which ought to be pursued, surprises me; for although it is the part of wisdom not to despise and not fail to profit by the conduct and acts of our enemies, it would be in the last degree, in my opinion, impolitic and dangerous to allow them to dictate the course it behooves us to follow.

Since my return to Louisiana from Washington, no officer of the Federal government, civil, military, or naval, with the exception of the U.S. Marshal and Naval Officer[3] has contributed in any way to aid in the reorganization of the State, or to make the arduous work of administering the civil government meantime practicable. On the contrary, the military authorities as represented by General Canby, and the quasi military of the Freedmens' Bureau, seem to have studied only how they could give trouble and cause vexation.

In this condition of our affairs, and failing to hear from you President, I issued a proclamation calling for an election on the 6th day of November next, for Congressmen, State officers and members of Legislature.[4]

This will cause no embarrassment if your commission of Provisional Governor yet comes; if it does not, I shall proceed and do the best I can.

To prevent all misconception likely to arise from correspondence however prolix, I concluded to request the Hon: Hu Kennedy, Mayor of this City, and Dr Cottman to go to Washington and to confer with you.[5] They are fully informed of the true state of affairs, and have full authority to act for me and in my place. Mr Kennedy has himself shared the vexations and annoyances to which I have referred in a very large degree, and he will be able to offer additional explanations to those he informs me he has already, with much fulness, given in writing.

Commending the Mayor and Dr Cottman to your confidence. . . .

J. Madison Wells

LS, DLC-JP.
1. See Johnson to Wells, Sept. 18, 1865.
2. See Wells to Johnson, Aug. 25, 1865, *Johnson Papers*, 8: 654–55.
3. Cuthbert Bullitt and Thomas M. Wells.
4. Wells issued his proclamation on September 21, 1865. *New Orleans Picayune*, Sept. 22, 1865.
5. Presumably Kennedy and Thomas Cottman were two of the four Louisianans who visited Johnson on September 26. *New York World*, Sept. 27, 1865; *Washington Morning Chronicle*, Sept. 27, 1865.

From Lafayette C. Baker

War Department, Washington City,
September 24, 1865

Sir—

D. N. Coleman[1] breakfasted at Willard's, Wednesday morning, September 20th, at eight o'clock and forty-five minutes. Went to the President's grounds (in the immediate vicinity of the White House) at ten o'clock and ten minutes. Remained around the White House until twenty-five minutes after. Returned to hotel, went to Attorney-General's office at eleven o'clock. Remained there until one o'clock. Went from Attorney-General's office to Dorsey's[2] livery stable, No. 122 Twelfth Street. Hired a small roan saddlehorse. Rode to Georgetown Heights; did not dismount or speak to any one. Returned to hotel at three o'clock and twenty-four minutes; did not leave hotel again that day. Retired at nine o'clock and thirty-five minutes. Thursday, September 21.— Breakfasted at eight o'clock and fifty-four minutes; went to President's grounds at nine o'clock and twenty-two minutes; remained until ten forty-five. Went to Attorney-General's office at eleven o'clock; remained until one. Returned to hotel at one-ten. Met a stranger near hotel. Stranger invited Coleman to call on him that evening at nine o'clock, at No. 9 Indiana Avenue (this is the residence of E. B. Edwards,[3] an old resident of this city, but decidely disloyal). Entered hotel; went to his room; remained until eight-twenty. Kept his appointment at No. 9 Indiana Avenue; remained until eleven-forty. Returned to hotel, and entered about twelve o'clock. Friday, September 22.— Arose at eight-twenty; breakfasted. Went to Attorney-General's office as usual at eleven o'clock; was there up to the time of the closing of this report.

Remarks.—Coleman seems to have but few friends among the numerous pardon-seekers now in this city. He has often met and conversed with one J. B. Fry,[4] who is comparatively a stranger here, but is said to be engaged in the business of procuring pardons (shall report further concerning this individual); also converses with John S. Hollingshead,[5] Commissioner of Deeds, corner of Eighth and E Streets.

The above is an extract from a police diary in the case of D. N. Coleman from Wednesday, September 20, four o'clock, to Friday, September 22, at twelve o'clock and forty minutes.[6]

L. C. Baker,

Brigadier-General and Provost-Marshal of the War Department

Lafayette C. Baker, *History of the United States Secret Service* (Philadelphia, 1867), 586–87.

1. Johnson had asked Baker two days earlier to place Nicholas D. Coleman, who was in Washington seeking a pardon, under strict surveillance. Coleman had early in the war written a letter denouncing Johnson "in the most bitter and scornful terms." Baker, *Secret Service*, 586.

2. Allen S. Dorsey (c1828-c1884) was variously listed in the city directories as clerk, horse dealer, foreman, and livery stable operator. 1870 Census, D.C., Washington, 3rd Ward, 217; Washington, D.C., directories (1862–85).

3. E. B. Edwards has not been otherwise identified.

4. Possibly John B. Fry (fl1870), a contractor who boarded at various addresses in postwar Washington. Washington, D.C., directories (1867–70).

5. John S. Hollingshead (c1814–1869), was also a notary public and local temperance leader. *Washington Evening Star*, Aug. 2, 1869.

6. Two days later Baker continued the surveillance report, noting Coleman's actions from Friday evening through Tuesday, including a Saturday morning visit at the White House reception room. On the 30th Coleman's departure on the previous day's 4:30 train was reported. Baker to Johnson, Sept. 26, 30, 1865, in Baker, *Secret Service*, 587–88.

From Peter J. Sullivan[1]

Metropolitan Hotel: Washington City, D.C.
Sept. 24th, 1865.

Sir.

I leave for my home in Cincinnati, this eveinging, and from thence to Memphis where I had Camd. for a long time; from there I pass over to Little Rock, on professional business: and as I have neither the time or opertunity to see you, I beg leave to Call your attention to the fact that my old chief—Lieut. General U. S. Grant is a Candidate for the Presidency IN the hands of THE Washburns[2] and that class of uncertain politicians. Sherman is promised the Lieut. General ship in the event of Grant's election. This I have learned from my friend Charles T. Sherman[3] Esq. brother of Genl. Sherman, a claim agent now in Washington.

My objection to Grant is, the company he is found in: I want no office. I am now a cripple and pensioner of the service; and I tell you, Mr. President, that THAT PORTION OF THE people who think & act with me, will close up the true patriotic columns around your honest standard, and will bid those boom proofs to demolish the solid square, if the can. My old friend, Hon. Fayette McMullin[4] of Va. I have entrusted with this sealed note, with the request to hand it to you. Discretion is every thing in the subject matter of this letter. All ears and CLOSE mouth, with studied action, will reveal this plot ere long. The great conservative people will surround and suport you.

Judge Chase, but a few weeks since wrote a caustic letter to Colonel (Judge) Key[5] of Cincinnati, late principal Judge Advocate on Staff of Genl. McLeelan,[6] stating that he wanted that officer to let Slavery go, and stand with him on the Duglas platform. I can, I think, furnish you, if desired, with a copy of that letter.

The Washburn platform for Grant, I will have on my return here from the South. I am determined to learn, from my brother lawyers and Army officers what Grant means by placing himself under the special guardianship of Washburn & Co.

I do not wish that this would go into the hands of one of your secretaries, for reasons which I may hereafter explain.[7]

Peter Sullivan
Late Col. 48th Ohio. Infty.
No. 447, West 4th. St.   Cincinnati, Ohio.

ALS, DLC-JP.
    1. Sullivan (1821–1883), a Mexican War veteran and former U.S. Senate stenographer, later became Johnson's minister to Colombia. *NCAB*, 5: 525–26.
    2. Israel, Cadwallader C., and Elihu B. Washburne.
    3. Sherman (1811–1879), a lawyer in Mansfield, Ohio, and later Washington, D.C., was briefly a government director of the Union Pacific Railroad before becoming the

U.S. district judge at Cleveland (1867-c72). *The Biographical Cyclopaedia and Portrait Gallery with an Historical Sketch of the State of Ohio* (6 vols., Cincinnati, 1883–95), 4: 1032–33; Washington, D.C., directories (1865–67).

4. McMullin had been a U.S. and Confederate congressman.

5. Thomas M. Key (c1820–1869), Ohio lawyer, legislator, and judge of the criminal court of Cincinnati, held the rank of colonel during the war. *Cincinnati Enquirer*, Jan. 19, 1869; Heitman, *Register*, 1: 595.

6. George B. McClellan.

7. Johnson's endorsement read: "in reference to the next presidency &c—Private package."

From James N. Lea[1]

Washington   Monday Septr. 25th [1865][2]

Sir

I respectfully ask on behalf of Mrs. Catherine M Pritchard[3] of New Orleans a pardon. She is a widow nearly sixty years of age, with five daughters dependent upon her and has not a male relative living to whom she can look for advice or assistance. She has never been outside of the Federal lines since the occupation of New Orleans by the Federal army. Her property which is under seizure by the Freedman's Bureau *could not* therefore have been abandoned by her. She has taken the amnesty oath. All these facts are within my personal knowledge and they are all known to the commissioner of the Freedman's Bureau in New Orleans who nevertheless refuses to deliver her property to her. Her case comes clearly within the class with reference to which the most positive instructions for restitution have been sent from the Government, and affords a striking illustration of the persistency with which those instructions are ignored and disobeyed. She applies for a pardon believing that it affords the readiest if not the only means of relief.[4]

J. N. Lea

ALS, DNA-RG94, Amnesty Papers (M1003, Roll 29), La., Catherine M. Pritchard.

1. Lea (fl1874) was a New Orleans attorney. During the war he served as administrator of the Charity Hospital in New Orleans for a time. New Orleans directories (1861–72); *OR*, Ser. 1, Vol. 15: 512–13.

2. Although no year was given by Lea, external evidence makes it clear that this is an 1865 letter.

3. Pritchard (fl1888) was the widow of George W. Pritchard. New Orleans directories (1859–88).

4. Johnson endorsed Lea's letter: "Let a pardon be filled up in this Case." Mrs. Pritchard was pardoned on September 26 and her property was restored on October 31, 1865. Amnesty Papers (M1003, Roll 29), La., Catherine M. Pritchard, RG94, NA; *House Ex. Docs.*, 39 Cong., 2 Sess., No. 116, p. 24 (Ser. 1293); *House Reports*, 40 Cong., 1 Sess., No. 7, p. 129 (Ser. 1314).

From Hylan B. Lyon [1]

Orizaba Mexico   September 25th 1865

I have the honor to respectfully request of his Excellency, The President of the United States, a pardon for my participation in the War waged by the insurrectionary States of the South against the United States government. I am a graduate of the United States Military Academy at West Point New York and was an officer of the United States Army at the beginning of the War. My resignation of my commission as 1st Lieutenant of the 3rd Regiment of Artillery U.S.A. was accepted by President Lincoln on the 30th of April 1861. I am a native of Kentucky.

All my acts during the war were governed by humane and civilized principles.[2] I desire to return to my home in Kentucky and if permitted to do so I will take the oath of allegiance to the United States Government and will conduct myself as a quiet and loyal citizen.

Please address your reply to this communication to me at Eddyville Lyon County Kentucky to the care of Judge F. H. Skinner[3] who will be advised in regard to my movements.

H. B Lyon   Late Brigadier General
Provisional Army of the Confederate States

ALS, DNA-RG94, Amnesty Papers (M1003, Roll 26), Ky., Hylan Benton Lyon.

1. Lyon (1836–1907), a West Point graduate of 1856, was a former cavalry commander in Kentucky, Tennessee, and Alabama and a veteran of the battles of Knoxville and Chattanooga. He had accompanied Tennessee's Gov. Isham G. Harris to Mexico. Warner, *Gray*; William H. Perrin et al., *Kentucky: A History of the State* (9 vols., Easley, S.C., 1979[1885–88]), 2: 859.

2. According to one correspondent, Lyon's last raid through Kentucky was "characterized by the worst species of outrages & robbery, house burning &c." Philip D. Yeiser to James Speed, July 8, 1865, Amnesty Papers (M1003, Roll 26), Ky., Two or more name files, RG94, NA. See B. L. Roberson, "The Courthouse Burnin'est General," *THQ*, 23 (1964): 372–78.

3. County Judge Frederick H. Skinner (1815-*fl*1885) forwarded his cousin's petition. Johnson did not pardon Lyon until June 11, 1866, after he had returned to the U.S. as required. Perrin et al., *Kentucky*, 2: 864–65; Skinner to Johnson, Oct. 27, 1865; L. S. Trimble to Johnson, June 11, 1866, Amnesty Papers (M1003, Roll 26), Hylan Benton Lyon, RG94, NA.

From Henry L. Stone

September 25, 1865, Bath County, Ky.; ALS, DNA-RG94, Amnesty Papers (M1003, Roll 73), Misc. Northern and Western States, Henry L. Stone.

A native Kentuckian, who was a law student in Greenville, Indiana, when the war began, asks for pardon under the 10th exception, having passed in September 1862 from Union to Confederate territory with the purpose of joining the Confederate Army. Captured in July 1863, he succeeded in escaping on four occasions, the last time to Canada, whence he made his way back to the South to rejoin his comrades and fight another year until surrendering in May 1865.

Stone concedes "there are no circumstances which you, Sir, would consider mitigating, except those which exist in the composition of my nature, or result from my early political training." Regarding his home state as part of the rebellion, he "did not want to sit idly by, and let the greatest war of modern ages pass away . . . without indulging my military aspirations." Stone did not join the Federals, "owing to an inborn prejudice in favor of the South and her institutions." [He was pardoned December 9, 1865.]

From Thomas B. Brown[1]

Washington   Sept. 26 1865

Dear Sir.

I have the honor to inform you that in accordance with your request, at the close of the present month I will tender the position of Physician to the Jail to Dr. Duhamel.[2]

It affords me *pleasure* in this particular to carry out your wishes.

The escape of several prisoners on the night of the 24th inst.[3] has rendered it important for me to remove some of the Guards and their places have been filled by men of stern loyalty and physical ability and who have been connected with the Union Army during the Rebellion.

I deem it proper to add that in the removal of Mr. Robinson[4] my reasons are that I am satisfied he was opposed to the election of your Excellency, as well as our late lamented President. I mention this case because I received a note from one of your private Secretaries, saying "that Mr. Robinson comes to you highly recommended["] and you would be glad if I could *consistently* retain him. I have other charges against him.

It will always give me *great pleasure* to serve you in any manner in my power.

T. B. Brown   Warden

ALS, DNA-RG48, Appts. Div., Misc. Lets. Recd.
1. Before the war Brown (c1818–1868) was a furniture dealer. Washington, D.C., directories (1858–69); *Washington Evening Star*, Nov. 28, 1868.
2. William J.C. Duhamel.
3. For accounts of the escape and recapture of prisoners, see *Washington Evening Star*, Sept. 25, 26, 28, 29, Oct. 3, 1865.
4. Thomas H. Robinson (c1832-fl1876) appears to have continued serving as a guard in the city jail, in spite of Brown's objections. 1860 Census, D.C., 5th Ward, 145; (1870), 102; Washington, D.C., directories (1860–77).

From Varina H. Davis

Mill View, Near Augusta Ga
Sept. 26th 1865.

Sir.

I have addressed some four or five letters to Your Excellency[1] begging a decision upon my case, without having recieved a reply.

I am not astonished that amidst your multifarious duties you cannot find time to examine, and act upon merely personal matters, but I think were you cognizant of all the suffering entailed upon me by the durance in which I am kept here, you would decide upon my case immediately.

When forcibly conveyed to Savannah I had not one friend in the city, had never been there, and knew of no place in which I could obtain shelter for myself and helpless little family but the hotel. And if I had known any one sufficiently well to claim hospitality, my family was too large to Justify me in doing so. I had $2500 in gold which being in my tent escaped the soldiers who captured us. Hoping from day to day to receive permission to leave Savannah I sold hundred after hundred of it to pay the extravagant board charged there until now a very few weeks longer of detention will throw me literally upon the charities of the public.

Finding the sensibilities of my children constantly wounded by depreciatory remarks, made of their Father, and the younger children taught derisive and ribald songs such as any kind hearted man would regret to hear a man's children repeat no matter what the prejudice against him might be—being told that my children would be educated for nothing there, at best schooled for the time, and with a hope that I might be permitted alone to go to their Father, when a large family would be denied the priviledge, I deprived myself of the only consolation now left to me, and sent my children to Canada.[2] The winter is coming on, I am staying about upon the suffrages of new friends, homeless, and nearly penniless. I have no protector, no one to stand between me and the wolf at my door—and all I love, and cherish torn from me to death in life consigned. Only let me go to him, and I will promise never to infringe upon your kindness by troubling you in any way. I am so racked by neuralgie from the confinement in a Southern climate in which I never could remain without great suffering that it seems as though my senses will desert me at times. You would not I am sure torture the helpless. May I not hope to be permitted to go to my Husband? I could go by sea, land at Old Point so as not to pass through any of the cities. I pray you decide the question in my favor. . . . [3]

                                                         Varina Davis.

ALS, DLC-JP.
    1. This letter was forwarded to Johnson by Francis P. Blair, Sr. Blair to Johnson, Oct. 8, 1865, Johnson Papers, LC. See Davis to Johnson, Aug. 30, 1865, *Johnson Papers*, 8: 672–73.
    2. See Ulysses S. Grant to Johnson, Dec. 28, 1865.
    3. Receiving no reply, Mrs. Davis repeated her plea the following January but it was not until May 1866 that Johnson permitted her to visit her husband at Fortress Monroe. *OR*, Ser. 2, Vol. 8: 874–75; Hudson Strode, *Jefferson Davis: Tragic Hero* (3 vols., New York, 1955–64), 3: 279–80.

From David X. Junkin[1]

Chicago Ill.   Sept 26. 1865

Sir,

When the U.S troops were approaching Huntsville Alabama, the secessionists fled, with most of their slaves and movable property, and kept within the Rebel lines. The Union men, originally a decided majority of the population, supposing the[sic] they had nothing to dread, as they both *felt* & had *voted* against secession, remained.

Amongst this number was Mr HENRY F HALSEY,[2] the proprietor of an extensive carriage manufactory. He is the brother of the Revd. Leroy J Halsey[3] D.D, professor in our Theological Seminary in this city. The military authorities took possession of Mr Halsey's factory and large stock of material, & used it for government purposes, *promising indemnification*. They still retain it, and Mr Halsey is thrown out of his business: reduced to poverty, & compelled, *by days works*, to try to get bread for a large family of his own, together with an aged & dependent mother, a widowed sister and niece.

There is now no military necessity for retaining his property, and it would seem but *just* that it should be restored to him, and this *great hardship* cease. It is a *very hard case* and demanding prompt relief.

The Revd. Prof. Halsey, who has to support a large family, in this expensive city, upon a small stipend, has been constrained to send relief to his suffering kindred, which would be needless if simple *justice* were done in the premises.

Profoundly convinced of your Excellency's desire to do justice, the undersigned, having become cognizant of the facts, volunteers this effort to bring them to your knowledge, assured that you will give the requisite orders to have *Henry F. Halsey*'s property restored to him, if the facts be found as above stated.

I know you to be the uncompromising foe of oppression; and feel confident that you will bid it cease, as promptly as your multiplied cares will permit.

The Halseys are *loyal people*, & it is hard they should longer suffer.[4] The undersigned has during this war, lost his own health, whilst serving on ship-board; and lost by death on the Frigate Potomac, a beloved son: & he would not ask your interposition in any case, unless profoundly convinced that it is *right*.

D X Junkin   Late Chaplain U.S. Navy
Now pastor North Presbyn. church Chicago

ALS, DNA-RG107, Lets. Recd., EB12 President 2594.5 (1865).

1. Junkin (1808–1880) formerly held pastorates in New Jersey, Washington, D.C., and Pennsylvania. Brown, *Am. Biographies*, 4: 468.

2. Halsey (c1816–1887), a native Virginian, died from injuries sustained in a carriage

accident. 1860 Census, Ala., Madison, 1st Dist., Hayes Store, 60; Gandrud, *Alabama Records*, 157: 22–23.

3. A graduate of the University of Nashville, Halsey (1812–1896) ministered to several Presbyterian congregations in Missouri and Kentucky before assuming the chair of "pastoral theology, church government and homilectics" at McCormick Theological Seminary. *NCAB*, 3: 517.

4. The President ordered the letter referred to Col. Lewis Johnson, commander of the post at Huntsville, who reported that Halsey actually rented the building in question and that his lease had expired sometime in 1864. Edwin M. Stanton to Johnson, Dec. 5, 1865, Lets. Recd., EB12 President 2594.5 (1865), RG107, NA.

From William Aiken

Charleston S.C   Sept. 27th 1865

My dear Sir

The Northern prints think you will pay a visit soon to the Southern sea port Towns.[1] Such an intention carried out would be highly gratifying to all of us here—as we desire most ardently to have you here. We wish you to see and judge for yourself—as to the state of affairs. Much and great good can be done by such a timely visit.

I wish now particularly to request the favour of you—if you come to Charleston—to make my house your home—as it will give me great pleasure to have you as my guest. Mrs Aiken requests me to say— if Mrs Johnson—your Daughter Mrs Patterson or any member of your family should accompany you—she will be most happy to receive them.[2]

William Aiken

ALS, DLC-JP.

1. For several weeks it had been rumored that Johnson was contemplating a fall southern tour. In fact, one newspaper reported that he had accepted an invitation to visit Richmond. Other southern presses reprinted a report from the *National Intelligencer* that the President had ordered the steamer *Rhode Island* to proceed to the nation's capital for the purpose of transporting him and some "distinguished officers" to the Carolinas. Andrew Jamieson to Johnson, Sept. 6, 1865, Johnson Papers, LC; *Augusta Constitutionalist*, Sept. 20, 1865; *Raleigh Standard*, Sept. 26, 1865; *Charleston Courier*, Oct. 17, 1865.

2. Johnson personally endorsed Aiken's letter thus: "Invitation from Gov Aiken of So Ca to stop at his house in Charleston." Later the mayor of Charleston forwarded resolutions passed by the city council which welcomed the President, but the visit was not forthcoming; in fact, a dispatch to the *Charleston Courier* denied that Johnson "had any intention of visiting the South at present." Ibid.; Charles Macbeth to Johnson, Oct. 11, 1865; Charleston, S.C., Citizens to Johnson, Oct. 10, 1865, Johnson Papers, LC.

From the Alabama Convention[1]

State Capitol, Montgomery, Alabama,
September 27, 1865.

The undersigned, Delegates to the Convention of the people of Alabama, now in session, respectfully and earnestly address your Excellency in behalf of Jefferson Davis, late President of the late Confederate States.

Mr. Davis is in confinement, as we are advised, under a charge of treason against the United States; which, if sustained, must be sustained upon the ground of acts performed by him as President of said Confederate States, or as Commander-in-Chief of its forces.

Mr. Davis was by the unanimous voice of the members of the Provisional Congress called to the Chief Magistracy, and by the unanimous voice of the people of the States composing said Confederacy was elected to the Presidency; and for a considerable portion of the term of his service he was sustained by the people with almost entire unanimity.

We do not propose to argue the question of the right of the States to secede, and to maintain that right by force if necessary. The argument on both sides is exhausted; the appeal to arms has forever settled the question, and the people of the South are daily giving unmistakable evidence of their acquiescence in the decision. State after State is wheeling into line; the authority of the United States is everywhere admitted and willingly conformed to; and the Southern people, with as great unanimity as they endeavored to dissolve the Union, are now willing and desirous to resume, in a fraternal spirit, their old relations.

In view of these facts, we respectfully submit that any additional punishment inflicted upon Mr. Davis is unnecessary to deter others from a like course. A Government and a people which overcame the united efforts of eleven States can well afford to be magnanimous.

Respectfully and earnestly we entreat that whatever power the Executive and Government of the United States can rightfully exercise may be used in favor of the eminent citizen in whose behalf this appeal is made.

Montgomery Advertiser, Oct. 3, 1865.

1. Seventy-nine names, headed by Benjamin Fitzpatrick, President, appear at the end of the document.

From Thomas C. Arnold[1]

Newport, R I   September 27th 1865.

Humbly represents the undersigned Thomas C. Arnold of Bryan County, Georgia—That he is the son of Richard J. Arnold[2] of Newport in the State of Rhode Island; that he was left by his Father in charge of a plantation in said county when his Father was obliged to leave that State in consequence of his union sentiments at the outbreak of the rebellion; that while there the undersigned cast the only union vote in his district upon the question of secession; and he has never taken the oath of allegiance to the so called confederate government;

that he was not engaged in the military service except when the militia was called out, and he then served in that county; that the property left in his charge by his Father was to a very great extent injured by the destruction of the mills & outbuildings together with all of the rice by order of the Confederate authorities and subsequently the dwelling house and other buildings were nearly destroyed and the plantation laid waste during the raid under General Kilpatrick;[3] that this affiant took the oath under the amnesty proclamation of President Lincoln upon the first oppertunity, to wit, upon the 31st day of May A.D. 1865.

And this petitioner further declares his intention to commence work upon the plantation with hired labor as soon as the pardon & release by your Excellency will enable him so to do, and hereafter to be & remain in all things a true & loyal citizen of the United States.[4]

Thos. C. Arnold

LS, DNA-RG94, Amnesty Papers (M1003, Roll 16), Ga., Thomas C. Arnold.

1. Not long after signing this, Arnold (1836–1875) returned to his family's winter estate, White Hall, Georgia's largest rice plantation, which he managed until his death. Charles and Tess Hoffmann, *North By South: The Two Lives of Richard James Arnold* (Athens, Ga., 1988), xi, xiii, 252, 257, 270.

2. A Rhode Island businessman and a Georgia rice planter for more than four decades, the elder Arnold (1796–1873) had in 1861 sold his plantation to his son in order to "avoid confiscation by rebel authorities." In November 1865, after having it temporarily exempted from Sherman's Special Field Orders No. 15, Richard Arnold repurchased the estate so that it would not fall prey to U.S. treasury agents. Ibid., xi, 255, 257; Samuel G. Arnold to William H. Seward, Aug. 7, 1865, Amnesty Papers (M1003, Roll 16), Ga., Thomas C. Arnold, RG94, NA.

3. Judson Kilpatrick (1836–1881), a West Point graduate of 1861, was by the war's end a major general of volunteers and commander of Sherman's cavalry. He soon became Johnson's minister to Chile. Warner, *Blue; OR*, Ser. 1, Vol. 44: 362–67; Vol. 47, Pt. 1: 857–63.

4. Supported by Governor Johnson of Georgia, Rhode Island senators Henry B. Anthony and William Sprague, and his brother-in-law and cousin, Samuel G. Arnold, Jr., a former senator, Thomas Arnold was ordered pardoned by the President on October 2, 1865. Amnesty Papers (M1003, Roll 16), Ga., Thomas C. Arnold, RG94, NA; *BDAC*; Hoffmann, *North By South*, 160.

From Neill S. Brown

Nashville   Sept. 27th 1865

Sir:

Before my return home from the South, and after your proclamation of the 29th of May last, my friends thought proper to present an application in my behalf, for pardon, which was endorsed by Gov. Brownlow. I took the oath of amnesty at Pulaski & on my arrival home, gave bail for my appearance at court to answer an indictment against me for treason, and am still under bond for my appearance at the Federal court in Nashville on the 3d Monday in Oct. next. Since then I have forwarded a formal application in my own name accompanied by a copy of my oath of Amnesty & asking that it be considered as a part of the original proceedings, then supposed to be on file.[1] I have recently been informed, that my application has not been acted on, for the want of the recommendation of Gov. Brownlow. In this state of the case I beg to submit this, as a repetition of my application, accompanied with a copy likewise of the oath of Amnesty, and the endorsement of Gov. Brownlow.[2]

Whatever may have been my status in the late lamented conflict, I find it necessary & proper to appeal to your clemency, & to ask to be restored to all the rights of a citizen of the united states. No man was more averse to the late war than I was, or would have made greater sacrifices to avoid it, or to arrest it in its progress, but I was powerless. And while I was decidedly opposed to some of the means & measures of the government employed to reduce the south to submission, I have no hesitation since the termination of the conflict to renew my allegiance, on the basis of union, & to do all in my power to restore harmony & peace, law & order. All this, I have done & shall do. In a word I mean to make as good a citizen as any one else.

I do not know to what exceptions in your proclamation I am necessarily subject. If my property, is to be computed as it was at the commencement of the war, I am worth more than twenty thousand dollars, but if the estimate is to include only what I had at the date of the proclamation, then I am worth less. I am under bond, as I have stated, for my appearance at court, and that I suppose is an exception to which I may be subject. I am not aware that I am under any other disability or exception. But however that may be, whether under any one or more or none, I am sincerely desirous of obtaining your Excellency's assent to my discharge, and a restoration to all the rights of a citizen of the united states, & I respectfully ask, that this supplementary application may be received & filed as a part of the former, so as to preserve all the benefits of time and prudence.[3]

Neill S. Brown

ALS, DNA-RG94, Amnesty Papers (M1003, Roll 48), Tenn., Neill S. Brown.

1. Included among Brown's Amnesty Papers are his letter to Johnson, July 13, 1865, and a copy of the oath dated June 19.

2. Brown's second amnesty oath is dated September 27. Brownlow not only endorsed Brown's letter, but also wrote a separate letter in which he asked for a "free and full pardon" of Brown, because "he has behaved well." Brownlow to Johnson, Sept. 27, 1865, Amnesty Papers (M1003, Roll 48), Tenn., Neill S. Brown, RG94, NA.

3. On October 26 President Johnson's secretary wrote to Attorney General Speed asking that he forward Brown's pardon to the Executive Mansion. Brown was in fact pardoned on that date. Ibid.; *House Ex. Docs.*, 39 Cong., 2 Sess., No. 116, p. 33 (Ser. 1293).

From Gazaway B. Lamar, Sr.[1]

Savannah   Sept 27 1865

Sir

When your Excellency placed me under parole on 28 July last, it was under three stipulations viz:

1st To return directly to Savannah

2d Not to leave the City, without permission of the ["]*Military Commandant of that City*"

3d To report in person, once in 3 months to the Military Commandant.

These conditions, I have religiously adhered to.

At that time, I told your Excellency my fear, that the Military Commandant would exercise his power arbitrarily & unreasonably & you
were pleased to say, that in such case I should apply to you.

Yesterday I recd. a message by *the Military Telegraph*, from New
York, saying that my creditors there, "deemed my presence there of
importance to them" (or words to that effect). I took the dispatch, to
Brevet Brig. Genl Davis,[2] *now Military Commandant*, respectfully
asked permission to go. He replied that *he* would not take the responsibility, but would refer to Maj Genl. Steedman at Augusta & this
morning he sent me the following Note viz

"Sir, I am directed by the Genl. Commanding to inform you, that
your application to visit New York has been disapproved by the Maj
Genl Commanding Department. Signed &c

W. H. Fold,[3]   Lt & AAAG"

I respectfully submit that under the parole Genl Steedman has nothing to do with me but that *the Commandant of this City*, and he alone
must deny or grant the pass—this being your own stipulation.

But it is plain, that if compelled to decide, Genl Davis, *would deny
me the pass* hence with all due respect, I make my application to you in
conformity with your promise—that if unreasonably refused, I ought
write to you, & you would act.

My creditors in New York, to whom I owe $260,000, request me to
go there as of importance to them. I have been denied a pass, & no
reason given.

May I not under these circumstances, respectfully ask to be relieved
from my parole altogether—as it is only annoying and injuring me—&
if not, that at least, I may go where my creditors request me.

As time may be essential to them, may I ask reply by telegram.[4]

G. B. Lamar

ALS, DLC-JP.

1. Earlier in the month the Confederate financier and blockade runner had met with
the President, who ordered that a copy of his July parole be given to Lamar. More
recently, Lamar had written Johnson asking that he be released unconditionally from his
parole. This letter was for some reason delayed in reaching the Executive Mansion,
where it was finally received on October 20 and marked "Filed" the next day. Thomas
T. Eckert to John M. Brannon, Sept. 12, 1865, Tels. Sent, Sec. of War (M473, Roll
89), RG107, NA; Lamar to Johnson, Sept. 19, 1865, Court-Martial Records, MM-
3469, RG153, NA; Ser. 4A, Vol. 3: 208, Johnson Papers, LC.

2. Edwin P. Davis (c1837–1890) was mustered out of service in early October 1865.
Afterwards he worked in real estate and the oyster business in New York City. CSR,
RG94, NA; *New York Tribune*, Oct. 24, 1890; New York City directories (1884–89).

3. By mid-October 1865, Lt. William H. Folk (c1837–1892) had been relieved from

duty as acting assistant adjutant general for the Savannah district. CSR, RG94, NA; Pension Records, Lydia A. Folk, RG15, NA.

4. The document is marked "Attended to Oct. 3, 1865." See William E. Chandler to Johnson, Dec. 21, 1865.

From Stephen R. Mallory

Fort La Fayette   27 September 1865

Permit me, Mr. President, to throw myself upon your generous Kindness and mercy.

Hearing nothing of my petition to you of the twenty first of June last,[1] I fear that I failed in the statement of my case. You are merciful and forbearing; and I know that you would not inflict one pang upon any human heart but from a high sense of duty. Let me assure you, therefore, that I deeply regret my participation in the rebellion, and earnestly desire, during my remaining life, to do all I can, as a good citizen, for the honor and glory of my country. Your efforts to raise up the South have my hearty thanks, and I pray you to release me that I may share the benifits they confer upon our people. If I seem importunate Mr. President I implore you to attribute it to my distress. I have been four months a prisoner; I am impoverished and ruined; My wife and children, helpless and dependent, are to me a constant source of mental anguish. Her anxiety led her to your presence recently in my behalf, but she had not the power to say to you what filled her heart.[2] I recognize fully your policy for the restoration of harmony to a united people, and I will pledge my good faith to aid it to the extent of my power. Your generous Kindness to my friend Mr. Robert Hunter[3] encourages the hope that you will not reject my prayer. I promise you Mr. President that you will never have cause to regret your clemency and magnanimity towards me; and that my good faith is pledged to show my appreciation of them.[4]

S R Mallory

ALS, DNA-RG59, Misc. Lets., 1789–1906 (M179, Roll 228).

1. See Mallory to Johnson, June 21, 1865, *Johnson Papers*, 8: 268.

2. Angela M. Mallory's mid-September interview with the President "had been unsatisfactory." While Johnson was courteous, he "had made no promises and had taken no action in behalf of her husband." Durkin, *Stephen R. Mallory*, 363, 365.

3. Three weeks earlier Hunter had been released on a temporary parole, which was made permanent in October. Johnson to Hunter, Sept. 6, Oct. 21, 1865, Johnson Papers, LC.

4. Despite a second visit from Mrs. Mallory in December and letters from Massachusetts Senator Henry Wilson and Florida's provisional Governor, William Marvin, Johnson delayed Mallory's parole. Durkin, *Stephen R. Mallory*, 378–79; Wilson to Johnson, Dec. 21, 1865, OFH; Marvin to Johnson, Oct. 22, 1865, Johnson Papers, LC. See Horace Greeley to Johnson, Nov. 16, 1865.

From Taliaferro P. Shaffner [1]

Washington D C   Sept 27th 1865.

In 1845, the Methodists of the United States divided into two jurisdictions, one for the Southern States, and the other for the Northern
States.

The Church of the South embraced all the Southern States, excepting Delaware, Maryland and a part of Virginia.

These grand jurisdictions are under legislative tribunals called Gen-
eral Conferences, and these are composed of delegates from Annual
Conferences, and these latter have jurisdiction over fixed territories,
bounded by Geographical, and not political lines: for example, the
Memphis Annual Conference embraces parts of Mississippi, Tennessee
& Kentucky.

All property of the Church is held in trust, subject to the General
Conference, either *mediately* or *immediately*, to be used for the spread
of Christian religion.

Of the property held and managed by the General Conferences, absolutely, are the Book Concerns; for the north it is in New York, for the
South, in Nashville, Tenn. These Book Concerns print the Bible, tracts
and religious books and sell them at nominal prices to the poor and for
the benefit of Missions.

In order to give "the Methodist Book Concern" at Nashville "sole"
powers in law, the Legislature of Tennessee about 12 years ago, passed
an act of incorporation, conformable to the Methodist system.

The General Conference appoint the Agents to manage the Book
Concern, and the whole Clergy act as distributing Agents.

The property in Nashville was seized in 1862 and has been libelled
for Confiscation. The property consists of real estate, printing presses,
books and perhaps some remaining stationery:—now valued at about
$200,000.

The seizure was made, as alledged, because a religious paper, printed
in the establishment disseminated dis-loyal sentiments: [2] The paper was
not under the authority of the General Conference, nor had the Trustees or Agents of the Book Concern, the right to dictate as to the contents of the paper. The paper was a weekly issue, published at the
request of several local conferences with its own editor, but not at the
expense, nor under the management of the Book Concern.

The officers of the Government were, perhaps ignorant as to the
ownership of the property, they supposing the property to be in common, and owned by the person who edited the paper.

The Book Concern, is the property of the whole Methodist Church
of the southern jurisdiction, including Kentucky, Missouri, part of California, several of the Territories &c.

The Methodist Church and the cause of religion now suffers by the above proceeding. The printing of the Bible, and tracts for the Missions and the poor has been thus unfortunately suspended.

The object of this Communication, made in behalf and by authority of the Methodist Church, is to request and humbly petition Your Excellency to issue an order to the proper officers of the Government at Nashville, to unconditionally release the property of the said Book Concern, and restore it to the possession of its Trustees.[3]

Tal. P. Shaffner

LS, DNA-RG60, Office of Atty. Gen., Lets. Recd., President.

1. Shaffner (1818–1881), an inventor, helped build several early telegraph lines, promoted the North Atlantic cable, and received a dozen patents for various methods of nitro-glycerine blasting. *NCAB*, 10: 482.

2. Following the arrest and release of editor James T. Bell, the offices of his *Gazette*, as well as other newspapers and the Southern Methodist Publishing House, were confiscated in May 1862. See Francis U. Stitt to Johnson, Feb. 19, 1862, *Johnson Papers*, 5: 150–52.

3. The President instructed Attorney General Speed to order the discontinuance of the proceedings instituted against the Southern Methodist Publishing House, "but at the cost of the claimants." The property was subsequently returned to its manager, John B. McFerrin. Speed to Horace H. Harrison, Oct. 21, 1865, Office of Atty. Gen., Lets. Sent, Vol. E (M699, Roll 10), RG60, NA. See Allen A. Hall to Johnson, Apr. 21, 1862, *Johnson Papers*, 5: 315–16.

From Joseph A. Wright

Berlin Prussia   Sept 27th 1865

My Dear President,

Permit me to return you my gratitude & thanks for the confidence you have placed in my hands in appointing my son[1] Secretary of Legation. I now feel as if my whole time can be fully given to my Country, and subsequent events will fully convince you of the propriety of the appointment.

I am looking with some anxiety for the reply to the letter I wrote you with regard to your son Robert.[2] I have only repeat, that any thing that lies in my power to advance his interests will be attended to with the greatest pleasure both by my good wife and myself. Do write me *fully* and *freely whatever* may be your *wishes*, reposing the fullest confidence that they will be faithfully carried out.

Your speech to the Southern friends[3] who called upon you, is printed in many of the leading journals in Europe, and has given your friends great Satisfaction.

The subject of returning Prussians to this Country is giving me some trouble,[4] but I am looking every mail for one of those matchless despatches from Seward (for which he is so distinguished) touching this question. Now is the hour in my judgment to strike. A pointed and direct issue will lead to the settlement of this vexed question for all coming time. It will distinguish your Administration as much or more as any subject of the present day, and will lead to great increase in Emigration from this vast Country.

Should any change be made of Consul to this place, please advise me.

Joseph A Wright

ALS, DLC-JP.

1. The minister to Prussia had requested a post for his son, John C. Wright (c1833–fl1875), in a note written to Johnson on July 8. 1850 Census, Ind., Marion, Indianapolis Centre Township, 444; Indianapolis directories (1870–75); Wright to Johnson, July 8, 1865, Johnson Papers, LC.

2. See Wright to Johnson, Sept. 7, 1865.

3. See Speech to Southern Delegation, Sept. 11, 1865.

4. The controversy involved Prussia's right to draft into military service American citizens returning to their native land. In early November Wright urged the President to incorporate in his first annual message to Congress "something *short, terse* & *emphatic*" that upheld the right of naturalized U.S. citizens to remain exempt from foreign military conscription. Johnson's address of December 4, however, did not include such a reference. See Wright to Johnson, ca. Aug. 25, Nov. 1, 1865, Feb. 7, 1866, Johnson Papers, LC. See also Wright to Johnson, Dec. 13, 1865, Misc. Lets., 1789–1906 (M179, Roll 231), RG59, NA.

From Joseph C. Bradley

Huntsville Alabama   Sept 28 1865

Ex Govr. Chapman[1] will or has sent you his petition for pardon. The Govr. has not been in the Military or Civil Service of the Confederate States. He beleived in the right of secession—but was opposed to its exercise. After his return from Europe in 1861 & found that his State had seceeded, his sympathies were with Alabama & the Confederacy. The Govr. acknowledges that the Institution of slavery was lost in the late rebellion, & accepts of its present Condition. He is now an old man, with a large familey of Daughters, and impoverished in fortune, and if you will grant him a pardon he will make a good and loyal Citizen of the United States Government.

R Jemison Jr[2] of Tuscaloosa Ala has also sent you his petition for pardon. I know that Mr Jemison was a union man and done all he Could to prevent secession. It is true he was a Senator in the Confederate Congress—but was elected by union men in our State Legislature. I recollect distinctly when we had to elect a Senator to the Confederate Congress at the expiration of C C Clay Jr term, that Jemison urged on me to try & have elected as his Colleague, a rabid secessionist, to divide the responsibility in the attempt that the union men intended to make in Ala to force the State back into the Union. He beleived that when our State was ready to act that it would be better to have one secessionist in the Confederate Congress or Senate than two unionist. I did not then beleive with him but voted first for Seibels & the Govr. Fitzpatrick.[3]

Jemison was so well satisfied with what would be the result of the late rebellion, that he would not attend the session of the senate of the

Confederacy in 1864–65. This man if pardoned by you can do much good in south Ala.

Judge Ormand & Mr. M Banks[4] of Tuscaloosa Ala will also send or have sent you their petitions. These men stand high with us—and from their known high character in the State, if pardoned will have much influence in settling our people down into posative loyalty to our Government.

The Four named gentleman have wrote to me, requesting that I would write to you in their behalf. I mention this fact, for the reason that I do not like to trouble you with letters, as I know how you are oppressed with business—and I fear you may consider me too forward in writing you letters.

I have wrote these men that they have influence & ought to go to work & send acceptable men to Congress that will be a benefit, instead of a clog or burthen to your Administration, or your policy of restoration, To elect men to our Legislature, who will vote for the amendment to the Constitution forever abolishing slavery in the United States, and who will vote for a Law giveing a Negro eaquel legal rights with the whites, who will not vote for any Law to oppress the Freedman.

I say to our people daily—and you must permit me to say it to you, that if our Convention adgourns without repudiateing the State rebel war debts that our Members of Congress ought not to be allowed to take their seats in Congress. This war debt is as much a part of the rebellion, as the Troops raised by the State. I was on the Committee of ways & means in our Legislature & told all of its members, that the debt we were then makeing to sustain the rebellion, would not be allowed to be paid, after the rebellion was suppressed, by the United States Government.

Joseph C Bradley

ALS, DNA-RG94, Amnesty Papers (M1003, Roll 8), Ala., Andrew B. Moore.

1. Prior to his single term as Alabama's chief executive (1847–49), Reuben Chapman (1799–1882) had served in Congress for a dozen years. His clemency petition already had been approved on September 12. Sobel and Raimo, *Governors*, 1: 13–14; Amnesty Papers (M1003, Roll 2), Ala., Reuben Chapman, RG94, NA.

2. A prominent businessman, planter, and politician, Robert Jemison, Jr. (1802–1871), was elected in August 1863 to fill William Lowndes Yancey's unexpired term. Finally taking his seat in late December 1863, he served only six months. Johnson pardoned Jemison on October 4, 1865. Amnesty Papers (M1003, Roll 6), Ala., Robert Jemison, Jr.; Warner and Yearns, *BRCC*.

3. John J. Seibels and Benjamin Fitzpatrick.

4. Cotton planter John J. Ormond (1795–1866) had stepped down from the bench in 1847 and retired from his law practice eight years later. Marion Banks (1813–1886) was a former director of the Alabama State Bank and general assemblyman. Both men had been pardoned on September 12. 1860 Census, Ala., Tuscaloosa, Tuscaloosa, 36, 37; Owen, *History of Ala.*, 3: 94; 4: 303; Amnesty Papers (M1003, Rolls 1, 8), Ala., Marion Banks, John J. Ormond, RG94, NA.

From Joseph C. Bradley

Huntsville Alabama   Sept 28 1865

I herewith send you a letter from Ex Govr. A B Moore of Ala[1] Which I received from him this day. The letter explains itself. He gives a truthful account of his political acts and in a fair & honest manner details his personal & familey matters. He is in feeble health, with his family affliction bareing on his mind, he is really an object of pity & a fit subject for a Magnanimous act of clemency on your part. I am the personal friend of Govr. A B Moore, differed from him widely in regard to the late rebellion, in which he was honestly mistaken or deceived, and I feel assured that you will not blame me for appealing to you in his behalf, or consider me officious in imploring you as President of the United States, to grant a pardon to this old enfeebled impoverished, distressed & unfortunate man. I know that Govr. Moore commited a high offence against the Government by ordering the takeing Fort Morgan & Mount Vernon Arsenal, when Govr. of Ala, but if consistent with your sense of duty to our Government, you will extend to him executive clemency. It will do more to restore loyalty among our people, than all of the other pardons you have granted in South Alabama. At the same time if you Can exercise the pardoning power in his behalf, and could only see him in his feeble health, and could see a part of his unfortunate familey (the beloved wife of his bosom) the Mother of his impoverished children, his Brother in Law Mr Gore,[2] to whom he is much attached, it would do you as much good in feeling as any other act of your life to turn him loose & let him go free the balance of the few days he has to live on earth.

Govr. Moore always belonged to the old school of Democracy in this State, (Jackson Democrats) until he was led off by the "Bogus" Southern Rights Democracy of our State. Public opinion had a good deal to do in makeing Govr. Moore part Company, with us union Democrats. He lived in one of the most populous negro counties in the State, and but few men could stand out against the overwhelming Pro Slavery influence that could be brought to bare against him in such a neighbourhood as Marion or County as Perry. I vividly recollect that the first time that Govr Moore was elevated to the speakership of our Legislature (many years past) when I was only a private Citizen, attending closely to buisiness, that I aided materially to his elevation, against a party forming to disseminate the doctrine of John C Calhoun in our State. Govr. Moore has always opposed proscription in our State for opinions sake. He has invariably refused to take sides against union men, and I will say to you with all the earnestness & honesty I possess, that if you will grant a pardon to Govr. Moore, and you should see proper to remove the Troops from this State, that he will do more if able to go about to prevent union men from being molested, than any other man in South Ala. Pardon him, & he can do more to keep peace between the whites & Blacks in South Ala.—for he lives in the most populous colored population in the State, than any other named man in South Ala. Govr. Moore does not know that I have sent you his letter to me.[3]

Joseph C Bradley

I herewith send you a press copy of my letter to Ex Govr. A B Moore to let you see what I wrote him for I do not wish to keep any thing from you.[4]

Joseph C Bradley

ALS, DNA-RG94, Amnesty Papers (M1003, Roll 8), Ala., Andrew B. Moore.

1. Andrew B. Moore (1807–1873) had been arrested and confined in Fort Pulaski for several months. He received an "indefinite parole" in August 1865 and returned to Marion to practice law. Moore to Bradley, Sept. 16, 1865, Amnesty Papers (M1003, Roll 8), Ala., Andrew B. Moore, RG94, NA; Brewer, *Alabama*, 490–91; Wakelyn, *BDC*.

2. Moore's wife Mary (b. c1817) and his brother-in-law, John Goree, currently resided in lunatic asylums. 1850 Census, Ala., Perry, Marion Beat, 740; Moore to Lewis E. Parsons, Feb. 20, 1866, Amnesty Papers (M1003, Roll 8), Ala., Andrew B. Moore, RG94, NA.

3. Moore's pardon was ordered on March 13, 1866. Andrew K. Long to James Speed, March 13, 1866, ibid.

4. Bradley assured Moore that Johnson was "the only man of weight & influence & position" whom southerners could count on to "save Republican Government & States Rights." Bradley to Moore, Sept. 28, 1865, ibid.

From Robert L. Caruthers

[Nashville][1]   Sept 28 1865

Three months ago I forwarded my petition for pardon by the hands of Judge Ridley.[2] It was accompanied by the amnesty oath,[3] but did not have the recommendation of the Governor, as he was then absent, & I was informed by Mr. East, just from Washington, that it was not regarded as essential where the petitioner was a Tennesseean, personally known to the President. Inasmuch as petitions filed at the same time, & since, by gentlemen who were ahead of me both as to time, & efficiency, in the southern movement, have received favorable action, I am induced to believe that some defect or informality existed in my application. For these reasons I feel it my duty to make this additional application with the endorsement of the Governor, with the amnesty oath attached, that my case may be placed on its merits before your Excellency. By reference to my former petition you will see the facts of my case, with the part I have acted in the rebellion, & my present determination to conform to the laws, & sustain the authorities, both State & National, in the restoration of law & order. Such has been my course since the termination of the conflict, & will continue to be so, in good faith, as a matter of patriotic duty. If your knowledge of my character since 1835, when we first met as members of the Legislature, does not satisfy you of my sincerity, & good faith, nothing that I, or others, could now say, would do so. I flatter myself that will be sufficient.

It may not be out of place to here, reiterate, that I was never an advocate of the doctrine of secession, but always opposed it. I did not approve the withdrawel of the southern members of Congress, nor the secession of the cotton states, but only espoused the southern cause when by the call upon the border states for troops, in April 1861, it became evident that they had to fight on one side or the other. I then thought we should join the side which were battling for the same rights & institutions, & therefore supported the resolutions of our Legislature, taking Tennessee out of the Union, & uniting her destiny with the newly formed Confederacy. Tho' my part has been obscure & ineffi- cient, yet it subjects me with others, to the consequences of the failure.

I am excluded from the benefits of your general amnesty because I am under bonds to answer a charge of treason. I may also fall under the exception of those who went south before the Federal army, & remained to the end of the war. But as this was to avoid arrest & not to "aid the rebellion" I presume it does not apply to me. The exception of all who held office under the Confederate Government would not apply to me unless being a member of the provisional Congress from August to December should be considered holding an "office". After the payment of liabilities I would not be excluded by the $20,000 exception. My estate consisted mainly in slaves. Their emancipation, which I consider complete & final, throws me upon my profession, at the age of sixty five, for a support. But this is immaterial as a pardon will cover many as well as a single offence.

If it comports with your sense of duty, to relieve me from my embar- rassment, by a pardon, in time, I desire to go to Mississippi, & make arrangements for the cultivation of my plantation under the new sys- tem, if it can be done.

It would perhaps not be indelicate, even in my situation, to say that your policy in restoring the southern states to their former position in the Union, & your entire southern policy so far as it has been devel- oped, has my cordial approbation & support, as highly patriotic, & evincive of the broadest statesmanship.

May God sustain & prosper you in this great work for the benefit of our whole country, & all mankind.

My case is before you. If consistant I would ask speedy action upon it, hoping it may be favorable.[4]

Robert L. Caruthers

ALS, DNA-RG94, Amnesty Papers (M1003, Roll 48), Tenn., Robert L. Caruthers.

1. This letter was presumably written from Nashville, because at this time Caruthers was engaged in the practice of law in that city, as indicated in a letter written a week later. Caruthers to Johnson, Oct. 4, 1865, Amnesty Papers (M1003, Roll 48), Tenn., Robert L. Caruthers, RG94, NA.

2. Presumably Bromfield L. Ridley.

3. The letter referred to here is probably the one written by Caruthers to Johnson, ca. July 6, 1865, Amnesty Papers (M1003, Roll 48), Tenn., Robert L. Caruthers, RG94, NA.

4. On August 20, 1866, Johnson's secretary wrote to the Attorney General requesting the immediate issuance of a pardon for Caruthers. Ibid. See also the "Amnesty Records," Ser. 8C, Vol. 3, Johnson Papers, LC.

From Lewis E. Parsons

Montgomery, September 28 1865

Sir

I have the honor to inform you that the Convention of Alabama has this day passed an Ordinance repudiating the War Debt and prohibiting any Legislature from assuming the same, both as regards the Confederacy and the State by a vote of sixty for and nineteen against the measure. The substance of the Ordinance with the vote thereon was sent you by telegraph at fifteen minutes before three o-clock this evening.[1]

The Convention has also abolished Slavery[2] by a vote of ninety to three, and amended the Constitution by striking out all provisions relating to Slaves and Slavery; and has also made it the duty of the Legislature at the next session to pass all laws necessary to give Freedmen full protection of the rights of person and property. They have also passed an Ordinance legalizing all marriages between persons of color, whether the same was valid or not, and to provide for the legality of future marriages, legitimizing the issue of former marriages.

Convention also passed an Ordinance declaring Secession null and void; the vote being unanimous, ninety three affirmative votes.

It will adjourn on Saturday next at six oclock P.M.

There is very little reason to doubt that it will adopt an Ordinance providing for the continuance of the arrangement entered into between Genl Swayne as Assistant Commissioner of the Freedmen's Bureau in this State and the Provisional Governor of the State,[3] by which negro evidence is made competent in all cases between negroes themselves and between negroes and whites, until the same is changed or modified by the Legislature of this State. A large number of the members were willing to incorporate in the constitution a provision making negro evidence competent or what is equivalent thereto giving to the negro the same rights as the non-voting population of the State are entitled to, and I had at one time strong hopes that this could be done, but the majority seemed to think that the people were not fully prepared for such a decided stand, and thought it best to wait for further developments.

The Convention will probably provide for its being called together before the first of March, if necessary, and in the mean time, it is probable the popular mind may more clearly discern what is necessary to be done, and sustain the Delegates in doing it.

Lewis E. Parsons   Prov Governor of Alabama

LS, DLC-JP.
1. This dispatch may be found in the Johnson Papers, LC. For an assessment of the legislation, see Joseph C. Bradley to Johnson, Oct. 13, 1865, Johnson Papers, LC.
2. Johnson was previously notified of this fact by special messenger and telegraph. Parsons to Johnson, Sept. 23, 25, 1865, ibid.
3. On August 4, 1865, Wager Swayne had authorized Alabama civil magistrates and judicial officers to serve as ex-officio Bureau agents responsible for ensuring the rights of black testimony. On August 18 Parsons issued a proclamation endorsing Swayne's order. *Huntsville Advocate*, Aug. 17, 31, 1865. See Carl Schurz to Johnson, Aug. 21, 1865, *Johnson Papers*, 8: 634–35, and Parsons to Johnson, Oct. 2, 1865.

From Margaret Donelson

Nashville Tenn   Sept. 29, 1865

I appeal to you for protection. This day my house has been entered by colored soldiers living on my place, my life and that of my family threatened, my daughters cursed, my dog shot in my dwelling.

Further violence is threatened tonight. From you alone can I expect justice.[1]

Margaret Donaldson[*sic*]

Tel, DNA-RG107, Tels. Recd., President, Vol. 4 (1865–66).
1. Upon receipt of Donelson's telegram on September 30, Johnson had a copy transmitted to General Fisk and ordered him to "immediately take steps to have the above corrected." Tels. Sent, President, Vol. 2 (1865), RG107, NA. See Fisk to Johnson, Oct. 3, 1865.

From Andrew J. Hamilton

City of Austin   29th Sept 1865.

Mr President

By the enclosed copy of a Newspaper, published in this City, you will see an address to the people of Texas, by John H. Reagan,[1] late Post Master General of the so called Confederate Government, written from his prison in Fort Warren, and forwarded to me for publication, through Major General Hooker[2] and the War Dept. There is but one opinion here, among Union men, as to the effect of this address. It comes at a time when many efforts are being made in different portions of the State, and especially in that portion of it, where Mr Reagan was best known, and most popular, to throw discredit upon the wisdom and justice of the Government, in the policy adopted for the restoration of regular Constitutional Govt. in the States lately in rebellion. These efforts go to the extent, of arguing, that Slavery is not dead—that it will be preserved in some form; and that the oath of amnesty, so far as it relates to this subject is not binding &c.

I have in every way possible, in the most public and solemn form, assured the people of the facts, as they exist, and of what was expected of them by the Government, but I have not been able to convince all, and perhaps least of any, those (and they are many) who dislike to be convinced by a political opponent. I know of no man who could accomplish as much with this class of persons in Texas, as Mr. Reagan. Aside from his high reputation for truth and honor, his full and public committal to the proper policy, to be pursued by our people, is, I think, a full guarantee for his future course, and I do not believe there is a single loyal citizen of the State, who would fear to trust him, but on the contrary, every one that I have heard speak upon the subject express an axious desire that he may be permitted to aid in the work before us. It is unnecessary, I hope, for me to labor to prove, that I would never ask favor for those, who I was not sure, would by their future conduct vindicate the magnanimity and mercy of the Govt. But supposing, that it is the general policy of the Government, to forgive all who are sincerely repentant, and anxious to give their aid in correcting the errors and repairing the injuries of the past, and believing there is nothing in Mr. Reagan's conduct, during the rebellion, which would exclude him from the general rule, and sincerely believing, that his restoration to liberty, and return to Texas, would greatly promote the general good I would most respectfully ask, that he be pardoned, if consistent with the views and feelings of your Excellency.[3] If there be anything in the policy of the Goverment, as applicable to Cabinet Officers of the late Rebel Govt., which precludes pardon at this time, then I pledge myself for the strict and faithful observance of the terms of any parole which you might choose to grant him.

In conclusion, Mr. President! allow me to declare, that in this application, I am actuated, more than from any other consideration, by a desire to promote the best interests of the Country, and especially of Texas.

A J Hamilton   Provl. Govr. of Texas

P S   I enclose herewith a letter upon the same subject from Ex Govr. Pease one of the leading Unionists of the State.[4]

Hamilton

I have also sent the enclosed to Mr. Reagan subject to your approval.[5]

H

LS, DLC-JP.

1. Reagan's "Fort Warren letter" of August 11, 1865, urged Texans to accept the result of the war, to renounce secession, to recognize the abolition of slavery, and to extend the franchise to qualified blacks. The copy Hamilton had published in the *Texas State Gazette* has not been found in the Johnson Papers. Walter F. McCaleb, ed., *Memoirs of John H. Reagan* (New York, 1906), 286–95; Hamilton to Reagan, Sept. 28, 1865, Johnson Papers, LC.

2. Joseph Hooker, commander of the Department of the East.

3. Although Reagan was freed two days after his parole on October 11, 1865, he was not pardoned until April 29, 1867. Ben H. Procter, *Not Without Honor: The Life*

of John H. Reagan (Austin, 1962), 174; Amnesty Papers (M1003, Roll 54), Tex., John H. Reagan, RG94, NA. See Order *re* Release of Prominent Confederate Prisoners, Oct. 11, 1865.

4. Pease applauded Reagan's address and asked Johnson to allow him to return to Texas, where "he cannot fail to be a useful and loyal citizen." Pease to Johnson, Sept. 28, 1865, Johnson Papers, LC.

5. Hamilton's letter congratulated Reagan for producing "a most welcome document," one that would "do much good . . . by inducing" Texans "to offer as a fit sacrifice upon the altar of our country, their prejudices and Idols of the past." Hamilton to Reagan, Sept. 28, 1865, Johnson Papers, LC.

From Lewis E. Parsons

Montgomery, Alabama   September 29th 1865

Sir.

I respectfully beg leave to call your attention to General Order No 38, by Major General Woods commanding the Department of Alabama issued "pursuant to directions from Major General Thomas commanding the Military Division of Tennessee" suspending the Rev Richard Wilmer[1] Protestant Bishop of Alabama, and the Episcopal Clergy of his diocese, from preaching or performing divine service, and closing their places of worship until they offer to "resume the use of prayer for the President of the United States and all in civil authority, and by taking the Amnesty Oath prescribed by the President."[2]

While in accordance with the rules of National law, the cessation of actual hostilities by, or the surrender of, the Confederate forces, does not terminate the war, and while until its termination, the belligerent country occupied by the forces of the United States, is still subject to martial law in its fullest and most comprehensive sense, still I must be excused for saying, that looking to the actual condition of things, I cannot but regard the order referred to as unwise and impolitic. I say the actual condition of things for the reason, that peace is really and in fact established. The people of the seceding States may be mortified and sore at their failure and their losses, but they accept the terms imposed on them as a legitimate consequence of such failure and as a people, will for the future, be found among the firmest defenders of the Union. There will be no differences, no division among them on this question.

By the intelligence of the State, I have good reason to believe, that the course of Bishop Wilmer is condemned.[3] Here it certainly is: and the Pastor of the Episcopal church at this place,[4] has for some time since the letter of the Bishop referred to in the order uniformly prayed "for the President of the United States and all in civil authority."

But while public sentiment may not approve the course, Bishop Wilmer has thought proper to pursue, yet now that peace is regarded as actually restored, and the people of Alabama in some senses more loyal than ever before; with the Constitution of the United States before them which secures the highest freedom to the exercise of religion, and with the knowledge that the act of the Bishop of Alabama, was not an offense under any law of the United States, I fear that the exertion of compulsion, to force pastors and their congregations to adopt a particular form of prayer, or to punish them for not doing so, will be regarded as following the example of monarchical or papal institutions, rather than those of our own free constitution.

With the existing feeling and temper of our people, the act of the Bishop is harmless. If he is ambitious of martyrdom let him be disappointed.

The Government of the United States is strong enough to be magnanimous and it will grow in the affections of the people by manifesting this spirit. Disapproving as I do of the letter of Bishop Wilmer, it is innocuous; while the course which General Thomas has adopted can scarcely fail to produce agitation, discussion and bitterness of feeling. If I may be allowed to make the suggestion, I sincerely believe that your public disapproval of the order, on the ground, that it was an encroachment on the right of religious liberty as asserted by our Constitution, will be warmly approved by a large majority of the people without distinction of party.[5]

Lewis E. Parsons   Provisional Governor of Ala

LS, DLC-JP.

1. Wilmer (1816–1900) served parishes in Virginia and North Carolina before his election as bishop of the diocese of Alabama in 1861. His June 20, 1865, pastoral letter had advised fellow clergymen and laity under his charge to exclude the usual prayer for the President from the liturgy until civil authority had been once more restored in the state. *DAB*; Fleming, *Alabama*, 324.

2. Here Parsons quotes directly from Woods's order of September 20, 1865, as it appeared in the *Montgomery Advertiser* on September 27.

3. See, for example, the October 1, 1865, editorial of the *Mobile Register and Advertiser*, in which "some gentlemen of the Federal Army" stationed in that city had "expressed a very marked dislike" for Wilmer. Despite this antagonism, the editor asserted that the Bishop had been clearly "wronged." See also Carl Schurz to Johnson, Nov. 22, 1865.

4. John M. Mitchell (c1824-fl1871) remained as rector of St. John's Church in Montgomery until 1868 when he assumed the rectorship of Christ Church, Savannah. For Mitchell's discussion of his position, see his letter published in the *Montgomery Advertiser*, Oct. 6, 1865. 1860 Census, Ala., Montgomery, 1st Dist., 180; Walter C. Whitaker, *History of the Protestant Episcopal Church in Alabama, 1763–1891* (Birmingham, 1898), 78, 96; Henry T. Malone, *The Episcopal Church in Georgia, 1733–1957* (Atlanta, 1960), 113, 121.

5. Parsons' letter was handed to General Thomas. From Washington, Thomas wired his adjutant in Nashville that the suspension of Wilmer would not be removed by the President, who had seen the pastoral letter and "comprehended fully the concealed treason." Nevertheless, Thomas finally revoked his order on December 22, one day before the Bishop's own appeal to Johnson arrived at the Executive Mansion. George H. Thomas to Robert H. Ramsay, Oct. 16, 1865, Tels. Sent, Sec. of War (M473, Roll 90), RG107, NA; Wilmer to Johnson, Nov. 27, 1865, Lets. Recd. (Main Ser.), File W-2212-1865 (M619, Roll 441), RG94, NA; Fleming, *Alabama*, 327–28; Ser. 4A, Vol. 3: 375, Johnson Papers, LC.

To Benjamin F. Perry

Washington, D.C., Sept 29th 1865.

I thank you for your dispatch of the (28") Twenty-Eighth instant, and have to congratulate your Convention upon its harmonious and successful amendment of the Constitution.

It affords great satisfaction here to all who favor a speedy restoration of all the States to their former relations in the Union. Let this work go on and we will soon be once more a United, a prosperous and a happy people forgetting the past, looking with confident hope to a prosperous and harmonious future.[1]

Andrew Johnson   Pres't

Tel, DNA-RG107, Tels. Sent, President, Vol. 2 (1865).
  1. See Perry to Johnson, Oct. 5, 1865.

To George Stoneman

Washington, D.C., 29 Sept 1865

Outrages & depredations in East Tennessee are reported[1] particularly the search of the house of John C Turnley[2] at Oak Grove 5 miles above Dandridge by an armed band in the U.S. uniform with threats of his assassination. Let proper steps of prevention be taken.[3]

Andrew Johnson   Pres

Tel, DNA-RG107, Tels. Sent, President, Vol. 2 (1865).
  1. The report originated from Mrs. Amanda Mahoney, as indicated in a dispatch sent by her brother. See Parmenas T. Turnley to Montgomery C. Meigs, Sept. 28, 1865, Johnson Papers, LC.
  2. Turnley (1792–1871), a farmer, attorney, hotelier, and postmaster, also had been, reputedly, an "intimate" friend of Johnson's for three decades. Ibid.; 1860 Census, Tenn., Jefferson, 255; Parmenas T. Turnley, *The Turnleys* (Highland Park, Ill., 1905), 128, 132, 134, 142; *U.S. Off. Reg.* (1865), 349.
  3. See Burr H. Polk to Johnson, Oct. 1, 1865.

From Bailey, Wedderburn & Co.

September 30, 1865, Richmond, Va.; Pet., DNA-RG94, Lets. Recd. (Main Ser.), File B-1806-1865 (M619, Roll 339).

The proprietors and editors of the *Commercial Bulletin* of Richmond complain that "their newspaper has been suppressed & their property taken in military possession" by order of Gen. Alfred H. Terry and that "one or more of the Editors and writers . . . have been imprisoned . . . upon an allegation . . . of disloyal or exceptionable matter published in their said newspaper." They ask that the President instruct General Terry "to reinstate petitioners in the right and use of their property . . . and to discharge from imprisonment any person connected with the paper" who has been detained, upon his posting reasonable bail, and that further action be transferred to a civil tribunal. [Despite Terry's claim that the paper "has continually manifested its sympathy with treason," Johnson's endorsement directed that the "parties be released from further arrest by General Terry after a conference with them upon the impropriety of the articles in question."]

From R. Weakley Brown[1]

Nashville   Sept 30th 1865.

My Dear Friend

I have several times read your late patriotic, & statesmanlike Address to the Southern Delegation.[2] It has stirred the very depths of my heart, and increased my respect and admiration for him who uttered such noble Sentiments. The speech does credit to your *heart* and *head*, and I hope you will pardon a few hasty lines from one who truly loves his country & people; honors and respects you as the head of his government,—the great representative man of the age—and the *true, tried friend* of the Southern *people*. Ah! well do I remember when immediately after your installation as Military Governor in 1862—I read for the *first* time your statesmanlike and prophetic speech of December 1860.[3] I saw tenfold more clearly how the Southern people had been misled from their true interest and safety, which was to have adhered to the Constitution and the Union. Your speech was very lengthy and at a time of so much passion & excitement was but little read or pondered. If it had only been generally *read* and *heeded*, how different the fate of your own *loved Tennessee*. The past cannot be changed. I only hope the people will act more wisely in the future. "'Tis *human* to *err*, and Godlike to forgive." You said in your letter to R. G. Payne & others in 1853,[4] "Let us stand by the people—and the people will stand by us." Right nobly are you redeeming that pledge—and the people are rallying to their true friend. When they were misled—you stood by their true interest and lasting good. It is now doubly the duty of every man who loves his country, and is the friend of *peace Law* and *Order*, to rally to the standard of Andrew Johnson, the Constitution and the Union. As you say "Let the *Constitution* be our *guide*. Let the preservation of that, and the Union of the States be our principal aim."[5] Let these be your guide and the rallying cry of the people. And I hope and believe the people will in 1868 honor you with a second term as they did Washington & Jackson. You mentioned the *Constitution* 8 or 10 times in your late Address. Oh! how it thrilled my heart when I read the words. "Let us look to the *Constitution*." You thought hard of me as a democrat, for my opposition to you in 1853 & 1855. You then proposed to amend the Constitution in several particulars.[6] I thought any kind of amendment would bring up the 3/5 slave basis—ending perchance in civil war and endless ruin. I then thought it my *duty* to oppose you, and had the courage and independence to do so. I acted on principle and would do so again—under similar circumstances. The *slaves* are now *free*—and that question belongs to the past. To day I regard you as the true faithful *friend* to the *Southern* people, aye the whole American people, also the friend of a *white* man's Government, and defender of Constitutional freedom. I therefore support you as warmly and earnestly as I opposed you in 1853 & 55. I did not vote for either of your competitors, although—one—Col. Gentry[7] was my relation, and I his devoted personal friend. I was a democrat and opposed to Knownothingism. I believe the only hope for the country, is for every patriot to stand by you in carrying out the principles enunciated in your late Address.

Some say you are President by accident. I beleive you are President by the will of God. You will remember that I predicted years ago you would be in all probability—both Military Governor and President of the United States. Having heretofore invoked the mantle of Washington and Jackson to fall on your shoulders. And as they were styled the first and second fathers of their country, I hope the name of Andrew Johnson will be handed down to posterity as the third father of his Country and the preserver of *Constitutional liberty* and *Republican Government*. Yes: thank God the friends of Consolidation or a centralized power will get no co-operation from you. The late Rebel Brig Genl T. B. Smith[8] a self made young man from Williamson County, says you have saved Republican government, and kept the Radicals from establishing a monarchy or Despotism. Smith was a brave soldier and is now your true friend. You are right in trusting the *southern people*. They are a *noble people*, they fought bravely, and have submitted in *good faith*. I beleive a *General Amnesty* would now rally the *whole south* to *your* support. The great majority of both *leaders* and *people went crazy* in 1861. And as the light of reason has been knocked into them by *very* hard knocks, and a terrible ordeal of suffering, They are fast learning wisdom by *sad experience*. How gratifying it must be to you—to see that those who thought *hate* or *revenge* was your ruling passion—now find that magnanimity—love for a united country and people and a true peace making—law and order policy—guides your actions. Your late speech contains the true spirit of christianity—which is love to God and *man*. The great mission of our Divine Lord and his apostles to do good to the people. The New Testament contains the truest and best principles of Democracy. Let us therefore labor for the good of our fellow men—and love God supremely—and our neighbor as ourself.

I must be brief. Gen. Geo Maney[9] is an outspoken Johnson man and one of the sickest of the Rebellion. Tom Henry[10] son of Hon G A Henry says you are the greatest man in America, and he wishes to vote for your re-election in 1868. My brotherinlaw Maj Wm Clare[11] occupies the same position. I told him of all *your kindness* to *myself* and *other members* of the *family*. F. C. Dunnington—J. C. Ramsey—Dr.

Menees[12]—my Uncle—Dr John M. Watson[13]—and thousands of other old Democrats now most cordially support you. In the old whig party Ex Gov N. S. Brown Maj Gen John C. Brown, Hon. R. L. Caruthers and others with whom I have talked most *cordially approve your policy*. How much men have misjudged you. You *love* the *southern people*. They made you by enabling you to develope the great powers with which God had endowed you. The Southern people are rallying to you as in days of *yore*. And the Radicals led by Sumner, Stevens and others would put down the peoples friend. Well perhaps they may—but I do not beleive it—but on the contrary beleive—The conservative Republicans—the Northern Democrats, and a United South will enable you by the blessing of God to put down the *Radical Destructionists*—and preserve law, order and constitutional liberty. The people of the south have suffered terribly—but they are noble and honorable and what they *promise* they will *perform*, but the presence & conduct of Coloured soldiers causes great irritation and does *more harm* than *good*. Many of them think they are better than White men. Slavery is dead—and I have no doubt you will disband all troops as rapidly as possible. I beleive the people can now be safely trusted—and the more they are trusted, the more they will prove they are worthy of being trusted, and will rapidly forget the past and the great majority of them love the Union as in days of *yore*. We all look to you as the *people's Tribune*. I beleive The civil authorities can now preserve law and order in Tennessee.

May God bless you and direct all your counsels for the good of our suffering people and country, is the prayer of your friend.

R. W. Brown

N.B. I know you must be worn out with your arduous official duties. Therefore to ask of you a long letter would be unpardonable, but if you have a few leisure moments, a few lines from you would be most highly appreciated by your old friend.[14]

R. W. Brown

2d N.B. The good effect produced by your late speech is still going on. Since writing this letter—I am informed by my friend Jas McLaughlin[15]—a man of strict veracity & honor—that the late rebel Gen'l W. B. Bate most cordially approves it and is zealous in support of the policy—enunciated in your address. Bate you know was an original secessionist and fought the battles of the rebellion with great gallantry—and if he can now be made a good friend of yours again and of the Constitution & Union—he can do great good for the cause, being a man of considerable talents & influence. I beleive a *general amnesty*, and removal of the colored troops, and the supremacy of the civil over the military authorities—will rally the entire South to you—as Tennessee democracy rallied in days of *yore*. Man was made in the image of God, and God will surely bless and direct the man who *loves him*, and loves and *labors* for the good of the people. Christianity and true conservative Democracy look to the elevation and *good* of the *people*. Religiously—morally, socially and politically—To do good to our fellow men is to obey the royal law. Let us then love God supremely and our neighbors as ourselves.

R. W. Brown

ALS, DLC-JP.

1. Brown (1825–1884) was a Nashville attorney, realtor and businessman. *Nashville American*, May 7, 8, 1884.

2. Speech to Southern Delegation, Sept. 11, 1865.

3. Speech on Secession, Dec. 18–19, 1860, *Johnson Papers*, 4: 3–46.

4. Johnson to the Democracy of Maury County, Sept. 18, 1853, ibid., 2: 170–72.

5. Brown quotes here from Johnson's September 11 speech.

6. Johnson's earlier proposals *re* amending the U.S. Constitution are found in his biennial legislative messages of 1853 and 1855. *Johnson Papers*, 2: 205, 335–36.

7. Meredith P. Gentry.

8. Thomas B. Smith (1838–1923) of Franklin, wounded at the Battle of Nashville, was later imprisoned at Fort Warren. Smith to Johnson, May 30, 1865, Amnesty Papers (M1003, Roll 51), Tenn., Thomas B. Smith, RG94, NA; Warner, *Gray*.

9. George E. Maney (1826–1901), a Nashville attorney who became a Confederate brigadier general, had been one of Brown's classmates at the University of Nashville. After the war he held several South American diplomatic posts. Ibid.

10. Thomas F. Henry (1835–1886), of Montgomery County, was variously a lawyer and a farmer. WPA, "Montgomery County, Tennessee Bible and Family Records Tombstone Inscriptions" (typescript, August 1938), 56; 1860 Census, Tenn., Montgomery, North & East of Cumberland River, 46; (1870), 3rd Dist., 3.

11. William H. Clare (c1840-c1873), Alabama-born attorney and former Confederate staff officer, settled in Nashville after the war and practiced law. Nashville directories (1867–70); *List of Staff Officers of the Confederate States Army, 1861–1865* (Washington, D.C., 1891), 32.

12. Frank C. Dunnington, John Crozier Ramsey, and Thomas Menees. Trained as a physician, Menees (1823–1905) practiced in Springfield, Tenn., but after the war moved to Nashville, where he became a member of the medical faculty. During the war he served one term in the Confederate Congress. Wakelyn, *BDC*; *BDTA*, 1: 514.

13. Watson (1798–1866), originally a Murfreesboro physician, was later a member of the medical faculty of the University of Nashville. Philip M. Hamer, ed., *The Centennial History of the Tennessee State Medical Association* (Nashville, 1930), 205–8. See Brown to Johnson, Nov. 25, 1865.

14. We have not found a Johnson reply. See Brown to Johnson, Oct. 16, 1865.

15. McLaughlin (c1834–1904) was a prominent Nashville businessman, first in the wholesale grocery business, then as president of the Merchants' Bank. He served on the Nashville city council for many years. *Nashville Banner*, Aug. 13, 1904.

From Abby Green[1]

[Washington, September 30, 1865][2]

Sir.

Richard B Winder[3] lately of the Confederate Army is now confined in the Old Capitol, and, as I am informed, there are no charges as yet preferred against him. His friends have endeavored in vain to obtain permission to see him. He has lately been very ill, and I respectfuly Submit that the public interest cannot scarcely be jeoparded by allowing this privilege. I am a refugee from Georgia, whence I was obliged to flee because of my strong attachment to the Union and especaially because I manifested that sympathy on all occasions. In my troubles there I received kindnesses & consideration from this young gentleman's relations & I am now desirous to manifest my appreciation of those kindnesses by ministering to him in his trouble. I therefore most respectfully solicit your Excellency to grant me permission to visit him in prison, pledging myself to do no act that can possibly give cause of offence to the Government, my sole object being to see that he does not suffer for want of whatever may be necessary to him.

I respectfully ask that Your Excellency will order the permission (if you deem it proper to grant it) to be addressed to me at No 375 Pennsylvania Avenue between 4th & 6th Streets.[4]

Mrs Abby Green

LS, DNA-RG107, Lets. Recd., EB12 President 2524 (1865).
1. While living in Richmond, Green (fl1884) had helped Federal officers escape from Libby Prison. Beginning in 1866, she worked as a clerk in the Treasury Department. Washington, D.C., directories (1866–84); *U.S. Off. Reg.* (1877, 1883); *Congressional Globe*, 39 Cong., 1 Sess., p. 2009.
2. This letter was received at the President's office on this date and was presumably written at Green's Washington residence.
3. Winder (1828–1894) had served as a quartermaster at Andersonville prison and was arrested in August 1865 as a co-conspirator with commandant Henry Wirz. Winder later was dean of the Baltimore Dental College and practiced dentistry in that city. *Baltimore Sun*, July 19, 1894; William B. Hesseltine, *Civil War Prisons* (New York, 1964[1930]), 240, 245–46; *House Ex. Docs.*, 40 Cong., 2 Sess., No. 23, p. 234 (Ser. 1331).
4. Although Holt endorsed Green's request, there is no record that it was granted. When the case against Winder failed to materialize, General Grant repeatedly urged his release. Although the specific date is unknown, Winder was probably freed soon after Grant won Holt's reluctant support in early April 1866. Hesseltine, *Civil War Prisons*, 245–46; Simon, *Grant Papers*, 15: 633–34.

From John M. Parkman[1]

Selma Ala   Sept 30 1865

John Hardy[2] U.S. Marshal for this District on the twenty eighth (28) inst seized a portion of my real estate in this City and today he refuses to allow the Warehouses here to deliver my cotton for shipment to New York and for which I hold the proper permits of the Treasury Agent here[3] having also paid to the Assessor of Revenue the tax on the said Cotton. I received my pardon in Washington dated twenty fifth July took the amnesty oath the same date accepted the conditions of the pardon in writing to Hon. Mr Seward.[4] I have the honor to ask you to order my property restored to, me, by telegraph.[5]

J. M. Parkman

Tel, DNA-RG107, Tels. Recd., President, Vol. 4 (1865–66).
1. Parkman (b. c1838) was president of the First National Bank of Selma. 1860 Census, Ala., Dallas, Selma, 41; *Montgomery Advertiser*, Sept. 20, 1865.
2. A former newspaper editor and U.S. consul to Havana (1847), Hardy (1823–

1883), whom Johnson appointed as marshal, later served in the state legislature and held several Selma municipal offices. Milo B. Howard, Jr., "John Hardy and John Reid: Two Selma Men of Letters," *AR*, 22 (1969): 44–52; *Cincinnati Enquirer*, July 10, 1865.

3. James P. Nimmo (*c*1831–1865), formerly of the Confederate quartermaster's department, a month earlier had been killed at the Gee House in Selma. 1860 Census, Ark., St. Francis, Franks Twp., Madison, 75; *Augusta Constitutionalist*, Sept. 8, 1865.

4. These facts Governor Parsons confirmed in his October 2 letter to Johnson. Office of Atty. Gen., Lets. Recd., President, RG60, NA.

5. The President referred the matter to Attorney General Speed, who in turn asked U.S. Attorney James Q. Smith for a report on the case against Parkman. The controversy dragged on until the spring of 1866, when Parkman once again requested executive intervention. Meanwhile, Speed ordered Marshal Hardy not to make any further unlawful seizures. Speed to Parkman and Speed to Smith, Oct. 2, 1865; Speed to Hardy, Oct. 21, 1865, Office of Atty. Gen., Lets. Sent, Vol. E (M699, Roll 10), RG60, NA; Parkman to Johnson, May 18, 1866, Office of Atty. Gen., Lets. Recd., President, RG60, NA.

From James Russell

September 30, 1865, Coweta County, Ga.; ALS, DLC-JP.

A "humble citizen," having in August written two twenty-page letters giving "part of a history of Southern & Northern troubles," and not having had a reply, now forwards twelve pages of ominous warnings concerning Georgia conditions. He expatiates on the grim economic scene and the homeless, starving, disorderly blacks. Russell sees only two ways to help them through their sudden freedom: "One is, by colonizing them in some Country to themselves" with white men to govern them, because "Negroes cannot govern themselves in their ignorant state"; the other is "to send them all back to their former masters, and let them go out by degrees." Of one thing he is certain: "the white man and negro cannot live together here in peace, in numbers as near equal as we are." As for the killing of blacks, "I have heard of as many negroes killing negroes, as I have heard of white men killing negroes." He refers to whites "standing picket" to protect themselves from blacks "pilfering and stealing" and concludes with a plea for forgiveness and for Johnson's intervention, asserting that "our people did not know what they were doing when they seceded."

October 1865

From Joseph F. Minter[1]

San Antonio Texas   October 1st 1865

The Undersigned being Excluded from the benefits of the Presidents Amnesty Proclamation of May 29, 1865, by reason of having been appointed in the Year A.D. 1855, an officer in the army of the United States with the rank of 2d. Lieutenant, and having served therein in the 2d. Regt. of Cavalry until on or about the 31st March 1860 at which time the Undersigned tendered his resignation from said army, which was very soon thereafter accepted, and having been abroad on duty as an officer of the late C.S. Government, and by reason of having served as a Quarter Master in the late Confederate states army, first, with the rank of Captain, and lastly with the rank of Major. To the end therefore that the undersigned Joseph F. Minter may obtain amnesty, and pardon, with restoration of all rights and property "Except as to Slaves," he makes this Special application.

The undersigned was born in Mathews County in the state of Virginia, and has resided in Texas since December 1838 and that San Antonio Texas is now his place of residence, and he respectfully represents that he has never been a politician, nor has he ever mingled, or taken an active part in political matters, that he entered, and remained, in the service of the Confederate states from a sense of duty, Conscienciously believeing that he was right in so doing, though the result of the war has Convinced him of his error. And regarding the question of Slavery, and Secession, as definitely, and finally, settled, it is his Earnest desire that they may never be revived again.

The undersigned further represents that he was prevented from makeing an Earlier application for pardon in consequence of his absence from this state, at the time of the surrender of the Confederate Armies, to which he returned at the Earliest opportunity after learning of such surrender,[2] that he has freely taken the amnesty hereto attached without any mental reservation and with the sincere determination to faithfully abide by and honestly carry out the same, and he further declares that it is his honest intention if permitted, to become, and remain a true, and loyal citizen of the United States; and to promote so far as he may be able the interests, integrity, and harmony of the whole Union. The undersigned would represent that he has never persecuted, or prosecuted any one for "Opinions sake," nor has he committed any acts of Violence, or oppression, against any one, because of Union sentiments; but conscious of his own honesty of purpose, he has ever accorded to others, like motives. No proceedings have been commenced against the undersigned under the Confiscation laws, nor is any of his property in possession of the United States Authorities. The undersigned would further state that he has never Engaged in any outrages, or wrongs upon any citizen because of his Union sentiments, nor has he belonged to any Vigilince Committee, or any secret organisation for the persecution of Union men; he is now, and ever has been opposed to mob law, or lawless proceedings, of any kind, he has no property of any kind belonging to the United States; or late Confederate States, in his hands—and that he is not excepted under any other clauses of the Presidents Amnesty Proclamation.

Wherefore the undersigned invokes the Clemency of the President of the United States; so liberally offered, and humbly prays that full pardon, with restoration of all rights; and property; "except as to slaves," may be granted to him.[3]

Joseph F. Minter

ALS, DNA-RG94, Amnesty Papers (M1003, Roll 54), Tex., Joseph F. Minter.

1. Minter (c1828–1885), who served as chief quartermaster for the Confederate Trans-Mississippi Department, later became city treasurer for San Antonio, then supervisor of the U.S. arsenal there. 1870 Census, Tex., Bexar, San Antonio, 3rd Ward, 52; Powell, *Army List*, 485; *Confederate Staff Officers*, 114; San Antonio directories (1877–85).

2. Minter had returned to Texas from Havana and applied for pardon at the direction of George Stoneman, with whom he had served in the 2nd Cavalry. Powell, *Army List*, 612; Stoneman to Minter, Aug. 8, 1865, Amnesty Papers (M1003, Roll 54), Tex., Joseph F. Minter, RG94, NA.

3. Despite the endorsement of Gov. Andrew J. Hamilton appended to this letter, we can find no indication that Johnson granted an individual pardon to Minter. Another copy of Minter's petition, which bore later endorsements from both Hamilton and Stoneman, apparently went astray and can be found in the Henry E. Huntington Library.

From Burr H. Polk[1]

Knoxville Tenn   Oct 1 1865.

Your telegram of 28 Sept referring to outrages & depredations in East Tenn and the search of the house of J C Tunley[*sic*] by men dressed in U S uniform just recd.[2] There are no troops in Tenn east of Chattanooga except four companies 4th U S C Infty at this place. They are kept closely at the post. All difficulties and outrages occuring in that vicinity now are brought about by citizens discharged Soldiers who live in the state. It has been claimed by Gov Brownlow and others that the civil authorities could correct these evils.

B. H. Polla[*sic*]   A A G
in absence of Gen Stoneman

Tel, DLC-JP.

1. Polk (1835–1886), a lawyer before the Civil War, enlisted in 1861 as a captain in the 33rd Ind. Inf. and remained in the military until early 1866, rising to the rank of brevet colonel. After the war he lived in Vicksburg, Miss., for several years. Theophilus

A. Wylie, *Indiana University, 1820–90* (Indianapolis, 1890), 327; Pension File, Burr H. Polk, RG15, NA.
2. See Johnson to George Stoneman, Sept. 29, 1865.

To Salmon P. Chase

Washington, D.C.   Oct. 2d. 1865.

Dear Sir,

It may become necessary that the Government prosecute some high crimes and misdemeanors committed against the United States within the District of Virginia.

Permit me to enquire whether the Circuit Court of the United States for that District is so far reorganized and in condition to exercise its functions that your-self, or either of the Associate Justices of the Supreme Court will hold a term of the Circuit Court there during the autumn or early winter for the trial of causes.[1]

Copy, DLC-JP.
1. See Chase to Johnson, Oct. 12, 1865.

From John T. Croxton[1]

Head qr. Dist of Columbus
Macon Ga.   Oct. 2nd. 1865

Dear Sir:

By Govt. order No. 13A. War Dept I was orderd to report for duty to Genl. Gilmore in South Carolina. I write now to ask your interposition to allow me to remain in Georgia, where Genl Steedman is anxious to have me—where I have been since the termination of hostilities. I consider myself in some measure responsible for the condition of things here when I have had control, & prefer working out the matter here, to taking the unfinished work of those who have gone before me in S. Carolina.

You know where & when & how I became a soldier; and, I think, the records of the War Dept. and the testimony of every officer I have served under will show I have done my duty.[2] I neiver was out of active service a day, save when wounded—nor did I ever apply until *now* to be relieved from orders or have them changed. I trust therefore you will find it consistent with the interests of the *public service* to direct as I request & have Genl Steedman so informed by telegram.[3]

I may say to you, that matters are improving very rapidly here. A month ago & I dont think there was a white man in my command who had any *positive loyalty* & in addition they were very bitter in their feelings toward their former Slaves. The *policy* of *trusting* them, as pursued in *Miss*—has magnetized the whole people & they really feel as if the Government was theirs; and that they could forgive their slaves for *freedom*, if the Government could forgive them for *Rebellion*. I do not think that matters could be progressing more favorably. As soon as the planting season arrives and thier is abundance of profitable employment, a rigid enforcement of the vagrant laws will make Georgia as peaceble as *Maine*.

Jno. T. Croxton, Brig. Genl Vols.

ALS, DNA-RG107, Lets. Recd., EB12 President 2522 (1865).

1. Commander, District of Southwest Georgia.

2. Several prominent Georgians agreed. See Joseph E. Brown to Johnson, Oct. 4, 1865; James Johnson to Johnson, Oct. 6, 1865, Lets. Recd., (Main Ser.), File C-1471-1865 (M619, Roll 345), RG94, NA; James H.R. Washington to Johnson, Oct. 9, 1865, Johnson Papers, LC.

3. Although the President granted the request, Croxton soon resigned. Johnson to Croxton, Oct. 13, 1865, Johnson Papers, LC; Warner, *Blue*.

From Charles J. Meng[1]

Louisville Ky   Octo. 2d. 1865

Sir,

You are the Chief Magistrate of this nation and as such you took an oath to support the Constitution of the U.S. & the laws of Congress made in pursuance thereof. Kentucky has not been in rebellion, has lost no right which she had before the war & yet her rights are invaded by a ruthlessness & atrocity, unparalleled in the history of this Country. I hope for the Credit of the nation & your Character as its Chief Magistrate that the Conduct of the Provost Marshal in Louisville has failed to receive your attention not from any desire on your part to Sustain him in his course, but from the pressing necessity & urgent demands upon your time to other matters.

Neither the Constitution of the U. States nor the Acts of Congress authorize the Provost marshal or any agent of the Government from you down to free the negroes of Kentucky and yet it is the daily practice of the Marshal or Commander here to give to all negroes man & woman letters of Manumission upon their application to him for that purpose.[2] It is true they are called passes, but they authorize the negro to go whither he pleases and enjoin it upon all persons not to interfere with him in the exercise of this privilege, the ostensible object being to enable the negro to escape from his owner and to defy his authority over him—and this he is presumed to do under your instructions or by your permission, which is the same thing in effect. Now sir, this Can be looked upon in no other light by all honorable & correct thinking men than as public robbery and that too (but I hope not) authorized by the Chief Magistrate. I can see no difference in principle between the course pursued by the Government towards the citizens of Ky in this respect & that of the highwayman who robs me of my purse while he holds a Pistol at my head.

No nation can stand long, no people can be respected abroad nor remain united at home when their agents to whom they have entrusted the execution of the laws for their protection, prosperity & happiness instead of acting in good faith under their oath & covenant become their oppressors & violate every sacred duty to the Nation. Whatever may be your views of negro slavery in the abstract the door is closed to your interference with it in Kentucky unless you become recreant to your oath & a violator of that Constitution which you have sworn to support.

No court of justice, unless the Judges are corrupt or *trucklers* (as too many are at the present day) could protect the negro in his right to freedom obtained in this way, the whole thing in the estimation of honorable men is a farce & a mockery. Any change made in the Organic Law of Kentucky without her consent other than the mode pointed out by the Constitution of the U. States is *revolution* and that is now going on in Kentucky at the point of the bayonet.

I lately saw published a petition[3] to you purporting to have been presented by some negroes of Kentucky setting forth their troubles & desiring the continuance of Martial Law here and that you received them *cordially* says the N.Y. Tribune and promised them all they desired. Now Sir, you Know enough about Ky & Kentuckians to Know that said petition was a lie & a slander (if negroes could slander any person) upon her Citizens. The laws of Ky are humane as much so as is consistent with the relations of Master & servant—a fact better Known to you than to those ignorant negroes. If the former Provost Marshal[4] was guilty of acts of cruelty to the negroes as they state without any mitigating circumstances he was wrong & should have been held to answer for it, but if he was, that don't justify the present Provost Marshall or Commander here in committing an outrage upon the rights of the Citizens in attempting to free the negroes and rob them of their property—and martial law seems to be retained in Ky by the Government for the express purpose of carrying on this state of things.

Another fact— A Freedman's Bureau has been established in this city[5]—yet there is no law to authorize it—it was intended for the benefit of such negroes as were freed by the Presidents proclamation in the states in Rebellion and should be confined to such states. Yet it is here & many negroes under its control are being supported I am told by the Government and I am also informed by reliable gentlemen that it is a grand *whore house for negro soldiers*—and so it will be wherever established. Sir—you are a southern man and you Know enough of the negro to Know that this is inevitable under the system inaugurated by the Govt.

Sir—If I were you I would put an end to these Bureaus in Ky—

establish them in the states that were in Rebellion—(although the whole thing if continued will prove a curse) require the negroes belonging there to return to their respective states if they wish Government protection—or establish them in the states North of the Ohio river where the negro will be among his *friends* and free from restraint & an opportunity afforded him for the full exercise of his faculties & his rights as a free man.

Again— I would remove Martial law in Ky—and let the civil power be exercised.[6] Order the Provost Marshal or Commander to give no more passes to negroes of Ky—nor to interfere with the civil rights of the citizens. Sir I know that the tide of fanaticism is pressing you heavily from the North and there is danger if yielded to that this nation will go down in blood. It is the same spirit which animated the grandfathers of these people to duck their grand mothers for witches. I hope you will have nerve to resist it. I hope you will take the Constitution as the Temple of Liberty for under its broad canopy as a nation we must alone expect to live.

Sir a moments reflection upon the history of our Government shows the danger & unsafety of relying upon Northern minds for the perpetuity of the freedom of this people. This Government has been in existence now nearly 90 years & yet during that long period no man was ever reelected to the Presidency from the North—except Mr. Lincoln and he did not survive it 60 days after his inauguration, showing in the judgment of this nation & the interposition of providence that Northern men & Northern minds won't do to administer this Government; they have been tried at intervals during our national existence but always condemned by the voice of the people. This nation owes mainly its establishment & preservation to southern intellect, honesty & influence. The South have never in their legislation attempted to trespass upon the local rights of the North a fact that can't be said of the North towards the South—the active & ingenious mind of the North has to be controlled or it becomes dangerous to the liberty of the citizen & the stability of the Government.

The infraction of one right opens the door for another and the liberty of the people is lost by degrees, their form of Government overturned & the dread serpent of despotism will be found ere long dragging its loathsome form over the ruins. Sir You have it in your power to remove the causes of dissatisfaction before stated and thereby do justice to the state & to yourself—the sooner the better for the welfare of the negro & for the quiet & good order of the citizens.

What I have here said to you is prompted by no spirit of disrespect but an ardent desire to see our Government in all its parts restored & our matchless institutions perpetuated.

Ch. J. Meng

ALS, DLC-JP.

1. Meng (c1810-fl1871) was an attorney and real estate agent. 1870 Census, Ky., Jefferson, 8th Ward, Louisville, 49; William H. Perrin et al., *History of Bourbon, Scott, Harrison and Nicholas Counties* (Chicago, 1882), 529; Louisville directories (1861–71).

2. On May 11, 1865, the "Provost Marshal of the Post of Louisville" had been authorized to issue passes to blacks for travel "to engage in or in search of employment." Since that time at least four captains had served as provost marshal in Louisville: George L. Swope, Leven M. Drye, Thomas Priestly, and George W. Lott. The post commander at Louisville was Louis D. Watkins (1833–1868), promoted to brigadier general for his cavalry service in the West during the war. Lets. Recd. (Main Ser.), M-2123-1865 (M619, Roll 385), RG94, NA; *Louisville Democrat*, July 15, Aug. 29, Sept. 6, 13, 1865; *Louisville Journal*, Oct. 12, 1865; Warner, *Blue*.

3. A reference to the June 9, 1865, petition presented by Kentucky blacks to Johnson. *Johnson Papers*, 8: 203–5.

4. Henry Dent (1819-fl1877), Louisville businessman and former police chief, during the first half of the war was colonel of the 34th Ky. Inf., USA, and Kentucky's provost marshal. In the spring of 1865 he was elected a councilman and later served as a magistrate. J. M. Armstrong et al., *The Biographical Encyclopaedia of Kentucky of the Dead and Living Men of the Nineteenth Century* (Cincinnati, 1878), 484–85; *Louisville Journal*, Apr. 2, 1865.

5. Although the Freedmen's Bureau was not formally established in Kentucky until after the ratification of the Thirteenth Amendment, in the fall of 1865 Gen. O. O. Howard authorized Clinton B. Fisk to extend his operations into that state. Howard to L. S. Trimble, Jan. 16, 1866, Records of the Commr., Lets. Sent (M742, Roll 2), RG105, NA; Howard, *Black Liberation*, 96–97.

6. See Meng to Johnson, Oct. 20, 1865.

From James L. Orr

Private

Anderson [South Carolina]   2d October 1865

My Dear Sir:

I have the honor to acknowledge the receipt of my pardon[1] from you for participation in the late rebellion and have notified the Secretary of State of its acceptance with the conditions therein contained.

I tender to you my grateful acknowledgements for your generous consideration and confidently trust that neither the country nor yourself will ever have occasion to regret your clemency. I am sure I will never lose any opportunity of attesting how sincerely gratefull I am to you for your kindness.

Our convention has adjourned and the result of its labors have doubtless reached you. The constitution is a vast improvement on its predecessor though not popularized as fully as in some of the states. The Parish system is broken up—the basis of representation in the house is white population and taxation. The property qualification for senators and representatives has been stricken out. Foreigners have been allowed to vote after two years residence coupled with a declaration of intention to become citizens. The election of Governor and Lieutenant Governor has been given to the people. The viva voce system of voting in all elections made by the legislature has been introduced and some responsibility at last fixed on the legislature in making elections. The constitution on the slavery question declares "that Slavery having been abolished by the military authorities of the U.S it shall never be re-established in this State."[2] The elections for Governor & members of the legislature takes place the 3d Wednesday of this month. The legislature will meet in special session on the 4th Wednesday to pass a law ordering the election of members of Congress. That election will perhaps take place about the 15th or 20th of November which gives ample time for the votes to be counted and the members elect to reach Washington by the first Monday in December.

The convention authorized the legislature to establish additional courts rendered necessary by the freed condition of the colored race. They authorized the Provisional Governor to appoint a commission of two persons to examine & report to the legislature what additional laws were necessary to give full protection to person & property of the freedmen. How far & in what class of cases their evidence should be received and also the best system of regulating labor, so as to give protection to the employer and employee. Under the existing laws of this state free persons of color can purchase & hold real as well as personal estate & can transmit to their children by descent will or deed and the law in that particular needs no amendment. The Governor has appointed Hon D L. Wardlaw one of our ablest judges & the Hon A Burt[3] Commissioners. They will report to the legislature at an early day and I have no doubt that such laws as the new relation of these people to society requires will be passed by the legislature.

Nearly all the members of the convention united in a written request to me to become a candidate for governor. I have consented to do so and think it likely that I shall be elected without serious opposition. If I am, I shall come on to Washington before the inauguration (which will take place the last of Nov.) and will have with your permission a full conference[4] so as to possess my self of your views & be prepared to cooperate heartily with you in carrying them out. Hon W. D. Porter[5] late President of the Senate will be the candidate for Lieut. Governor.

I am glad to see that most of the conventions at the north have endorsed you and your reconstruction policy notwithstanding the radical views of Mr. Thaddeus Stevens.

This letter will be handed to you by the Hon. Wm Henry Trescott[6] late Asst. Secy of State under Genl. Cass.[7] He goes to Washington by appointment of Govr. Perry & I beg to commend him to your kind consideration.

James L Orr

P.S. The convention passed resolutions which were directed to be transmitted to the legislature expressing an earnest desire that the election of Presidential electors should be given to the people by that body and I have but little doubt that it will be promptly passed by that body.

ALS, DLC-JP.

1. Johnson had recently notified Orr that his pardon had been granted. Johnson to Orr, Sept. 16, 1865, Tels. Sent, President, Vol. 2 (1865), RG107, NA.

2. Article IX, section 11 of the South Carolina constitution of 1865 actually read: "The slaves in South Carolina having been emancipated by the action of the United States authorities, neither slavery nor involuntary servitude, except as a punishment for crime, whereof the party shall have been duly convicted, shall ever be re-established in this State." *Senate Ex. Docs.*, 39 Cong., 1 Sess., No. 26, p. 163 (Ser. 1237).

3. Armistead Burt (1802–1883) was an Abbeville lawyer, prewar U.S. congressman, and later a delegate to the Democratic convention of 1868. *NCAB*, 12: 203.

4. See Orr to Johnson, Dec. 23, 1865.

5. William D. Porter (1810–1883), an ardent secessionist, served as lieutenant governor until his removal by Gen. Edward R.S. Canby in June 1868. Bailey et al., *S.C. Senate*, 2: 1302.

6. Appointed state agent to recover confiscated property, Trescot (1822–1898), an attorney, planter, historian, and state legislator, later held minor posts in the U.S. foreign service corps. *Cyclopedia of the Carolinas*, 1: 676; Robert N. Olsberg, "A Government of Class and Race: William Henry Trescot and the South Carolina Chivalry" (Ph.D. diss., University of South Carolina, 1972), iii, vii, 23, 73, 222, 309.

7. Lewis Cass, President Buchanan's secretary of state.

From Lewis E. Parsons

Montgomery   October 2nd 1865

Sir

The adjournment of the convention of the State of Alabama, on the evening of September 30, renders it proper that I should make a statement of the action of the provisional government of the State, and of myself as governor, invested by you with certain powers and authority under your appointment and your proclamation of June 21, 1865.[1]

That proclamation and your instructions looked to an early resumption of the civil authority, so far as was consistent with the order of things then in existence, and the disposition, character, and tendencies of the people of the State. To that end I have looked and labored, endeavoring, by a course modelled by my own convictions of right and propriety, and what I deemed your just and wise views of conciliation, as expressed in your proclamation, to cause the sway of law to be resumed, and the regularity and order of its supremacy to give confidence to the people of the State, that their action might evidence to the government the returned loyalty of the citizen. With these views, immediately upon my return to this city, I made appointments of the civil officers of the State necessary for the proper administration of its civil affairs at the capital, and on the 20th day of July, A.D. 1865, a copy of which has been forwarded to you,[2] after mature consideration, I issued my proclamation to the people of Alabama, appointing, temporarily, to discharge the duties of county officers, such as were then incumbents, and not excepted from the terms of amnesty contained in your proclamation of May 29, 1865, reserving to myself the right of removal for disloyalty, disaffection, incompetency, perversion of justice, or abuse of office or powers with which invested.

The condition of the people imperatively demanded immediate action. Society was disorganized, military courts decided grave questions of laws and equity upon ex parte statements, personal rights were the subject of captious and uncertain regulations, the tenure of property was uncertain, and life held too cheaply for its security. Fear and uncertainty possessed the public mind; and action immediate, and tending to resumption of civil functions, was necessary to quiet feeling and add something of certainty to the gracious assurances given and the hopes incited by your proclamation.

These evidences of the disposition of the government were favorably received by the people, and I have every reason to believe that they have done much to harmonize and to restore loyalty.

Upon the various measures intended to secure the supremacy of the civil authority, I deemed it my duty to consult with the Major Generals in command, and I am pleased to say that on the part of major general A. J. Smith,[3] commanding 16th army corps, and Major General Charles R. Woods, commanding department of Alabama, I have met a generous acquiescence and support.

The qualifications, prescribed in my proclamation, for electors and for delegates to the convention,[4] were such as to secure the return of none but loyal men; and the number of votes cast will give assurance of the fidelity of the people to the conditions of your proclamation, and the principles of loyalty to the government of the United States. The character, talent, and political influence of the delegates are also an earnest of the desire of the people to maintain their allegiance and place themselves among the States of the Union.

The important changes in the constitution of the State upon the question of slavery, and the ordinances affecting the social and political standing of the freedmen of the State, will, I think, evidence to your excellency the same fact. Copies of those ordinances and of the amendments of the State constitution effecting these great political and social changes are herewith transmitted to your excellency.[5]

By them you will observe that the social privileges and rights of the freedmen are secured in the family relation; that the acquisition disposal, and tenure of property are made secure to them by organic law; and that the courts of law and equity are opened to them for enforcement of rights and redress of injuries to their persons or property, and that in all cases affecting themselves alone, or between them and the whites, their evidence is admissible. Upon the latter subject I had previously to the assembling of the convention, approved an order of Brigadier General Swayne, assistant commissioner of freedmen, constituting the civil officers of the State agents of that bureau for the trial of causes between freedmen themselves, and between them and whites, upon the same rules of testimony. This order received almost universal acquiescence by the magistrates of the State, and I have reason to believe that the new duties thus imposed are discharged with fidelity and uprightness.

To the extent to which I have exercised the powers with which I was invested by your excellency, I have every assurance of the approbation of the people of the State, and they generally acquiesce in the propriety and justice of the measures adopted. Four years of almost anarchy and of military oppression have made them desirous of the restoration of civil law, and, while willing to abide patiently the decision of the government, they anxiously await a full return to its protecting and fostering care.

The announcement in my proclamation of the 20th July last, that "from and after this date, the civil and criminal laws of Alabama, as they stood on the 11th day of January, 1861, except that portion which relates to slavery, are hereby declared to be in full force and operation, and all proceedings for the punishment of offences against them will be turned over to the proper civil officers, together with the custody of the person charged, and the civil authorities will proceed in all cases according to law," was induced by what I deemed your wishes and intention, as expressed to me in person, and in your proclamation providing a provisional government for the State, that the civil authority should be restored as soon as was consistent with the disposition and condition of the people, and a just regard to the rightful authority of the government.

I regret, however, to state that, in some instances, the military authorities have continued, and in others assumed, jurisdiction. They have withdrawn from a chancery tribunal and adjudicated before a military commission a case in which the civil rights of citizens, under the laws of Alabama, were alone at issue. Copy of letter in reference thereto is appended,[6] marked A, and your attention respectfully invited.

I beg leave, also, in this connexion, to refer your excellency to the accompanying papers[7] in reference to the claim of John Grant, of Mobile, to fees against the Steamer Eleanor Carrel, under a grant of the legislature of the State of Alabama, approved February 2, 1839; in which case the military authorities assume not merely to adjudicate a question then pending in the circuit court of Mobile county, but also to remove from the jurisdiction of the court a security given by consent of parties.

And I would also respectfully state, that instances of like assumption of authority, in respect to municipal regulations, have occurred in issuing military licenses to retail ardent spirits in the city of Mobile and our inland towns, taking from the municipal authorities the right to regulate and restrain, as well as the right to prevent and repress, disorder and the vices which naturally attend the unrestrained traffic in liquors.[8]

In like manner, in contravention of municipal regulations, the military authorities assume in the city of Montgomery, and, I am informed, in Mobile and other places, to license houses of prostitution and ill fame, to the detriment of morals, the annoyance of good citizens and their families, and the spread of corruption among the young of both sexes. The harlot thus shamelessly and openly plies her vocation, and opens wide the door of licentiousness through which the crafty and the unwary alike enter the chambers of her whose steps lay hold on death. I am well satisfied that it is not the desire of your excellency to give the sanction of the government to pursuits upon which the laws of every State have pronounced a ban, nor to encourage the licentiousness which these orders legalize. I have but to refer your excellency to the copy marked C, herewith enclosed.[9]

I refer to this action of the military authorities with great reluctance, because I have in other matters found a willingness on their part to aid in the administration of the law, and, as I thought, a desire to allow the civil administration of the government to be resumed in all its forms and force, in accordance with your proclamation. But if questions of titles to land, already too complicated or uncertain to be determined by the common law, and awaiting the more cautious and equitable decision of a court of chancery, are to have the Gordian Knot cut by the sword; if the agreement of parties in matters of dollars and cents, awaiting the decision, is to be set aside without consent or legal arbitrament, and the security for eventual payment dissipated by a military order; if time-honored municipal regulations affecting public morals are to be placed the control of provost marshals and at the pleasure of officials liable to change, and uninterested in the permanent welfare of the community, your excellency's manifest intention cannot be properly carried into effect, and loyal citizens must feel insecure in the enjoyment of their rights of person and property. Thus energy will be repressed, evil encouraged, and doubt and uncertainty prevail; and while the efforts of the good and loyal to build up the prostrate interests of the State are discouraged, the evil, the vicious, the dissolute, and the crafty will be emboldened, and their deeds, if not sanctioned, will fail to meet their due punishment.

In the administration of the provisional government, my attention has been called to the prevalence of lawlessness in theft and robbery of cotton. Under cover of pretended or assumed authority, evil minded persons have claimed and exercised the right of seizing and taking away from the owners or proper custodians cotton said to have belonged to the confederate government; and, emboldened by impunity and success, they have proceeded by stealth and flagrant outrage, in armed and disguised bands, as well as by fraud and device to take cotton from loyal and peaceable citizens of the State. Violence and bloodshed have resulted in some instances, and further evil may well be apprehended.[10]

The general confusion which reigned upon the surrender of the confederate armies, the unprovided condition of that soldiery, the destitution of families, the hopelessness of support, and the habits of improvidence induced by protracted and in many cases undisciplined and unrestrained camp life, have led to the commission of many deeds of wild lawlessness, engendered and encouraged by a laxity of morals, the invariable accompaniment of war. To these were superadded the suppressed grudge, revenge for real or supposed injuries, nursed and cherished for months and years, the greed of the unscrupulous seeking to appropriate something to themselves from what they deemed a wreck, and the general conviction that the civil law with its remedies, and the criminal with its punishments, could not assert their supremacy. In many instances the military force which might have aided to suppress violence or arrest offenders was far distant or too small in number to be effectual, the civil authorities inefficient or unprepared for an emergency, the orderly citizen unarmed, while the disturbers of the public peace and the violaters of law were reckless men, protected by their arms and surrounded by others as lawless and desperate as themselves, and instigated by hope of gain and the impunity of previous offences.

Anticipating resistance to the law from these and other sources, in my proclamation of 20th July, 1865, as provisional governor, I directed the several sheriffs, continued or newly appointed, to provide a sufficient number of deputies, to be well armed, for the purpose of executing processes committed to them, and preserving the public peace within their respective counties.

To the same end the convention recently assembled passed a resolution requesting the provisional governor to cause to be organized and called into service one or more companies of militia in each county in the State "for the purpose of repressing disorder and preserving the public peace." In accordance with that resolution, I have appointed commandants of militia in each county in the State, with the rank of colonel, and issued instructions to them, of which I enclose a printed copy.[11]

I trust that those instructions and my action herein will receive your approbation, as I feel that in it I have followed what I believed to be your intention and to conduce to the security of the people of the State in person and property. This force is merely constabulary, and the military form given it only intended to render it more efficient in power and readiness for service. It will bring to the support of laws and order the moral force of the *posse comitatus* with a readiness which I trust will sufficiently deter evil-doers without resort to actual force.

In the proceedings of the convention I trust it will be manifest to your excellency and the people of the loyal states that the people of Alabama desire in good faith to renew their allegiance to the government of the United States, and that while the circumstances surrounding their social and political condition are novel and embarrassing, they are willing to meet embarrassment, surmount difficulties, and adapt themselves to the condition into which events have thrown them. The calamities of war have pressed them to the earth; the fruits of long-continued industry have been swept away; the blessings of a state of peace and prosperity, which had been theirs under a genial and fostering government, have been swept away and lost; they have tasted of rebellion and its effects have been like the apples of Sodom—ashes upon their lips.

To all this has been added, in many parts of the State, a long-continued drought, and scorched and•barren fields offer but a scanty reward to the labors of the husbandman.

Yet with those and many other discouragements, blessed with a return to allegiance and a position among the loyal States of the Union, I doubt not the recuperative energies of the people, and, if they bring sadder hearts to the work of restoration, the chastening will carry wiser heads and more earnest minds to the great labors necessary for the prosperity of the nation and the perpetuity of its government. Already has that great work commenced in the resumption of agricultural and mechanical industry. The merchants and bankers of the State are redeeming their faith, plighted before the late unhappy troubles, and entering again upon their accustomed pursuits, assured in the policy and strength of the government that trade will soon be placed upon strong and firm foundations, while the great arteries of the commerce of the nation are striving with every nerve to connect the States with their iron bands. And I would especially refer to this probity, confidence, and energy on the part of the directors and rulers of the commerce of the land as an evidence of their opinion that a common loyalty will soon make us, as before, a united people.

You will find that the convention has approved the provisional government and passed the necessary appropriations for its support. It has also expressed its approval of my action as provisional governor, and thus endorsed your policy and selection. Grateful as I feel for this proof of confidence, I rejoice rather that it affords evidence that the wisdom of your policy has found a response in the hearts of a people, erring but repentant, and ready and willing to return to an allegiance broken but not destroyed.

Assuring your Excellency of my earnest desire to carry out that policy, and that in the humble but important part which I have borne I have been actuated by a desire for the good of the whole country, and that I have sought rather the approval of my own conscience than the praise of men. . . .

Lewis E Parsons   Provisional Governor of Alabama

Senate Ex. Docs., 39 Cong., 1 Sess., No. 26, pp. 97–101 (Ser. 1237).

1. Richardson, *Messages*, 6: 323–25.

2. A letterbook copy in the Alabama Department of Archives and History reads: ". . . July A.D. 1865 after mature consideration I issued my proclamation to the people of Alabama, a copy of which was duly forwarded. . . ." Parsons' address restoring civil

government in Alabama has not been found in the Johnson Papers or other Washington records.

3. Andrew J. Smith (1815–1897) had participated in the Battles of Nashville and Mobile. Warner, *Blue*.

4. Parsons mandated that only those who had sworn an oath of allegiance or had received a presidential pardon could hold these positions. Fleming, *Alabama*, 353.

5. Although not found in the Johnson Papers, copies of these documents are published in *Senate Ex. Docs.*, 39 Cong., 1 Sess., No. 26, pp. 105–8 (Ser. 1237).

6. See Peter M. Dox to Parsons, Oct. 3, 1865, ibid., 101.

7. Ibid., 101–4.

8. Effective September 30, the right to license and tax drinking establishments reverted to municipal authorities. *Mobile Register and Advertiser*, Sept. 9, 1865.

9. *Senate Ex. Docs.*, 39 Cong., 1 Sess., No. 26, pp. 101–4 (Ser. 1237).

10. By now similar allegations had already reached Johnson's office. See James Q. Smith to Edward H. East, Sept. 4, 1865, in which the Alabama district attorney reported that treasury agents "deeply versed in thievery and rascallity . . . swarm each county in large numbers" stealing cotton and other property. East called the President's attention to the letter. Johnson Papers, LC.

11. For the instructions to the militia officers, dated September 28, 1865, see *Senate Ex. Docs.*, 39 Cong., 1 Sess., No. 26, pp. 108–9 (Ser. 1237).

From Charles H. Patton [1]

Washington   Oct 2 1865

Your petitioner Charles H Patton, a citizen of Madison County Ala, respectfully asks your Excellency to grant a special pardon to his wife Martha L. Patton, and his step-daughter Kate Moore,[2] both of whom reside in said County of Madison. Your petitioner states that neither of said parties ever participated in the late rebellion, but each of them owns taxable property of more than the value of twenty thousand dollars—his said wife, owning a separate estate under the laws of Alabama. He further states that no proceedings have been instituted against either of said parties for treason or conspiracy against the laws of the United States. Nor has any portion of their property been taken possession of by the United States authorities as abandoned. The said Kate Moore is your petitioners ward.

He further states that his said wife and ward will be loyal citizens of the United States. And he, therefore prays your Excellency to grant to each of them a special pardon, under your proclamation of May 29 1865.[3]

Charles H. Patton

LS, DNA-RG94, Amnesty Papers (M1003, Roll 12), Ala., Charles H. Patton.

1. The brother of Alabama's next governor, Patton (1806–1866) was a retired U.S. Army surgeon, planter and cotton mill owner. Owen, *History of Ala.*, 4: 1327; Gandrud, *Alabama Records*, 64: 94, 99.

2. Patton's second wife Martha (1811–1881) and her daughter Catherine Moore (c1847–fl1870). 1870 Census, Ala., Madison, Huntsville, 3rd Ward, 19; Owen, *History of Ala.*, 4: 1327; Gandrud, *Alabama Records*, 129: 23; 161: 63.

3. The pardons of Martha L. Patton and Kate Moore were dated September 29, 1865, the same date that Charles H. Patton was granted his. *House Ex. Docs.*, 40 Cong., 2 Sess., No. 16, pp. 25, 28, 29 (Ser. 1330).

From Moses Bates[1]

Boston Mass.   October 3d 1865.

Dear Sir

The motives which prompted the Democracy of Mass.—at their Convention on Thursday last to pledge their unqualified support to your administration in bringing the States lately in rebellion back to their true position in the Union, having been so generally misrepresented by the radical press of New England, I deem it my duty to my associates in the democratic party,—as the author of, and chairman of the committee reporting the *resolutions*, and moreover as Chairman of the Democratic State Central Committee of this State, to say that our endorsement was not only honest and sincere, but it was *unanimous*,—and prompted only by an entire appreciation of the broad, Statesmanlike view you have taken of the complicated questions which have grown out of the late rebellion. During the Session of Congress in 1859–60 it was my fortune, as *then* the representative of the Boston *Post* in Washington, to see much of your own political action, having then been introduced to you by Warren Winslow of N.C. who with Miles Taylor[2] of Louisiana, were true *Union men*; and from that time to the present I have found your political career so entirely consonant with my own views, that I am *compelled*, from a sense of justice to yield the support of the press with which I am connected. Having been engaged by Gen. Butler to precede him upon Ship Island, and remain with him in Louisiana until his recall in December 1862, I saw the South under his administration then; and subsequently having remained for nearly three years, in Mercantile business, in New Orleans, I have seen affairs there from a disinterested stand-point, and having given to the South and her institutions much thought and attention, I am fully satisfied the course you have adopted is the just one, and one which will ultimately receive the entire approval of the *people of the North*, in spite of the predictions to the contrary by Mr Sumner and his adherents.

With no wish for office or distinction,—independent of administrations or of parties, but with an honest desire to serve in the *ranks* of an Administration seeking to restore our glorious Union. . . .

Moses Bates   Chairman Dem State Cent. Committee

ALS, DLC-JP.

1. Bates (c1805–1873), a Connecticut native, was superintendent of the Louisiana penitentiary in 1862 and speculated in land in New Orleans after the war. He later returned to Massachusetts, where he worked as an engineer, as a "conveyancer," and as editor of the *Plymouth Sentinel*. 1860 Census, N.H., Strafford, Somersworth, 64; Jessie A. Marshall, ed., *Private and Official Correspondence of Gen. Benjamin F. Butler During the Period of the Civil War* (5 vols., Norwood, Mass., 1917), 1: 586; Boston directories

(1871–72); *Boston Advertiser*, June 17, 1873; Bates to Johnson, Dec. 14, 31, 1867, Nov. 16, 1868, Johnson Papers, LC.
2. Winslow (1810–1862) and Taylor (1805–1873) both served three terms in Congress (1855–61). *BDAC*.

From Joseph E. Brown

Milledgeville Ga   Oct 3d 1865

Genl Croxton sends me order for transportation to Washington as witness in Wirz case. Such is the condition of my wife[1] that to leave home at present would probably endanger life. Please hand this to proper officer as my excuse for delay and say by telegraph whether I will be required to leave under the circumstances. I never saw Capt Wirz, was never at Andersonville prison, do not believe I know any fact important in the case. There are other important reasons with which you are acquainted why I regret to leave Georgia at present.[2]

Jos E Brown Gov

Tel, DNA-RG107, Tels. Recd., President, Vol. 4 (1865–66).
1. Elizabeth Grisham (1826–1896), whom Brown had married in 1847, was expecting a baby. Joseph H. Parks, *Joseph E. Brown of Georgia* (Baton Rouge, 1977), 4, 341; *NUC*.
2. The President responded on October 4: "You need not come here to attend the Wirz trial until further orders." Johnson Papers, LC.

From John Cessna[1]

Philadelphia   Oct 3d 1865.

The leading politicians in Pennsylvania who opposed the election of Abraham Lincoln & yourself last year for some days past claim that you are a Convert to their views. That you desire the success of their ticket next tuesday, that in a short time you will dismiss from office all the appointees of Mr Lincoln who have been true to the Union & the Principles of the platform upon which you were elected and appoint in their stead men who uniformly opposed his administration that should Congress refuse to admit members from the South that our political opponents will withdraw & unite with such rejected delegations & that you will recognize that body. These declarations are made partly in conversation partly from the stump & partly in printed Circulars. Will you authorize me to deny in writing any, or all, or which of these allegations?[2]

John Cessna   Chairman
Union State Central Committee

Tel, DLC-JP.
1. Cessna (1821–1893), a former Democratic legislator, later served two terms in Congress (1869–71, 1873–75) as a Republican. *BDAC*.

2. Rumors of impending changes in Pennsylvania patronage "spread like wildfire" in the fall of 1865, as various factions vied for the President's support. Although Johnson apparently did not reply to Cessna's inquiry, the President abstained from making any significant changes in Pennsylvania patronage until 1866. Bradley, *Militant Republicanism*, 231–32, 241–42.

From Clinton B. Fisk

Nashville Tenn   Oct 3d 1865

Dear Sir—

I have the honor to report that on the 1st inst. I received the following telegram from yourself.[1]

In obedience to your order I proceeded immediately to Mrs Donelson's plantation in person—and thoroughly investigated the serious charges contained in her telegram to yourself. I found that no colored soldier had entered Mrs Donelson's house. Neither her own, or the lives of her family had been threatened. Her daughters had *not* been cursed. Her dog had not been shot in her dwelling. No violence had been threatened—and she had no reason whatever to fear that she would be disturbed. Mrs Donelson's family—her neighbors and the troops all agree in this finding. There was a slight disturbance between Mrs D. and a guard in charge of Quarter-Master's property, but Mrs D. was the only party at fault. Her dog was shot & slightly wounded in her yard. The dog was a vicious negro dog, & was undoubtedly set upon the guard.

Mrs Donelson is herself greatly at fault in all this matter—and she now sees it. Her Children and her adviser in this City (Atty White)[2] all counseled her against the course she pursued—and she promised them she would not telegraph you.

I have finally succeeded in disposing of the crops on the place, and the troops are withdrawn. A guard of three men only being left in charge of a Government saw-mill yet on the place. Mrs Donelson's Sons-in-law, Dr. Williams and Mr Martin[3] were with me during the investigation, and aided me materially in the final adjustment of the matter. Mrs D. had prevented the Sale of the crops by threatening prosecution of all persons who might purchase. She has made me more trouble than all the other returned prodigals in Tenn. I regret she should have thought it necessary to annoy you with her complaints.[4]

Clinton B. Fisk   Brig Genl   Asst. Commr.

ALS, DLC-JP.

1. Fisk follows here with the contents of Margaret Donelson's telegram to Johnson, Sept. 29, and Johnson's to Fisk, Sept. 30, 1865.

2. Jackson B. White.

3. Dr. William Williams (b. c1820), who married the Donelsons' eldest daughter, and James G. Martin (1823–1904), the second daughter's husband, who had served as aide to General Donelson. 1850 Census, Tenn., Sumner, 7th Dist., 487; Margaret C.

Snider and Joan H. Yorgason, comps., *Sumner County, Tennessee Cemetery Records* (Owensboro, Ky., 1981), 5–8; *BDTA*, 1: 206; CSR, RG109, NA.

4. On the same day that Fisk wrote his letter to Johnson, he also sent a telegram to the President, in which he stated: "I have the honor to report that I have visited Mrs Donaldson's[*sic*] plantation & corrected the evils complained of. Particulars by letter today." Fisk to Johnson, Oct. 3, 1865, Johnson Papers, LC.

From Walter N. Haldeman[1]

Louisville, Ky., Oct. 3d 1865.

Respected Sir;

I know your time is precious, but I feel sure you will be well repaid in reading the enclosed Extract[2] which I clipped from a Georgia paper.

I have but recently returned home from a four years visit to the South. Most of that time I spent in Georgia and South Carolina, and having had the best opportunities for becoming familiar with public sentiment, I beg to assure your Excellency that the feeling in regard to yourself is very correctly expressed in the extract referred to.

I *know* you have secured for yourself the respect and confidence of the people of the South. A continuance of your policy will win their Everlasting love and gratitude. You are Knitting the people to you as with hooks of steel. Although during my twenty years connection with the public press in this city, I had always acted with the party that opposed you until the campaign which resulted in the election of Buchanan, (since which time I have co-operated with the Democratic party) yet I beg to say it gives me unfeigned pleasure to say and know this. And I beg further to add that whether in the capacity of a private citizen or as a public journalist (in which vocation I may find it necessary again to engage) I shall feel it my privilege and duty to accord to you and your administration and policy a hearty and an earnest support.

W. N. Haldeman

Hon. Jas. Speed, of this city, your Attorney General, can tell you who I am.

ALS, DLC-JP.

1. Haldeman (1821–1902) edited the *Louisville Courier*, a former states' rights and pro-Confederate paper. After the war he resumed publishing in Louisville. Perrin et al., *Kentucky*, 799; *NUC*; *Chicago Tribune*, Aug. 26, 1865; *Nashville Press and Times*, Aug. 24, 1865.

2. Not found.

From Henry Hays[1]

October 3rd 1865

The Petition of Henry Hays of Madison County, Arkansas; humbly sheweth, that on, or about the 15th day of March 1864, he took the amnesty oath required by the President of the United States in his

Proclamation of 8 December, 1863, before the Commissioner of election at Huntsville, Ark. On or about the 10th of October, thereafter, a party of rebels come to the house of your petitioner in the night, and robbed him of all the money he had, (about seven hundred dollars,) together with some valuable papers, amongst them, vouchers against the United States amounting to about seven hundred dollars and then threatened to hang him, and said if he did not have more money when they returned that they would kill him. Your petitioner could not move North, safely, on account of robbers &c. On the 8th November, 1864, he left his home in Madison County, Ark., with an escort of Confederate soldiers and moved to Red River County, Texas, where he remained quietly until August, 1865, when he left Texas, and on the sixteenth of September last, returned to his home in Madison County, Ark.

Your petitioner did not pass into the so-called confederate lines for the purpose of aiding the rebellion, he never has borne arms against the United States Government, he left his home, and passed the Federal lines, and went into Texas because he believed, at that time, that that was the only means by which he could avoid being murdered by robbers. His age is sixty-three years.

The estimated value of his property is about four thousand dollars.

Your petitioner, therefore, prays that your Excellency will grant unto him full amnesty and pardon (if he has erred) and restore unto him all the rights and privileges that he possessed previous to the rebellion, and under such terms, as your Excellency shall prescribe and direct.

And your petitioner will ever pray &c.

his
Henry X Hays
mark

LS(X), DNA-RG94, Amnesty Papers (M1003, Roll 13), Ark., Henry Hays.

1. Hays (c1802-fl1870), who took the oath of allegiance under the May 29, 1865, Amnesty Proclamation before Elias Harrell, judge of the Arkansas 8th judicial circuit, received Governor Murphy's support: "The within petitioner is a very ignorant man not politically responsible. He ought to be pardoned." On November 4, 1865, President Johnson pardoned Hays, who had come under the 14th exception. Amnesty Papers (M1003, Roll 13), Ark., Henry Hays, RG94, NA; 1870 Census, Ark., Madison, War Eagle Twp., 9; *House Ex. Docs.*, 39 Cong., 2 Sess., No. 116, p. 82 (Ser. 1293).

Interview with George L. Stearns

Washington, D.C., Oct. 3, 1865—11 1/2 A.M.

I have just returned from an interview with President JOHNSON, in which he talked for an hour on the process of reconstruction of rebel States. His manner was as cordial, and his conversation as free, as in 1863, when I met him daily in Nashville.

His countenance is healthy, even more so than when I first knew him.

I remarked, that the people of the North were anxious that the process of reconstruction should be thorough, and they wished to support him in the arduous work, but their ideas were confused by the conflicting reports constantly circulated, and especially by the present position of the Democratic party. It is industriously circulated in the Democratic clubs that he was going over to them. He laughingly replied, "Major, have you never known a man who for many years had differed from your views because you were in advance of him, claim them as his own when he came up to your stand-point?"

I replied, I have often. He said so have I, and went on; the Democratic party finds its old position untenable, and is coming to ours; if it has come up to our position, I am glad of it. You and I need no preparation for this conversation; we can talk freely on this subject for the thoughts are familiar to us; we can be perfectly frank with each other. He then commenced with saying that, the States are in the Union which is whole and indivisible.

Individuals tried to carry them out, but did not succeed, as a man may try to cut his throat and be prevented by the bystanders; and you cannot say he cut his throat because he tried to do it.

Individuals may commit treason and be punished, and a large number of individuals may constitute a rebellion and be punished as traitors. Some States tried to get out of the Union, and we opposed it, honestly, because we believed it to be wrong; and we have succeeded in putting down the rebellion. The power of those persons who made the attempt has been crushed, and now we want to reconstruct the State Governments and have the power to do it. The State institutions are prostrated, laid out on the ground, and they must be taken up and adapted to the progress of events. This cannot be done in a moment. We are making very rapid progress; so rapid I sometimes cannot realize it; it appears like a dream.

We must not be in too much of a hurry; it is better to let them reconstruct themselves than to force them to it; for if they go wrong, the power is in our hands and we can check them at any stage, to the end, and oblige them to correct their errors; we must be patient with them. I did not expect to keep out all who were excluded from the amnesty, or even a large number of them, but I intended they should sue for pardon, and so realize the enormity of the crime they had committed.

You could not have broached the subject of equal suffrage, at the North, seven years ago, and we must remember that the changes at the South have been more rapid, and they have been obliged to accept more unpalatable truth than the North has; we must give them time to digest a part, for we cannot expect such large affairs will be comprehended and digested at once. We must give them time to understand their new position.

I have nothing to conceal in these matters, and have no desire or willingness to take indirect courses to obtain what we want.

Our government is a grand and lofty structure; in searching for its foundation we find it rests on the broad basis of popular rights. The elective franchise is not a natural right, but a political right. I am opposed to giving the States too much power, and also to a great consolidation of power in the central government.

If I interfered with the vote in the rebel States, to dictate that the negro shall vote, I might do the same thing for my own purposes in Pennsylvania. Our only safety lies in allowing each State to control the right of voting by its own laws, and we have the power to control the rebel States if they go wrong. If they rebel we have the army, and can control them by it, and, if necessary by legislation also. If the General Government controls the right to vote in the States, it may establish such rules as will restrict the vote to a small number of persons, and thus create a central despotism.

My position here is different from what it would be if I was in Tennessee.

There I should try to introduce negro suffrage gradually; first those who had served in the army; those who could read and write, and perhaps a property qualification for others, say $200 or $250.

It will not do to let the negroes have universal suffrage now. It would breed a war of races.

There was a time in the Southern States when the slaves of large owners looked down upon non-slaveowners because they did not own slaves; the larger the number of slaves their masters owned, the prouder they were, and this has produced hostility between the mass of the whites and the negroes. The outrages are mostly from non-slaveholding whites against the negro, and from the negro upon the non-slaveholding whites.

The negro will vote with the late master whom he does not hate, rather than with the non-slaveholding white, whom he does hate. Universal suffrage would create another war, not against us, but a war of races.

Another thing. This Government is the freest and best on the earth, and I feel sure is destined to last; but to secure this, we must elevate and purify the ballot. I for many years contended at the South that slavery was a political weakness, but others said it was political strength; they thought we gained three-fifths representation by it; I contended that we lost two-fifths.

If we had no slaves, we should have had twelve representatives more, according to the then ratio of representation. Congress apportions representation by States, not districts, and the State apportions by districts.

Many years ago, I moved in the Legislature that the apportionment of Representatives to Congress, in Tennessee, should be by qualified voters.

The apportionment is now fixed until 1872; before that time we might change the basis of representation from population to qualified voters, North as well as South, and in due course of time, the States, without regard to color, might extend the elective franchise to all who possessed certain mental, moral, or such other qualifications, as might be determined by an enlightened public judgment.

New York Times, Oct. 23, 1865.

From James H. Lane

Wyandotte [Kansas]   Oct 3d 1865

Col Simpson[1] arrived here this morning to meet two other commissioners[2] to re examine the Union Pacific Road, Eastern Division.[3] Col Simpson is accompanied by one of the Chief Engineers of the Omaha line[4] who is in the employ of person[5] deadly hostile to all the Rail Road interests of Kansas. Respectfully ask you suspend the action of this commission for thirty days by telegraphic order to Col Simpson. I will see you in Washington early next week and give you very satisfactory reasons for this course.

Please reply to me at Wyandotte and if you grant my request telegraph me copy of order to Col Simpson.[6]

J H Lane   U.S Senator

Tel, DNA-RG107, Tels. Recd., President, Vol. 4 (1865–66).

1. James H. Simpson (1813–1883), a West Point graduate who had served for many years in the Corps of Engineers, was chief engineer for the Department of the Interior (1865–67). *DAB*.

2. Samuel J. Crawford (1835–1913) was governor of Kansas (1865–68) following a distinguished career as a Union officer. Chauncey Rose (1794–1877) was an Indiana railroad developer. Ibid.

3. This inspection was undertaken on Johnson's order after Harlan reported that faulty railroad bridges built by the Union Pacific Railroad Company were collapsing. *House Ex. Docs.*, 39 Cong., 1 Sess., No. 1, p. 963 (Ser. 1248).

4. Presumably Silas Seymour (1817–1890), who was a consulting engineer for the Union Pacific. Wallace, *North American Authors*, 409; John D. Galloway, *The First Transcontinental Railroad* (New York, 1950), 246.

5. Probably a reference to Thomas C. Durant (1820–1885), vice president in charge of construction for the eastern division of the Union Pacific, who was accused of various illegal activities. Ibid., 247; *DAB*.

6. The President apparently ignored Lane's request. On October 28, 1865, Harlan forwarded the commissioners' report, commenting that he was "fully satisfied" that the railroad was "under the control of gentlemen of the highest respectability." Johnson subsequently endorsed the bond issue to which the company was entitled for properly completing the first section of its transcontinental line. *House Ex. Docs.*, 39 Cong., 1 Sess., No. 1, pp. 976–77 (Ser. 1248).

To Lewis E. Parsons

Washington, D.C., Octo. 3d 1865.

Your dispatches have been received and acknowledged.[1] The proceedings of the convention has met the highest expectations of *all* who desire the restoration of the Union. All seems now to be working well, and will result as I believe in a decided success.

Andrew Johnson   Prest. U.S.

Tel, DNA-RG107, Tels. Sent, President, Vol. 2 (1865).

1. Earlier in the afternoon the governor had inquired whether the President had received "several telegrams" and "full reports of all important questions" which had been discussed during the convention that adjourned on September 30. Parsons to Johnson, Oct. 3, 1865, Johnson Papers, LC.

From James M. Tomeny[1]

New Orleans   Oct 3d 1865.

Melton[2] decides not to remove Dexter[3] at Mobile. The investigation was no investigation. No witnesses were summoned no testimony whatever taken. The whole thing was a bad farce. Melton should be released instead—he is the key stone of a corrupt combination defrauding the government of millions. It should be broken up at once.[4] Were you here you would not hesitate a moment. I write fully.[5] Am going to Nashville.

J. M. Lowry[6]

Tel, DLC-JP.

1. A former Memphis treasury agent.

2. William P. Mellen, who was responsible for investigating reports of fraud in the Mobile agency.

3. Thomas C.A. Dexter (*c*1819-*fl*1881), a prewar cotton factor and former treasurer of Louisiana, had obtained an appointment as special treasury agent at Mobile in May 1865. *Richmond Whig*, June 8, 1865; *OR*, Ser. 1, Vol. 49, Pt. 2: 893; Boston directories (1859–82); 1860 Census, Mass., Suffolk, 11th Ward, Boston, 100; 1860 Census, Ala., Mobile, 2nd Ward, Mobile, 31.

4. Johnson forwarded Tomeny's telegram to acting secretary William E. Chandler, asking him to "read this dispatch and return." Chandler met with the President, who insisted that Mellen remove Dexter and appoint Tomeny as Dexter's replacement. Immediately Chandler advised Mellen "to proceed as directed, and carry out, in good faith, the views of the President." See Chandler's official dispatch and his confidential letter to Mellen, both dated Oct. 7, 1865, in Records of Gen. Agent, Lets. Recd., RG366, NA.

5. See Tomeny to Johnson, Nov. 7, 1865.

6. This is the name the telegrapher assigned to the dispatch. Below the name, in another hand, is written "J. M. Tomeny," obviously a clerk's correction. Internal evidence and Tomeny's letter of November 7 indicate that Tomeny was the correspondent.

To Michael Burns

Washington, D.C.   Octo 4 1865.

Will you please see that the Body of Col Daniel Stover,[1] now in the Vault of Mr John Johnston,[2] at M't. Olivet Cemetery, is properly forwarded to Carter Depot, Carter County, East Tennessee.[3] Mrs Stover has left here,[4] and will meet it at that place. See Andrew Johnson, Jr. at the Penitentiary—he has been written to upon the subject.[5]

Andrew Johnson   Pres

Tel, DNA-RG107, Tels. Sent, President, Vol. 2 (1865).

1. Stover, Johnson's son-in-law, had died in 1864.
2. Not identified.
3. Nashville undertaker W. R. Cornelius (who in 1863 had interred Charles Johnson) a few days earlier had written to Robert Johnson in Washington concerning his interest in a burial plot in Mt. Olivet cemetery, "near the vault where the remains of your brother & Col Stover is deposited." Cornelius promised to purchase the cemetery lot, if it met the approval of the Johnsons, and also to "attend to the burial of the bodies." Apparently the family was considering permanent burial in Mt. Olivet for Stover before deciding to send his remains to Carter County. Cornelius to Johnson, Sept. 28, 1865, Johnson Papers, LC.
4. Mary Johnson Stover had gone to Washington in August 1865 to live at the White House. She left for Tennessee on October 3 (the date her late husband's property was sold), accompanied by Robert Morrow and also probably Robert Johnson. Mrs. Stover returned to Washington in late October. *Washington Morning Chronicle*, Oct. 5, 1865; *Nashville Press and Times*, Oct. 6, 23, 1865; Andrew Johnson Project files.
5. No correspondence with the President's nephew relative to the Stover matter has been found. Burns telegraphed Johnson to assure him that "all will be attended to." Burns to Johnson, Oct. 5, 1865, Johnson Papers, LC.

From Mary L. Carter[1]

[Mobile, Ala., ca. October 4, 1865][2]

The petition and application for special pardon of Mary L. Carter, would respectfully shew unto your Excellency that she is the wife of Dr Jesse Carter of the city and county of Mobile and State of Alabama, that she is of the age of fifty years and has a family of seven children.

Your petitioner would further shew that by inheritance she became and so possessed in her own right, of property principally real estate in the city of Mobile the value of which is probably more than twenty thousand dollars, and which for the purpose of this petition is admitted to be worth more than that sum.

In regard to her participation in the late war or the proceedings connected therewith, your petitioner begs leave to state that although she was opposed to the war in the beginning, and did not approve of the acts of the South that led to it, yet after the war had already broken out, her sympathies were with her own people, and she openly expressed her feelings, and extended her sympathies to the soldiers who were suffering from wounds and sickness in the cause of the South and she assissted such soldiers by helping to nurse, feed and take care of them, and by assisting to furnish them with clothing. She would further state that whenever she found in the course of her visits to the hospital Federal prisoners she extended to them also such aid and comfort as was in her power to bestow. Your petitioner had no further connection with the war. She has now taken the oath of amnesty in good faith and believes it to be her duty, and intends to keep and observe the same.

She would further state that her property has been very much diminished by the war, having lost about thirty five slaves, and besides other diminutions, the improvements upon her real estate were very badly damaged by the explosion of the Federal powder magazine in Mobile in May last.[3]

Your petitioner would further state that her husband is now nearly sixty years of age, has retired from the practice of his profession, and has but little property, and that the property and estate owned by her is the sole source of income for the support and maintenance of her family: that her said husband has taken the oath of amnesty and is not within any of the excepted classes.

Your petitioner would therefore respectfully pray your Excellency to extend to her amnesty and pardon promised in your proclamation of 29th May last.[4]

And as in duty bound your petitioner will ever pray &c.

Mary L Carter

L, DNA-RG94, Amnesty Papers (M1003, Roll 2), Ala., Mary L. Carter.

1. Mrs. Carter (c1815–1867) was long survived by her husband (c1808–1884), a prominent physician. 1860 Census, Ala., Mobile, Mobile, 1st Ward, 28; Thompson, *Magnolia Cemetery*, 3.

2. The document's internal evidence, as well as the date Mrs. Carter's petition was notarized, provide the date we have assigned to the letter. We assume that she wrote from Mobile, her hometown.

3. On May 25, 1865, an accident in the handling of captured Confederate percussion shells caused the explosion of twenty tons of powder at a warehouse in northeast Mobile. *OR*, Ser. 1, Vol. 49, Pt. 1: 566–67.

4. Her pardon was issued October 30, 1865. *House Ex. Docs.*, 40 Cong., 2 Sess., No. 16, p. 8 (Ser. 1330).

From James W. Moore[1]

Richmond, Va.   October 4th 1865.

Sir.

Early in last June my petition for pardon was forwarded to *you*, by the Honl. H S Lane of Ia: with his recommendation.[2] Also another letter from him, containing a statement from Judge Peters[3] of the Supreme Court of Ky. who resides in Mt Sterling Ky my home and who made in said statement no reference to my departure from my home in

1861. Also I have forwarded to you the requisite oath, and letters from Gov Pierpont & Genl. Mulfurd[4]—All of which I presume are on file in the department. I was a member of the Confederate Congress, and stated fully in my petition all the facts which connected me with the rebellion.

Sir I was no speculator during the war, and acquired no money. I have my family to support[5] & no means to do it with except my exertions in business. I have not the means to spare from my family to incur the expences of a visit to Washington to present my case in person. I have given every proof in my power of my loyalty to the government of the United States, since I took the oath and accepted the terms of your amnesty proclamation.

May I not ask; and hope that you will grant my pardon and cause the same to be forwarded to me at Danville Virginia, as my time and means are *all* required to support my family & I have none to spare from them to come to Washington.[6]

J. W. Moore

ALS, DNA-RG94, Amnesty Papers (M1003, Roll 26), Ky., James W. Moore.

1. Moore (1818–1877), a former circuit court judge (1851–58) and Confederate congressman (1862–65), after the war returned to Mt. Sterling to practice law. Warner and Yearns, *BRCC*.

2. In addition to Moore's letter to Johnson of June 8, he also wrote a letter to the President on July 31. Henry S. Lane of Indiana wrote an undated recommendation in behalf of Moore. All of these documents are found in Amnesty Papers (M1003, Roll 26), Ky., James W. Moore, RG94, NA.

3. Belvard J. Peters (1805–*fl*1897) retired to private practice in 1876 after serving sixteen years as a state court of appeals judge. H. Levin, *The Lawyers and Lawmakers of Kentucky* (Chicago, 1897), 81–83.

4. The Union commissioner for the exchange of prisoners, John E. Mulford (*c*1829–1908) was, after the war, collector of internal revenue at Richmond, Va., before heading a New York tool company. *New York Times*, Oct. 20, 1908; Richmond directories (1869–71).

5. According to Moore's biographers, he was "a lifelong bachelor" who "left no descendants." Warner and Yearns, *BRCC*.

6. Moore was pardoned by the President on September 28, 1866. Amnesty Papers (M1003, Roll 26), Ky., James W. Moore, RG94, NA.

From Lewis E. Parsons

Montgomery   Oct. 4 1865.

Sir:

Allow me to introduce to you my friend Mr J. C. Gibson[1] one of the Editors of the "Montgomery Daily Mail" (Newspaper). The "Mail" has rendered efficient service in the cause of reconstruction in Alabama. It is an old established, widely circulated Journal, & an ardent & *sincere* supporter of the Presidents policy.

Mr Gibson is in every way reliable & I trust your Excellency will find it convenient to aid him or the Mail in the matter of printing the laws. I have recommended *two* papers, one in Huntsville & the other in Mobile[2] but we really need one at this place.[3]

Lewis E. Parsons   Pro Gv. Ala.

ALS, DNA-RG59, Entry 149, Lets. Recd. *re* Publishers of Laws.

1. Not otherwise identified.
2. Presumably the *Advocate* and the *Register*, respectively.
3. After obtaining the President's endorsement, Gibson applied directly to Seward, who evidently approved the request. Gibson to Seward, Oct. 16, 1865, Lets. Recd. *re* Publishers of Laws, RG59, NA. See Joseph C. Bradley to Johnson, Nov. 15, 1865.

From Lewis E. Parsons

Montgomery, October 4th 1865

Sir:

In referring to your consideration and action the application of Abram Martin[1] of the city of Montgomery for amnesty and pardon, it is proper that I should state that the application and the answers to the interrogations, contained in my Circular of July 25, 1865, disclose the fact that the applicant was Chairman of a Vigilance Committee[2] established in the city of Montgomery Ala, on the 8th day of August 1861.

It does not appear at whose instance the meeting was called that appointed the Committee—nor have I been able to ascertain after a thorough examination of the numerous affidavits and statements in writing which have been submitted by friends of the applicant who were the prime movers and active parties in getting it up. The meeting which appointed the Committee instructed them to stop all intercourse between citizens of this place and the Lincoln Government and to carry out this purpose to the utmost of their ability and to that end empowered them to institute inquiries and make examination of all suspicious persons and strangers coming to or leaving the city and arrest and bring before the Vigilance Committee all persons against whom evidence of suspicious actions may be found. The police and the military companies of the city were empowered and requested to arrest all suspicious persons and bring them before the Committee for trial and their decision should be final. And the Chairman was empowered to call a meeting whenever he thought proper, and on information of any respectable person to order the arrest of any person charged by the City Marshal, City police or any one of the Military companies in the city. It also appears that the Committee kept a record of their actings and doings but that it was destroyed shortly before Genl Wilson[3] occupied the city on April last.

It further appears that the applicant left the chair on several occasions and spoke in defense of several persons who were on trial before it, and that no one was punished by the judgment or sentence of the Committee.

It appears further that "he was from the first as Conservative in his course as any man could be who was acting on such a Committee."

I can also state of my own personal knowledge that I have known the applicant for many years and I am well satisfied he is a just and good man and one whose leading trait of character is *kindness of action* and violence of opinion.

I thus recommend the application.

Lewis E Parsons   Prov Governor of Alabama

LS, DNA-RG94, Amnesty Papers (M1003, Roll 7), Ala., Abram Martin.

1. Martin (1798-*fl*1872), a lawyer and resident of Montgomery since 1832, had been an antebellum circuit judge and later a state tax collector for the Confederacy. Brewer, *Alabama*, 453.

2. In a lengthy response to the third question of Parsons's circular ("Have you served on any 'Vigilance Committee' during the war . . . ?"), Martin stated that in his absence he had been appointed chairman of such an organization. He remembered thirteen persons who were brought before the committee, and claimed to have voted for the discharge of eleven. Martin to Parsons, ca. Aug. 8, 1865, Amnesty Papers (M1003, Roll 7), Ala., Abram Martin, RG94, NA.

3. James H. Wilson.

4. Martin's pardon was issued October 18, 1865. *House Ex. Docs.*, 40 Cong., 2 Sess., No. 16, p. 23 (Ser. 1330).

From Thomas W. Turley[1]

Nashville Tenn.   Oct. 4th 1865

The petition of T. W. Turley a citizen of the county of Jefferson in the State of Tennessee respectfully represents that at the breaking out of the late civil war and for several years previous to that time he was and had been one of the Judges of the circuit courts of said State and assigned to hold the courts in the second judicial circuit thereof. The life of petitioner has been one devoted exclusively to his professional pursuits, with but little interference with political affairs further than to express his opinions on the leading questions which have been agitated in his native state. This he always did with candor but with deference and respect for those who entertained different views. Especially after his elevation to the Bench did petitioner refrain from active participation in political strife but could not avoid becoming identified with one or the other of the parties when the whole country became involved in war. Petitioner was uniformly opposed to secession and every measure set on foot by the southern states having for their object a dissolution of the Union. After however the war had been fully inaugurated, petitioner regarded dissolution as an accomplished fact, and, acting on this erroneous belief from that time to the close of the war expressed himself in sympathy with the insurgents, under the honest conviction that in doing so he was but giving his voice to the cause of his country and for the best interest of his native land. The result has proven these ideas to have been fallacious, but petitioner has the happiness to know that his errors as to public right and policy never betrayed him into individual wrong. On the contrary petitioner believes that for the first two years and a half of the war during which time he was constantly surrounded by numerous and outspoken friends to the Union cause he never gave any one of them offense by even an expression calculated to wound their sensibilities. It is not to be denied that during the occupancy of East Tennessee by the Confederate authorities many unwarrantable things were done by the party with which petitioner was identified, but for none of them does he feel himself responsible as he uniformly opposed all infringment on the rights of liberty or property of Union men, both officially and as a private citizen. Petitioner will not specify any of his official transactions in this regard as they were merely acts of positive duty, and are preserved in the records of the country, yet he deems it not amiss to state that on many occasions he interceded for Union men whom he believed to have been improperly arrested, sometimes succeeding and at others failing to procure their release. On one occasion petitioner having heard of a lot of poor men being arrested and sent without trial and without cause as petitioner believed to the city of Mobile and there imprisoned, petitioner went at his own expense to Richmond and after much difficulty and delay obtained an audience and procured from Mr. Benjamin[2] an order for their release. Not one of these men was a man of property or in any way related to petitioner. The course of petitioner altogether had been such that he could see no cause why he should leave his home when the country was occupied by the United States forces and he accordingly remained. Although petitioner was not arrested yet his stock and grain were taken and he was assured by his Union friends that an indictment for treason would be prefered against him so soon as the Federal Court commenced at Knoxville. This petitioner believed would inevitably be followed by imprisonment, and that if long continued petitioner was satisfied would endanger his life. Petitioner's family consisted of a timid wife in delicate health and two small children who would in his absence have been exposed without protection in a country likely to be and afterwards was the scene of protracted and bloody strife. In view of these facts petitioner availed himself of the temporary absence of the Federal forces during the seige of Knoxville and passed with his family beyond the limits of the state. Petitioner asserts distinctly that he left his home not with any purpose of giving aid or assistance to the rebellion but alone for the reason just stated. Petitioner has never taken up arms or engaged in any active hostility to the authority of the United States government. His family is now temporarily residing in Cleveland County in the state of North Carolina, but it is his purpose soon to return to his native state. Petitioner further states that immediately after the promulgation of your Excellency's Amnasty Proclamation bearing date

29th May 1865 he attempted to avail himself of its benefits by taking and subscribing the oath therein prescribed before the Commander of the post at Shelby N.C. on the 12th day of June thereafter. But this being somewhat informal petitioner on the 24th of the same moth again took the oath before Wm. Heiskell Esqr. Com. &c. at Knoxville E. Tenn. the original whereof is hereto attached as part of this petition.[3] Petitioner however is debarred from the full benefits of said oath by reason both of indictment having been prefered against him in the Federal Court at Knoxville and his property having been seized as abandoned, the personalty sold and the realty rented out and libeled for confiscation. Petitioner believes he is not embraced under any of the exceptions in the amnasty Proclamation unless it may be the $20,000 clause and whether under this or not future events must determine and petitioner cannot now certainly state.

Petitioner states it is his fixed purpose to keep and perform in good faith his aforesaid oath and to bide by and support the constitution and laws of the United States. He therefore prays your Excellency would grant unto him that special pardon reserved for such as may be deemed worthy of such favor and will ever pray &c.[4]

T. W. Turley

ALS, DNA-RG94, Amnesty Papers (M1003, Roll 51), Tenn., T. W. Turley.

1. Turley (1820-*fl*1888), a Rutledge lawyer, later in the fall moved to Franklin, Tenn., where he resumed his practice. William S. Speer, *Sketches of Prominent Tennesseans* (Nashville, 1888), 254–56.

2. Judah P. Benjamin.

3. The oath is enclosed in Turley's Tennessee file in the Amnesty Papers.

4. On October 5 Gov. William G. Brownlow forwarded Turley's petition and accompanying documents to Washington with his endorsement of pardon for Turley. Two days later David T. Patterson also endorsed Turley's petition, saying that Turley "is a fit person for Executive Clemency." Both endorsements are found attached to Turley's October 4 letter. The file sheet indicates that Turley was pardoned on October 9, 1865. Earlier, on September 21, Turley had written from North Carolina seeking pardon as a citizen of that state. This petition was eventually forwarded by Governor Holden to Washington in late October and a second pardon evidently was issued to Turley on November 7, 1865. See Turley to Johnson, Sept. 21, 1865, Amnesty Papers (M1003, Roll 43), N.C., T. W. Turley, RG94, NA.

From Jacob Collamer[1]

Woodstock, Vt.   Oct. 5. 1865.

Dear Sir,

The definitive, entire & unquestionable abolition of slavery in this country, will never be complete & beyond dispute until the adoption of the amendment to the United States Constitution proposed by Congress, by the legislatures of twenty seven states.[2]

The constitution provides that amendments proposed by Congress may be adopted by the States in convention or by their legislature, as

Congress shall direct. In this case Congress has directed the adoption to be by the legislatures, and therefore all proceedings in the State Conventions on this Subject are inoperative.

All the proceedings in the State Conventions abolishing Slavery or declaring it forever ended in the State, will be unsatisfactory in reconstruction; Such proceedings being always Subject to revision or repeal in State Convention. The neglect by any State to adopt effectually, by its legislature, this proposed amendment, is a distinct implication that Such State intends to hold itself in a position to restore Slavery at its own pleasure.

It seems to me quite obvious that whatever questions or differences of opinion may be held in Congress by the loyal states on this subject of reconstruction, there can be none on this point, and that no state can be accepted as restored to regular & reliable reorganization which declines or neglects to ratify the proposed amendment by its legislature. Nor is this to require of them anything we have not done ourselves.

As this point seems to have been overlooked in some cases I have felt it my privilege briefly to suggest it to you. I have no doubt of your concurrence in this opinion and therefore do not elaborate it, but desire the people of Seceded States Should reasonably understand it, & which if, you concur, you will best know how to effect, if not already done.

I respectfully request information of the receipt hereof.

J. Collamer

ALS, DLC-JP.
1. Senator Collamer died five weeks after writing this letter.
2. Seward declared the Thirteenth Amendment to be ratified by the requisite number of states on December 18, 1865. James G. Randall, *Constitutional Problems Under Lincoln* (Urbana, Ill., 1951[1926]), 397–98.

From Francis H. Peirpoint

Richmond, Oct 5 1865.

Dr. Sir.

Most respectfuly I desire to call your attention to the case of Judge Haliburton[1] of this city. He was U S. Judge of this district before the rebellion, resigned and became judge in the Confederacy. He is one of those earnest simple-minded learned pure legal men. Every body concedes him to have been a very pure minded good judge. He is poor. Wants to do some thing for the support of his family—but is filled with the idea that he can do nothing without a pardon. This itself is evidence of the purity and sincerity of the man. He has a helpless family. The very condition of the man and his family induces me to ask for an exception in his case. I therefore seriously ask you to pardon him with understanding that his case shall not be a precedent for one of his class.[2]

F. H. Peirpoint

ALS, DNA-RG94, Amnesty Papers (M1003, Roll 62), Va., James D. Halyburton.
    1. James D. Halyburton (c1803-c1876) later resumed the practice of law. 1860 Census, Va., Henrico, Richmond, 3rd Ward, 40; NUC; Richmond directories (1869–77).
    2. The judge's pardon was not ordered until November 23, 1866. House Ex. Docs., 39 Cong., 2 Sess., No. 31, p. 14 (Ser. 1289).

From Benjamin F. Perry

Greenville S.C.   October 5th 1865

My Dear Sir

I received your telegram of the 29th ult. and was very much gratified to learn that you were pleased with the amendments to our Constitution and hoped to see all the Southern States restored to the Union in a short time.

There is one matter about which I wish your free expression of opinion to me. Will the members of the Confederate Congress, members who resigned their seats in the United States Congress, and prominent Generals in the Confederate Army, be acceptable as members of the next Congress? Will they prejudice, by their election, the restoration of South Carolina to the Union? In other words, will they be allowed to take their seats in the United States Congress?[1]

The present Oath of Office is such that no one can take it in South Carolina. Will this oath be required of all the Southern members? If so I do not see how the Southern States are to be represented. Every one has either held office under the Confederate States or been in the army or countenanced in some way the Rebellion. No one could have lived in South Carolina and done otherwise. The State Governments and the Confederate Government were *de facto* Governments, having control of life and property with the power of enforcing their laws.

I am very much in favor of returning, so far as is possible old union men to the present Congress. But in some of the Congressional Districts there are none such to send. In every instance, however, we ought, in my opinion to elect the most conservative men we can get, men who have not been prominent in the Rebellion and made themselves offensive to the North.

I must say that I believe all are now loyal and will prove true to the Union hereafter, no matter how prominent they may have been in the Rebellion either in the army or in civil life.

In this Congressional District we now have as Candidates, Col Farrow,[2] who was a member of the Confederate Congress, and Col. Ashmore[3] who resigned his seat in the United States Congress to take a part in the rebellion. In the adjoining District General McGowen is a candidate, who was a General in the Confederate Army. In the third District C W Dudley, an old union man is running without opposition.[4]

I shall probably be elected to the United States Senate, and the Candidates for the other seat are W. W. Boyce, who resigned his seat in the U.S. Congress and became a member of the Confederate Congress. He is well known to you. Governor Manning, an old Union man is also a Candidate. Who will be elected is very doubtful.[5]

Ben. F. Perry.

LS, DLC-JP.

1. Perry had to repeat this question before he received an answer. See Perry to Johnson and Johnson to Perry, Nov. 27, 1865.

2. James Farrow (1827–1892), a former Spartanburg attorney, was elected but not seated. He later moved to Kansas City, where he was elected city judge, then returned to South Carolina to serve as president of Laurens Female College before resuming his law practice. Warner and Yearns, *BRCC*.

3. John D. Ashmore (1819–1871), planter, merchant, and former state representative, was by his own admission a strong unionist before the war. *BDAC*; Ashmore to Johnson, Aug. 3, 1865, *Johnson Papers*, 8: 536.

4. Perry is mistaken here. Samuel McGowan won the congressional race in the third district, while John D. Kennedy won in the first district, where Dudley resided. Both were refused their seats. John S. Reynolds, *Reconstruction in South Carolina* (Columbia, S.C., 1905), 20.

5. John L. Manning won the second Senate position but was not allowed his seat. Sobel and Raimo, *Governors*, 4: 1408.

From Abraham K. Allison

Fort Pulaski   Oct 6 1865.

Sir,

As an opportunity offers I have concluded to take the liberty of calling your attention to my application for Pardon & amnesty filed in the Atty Genls. office, and recomended by our Provisional Governor, Marvin.[1]

As it is somewhat lengthy I will simply state that I was Prest of the Senate of Fla at the time of the decease of the Governor John Milton on 1 April 1865. That the Constitution made it my duty to discharge the duties of that office until a successor could be elected.

That in accordance with the then law I issued a proclamation as Actg Gov. for that election to take place on the 7' day of June last. That I issued no orders of any kind except such as were necessary to carry on the Gov. of the State until the election of Gov could be held. That I never held office of any kind in the Confederate service. Was never a contractor or agent in any department of it. I have not twenty thousand Dollars worth of property left. I have a large family of small children dependent upon me for support.

I have always been a Democrat am yet, & am a firm supporter of your views in regard to the reconstruction of the Southern States. Am fifty four years old, and to wind up am extremely anxious to get home. Not that I am sick or an invalid, nor that I have not been well treated since I have been in prison for I have been kindly & humanely treated.

I send you Gov Marvin's last letter to me.[2] Please give this your immediate attention, as I believe you will, and do in the premises that which is just & right to the country & myself.[3]

A K Allison

ALS, DNA-RG94, Amnesty Papers (M1003, Roll 15), Fla., A. K. Allison.
1. William Marvin (1808–1902), a native New Yorker, had served as Florida's territorial district attorney and later U.S. district judge. He was appointed provisional governor in July 1865. Roller and Twyman, *Encyclopedia of Southern History*, 783–84. For Allison's earlier application, see Allison to Johnson, June 22, 1865, Amnesty Papers (M1003, Roll 15), Fla., A. K. Allison, RG94, NA.
2. Possibly the note from a private secretary indicating that the governor had approved and forwarded Allison's petition to the President. Samuel J. Douglas to Allison, Sept. 27, 1865, ibid.
3. The reverse of this document bears the endorsement "Issue a pardon in this case A J Pres." In November, when the matter of Allison's clemency was referred to the judge advocate general, Holt advised against it. Allison was released on parole in January 1866 and was apparently pardoned on October 19, 1866. Dorris, *Pardon and Amnesty*, 262–63; Amnesty Papers (M1003, Roll 15), Fla., A. K. Allison, RG94, NA.

From Adele Petigru Allston[1]

Charleston   6th Oct 1865

Being a widow greatly reduced in circumstances by the war, and having two children whose education is unfinished, I take the liberty of applying to you for an appointment for my son Petigru to the military academy West Point.[2] He has just completed his seventeenth year, and would I believe do credit to the appointment. I am the sister of the late James L Petigru[3] brought suddenly from wealth to poverty. Your compliance with this request will be cause for lasting gratitude to me and my family.[4]

Adele Petigru Allston

ALS, DNA-RG94, USMA Appls. (M688, Roll 237).
1. Allston (1810–1896) was the widow of Robert F.W. Allston, governor of South Carolina in the 1850s. *DAB*; J. H. Easterby, ed., *The South Carolina Rice Plantation, as Revealed in the Papers of Robert F.W. Allston* (Chicago, 1945), 19.
2. Following his graduation from the College of Charleston in 1869, Charles Petigru Allston (1848–1922) became a successful rice planter. Ibid., 18.
3. Petigru (1789–1863) had been a staunch unionist, initially during South Carolina's nullification crisis, and some three decades later when the state seceded. *DAB*.
4. Johnson endorsed the letter, "Let the name of this young man be entered as an applicant from the congressional district embracing Charleston." Allston did not receive an appointment.

From John Jay Anderson[1]

Maysville, Ky   Oct 6th 1865

My Dear Sir
Without the least thought of advising or dictating as to any policy in regard to the removal of the troops from the States I would suggest that as Collector of the 6th Dist Ky In the Cos of Morgan Floyd & Pike

there is a large population who are disaffected and nothing but Military force will keep them under. Three weeks ago the Assessor of Morgan[2] was arrested by Jno T Williams[3] and his gang and made sign his name to paper that he would release certain claims he had also that he was oppressing his people in Morgan and he must cease his labors in that quarter. In those counties there is considerable Tax due on distilled spirits. If it was not for the class of Politicians known in our state as Conservatives all these things would have ceased long since. They are to day more bitter and unrelanting than the greatest Rebel in Dixie. This Class of Judges are now instructing the Grand juries to indict union men for zeal in the late elections. In some counties as high as Fifty have been presented. If the election of Judges was next year this could be borne but they have Two & Three years yet to serve. By all means if an small army is to be kept up let a few stay in Ky as I verily believe there is more disloyalty in the Blue grass region of Ky than in South Carolina. This part of the state has furnished thousands to the Rebel cause and but few hundreds to the cause of their Country. There will be great suffering with the negroes in the state this winter. By a law of the Legislature any one who hires a negro made Free by the Husband being in the army[4] is indicted and the Law in such cases is trampled under Foot and Judge Andrews[5] of this Circuit has decided its unconstitutional and no one will hire them for fear of being prosecuted. If there is any power on earth to declare all Free for Heavens sake Issue the Fiat For the peace of the Country requires it.[6]

Jno Jay Anderson

ALS, DLC-JP.

1. Later reappointed collector, Anderson (1819–1894), a planter, resigned before January 1867. 1860 Census, Ky., Montgomery, Mt. Sterling, 84; Emma J. Walker and Virginia Wilson, eds., *Some Marriages in Montgomery County, Kentucky Before 1864* (n.p., 1961), 3; Ser. 6B, Vol. 4: 241–42, Johnson Papers, LC.

2. Joel W. Gordon.

3. Williams (c1824–c1884), who once held a Confederate officer's commission, reportedly threatened to resist any further attempts to collect U.S. taxes "in the country while he is in it." *Cincinnati Gazette*, Oct. 4, 1865; 1860 Census, Ky., Morgan, 2nd Div., West Liberty, 75; J. Wendell Nickell et al., comps., *Will Abstracts (And Related Records), Morgan Co., Ky., Before 1900* (West Liberty, Ky., 1982), 55; *OR*, Ser. 1, Vol. 20, Pt. 1: 113; Vol. 39, Pt. 2: 741.

4. Congressional legislation on March 3, 1865, had granted freedom to the dependents of black enlistees. Howard, *Black Liberation*, 79–80.

5. In April 1865 Judge L. Watson Andrews (1803–1887), a former Whig congressman, had ruled that the federal law was unconstitutional because Kentucky did not sanction slave marriages. The state court of appeals upheld Andrews's decision until the Thirteenth Amendment had been ratified and Kentucky's slave codes were repealed. Ibid., 120–22; *BDAC*.

6. See Green Clay Smith to Johnson, Oct. 7, 1865.

To James Gordon Bennett

Private

Washington, D.C.   October 6th 1865

Dear Sir,

Your note of recent date,[1] by the politeness of Mr Wikoff,[2] was received and read, and the Suggestions made in reference to our Foreign policy considered.

This is a subject, I would be pleased to confer with you upon freely and fully. This letter, however is not written for that purpose, but simply to tender you my thanks, for the able and disinterested manner in which you have defended the policy of the Administration since its accession to power. It is the more highly appreciated, because it has not been Solicited, but Voluntarily tendered. I feel grateful for your timely help, and confidence, and hope to prove in the end that they have not been misplaced. The *people proper*, who need friends—who need honest and able advocates to defend their rights and interests, in all Governmental affairs, will in due time appreciate those, who firmly and faithfully stand by them, while passing through this dreadful Ordeal!

If the patriotic impulse of the National heart is consulted, obeyed and carried out in good faith, regulated by Law and the Constitution, which should be held Sacred and dear by all true friends of free Government—All the former relations of the States in the Union, will be restored, with all the avocations of peace, and sincere devotion to a Union, that will be as enduring as time. This will be so, if we perform our parts as patriots.

I entered upon this Presidential term with a fixed and unalterable determination to administer the Government upon the principles, which will bring the people, as near as may be, in close proximity with all the acts and doings of their public Servants; thereby enabling them to determine understandingly all questions of public policy. So far, in public life, the people have sustained me. I have never deserted them, and if I know my own heart, I will stand by them now. Hence in the peoples' cause, I need, and ask your aid. You can now indelibly fix upon the hearts of this people, who will be grateful, that you are their friend and benefactor.

Now is the time for the principles, upon which the Government is founded, to be developed, discussed, and understood. There is no man in America, who can exercise more power in fixing the Government upon a firm and enduring foundation than you can—with such aid, the task will be made easy in the performance of this work. I do not intend to be driven from my purpose by taunts or jeers, coming whence they may. Nor do I intend to be overawed by pretended or real friends, or bullied by Swaggering or presuming enemies. "If truth is made our guide, the public good our aim," the Union will be restored, attended with all the blessings of a prosperous peace.[3]

Andrew Johnson

N.B. By the meeting of Congress the work of restoration will I think be nearly Complete—Post offices, Federal Courts, [Navy?] &c &c will be established.[4]

LS, NjMoHP-L. W. Smith Collection.
    1. See Bennett to Johnson, Aug. 26, 1865, *Johnson Papers*, 8: 656–58.
    2. Henry Wikoff.
    3. Bennett's laudatory reply was delivered by his son, James Gordon Bennett, Jr. Bennett to Johnson, Oct. 15, 1865, Johnson Papers, LC.
    4. This note and the signature are in the President's hand, although the body of the letter was written by someone else.

From William W. Holden

Raleigh   Oct 6th 1865.

Sir,

The convention has just passed the following by an unanimous vote.[1] That the ordinance of the convention of the state of North Carolina ratified on the twenty first day of November seventeen eighty nine which adopted & ratified the constitution of the united States & also all acts & parts of acts of the general assembly ratifying & adopting amendments to the said constitution are now & at all times since the adoption and ratification thereof have been in full force & effect notwithstanding the supposed ordinance of the twentieth of may eighteen sixty one declaring the same to be repealed rescinded & abrogated & the said supposed ordinance is now & at all times hath been null & void.

The convention will dispose of the slavery question tomorrow.[2]

The state elections will be fixed on the first thursday of november.[3]

W W Holden   Prov Gov

Tel, DLC-JP.
    1. Actually, several delegates voted against the repeal ordinance, while others simply abstained from voting. Harris, *Holden*, 188.
    2. The following day Holden wired Johnson that the convention had passed "unanimously" an ordinance prohibiting "Slavery & involuntary servitude," and would "in all probability ignore [repudiate] the rebel state debt." Ibid.; Holden to Johnson, Oct. 7, 1865, Johnson Papers, LC.
    3. In a separate telegram also transmitted and received on October 7, Holden informed Johnson that the state election would take place on November 9 and the legislature would meet on Sunday, the 19th; it actually convened on Monday, the 27th. Johnson Papers, LC; Raper, *Holden*, 83; *Raleigh Standard*, Nov. 27, 1865.

From John Bell Hood

Galveston Texas   Oct 6, 1865

The undersigned finding himself embraced by the exceptions made by your proclamation of 29th of May 1865 to the amnesty which is granted to others who were complicated in the effort to establish the Southern Confederacy, Avails himself of the suggestion of the proclamation to ask your Excellency to extend a special amnesty in his case.

With this view he has complied with the requirements of said proclamation; and submits herewith the amnesty oath which was administered to him by the Provost Martial Gen'l of the Depmt. of Texas.[1] He is a native of the State of Ky. and during the war has been in the Confederate Army—in which he held the rank of Lt General and temporary General.

Prior to the war he was an officer of the U.S. Army. He submits his action in accordance with the requirements of your proclamation as evidence of his willingness to return to his allegiance to the U States, of which he believes he can make a loyal citizen.

He submits his case to your special consideration, asking special amnesty.[2] He had nothing to do with bringing on this war—but being a soldier by education, he deemed it necessary & right, that he should take part in the struggle, and accordingly fought earnestly, for what he considered to be right & just. He thinks he can now be as earnest in his efforts to restore the union as he was in his attempts to tear it asunder.

J. B. Hood

ALS, DNA-RG94, Amnesty Papers (M1003, Roll 53), Tex., John Bell Hood.

1. Hood's amnesty oath, which has not been found, was presumably taken before Lt. Col. Rankin G. Loughlin (c1828–1878) of the 94th Ill. Inf., provost marshal general of the Thirteenth Corps. After the war, Loughlin resumed the practice of medicine in Illinois. 1860 Census, Ill., McLean, Randolph Twp., 92; Pension File, Rankin G. Loughlin, RG15, NA; OR, Ser. 1, Vol. 49, Pt. 2: 991.

2. There is no record of an individual pardon.

From James Johnson

Macon Ga.   Oct. 6, 1865.

Some of the Treasury agents are seizing & carrying off cotton of citizens which never belonged to Confederate States.

It is creating much discontent. Please stop them until you can be furnished with details.

J. Johnson   Prov. Govr Ga

Tel, DNA-RG107, Tels. Recd., President, Vol. 4 (1865–66).

From J. Madison Wells

New Orleans, October 6th 1865

To President Johnson

I have the satisfaction to enclose you the platform adopted by the national democratic convention which convened in this city on the 2d inst. Also the list of candidates nominated for State offices and my letter of acceptance.[1]

As the first democratic convention in the south under the new order of things, I attach considerable importance to the success of the convention in resuscitating the democratic creed on the broad principles of nationality and constitutional rights. How far the resolutions embody these principles, you can judge by reading them. The convention itself was respectable in numbers and composed of quite a Superior class of men generally—many of them distinguished for talent and for their public Services. Past party divisions was entirely ignored in the composition of the convention. The old whig element I think largely predominated and as you have some Knowledge from experience of the tenacity with which an old whig clings to his creed and his horror of democratic principles heretofore, I believe you will appreciate the sacrifice made, in sitting in a democratic convention and giving in their adhesion to the saving principles of democracy to uphold and preserve the constitutional rights of the States.

I am further gratified to be able to state that the convention was entirely harmonious in its proceedings and results. Notwithstanding this and the conservative tone of the resolutions, you may expect to hear through the northern radical press, and from disappointed politicians here, the usual charges and denunciations, of treason, rebellion— secession &c both against the material of the Convention, and the character of the candidates nominated. This has become so customary and stale, that it is hardly worth noticing and particularly to you, who I beleive Know the motives of such charges and what weight to attach to them. As regards the animus of the convention, you have the evidence before you. In relation to the candidates, I will say that in point of capacity, talents, honesty and experience, no other men could have been selected, always excepting the head of the ticket. Whatever may have been their antecedents, I regard them as true, sincere and loyal men, who have renewed their allegiance in good faith—who realize and accept the new order of things and will prove faithful to the Government and the trust reposed in them, if elected. I am willing to trust them, and God knows, I have no particular reasons for loving or countenancing rebels, if I Knew them to be such.

All reports and clamor therefore you may hear, affecting their status as loyal men, you may safely disregard as originating in selfish and political designs of a few men who wish to monopolize the power of the state.

There will probably be an opposition ticket under the name of "Union Conservative,"[2] which is desirable in one sense, as tending to bring out a large Vote.

I will further mention that efforts have been made by this party to induce Gen'l Canby to interfere with the elective franchise—but against this, I have and shall continue to remonstrate, entertaining perfect Confidence in the ability of the civil authority to enforce the law. I have however too high an opinion of the good sense of that officer and his respect for your orders, to suppose that he will depart from his instructions.

J Madison Wells   Governor of Louisiana

ALS, DLC-JP.

1. Not found. An editorial supporting the National Democratic ticket and its platform, which "emphatically" endorsed Johnson's administration while condemning proposals for racial equality, was published in the *New Orleans Picayune*, Oct. 4, 1865.

2. The "National Conservative Union" party differed from the National Democrats primarily in its support for the 1864 Louisiana constitution, which the latter condemned. Both parties, however, nominated Wells for governor. Ibid., Sept. 12, Oct. 10, 1865; Taylor, *La. Reconstructed*, 72.

From Charles Hening[1]

Augusta [Ga.]   Octo 7. 1865

Mr President

Permit me an humble man to implore you in the name of our bleeding Union, and of common justice not to pardon Gen Humphry[2] Gov. elect of Mississippi. If you do and he is made Gov. who would have hung you to the first tree as he would a dog, who would have trampled on the old flagg and the Union, will crush to powder every Union man in his state, and liberty will be lost to us, and to them. It should not in my humble opinion be done for many reasons. First it would seem to [be] done, if done at all, at the demand of the Disloyal men of the state, who would not vote for a man who seemed to have any regard for the old flagg & Union but thrust upon us a man whose hands are red with the blood of Union men. Second it will encourage all the late rebelous States to do the same thing, and the true Union men will every where be crushed and the rebbel, will be king as of old. Make these States to know I humbly prey you that none but Union men can be entrusted with Political power. In the name of outraged Union and freedom I humbly ask this.[3]

Chas. Hening

ALS, DLC-JP.

1. Not identified.

2. Benjamin G. Humphreys (1808–1882), a planter and former Whig legislator, had been a brigadier general in the Army of Northern Virginia before being wounded and reassigned to southern Mississippi. Sobel and Raimo, *Governors*, 2: 815–16.

3. Humphreys had already been pardoned. See Humphreys to Johnson, Oct. 26, 1865.

From Mifflin Kenedy[1]

Brownsville Texas   Oct. 7th 1865

MIFFLIN KENEDY, a citizen of the state of Texas and the United States of America, residing at Brownsville, respectfully represents:

That he was born in the state of Pennsylvania and has been engaged since his youth in the managment of Steamboats on the Southern rivers; in the year 1846 he came to Texas and was employed during the Mexican War in transporting supplies for the Army on the Rio Grande. When peace was concluded he remained at Brownsville and formed a partnership under the style of M Kenedy & Co. for the purpose of navigating the Rio Grande with steamboats. He continued in this business as managing partner until the year 1861 and then had under his charge on the Texas side of the Rio Grande six valuable Steamboats and a large amount of material for their repair. He was also interested with Richard King, in a stock rancho called Santa Gertrudes,[2] situated in Nueces County in Texas, about one hundred and twenty five miles from Brownsville, on which in 1861 was a large stock of cattle, sheep, goats, horses and mules, valued at that time at about $300,000. He and Richard King were then and still are general partners in all business, as well in the steamboats as the stock, but the real estate held by them, consisting of pasture lands and houses and lots in Brownsville, was of small comparative value the great bulk of their property being moveable.

That the secession movement in 1860 and 1861 and the war consequent thereon, was so unexpected and sudden, that your memorialist could not remove his property from Texas before the seceding government was established—and after that, it was impossible to obtain permission to remove the stock, and only after long delay could he transfer the steamboats to the Mexican side. He and his partner were therefore obliged to decide whether they would abandon their moveable property, or remain in the state under the new organisation. They were not politicians but simply steamboatmen and stock raisers, who by a lifetime of industry had accumulated this property and desired to preserve it honorably for their children. They did not anticipate a long war, but felt persuaded that it would soon close under some amicable arrangement, and they decided therefore, to remain and protect what they would otherwise lose.

After thus deciding to remain, they felt it their duty to act honorably and sincerely as citizens of the seceding government, under whose protection and laws they came, and they did so during the war, but without any feeling of hostility or enmity to the citizens of the northern states or to those who took a different course. On the contrary, on every occasion in their power, they assisted and protected individual citizens of the United States who needed their aid. As a matter of business, they invested their surplus means in Cotton in Texas and exported it by the Rio Grande, and they were induced to take general contracts to supply the Confederate forces on that river and in western Texas. Their motive for taking these contracts was not so much to obtain profit (because they actually proved unprofitable) as to insure protection to their property on and near the Rio Grande during the war, the Confederate troops posted there not being designed originally to oppose the armies of the United States but to preserve order on the Mexican frontier. Notwithstanding all these efforts a large portion of their stock was appropriated by both parties during the war, or dispersed; and they were obliged to sell their steamboats then belonging to M. Kenedy & Co to Mr. J. Galvan,[3] who transferred them to the United States at the time of the occupation of the Rio Grande by Genl. Banks. Their losses have thus been very heavy and they desire to collect and preserve what remains of their property.[4]

That in all their acts during the war, they have not been influenced by motives of hostility to the United States, and on the contrary sincerely desired at the commencement, that secession could be prevented; but being compelled either to remain in Texas, or abandon every thing, they thought it right to remain, and in that case, felt it their duty not to deceive their old friends and associates by taking a doubtful or insincere course, but to give their candid concurrence to the measures of the new government.

Your memorialist is aware that it may be considered that they failed in the higher duties of allegiance to the United States, and that they should have sacrificed everything to this; but he desires your Excellency to consider the circumstances of the times—the general expectation that the war would last but a few months—the fact that the United States never seriously attempted to recover Texas—the novelty of the political questions—and the character of your memorialist and his partner—as simply men of business and industry without the power or means of judging of these questions in so sudden an emergency.

And your memorialist, after carefully reading your Excellency's Proclamation of the 29th of May 1865 states emphatically that he is not embraced within any of the fourteen exceptions to the general amnesty declared therein except in the *thirteenth*, and in that only so far as his taxable property is over twenty thousand dollars in value. As to a voluntary participation in the rebellion, he refers your Excellency to the preceding statement to determine whether his action was such as to establish this fact according to the meaning of those words and the intention of your Excellency.

Your memorialist has taken the Oath prescribed in the Proclamation (a copy of which is hereto annexed) and is ready and desirous to resume his position as a citizen of the United States and to conform to all the laws and requirements of the constituted authorities of the nation.

He therefore respectfully requests your Excellency to be pleased to extend to him the benefit of the Amnesty under your proclamation above mentioned.[5]

M Kenedy

LS, DNA-RG94, Amnesty Papers (M1003, Roll 55), Tex., Two or More Name File.
1. Kenedy (1818–1895) prospered in steamboating, ranching, and railroad development in Texas. Webb et al., *Handbook of Texas*, 2: 947.
2. King (1824–1885), a New York native, was a partner with Kenedy in steamboating until 1874. He sold Kenedy a half-interest in the Santa Gertrudis land grant of 75,000 acres in December 1860. Ibid., 2: 959; 3: 476.
3. Not identified.
4. Kenedy and King actually profited from their wartime activities. They used the proceeds to enlarge their ranches, including the Santa Gertrudis, which became the nucleus for the 1.25-million-acre King Ranch. Ibid., 2: 959; 3: 475.
5. Both Kenedy and King, who submitted almost identical applications on the same date, were pardoned on November 25, 1865. *House Ex. Docs.*, 39 Cong., 2 Sess., No. 116, pp. 63–64 (Ser. 1293); Amnesty Papers (M1003, Roll 55), Tex., Two or More Name File, RG94, NA.

From John G. Ryan

October 7, 1865, Vicksburg, Miss.; ALS, DNA-RG94, Lets. Recd. (Main Ser.), File G-774-1865 (M619, Roll 359).

A Confederate captain protests that, in spite of his parole, he was arrested in Memphis in July 1865 and placed in prison, "where I was *ironed* DOWN to the *floor*, with a *ball* and *chain* on *each leg*." Subsequently transferred to Old Capitol Prison in Washington, D.C., Ryan was again kept in "*irons*" and spent a week "in a *filthy dungeon*, called the *Sweat Box*." In late August he was sent to Vicksburg Prison Number 1, whence he writes "merely to get *justice*" for this "*gross violation* of the *laws* of the *United States*." He has had "*no trial*, or the *shadow* of a *hearing*, and NO REASON has been OFFICIALLY communicated" to him for his incarceration. [Anonymously accused of having been an "accomplice" in the assassination of Lincoln, Ryan was initially detained on the formal charge of "stealing Government mules." After Joseph Holt exonerated him from any complicity in Lincoln's death, Ryan was sent to Vicksburg to be tried for writing an incendiary article some time after his parole. Gen. Henry W. Slocum hesitated to try Ryan, because the said article had been written *prior* to his surrender. Sharkey forwarded Ryan's appeal with an endorsement and Ryan was released on November 4, 1865.]

From Green Clay Smith [1]

Washington, D.C.   Oct. 7 1865

Sir,

I called to see you the other night on matters which I conceived and so did others, of the most vital importance to the support of your Administration. I did wrong no doubt in leaving so soon, before you could find time to see me. I beg pardon. I have been here all day, and failed again. I make no complaint, but satisfy myself by this note to submit my propositions.

First—If you would secure the peace and quiet of Ky. and save the lives and property of her people, do not I beseech you, now, let the order of Martial law be revoked; there is no safety for Union Men, such as voted for, and now support you—but all are endangered and subjected to the grossest prosecutions. [2]

I agree to the removal of negro troops only because, we have such a large negro population outside to deal with, otherwise I should not ask it. [3]

I do not wish any negro in the state to be a slave, none who have been freed by *any process* to be returned to bondage—but am exceedingly anxious for the Constitutional Amendment to be adopted by which all shall be made free. My party I believe are its only friends—and upon us must depend its success. I am satisfied my plan alone will secure this end.

Genl. Palmer should be removed at once and Genl. Granger appointed to command. My reasons for this were given in full to you in person, and to the Sety. of War in writing. [4]

Enough on this subject.

Second—It seems to me altogether important that the New York election should go for the support of your administration. Twenty thousand votes may decide this point—and I believe it is within your power to secure it. The man condemned and now in prison, [5] whose case I presented a few days ago, for pardon belongs to a peculiar class of people, *Jews*, twenty thousand are in that City, and legal voters—they are clanish, and have the impression that he, Konstarm, is being persecuted, and consequently they will act just as they are made to believe their class is treated. These facts have been presented to me by some of the most prominent men of New York—and clemency is asked by many whose letters you have on your table. My only interest in the matter is to assist my friends of that city; & the cause of the Govt. which I believe can be materially affected by his pardon.

I will not argue this matter now, but merely throw out this suggestion as of great importance. I hope you will pardon the man, and rest assured you will secure this force in New York. [6]

I shall not call to see you any more as I know it would be use-less—indeed I will be pardoned if I say, I shall not hereafter ask a moment of your time—but you shall find now & in the future, in Congress and out a warm and faithful friend of your Administration.

G. Clay Smith

ALS, DLC-JP.

1. The congressman headed one of three different Kentucky delegations which hoped to confer with Johnson. Smith's group evidently was not successful. *Louisville Journal*, Oct. 17, 1865.

2. See Charles J. Meng to Johnson, Oct. 20, 1865.

3. Gov. Thomas E. Bramlette, who headed another Kentucky delegation which had met with Johnson in late September, left Washington with the President's assurances that black troops would soon be removed from the state. Afterwards black regiments were gradually mustered out in Kentucky, but it was April 1866 before all had been demobilized. Coulter, *Civil War Kentucky*, 265; *Washington Morning Chronicle*, Oct. 6, 1865; *Louisville Journal*, Oct. 17, 23, 1865.

4. On the morning of September 27, Smith and Bramlette had an interview with Secretary Stanton, during which Gordon Granger was recommended as a replacement for John Palmer as department commander of Kentucky. Ibid.

5. Solomon Kohnstamm (b. *c*1831), a German-born merchant and owner of a large importing firm in New York City, was convicted in May 1864 of intent to defraud the U.S. government for the lodging and subsistence of soldiers and was ordered imprisoned for ten years. New York City directories (1854–64); *New York Times*, Jan. 17, 1866; James Speed to Johnson, Sept. 29, 1865, Office of Atty. Gen., Lets. Sent, Vol. E (M699, Roll 10), RG60, NA.

6. Kohnstamm's case evidently generated some dissension among Johnson's cabinet members. His petition for pardon and supporting affidavits had already been forwarded from the Executive Mansion to the Attorney General who, on September 29, advised the President against granting executive clemency. Secretary McCulloch had recommended leniency and at least through early December 1865 continued to press for the New York merchant's release. Kohnstamm, however, remained an inmate of Sing Sing Prison until Johnson pardoned him on April 30, 1867. Ibid; McCulloch to Johnson, Dec. 4, 1865, Lets. Sent to President (Letterpress Copies), RG56, NA; Pardon Case File B-117, Solomon Kohnstamm, RG204, NA.

From Francis P. Blair, Sr.

Silver Spring   8 Oct '65

My Dear Mr. President:

I send all my correspondence with the Rebels to you that I may have a clear conscience.[1] I beg you to read & take to heart the enclosed.

"The chivalry of the South" have really a great deal of gallantry & some magnanimity mixed up with meaner material. Your duty & the deep rooted interests of the Country may demand some sternness in your dealing with Jef Davis. I think your purpose of bringing him to trial before a civil tribunal will meet the approbation of the people. But tenderness to his wife on your part, will touch the finer chords in the hearts of the Southern to reconcile them to the course taken to him and will give you a strong hold on the high traits in their character to which I have adverted. I do hope you will listen to her prayer which marks her troubled spirit.

F. P. Blair

ALS, DLC-JP.
1. Blair forwarded two letters from Varina H. Davis. The first was an impassioned plea for his intervention with the President, with which she enclosed a photograph of herself and her infant daughter, Varina A.J. "Winnie" Davis. Davis to Blair, Sept. 26, 1865, Johnson Papers, LC. For the second, see Davis to Johnson, Sept. 26, 1865.

From James M. Campbell[1]

Atlanta Geo   Octo 8th 1865

Dr Sir,
If the appointment of U S. Marshal for the District of Geo in which Atlanta is Situated has not been made[2] I respectfully Solicit the appointment. I have Settled here, and would be pleased to get the situation. I respectfully refer you to Hon D T. Patterson and Col Robert Johnson with both of whom I am personally acquainted, having myself formerly been a resident of Evan's X Roads Greene Co Tenn.

James M. Campbell

ALS, DNA-RG60, Appt. Files for Judicial Dists., Ga., James M. Campbell.
1. Campbell (c1824–1892) formerly worked as a clerk for James Evans, a Greene County, Tenn., merchant. 1860 Census, Tenn., Greene, 25th Dist., Timber Ridge, 114; Reynolds, *Greene County Cemeteries*, 414.
2. Johnson had already appointed William G. Dickson to fill the position. Ser. 6B, Vol. 4: 162, Johnson Papers, LC.

From James Dixon[1]

Hartford   Oct 8, 1865

My dear Sir,
As the period approaches for the meeting of Congress public attention is more and more called to the policy of your administration on the great question of the day. I have hertofore taken the liberty to say to you that your course, thus far, meets the approbation of a large proportion of the Republican party of Connecticut. In this opinion I am daily strengthened & in my intercourse with the people I find the sentiment of approbation growing into the warmth of admiration. It is not, however, to be denied, that there is a element which would gladly denounce your policy. Prudence and discretion may check it for a time, but it cannot be denied that the radical and fanatical element in our party, is mortified to find that its own bitterness and malignity does not control your official action, & fire your heart with its own passionate hatred of the South. But I am convinced that those who share this sentiment are few in number—though from their position they are not without influence. The great heart of the people is full of noble and patriotic feeling, & longs for the day when our Country shall again be united and harmonious. I think I may safely say that three fourths of the Republican party, here, most heartily approve your course.
Of course the entire Democracy are with you, and thus you have the

ardent support of an immense majority of the entire people. This results from the fact that you have done, & so far as we can see, are doing right, for as a general rule the people instinctively see and understand what is & what is not right. They are impressed with the great idea that you favor the early return of the lately rebellious states to their constitutional relation to the government, and that you propose to leave all matters of internal state policy to the decision of the people of the several states. They also understand that you propose, by a wise & magnanimous exercise of the pardoning power, to sooth and calm the disturbed and impassioned feelings of the people of the South and revive in their hearts the love of the Union, which once prevailed there as well as here. Of all this they earnestly approve. They thank God that he has inspired you thus to act. Their enthusiastic gratitude to you would move your feelings, could you see and appreciate it, as it is. Nothing that I have ever seen has equalled it, and I do not hesitate to say that to-day you are, throughout the North, the most popular President since the days of Washington.

The truth is the day of radical fanaticism is over. The People desire justice to the Negro, but they are tired of the perpetual reiteration of his claims upon their attention to the exclusion of all other interests. Moreover, as you will see by the recent vote of Connecticut on the question of extending suffrage to the colored population,[2] there are very grave doubts as to his fitness to govern the country, even *here*; much more doubtful is it, whether the black race, at the South, have yet reached that degree of intelligence which would justify us, even if we had the power so to do, in *forcing* negro suffrage upon the Southern states. The prevailing sentiment, here, therefore, is that this and other domestic questions, should be left entirely to the people of the several States, and that their decision must be accepted by the Government.

My hope is that the next Congress will sustain what I understand to be your policy. Yet I do not think it certain. One thing however is sure, *viz* that if the Southern Senators & Representatives are refused admission to their seats at the next session, the subsequent Congress will be composed of men of another school of politics. An indignant people will set the matter right as soon as they can constitutionally act upon the subject. So that in the end your policy is certain to be adopted whatever the next Congress may do.

I trust you will pardon the length of my letter. This is so important a crisis and the intent I feel in it is so deep, that I could not very well refrain from a free & full expression of my opinions.

James Dixon

P.S. I open my letter to add a word. Can you not consistently release or parol Alexander H. Stephens? That you should do is the ardent wish of *all* your friends.[3]

J. D.

ALS, DLC-JP.
1. U.S. Senator from Connecticut.
2. In a public referendum Connecticut voters rejected black suffrage by a majority of 6,000 votes. Representative John Law of Indiana, a native of Connecticut, also wrote to congratulate Johnson on the referendum in that state. Eric Foner, *Reconstruction: America's Unfinished Revolution, 1863–1877* (New York, 1988), 223; Law to Johnson, Oct. 10, 1865, Johnson Papers, LC.
3. See Order *re* Release of Prominent Confederate Prisoners, Oct. 11, 1865.

From Braxton Bragg

New Orleans.   9th October 1865.

Your memorialist respectfully represents that he has been a citizen of the state of Louisiana and by occupation a planter from the first of January 1856, when he resigned his commission in the United States Army.

That he acknowledged the government *de facto* of the state upon the passage of the Ordinance of Secession; and soon thereafter accepted the command of the military forces, unexpectedly tendered him.

That shortly after the organization of the government of the Confederate States he accepted office as a general in the Army thereof, and continued as such until the close of the war.

That he owned property valued at more than *Twenty thousand Dollars* before the war, which has been in the military possession of the United States since October 1862; but that he believes all that is now left would not be assessed at this time for more than half that amount. He has received no notice of any legal action having been taken for the confiscation of that property.[1]

Finally your memorialist respectfully asks that he may receive the benefits of the amnesty from which he is now excluded, in order that he may be restored to such civil status as will enable him to procure employment and the means of living.[2]

Braxton Bragg.

ALS, DNA-RG94, Amnesty Papers (M1003, Roll 27), La., Braxton Bragg.
1. Bragg's plantation, "Greenwood," was subsequently seized by the United States District Court and sold at auction on January 3, 1866, whereupon he was "forcibly ejected" from the premises in favor of the new owners. He sued for restoration of his property following his pardon under the general amnesty of July 4, 1868, but the Circuit Court denied his appeal, ruling that, as he had not yet been pardoned at the time of the confiscation, the procedure was lawful. Dorris, *Pardon and Amnesty*, 414; *Bragg v. Lorio et al.*, in *The Federal Cases, Comprising Cases Argued and Determined in the Circuit and District Courts of the United States* (31 vols., St. Paul, Minn., 1894–98), 4: 2–4.
2. Despite Governor Wells's endorsement of this application, Bragg received no individual pardon.

From John B. Castleman

Toronto, Canada West.   Oct. 9th 1865—

Sir;

On the 30th day of September 1864, being then in the service of the late Confederate States, in which I held the rank of Captain, I was arrested in the State of Indiana, and for some months held a prisoner under charges arising from the circumstances of my arrest within the Federal lines.

From Indianapolis Indiana, I made an application to your Excellency dated June 7th 1865,[1] asking to be permitted to take the Oath of Allegiance to the United States, and in the event this should not be granted, that permission be given me to become a voluntary exile for such time as might be specified, and subject to such restrictions as you might deem proper to impose.

On the 27th day of June 1865, in accordance with instructions from your Excellency, I was released from Prison upon giving my parole of honor to leave the United States within seven days and not return to the same without permission from the President.

Since my release, with the view of remaining as near my family as was consistent with the requirements of my parole, I have been in Canada, hoping soon to be allowed to return to my Native Country, to which I am bound by the strongest ties of affection and by every feeling of sympathy and of interest. With this preliminary statement, I desire now to ask that I may be granted a pardon by your Excellency, and the privilege of returning to my friends, family and Country, where by faithful efforts to discharge the duties devolving on me as a citizen, I shall prove worthy of Executive clemency.

I most earnestly hope that it will be found consistent with your views of duty and with the public interest to grant my request.[2]

J. B. Castleman

ALS, DNA-RG94, Amnesty Papers (M1003, Roll 25), Ky., John B. Castleman.

1. See Castleman to Johnson, June 7, 1865, *Johnson Papers*, 8: 195–96.

2. Castleman's request for clemency apparently was not forwarded to Johnson until the summer of 1866, after it had been endorsed by Gov. Thomas E. Bramlette of Kentucky, eight members of the 39th Congress from that state, former Kentucky congressman George Robertson, and six prominent Lexington citizens who were associates of Castleman. In response, the President said that if Castleman would return to the United States and apply for pardon, he would "consider the case." Castleman did so, and Johnson revoked his exile on August 27, 1866. John B. Castleman, *Active Service* (Louisville, Ky., 1917), 203–5; Madison C. Johnson et al. to Johnson, June 12, 1866, Castleman to Andrew K. Long, July 30, 1866, Amnesty Papers (M1003, Roll 25), Ky., John B. Castleman, RG94, NA; *Memphis Appeal*, Jan. 5, 1867.

From Richard H. Johnson

Little Rock Arkansas   October 9th 1865—

Mr President

On the accompanying papers,[1] I respectfully ask your Excellency to grant an order for the restoration to me of the property in this city, that is to say my half interest in the same, known as the True Democrat Office.[2]

I have lost nearly all I possessed during and in consequence of the war, and am moreover embarrassed by debts. Outside of my interest in that printing establishment, 560 acres of wild land is all the property I own—my interest in the printing establishment, which has been libeled for confiscation, not being worth more than three or four thousand dollars.

At the close of the war I acquiesed in the result, and have availed myself of your Amnesty proclamation in entire frankness and good faith. The accompanying papers will show, that although indicted for treason I voluntarily returned to Little Rock, and appeared before the Circuit Court of U.S. where I have been acquitted.[3]

One of my creditors has sued out a writ of Error from the decree of confiscation, and the case is now pending in the United States Circuit Court, and my condition is this, that while it is desireable on many accounts for the publication of the paper to be resumed, there may not be an Associate Justice of the Supreme Court of the United States in attendance in this District, so as to try the Errors, for several years to come; and in the meantime the property is daily deteriorating and going to waste.

If your Excellency shall think favorably of this application, I shall have more abundant cause than I already feel that I have for being under obligation to you.[4]

Richd. H. Johnson

ALS, DNA-RG60, Office of Atty. Gen., Lets. Recd., President.

1. Not found. In a subsequent letter Johnson submitted a second application for amnesty, expressing some doubt that the President had received the first petition. Richard H. Johnson to Johnson, Oct. 12, 1866, Office of Atty. Gen., Lets. Recd., President, RG60, NA.

2. Johnson, as editor of the *True Democrat*, had been instrumental in the dominance of his brother, Sen. Robert W. Johnson, in Arkansas Democratic politics during the 1850s and had strongly supported secession. His press was confiscated by the United States District Court in April 1865, at which time he was also indicted for treason. Ibid.; James N. Woods, *Rebellion and Realignment: Arkansas's Road to Secession* (Fayetteville, Ark., 1987), passim; Michael B. Dougan, *Confederate Arkansas* (University, Ala., 1976), passim.

3. Johnson enclosed a copy of the amnesty oath he had taken before the clerk of the United States Circuit Court in Arkansas on October 6, 1865. He later forwarded a duplicate of an oath he took in Galveston, Texas, on August 5, 1865, claiming that he had misplaced it at the time he wrote this letter.

4. The President referred this matter to Stanton, who replied that he had submitted the case to Gen. Joseph J. Reynolds, commander of Arkansas, "for such action as he deems proper and a report." The case was continued by the Circuit Court through the spring term of 1867, when the judge decreed that Johnson would have to obtain an executive pardon even though he came under no exception of the Amnesty Proclamation. In response to yet another appeal from Johnson, the President ordered that he be issued a pardon on August 21, 1867. Stanton to Johnson, Mar. 16, 1866, Lets. Sent to President, Vol. 8 (M421, Roll 3), RG107, NA; Richard H. Johnson to Henry Stanbery, April 1867, Amnesty Papers (M1003, Roll 13), Ark., Richard H. Johnson, RG94, NA.

From John Van Buren[1]

Private—

Willow brook [New York]   Octo. 9th. 65

Dear Sir,

I see you are pressed by Mrs. Le Vert[2] to pardon Beauregard. He is a brother in law of Slidell[3] whom people this way would like to hang. Genl. B. announced that if the Confederacy collapsed he would buy his way to a Foreign Port to save *him* from this humiliation & *you* from the consequences of pardoning him.[4] I will pay his expenses to any Foreign Port he may select.

I have been asked to write you about A. H. Stephens. He is as you know a self made man of great ability & has no affiliation with the high bred Traitors who started this Rebellion. His speech in favor of the Union was the ablest ever delivered.[5] He never attempted to answer it, & nobody else could. His conduct after the conference at Hampton Roads[6] was in the highest degree commendable. Instead of going South as the Rebel press pretended he did to fire the Southern hearts he acted more as if he was going home to break his own.

I have no doubt his unconditional pardon would be well received at the North & do great good at the South.[7]

J. Van Buren

ALS, DLC-JP.
    1. Van Buren (1815–1866), the son of President Van Buren, was a prominent attorney and Democratic partisan in his native New York. Although he bitterly opposed conscription and Lincoln's wartime suspension of habeas corpus, he lent his support to Johnson after the war. *DAB*.
    2. Octavia Walton Le Vert travelled to Washington to ask Johnson to pardon several prominent Confederates. T. Harry Williams, *P.G.T. Beauregard: Napoleon in Gray* (Baton Rouge, 1955), 260.
    3. John Slidell.
    4. Although Beauregard periodically considered self-exile for ten years after the war ended, he remained in New Orleans and had already applied for pardon. Ibid., 258–62. See Beauregard to Johnson, Aug. 12, 1865, *Johnson Papers*, 8: 569–70, and Beauregard to Johnson, Sept. 16, 1865.
    5. Presumably Van Buren refers to Stephens's address to the Georgia legislature on November 14, 1860, the text of which was printed in many northern newspapers. Thomas E. Schott, *Alexander H. Stephens of Georgia: A Biography* (Baton Rouge, 1988), 305–9.
    6. On February 3, 1865, Lincoln and Seward conferred with Stephens, John A. Campbell, and Robert M.T. Hunter aboard the *River Queen* in Hampton Roads. Their

attempt to negotiate a peace settlement floundered on the Confederates' refusal to accept Lincoln's demand for reunion as a precondition for further discussion. James G. Randall and David Donald, *The Civil War and Reconstruction* (Lexington, Mass., 1969), 524–25.

7. Stephens received no individual pardon, but he was released on parole two days after this letter was written. See Order *re* Release of Prominent Confederate Prisoners, Oct. 11, 1865.

From Leroy P. Walker

New York   Oct 9 1865—

Sir;

I leave for Alabama to-night,[1] but cannot do so without first expressing my obligations to you for the pardon you granted me, which, I feel was purely a personal kindness, and not, in any sense, a political necessity.

How very much I appreciate it, the future, now open to me, by this act of clemency, will, I trust, to some extent, at least, demonstrate.

Wishing that your life may long be spared for the benefit of the country which honors you with its confidence and trusts you with its hopes.

L. P. Walker

ALS, DLC-JP.
1. Walker had been in Washington meeting with the Attorney General and the President, who had pardoned him in late September. See Walker to Johnson, Sept. 11, 1865, Amnesty Papers (M1003, Roll 11), Ala., Leroy Pope Walker, RG94, NA.

From J. Madison Wells

New Orleans   October 9th 1865.

To President Johnson

Enclosed you will please find a printed Copy of a memorial[1] adopted by a convention of Planters which lately met in this city, addressed to major Genl Canby through the Governor of the state, with reference to the rebuilding and repair of the Levees. This memorial was presented to Major Gen'l Canby in person by a committee, at which I was present. The committee was politely received on the part of the General, the memorial was read, duly presented to him, graciously received and an early answer promised. On yesterday you may judge of my surprise in having the document returned through me to the memorialists, with the following endorsement.

H'd Quarters Dep't of La. N Orls   Oct 6/65

By direction of the Major Gen'l Commd'g the division of the Gulf, this memorial is returned to the memorialists. I send it through His Excellency the Governor as the readiest means of reaching its destination. Very Respectfully

Signed.   Ed R.S. Canby   M.G.C.

As the proper and only inference to be drawn from this refusal to receive the memorial, was that there was something in it disrespectful,

either to the United States Government or to the military officer to
whom it was addressed, I have carefully read the memorial to discover
in what the offence consisted. After reading and rereading it, I must
confess my inability to detect wherein it is—unless the remarks relating
to acts of the Military in cutting or damaging the Levees, is so construed. If I am correct in this surmise, all I have to say is that the
Commander of the Division of the Gulf Knows very little of the military
operations on the mississippi, if he doubts the truth of what is charged
under that head. Gen'l Canby himself has admitted it by stating in a
previous letter that he would apply to the War Department, to be allowed to expend the sum of $200,000 to rebuild the Levees destroyed
by the military. I always thought the fact was admitted and beyond
dispute. My chief concern in the matter however is not with reference
to the wounded pride of General Sheridan or Gen'l Canby, but the
almost hopeless prospect of having the Levees repaired in proper time
without the aid and assistance of the General Government, which as far
as dependent on the Exertions and agency of the aforesaid Generals, in
view of the rejection of the memorial, may be I suppose finally dismissed. Under these circumstances Mr President I appeal to you in
behalf of my unfortunate and almost ruined State to do something toward rebuilding our destroyed levees, to save it, I may truly say, from
total ruin, for the alluvial lands of Louisiana constitutes her wealth and
fertility. Allow the 8,000,000 of acres as estimated by the Committee
to become a waste and a wilderness, and there is little left, to be worth
struggling for in the way of our political rights under the constitution.
As regards the present bankrupted condition of the State, the impoverished state of the people, and the utter impossibility of the Levees
being restored through such agencies, I take it for granted no proofs is
required to convince you of so patent a truth.

It is sufficient for me to say the State has not one dollar in the Treasury. The idea has occurred to me to raise money by the issuing of
bonds on short time payable from a tax to be levied on the lands benefitted—but such power belongs only to the Legislature, which is not
yet elected. There was one other resource and which I confidently expected would be realized by which the State would have had sufficient
means to have taken the building of the Levees in her own hands. I
refer to the proceeds of the cotton purchased in the Confederacy by the
Louisiana State Bank by a permit from Major Gen'l Butler, on condition that the Bank paid to the state in current funds the sum of $462,
000, then held on deposit in Confederate notes. A sufficient amount of
the cotton so purchased to have satisfied this claim was received by the
Bank in the month of June. I immediately sequestered the same but
Gen'l Canby intervened and took possession of the Cotton as captured
property and belonging to the United States. If that sum could be realized by the state now, I would take the responsibility of using it solely

for the construction of the Levees. If you can do nothing else to assist us Mr President, you can order Gen'l Canby to release that cotton and to that extent contribute to save our State from utter desolation.

I hope sir you will carefully read the memorial I enclose—that you will seriously consider the impending danger and save our people from the threatened ruin.[2]

Madison Wells   Governor of Louisiana

ALS, DNA-RG107, Lets. Recd., EB12 President 3008 (1865).

1. Enclosed was an unidentified newspaper clipping that contained the text of a memorial to Wells and Gen. Edward R.S. Canby. The missive, which asked them to repair the Mississippi River levees, was signed by nineteen men, each representing an "overflowed parish."

2. This letter was forwarded to Stanton. He sent it to Grant, who replied in an endorsement that the national government was not responsible for repairing the levees and that the release of the captured cotton was a matter to be decided by McCulloch. Wells continued to press for presidential intervention in this matter. See Johnson to Wells, Nov. 1, 1865.

From Montgomery Blair

Washington   Oct 10. 1865

My dear Sir

I recommend the pardon of Robert Ould.[1]

In doing so I take the opportunity to submit for your considerations a few observations bearing on all such cases.

Ould is a man of good heart & fair abilities but never a leader in public affairs. He belongs to that subordinate class who were dragged into the Rebellion by those controlling the Govt & in fact by the use of its prestige power and authority.

It seems marvellous to people who look at the rebellion from a distance how so many people who had flourished & thriven under the Union so long should without receiving any injury whatever from the Govt fly to arms—& the enemies of popular institutions draw their customary conclusions that it shows the fallacy of the Republican idea.

But a closer scrutiny explains all this & shows that so far from the wonder being that so many of our people were involved in the Rebellion into which they were united both by passions diligently fomented for a generation, & by duty even as taught by those clothed with the highest authority by the people of the United States, the wonder is that so many refused to follow.

You know the duress put upon our people, tho you yourself withstood it. I beg you however not underrate that pressure because you were proof against it. It is because you with stood it & were able to do so that you have acquired distinction & I trust have still greater in store. That others succumbed was because they had not the nerve & independence to withstand the "constituted authorities."

Is it just mr. President to doom subordinate men—men who op-

posed the Rebellion openly & warmly till overcome whilst Buchanan
& those who held power here with & inaugurated the rebellion go scot
free? It was brought on simply by an effort to continue to hold power
by these men.

M Blair

ALS, DNA-RG94, Amnesty Papers (M1003, Roll 66), Va., Robert Ould.
1. The Confederate agent for prisoner exchange applied for presidential pardon in
September, and it was granted on October 30, 1865. Ould to Johnson, ca. Sept. 5, 1865,
Amnesty Papers (M1003, Roll 66), Va., Robert Ould, RG94, NA.

From Anthony M. Branch[1]

Huntsville Walker County Texas
October 10th 1865.

Your petitioner A. M. Branch a citizen of Walker County Texas,
most respectfully solicits special pardon and amnesty for all offences
that he may have committed in connection with the late rebellion
against the government of the United States, he being excluded from
general pardon by the 1st exception of your Excellency's proclamation
under date of May 29th 1865, by having been a member of the so called
Congress of the Confederate States from the third district of Texas, and
which he solemnly avers is the only circumstance which excludes him
from such general pardon.

Your petitioner states that although he did give aid and support to
the rebel authorities, yet he was never a violent man, and he always
endeavored to treat those who differed with him in political opinion
with kindness and courtesy, and further that since the disbanding of
the rebel armies he has opposed all resistance to the authorities of the
United States and has endeavored to the best of his ability to aid and
assist them in their efforts to restore and reestablish civil government
in the country, and he promises in the future in good faith and to the
best of his ability to support, sustain and abide by, the Constitution and
laws of the United States and all proclamations issued during the late
rebellion having reference to the emancipation of slaves.

Your petitioner further states that he has never been a member of
any vigilance committee organized for the purpose of trying persons
charged with disloyalty to the government of the so called Confederate
States.

That he has never ordered advised or participated in the unlawful
hanging of any man for political offences.

That he has never hunted or advised the hunting down any man with
dogs for offences or alleged offences against the Government of the so
called Confederate States, but has on the contrary alway opposed all
such violent and illegal proceedings.

That he has not in his possession any property belonging to the late so called Confederate States.

That no proceedings have been instituted against his property under the Confiscation act, and that he is not under arrest or in confinement.

He further represents that he earnestly desires to renew his allegiance to the Constitution and laws of the United States, and to conduct himself in all things thenceforth becoming a good and loyal citizen, without reserve or evasion, all of which he solemnly avers to be his earnest intention, that he has taken the amnesty oath as required by said proclamation a copy of which is hereto appended.

He therefore prays for special amnesty and pardon and to be restored to all of his civil and political rights.[2]

A M Branch

LS, DNA-RG94, Amnesty Papers (M1003, Roll 52), Tex., A. M. Branch.

1. Branch (1823–1867) commanded a company in the 21st Tex. Cav. before his election to the Confederate Congress in 1863. He was elected to the 39th and 40th U.S. Congresses, but was refused his seat on both occasions. Warner and Yearns, *BRCC*.

2. On June 6, 1866, "By order of the President," a pardon was issued for Branch. The following summer, after he complained that he had never received his pardon, a second order was sent to the Attorney General's office on July 27, 1867. Andrew K. Long to Matthew F. Pleasants, June 6, 1866, Branch to Lemuel D. Evans, July 9, 1867, Amnesty Papers (M1003, Roll 52), Tex., A. M. Branch, RG94, NA; *House Ex. Docs.*, 39 Cong., 2 Sess., No. 31, p. 11 (Ser. 1289).

From Joseph L. Burts[1]

Bluntville Tennessee   Octr 10th 1865

Dear Sir

I wrote you last spring[2] siting forth my position and the deplorable condition in which I find myself placed in these times of trouble. I informed you that the cruelty perpetrated upon me by union men so called, is not for any crime commited against the government or individuals, but for my opinions sake. I profess to have ever been as loyal as any man living to the government of the united whilst administered according to the letter and spirit of the constitution, but in this horible war, which I believed sincerely was an abolition Crusade against southern rights and property, my sympathies ware with my home & my section of country. But the decision of that strugle has been against us, and I have submitted, have taken the Amnesty oath, and have no other desire than to be a peaceful loyal citizen of the government. But insted of peace the Very foundations of society are rooted up. Their is a set of men spread over this country, called discharged union soldiers, who are commiting all maner of cruelty against the peaceful & very best citizens of the country calling evry man a Rebel, who dont incourage them in their lawless conduct. The men ingaged in these cruelies ware before the war the Very dregs of society, restrained only by the strong arm of the civel law, but now millitary power is removed & the civel in the hands in which it placed is entirely powerless, & Brigandism & mob law conroul the country. The union Flag[3] *so called* published in Jonesboro the Knoxville Whig (& that man with all the influence now in his hands,[4] who once said that you would be sunk so deep in Hell that a canan ball couldent reach you in an age) are all combined to inflame and incourage these deluded and wicked men, in their lawless conduct. In conclution I will say that a large majority of these men have ever been your bitter political Enemies whilst myself and the most of my suffering friends ware sustaining you & building up your political fortunes. You alone have the power to restore peace & order in our land. Will you do it or must our country, be utterly ruined. I would not presume to dictate but will give it as my opinion that if you will place a police in each of these Town under the right sort of officers with orders to make a few examples of these lawless men it will stop it or if the Execution of the state government & laws ware returned to the hands of those who have been disfranchised they will restore peace & order or if neither of these modes will do, if you will give us arms & tell us to protect ourselves I think it will be stoped. I am now a refugee from my once peaceful home driven by these lawless Brigands. The whole country side is anxiously looking to you for relief. Will you grant it?

Joseph L Burts

P S I might send a long list of your old and friends such as Joseph Henderson his sons & hundreds of others but deem it unnecessary to trouble with it.

J.L.B

ALS, DLC-JP.

1. Burts (1798–1881), a long-time Washington County resident, was a farmer and former postmaster who had served briefly in a Confederate home guard unit. Bennett and Rae, *Washington County*, 1: 132; 1860 Census, Tenn., Washington, Brush Creek Dist., Jonesboro, 15; Burts to Johnson, ca. June 1865, Amnesty Papers (M1003, Roll 51), Tenn., Joseph L. Burts, RG94, NA; CSR, RG109, NA.

2. This is perhaps a reference to Burts' letter of ca. June 1865.

3. The *Union Flag* was a newspaper founded by G. E. Grisham, who published it until 1873. Goodspeed's *East Tennessee*, 899.

4. The reference here is undoubtedly to William G. Brownlow.

From James R. Doolittle
Private

Racine   Oct. 10, 1865

Dear Sir

To enable you to comprehend our situation, I send you two of my speeches,[1] out of four, which I have made, in the last 10 days, in defending myself, and the Convention of the Union party, in our state, for standing square up to your policy.

I will send the other two as soon as they are published.

The four taken together Constitute One whole, and in my judgment constitute a triumphant,—a crushing vindication of your policy, and demolish Sumner and Thad Stevens' infernal policy toward the southern states. I hope you will read these two and when I send them, the other two also. I deem it very important to have the four speeches pamphletted together and give them a very broad circulation *before Congress* meets.

Sumner & Stevens are flooding the Country with theirs and the whole of that class, who follow them. It is wrong for us to wait until prejudices and passions, and hate of the south, and avarice, and ambition shall all be joined together hand in hand, before wise statesmanship Magnanimity and returning affection and loyalty can have a fair chance to be heard.

We are breasting the shade of battle here for the Constitutional Union of the states against Concentration of power, *Republicanism* against Imperialism.

When the others appear I will write you again. They should be published at Washington.

J. R. Doolittle

Let those appointments rest until you hear from me again. I mean those Judicial appointments for New Mexico & Colorado.[2]

ALS, DLC-JP.
1. Not found. Doolittle's speech at Madison was published serially in the *Chicago Tribune*, October 11, 12, and 14, 1865.
2. See Doolittle to Johnson, Sept. 23, 1865.

From Robert J. Ker and John R. Conway[1]

Washington City, 10th October 1865

Mr. President,

Delegated by the Democratic Party of Louisiana and representing as we believe, the almost unanimous opinion of the people of Louisiana, we approach you animated with profound admiration of your wise and patriotic administration.

The policy which you have indicated for the rehabillitation of civil government in States which, like our own have been deprived during the conflict of arms of its inestimable benefits, meets with a hearty response from the great mass of our people.

We feel assured they are anxious and ready in good faith to accept all the conditions which, you consider essential to that end: but to accomplish that purpose, it becomes necessary that the people of Louisiana should have the same facilities as the people of States similarly situated, of remodelling their government in conformity with past events; and yet to secure a true and fair expression of the popular will through a

Convention chosen by the people of the whole state, and not by an insignificant faction in a part of the state, which faction, was composed of persons who were not citizens of our state, and of others who were influenced and controlled by military power—for it should be understood that the order convening the members elect of the so called *Convention* of Louisiana of 1864 issued from Major General Banks and *commanded* them to assemble, and that the order appears at the Commencement of their proceedings as their warrant.

The people of Louisiana throughout her several parishes by reason of the notorious fact, that by far the greater portion of her territory was in the possession of an adverse military power, having had no voice in that Convention, rendered any Constitution it could adopt for the state, a nullity.

That Constitution was a paper project, without popular sanction and a nullity, and as such it cannot be ratified: but the time for ratifying it (if such an absurdity were possible as ratifying a void act) by its own provision, passed away on the *1st September 1864.*

The position of the State of Louisiana with this pretended Constitution must not be confounded with the position of the State of Tennessee. The State of Louisiana was only partially within the Federal lines of military occupation when that instrument was formed. A more odious mode of foisting a government on an intelligent people cannot be conceived.

We are aware that, it may be said, this matter of a Constitution for the State of Louisiana is a local affair. We are willing so to consider it, but the so-called Constitution of 1864 is a grievous wrong, and the people can have no redress other than by the interposition of the Federal government.

The people of Louisiana are desirous of resuming their former loyal relations with the Federal government under the provisions of the Constitution, guaranteeing to them a republican form of goverment and are a unit, that is to say, the entire voting population with but few exceptions are ready to accept the results of the late unfortunate struggle; to accept emancipation and assume all its responsibilities.

Knowing the incessant demands upon your time we shall refrain from further arguement, further than, that the people of Louisiana have been deluded and deceived by interested parties who have from time to time, held out to them that it was your intention to appoint a Provisional Governor.

The proclamation of Governor Wells recently issued, ordering an election for State Officers under the socalled Constitution of 1864, taken in connection with other significant facts, would seem to indicate a disposition to accept that Constitution, notwithstanding it has been reprobated by Democratic and Republican opinion of the highest authority.

In this position of our affairs, we have been delegated to make an appeal to you for the appointment of a Provisional Governor of Louisiana, in order that the people, relieved of the rubish of the Convention of 1864, may proceed to form a government consonant with their wishes and which will conform to existing facts and respond to your patriotic intentions.

Robert J. Ker.
John R. Conway

ALS (Conway), DLC-JP.

1. Ker (c1814-fl1887), a New Orleans printer and attorney, had been a candidate for the nomination of the National Democratic Party for the lieutenant governorship. Conway (1825–1896), a wholesale grocer and commission merchant, was later mayor of New Orleans (1868–70). 1860 Census, La., Orleans, New Orleans, 6th Ward, 163; Thomas Cottman to Johnson, July 20, 1865, *Johnson Papers*, 8: 391; New Orleans directories (1861–87); *New Orleans Picayune*, Oct. 4, 1865; Melvin G. Holli and Peter d'A. Jones, eds., *Biographical Dictionary of American Mayors, 1820–1980* (Westport, Conn., 1981), 77. See Wells to Johnson, Oct. 6, 1865.

From John P. Pryor[1]

Memphis, Tenn., Oct. 10th 1865.

Dear Sir:—

Your friends here would be infinitely pleased to have some intimation of your views on the subject of *Negroes testifying in the Courts*.[2] I think I can safely say that throughout all this region there is almost perfect unanimity among the people in support of the policy you are pursuing; and I am quite confident that the expression of your views on the subject referred to, at this time, *would save infinite trouble*.

The enthusiasm you have kindled among the people, would *be very likely to* lead them to harmonize upon the policy you might indicate.

J. P. Pryor.

ALS, DLC-JP.

1. Pryor (b. c1824), a Memphis newspaper editor most recently associated with the *Argus*, had been a Confederate private and captain. In 1868, he and Gen. Thomas Jordan were joint authors of a biography of Nathan Bedford Forrest. CSR, RG109, NA; J. M. Keating and O. F. Vedder, *History of the City of Memphis and Shelby County Tennessee* (2 vols., Syracuse, 1888), 2: 213, 225; J. P. Young, ed., *Standard History of Memphis, Tennessee* (Knoxville, 1912), 446; Pryor to Johnson, Sept. 15, 1865, Johnson Papers, LC.

2. See Johnson to Andrew J. Fletcher, Dec. 9, 1865.

Speech to First Regiment, USCT

October 10, 1865

My Friends:

My object in presenting myself before you on this occasion is simply to thank you, members of one of the colored regiments which have been in the service of the country, to sustain and carry its banners and its laws triumphantly in every part of this broad land. I repeat that I appear before you on the present occasion merely to tender you my thanks for the compliment you have paid me on your return home, to again be associated with your friends and your relations, and those you hold most sacred and dear. I repeat, I have but little to say. It being unusual in this government and in most of the other governments to have colored troops engaged in their service, you have gone forth, as events have shown, and served with patience and indurance in the cause of your country. This is your country as well as anybody else's country. (Cheers.) This is the country in which you expect to live, and in which you should expect to do something by your example in civil life as you have done in the field. This country is founded upon the principles of equality, and at the same time the standard by which persons are to be estimated is according to their merit and their worth; and you have observed, no doubt, that for him who does his duty faithfully and honestly, there is always a just public judgment that will appreciate and measure out to him his proper reward. I know that there is much well calculated in the government and since the late rebellion commenced, to excite the white against the black and the black against the white man. There are things you should all understand, and at the same time prepare yourself for what is before you. Upon the return of peace and the surrender of the enemies of the country, it should be the duty of every patriot and every one who calls himself a Christian to remember that with the termination of the war his resentments should cease, that angry feelings should subside, and that every man should become calm and tranquil, and be prepared for what is before him. This is another part of your mission. You have been engaged in the effort to sustain your country in the past, but the future is more important to you than the period in which you have just been engaged. One great question has been settled in this government, and that is the question of slavery. The institution of slavery made war against the United States, and the United States has lifted its strong arm in vindication of the government and of free government; and in lifting that arm, and appealing to the God of Battles, it has been decided that the institution of slavery must go down. (Cheers.) This has been done; and the Goddess of Liberty, in bearing witness over many of our battle-fields since the struggle commenced, has made the loftiest flight, and proclaimed that true liberty has been established upon a more permanent and enduring basis than heretofore. (Applause.) But this is not all; and as you have paid me the compliment to call upon me, I shall take the privilege of saying one or two words, as I am before you. I repeat that it is not all. Now, when the sword is returned to its scabbard, when your arms are reversed, and the olive branch of peace is extended, as I remarked before, resentment and revenge should subside. Then what is to follow? You do understand, no doubt, and if you do not, you cannot understand too soon, that simple liberty does not mean the privilege of going into the battle-field, or into the service of the country as a soldier. It means other things as well; and now, when you have laid down your arms, there are other objects of equal importance before you. Now that the government has triumphantly passed through this rebellion, after the most gigantic battles the world ever saw, the problem is before you, and it is best that you should understand it; and, therefore, I speak simply and plainly. Will you now, when you have returned from the army of the United States, and take the position of the citizen; when you have returned to the associations of peace, will you give evidence to the world that you are capable and competent to govern yourselves? That is what you will have to do. Liberty is not a mere idea; a mere vagary. It is an idea or it is a reality; and when you come to examine this question of liberty, you will not be mistaken in a mere idea for the reality. It does not consist in idleness. Liberty does not consist in being worthless. Liberty does not consist in doing all things as we please, and there can be no liberty without law. In a government of freedom and of liberty there must be law and there must be obedience and submission to the law, without regard to color. (Cheers.) Liberty (and may I not call you my country-men) consists in the glorious privilege of work; of pursuing the ordinary avocations of peace with industry and with economy; and that being done, all those who have been industrious and economical are permitted to appropriate and enjoy the products of their own labor. (Cheers.) This is one of the great blessings of freedom; and hence we might ask the question, and answer it by stating that liberty means freedom to work and enjoy the products of your own labor. You will soon be mustered out of the ranks. It is for you to establish the great fact that you are fit and qualified to be free. Hence, freedom is not a mere idea, but is something that exists in fact. Freedom is not simply the privilege to live in idleness; liberty does not mean simply to resort to the low saloons and other places of disreputable character. Freedom and liberty do not mean that the people ought to live in licentiousness, but liberty means simply to be industrious, to be virtuous, to be upright in all our dealings and relations with men; and to those now before me, members of the first regiment of colored volunteers from the District of Columbia and the Capital of the United States, I have to say that a great deal depends upon yourselves. You must give evidence that you are competent for the rights that the government has guaranteed to you. Henceforth each and all of you must be measured according to your merit. If one man is more meritorious than the other, they cannot be equals; and he is the most exalted that is the most meritorious without regard to color. And the idea of having a law passed in the morning that will make a white man a black man before night, and a black man a white man before day, is absurd. That is not the standard. It is your own conduct; it is your own merit; it is the development of your own talents and of your own intellectuality and moral qualities. Let this then be your course: adopt a system of morality. Abstain from all licentiousness. And let me say one thing here, for I am going to talk plain. I have lived in a Southern State all my life and know what has too often been the case. There is one thing you should esteem higher and more supreme than almost all others; and that is the solemn contract with all the penalties in the association of married life. Men and women should abstain from those qualities and habits that too frequently follow a war. Inculcate among your children and among your associations, notwithstanding you are just back from the army of the United States, that virtue, that merit, that intelligence are the standards to be observed, and those which you are determined to maintain during your future lives. This is the way to make white men black and black men white. (Cheers.) He that is most meritorious and virtuous and intellectual and well-informed, must stand highest without regard to color. It is the very basis upon which heaven rests itself. Each individual takes his degree in the sublimer and more exalted regions in proportion to his merits and his virtue. Then I shall say to you on this occasion in returning to your homes and firesides after feeling conscious and proud of having faithfully discharged your duty, returning with the determination that you will perform your duty in the future as you have in the past, abstain from all those bickerings and jealousies and revengeful feelings which too often spring up between different races. There is a great problem before us, and I may as well allude to it here in this connection; and that is, whether this race can be incorporated and mixed with the people of the United States, to be made a harmonious and permanent ingredient in the population. This is a problem not yet settled, but we are in the right line to do so. Slavery raised its head against the government, and the government raised its strong arm and struck it to the ground. So that part of the problem is settled: the institution of slavery is overthrown. But another part remains to be solved, and that is, Can four millions of people, raised as they have been with all the prejudices of the whites, can they take their places in the community and be made to work harmoniously and congruously in our system? This is a problem to be considered. Are the digestive powers of the American Government sufficient to receive this element in a new shape, and digest and make it work healthfully upon the system that has incorporated it? This is the question to be determined. Let us make the experiment, and make it in good faith. If that cannot be done, there is another problem before us. If we have to become a separate and distinct people, (although I trust that the system can be made to work harmoniously, and the great problem will be settled without going any further) if it should be so that the two races cannot agree and live in peace and prosperity, and the laws of Providence require that they should be separated—in that event, looking to the far distant future and trusting that it may never come; if it should come, Providence, that works mysteriously but unerringly and certainly, will point out the way, and the mode, and the manner by which these people are to be separated, and to be taken to their lands of inheritance and promise; for such a one is before them. Hence we are making the experiment. Hence let me impress upon you the importance of controlling your passions, developing your intellect, and of applying your physical powers to the industrial interests of the country; and that is the true process by which this question can be settled. Be patient, persevering and forbearing, and you will help to solve the problem. Make for yourselves a reputation in this cause as you have won for yourselves a reputation in the cause in which you have been engaged. In speaking to the members of this regiment I want them to understand that so far as I am concerned, I do not assume or pretend that I am stronger than the laws, of course, of nature, or that I am wiser than Providence itself. It is our duty to try and discover what those great laws are which are at the foundation of all things, and, having discovered what they are, conform our actions and our conduct to them, and to the will of God who ruleth all things. He holds the destinies of nations in the palm of His hand; and He will solve the question and rescue these people from the difficulties that have so long surrounded them. Then let us be patient, industrious and persevering. Let us develop any intellectual and moral worth. I trust what I have said may be understood and appreciated. Go to your homes and lead peaceful, prosperous and happy lives, in peace with all men. Give utterance to no word that would cause dissensions; but do that which will be creditable to yourselves and to your country. To the officers who have led and so nobly commanded you in the field, I also return my thanks for the compliment you have conferred upon me.

New York Times, Oct. 11, 1865.

From Joseph E. Brown

Milledgeville Ga   Oct 11th 1865

Dear Sir

The object of this letter is to invoke your aid by the exercise of the pardoning power in the case of my friend Gov Lowe[1] formerly of Maryland. Gov. Lowe left that state in the summer of 1861 and removed his family to this state where Mrs Lowe,[2] who is a relative of the late President Polk as I understand, has highly respectable relatives. I have know Gov Lowe intimately since 1861 and I know that he has taken little or no active part in the war. He has been generally at home with his family and has taken no part in political matters. The Gov. is a gentleman of fine talent and as you know was once a leading democrat of Maryland.

He filed his petition for pardon in the Executive office in this state, and it received as I am informed, the sanction of the Provisional Governor of the state.[3] At Washington I learn it was given to some Maryland frinds[4] to try to inlist influences in that state in his behalf and in that way it is said it is filed as a Maryland application.

Owing to past political and other differences the Gov. of that state[5] will not recommend his pardon, and other men there may do all they can to prevent it.

In this state of the case I ask that the case be transferred to the list of Ga applications and so considered. Here it has received the necessary indorsemts.

I feel a deeper interest in this case on account of the condition of Gov. Lowe's family. He has a large dependant family of children. Mrs Lowe is a Very amiable and highly cultivated lady. They once had a handsome property, and have lost nearly or quite all of it by the war. The family are left dependant on his exertions and labor for a living. They are my near neighbors, and I feel a deep sympathy for them. If you knew the family as I do, I am quite sure your kind heart would be moved in their behalf, and however much you may disapprove of the course of the Gov. in leaving his state under the circumstances you would extend to him a pardon, and leave him at liberty to resume business in the practice of his profession, in the hope that he may accumulate a competency and make them comfortable and contented.

I trust you will excuse me for troubling you, in the midst of so much care, with this letter. The case is one in which I feel a deep interest.[6]

Joseph E. Brown

ALS, DNA-RG94, Amnesty Papers (M1003, Roll 21), Ga., Enoch Louis Lowe.

1. One of Brown's wartime aides, Enoch L. Lowe (1820–1892) served as Maryland's chief executive in the early fifties. In 1866 Lowe commenced practicing law in Brooklyn, N.Y. James Polk to Simon Cameron, ca. Aug. 1865, Amnesty Papers (M1003, Roll 21), Ga., Enoch Louis Lowe, RG94, NA; Sobel and Raimo, *Governors*, 2: 665–66.

2. Esther W. Polk (c1824-*fl*1901), a distant cousin of the former President, married Lowe in 1844. *NCAB*, 4: 305; Brooklyn directories (1891–1901); 1860 Census, Md., Frederick, Frederick City, 119.

3. James Johnson's endorsement of Lowe's pardon petition is dated August 7, 1865. Amnesty Papers (M1003, Roll 21), Ga., Enoch Louis Lowe, RG94, NA.

4. Former governor Hershel V. Johnson delivered the application to Lowe's father-in-law, James Polk, of Somerset County, Md., who in turn requested Montgomery Blair's aid. Polk to Cameron, ca. Aug. 1865, ibid.

5. Unionist Augustus W. Bradford (1806–1881) was later appointed by Johnson surveyor of the port at Baltimore. After his removal in 1869 he resumed his law practice. Bradford did refuse to recommend Lowe's pardon. *Washington Evening Star*, Oct. 2, 1865; *DAB*.

6. Despite newspaper claims that Lowe received a pardon in late October 1865, he was not actually pardoned until March 14, 1866, the delay being caused partly by Bradford's opposition. *Nashville Republican Banner*, Oct. 27, 1865; *Augusta Constitutionalist*, Nov. 3, 1865; *House Ex. Docs.*, 40 Cong., 2 Sess., No. 16, p. 127 (Ser. 1330).

From Champ Ferguson

Nashville Tenn.   Oct. 11, 1865

Sir:

Please permit me to appeal to you for commutation of sentence in my case.

I have been Sentenced, by Military Commission, to be hanged on the 20th of October instant.[1]

I only ask that my life may be spared: and will humbly submit to such other punishment as you in your clemency may deem fit.

My case is too long for me to recite to You; nor could you among your many and great duties afford the time for an examination.

I desire to state, only, that I delivered myself up by reason of a letter from General Thomas to Genl Rousseau, directing him to receive, a prisoner of War, all independent bands, and their leaders. Others as your excellency is aware, having commanded, during the war, similar bands, to organizations have been jailed and pardoned.

I therefore trust my case may be as mercifully considered. Life is ever desirable! death always terrible. I beg you, in your goodness to save my life! Your power is great, and I feel that your heart is warm.

I pray you to consider my prayer earnestly, and grant me that which no mortal can restore.[2]

Champ Ferguson

LS, DLC-JP.

1. Col. William R. Shafter had gone to the prison the day before Ferguson's letter was written to inform him of the decision to uphold the recommendation of the Military Commission and the date for execution. Thurman Sensing, *Champ Ferguson: Confederate Guerilla* (Nashville, 1942), 247.

2. Although President Johnson also received other entreaties for delaying the appointed execution, he disregarded them, and Ferguson was hanged on October 20. Ibid., 251–53. See also R. M. Goodwin to Johnson, Oct. 9, 1865; M. Winbourn et al. to Johnson, Oct. 16, 1865; John W. James, Jr., to Johnson, Oct. 14, 1865; Maclain L.J. DeVillia to Johnson, Oct. 14, 1865, Johnson Papers, LC.

From Stephen Miller[1]

St Paul   Oct 11 1865.

Hundreds of our best citizens including Supreme Court & State officers ask for commutation of sentence of John Pryor[2] to be executed at Fort Snelling next friday. Please suspend execution till petition reaches you.[3]

Stephen Miller   900 Minnesota St

Tel, DLC-JP.

1. Governor of Minnesota.

2. Pryor (*c*1835-*fl*1889), a native of Ireland, had served in the 3rd Mo. Inf., CSA, until its surrender at Vicksburg. He subsequently joined the 6th Ind. Cav., USA, then

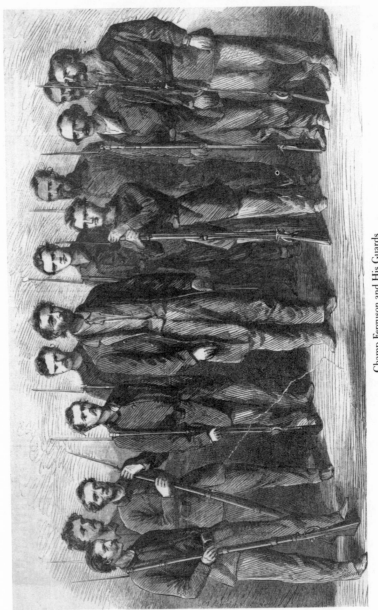

Champ Ferguson and His Guards
Harper's Weekly, September 23, 1865

was transferred to the 1st Vol. Inf., USA, for service in Minnesota. On September 16, 1865, he was condemned for killing a fellow private, who Pryor claimed had robbed him. CSR, RG94, NA; Edmund N. Morrill to Adjutant General, Jan. 10, 1889, Enlisted Branch, File P-1511-PR-1865, John Pryor, RG94, NA.

3. On October 10, 1865, Johnson, at the request of former U.S. senator Henry M. Rice, had already postponed the execution of Pryor. After Miller forwarded petitions, signed by 837 persons, on October 15, the President commuted Pryor's sentence to "imprisonment at hard labor for life." Pryor was sent to the penitentiary at Jefferson City, Mo., whence he forwarded several applications for pardon. Appeals on his behalf from the Missouri legislature and Francis P. Blair availed little, but Pryor was freed in January 1873 after his physician wrote that, due to "consumption," the prisoner had only "a very few months to live." Sixteen years later, Pryor employed U.S. representative Edmund N. Morrill in a futile attempt to have any reference to his murder conviction removed from his discharge certificate. Ibid.; Rice to Johnson, Oct. 10, 1865, Johnson Papers, LC; Johnson to Miller, Oct. 11, 1865, Tels. Sent, President, Vol. 2 (1865), RG107, NA.

Order re *Release of Prominent Confederate Prisoners*

Executive Office   October 11 1865

Whereas the following named persons, to wit: John A. Campbell of Alabama; John H. Reagan, of Texas; Alexander H. Stephens, of Georgia; George A. Trenholm, of South Carolina; and Charles Clark, of Mississippi, lately engaged in rebellion against the United States Government who are now in close custody, have made their submission to the authority of the United States, and applied to the President for pardon under his proclamation;[1] and whereas the authority of the Federal Government is sufficiently restored in the aforesaid states to admit of the enlargement of said persons from close custody, it is ordered that they be released, on giving their respective paroles to appear at such time and place as the President may designate, to answer any charge that he may direct to be preferred against them; and also, that they will respectively abide, until further orders, in the places herein designated, and not depart therefrom: John A. Campbell, in the State of Alabama; John H. Reagan, in the State of Texas; Alexander H. Stephens, in the State of Georgia; George A. Trenholm, in the State of South Carolina, and Charles Clark,[2] in the State of Mississippi; and if the President should grant his pardon to any of said persons, such person's parole will be thereby discharged.

(Signed) Andrew Johnson.[3]

Copy, DLC-JP, Ser. 7A, Vol. 2: 42–43.

1. See Campbell to Johnson, June 22, 1865, Amnesty Papers (M1003, Roll 2), Ala., John A. Campbell, RG94, NA; Trenholm to Johnson, June 6, 1865; Stephens to Johnson, June 8, 1865; Reagan to Johnson, July 18, 1865, *Johnson Papers*, 8: 193, 202, 431; Clark to Johnson, Sept. 12, 1865.

2. Clark had already received a parole from the President. Johnson to Clark, Sept. 28, 1865, Johnson Papers, LC.

3. A slightly different version of this proclamation, which appears in Richardson, *Messages*, 6: 352, may have been reprinted from a newspaper, as this document was widely disseminated.

From Frederick Steele[1]

Brownville. Texas.   Oct. 11. 1865.

I have information deemed reliable that Isaac Surratt,[2] whose mother was executed, left Monterey Mexico, a few weeks ago, with the intention of going to Washington for the purpose of assassinating the President. He has changed so much since he left home that his sister would not recognize him.

He is a desperate character. I have made a report to General Sheridan[3] giving a discription of Surratts person.

(Sgd) F Steele. Major General Comdg.

A true copy. O H Howard[4]
Bvt Maj. Chf Sig officer

Copy, DLC-Philip H. Sheridan Papers.
   1. Steele (1819–1868), a West Point graduate, served continuously in the army from 1843 until his death. During the Civil War he commanded troops through most of the major campaigns in the Trans-Mississippi. Warner, *Blue.*
   2. Isaac D. Surratt (1841–1907), the eldest son of Mary E. Surratt, went to Texas after the election of Lincoln and there enlisted in the 33rd Tex. Cav., CSA. He fled to Mexico after the war, but returned and gave his parole at San Antonio on September 18, 1865. Helen J. Campbell, *Confederate Courier* (New York, 1964), 21–22, 143; Joseph George, Jr., "'A True Childe of Sorrow': Two Letters of Mary E. Surratt," *MdHM*, 80 (1985): 405n.
   3. Philip H. Sheridan, commander of the Department of the Gulf, relayed Steele's warning to Stanton. The War Department monitored Surratt's activities closely for awhile, but he eventually settled peacefully in Baltimore. Ibid.
   4. Ocran H. Howard (1838–1888), a former midshipman in the United States Navy, served with the 2nd Mass. Inf. during the Civil War and remained in the regular army until 1876. Powell, *Army List*, 383; Heitman, *Register*, 1: 546; Pension File, Sarah Howard, RG15, NA.

From Charles W. Webster[1]

Westminster, Carroll Co., Md., Oct 11th 1865
Sir:

A pardon, signed by your Excellency, for a certain W. D. Hartley,[2] was this morning placed in my hands. Hartley has been indicted in this State upon two separate charges of treason against the State under an Act of the General Assembly of Maryland passed March 6, 1862, Chap. 235, to which I beg leave to refer your Excellency. By this Act you will perceive that treason is an offence under our Criminal Code. It is not necessary for me to advert at present to the particular circumstances in this case. Hartley, however, is now held in our jail to answer the charges above referred to, as offences against the State of Maryland.

Presuming that your pardon was not intended to operate as a release of Hartley from prison while there held under charges for offences against the State, I have directed the Sheriff not to release Hartley, knowing of no law which would justify that officer in so doing. There are many other former citizens of Maryland in the same condition as Hartley; some fifty in this county; who are either under bail or in prison, and I should be pleased to know the policy and views of the Government in regard to all their cases.

Has the President of the United States power and authority to pardon criminals for offences against the laws of a particular State?

And will pardons granted by the President of the United States be considered as a release, from bonds and imprisonment, of persons now held under the State laws punishing treason?[3]

By informing me fully upon this subject your Excellency will confer a very great favor upon. . . .

C. W. Webster,
"The State's Attorney," for Carroll County Md.

ALS, DNA-RG94, Amnesty Papers (M1003, Roll 30), Md., William D. Hartley.
1. Webster (b. c1810) was a Maryland native and longtime resident of Carroll County. 1860 Census, Md., Carroll, Westminster Dist., 166.
2. William D. Hartley (b. c1848) had "absconded from the home of his parents" and joined Company B, 35th Va. Btn., CSA. On April 22, 1865, he took the oath of allegiance and returned home, where he was soon arrested by civil authorities. He had been pardoned on September 11, 1865. Amnesty Papers (M1003, Roll 30), Md., William D. Hartley, RG94, NA; *House Ex. Docs.*, 39 Cong., 2 Sess., No. 116, p. 3 (Ser. 1293).
3. There is no record of a reply or subsequent executive action, inasmuch as presidential pardons were constitutionally restricted to offenses against the United States.

From James B. Campbell

Charleston So Ca   Oct 12" 1865.

Dear Sir.

I venture respectfully to ask your attention to the following matter. On the premises of Messrs J. M. Eason & Bro[1] Machinists and Iron Founders in this City, is posted on the principal door, the following.

Notice.
Proposals will be received for the purchase of this Foundry and its contents,
For particulars apply to
Comdr H.N.P. Arnold[2] U.S.N.
Officer in Command Naval Forces Present.

Mr Eason on seeing this applied or caused an application to be made to the Naval Commander here by which he obtained an extract from an order of the Admiral, explaining the action of Capt Arnold, as follows.

Capt H.W.T. Arnold will associate with Chief Engineer Chasang and Mr Moran(?)[3] and cause to be posted on the Naval Machine Shops in Charleston, an advertisement for sale of the premises.

Sealed proposals shall be endorsed—Proposals for the purchase of the Naval Machine Shop, Charleston S.C. by Messrs——— or Mr——— and forwarded to Secretary of Navy Washington D.C.

W. Radford[4]   Admiral   Hampton Roads.

I do not doubt there is some strange mistake in this matter, which will be explained upon enquiry. It is not to be readily assumed that any Military or Naval officer, or any department of the Government would intentionally undertake this short method of confiscation, in the face of your official declaration to the effect that property cannot be confiscated, except by judicial decision. Yet the facts of the case are as they appear above. They make one thing clear, that the retention of Mr Eason's property is not a Military or Naval necessity. Your Excellency will perhaps recollect, I had the honor to present to you the application of a number of our citizens[5] to have their property put into their possession for the purpose of repairing the damages done to it, at their own expense, to be held just as liable to confiscation in their possession as while in possession of the Government—the claims of which were in no wise to be waived or prejudiced. A considerale portion of the property—such as wharves and ware houses are essential to the revival of trade in Charleston. I thought the proposal very creditable to the signers, and likely to be approved by the Government. I was not mistaken I believe, as to your approbation—but the matter has been delayed at the War Department, and more than three months have elapsed without any decision. The property the use of which is essential to the Commerce of Charleston continues useless and day by day is falling into irreparable ruin.

Mr Eason's work shops were a part of the property applied for and he was among the signers of the application. His premises have continued unused and useless to the public, which greatly needs his sort of work, and are going to ruin greatly to his injury. They were taken possession of by the Military at first, and afterwards turned over to the Naval forces. They were of course used by the Rebel powers in their day.

Mr Eason is a man of Sterling character—a hard working enterprising man who has made his own way in the world—has been and is likely to be again a member of our Legislature. Has in good faith taken the Amnesty Oath and practices in that respect, as in all others, what he promises—has applied for pardon under the 13th exception—his petition has been approved by Gov Perry and is in the Attorney Generals Office or before your Excellency. Is it too much for me to ask and hope of you, to relieve him? I shall be personally obliged for the act of Clemency and justice which restores him to his rights and usefulness to the public.[6] I am constrained to report that there is great difficulty in obtaining from the Military—especially the Quarter Masters Department the property of pardoned persons, even when such persons are willing to meet the convenience of Government and expect only a moderate compensation for its use. They the (Quarter Masters) still seem to *claim everything* as "Prize of War.["]"[7] On the other hand, greatly to the gratification of our people, Genl Saxton (Freedmans Bureau) appears to be executing in perfect good faith and promptly your policy as I understand it. Everything in South Carolina has gone on and will continue as I predicted. There is one thing in which I believe our people can be always relied upon. I mean the practice of *good faith*. When they say peace they mean it. They went in for the square open fight. They are now in for a square open peace.

Jas. B. Campbell

P.S. My attention has just been directed to the printed notice appended to the margin of this, published in this mornings papers.[8]

ALS, DLC-JP.

1. James M. (*c*1820-*fl*1881) and Thomas D. Eason (*c*1822–1872). The elder Eason was also a state legislator (1860–66, 1878–80). 1860 Census, S.C., Charleston, Ward 7, Charleston City, 46; Charleston directories (1852–81); *Charleston Courier*, Dec. 28, 1872; Joan S.R. Faunt et al., comps., *Biographical Directory of the South Carolina House of Representatives* (2 vols., Columbia, 1974), 1: 384, 389, 392, 398, 430.

2. Henry N.T. Arnold (*c*1825–1881) was naval officer from 1839 until his retirement in 1871. 1880 Census, D.C., Washington, 39th Enum. Dist., 29; Edward W. Callahan, ed., *List of Officers of the Navy of the United States and of the Marine Corps from 1775 to 1900* (New York, 1969[1901]), 28; Abstracts of Service Records of Naval Officers, 1798–1893, Vols. J-1, L-1 (M330, Rolls 7, 11), RG24, NA.

3. Benjamin E. Chassaing (*fl*1867), a Maryland native and naval engineer since 1857, was "Superintendent of Vessels" at the Charleston machine shop. William Moran (*c*1819–1903), an occasional sailor from 1841 until 1886, was at this time acting third assistant engineer. *U.S. Off. Reg.* (1865), 247; *OR Navy*, Ser. 1, Vol. 16: 378–79; Register of Engineer Corps (Officers), 1842–61, Vol. 1: 123, RG45, NA; Abstracts of Service Records of Naval Officers, 1798–1893, Vol. L-1 (M330, Roll 11), RG24, NA; Pension File, William Moran, RG15, NA.

4. A career navy man, William Radford (1809–1890) retired in 1870 and settled in Washington, D.C. *DAB*; *NCAB*, 4: 294–95.

5. A reference to the petition which Johnson had received and referred to Stanton on August 19. Johnson endorsed the petition: "I am inclined to recommend that the property in question should be restored to the claimants." Robert Adger et al. to Hugh McCulloch, June 30, 1865, Lets. Recd. (Main Ser.), File P-1544-1865, RG94, NA; Ser. 4A, Vol. 1: 64, Johnson Papers, LC.

6. James M. Eason, who admitted to having manufactured at least two "Iron Clad Gun Boats—for the State," was pardoned on October 16, 1865. Amnesty Papers (M1003, Roll 45), S.C., James M. Eason, RG94, NA. For further developments concerning the status of Eason's Foundry, see Gideon Welles to Johnson, Oct. 24, 1865; James B. Campbell to Johnson, Nov. 5, 12, 1865, Johnson Papers, LC; *Charleston Courier*, Oct. 21, 1865, Jan. 26, 1866.

7. See, for example, Michael Powers to Johnson, Oct. 25, 1865.

8. Not found. This was probably a copy of Commander Arnold's order. *Charleston Courier*, Oct. 12, 1865.

From Salmon P. Chase

Washington   Thursday Evg. Oct 12th 1865

Dear Sir,

Your letter of the 2d directed to Cleveland, & forwarded to Sandusky reached me there night before last.[1] I left for Washington yesterday morning and am just arrived.

To your enquiry whether a term of the Circuit Court of the United States for the District of Virginia will be held by myself or one of the

Associate Justices of the Supreme Court during the autumn or early winter, I respectfully reply in the negative.

Under ordinary circumstances the regular term, authorized by Congress would be held on the 4th Monday of November which this year will be the 27th. Only a week will intervene between that day and the commencement of the annual term of the supreme court when all the Judges are required to be in attendance at Washington. That time is too short for the transaction of any very important business.

Were this otherwise I so much doubt the propriety of holding Circuit Courts of the United States in States which have been declared by the Executive and Legislative Departments of the National Government to be in rebellion & therefore subjected to martial law, before the complete restoration of their broken relations with the nation & the supercedure of the military by the civil administraton, that I am unwilling to hold such courts in such states within my Circuit, which includes Virginia, until Congress shall have had an opportunity to consider and act on the whole subject.[2]

A civil Court in a district under martial law can only act by the sanction and under the supervision of the military power; and I cannot think that it becomes the Justices of the supreme Court to exercise jurisdiction under such conditions.

In this view it is proper to say that Mr. Justice Wayne,[3] whose whole circuit is in the rebel states, concurs with me. I have had no opportunity of consulting the other Justices; but the Supreme Court has hitherto declined to consider cases brought before it by appeal or writ of error, from Circuit or District Courts in the rebel portion of the country. No very reliable inference, it is true, can be drawn from this action for circumstances have greatly changed since the Court adjourned; but so far as it goes it favors the conclusion of myself & Mr. Justice Wayne.

S. P. Chase

ALS, DLC-JP.
    1. See Johnson to Chase, Oct. 2, 1865.
    2. Johnson forwarded his inquiry and this response to the Senate in February 1866, after it had requested copies of presidential correspondence with the Supreme Court regarding treason trials in the South. On April 2, 1866, Johnson issued an executive proclamation declaring the rebellion at an end in all southern states except Texas, but Chase did not convene a circuit court in the South until May 1867. *New York Times*, Feb. 3, 1866; Richardson, *Messages*, 6: 429–32; Blue, *Salmon P. Chase*, 263–66.
    3. James M. Wayne (c1790–1867), a former congressman from Georgia, served as an associate justice of the Supreme Court from 1835 until his death. *DAB*.

From Sarah J.C. Whittlesey[1]

Alexandria [Va.]   Oct. 12th. 1865

President of the United States:

I respectfully enclose a copy of an order issued by "the Major General commanding this department,"[2] believing from past proclamations, you are not aware of the astounding fact that one of your subordinates defies your authority. Years ago, I met you in the Senate, and subsequently in the State Department; and as a native of my own dear State; as an *honorable man*, and great head of this people, I come to you, as a child to a father, and ask you, with humble boldness, by all that is good and merciful to help us, or we shall be driven to desperation, by such men as the "General commanding this department."

Our town is overrun with negroes, and they are daily coming in by scores—they are a lying, lazy people, in their present ignorant state, who will not work so long as they can steal, be supported by the Government, and protected by Northern men, who treat them cruelly, except where kindness enables them to gratify their hate for Southern white men. They will not engage for service for less than an exorbitant sum, which our people in their poverty, which *abolition first* and *secession second* have wrought, are not able to pay; they rent rooms, and run off, between two days to avoid paying for them—they cry "poor white trash" in the streets; carry guns and pistols, and threaten white men at pleasure; and if the white man, in self-defense turns upon his assailant, he is arrested by the *military authorities* and committed to jail, while the negro is left free. You are a southern man, sir, and well know what is absolutely necessary for a negro—they cannot be left to run wild, and behave decently; we should get along smoothly together, if Northern men, who being "clothed with a little brief authority" are "playing such fantastic tricks before high heaven, as make the angels weep!",[3] would not interfere with our civil authorities, and trample upon State laws; and that too, against *your* command! I am a well known loyalist, sir, together with my father and brother,[4] and do not bring to you the complaints of a rebel and prejudiced heart; but I come to you as one who *knows* our people have been imposed upon, tormented and tortured by Yankee officials, for the last four years, who have professed to be fighting from *patriotism*, when their sordid small soul is in their *pocket*, until the word UNION has an unsavory smell to the most faithful Southern heart to the Government. Now that war is ended, and our Southern people are returning to their allegiance—and I assure you, sir, they are more reliable than those who wear the livery of the United States, and steal from its Treasury—shall our State laws be crushed under *military* heels, and our city authorities driven before *military* commands? We are in frequent dread of an insurrection among the negroes, they are so ignorant and easily led by those who *profess* to be their *best* friends, and if they are permitted to supply themselves with guns and pistols, another and worse war, we believe to be inevitable. The northern men we firmly believe will *secretly* lead them on to destroy the Southern people, and then *openly* turn and exterminate them (for in their hearts they hate the race)—and take full possession of the coveted Southland.

Last Summer, in Connecticut, I heard a Yankee say, who wears the prefix of Rev to his name: "Virginia has got to have her nose put to the grindstone, and then pay for the turning"—and "*we* must give the negroes the right to vote in order to *keep the Southern people down.*" President Johnson, *you* are a *Southern man*; *I* am a *Southern woman*, and those remarks burned my brain like livid lightning! I found *that* was the spirit that prevailed wherever I went, and I did not remain there through the summer, as I contemplated. I left the State in disappointment and disgust. That same *Rev.* rejoiced at the assassination of President Lincoln because, he said "Andy would hang the rebels"—as you did not, he abused you in my presence. Sir, are such men ["]to keep the Southern people down," with the force of a *negro's* foot?

Pardon me for presuming to address you—I do it without the knowledge of any one, believing you will sympathize with a suffering people, and reward their oppressors according to their deeds, when you are appraised of their mischievous tendency. Your position is such that you cannot know all the torments to which our people are subjected by those in authority under you, without private information; and I know you have ever done justly when appealed to by an oppressed and almost despairing people.

Sarah J.C. Whittlesey

ALS, DNA-RG105, Records of the Commr., Lets. Recd. from Executive Mansion.

1. Whittlesey (1825–1896) was a poet and a novelist. Oscar F. Adams, *A Dictionary of American Authors* (Detroit, 1969[1904]), 422.

2. The order had actually been issued by the provost judge's office under the authority of Gen. Alfred H. Terry, commander of the Department of Virginia. It sought to guarantee and protect the civil rights of blacks recently arrested for having violated a local curfew.

3. From Shakespeare's *Measure for Measure*, Act II, sc. ii.

4. Lunar Whittlesey (b. *c*1795), a Connecticut-born tutor, and Oscar C. Whittlesey (1826-*fl*1871), an attorney and state printer. 1850 Census, Va., Alexandria, Alexandria, 661; *NUC*; Alexandria directories (1867–71).

From Samuel D. Baldwin

Nashville Tenn   Oct 13/65

Dear Sir.

I owe you thanks—thanks a thousand times over; and I am formally instructed by the trustees of McKendree and by the congregation to return you heartfelt, glowing thanks for your kindness in the restoration of their church property and house of worship.[1] On the day of their reunion,[2] the vast assembly gave utterance to their grateful emotions in streaming tears and rapturous songs and fervent prayers, in all of which you were remembered as God's chosen minister of mercy to them and to our people. Their prayer for you is noteworthy. It was that you might long live, the prosperous *president of the nation*; the *guardian* of the *States*; the *representative* of the *people*; the *conservator* of true *democracy*; the *foe* of *aristocratic & financial despotism* and of *autocratic* and *Puritan* politics; and become immortal as the *pacificator of the Continent* and "the *iron rod*" to *European ambition* and *encroachments*.

Your order of relase to us has created an admiration & love for you & a trust in your, which no political decree could ever accomplish; and while my pen & tongue are free, you will never lack a publisher of your noble deeds to distressed humanity & christianity.

Saml. D. Baldwin.

P.S. The pen portrait of yourself (brought to your notice by McClellan)[3] was sent to the *Missouri Democrat*, and was to have been published by that paper & through the North West. They said it would do you vast good; but they deceived your friends & destroyed the article to prevent your growth of popularity in that region—so I learned on yesterday. Another copy of the original has been sent for by other papers in St. Louis and will be furnished in a few days.[4] I can do but little to repay you for kindness to our people, yet as far as my influence can reach it shall be used to make your fame as *permanent* as it is merited. Excuse so long a letter.

S.D.B.

2. P.S. The Missouri Democrat is not your friend, but your hypocritical foe.

S D B

3 P.S. General Thomas has not executed your order in full, hence the delay in the acknowledgement of your kindness. I waited to thank you for a *fully* executed purpose of liberality.

B.

ALS, DLC-JP.

1. The problem of the McKendree Church had already received an inordinate amount of attention from President Johnson. He had been in office scarcely a month when he telegraphed Baldwin to ask why the church had not been turned over to its original owners. Baldwin replied about two weeks later. Following that there were various exchanges of communication between the President and Methodist officials. Finally on August 23, the Rev. Allen A. Gee notified Johnson that he had given the church keys to General Thomas's secretary that day. Johnson to Baldwin, May 15; Baldwin to Johnson, June 5; Gee to Johnson, Aug. 23, 1865, *Johnson Papers*, 8: 72, 180–81, 645–46.

2. Evidently Baldwin here is referring to the last Sunday in August, when he first assumed the pulpit of McKendree Church.

3. Probably John McClelland (1814–1885) of Nashville, who worked for the Nashville and Chattanooga Railroad and was also U.S. internal revenue assessor for Nashville during the Johnson administration. *Nashville American*, Aug. 2, 1885; *Nashville Banner*, Aug. 1, 1885; *U.S. Off. Reg.* (1865–67).

4. A pen portrait of Johnson was in fact published in the *Missouri Republican* on November 3, 1865, three weeks after Baldwin's letter. The document is reprinted in full in *Johnson Papers*, 7: 679–85.

Exchange with South Carolina Convention Delegates[1]

October 13, 1865

The President inquired the object of the memorials. Judge Wardlaw informed him that one of them was in behalf of Jefferson Davis, A. H.

Stephens, George A. Trenholm, and Geo. Magrath. He said they had understood that by the late interference of the President, Messrs. Stephens and Trenholm had already been released from close confinement, and permitted to return to their homes.[2] He would ask for George Magrath either a pardon or that he might be released on parole.[3] They could assure the President that no harm would result from such an act of clemency.

The President replied that all could not be pardoned at once. The business must be proceeded with gradually, and an effort made to execute the law. A discrimination was necessary as we went along. It was a too common expression, by way of argument in regard to clemency, that such a one had been pardoned, and that he was just as bad as another who had not been pardoned.

Judge Wardlaw replied that the delegation presented no such argument as that.

The President said sometimes the peculiar locality had much to do with pardons. Like many other things in human affairs, we cannot have a fixed rule. Much depends on discretion and circumstances. If we know ourselves, we want to do what is best and just, and to show a proper degree of humanity on the part of the government.

Judge Wardlaw remarked that they had not come hither to express their own hopes and desires, but as delegates from the South Carolina Convention to present the memorials of that body in a formal manner.

The President—We will, gentlemen, extend all the facilities and courtesies which the questions require. We would prefer to pardon twenty men than to refuse one.

Judge Wardlaw replied that they did not design to say anything with reference to Gov. Magrath further than that they believed much good would result by the exercise of the Executive clemency toward him.

Col. Dawkins said if we can get Gov. Magrath paroled, it would be a great relief to him at the present time.

Judge Wardlaw thanked the President for having released Messrs. Stephens and Trenholm.

The President—We have that far, then, anticipated your memorial.

Mr. Huger said Mr. Trenholm was one of their most useful men, and there was no doubt he would exert all his power with a view to entire harmony between the State and the government.

The President replied that he understood that was so; adding if treason was committed there ought to be some test to determine the power of the government to punish the crime. He was free to say that it was not a mere contest between political parties, or a question as to *de facto* government. Looking at the government as we do, the laws violated and an attempt made at the life of the nation, there should be a vindication of the government and the constitution, even if the pardoning power were exercised thereafter. If treason has been committed, it ought to be determined by the highest tribunal, and the fact declared, even if clemency should come afterward. There was no malice or prejudice in carrying out that duty.

Judge Wardlaw remarked they were well aware of that.

The President, resuming, said there may be some unkind feeling on the subject, but it did not exist to any great extent.

Judge Wardlaw said although not instructed by the convention, he was induced to ask whether Mrs. Jefferson Davis, who was now confined to Georgia, could not cross into South Carolina to see her friends.

The President replied that he had received letters from Mrs. Davis,[4] but they were not very commendable. The tone of one of them, however, was considerably improved, but the others were not of the character becoming one asking leniency.

Judge Wardlaw interposed by saying she was a woman of strong feeling.

The President—Yes; I suppose she is a woman of strong feeling and temper; but there is no intention to persecute her. There is as much magnanimity and independence and nobleness of spirit in submitting, as in trying to put the government at defiance. True magnanimity takes things as they are; and when taken in the proper way I disconnect them from humiliation. Manifestations of temper and defiance do no good.

Mr. Huger remarked that they had a deep consciousness of the truth of all the President said.

The President, resuming, observed that the character of an individual may characterize a nation, which is nothing but an aggregate of individuals, and when a proper spirit is manifested, all can act harmoniously. The man who goes to the stake, is almost dignified by his bearing; it lifts him above humiliation. In these cases, gentlemen, we will do the best we can. While there is sympathy, there is a public judgment which must be met. But I assure you, gentlemen, no disposition exists for persecution, or thirst for blood.

Judge Wardlaw remarked that the tone of the newspapers was more favorable and different from what it was. He then asked if the President had seen a copy of the amended constitution of South Carolina. Of course he had seen that we accept emancipation. He felt perfectly satisfied that the person and property of the negro will be protected, and spoke of the great difficulties of regulating labor, and of restraining vagrancy, &c.

The President thought many of the evils would disappear if they inaugurated the right system. Pass laws protecting the colored man in his person and property, and he can collect his debts. He knew how it was in the South. The question when first presented, of putting a colored man in the witness stand, made them shrug their shoulders. But the colored man's testimony was to be taken for what it was worth by those who examine him and the jury who hear it. After all there was not so much danger as was supposed. Those coming out of slavery cannot do without work. They cannot lie down in dissipation; they must work. They ought to understand that liberty means simply the right to work and enjoy the products of labor, and that the laws protect them. That being done, and we come to the period to feel that men must work or starve, the country will be prepared to receive a system applicable to both white and black—prepared to receive a system necessary to the case. A short time back you could not enforce the vagrant law on the black, but could on the white man. But get the public mind right and you can treat both alike. Let us get the general principles, and the details and collaterals will follow.

A conversation of some length ensued between the President and Judge Wardlaw and Mr. Trescott,[5] as to the legislation of the State necessary in reference to the condition of the freedmen, and to the scope and consequences of the Circular No. 15 and General Orders No. 145, from the Adjutant-General's Department, relative to abandoned lands in South Carolina and other Southern States.[6] The examination of these subjects, it is understood, is to be continued at another interview.

The President said: "We must be practical, and come up to surrounding circumstances."

Judge Wardlaw, Col. Dawkins and Mr. Huger, all expressed to the President their conviction that the State had accepted in good faith the result of the issue which had been made; that the people felt that the President had stood between them and a harsh use of the power of the government; that they felt entire confidence in his purposes and actions, and hoped in return to entitle themselves to his confidence as to their feelings and actions.

The President replied he was glad to hear it; that whenever such mutual confidence existed, there would, he thought, be an open road to the restoration of good feeling and a prosperous condition; and that, if he knew himself, and he thought he did, he would recommend nothing but what would advance their interests. So far from pandering or looking to future elevation, he must be believed when he said he had not an eye single to such preferment. If, he continued, I could be instrumental in restoring the government to its former relations, and see the people once more united and happy, I should feel that I had more than filled the measure of my ambition. If I could feel that I had contributed to this in any degree, my heart would be more than gratified, and my ambition full.

New York Times, Oct. 14, 1865.

1. Convention president David L. Wardlaw with fellow delegates Alfred Huger (1788–1872), a Cooper River rice planter, former state senator, and longtime Charleston postmaster, and Thomas N. Dawkins (1807–1870), attorney, state legislator and formerly a governor's aide, had been appointed a committee to present memorials to Johnson. Brown, *Am. Biographies*, 4: 218; *Cyclopedia of the Carolinas*, 1: 253.

2. See Order *re* Release of Prominent Confederate Prisoners, Oct. 11, 1865.

3. Issued a parole in late November, Andrew Gordon Magrath was finally pardoned by order of the President on January 19, 1867. Amnesty Papers (M1003, Roll 46), S.C., A. G. Magrath, RG94, NA.

4. See Davis to Johnson, Aug. 30, 1865, *Johnson Papers*, 8: 672–73; Davis to Johnson, Sept. 26, 1865.

5. William H. Trescot.

6. See Edisto Island Freedmen to Johnson, Oct. 28, 1865.

From Philip H. Sheridan

New Orleans La   Oct 13 1865.

J. B. Hood late General in the Rebel Army is desirous of a personal interview with Mr. Davis to get at some military information in connection with his military career.[1] He has made a full statement to me of his object, which would require an interview of a few minutes. May I respectfully ask your permission for this interview?[2]

He has made his application for pardon.[3]

P. H. Sheridan   Maj Genl

Tel, DLC-JP.

1. In the fall of 1865 Hood was eager to write his memoirs and had asked Sheridan, his West Point classmate and fellow officer in the 4th U.S. Inf., to request permission for a visit with Jefferson Davis to collect information. Richard M. McMurry, *John Bell Hood and the War for Southern Independence* (Lexington, Ky., 1982), 193, 196.

2. Johnson forwarded this inquiry on October 16 to Stanton "for his consideration and action," adding in his endorsement that "There may be some reason not known to me why he should be permitted to visit and have an interview with the prisoner." Although another endorsement indicates the request was refused "By order of the Sec'y of War," Stanton telegraphed Sheridan that the President had turned down Hood's application. Hood subsequently travelled to Washington that fall, but with no success. John P. Dyer, *The Gallant Hood* (New York, 1950), 310; *OR*, Ser. 2, Vol. 8: 766, 767.

3. See Hood to Johnson, Oct. 6, 1865.

From James A. Stewart

Rome Ga   Oct 13th 1865

Dear Sir:

Enclosed you will find my circular letter as candidate for Congress;[1] also an editorial from the Rome Enquirer in reference to oath of office &c.[2] You will readily perceive from them, that true Union men here, are stil to be the objects of bitter persecution by Secessionists who have purjured themselves in taking the amnesty oath. Their only object in taking the oath is to qualify themselves to controll elections, so as to keep themselves in power. They are even now, (some of them) boasting what they will do with Union men when the once more get power in their hands. We are to be driven out of the South. I think any modification of the congressman's oath of office for the ensuing congress, would do gross injustice to true Union men of the South.[3]

J. A. Stewart

ALS, DLC-JP.

1. We have been unable to find the circular in the Johnson Papers, though a copy did appear in the *Rome Courier* of October 12, 1865. Although acquiescing in emancipation, Stewart pledged that he would "work in Congress" to secure for his constituents "just compensation for private property taken for public use by the Federal Army."

2. The editorial has not been located in the Johnson Papers.

3. In early November Stewart withdrew from the race which Gen. William T. Wofford eventually won. *Rome Courier*, Nov. 9, 1865. See Alexander N. Wilson to Johnson, Nov. 25, 1865.

From Jacob R. Shipherd[1]

American Freedmen's Aid Commission
Washington, D.C., Oct 14th 1865.

Sir;

I have the honor to submit to your Excellency, a copy of a communication from Genl. Wager Swayne,[2] Commissioner of the Bureau of Refugees, Freedmen, and Abandoned Lands, for the State of Alabama.

While it forms no part of the purpose of the American Freedmen's Aid Commission or any of its officers, to delay by one moment the earliest restoration of the conditions of peace, consistent with the National welfare, it is not, perhaps, improper that we should appear before your Excellency in the interest of a class who certainly have occasion for a next friend, if their case is to be fairly stated.

The case represented by General Swayne, chances to be personally familiar to me; and I am able to attest the accuracy of his statement in every essential particular.

The Medical College belonged to the State of Alabama:[3] had been liberally aided from the United States Treasury, as I am informed; was vacant during the war; was found unoccupied when our forces entered the city; has been occupied with the sanction of Genl. Andrews and Gen Woods[4] by teachers and pupils who have preserved the premises with the utmost care, and who have not only preserved, but improved them at an outlay of over a thousand dollars, chiefly contributed by the industrious colored citizens of Mobile.

The Trustees have no present use for the building, and do not expect to have for fully two years to come; while the Genl. proposes, with the co-operation of this Commission to expend some $3000—in needed repairs, and to restore the building and contents at the end of two years, unharmed.

The issue, therefore, cannot be disguised.

The Dean himself,[5] who proposes to apply to Your Excellency for the restoration of this building to the custody of the Trustees, declares, in a letter dated as recently as the 20th of September, that he is "hoping to save enough from the wreck of his property to get out of a *Free Country*", and upon the same page makes wholesale charges of the most grossly slanderous character upon the representative friends of the freed people whose endeavors to render these unfortunate outcasts less un-worthy members of society have provoked his temper, and thus betrays what cannot be concealed under pretentious phrases.

The white citizens of Mobile, displeased that negroes should desire to improve their intellectual condition, and yet more displeased, it would almost seem, that any white persons should be found, perverse enough to encourage these improper aspirations, have by threats and actual violence, and incendiarism, driven the schools from every other shelter, and now besiege six hundred (600) cowering children, in their last and only fortress.

Sheltered by the right hand of the Government, that has been up-lifted to declare that having decreed, it would *maintain* and *defend* their freedmen, they are safe from their unnatural neighbors.

Shall they, may it please Your Excellency, continue safely sheltered, until the first violence of this storm of indignation is overpast?

It cannot be doubtful with us, that the President of the United States will esteem it a rare and precious privilege, in so clear a case of simple kindness to the weak, without injustice to the strong, to secure for himself a harvest of benedictions from the lowliest of the land, who even because they are the lowliest have a first claim to generous justice.

The rapid return of estates in all parts of the South to their former owners has already almost estopped schools in many places; and the violent antipathy of the already dominant classes will all but extinguish them elsewhere, as now at Mobile, unless the potential aid of Executive favor shall stay them in instances like the present.

In conclusion, it might be observed that the finest school in Louisi-ana is held, as it has been for two years past, in a Medical College building like that at Mobile, selected and fitted for school purposes by Maj Genl. Banks, and was, when I inspected it in March last, in as perfect order and repair as it could have been if no African child had ever passed the portals of intellectual life in crossing its threshhold; and that the Superintendent[6] in charge of the school at Mobile is intimately and personally known to me as eminently fitted for the conscientious discharge of the delicate and difficult trust at present confided to him.

Gen Swayne is doubtless known to Your Excellency as the son of Justice Swayne[7] of the Supreme Bench, a Kentuckian, and with no prejudice in favor of the negro as such.

Trusting that no apology is necessary for this frank, and direct ad-dress to the President, upon a test case of great moment, I hasten to releive the President's patience by subscribing myself, upon behalf of the Commission,[8]

Jacob R Shipherd   Secretary.

LS, DNA-RG105, Records of the Commr., Lets. Recd. (M752, Roll 23).

1. A graduate of Oberlin College, Shipherd (c1837–1905) later served as pastor of a Congregational church in Chicago until shady business dealings allegedly forced him to resign. Afterwards he engaged in banking and real estate development before returning

to his native New York, where he took up law and established a Peruvian investment firm. *Atlanta Constitution*, Mar. 25, 1882; Louis D. Hartson, ed., *Alumni Register* (Oberlin, Ohio, 1960), 8.

2. See Swayne to Shipherd, Sept. 30, 1865, Records of the Commr., Lets. Recd. (M752, Roll 23), RG105, NA.

3. The college began in 1859 without state aid but during its first winter the state legislature provided money to buy a building. Reginald Horsman, *Josiah Nott of Mobile: Southerner, Physician, and Racial Theorist* (Baton Rouge, 1987), 239, 245.

4. Christopher C. Andrews and Charles R. Woods.

5. Josiah C. Nott (1804–1873) had been instrumental in establishing the Medical College and had served as its professor of surgery and also its dean. Although Nott's biographer implies that the doctor presented petitions to Johnson, we have been unable to substantiate the claim. Swayne to Shipherd, Sept. 30, 1865, Records of the Commr., Lets. Recd. (M752, Roll 23), RG105, NA; Horsman, *Josiah Nott*, 238–39, 245, 296–97, 304; *DAB*.

6. E. C. Branch (*fl*1867), who had taken possession of the college on October 12, was in 1866 appointed superintendent of schools for the Mobile district of the Freedmen's Bureau. Branch to Wager Swayne, Oct. 12, 1865, Aug. 20, 1867, Asst. Commr., Ala., Unregistered Lets. Recd., RG105, NA; Special Orders No. 53, Mar. 28, 1866, Recs. of the Commr., Lets. Sent (M742, Roll 7), RG105, NA.

7. Noah H. Swayne.

8. Shipherd's letter was referred to the Freedmen's Bureau, where General Howard directed the agent at Mobile to take action to return the buildings to the trustees of the Medical College as soon as possible. Yet, in November when Howard visited Mobile and conferred with Nott, he reversed his position. By the fall of 1866 the College had been returned to the trustees, though it did not resume its original operations until two years later. *Senate Ex. Docs.*, 39 Cong., 2 Sess., No. 6, p. 12 (Ser. 1276); Horsman, *Josiah Nott*, 296–97; Max Woodhull to Johnson, Oct. 26, 1865, Records of the Commr., Lets. Recd. from the Executive Mansion, RG105, NA.

From John H. Almond[1]

Nashville, Tenn., Oct. 15th 1865.

My Dear friend;

A feeling that I cannot repress impels me to intercede for and in behalf of a gentleman whose self and family have always been kind to me and mine. It pains me to witness his distress and that of his family. The Rebellion is the cause of his trouble, but I think that his proverbial abstinence from politics before the war, should be taken as evidence in his favor. He is perhaps less guilty than many I might mention, who now, by the exercise of your clemency, are restored to the full posession of their property. I do not know positivly whether his application for pardon has been rejected or not, but he has not yet obtained it. I make this application on my own responsibility, without his, or his families knowledge. If you will grant him pardon, and allow me the privilege of delivering it to him, you will confer a favor upon us both, that a life of gratitude cannot sufficiently compensate you for. I refer to the case of John Overton of Davidson County Tennessee.[2]

Our Paper is in a healthy condition. We have been with you in your "Reconstruction Policy" from the beginning, and will continue in that faith to the end of the Chapter. Though you have been elevated to the highest Office in the gift of the American people, I trust you will never have cause to regret your action with the "Association of Printers," of which I am a member, in starting the Nashville Union. In our course we will endeavor to merit your approbation.

Hoping that God may impart to you, the wisdom, the will, and the physical strength, to discharge the duties that devolve upon you as President of our great Republic. . . .

John H. Almond.

ALS, DNA-RG94, Amnesty Papers (M1003, Roll 50), Tenn., John Overton.

1. Although affiliated with the *Nashville Union* at the time of this letter, Almond (c1834-fl1889) soon moved to Louisville, where he worked for the *Louisville Journal.* 1870 Census, Ky., Jefferson, Louisville, 3rd Ward, 57; Nashville directories (1865–66); Louisville directories (1868–89).

2. See Frank C. Dunnington to Johnson, Nov. 2, 1865, and William G. Brownlow to Johnson, Nov. 20, 1865.

From John McClelland

Nashville   Oct 15th/65

Dear Sir & Friend

Last night, Just after supper, a poor fellow came to my door and asked one of the children for something to eat. She went to get it for him. It was dark, I went to the door to invite him in, he stepped back & stood away from the door as if to avoid the light. I told him to come in and be seated in the Hall, but he refused. My Daughter then came up with a cup of coffee some victuals and a light. He abruptly excused himself, left the door and passed out of the gate into the street and disappeared.

Of course there was a great deal of speculation as to motives which prompted his strange conduct. Some thought he was an escaped prisoner, and one of the children said "Pa, may be it was Champ Ferguson who is making his escape." My thoughts at once turned to the condition of the forgotten, helpless, friendless man, in his cell whose days of existence are numbered by 6 for on Friday the 20th inst he dies— forgotten by all except his wife and family, and the officers of the Law, who are too sure to see that the sentence shall be executed. I could not sleep untill I had determined to write you, and ask for a respite, untill his attorneys & friends can get forward a statement of his case. There can certainly no harm arise by a little extension of time. He has done no more than thousands of others, who have never been arraigned at all. "Tinker Dave"[1] as he is called has been guilty of as many enormities as Ferguson. Humanity has been as much outraged by Payne[2] as by the worst Brigand in the country. Then let us try heal the sores of the nation, so as to leave no more scars than the War has already made. Would it not be better to commute his sentence to 20 years imprisonment, and then in a year, or 2 or 3 let him out. For God sake send the order for a respite, over the wires, for on Friday he dies. I have no doubt of his guilt, but look at the surroundings—The feuds in his section— the entire want of all law—the raids by irresponsible bodies of men, of both sides through that portion of country, and we can more properly estimate the temptation to crime.

But we want peace, and the restoration of social order in our neigh- borhoods, especially in East Tennessee. The Divine Virtue of forgive- ness should be taught by precept and example, by all our state officials. The words "Traitors Rebels" &c should be discarded in all discussion and news paper controversy, and if possible teach the people to forgive & forget all injuries.

Rev S D Baldwins remarks, a few Sundays since, on the subject of restoring the churches, were most appropriate and beautiful. The churches are crowded every Sunday, and the ministry are doing their duty, nobly.

Mr Burns[3] is bussily engaged with his Rail Roads, and I think is managing them well.

Since the death of slavery, Rail Roads are destined to be the great influential interest of the state and I am glad our Friend Burns has so large a share in their management. His well known integrity of char- acter—His liberal support and encouragement of all the industrial pur- suits of the state—His personal friendship for you, all combine to make him one of the most influential supporters of the administration, in the state.

The Tennessee Conference has just closed its session.[4] All was har- mony. All were pleased and no lack of prayers for the President of the United States. It was a noble policy which restored the churches to the people.

Jno McClelland

ALS, DLC-JP.
1. See David C. ("Tinker Dave") Beaty to Johnson, *Johnson Papers*, 6: 666–67.
2. Eleazer A. Paine, Union general at Gallatin, who was notorious for his atrocities in the Middle Tennessee area. Walter T. Durham, *Rebellion Revisited: A History of Sum- ner County, Tennessee From 1861 to 1870* (Gallatin, Tenn., 1982), 186–92.
3. Michael Burns.
4. For contemporary accounts of the October meeting of the Tennessee Conference of Methodists, see *Nashville Press and Times*, Oct. 5, 8, 14, 1865.

From R. Weakley Brown

Nashville Ten   Octo 16, 1865
My Dear Friend
Your very kind and to me most welcome gratifying favor of the 9th ult has been rec'd.[1] The truly patriotic—and I may say Christian spirit pervading the entire letter, filled my heart with joy and increases my admiration and friendship for its author. God grant that the present

State Executive and members of the Legislature may be hereafter animated by the same noble spirit and statesmanlike views. Unfortunately
for the Country a very large majority of the ablest and best men in the
South despairing of the Union in 1861—joined the rebellion—and the
times have unfortunately brought into public life many men of smaller
minds and smaller hearts. But nevertheless I cannot beleive that God
created this government and placed George Washington as its head in
vain. The Govt has put down the most gigantic rebellion every arrayed
against any nation, and you the peoples Tribune—and the man of Destiny—are called by the Great Ruler of the Universe—to proclaim peace
to the nation, and restore *good will* among the people. Though the
clouds are loosening—and the destructionists and radicals are gathering their hosts to crush you—I cannot—will not beleive they can
succeed—for the rebellion was wrong and it went down. So is consolidation wrong—and God grant Republican government may stand.
The war the radicals are waging against you is wrong. You are in the
right—and my faith is strong that you will triumph—and the good and
true men everywhere should rally to you and save our glorious heritage
of freedom from the madness of fanaticism. I will enlarge on this theme
at another time. I must come to specialities now. Since writing to you
about 2 weeks since—I have not been idle.[2] Our old friend Genl Frank
Cheatham tells me "you are the Saviour of the Country." Your old
friend & Adj Gen' Granville P. Smith says "The salvation of the Country depends on you." A short time after receiving your letter I met our
old friend Hon' Geo W. Jones—and knowing the warm friendship that
has so long existed between you & him—I deemed it no breach of your
injunction in your letter *"Private"*—to read it to him. We talked over
the past, and he was affected almost to tears. He fully concurs with me,
that the only hope for the Country is for every man to rally to you.
There is a magnetic attraction or affinity between Democrats, which
though parted by circumstances for a time will reunite them again. And
I beleive that your truest and best friends in the future as in the past
previous to the rebellion will be found in the old Democratic party. But
you know I am a thorough beleiver in the principles of Washington's
farewell Address—and having witnessed the baleful effects of party
spirit which the father of his country so much deplored—I earnestly
desire—and my ardent prayer is that all Tennesseans—irrespective of
past party associations—should now especially in this trying crisis rally
as one man to Andrew Johnson, the Constitution and the Union. Now
is the time for Unity of action—and no discord. Regarding you as the
great intellect of the age and the conservative Head of the Government
(This I say as no empty compliment but the solemn conviction of my
mind) I of course have more confidence in your superior intellect and
political sagacity than my own. While I concede this much, I know
there are many things taking place here which you cannot see, and can

only hear of through a *friend.* There is an idea prevailing here to some considerable extent that you are pardoning many of the most solidly rebilious Democrats and passing over whigs who were far less guilty. I mentioned to you in my last letter that my relative Hon R L Caruthers, Hon N. S. Brown Gen John C. Brown most cordially endorsed your late Address to the Southern Delegation. Ex Gov N.S.B. made a most stirring patriotic speech to the meeting at the Court House called to respond to your address.[3] I think that immediate pardon granted to these gentlemen and some other whigs would have a most happy effect upon the old whig party. You know you have made me your firm personal friend by kindness. The same cause will have the same effect upon most other men. And I tell you truly that John C Brown and many other men I could mention—are much better men than I am in many respects. Kindness to and confidence in the honor of the brave is the way to make firm friends of them. If these gentlemen—are pardoned—immediately they will be released from the penalties of the U S District Court—which convened to day—has the power to inflict on them. I think they have suffered enough already. Judge Caruthers was imprisoned in the penitentiary in July last and remained there until my cousin Judge Trigg[4] came to Nashville—and released him on bail. His property has been swept away by the war and his good christian wife[5] is in great distress about him—so much so—that I thought some months since there was great danger of her mind's giving way. Judge C was blinded in 1861—himself—Gov B and others thought the Union was gone forever after the fall of Fort Sumter. I never saw any man die—over the Union harder than Gov B. His mental anguish was torturing.

Again Dr Granville P Smith is bound over to the Court in a bond of $10,000. He told me last evening—that he went into the war from an honest conviction of duty—that he accept the result had taken the *amnesty oath* in *good faith*—and was as *loyal* as *any man* to the *government*, and I solicit you to pardon him immediately—at *his earnest solicitation.*[6] The motives that actuate me in behalf of these men—are personal friendship—patriotism, and christian love or charity. They put no money in my purse. No thank God—I am governed by higher—purer motives. If I know my own heart I am laboring—for the good of my country—my fellow men—and for your own good—*politically* and *spiritually.* I met with Brother A L P Green[7] today. He was delighted with his interview with you recently. You made the right impression on him. Some days ago—I met Brother Adam S Riggs[8] P E. in the Shelbyville District. He is one of best christians I ever saw—and warmly approves your policy. I have more influence with my Methodist brethren than any other persons. I tell them plainly it was wrong to join the rebellion—although they were forced to separate from the Northern Church in 1844. I shall impress upon them the fact that you are the friend of *religion* as well as constitutional liberty—and 'tis *their duty* to *rally* to *you* as *one man*. Pardon this long letter—and I close with my prayers & blessing.

R. W. Brown

Please excuse bad writing—and inaccuracies—as I have not time to copy this—besides I know you will pardon it on the score of bad health. N.B. I causally met Ex Gov N. S. Brown in the street to day—had a short conversation. He remarked to me "that as long as you pursued the policy you were pursuing—he would support you as ardently as he ever did Henry Clay." I thought that was to the point and covered the whole ground.

R.W.B

ALS, DLC-JP.
   1. We have been unable to locate a September 9 document from Johnson to Brown.
   2. See Brown to Johnson, Sept. 30, 1865.
   3. Reports of the September 23 meeting in Nashville at which Neill S. Brown, along with others, spoke are found in the *Nashville Union*, Sept. 24, 1865.
   4. Connally F. Trigg.
   5. Sarah (Sally) Saunders (1807–1870) had married Caruthers in 1827. Jeannette T. Acklen, comp., *Tennessee Records* (2 vols., Baltimore, 1967[1933]), 1: 287; *BDTA*, 1: 132.
   6. Smith's quest for a pardon had something of an involved history, beginning in mid-summer when he first took the oath and forwarded to Johnson a request for a pardon. Because it was rejected on a technicality at the time, Smith remained unpardoned until the fall months. Apparently Brown influenced Smith to seek a pardon again, for on October 19 Smith wrote to the President requesting such. Johnson personally endorsed the letter: "Issue pardon in this case." Smith was pardoned on October 25, but not realizing this development he again took the oath and wrote to Johnson on October 27. Smith to Johnson, Oct. 19, 27, 1865, Amnesty Papers (M1003, Roll 51), Tenn., Granville P. Smith, RG94, NA; *House Ex. Docs.*, 39 Cong., 2 Sess., No. 116, p. 50 (Ser. 1293).
   7. Alexander L.P. Green.
   8. Riggs (c1817-fl1870) was a Methodist minister. 1860 Census, Tenn., Bedford, 21st Dist., 60; (1870), Shelbyville, 20.

From David G. Burnet[1]

Washington   October 16th 1865

Sir

In presenting to your consideration the accompanying documents, alluded to in my note of 13th inst.[2] I beg leave to remark:

The issues of battle, which are ever the dispensations of a divine Providence, have placed in your control the person of the late Chief Magistrate of the subdued and extinct Confederacy, Jefferson Davis.

That we, the pioneers of Texas whose labors and privations were the first instrumentalities in introducing the great "Lone Star" State into this illustrious constellation, in common with the entire South regard Mr. Davis with profound veneration and affectionate sympathy, is a natural sequence of our late political connection with him and of our knowledge of his eminent political and moral virtues. We consider him, in his present sufferings, as a vicarious sacrifice and no more justly obnoxious to the vengeance of the laws alleged to have been violated by the recent effort to establish a separate nationality in the South, than any one of ourselves. His exalted position was imposed upon him by the unsolicited suffrages of his compatriots and can attach no more of guilt to him personally (if guilt is to be ascribed to any) than to either one of the many ten thousand brave men who placed him there. But wherefore impute *guilt* to a political offence, by a similitude to which, in all its essential properties, our immediate ancestors constituted you and all of us members of a free and independent government? The whole moral difference in the two series of events is involved in the one simple fact of failure!! While success consecrates revolution and converts its actors into heroes, failure brings odium upon every motive however pure and disrepute upon the most illustrious of those who sought to accomplish the highest good for that region of country which peculiarly enlisted and intensified their every statement of patriotism. If on this basis of failure the jealousies of political power have erected the authority to punish the higher and holier principles of humanity have established and the laws of God have enjoined the exercise of a glorious clemency.

Although specially commissioned by a few pioneers of Texas, I feel authorised to assume that the entire population, with a few inconsiderable exceptions, concur cheerfully and ardently in the beneficient purpose of the memorial. I will avail myself of this opportunity, to say to Your Excellency that, there is no intelligent, rational man in Texas and probably in the South who entertains a thought of renewing the unhappy controversy, the gratuitous assumptions of a partizan press to the contrary notwithstanding. Having been decisively overpowered in arms, they frankly yield the contest and have good sense and magnanimity enough to return with full purpose of fidelity, to their first allegiance recognising the law of a sovereign God, the Judge of all the Earth, in the inevitable issue. That they regard the instant emancipation of their slaves as a grievous measure it would savor of dissimulation to deny. They know it to be fraught with immense loss to themselves and with disastrous results to the ignorant, improvident race whose well being was the professed object of it. One consequence already developed by a brief experience is, a very general and gross demoralization of that ill-fated, indolent race.

That there is a prevailing desire to render to the freed man full protection in person and in property and such equality as these import, is generally true and is by no means impugned by a conviction that all persistent artificial and compulsory efforts to elevate the negro to a social and political equality with the white man must enure to the proximate extinction of the inferior race, while it will debase the superior in the precise ratio of its practical operation. The heritage of the son of Ham precludes such equalization.

David G Burnett.

ALS, DNA-RG94, Amnesty Papers, Jefferson Davis, Pets. to A. Johnson.
1. Burnet (1788–1870), former president of the Republic of Texas, was elected to the United States Senate in 1866, but was not allowed to take his seat. Webb et al., *Handbook of Texas*, 1: 252–53; 3: 127.
2. Burnet had requested, and later obtained, an interview to present petitions on behalf of Jefferson Davis from seventy-five settlers of Stephen F. Austin's colony (who asked Johnson to extend the same mercy that Burnet had to Santa Anna) and from the "Ladies of New Orleans." Burnet to Johnson, Oct. 13, 1865, Johnson Papers, LC; Dorris, *Pardon and Amnesty*, 286–87; *Lynchburg Virginian*, Jan. 29, 1866.

From Thomas C. English

October 16, 1865, Monroe County, Ala.; LS, DNA-RG94, Amnesty Papers (M1003, Roll 3), Ala., Thomas C. English.

Gen. George B. McClellan's brother-in-law has just taken the amnesty oath, though he does not feel "in conscience that he falls within any of the exceptions" in the President's proclamation, estimating that "his property over and above his just debts is considerably less than $20,000." But "others might value the same higher"; hence, his application. During the war English remained on his plantation "pursuing his usual round of duties," though when the state militia was organized, he served as a captain, active only in the county, from October 3, 1864, until war's end. Having satisfactorily answered Governor Parsons' interrogatories for pardon applicants, English assures Johnson that to the best of his ability he will "be a peaceable & loyal citizen in the future." He asks the President to grant him "a special pardon and reinstate as perfectly as it ever was his right of person and property." [English was pardoned December 15, 1865.]

From John H. Gilmer[1]

Richmond, Va.   Oct. 16th 1865

Dear Sir

I very respectfully enclose you a copy of the remarks made by me—at the close of the Polls, in this city—on the 12th Inst.[2] I can in good faith, assure you, that my words, echoed the real sentiments of my constituency, and indeed that of the People of Virginia.

I understand ungenerous and disingenuous efforts are being made to induce *you* to believe that my election, is an evidence of disloyalty in this community. There is no foundation for this. The people of this city are loyal—and will sustain you, in your firm, wise, sagacious and patriotic efforts, to restore harmony, rebuild the legal and constitutional basis of the Federal government, and restore the *states* to their original position.

John H Gilmer

ALS, DLC-JP.
    1. Gilmer (1812-*fl*1879), a Richmond attorney, had just been elected to the Virginia senate. Richmond directories (1866–79); *NUC.*
    2. Not found.

From Henry W. Hilliard[1]

Washington City, October 16th 1865.

I cheerfully comply with the President's suggestion and make the following statements:

I was decidedly opposed to the measures that brought about the secession of Alabama and other Southern States from the Union.

I was ardently attached to the Union, and endeavoured to perpetuate it. After the secession of the States I refused to participate in any of their measures or to approve their policy, until Virginia & Tennessee manifested a disposition to oppose the threatened coercion of the States.

My first act of actual participation in the measures of the so-called Confederate government was to accept the appointment of Commissioner to Tennessee.

The appointment was unsolicited by me. It was tendered to me by Mr. Davis himself who invited me through a member of his Cabinet to call on him. The invitation took me by surprise. I had made a public speech in Montgomery—(the only one delivered in opposition to secession in that place) at the risk of my personal safety—denouncing the scheme of secession. When then the invitation of Mr Davis was recieved, it found me engaged in my library in literary labors, unconscious that the Confederate Administration had any such purpose. Upon calling on Mr. Davis he urged me to consent to go to Nashville as the representative of the government & I accepted the mission regarding the state of the country as such that I could not decline it.

I desired to settle the unhappy dispute which threw its portentous shadows over the country, by *negotiation*—and to avoid a conflict of arms.

For some eighteen months previous to the close of the war, I felt it to be my duty to oppose the measures of Mr. Davis' Administration. I ardently desired the restoration of peace upon terms that he would not accede to. I exerted all my energy and influence to bring about a reconciliation between the United States and the States that had revolted against it. By my pen constantly employed either in writing articles for the public journals, or in correspondence with gentlemen throughout the South, I sought to end a war that had been already too protracted.

I rejoiced at the restoration of peace—and can in perfect sincerity say, that I glory in being able to claim this *whole country* in its widest extent—as *my country.*

I need hardly assure the President how heartily I approve the comprehensive and statesman like measures by which he is conducting the Government to tranquillity—fraternal mind—and national strength. I trust that I shall be permitted to take part in the great work of reconciliation, with the confidence of the President—with his continued regard—and with the consciousness of owing to his clemency my exemption from any further trouble on account of my participation in the unhappy convulsion which is just ended. Having frankly made this statement, I shall now hope to recieve from the President the *paper* so *anxiously*—yet *patiently* sought—and the *autograph* to which I referred in a late friendly conversation.[2]

Henry W. Hilliard.

ALS, DNA-RG94, Amnesty Papers (M1003, Roll 19), Ga., Henry W. Hilliard.

1. Already an applicant for executive clemency, the former Alabama congressman had journeyed from Georgia to Washington and obtained an interview with Johnson on August 24. Hilliard to Johnson, July 1, 1865, Amnesty Papers (M1003, Roll 19), Ga., Henry W. Hilliard, RG94, NA; *Augusta Constitutionalist*, Aug. 31, 1865; Evans C. Johnson, "Henry W. Hilliard and the Civil War Years," *AR*, 17 (1964): 112.

2. Hilliard's pardon is dated September 14, 1865. *House Ex. Docs.*, 40 Cong., 2 Sess., No. 15, p. 123 (Ser. 1330).

From Reuben D. Mussey[1]

[Washington]   October 16" 1865.

My dear Mr President.

May I crave your indulgence for a few moments to read to you this which I could hardly trust myself to speak?

Accompanying this is an official paper which I beg you to read, and if you can, act favorably upon.[2]

I would not tresspass thus on your time and kindness had you not been so uniformly kind to me in the past and had you not honored me with so many honors and so many marks of your confidence.

You know very well dear Sir how I did my work at Nashville; you know very well my way of life and I believe, I may say, you know me well enough to know that I was not dishonest.[3]

Had you not had that opinion of me I am sure you would never have placed me on duty so near you—in a relation so confidential and honorable.

It is not necessary for me to say to you that I did not convert to my own use the money with the disbursement of which I was charged and the failure to account for which has caused me to write this letter, and the accompanying one.

I expended it as seemed to me proper in recruiting Colored troops according to the instructions of Major Stearns[4] (who acted upon an understanding with the War Department) and of the Recruiting Regulations. That some of the money thus disbursed may not have been in accordance with the strict Regulations is probably true. Few disbursing officers have all the accounts allowed.

There are some $600,000 or $700,000 charged against our friend General Webster[5] who at one time had charge of Rail Roads in Tennessee and General Grant has some $5,000,000 charged against him as I am reliably informed.

My offence consists in having failed to render the monthly returns called for by law. I did wrong not to do so. My only excuse is—I was too busy to do it properly and when, at last, my vouchers were got into some sort of shape they were stolen from the Officer who had them in his keeping. This I told General Fry[6] and promised to produce his Affidavit to the fact. I suppose it is on the way here now.

When you placed me on duty with you and often since the thought of the possible suspicion that might attach to me has made me sad and troubled and it occurred to me more than once whether I ought not to tell you all about it and say to you that perhaps you had better relieve me so that by no possibility might any suspicion attach to you or persons of your official household. But the thought that I might be useful to you—the belief that the failure to render accounts on my part was known only to the War Department and that, there, it was understood—and further the knowledge of my innocence of actual guilt save the guilt of negligence—and yet again the desire to spare you annoyance and pain—you who had so very, very much to annoy and pain you—led me to keep still and I didn't speak to you. I spoke once of this matter to my personal, as well as public friend Mr Dennison[7] and he told me to wait till Congress met and then apply to it for "relief" saying kindly he had no doubt it would be granted readily.

And so I worked on, Dear Sir, trying to do my duty to you—waiting for Congress to meet and then present my case.

Recently—that is within three or four months—I have seen that the War was thoroughly over and have felt, as I once told you, very anxious to be in some place where I could be earning my livelihood, looking to a future and rearing my family. And I have been delayed by this unsettled account from resigning—when I saw an opening.

After the first dispatch from General Stoneman[8] I looked about and found a "lead" which I have been "prospecting" at since. And I was determined when this matter took definite shape to present it to you, as I said on Saturday, in all its fullness. Probably, my "Emigration" will be advantageous in a month or less and the Lieutenant General has told me that he not only does not object to my having a "Leave" but favors it.[9]

In one month I could probably collect all that ever can be collected of the papers &c relating to my accounts and can prepare the case, for the action of Congress.[10]

The "Leave" will allow me to show that I have no desire to shirk danger or evade duty and will so enable me to silence all babblers. And it promises moreover to open the way to my personal advantage and the advantage of others.

Feeling that there ought not to be the breath of suspicion attaching to you or to those about you I have made the request to be relieved from duty with you.

I have not done so without regret. For duty with you suited me. I liked to be near you—like to study your character and see how you had hewn out your own fortune what tools you had used and how you had labored. For thereby I learned how to work for myself.

And I admired your Honesty, your Frankness, your Justice, your Kindness, your Faith in the People—your Democracy.

I have tried to save you labor and pain; I have felt for you so keenly when others whom you loved and trusted abused that love and trust; your honor has been dearer to me than my own. Pardon me this confession. I have *loved* you with an affection which few men ever feel for each other—and sinner though I am I have prayed the Almighty always specially to bless you and guide you. And from my Father whose feet almost touch the golden streets—to my little baby whose mother holds it up to kiss your photograph—all of us have been grateful to you for your kindness to me and have prayed God to reward you.

My dear Sir—I have written a long letter. It is not theatrical and assumed. It is felt more deeply than my pen can tell it.

May God bless you.

R Delavan Mussey

ALS, DLC-JP.

1. Johnson's military secretary since April 1865.

2. Not found, but perhaps a paper pertaining to the stoppage of Mussey's pay. See Mussey to Johnson, Dec. 7, 1865.

3. When Mussey's accounts as a disbursing officer for recruitment were settled, a "deficiency" of $28,600 was discovered. Vouchers for a portion of the shortage were later recovered, but Treasury Department proceedings against Mussey were initiated in March 1866. *Washington Evening Star*, Mar. 8, 1866; *Nashville Union*, Mar. 10, 1866.

4. George L. Stearns.

5. Joseph D. Webster, former chief of staff for Gen. George H. Thomas.

6. James B. Fry, provost marshal general.

7. William Dennison, postmaster general.

8. Gen. George Stoneman had wired Johnson an extract of Special Orders Number 94 by which, "subject to the approval of the President," Mussey was ordered to report "without delay" to his regiment in Tennessee, the 100th Inf., USCT. Stoneman to Johnson, Oct. 9, 1865, Tels. Recd., President, Vol. 4 (1865–66), RG107, NA.

9. On October 27 the President granted Mussey thirty days' leave, effective November 1. On December 2 the War Department ordered him to Nashville to be mustered out of the 100th Inf., USCT, and to "join at once" his original unit, the 19th U.S. Inf. Johnson to Mussey, Oct. 27, 1865, Johnson Papers, LC; CSR, RG94, NA.

10. No congressional action in Mussey's case has been discovered.

From Howell Cobb

Athens Ga.   17 Oct 1865

Dr. Sir

This letter will be handed to you by my near relative and friend Genl Henry R Jackson[1] of this state. I respectfully request that you will grant him a private interview, on the subject upon which I now address you. When summoned to Washington as a witness[2] I directed my application under your amnesty proclamation (which was then before Gov Johnson) to be forwarded to me under cover to Mr. Seward at Washington. My summons was revoked, but the paper with the approval and favorable recommendation of Gov Johnson was forwarded as directed.[3] I have since addressed Mr. Seward requesting him to present it to you, with an additional word of explanation in my letter to him. Disappointed in the hope of seeing you personally, I had intended to leave the matter in your hands, with the recommendations of Gov Johnson and General Steedman, until my good friend Genl Jackson, purely from his feeling of affection and friendship, offered me the opportunity of saying to you through him what I had been very anxious to say to you with my own lips.

My application now before you contains a frank statement of my case, as strongly presented against myself as it can be truthfully made. Any and every charge beyond what I have frankly stated against myself is untrue, and especially any imputation that I ever treated a prisoner unkindly myself or countenanced it in another. I believe you know me well enough, to know, that such conduct would be at war with every impulse of my heart.

The request I now make for a private interview, with Genl Jackson, is to enable him to place before you, the facts in reference to these matters, that my case when truly presented shall receive your calm and deliberate judgement.

I have employed no intermediate to approach you in my behalf, because you know me as well as any one, and I only availed myself of the kind & friendly offer of Genl Jackson, when it became impracticable for me to see you myself. I trust I have not, in doing so, trespassed too much, upon our former kind, and friendly relationship.

Howell Cobb

ALS, DNA-RG94, Amnesty Papers (M1003, Roll 17), Ga., Howell Cobb.

1. Cobb's cousin, Jackson (1820–1898), a prewar federal district attorney, state superior court judge, and U.S. minister to Austria, had been captured at the Battle of Nashville (1864) and imprisoned at Fort Warren, Mass., until July 1865. Resuming his law practice after the war, Jackson later served as U.S. minister to Mexico. Warner, *Gray*; Jackson to Johnson, June 6, 1865, Amnesty Papers (M1003, Roll 20), Ga., Henry R. Jackson, RG94, NA.

2. As Confederate commander of the district of Georgia, Cobb had been implicated in the Henry Wirz trial. See Cobb to Johnson, Nov. 20, 1865.

3. In his petition for pardon, Cobb admitted that he had been a secessionist and had believed it his duty to enter Confederate military service, but since Johnston's surrender he had "counselled an unconditional submission to the result of the war." Governor Johnson endorsed Cobb's application on September 29, 1865. Cobb to Johnson, Sept. 25, 1865, Amnesty Papers (M1003, Roll 17), Ga., Howell Cobb, RG94, NA.

From William W. Holden

Raleigh   Oct 17th, 1865

Sir,

Contrary to my expectation the convention has involved itself in a bitter discussion of the state debt, made in aid of the rebellion. A continuance of this discussion will greatly excite the people and retard the work of reconstruction. Our people are believed to be against assuming this debt by a large majority. Is it not advisable that our convention like that of Alabama should positively ignore this debt now & ever? Please answer at once.

W. W. Holden   Pro Govr

Tel, DNA-RG107, Tels Recd., President, Vol. 4 (1865–66).

From William C. Jewett

London   Oct 17 1865

President Johnson,

Heed within[1] & fear not the threatened impeachment. God will protect you under a wise & humane policy.

W. C. Jewett

ALS, DLC-JP.
    1. Not found, though this may have been a copy of the *New York Herald* article of October 1, 1865, the "Impeachment of President Johnson by the Radicals." See Hans L. Trefousse, *Impeachment of a President: Andrew Johnson, the Blacks, and Reconstruction* (Knoxville, 1975), 48; Hans L. Trefousse, *Andrew Johnson: A Biography* (New York, 1989), 281.

To William W. Holden

Washington, D.C., October 18th 1865.

Every Dollar of the Debt created to aid the rebellion against the United States should be repudiated, finally and forever. The great Mass of the people should not be taxed to pay a debt to aid in carrying on a rebellion, which they in fact, if left to themselves were opposed to. Let those who have given their means for the obligations of the State, look to that power they tried to establish in violation of Law, Constitution and the will of the people. They must meet their fate. It is their misfortune and cannot be recognized by the people of any State professing themselves Loyal to the Government of the United States, and in the

Union. I repeat that the Loyal people of North Carolina, Should be exonerated from the payment of every Dollar of indebtedness created to aid in carrying on the rebellion.

I trust and hope that the people of North Carolina, will wash their hands of every thing that partakes in the slightest degree of the rebellion, which has been so recently crushed by the Strong Arm of the Government in carrying out the obligations imposed by the Constitution of the Union.

Andrew Johnson   Pres't.

Tel, DNA-RG107, Tels. Sent, President, Vol. 2 (1865).

From Green T. Henderson

Murfreesboro, Tenn.   Oct. 19th. 1865.

Dear Sir.

Months ago, I addressed you on the subject of restoring to the Methodist E. Church South, or its members here, their House of worship.[1] The house has not been restored. Rumor says that I was represented to you as its intended paster, and that I had been the editor here of a Secession newspaper &c.[2] I sold my printing office about the time of Mr. Lincoln's first election to Dr. Fain,[3] who became the sole editor and publisher of the paper, and you know it was not a secession paper while under my control. I am not the pastor of the church here, and never expect to be. I, being an acquaintance and friend of yours wrote for the benefit of others.

At the time I wrote to you the church was used as a hospital. It is not so used now—nor has it been for months. A gentleman by the name of Prettyman,[4] claiming to be a preacher, but unknown to the church here, has taken possession of the house, and holds it by direction of some Bishop, probably Simson, or Ames,[5] neither of which are recognized by the Church here as having authority in this case.

Now my dear Sir; as it appears to be the policy of your fair and excellent administration to restore to the proper owners all property of this kind, once held by the military; Why has this house not been restored? I dislike to trouble one of your vast business with so small a matter, but the case of the church is urgent. A pastor—Mr. Plummer[6]—a loyal man—has been appointed by Bishop Kavanaugh[7] to serve the church here. He is now seated by me: but he is not permitted to preach in the House belonging to his own church, nor has he a house in which to place his family, all here with him.

I once more ask you, as commander in chief, to order the restoration of the church building, and the parsonage house, to the trustees to whom they were deeded for the use of the Methodist Episcopal Church

South, that they may be used as heretofore. The people confident look for their early restoration.[8]

As in gone by days, I remain your friend.

G. T. Henderson

ALS, DNA-RG107, Lets. Recd., EB12 President 2520 (1865).

1. See Henderson to Johnson, July 31, 1865, *Johnson Papers*, 8: 506–7.

2. Gen. Richard W. Johnson had claimed in an endorsement on Henderson's letter of July 31 that Henderson was the "editor of a vile rebel sheet." See ibid., 507n.

3. Richard W. Fain (1807–1876), Primitive Baptist preacher and formerly editor of the *Herald of Truth*, published at Shelbyville, became owner of the *Murfreesboro News* in 1861. During the 1870s he co-edited the *Baptist Watchman*, published in Nashville. *Nashville American*, Feb. 4, 1876; *Nashville Patriot*, Dec. 14, 1860; Nashville directories (1873).

4. Wesley Prettyman (*fl*1876), a missionary from the Ohio conference of the Methodist Episcopal Church, North, later established a church and worked as an agent for the Freedmen's Aid Society in Atlanta. He campaigned unsuccessfully in 1871 for election to the school board in Marietta, where he served as postmaster from 1869 until his removal in 1874. Harold Lawrence, ed., *Methodist Preachers in Georgia, 1783–1900* (Tignall, Ga., 1984), 435–36; Sarah B.G. Temple, *The First Hundred Years: A Short History of Cobb County in Georgia* (Atlanta, 1935), 398; Jerry H. Brookshire, "Methodists and Murfreesboro in the Mid-Nineteenth Century," RCHS *Pubs.*, 10 (1978): 75; *U.S. Off. Reg.* (1869–75); *Philadelphia Evening Bulletin*, Sept. 22, 1874.

5. Matthew Simpson and Edward R. Ames (1806–1879), who became bishop in 1852 and resided in Indianapolis. During the Civil War Ames was appointed as a special commissioner to visit Union prisoners at Richmond, but was not permitted to enter the city. His later years were spent in Baltimore. *DAB*.

6. James R. Plummer (*c*1823–1885), native Tennessean and Methodist clergyman, before and during the war lived in Madison County, Ala. In Murfreesboro he directed a female school as well, and later apparently moved to Clarksville, where he also pastored a Methodist church and supervised a school. 1860 Census, Ala., Madison, SW Div., Madison Station, 19; *Nashville Banner*, Apr. 20, 1885; *Huntsville Advocate*, Oct. 4, 1865; Goodspeed's *Rutherford*, 835.

7. Hubbard H. Kavanaugh (1802–1884) was elected bishop in 1854 and served for over twenty-five years. He died in Columbus, Miss. *NCAB*, 9: 246.

8. No action by Johnson has been uncovered.

From Joseph N. McDowell[1]

[Washington]   Oct 19 1865

My Dear Sir

In presenting myself before you for Pardon I was *unfortunate*. Dr Andros[2] of Boston, introduced me and you supposed him my attorney and would not listen to me. *Such never was my intention.*

I persued the course advised by you and presented my claim to the Att General who said it was all right *but* I must have the endorsement of the Gov of the state which is equivalent to a *rejection. Gov* Fletcher[3] is *my enemy* as he is yours, and would *not* endorse *either* of *us you particularly.*

I can not apply to *Gov.* Fletcher for pardon. I *came* to the President of the *United* States that I have *swornt* to support. Gov. Fletcher, is bound by oath, to exclude *me* from the state by her *late constitution.*[4]

I have taken your oath of Amnesty and will return to Missouri to, take the *stump agaenst* the constitution that would exclude me and *agaenst* your enemies *even* though you refuse *me pardon* which I again *Humly* ask.[5]

Dr. Jos N McDowell

ALS, DNA-RG94, Amnesty Papers (M1003, Roll 36), Mo., Joseph N. McDowell.

1. McDowell (1805–1868) founded Missouri Medical College, the "first medical school west of the Mississippi River," and served as "inspecting surgeon" for the Confederate Army of the Trans-Mississippi. He subsequently reopened the College, where he remained as dean and professor of anatomy until his death. John J. Anderson to Johnson, Aug. 19, 1865; McDowell to Johnson, Oct. 15, 1865; Parole of Joseph N. McDowell, June 21, 1865, Amnesty Papers (M1003, Roll 36), Mo., Joseph N. McDowell, RG94, NA; Martin Kaufman et al., eds., *Dictionary of American Medical Biography* (2 vols., Westport, Conn., 1984), 2: 476–77.

2. Richard S.S. Andros (1817–1868), a former newspaper editor, served as deputy collector of the port at Boston and was assigned after the Civil War as a special agent for reorganizing customs houses in the South. *Appleton's Cyclopaedia*; Wallace, *North American Authors*, 12.

3. Thomas C. Fletcher of Missouri.

4. The Missouri constitution adopted in 1865 required all teachers—as well as voters, lawyers, jurors, corporate officials, trustees, ministers, and candidates for public office—to take an oath affirming that they had never committed one of eighty-six specific acts of disloyalty against the state or the Union. William E. Parrish, *Missouri Under Radical Rule, 1865–1870* (Columbia, Mo., 1965), 27–29.

5. McDowell's formal petition for amnesty stressed that, as the son of a Revolutionary War soldier, he had "early learned the value of a free government." Johnson pardoned him on October 20, 1865. McDowell to Johnson, Oct. 15, 1865, Amnesty Papers (M1003, Roll 36), Mo., Joseph N. McDowell, RG94, NA.

From R. Weakley Brown

Nashville   Oct 20, 1865

My Dear Friend

So many letters are written you that the one my father refers to may not have reached you.[1] I know you will appreciate my feelings as a son—and as the Federal Court is now is session—hope my fathers pardon will be *forwarded* at as early a *day* as *practicable*.[2]

Mr. East informs me that he left my Uncle Doct. John M. Watson's papers (amnesty oath etc) with you, or on your table, and requests me to write on the subject. My Uncle's property was taken possession of by military order notifying him to vacate in a day or two. It has been greatly damaged—and he has only partial possession of it now. He has been a great sufferer by the war and has had an unusually hard time. You may remember the cordial support he gave you in 1855 although his wife was a sister of Col Gentry's[3] and you can readily apprehend how your present wise and statesmanlike policy—commends itself to his approbation. As a physician he has twice providentially saved my life—and seems as a second father to me.

Your early attention to his case will only increase the many obligations I am under to you.[4]

R. W. Brown

ALS, DNA-RG94, Amnesty Papers (M1003, Roll 48), Tenn., John L. Brown.

1. John L. Brown wrote to Johnson on October 19, 1865, saying that his pardon had been applied for by his son. We have not found that letter of application. The elder Brown indicated in his letter that he did not want to go through Governor Brownlow "on account of his bitter denunciations of Genl Andrew Jackson and other great and good men" and therefore chose to deal directly with the President. Amnesty Papers (M1003, Roll 48), Tenn., John L. Brown, RG94, NA.

2. President Johnson endorsed R. Weakley Brown's letter thus: "Issue Pardon." John L. Brown was in fact pardoned on October 25, 1865. Ibid.; *House Ex. Docs.*, 39 Cong., 2 Sess., No. 116, p. 35 (Ser. 1293).

3. Lockey S. Brown (b. c1815), who married Watson in 1831, was actually the sister of Meredith P. Gentry's second wife. Byron and Barbara Sistler, trs., *1850 Census, Tennessee* (8 vols., Evanston, Ill., 1974–76), 7: 18; Silas E. Lucas, Jr., comp., *Marriages from Early Tennessee Newspapers, 1794–1851* (Easley, S.C., 1978), 50, 155.

4. Watson, recommended by Brownlow and East, had already been pardoned by the President on October 2, 1865. *House Ex. Docs.*, 39 Cong., 2 Sess., No. 116, p. 53 (Ser. 1293). For Watson's file, see Amnesty Papers (M1003, Roll 51), Tenn., John M. Watson, RG94, NA.

From Alcibiade DeBlanc[1]

St. Martinsville, October 20, 1865.

Sir,

Two hostile causes and the armies by which they were supported, were—for upwards of four years—in presence of each other; the confederate armies have surrendered and their cause is lost.

There is no tribunal, on Earth, before which thirteen independent states can be tried for, and convicted of rebellion. If it were treasonable to resist the authority of the United States, we were ALL traitors and, to but a few exceptions, the South ought to be exterminated.

If our only crime be our failure, the most sacred and most pleasant duty imposed on you by the triumph of your arms, is to extend a generous hand to the vanquished and respect the greatest and most respectable misfortune of the nineteenth century.

We have sworn allegiance to the federal government—ratified the abolition of slavery in our midst, and the price of that allegiance & that sacrifice cannot be less than the restoration of the liberty we hold from God and that of our rights under the american Constitution.

I, then, ask of you—as an act of justice—the release of those confederates you still retain as prisoners, and the amnesty of the many who linger in distant and foreign localities. They have done nothing more than any of us. Your victory shall not be complete until our President, our Governors and those that are proscribed for the reason that they were engaged in the late Revolution, shall have been allowed to enter the desolated homes, where their return is anxiously awaited by a mother, a wife, a child or a friend.

When that is done, you can unhesitatingly order every musket to be unloaded, from the banks of the Rio Grande to the memorable banks of the Potomac; for, then, we shall again be one nation and the first among the proudest of nations, and your soldiers and those—at the North and in the world—that are good & honorable, will bless the hand that shall have demolished, in our States, the political scaffolds, emptied the political dungeons and reopened to the exiled the gates of their country.

The blood has ceased to flow—now the tears: dry these and God will smile on you, those who are dear to you and on our distracted land—and, more than any of the brightest and most glorious days of our Republic, the people would cherish the day that could be so well illustrated by your clemency.

Alcibiade DeBlanc,

Heretofore a colonel in the 1st La Brigade C.S.A.

ALS, DNA-RG94, Amnesty Papers (M1003, Roll 27), La., Alcibiade DeBlanc.

1. DeBlanc (1821–1883), a native Louisiana attorney, commanded the 8th La. Inf. before wounds compelled him to accept service with the reserves. After the war he was the first commander of the Knights of the White Camellia in Louisiana, and in 1873 he was arrested for leading a bloody rebellion against the state government. After his release, he was active in organizing the White League and subsequently served as a Louisiana supreme court justice from 1877 until his death. Conrad, *La. Biography*, 1: 222; Taylor, *La. Reconstructed*, 62–63, 162, 274–75, 283, 285.

From William W. Holden

Raleigh N.C   Oct 20" 1865

Sir:

The convention has adjourned. It has promptly repudiated every dollar of the rebel debt and bound all future Legislatures not to pay any of it. Your telegram had a most happy effect. The Worth faction[1] is working hard, but will be defeated by a large majority.

Turner[2] and other contumacious leaders ought to be handled at the proper time. Please pardon no leading men unless you hear from me.[3]

W. W Holden   Pro Gov

Tel, DNA-RG107, Tels. Recd., President, Vol. 4 (1865–66).

1. Gubernatorial candidate Jonathan Worth and his ex-Whig coalition of Graham-Vance conservatives. See Holden to Johnson, Nov. 2, 1865.

2. Holden's chief nemesis, Josiah Turner, Jr. (1821–1901), was a member of the Confederate Congress and one of Worth's campaign managers. Turner had a subsequent career as a state legislator, constitutional convention delegate, and newspaper publisher. Warner and Yearns, *BRCC*; Raper, *Holden*, 81. See Elizabeth G. McPherson, ed., "Letters from North Carolina to Andrew Johnson," *NCHR*, 27 (1950): 486–87.

3. In reference to Turner's twenty-three-page clemency request, Holden had in late September recommended suspension. In a telegram and letter, both dated October 5,

Holden again urged the President not to pardon Turner. He was not pardoned until February 17, 1866, long after the election. Ibid.; Holden to Johnson, Oct. 5, Johnson Papers, LC; Amnesty Papers (M1003, Roll 43), N.C., Josiah Turner, Jr., RG94, NA.

From Charles J. Meng

Louisville Ky   Octo. 20th 1865

The people of Kentucky for several days have been congratulating themselves upon the removal of Martial law in this state by your proclamation a few days since,[1] but it seems they were too fast judging from the Order issued on the 18th inst. a copy of which is herewith enclosed.[2]

This is a remarkable order both for its falsity & its arrogance and certainly can't be countenanced or permitted by you without laying your self liable to the imputation of deception. You surely meant what you said in your proclamation & it can't be possible that secret orders in contravention have been given to the commander of this department, and yet this seems to be the feeling of the citizens of Ky, which is damaging to your character for independence & manliness.

It is interfering with the purposes of the Goverment and I am confident that it will be promptly rebuked by you; the question here seems to be whether you or Palmer is President U.S. & Palmer seems to have it. This is mere trifling and can do you no good & the state great harm. I would mean what I said in my proclamation or withdraw it and let Palmer reign.[3]

Ch. J. Meng

ALS, DLC-JP.

1. Johnson had declared an end to martial law in Kentucky on October 12. *OR*, Ser. 3, Vol. 5: 125.

2. Not found, though a secretary's note on the reverse side indicates that Meng had enclosed "an order of Gen'l Palmer in regard to the negro population of Kentucky." This may have been Palmer's declaration to the post commander at Lexington that all Kentucky blacks were presumed to be free "until orders are received to the contrary." Clipping, n.d., in Madison C. Johnson to Johnson, Oct. 21, 1865, Lets. Recd. (Main Ser.), File J-405-1865 (M619, Roll 368), RG94, NA.

3. By the time this reached the Executive Mansion (October 25), Johnson had already decided to allow Palmer to remain in command "for a little while longer," or at least until most of his troops could "safely be withdrawn." George H. Thomas to Palmer, Oct. 19, 1865, Tels. Sent, Sec. of War (M473, Roll 90), RG107, NA; *Louisville Journal*, Oct. 22, 1865.

From J. Madison Wells

New Orleans, October 20th—1865

To President Johnson

The enclosed letter[1] is from the pen of a highly intelligent and respectable citizen of North Louisiana and is couched in such candid language and presents so true a picture of the baneful influence exercised by the presence and insubordinate conduct of colored troops on the surrounding population of the same color, that I am induced to send it to you for your perusal, in preference to anything I could say of my own in the matter. I will merely remark that his testimony is corroborated from every part of the state, wherever the colored troops have appeared. Their very presence demoralizes the negroes for all purposes of useful industry. I am aware you are getting rid of them as fast as you can, but as civil government is completely restored in our state, I trust I may be excused for suggesting to you the importance, for the interests of the black race, as well as the white, that the day may be hastened when their baleful influence may no longer be felt in the South.[2]

J. Madison Wells   Governor &c

ALS, DLC-JP.
1. Not found. The governor may have forwarded the letter from a citizen of Homer published anonymously in the *New Orleans Picayune*, Oct. 19, 1865.
2. See Isaac E. Morse to Johnson, Sept. 5, 1865.

From Andrew J. Hamilton

Austin Texas   21st Oct 1865

Mr President.

This will be presented to you by the Hon James. H. Bell my Secretary of State and formerly an associate Justice of our Supreme Court. I present him to your acquaintance as a man who has no superior in Texas in point of *moral worth, ability and patriotism*, and to whose suggestions and representations I beg most respectfully, but earnestly, you will lend an attentive ear. He is a native Texan deeply interested in the present and future of the State, known to, and thoroughly knowing her people. He has my *entire confidence* and knows my views and opinions upon all the questions growing out of the late rebellion and which have to be met and adjusted in the reconstruction of State Governments in the South.

You will perceive at once that he is no ordinary man; and because of his eminent ability his integrity and loyalty to the Government I have sent to confer freely and fully with you; to give you a correct idea of affairs, as they at present exist in this State, and to learn, as far may be proper, what is expected of us. I pray you therefore Mr President hear him for *himself*, for *me* and for *Texas*.

In my former communications[1] I believe I gave you the reasons, briefly, why I did not deem it best to call a Convention as early as was done in the other Southern States: I feel well satisfied that I have not acted unwisely in this matter, and if the question effected only Texas, I would delay action still longer. But I regard the question as one of National proportions which will not Justify me in limiting my views alone to the interests of Texas. And believing that the policy of the General Gov't demands it, I will, in a day or two, issue a Proclamation for the election of delegates and the assembling of a Convention.

Oweing to our immense territory and entire absence of Mails the election can not be provided for, by proper notice, earlier than the 15th or 20th of December—And the meeting of the Convention say thirty days later.

I will telegraph to you the time as soon as fixed and forward by mail the Proclamation.[2] The great body of the people of Texas have, since my return to the State, behaved with the most commendable propriety, far exceeding in this respect any thing which I had hoped. I think I can say very truthfully that the great mass of the people—all the good and thoughtful men, are earnestly seeking truth and wise Counsels to enable them to do right, and considering the extent to which their minds and hearts had been perverted and abused by the miseducation and despotism of the rebellion and its leaders, their progress is cheering and hopeful. There are some sections of the State remote from any Military force where I am informed late Slave owners stoutly deny the power of the Gov't to free the Negros and who still claim and control them as property and in two or three instances have recently bought and sold them as in former years. The Military authorities will be furnished with proper information in these cases which will doubtless cause them to be properly dealt with.

The great body of the late Slave owners realize not only the fact that Slavery is dead, but let it be said to their credit many, very many of them are deeply concerned for the welfare of the freedmen.

There are however some who in the littleness of their minds and selfish dispositions are in a great passion because the Negro has been made free and not being able to revenge themselves upon the Gov't gratify their malice by abusing the freedmen. A few such men can do, and have already done much harm, by producing distrust of white men in the minds of the Negroes. It is but too true that many of this unfortunate race have been murdered within the past three months.[3] This however is not the only reason I have for fearing a very unpleasant state of things towards the approach of Christmass.

I have information from many and undoubted sources that in the Counties in the lower or Coast Country where the blacks are most numerous they stubbornly refuse to hire to labour for wages and openly declare that they will not work for white men—that they will be furnished with farms and whatever else they may need by the U S Gov't and that this will be done by causing a division of property between the whites and blacks. It is impossible for me to say who has caused this foolish notion to take hold of the minds of the blacks; but there is no doubt of the fact that the impression has been made and will have to be met and dealt with. I shall issue an address to them as soon as it can be prepared, undeceiving them in regard to this matter,[4] in which I shall try to impress upon them, that while the Govt has made them free and will protect them in their freedom it will never protect them or others in idleness, viciousness and robbery—that liberty for them means just what it means for all; the right to labour for an honest living; that if they fail to deserve it they will not have the friendship of the Govt, that it will treat all people white or black as friends or enemies according to their conduct.

If the danger becomes imminent I will resort to such means as may suggest themselves to my mind to avert it. I have called Major Genl Wrights[5] attention to the matter and have made such suggestions to him as in my judgment were necessary on the part of the Military Authorities.

Judge Bell will give you a full account of this threatened trouble and will also present to you what I propose to do should action on my part become necessary.[6]

As to the Provisional Government which I have organized I think I may say that it was not only necessary considering the condition in which I found the people, of Texas, but well calculated to quiet the apprehensions of many who seemed to think that a most rigid and oner-ous Military rule would be kept over them for an indefinite time. And I trust I may not be considered egotistical in expressing the belief that, so far, I have not only met the just expectations of the loyal people of the State but have challenged the respect and even confidence of the most virulent rebels.

The question of meeting the expenses of the Provisional Govt gives us no unesiness provided the Bonds of the U S which Texas ownes are paid at the National Treasury.[7] This matter Judge Bell will fully ex-plain to your Excellency and I trust to your entire satisfaction so that Texas may be rèlieved from all embarrassment on account of present means. We propose to defray our own expenses in all that is to be done in returning to the fold of the Union.

My brother,[8] who is on his way to England to try to recover some of the Securities belonging to the State accompanies Judge Bell to Wash-ington and they together will explain to you how important it is to Texas that he shall succeed in his mission.

The pardon business is to me a source of great responsibility and labour. I have acted on the idea that it was the policy of the Govt to forgive all sincerely repentant rebels whose sins are pardonable. I have refused where I could not in conscience do so, to recommend. I will not recommend to you for pardon any man that I would not be willing to pardon myself were the power mine. As a class I have and shall con-tinue to refuse to recommend the pardon of those who were educated at the National expense to be the soldiers of the Republic but betrayed her in her hour need.

I have laboured incessantly since my return to the State, and feel greatly the want of rest but this I cannot hope until the task which I have undertaken shall have been completed. It shall be completed in such manner that one reward will be secure—the consciousness of having aimed at the best and most lasting interests of Texas and the United States.

You have Mr President not only my sympathy in the performance of your great labours but my prayers for your health and complete success.

A J Hamilton

ALS, DLC-JP.

1. Hamilton to Johnson, Sept. 23, 1865.
2. See Hamilton to Johnson, Nov. 27, 1865.
3. According to a special report submitted to Congress in 1868, there had been at least thirty-eight freedmen killed in Texas during the latter half of 1865. *Senate Misc. Docs.*, 40 Cong., 2 Sess., No. 109, p. 2 (Ser. 1319).
4. See Hamilton to Johnson, Nov. 27, 1865.
5. Horatio G. Wright, commander, Department of Texas.
6. See Hamilton to Johnson, Nov. 27, 1865.
7. See George W. Paschal to Johnson, Sept. 20, 1865.
8. Staunch Republican Morgan C. Hamilton (1809–1893), formerly secretary of war for the Republic of Texas, later served as a U.S. senator (1870–77). *BDAC.*

From Sam Milligan

Greeneville Ten   Oct. 21, 1865

Dear Sir:

Did I not know your time was taxed so severely with the cares and responsibilities of the high position you occupy, I would be greatly pleased to give you a full history of Tennessee affairs. But I must forego the pleasure, and confine myself to what I conceive to be a matter of the highest public interest.

At the last session of the Supreme Court, at Knoxville, which has just closed, the question was presented for the determination of the Court; Wether the Confederate Government, was a government *de facto*, or not? At my instance, perhaps more than the other judges, the case was held under advisement. My object in this was not to avoid responsibility, but to gain time, so as to be able to make at least a just and respectable descision of the case.

The question to my mind is of the highest interest to the country, and involves more perhaps than any other question growing out of the war. A *"de facto"* Government, differs widely from a *"Belligerent Power."* And the recognition of the one, does, by no means, involve the recognition of the other. The former is an existing government in fact, with the ordinary powers of a government *de jury*; while the latter is only a rule of war, designed simply to soften and humanize—so to speak, the rigors of the existing contest. Their objects and purposes are widely different.

The recognition of the Rebel Government as a government *de facto*, would, as it appears to me, without intimating my opinion in advance of a full investigation, go very far to justify the rebellion, and render all its infamous legislation valid, and thereby impose upon the Government, the settlement of the most perplexing questions imaginable. Such as the conflict of civil authority in the same state, and under the same General Government, as when the jurisdiction was claimed by both parties, and the validity of contracts, and debts created under the Rebel authority &c &c.

I only mention a few of the most obvious consequences that must flow from such a recognition, in order that it may the more fully appear, that the General Government is interested in the decisions which even the State Courts may make of this question.

But the strong inclination of my mind is, that the question is a *political one*, and not a *judicial one*. It is a matter, as it appears to me, which ought to be decided by the political power of the nation; and if so, what power or department of the Government, can rightfully exercise the power? Does it belong to Congress, or to the Executive?

I feel so much interest in the question, I would be greatly pleased, if it was not improper, to have your opinion, and also Mr Secretary Seward's.[1] I do dislike to trouble any one, but as this must be one of the first cases that is decided of the kind in the rebellious States, it certainly is important it should be decided correctly.

I am more importunate because the books and papers are not accessible here, necessary to an enlightened decision of the case. To obviate that I am willing to come to Washington and consult the Library there, and especially if I felt I could be so far assisted by the Officials of the Government, as to make the decision in conformity to the policy of the Government. A conflict between the State Courts & the nation Government would be, as I think, highly improper, not to say injurious in any respect.

Please excuse this long letter and let me hear from you.[2]

Sam Milligan

ALS, DLC-JP.

1. So concerned about this issue was Milligan that in a letter to the President's son he asked Robert to have his father send information to Milligan about the de facto status of the Confederate government. Milligan to Robert Johnson, Oct. 25, 1865, Johnson Papers, LC.

2. This letter was received at the President's office on October 26 and filed on the 30th. One day after the receipt of the letter the President telegraphed Milligan asking him to come to Washington. Evidently receiving no response, Johnson sent a second telegram, this one on November 2, inquiring whether Milligan had received the request. Two days later Milligan assured the President that he would be in Washington the following week. Ser. 4A, Vol. 3: 237, Johnson Papers, LC; Johnson to Milligan, Oct. 27, Nov. 2, 1865, Tels. Sent, President, Vol. 2 (1865), RG107, NA; Milligan to Johnson, Nov. 4, 1865, Johnson Papers, LC.

From Robert J. Powell

Washington, D.C.   21st. Oct. 1865.

To the President:

I would respectfully state in reference to the Internal Revenue officers appointed in N. Carolina, that *not a single one* has been appointed upon the recommendation of Gov. Holden.[1]

A few weeks ago, I had a *distinct and positive understanding* with Commissioner Orton,[2] to the effect that all action in reference to the Districting this state, and appointing Collectors and Assessors, should be suspended till the state should be districted for Congress, when those districts seven in number should be adopted as the Internal Revenue districts, and that no appointments would be made save on the recommendation of Gov. Holden.

I say such was our *positive* agreement, and of which I immediately informed the Governor.

Yet within three days thereafter an appointment was made.

Two days ago I received a telegram from the Governor, saying the state had been districted and asking that my understanding would be rigidly observed. I called on Mr. Orton, and learn from him and his Chief Clerk that a Commission for a Mr. Thompson,[3] as Collector of the old 2nd district had been prepared—notwithstanding another had been recommended for that position—by Gov Holden. I then called on Mr. Chandler,[4] who ordered a suspension of action for a few days.

I again called on Mr. Whitman[5] Chief Clerk of the Internal Revenue Bureau yesterday—and learned that he regarded Hedrick[6] as the representative of *our party* in N.C. and said it was but fair that the offices should be divided between the *two parties* there. I informed him that there ought not to be but one party there. I objected to the production of parties there by favoring opposition to Gov. Holden.

I will here remark that in all of the Departments, as a general thing, I find the *National men*, friendly disposed, and desirous of sustaining Gov. Holden, whilst the *radicals*, are disposed to a contrary course.[7]

R. J. Powell   State Agent for N Carolina

ALS, DLC-JP.

1. In his dispatch of October 19 the governor had requested Johnson to suspend further appointments until "I can make nominations." *Senate Ex. Docs.*, 39 Cong., 1 Sess., No. 26, p. 226 (Ser. 1237).

2. William Orton (1826–1878), a former New York revenue collector whom Johnson had only recently appointed commissioner, resigned in November to become president of the United States Telegraph Company. When his company merged with Western Union in the spring of 1866, Orton became vice president and a year later president. *DAB; Washington Evening Star*, Oct. 21, 1865.

3. Probably William H. Thompson (*c*1824-*fl*1870), a dentist who was eventually commissioned collector of the new 5th district and who held that post until March 1867. 1860 Census, N.C., Alamance, Graham, 164; (1870), Thompson's Township No. 9, Saxapahaw, 7; Ser. 6B, Vol. 2: 140–41, Johnson Papers, LC.

4. Assistant secretary of the treasury William E. Chandler (1835–1917), of New Hampshire, later served as secretary of the navy (1882–85) and U.S. senator (1887–89). *BDAC*.

5. Later appointed deputy commissioner, Daniel C. Whitman (*c*1820-*fl*1874) resigned from government service in July 1866 and went into banking. 1860 Census, N.J., Essex, 7th Ward, Newark City, 232; *National Intelligencer*, June 30, 1866; Hugh McCulloch to Whitman, Aug. 15, 1866, Lets. Sent *re* Internal Revenue Service Employees (QD Ser.), Vol. 1, RG56, NA; Newark directories (1855–75).

6. Benjamin S. Hedrick.

7. See McCulloch to Johnson, Jan. 31, 1866.

From John W. Forney

Philadelphia, October 22d 1865.

Dear Mr. President—

You will recollect that on the occasion of my last interview with you I stated that when you had determined to make a change in the office of United States assessor under the Internal Revenue bill, for this the first Congressional District of Pennsylvania, (in which I reside,) I would take the liberty of presenting to you the name of my personal friend Edward G. Webb,[1] Esq. as entirely worthy of your confidence. I now learn that there is some probability of such a change; indeed a gentleman yesterday informed me it was determined upon. As among all the Federal appointments although I have recommended several, you have not appointed one of my personal friends but have frequently expressed a desire so to do, I now lay before you the claim of Mr. Webb for the post of United States Assessor in this District. Mr. Webb opposed the aggressions of the Democratic organization during the rebellion and acted with the National Union party with signal efficiency and ability; not only as a writer and a public speaker has he shown his devotion and influence, but among a large circle of friends he has wielded a great and conclusive power. Should you feel disposed to confer this appointment upon him, he will lay before you such testimonials as will prove him to be abundantly worthy of this mark of distinction. I ought to remark that Mr. Webb ran as the Union candidate for Congress against the Democratic incumbent Randall,[2] three years ago.

I ask my friend Jones[3] to present this letter in person to you and to obtain your answer.[4]

J. W. Forney

LS, DNA-RG56, Appts., Internal Revenue Service, Assessor, Pa., 1st Dist., Edward G. Webb.

1. Webb (*c*1808–1866), a former Philadelphia newspaper editor and reporter, served one term as prothonotary of the local court of common pleas. 1860 Census, Pa., Philadelphia, Philadelphia, 2nd Ward, 77; *Philadelphia Evening Bulletin*, July 5, 1866.

2. Samuel J. Randall (1828–1890), a Philadelphia merchant, city councilman, and state senator, served as a Democratic congressman from 1863 until his death. *BDAC*.

3. Not identified.

4. Webb was nominated as assessor of Pennsylvania's 1st district on March 20, 1866, and was confirmed by the Senate three weeks later. Ser. 6B, Vol. 2: 353, Johnson Papers, LC.

From Henry Ward Beecher

Brooklyn   Oct 23, 1865.

Dear Sir:

Will you allow me to express the great satisfaction which I have felt in reading you remarks to Mr. Stearns.[1] Every act of your administration, as far as I had been able to judge, seemed wise and patriotic. It only needed some deffinite annunciation of your views and policy on a few critical points to unite in confidence and admiration, toward you, that large body of intelligent men, in the north, who, without beeing politicians, have the liveliest interest in public affairs, and who seek to infuse into the life of the nation moral purity and essential Justice.

I think I may assure you that the religious men of the north and west are rapidly growing into a confidence in your patriotism, and wisdom, second only to that which they felt for Mr. Lincoln; a confidence which I am sure will increase.

I hope it will not seem presumptous, if I mention, with especial satisfaction, your kindness and sympathy toward those who have been wrecked by this terrible war; your firmness in securing to the Nation all the fruits which it had ought to gotten from so much suffering, Viz, the utter eradication of slavery. However wise it might have been before the war to get rid of slavery gradually, it can scarcely be doubtful to any, that *now* the sooner, and more utterly it is extirpated the better will it be for all concerned. But your clear perception that the welfare of the freedmen depends far more upon the good will of their white neighbors than it does upon northen philanthopy or Governmental protection, is eminently sagacious. We, at a distance, can do much, and the Government much for the Black men. But if it shall have the effect of relieving the white people of the south from all responsibility toward the African, and even exciting their animosity, it will do little to prevent the liberty of the slaves from becoming a disaster to them.

I am heartily thankful to you for the statesman like caution with which you touch the essential affairs of *States*. State sovereignty is a heresy but state-rights, is a reality of transcendent value. And the temptation is very great to employ Federal power in such a way as to make a precedent which bad or weak men, by & bye will use with most disasterous effect. Much as I desire to see the *Natural* right of Suffrage given to the freedmen, I think it would be attained at too great a price if it involved the right of the Federal Government to meddle with State affairs. It is true, that a certain absolute power had to be exercised in the reformation of States, and in preparing them again to take part in national affairs. But, just how far to go, and where to stop, was the very test of statesmanship, and I think you have hit it exactly. If a man is drowning I have a right to seize him by the hair & pull him out, & then to take liberties with his person, which, as soon as he begins to recover, would no longer be permissable. The Government *must* exercise extraordiy power in restoring the suspended states animation. But not a whit more than is needed for that, in connection with the safety and stability of the National Govt.

I pray your pardon for so many words and yet I have not half expressed the great thankfulness which I feel that God has raised you up for such a crisis endued you with the ability and disposition, to serve the Nation rather than yourself or any mere party. And your reward will be in having your name intimately associated with a Nation the Grandeur of whose History even the most lively imagination cannot estimate or conceive.

Henry Ward Beecher

ALS, DLC-JP.
1. See Interview with George L. Stearns, Oct. 3, 1865.

From Robert P. Dick[1]

Greensboro   Oct 23 1865.

Govr Vances wife[2] is here with a friend very dangerously ill with Consumption. I think she will die. Please allow Gov Vance to attend his wife during her illness wherever it may be necessary for her to go in the state.[3] I know He will do nothing wrong. Please answer.[4]

R P Dick

Tel, DLC-JP.
1. State legislator and delegate to the state convention.
2. Harriet N. Espy (1832–1878), who had married Vance in 1853, had been "seized with hemorrhage of the lungs and came near dying." Clement Dowd, *Life of Zebulon B. Vance* (Charlotte, 1897), 213; Glenn Tucker, *Zeb Vance: Champion of Personal Freedom* (New York, 1965), 429.
3. In strict compliance with the conditions of his July 6 parole from Old Capitol Prison, Vance had returned to Statesville, N.C., where he resumed his law practice. Dowd, *Life of Vance*, 100, 103; Tucker, *Zeb Vance*, 430.
4. Receiving the dispatch before noon on the 24th, the President replied on the same date: "Zebulon Vance is hereby authorized to visit and remain with his wife during her illness without regard to location." Johnson Papers, LC.

From Milo A. Holcomb[1]

Hartford County Conn.   Burlington   Oct 23d 1865

Dr Sir

Since writing my first letter I have given to this subject of disposing of the freed men further consideration and became more convinced than before of the merits of the plan of sending them into the congressional districts.[2]

If the Southern States offer to sell to northerners their surpluss tilable land at fair prices lots of the laboring classes from New England, and the northern states will emigrate there, hence farm labor in New England will be wanted, and the negroes will find ready employment here. Politicians and Congress men will not be likely to favor the project. But the plan is a fair one and once reduced to trial will give general satisfaction. Tis the best disposition that can be made of the Negroes. If it should appear that the negroes could not be made to sustain themselves the Deposit fund[3] could be appropriated towards aiding them to do so.

A proportionate distribution to Each Congressman would probably Amount to about 13,000 to Each congressional district. But a great diminution may be expected by reason of many causes. So that an assignment of ten thousand to Each congressional district would fully equal all that would be required. Now that number could find ample Employ in any one the most populous district in New England.

I am fully satisfied that You are as nearly equal to your task as any man can be to any task. But heretofore no one individual was ever called to a task of half the difficulties that have fallen to your lot and please pardon me if suggest caution.

If Enough Military power is retained it may have a tendency to pass difficulties by without showing themselves which otherwise might prove disasterous. In plain words, I would Keep the power to sustain my opinions. The Executive power should be backed for four years at least, by a sufficient force to command the respect of all classes no matter whether that respect be the result of love or fear.

I have known Thad. Stevens Chas Sumner Wilson &c, and I have no confidence in them. May you have the counsel and influence of divine wisdom to aid you is the sacred wish. . . .

Milo A. Holcomb

ALS, DLC-JP.

1. Holcomb (b. c1799) during the late 1850s had been a clerk in the pension office at Washington. 1860 Census, Conn., Hartford, Granby, 49; *U.S. Off. Reg.* (1859), 96.

2. A week earlier he had proposed a scheme whereby the recently freed slaves were to be held by national authority, apportioned to each representative district, and governed by martial law. In time, they could "become citisens of the states when they become possessed of a specific estate and proper inteligence." Holcomb to Johnson, Oct. 16, 1865, Johnson Papers, LC.

3. Perhaps a reference to the Freedmen's Savings Bank, chartered in March 1865, when the Freedmen's Bureau was created. McFeely, *Yankee Stepfather*, 323.

From James Q. Smith

Montgomery, Ala.   October 23d 1865

Respt. Sir

I have just learned that certain persons in this Section particularly in this city have drawn up and propose to present to Your Excellency a petition containing charges against me.[1] What those charges are I can only collect from information of persons who had the petition presented to them for signature but refused, and that a combination of Secessionists were determined if possible to have me removed from office and in order to give this proceeding an appearance of honest intentions alleges That "I have instituted proceeding for Confiscation against property after the owners were pardoned"—"That I have instituted proceedings unnecessarily for Confiscation"—And "That when persons were pardoned and desired to have their causes dismissed I have charged unreasonable costs."[2]

Your Excellency will pardon me for giving the true version of this matter, what has been done by me officially since my arrival in Montgomery and the real cause of these exceedingly disafected persons.

My only instructions as to proceedings under the late acts of Congress for the Confiscation of property of persons engaged in rebellion and of property employed and used for rebel purposes, are contained in Your Excellancies proclamation dated 21th June 1865 appointing a provisional Governor for Alabama—Sect 5 of which reads as follows.

That the District Judge for the Judicial District in which Alabama is enclosed, proceed to hold Courts within said State in accordance with the provisions of an Act of Congress. And the Attorney General will instruct the proper Officers to libel and bring to Judgment, Confiscation, and Sale, property subject to Confiscation, and enforce the administration of Justice within said State in all matters within the Cognizance and jurisdiction of Federal Courts.

The District Court being fully organized I proceeded to libel for Condemnation and Sale property used for rebel purposes, and where the owners thereof were excluded from your Excellencies proclamation of Amnesty. This Section of Country and particularly the City of Montgomery being the *first Capitol*, and *"last ditch"* of the rebel States much property was Subject to Condemnation under the late acts of Congress. This property encluded Conft. States, Cotton Yards, Gun Factories, Pistol factories, sword factories, Machine Shops for casting Cannon Shot & Shell, Foundries, Rolling Mills, Coal, Iron & lead Mines, clothing Establishments, and hospital Nitre and other buildings most of which were put in opperation by funds furnished from Richmond. All this property (clearly liable to Condemnation) is now claimed by wealthy educated precipitators who have Some Stock interest, and attempt to cover all by Your Excellencies pardons to them. I am directed by the Attorney General[3] that a pardon does not nor can it cover property which belonged to the late so-called Conft. States and now held by private citizens.

The owners of other property which has been libeled because they were engaged in rebellion, or because they permitted property to be used for rebel purposes, a few weeks Since paid from two to twenty five hundred dollars to lawyers who drew up their applications for pardon, and in fact would have given half their estate for a pardon, are now, that they have obtained pardon, exceedingly indignant in Complying with Your Excellencies pardon in the payment of any Costs due the officers of Court and insist that a pardon relieves them entirely. I have been told by Such persons that they Committed no offence and would under the Same circumstances do what they had done over again, that "they only applied for pardon because others Seem to be doing so."

As to my having informations for libel executed after I knew the parties were pardoned, it is not true. I have directed the clerk of the Court[4] to make a list of names of pardoned persons as they were published, and the Marshal[5] to execute no process where the party against whom the process was directed had obtained pardon, and so careful was I after seeing Your Excellencies policy of pardoning, and fearing that those pardoned and those expecting pardon may be embarrassed as to how they should act and to relieve them I published the following notice in the City papers.[6]

It may be as I have had no official lists of persons pardoned and as the Marshal has papers unexecuted Sometimes for 10 or 12 days that during the issuance of the process and its execution the parties may have recd. pardons. In Such Cases the matter was unavoidable, and when represented to me I have immediately stopped all proceedings. Such mistakes were also caused by the fact that many prominant rebel leaders caused the publication of their pardons to be made in Newspapers when no Such pardons were granted, and done expressly to deceive. They now boast of this sharp trick on the U.S. District attorney who failed to proceed after seeing the announcement that they were pardoned.

Under the Confiscation act of July 17 1862 Section 8 U.S. Statutes at large Vol 12 in reference to fees and charges in Confiscation cases Says—"And the Said Courts shall have power to allow Such Costs and Charges of its officers as shall be reasonable and just in the premises." The Judge therefore would have the allowance of fees & charges. The Court not being in Session this could not be done. The pardoned parties were unabled to accepet the pardon not having paid all costs of proceedings against them—Twenty thousand dollars being the lowest amount in any Case. I at the Special request of persons against whom Informations were filed fixed the Costs Conditionally to be ratified by the Judge at the lowest estimate at which I have known Such Cases disposed of in Tennessee, being 150.00 Dols for Attorney Marshal Clerk Advertising &c &c. When parties are worth 75 100 or 300 thousand dollars and all this property Subject to Condemnation the fees & charges are in proportion. In this way ten Cases have been disposed of the form of whose receipt I hereto attach.[7] At the time Such applications were made I distinctly informed the parties. This was only done at their request and for their accommodation.

Now I will State to your Excellency the object to be attained by those persons complaining. It is simply to oust a man who has fought Secession in all its forms, to get out of the way a man who knows all about their actings and doings for four years past, and where they have hid property belonging to the late So-Called Conft. States—and now claimed as their individual property. They are persons who have persecuted union men, original precipitators prominant and wealthy, and who now wish to control not only the State but the Federal offices. No man here can possibly be elected to a State office unless he is a Secessionist and has gallantly fought four years against the Flag of his Country. They want also to have their associates in Federal offices. The names attached to the petition and charges against me, also appear on Vigelence Committees, are Cotton agents, Conscript officers, Judges who have with military force held Court in the Woods and hung union men.

I feel that I aught not to permit Such charges to be made against me ex parte, without a statement from me as to the facts, and also as to the motives actuating those men. I have a difficult time with the Yancy precipitors. They are precipitators yet if they could precipitate, and having laid the whole matter before your Excellency, I leave the case in your hands, fearing nothing from a President who knows and have suffered from such "educated intelligent precipitating rebels.["]

This will be presented by my friend Gov Lewis E Parsons,[8] who will further explain if necessary.[9]

James Q Smith

ALS, DNA-RG60, Office of Atty. Gen., Lets. Recd., President.

1. In an undated petition nineteen Montgomery, Ala., citizens alleged that, though they had been pardoned, the district attorney had forced them to pay "excessive & onerous" fees before their property could be restored. Treasury agent Joseph R. Dillin also wired the President that Smith was "acting very badly. Very rashly pursuing the people." William C. Ray et al. to Johnson, Office of Atty. Gen., Lets. Recd., President, RG60, NA; Dillin to Johnson, Oct. 9, 1865, Johnson Papers, LC.

2. This quoted material is not from the petition per se.

3. See James Speed to Smith, Sept. 28, 1865, House Reports, 40 Cong., 1 Sess., No. 7, p. 431 (Ser. 1314).

4. William T. Harris (b. c1816) was a planter. 1860 Census, Ala., Greene, Pleasant Ridge, 57; Gandrud, Alabama Records, 140: n.p.; Macon Telegraph, Aug. 30, 1865.

5. John Hardy.

6. The notice issued on October 3, which was attached to the document, permitted those whose property had been seized and who had applied for a pardon to request that their cases be continued at the next term of the district court.

7. Smith enclosed a blank "Copy Receipt," which he evidently issued to litigants whose cases had been dismissed.

8. Parsons met with the President on several occasions during the next few weeks. This document bears a receipt stamp of November 2, 1865. *Cincinnati Gazette*, Oct. 31, 1865; *Huntsville Advocate*, Nov. 9, 1865.

9. The President referred the letter to the Attorney General.

From J. Madison Wells

New Orleans, October 23/—1865

Dear Sir

Some time since, a petition was presented for my approval in behalf of amnesty and pardon, being granted to Henry Watkins Allen[1] late Governor of a portion of this State, under the reputed Confederacy, and now a fugitive in Mexico. I endorsed my approval thereon,[2] so far as my knowledge embraced his general Character in connection with the rebellion, which went to show that he was a kindhearted, honest man, was not guilty of peculation and taken altogether, his acts tended to plead in his favor. I have within a few days learned that the true reason why Allen fled the Country is, that in the year 1860, he was one of the principals engaged in the importation of slaves from africa on the Louisiana and Texas Coast and that bills of indictment for that offence in both States, are now pending against him.[3] In view of this knowledge, I feel it incumbent on me to revoke my approval of the said application, not that I deem it a matter of importance, because I believe Henry W Allen will never return to this country, and I am so assured by his most intimate friends—but to place myself right before you.[4]

J Madison Wells   Governor of Louisiana.

ALS, DNA-RG94, Amnesty Papers (M1003, Roll 27), La., Henry W. Allen.

1. Allen (1820–1866) had risen to the rank of brigadier general in Confederate service before being elected governor of Louisiana in 1863. *DAB*; Conrad, *La. Biography*, 1: 9–10.

2. Wells had endorsed a petition submitted on Allen's behalf by four citizens of New Orleans. William S. Pike et al. to Johnson, Aug. 9, 1865, Amnesty Papers (M1003, Roll 27), La., Henry W. Allen, RG94, NA.

3. No evidence has been found to substantiate this allegation.

4. Allen did not return from Mexico and therefore did not receive a pardon before his death.

To George Bancroft

Washington, D.C., October 24 1865.

I would be pleased to see you on important business in Washington.[1]

Andrew Johnson

Tel, DNA-RG107, Tels. Sent, President, Vol. 2 (1865).

1. See Johnson to Bancroft, Oct. 29, 1865.

From Milledge L. Bonham [1]

Columbia   Oct 24 1865.

President Johnson

I have been elected to the Legislature which meets here tomorrow. My application for pardon is before you.[2] I should be glad to receive a favorable reply before the hour of meeting. I shall otherwise be much embarrassed.[3]

M A Bonham

Tel, DLC-JP.
1. A former U.S. and Confederate congressman, brigadier general, and wartime governor of South Carolina, Bonham (1813–1890) was also a cousin of Preston Brooks. Warner and Yearns, *BRCC*.
2. Bonham had originally submitted his petition in late August. Amnesty Papers (M1003, Roll 44), S.C., Milledge Luke Bonham, RG94, NA.
3. The telegram reached the War Department at 10:30 the next morning; before 12:50 that afternoon Bonham's pardon had been granted. Johnson to Bonham, Oct. 25, 1865, Johnson Papers, LC.

From Augustus H. Garland

Little Rock, Arks.   Octr. 24/65

Mr. President:

Circumstances connected with the public good, and nothing else, suggest to me the propriety of writing you at this time.

By way of some kind of an introduction, if any be needed, I state that on the 15th of last July you gave me a full pardon & amnesty, for all offences by me committed in the late rebellion: and to the papers on file with my application for pardon, I refer you for my position, sentiments &c.[1]

Some efforts are being made for a provisional Govr. of this state, & a setting aside of the present government. I believe, to secure a reconstruction, or reorganization consistent with your views, which three fourths or four fifths of our people endorse, it will be necessary to set aside the government & give us a Provisional Govr. until the people can meet in convention & form a new constitution. I am now satisfied the present government will not work to the public advantage. And can we not be placed on the same footing that N C, S C, Ala., Geo, Miss &c occupy? Matters could be brought to your attention that would convince you at once, that the present government is a failure—represents nobody—is nothing in fact. And a government should suit, or fit, the people, this does not. No people, on earth, were ever more ready, or willing to submit to, & obey what is required of them, than ours—but now, unfortunately they know not to-day what will be required of them to-morrow. And your policy is thoroughly & fully endorsed here—there is no doubt of this.

This state was never in favor of secession, & the day an ordinance of secession was passed (6th May/61) there was a popular majority then against it of 20,000—and throughout the war union men or conservative men managed & controlled our councils. I went first to the Provisional Congress, & then to both the others, & was finally elected to the Senate, and in every instance I know I was elected by conservative men, & their influence.

And if you will appoint a Governor here, let me urge you for the people, to give the place to no radical, or ultra man, on any side. There are men in this state, who, like Sharkey, Perry, Holden, Parsons[2] &c stood their ground all the time, & breasted the storm, that would make us good & competent Governors—and the appointment of any ultra man would ruin us forever.

I hear, & believe it is true, that F. W. Compton[3] of this state has been recommended for Governor—a Breckenridge-Secessionist! This will not do—& it will look like trifling, in the eyes of the people. He was warm, earnest, zealous and anxious for the "*break up*"—and he will not suit our people or their views. And for the sake of the country, let me urge you not to hear to his appointment or that of any other of the kind.

If conservatism does not save this country, it will not be saved. We can certainly select men, to whom the country can, & will look, for support, & in confidence, from their previous record—and if a change is to take place, let us have one of this sort.

If a conservative man is chosen, the country will gather hope, reorganize & reunite at once, and there will be no disturbing voice to the wise & patriotic policy of Your Excellency, & among them, you have no more earnest & faithful supporter than. . . . [4]

A. H. Garland

I refer Your Excellency to Reverdy Johnson of M'd—Mr. Pennebaker of K'y (411 Penn Avenue, Washington D C) W. D. Snow of this State—Mr. Middleton & officers of the Sup. Court,[5] for my status &c &c.

A.H.G.

ALS, DLC-JP.

1. See Edward W. Gantt to Johnson, June 29, 1865, *Johnson Papers*, 8: 313–14.

2. The provisional governors of Mississippi, South Carolina, North Carolina, and Alabama, respectively.

3. Freeman W. Compton (1824–1892), first elected to the Arkansas supreme court in 1856, was reelected in 1866 and served until his removal two years later. Fay Hempstead, *Historical Review of Arkansas* (3 vols., Chicago, 1911), 1: 455.

4. See Johnson to Isaac Murphy, Oct. 30, 1865.

5. Charles D. Pennebaker (c1826-fl1888), a Louisville legislator, commanded the 27th Ky. Inf., USA, then moved to the national capital after the war to serve as "Kentucky state agent"; William D. Snow, senator-elect from Arkansas; and Daniel W. Middleton (1805–1880), clerk of the United States Supreme Court from 1863 until his death. *NUC*; Lewis and Richard H. Collins, *History of Kentucky* (Louisville, 1877), 357; *Off. Army Reg.: Vols.*, 4: 1281; Washington, D.C., directories (1869–89); 1860 Census, D.C., 5th Ward, Washington, 157; (1870), 2nd Ward, Washington, 128; Fairman, *Reconstruction and Reunion*, 80.

From Samuel B. Maxey[1]

Paris, Texas, Octr. 24th, 1865

Sir:

I have the honor to present herewith my application for Special Pardon, with the endorsement of A. J. Hamilton, Prov. Govr. of Texas, together with his letter saying that it "is a rule of action in his office not to recommend any man who was educated at West Point to the President of the U.S. for pardon."[2]

This is the only objection assigned, and I have no reason to believe that any other exists.

I respectfully submit that I was born and raised in a Slave State, appointed a Cadet therefrom, and never lived out of a Slave State, and for years before the act of Secession of Texas, had been a private citizen.

When the War broke out, and not till then, did I hold any position, Civil or Military, under the late Confederacy.

I acted with my State. In this I am neither more nor less guilty than the mass of the people South. The fact that I was educated at West Point, did not, in my judgment, require me to take up arms against my state. Whether this view was right or wrong, it was honest.

By the 4th par. of a proclamation of Gov. Hamilton, issued Septer. 8th (ult) I, together with all other Lawyers falling within any of the exceptions to the President's proclamation of May 29th last, am prohibited from practising law.[3]

A careful comparison of the Constitution, the proclamation, and my parole, has led me to conclude, that my Political rights are held in abeyance, subject to the future action of the President, or of the Courts, and that I am not to be disturbed in my civil pursuits and the ordinary avocations of life, pending the determination of my political rights. In the note of the Govr. returning my application, he leaves my case to the direct action of the President.

I therefore respectfully ask of the President,

1st That I be pardoned, and restored to my Political and Civil rights.[4]

2d That I be, (in the event he does not pardon me,) permitted and authorized to pursue my profession of the law.[5]

In conclusion I beg to say, that whatever decision may be made by the President, I shall not cease to exert my influence in favor of law and order, and the restoration of harmony.

I went into the War in good faith, and the South having fairly yielded, after a submission of the issues to the sword, I consider it my honorable duty, faithfully to abide the award.

S B Maxey,
Late a Major Genl Prov. Army, C. States.

ALS, DNA-RG94, Amnesty Papers (M1003, Roll 54), Tex., Samuel Bell Maxey.

1. Maxey (1825–1896), a native of Kentucky, fought in the Mexican War after graduating from West Point, then in 1849 resigned from military service to practice law. Declining a seat in the Texas senate at the outbreak of the Civil War, he commanded the 9th Tex. Inf. and subsequently was brevetted a major general for his services in the Trans-Mississippi. In 1875 he was elected to the first of two consecutive terms in the U.S. Senate. Warner, *Gray.*

2. Maxey refers to his August 22, 1865, application, which he had earlier submitted to Hamilton for endorsement and submission to the President. He cites an October 11, 1865, letter from Livingston Lindsay, who returned his petition to him with an explanation of Hamilton's action. Amnesty Papers (M1003, Roll 54), Tex., Samuel Bell Maxey, RG94, NA.

3. Hamilton, in a proclamation on September 18, 1865, had extended to the Texas state courts Congress's requirement of a test oath for attorneys practicing in federal courts. Fairman, *Reconstruction and Reunion*, 58; Waller, *Hamilton of Texas*, 73.

4. Maxey entrusted this letter and other documents to Benjamin H. Epperson, who in turn enlisted the aid of the Kentucky congressional delegation. In spite of additional endorsements from a delegation from the Indian Territory, Kentucky Gov. Thomas E. Bramlette, and General Grant, Johnson did not act on the application until 1867. In March of that year Grant forwarded letters from Maxey and Texas Gov. James W. Throckmorton and again recommended clemency. The President's office referred the matter to Attorney General Stanbery, who approved a pardon on July 20, 1867. Amnesty Papers (M1003, Roll 54), Tex., Samuel Bell Maxey, RG94, NA.

5. In November 1865, upon the advice of influential unionist and former governor Elisha M. Pease, Hamilton allowed attorneys who had taken an oath of allegiance to practice at the discretion of the state district judges. Although the federal requirement was not declared unconstitutional until 1867, Johnson in January 1866, after a visit from Maxey, ordered Attorney General Speed to inform the Texan that he was "permitted to practice law in all the courts in Texas before which you have licens to practice." Waller, *Hamilton of Texas*, 73; Fairman, *Reconstruction and Reunion*, 59; Louise Horton, *Samuel Bell Maxey: A Biography* (Austin, Tex., 1974), 46; Speed to Maxey, Jan. 17, 1866, Amnesty Papers (M1003, Roll 54), Tex., Samuel Bell Maxey, RG94, NA.

From Thomas Corwin[1]

W[ashington] City   25th Oct, 65

To the President

I am requested by the gentleman[2] whose letter I inclose herewith, to hand to yr. Excellency the petition of the Members of the N Carolina convention,[3] praying the enlargement of the parole of the late Confederate Gov Vance.

It seems his Parole confines him to his own home in N Carolina. I wrote him some time since, advizing him to come to Washington & seek a personal interview with the President, as the best method of obtaining his pardon. I suppose he wishes to visit W City for that purpose.[4] The letter I inclose relates in part, to the petition of a Mr Ashe,[5] of whom I know nothing.

Thomas Corwin

ALS, DLC-JP.

1. Vance's old Ohio friend, a former senator, cabinet member and U.S. minister to Mexico, died on December 18, 1865. *BDAC.*

2. Richard H. Battle (1835–1912), a son of Vance's law professor, was the governor's former private secretary and a Raleigh attorney. Johnston, *Vance Papers*, 156–57; Battle to Corwin, Oct. 21, 1865, Johnson Papers, LC.

3. The petition is dated October 14, 1865, and found in the Johnson Papers, LC.
4. See Vance to Johnson, Nov. 29, 1865.
5. Thomas S. Ashe (1812–1887) was a Confederate representative whose pardon had already been granted on October 14. After losing to Holden in the 1868 gubernatorial election, Ashe served in Congress (1873–77) and as a state supreme court justice (1878–87). Warner and Yearns, *BRCC*; Amnesty Papers (M1003, Roll 37), N.C., Thomas S. Ashe, RG94, NA.

From Quincy A. Gillmore

Hilton Head S.C.   Oct. 25th 1865.

Sir

I would most respectfully urge, if there exist no special reasons to the contrary, that the application for pardon of Mr. Stephen Elliott,[1] late a Brigadier General in the rebel army, receive early attention.

Mr. Elliott is now residing in this vicinity, supporting himself and family as best he can, by fishing. He was, at the beginning of the war, the owner of considerable land in the neighborhood of Port Royal, which is now in the custody of the agents of the Freedmen's Bureau, and he would probably soon be restored to the possession of some of it, were he to receive pardon. I know of no more worthy object of executive clemency, among the officers lately arrayed against the Union, than himself.

He is a high toned gentleman, & a man of truth and probity, and I earnestly recommend his case for early consideration.[2]

Q. A. Gillmore   Maj. Genl.

ALS, DNA-RG94, Amnesty Papers (M1003, Roll 45), S.C., Stephen Elliott, Jr.
1. Seriously wounded during the Battle of the Crater, Elliott (1830–1866), the son of the eminent Episcopal bishop, was a newly-elected member of the state legislature. His two applications on file are dated June 14 and August 5, 1865. Warner, *Gray*; Robert M. Myers, ed., *The Children of Pride: A True Story of Georgia and the Civil War* (New Haven, 1972), 1514; Benjamin Perry to Johnson, Nov. 3, 1865, Johnson Papers, LC; Amnesty Papers (M1003, Roll 45), S.C., Stephen Elliott, Jr., RG94, NA.
2. Gillmore's letter was personally retrieved from the President and handed to the Attorney General by the Rev. Richard Fuller, a Baptist divine from Baltimore, who, following an interview with Johnson, succeeded in obtaining a pardon for his cousin. Fuller to Johnson and Robert Johnson to James Speed, Nov. 4; Fuller to Speed, Nov. 11, 1865, ibid; *DAB*. See Johnson to Perry, Nov. 4, 1865, Johnson Papers, LC.

From John B. McGehee[1]

La-Grange Ga   October 25th, 1865

Sir,

Permit me, most respectfully, to submit the accompanying documents[2] as furnished Major General Thomas and showing reasons why the enclosed "Special Order No 79["][3] should be revoked.

I do this 1st Because the General, after injuring me by an order issued on a mere ex-parte application, has (so far as I know) taken no steps to repair that injury. Perhaps he has never received my communications, or he may have suppressed them because they were not sent via Military channels.

2 Because the churches at Newnan and Palmetto are *now* suffering for a Pastor. The Rev J H Caldwell, although "reinstated," prefers to remain at the North.[4]

3 Because the Annual Conference, when the *merits* of this case will be tried, is rapidly approaching, and it is proper, and becoming the genius of our Government, that such a body should be allowed to deliberate without any military dictations or decisions.

I had thought, Mr President, of furnishing you with numerous certificates (now in my possession) touching the Antecedents of Rev Mr Caldwell, his very extraordinary course, and my treatment of him—but deem it wholly unnecessary.

For the present, I submit the above and the accompanying. Should you see proper to take any action, I beg that your action be forewarded before the 15th of Nov.[5] Thanking you for your very kind indulgence. . . .

J B. McGehee   Presiding Elder
La Grange Dist Ga Conference.

ALS, DNA-RG107, Lets. Recd., EB12 President 2709.5 (1865).

1. Entering the ministry at age nineteen, McGehee (1833–1917) superintended numerous Methodist districts throughout Georgia. Lawrence, *Methodist Preachers*, 341.

2. Copies of the following documents relating to McGehee's removal of John H. Caldwell as pastor of a Newnan church were included: McGehee's September 25 letter of complaint to Gen. George H. Thomas; an October 9 report to Thomas from the commander at Newnan; an October 7 petition signed by various Newnan citizens; and several affidavits. Lets. Recd., EB12 President 2709.5 (1865), RG107, NA. See Caldwell to Thomas, Nov. 6, 1865, ibid.

3. Issued on September 13, 1865, the order stated that Caldwell, who had been removed for delivering sermons denouncing slavery, should be "immediately reinstated . . . protected and upheld . . . by the United States military authorities." *Cincinnati Gazette*, Sept. 20, 1865.

4. After a brief tour of the North, Caldwell (1820–1899), a former secessionist, returned to Georgia, replaced McGehee as presiding elder of the LaGrange district, worked with the Freedmen's Bureau, served as a Republican in the state legislature, and in 1871 was appointed as a federal judge. Lawrence, *Methodist Preachers*, 83; Ralph E. Morrow, *Northern Methodism and Reconstruction* (East Lansing, Mich., 1956), 47, 225; *NUC*; Ruth Currie-McDaniel, *Carpetbagger of Conscience: A Biography of John Emory Bryant* (Athens, Ga., 1987), 89, 208.

5. Received by the President on November 3, McGehee's letter was referred to General Thomas "for such action as in his judgment, the facts of the case may justify." After further investigation Thomas concluded that his "order was right" and would stand until the November 15 meeting of the Georgia Conference, which ultimately censured Caldwell and upheld his dismissal. Harold W. Mann, *Atticus Greene Haygood: Methodist Bishop, Editor and Educator* (Athens, Ga., 1965), 55–56. See endorsement by Robert Johnson, Nov. 3, 1865, and Thomas's undated decision, Lets. Recd., EB12 President 2709.5 (1865), RG107, NA.

From Benjamin F. Perry

Executive Department   South Carolina
Oct 25" 1865

My dear Sir

I have just received a beautiful, & most affecting letter from Mrs Lubbock,[1] wife of Ex Governor Lubbock of Texas,[2] in behalf of her husband, now confined as a Prisioner. She appeals to me to address your Excellency requesting that her husband may be released on parole, & permitted to see & visit his family once more.

I know how much you are annoyed with similar applications, & am therefore reluctant to trespass on your time. But I cannot resist this gushing overflow of affection on the part of a loving wife for a noble & gallant husband, whose only crime has been one of judgement, honestly & sincerely entertained, under the impression that his state was to be benefitted, & never anticipating the terrible calamities he was bringing down on his country, himself & his family. Punishment, terrible and wide spread & permanent has followed this Rebellion. Sight & knowledge have overtaken its leaders—they have sincerely repented of their errors—and this day would prove as true & loyal to their country in council or in battle as any of her sons.

I know the government has a course to pursue & certain great principles to establish. May this not be done most effectually by kindness and clemency? Will not the release of Ex Governor Lubbock & others like him on their parole have a salutary influence on public sentiment after their long & painful imprisonment? As honorable men, loving their poor country which they have brought to ruin, will they not exert themselves to restore peace & security to the Republic? Will not their example have its influence on others? I think so. Mercy & policy unite.[3]

Ben. F. Perry

ALS, DNA-RG94, Lets. Recd. (Main Ser.), File S-2492-1865 (M619, Roll 401).

1. Adele Baron (c1818–1882) married Francis R. Lubbock in 1835. C. W. Raines, ed., *Six Decades in Texas: The Memoirs of Francis R. Lubbock, Confederate Governor of Texas* (Austin, 1968[1900]), 23, 630.

2. Francis R. Lubbock (1815–1905), former comptroller of the Republic of Texas and an ardent secessionist, had been elected governor in 1861. Late in the war he became an aide-de-camp to Jefferson Davis and was captured with him in Georgia. Webb et al., *Handbook of Texas*, 2: 89.

3. Johnson forwarded this letter to Edwin M. Stanton who, by way of reply, returned it with a report from Joseph Holt. Despite the latter's assertion that Lubbock was "among the most vindictive and bloodthirsty of all the traitors in arms against the government" and "should not escape severe and retributive punishment," Lubbock was released on parole from Fort Delaware on November 24, 1865, upon the President's order. Holt to Stanton, Nov. 4, 1865; Albin F. Schoepf to Edwin D. Townsend, Nov. 24, 1865, Lets. Recd. (Main Ser.), File S-2492-1865 (M619, Roll 410), RG94, NA.

From Michael Powers[1]

Charleston South Carolina   October 25th 1865

Sir.

With unbounded confidence in Your Honor & Justice I make bold to approach you and state truthfully my own case in my own simple way. I am a poor hardworking laboring man, my name *Michl. Powers*. I am the owner of only one horse and cart with which I Labor to support my wife and children. Last February in this city I was the owner of some yellow Pine plank which I received in payment for work done with my horse and cart. This plank was piled in my own yard in front of my house. The Qr. Mr. Waggons come and took this plank away for Govmt. use. I sent a Bill to the Chf. Qr. Master. for the amount puting the price of this plank lower than it could be purchased for at that time in Charleston viz $20.00 per thousand ft. It is now selling here for *$40—per Thousand*. After numerous delays, and refering my little Bill from one office to another (the amt of which was only $40.00) it was at last sent to washington City to the office of the Quarter Master General[2] for him to decide whether I should get paid for my lumber or not.

That Hon. Gentleman has decided that my little parcel of lumber was prize of war it being captured in a Hostile city &c. and that I could not be paid by the military authoritys.

May it please your Excellency I am now and always was a Loyal citizen of the United States. I have not been engaged in the late war at all. I am too old for such purpose. I have renewed my allegiance to the U.S. and took your amnesty proclamation oath. I am too poor to loose this amount of $40. It may be a very small amount to some people, but to me it is considerable money at this time. I therefore pray your Excellency will refer this matter back to the Qr. Master Genls office with directions that he will order payment for my Lumber.

Col J. J. Dana[3] in the Quartermaster Generals departmt. is in possession of the papers apertaining to this matter and I have no doubt will remember this case. And in conclusion I shall ever pray that almighty God may always have your Excellency in his holy keeping.[4]

Michael Powers

ALS, DNA-RG107, Lets. Recd., EB12 President 2744 (1865).

1. Powers (c1820-fl1880) held a variety of occupations, including carter, carpenter, carpet layer, cotton pressman, drayman, and "scavenger." 1860 Census, S.C., Charleston, 2nd Ward, Charleston City, 26; Charleston directories (1859–81).

2. Montgomery C. Meigs.

3. Commissioned in 1855, James J. Dana (c1821–1898) was a career soldier, devoting nearly thirty years to the quartermaster general's office at numerous military posts scattered across the continent. Powell, *Army List*, 271; ACP Branch, File D-2/95–1885, James J. Dana, RG94, NA.

4. Received by the President on October 30, routinely forwarded the following day

to the Secretary of War, and referred on November 1 to the Adjutant General's office, the claim eventually wound up for a second time on Meigs's desk, where it was flatly "rejected." Lets. Recd., EB12 President 2744 (1865), RG107, NA.

From Emma Willard[1]

Troy [N.Y.]   Oct. 25th. 1865.

Respected and dear Sir,

Having regarded with the deep feeling of an anxious patriot, your difficult official course, I have become impressed with the belief, that the Almighty has given you the wisdom and virtue to do a great and good work in the reconstruction of our broken country. The confidence which arises from this belief, impels me to appeal to you, some thoughts which have come to my mind on the grand problem now laboring noble the whole country; as remarked by yourself in your address to the colored troops.[2] To avert the dangers which beset this problem (a servile war lowering in the dark distance) you allude to Colonization in Africa.

But there is an obstacle—in its unpopularity with the colored race. And it is to point out, (what others do not appear to have thought of) measures, by which this unpopularity may be overcome that I presume to write to your Excellency: in advance, however, of suggesting what appear to me means which might change the current of their thoughts and feelings. I would premise, that the evils these measures promise to prevent, are of such magnitude, as to justify a grand national experiment, in which the different branches of the general government would be called into action, with cooperating aids from states and individuals. That the plan of Colonization in Liberia would be approved by the nation, North and South, we have this pledge,—our dearest patriots, and our Christian philanthropists have given it their sanction. The experiment, should it succeed, would infuse life and healthy action into the yet living and noble skeleton of the first Republic ever attempted in Africa; and if we were truly bent on doing good to the family of man, the experiment would for that cause alone justify the trouble and expence of the trying; while at the same time, its object is urged imperatively upon us, as a resort from appalling calamity.

We come now to state what it is, which we believe would make Liberia a desirable home to the American Africans. We propose that the American government should send to Liberia an Envoy extraordinary, and Minister plenetitentiary; thus setting this first of negro Republics, on an equal national level with our own—our Envoy to be understood as our agent to promote and regulate emigration, and to be supplied with money accordingly. He would want to hasten on all those national improvements in Liberia, on which its healthy growth depends; and from which *offices* would arise in government, in education, in financial affairs &c, worthy the ambition of our most intelligent and best educated colored aspirants. Produce a state of things in Liberia, where a resident American Minister might be found by our African emigrants—a man known to all for superior abilities, and specially confided in by the colored race for former services to them—suppose him there, ready to receive and find them employment,—would there not be an immediate rush thither?

We cannot doubt that the American Africans already qualified, would be at once attracted; and further that a state of things would be superinduced, which would lead to measures that would keep up the emigration. For example, let us suppose some southern man who has been a large slave-owner with a great plantation. It is desirable that he make the most of all the home-feeling, that his freedmen now have in their hearts; and by fair agreement give them money and such other coveted privileges as to attract them to cultivate his lands, and perform his domestic services. Suppose he calls his people together and says to them, 'You are no longer slaves; you are now free men. Behave as our good President has advised you, and you may depend on me, as well as him for your friend. Indeed, I have already shown myself the friend of your race, by supporting our government to help build up an equal nation with our own in Africa; where colored people may go, and in their native climate if they are qualified, may have the same chance to be senators and representatives there that white people have here. I will have a school set up, where all your children may be taught, and those who show themselves sufficiently capable, be fitted for Liberia; and for those who wish to go I will see to it that they shall not lack a conveyance thither, nor care for their welfare when there; and crossing the ocean is not such a mighty matter; but that if you were not contented you might after making a fair trial return.[']

The Colonization Society now stand ready to accommodate all who wish to emigrate; but if the movement we have supposed, were once inaugurated, Liberia would soon have her wants to be supplied, and her products to dispose of, and commerce would be invited to her shores; and merchant ships could carry emigrants.

Of course, the Liberian government could not but be gratified, and give their hearty cooperation; and we see not but an agreement might be made, by which our emigrants should be at once received in Liberia, as if they were native-born citizens of that Republic; they being such, of one, which would have constituted itself their ally; and thus I know they would at once be eligible to the highest offices and honors of a fast rising state.

The Christian world would look with an exciting joy and admiration on the elevation of Liberia; and our religious community would, by their voluntary gifts and exertions, go hand in hand with the secular authority; and thus make that country a delightful home to a naturally religious race. Whole churches with their ministers would be likely to emigrate. And should the way be opened by the agency of President Johnson, their prayers, like mine, would be for him, that his life on this earth, may be long; and his happiness never-ending.

Emma Willard

ALS, DLC-JP.
1. Willard (1787–1870) was an educator, having founded Troy Female Seminary in 1821, and a literary artist. Her letter was actually forwarded later by Abram B. Olin. *DAB*; Olin to Johnson, Nov. 11, 1865, Johnson Papers, LC.
2. See Speech to First Regiment, USCT, Oct. 10, 1865.

From Alexander N. Wilson

Savannah, Georgia. Oct 25th 1865

My Dear Sir,

I have been here on duty as Collector of Internal Revenue for two months, trying to serve the Government, at the same time, give the least possible trouble to the people.

The Secessionists in lower Geo. are still full of venom and hang together like a pack of thieves. None entertain the idea of resistance, but the feeling is almost universal to "*play Possum*," till the Delegates from the Southern States are admitted into Congress, then make such combinations as will enable them to control the Government, repudiate the National Debt and play the mischief generally. A majority of the Delegates to the State Convention from the up Country are good men, the low Country sends Gasbags or toads generally. Your lenience toward Rebels is having a softening effect upon even the worst. All speak in your praise, but the hard headed Union men, who suffered persecutions are a little *Soured*. They say treason is not a crime when such men as Henry R. Jackson of Savannah, Ben C. Yancey of Athens can get pardoned and restored to all their original privilleges.[1] I think this is more from a desire to see such men punished through pride than patriotism, but it is a fact in Geo. that those who have been the best Union men during the War are taking a position against the Administration. Men ordinarily from their selfish stand point lose sight of the fact that a *Statesman* is actuated by one principle, vis: "The greatest good to the greatest number." United States troops are an excellent medicine all through this Country.

Alex. N. Wilson

ALS, DLC-JP.
1. General Jackson had been granted amnesty on September 7 and Yancey on August 28, 1865. The younger brother of the Alabama secessionist, Yancey (1817–1891) was an attorney, editor, state legislator, minister to Argentina (1858–59), and agricultural reformer. *House Ex. Docs.*, 39 Cong., 2 Sess., No. 31, p. 9 (Ser. 1289); *NCAB*, 13: 560; Yancey to Johnson, ca. Aug. 2, 1865, Amnesty Papers (M1003, Roll 24), Ga., Benjamin C. Yancey, RG94, NA.

From John Adriance

Houston   Oct 26th 1865

I deem it my duty as an act of justice to Col J C DeGress[1] Provost Marshal General of the Eastern District of Texas, to state that I was traveling in Company with him on the 15th inst in Brazoria County, when a Messenger came to the place where we were stopping and asked for a Doctor. Col DeGress asked him what he wanted a Doctor for, to which he replied that Mr Wm P Johnson had accidently shot himself through the Arm, and they could not arrest the bleeding—that he had tried to get a Surgeon to go down and attend to him but was unable to procure the services of any one. Col DeGress then made an endorsement on the paper which the messenger had, ordering the Provost Marshal at Columbia Brazoria County[2] to send a Surgeon to Mr Johnson *at once*, even if he had to do so by force of Arms, and send a Soldier with said Surgeon and have him repeat his visits as long as Mr. Johnson required his services. The Messenger went to Columbia and procured a Physician who went down in conformity with the order of Col DeGress. A few days after the Post Surgeon went down (he being absent on the day the Messenger arrived) and has been in attendance as I am informed until Mr Johnson died.[3] Col DeGress manifested the greatest anxiety to serve Mr Johnson, and if he had been his Father, he could not have done more for him.[4]

John Adriance

ALS, DLC-JP.

1. Prussian native Jacob C. De Gress (1842–1894), formerly lieut. col. of the 6th Mo. Cav., had come to Texas in June 1865 as provost marshal and agent for the Freedmen's Bureau in the eastern district. Upon the recommendation of many correspondents, including William P. Johnson's widow, the President personally ordered De Gress reinstated after his routine dismissal from volunteer service. He served intermittently in the regular army until 1870, then became active in Texas Republican politics, holding several public offices. Powell, *Army List*, 278; Webb et al., *Handbook of Texas*, 1: 482; William C. Nunn, *Texas Under the Carpetbaggers* (Austin, 1962), 241–42, 252n; Sarah G. Johnson to Johnson, Nov. 23, 1865; Andrew J. Hamilton to Johnson, Jan. 6, 1866; Thomas E. Noell to Johnson, Mar. 1, 1866; John Hogan to Johnson, May 25, 1866; Thomas C. Fletcher et al. to Johnson, Apr. 3, 1866, ACP Branch, File D-359-CB-1866, Jacob C. De Gress, RG94, NA.

2. Captain Andrew M. Cochran (1834–1904) of the 48th Btn. Oh. Inf. commanded the post at Columbia. He may have served as provost marshal as well, for he sent surgeons to attend William P. Johnson as De Gress had ordered. Pension Record, Mary E. Cochran, RG15, NA; Cochran to De Gress, Oct. 25, 1865, Johnson Papers, LC.

3. The President's brother died on October 24, 1865, after gangrene developed in a wound suffered during a hunting expedition. Ibid.; *Johnson Papers*, 3: 683–84n.

4. Texas Secretary of State James H. Bell endorsed this letter, praising Adriance as a "man second to none as a citizen in point of respectability and moral worth," adding, "I should desire every statement he might make as entitled to the fullest credence." Although allegations surfaced that William P. Johnson had died of neglect because he was a unionist and the President's brother, Andrew Johnson apparently accepted the testimony of Adriance and others that nothing more could have been done. Cochran to De

Gress, Oct. 25, 1865, Johnson Papers, LC; *Cincinnati Commercial*, Mar. 3, 1866. See Harris T. Garnett to Johnson, Oct. 31, 1865.

From William G. Brownlow
Nashville, October 26th, 1865.

President Johnson:

If you have not appointed the Cadet for the Memphis District, allow me to suggest that it cannot be conferred upon a more worthy young man than Charles S. Collins.[1] If the District appointment has been agreed upon, could not young Collins be appointed for *the State at large*?

He is the son of the former President of Emory & Henry College, who, for the last several years, has been at the head of the State Female College at Memphis.[2] Doct. Collins is my old *Methodist* friend, and your old *Democratic* friend. His son would set in with a good education, for one of his years, and come out with honor to himself and those appointing him.

W. G. Brownlow   Governor of Tennessee.

ALS, DNA-RG94, USMA Appls. (M688, Roll 237).

1. Instead of embarking on a military career, young Collins (c1847–fl1871) became an attorney. 1870 Census, Tenn., Shelby, 14th Dist., 10; *Edwards' Annual Director . . . City of Memphis* (1871), 125.

2. Charles Collins (1813–1875), an educator and Methodist minister, also had been president of Dickinson College (1852–60). *NCAB*, 6: 464.

From Benjamin G. Humphreys
Jackson, Miss., Oct 26th 1865.

Sir—

I received by the hand of Govr Sharkey to day your pardon for my participation in the rebellion just terminated.[1] A majority of my fellow citizens, believing this clemency would be extended to me—and in view of my political anticedents, elected me to the office of Governor, at the recent election. I was installed in office on the 16th inst, by Governor Sharkey, under the sanctions of an oath to maintain the Constitution of the United States, and of the State of Mississippi; and am now endeavouring to do my duty to both Governments.[2]

The people of Mississippi, during the rebellion, displayed that martial prowess that no American can be ashamed of; and is a guaranty of their fidelity to professions of honor. But, over powered and exhausted, they have surrendered; and have laid down their arms, as they believe, to a magnanimous foe. The magnanimity already shown by the Federal Government, in the liberal amnesty granted by your proclamation, assures them that it will be paternal and just, and they now desire in good faith to return to their allegiance, and the protection of the Constitution and the Union. I feel safe in pledging their unwavering fidelity to your administration in your policy of reconstruction, and restoring Mississippi to the sisterhood of states—and removing those restraints that the necessities of war has imposed upon her.[3]

I thank you for your kindness to me personally, and to my family, and beg to assure you of my high consideration.

Benj G Humphreys

ALS, DLC-JP.

1. Although Humphreys was elected governor on October 2, 1865, it was not until three days later that Johnson granted him a pardon, which was dated September 21, 1865. Amnesty Papers (M1003, Roll 33), Miss., Benjamin G. Humphreys, RG94, NA; *House Ex. Docs.*, 39 Cong., 2 Sess., No. 31, p. 19 (Ser. 1289).

2. Johnson did not officially relieve Sharkey from his duties as provisional governor and recognize Humphreys as governor of Mississippi until December 25, 1865. Seward to Sharkey, Dec. 25, 1865, Tels. Sent, Sec. of War (M473, Roll 90), RG107, NA. See Johnson to Sharkey, Nov. 17, 1865.

3. See Johnson to Humphreys, Nov. 17, 1865.

From Madison C. Johnson[1]

Lexington, Oct 26. 1865

Mr. President

I beg leave to call your attention to the inclosed extract of a letter of Genl. Brisbin published in the Cincinnati Gazette of today,[2] with the view of your determining, whether a Genl. animated with such a desire of "blood-letting" in the region in which he commands is a suitable commander for that District.

It does not seem proper that your subordinates should be predicting the certain failure of your great policy on the success of which so much of national blessing depends. The wish is the father to the prophesy. It may be said with certainty that such an officer will work ardently both to bring about the bloodletting which he thinks so necessary, and for the fulfilment of the prophesy he so confidently makes.

M C Johnson

ALS, DLC-JP.

1. Johnson had recently addressed a convention endorsing the President and his restoration policy. His letter was enclosed in a missive of the same date to Francis P. Blair, with the proviso: "If you agree with me the President should see it please see to it that he does quickly." *Louisville Journal*, Oct. 20, 1865; Madison C. Johnson to Blair, Oct. 26, 1865, Johnson Papers, LC.

2. James S. Brisbin (1837–1892) was an abolitionist and the controversial superintendent of black troops in Kentucky. Mustered out of volunteer service in January 1866, he served with distinction in the postwar army while continuing to speak in favor of black rights. The extract has not been found in the Johnson Papers, but the newspaper reported that Brisbin had written, "I think a little blood letting would do good, especially here in the blue grass region, where the people seem determined to be troublesome." Warner, *Blue*; Howard, *Black Liberation*, 73, 139; *Cincinnati Gazette*, Oct. 26, 1865.

From Louis Schade[1]

Washington, D.C., October 26, 1865.

Sir:

One of the principal prerogatives of your high position is that of mercy and pardon. It becomes still more important in dubious cases, where it is not quite clear whether justice has been done or not. Such one, I regret very much to say, is my duty not only as counsel for the defendant, but as friend of humanity, to lay before Your Excellency to-day.

Captain Wirz,[2] my client, has been tried, and, as I apprehend, condemned to die. In your hand it rests whether this sentence shall be carried out or not. It is true that if you are solely guided by the evidence which will be or has been laid before you, little or no hope is to be entertained; but there is something else which cannot fail to command Your Excellency's regards, and that is the following:

1. That this commission, before which the prisoner has been tried, has in many instances excluded testimony in favor of the prisoner, and, on the other hand, admitted testimony against the prisoner, both in violation of all rules of law and equity. That the whole country knows. Every lawyer in this city and elsewhere has regarded this and the treatment the counsel suffered at the hands of the president of the commission and the judge-advocate with indignation and as an insult to the profession. My former colleagues, Messrs. Hughes, Denver, and Peck,[3] left for that reason, and then I would have followed their example had not the prisoner had my word of honor not to forsake him.

2. The testimony for the prosecution is loose, indefinite, and in the most part contradictory. Before any other court but that military commission it would have been an easy matter to uncover and bring to light a tissue of perjuries as the world has seldom seen. Time will show that this assertion of mine is no empty one.

Captain Wirz was almost a prisoner himself at Andersonville. If permitted we could have proven by our witnesses that at different times he requested to be discharged, or to be sent to the Trans-Mississippi Department away from Andersonville. He took the responsibility of enlarging the stockade against the orders of his superiors, as appears from Colonel Persons' testimony,[4] a witness for the prosecution; and "worked indefatigably" for the benefit of the prisoners. Colonel Persons, commandant of the post, in harmony with Wirz, approved what the latter had done. Both sent remonstrances to Richmond, and the consequence of these remonstrances was that General Winder[5] was sent to Andersonville to stop them. It was Captain Wirz who complained of the bad bread (see his letter published in the testimony);[6]

who asked for shoes or leather from the rebel authorities for paroled Union prisoners; who paroled about fifty young Union drummer boys in order that they might escape the horrors of the stockade; who remonstrated against having so many prisoners sent there; who gave writing material to our boys to prepare a petition for exchange to Washington, and permitted six of our men to go North for that purpose in order to see the President and the Secretary of War; and when all hopes for exchange were gone he told Judge Hall,[7] one of the witnesses for the prosecution, that he (Wirz) would wish all the prisoners paroled and set at large, instead of letting them die in the stockade. All that and many other facts prove that Captain Wirz did certainly not conspire to kill the prisoners.

Thirteen cases of acts of personal cruelty and murder alleged by the prosecution to have been committed by Captain Wirz are located in the month of August, 1864. About sixty witnesses (thirty-four for the defense and over twenty for the prosecution) have positively sworn that Captain Wirz was not at Andersonville and Lieutenant Davis[8] in command of the prison during that time. Not a single one has contradicted that statement. That proves sufficiently how much stress is to be laid upon such testimony. Some ten to twelve on both sides swear that he was sick in the latter half of July and most part of September; that he was fetched in an ambulance from his residence to his office, and was unable to ride on horseback, &c. And almost all the alleged cruelties and murders are said to have been committed in July, August, and September, 1864.

Among the 35,000 prisoners were many bounty-jumpers and bad characters. Some six of them were hung by their own comrades. If I have the Government's patronage, and perhaps the prospect of an office or two (as actually has been the case with some of the witnesses for the prosecution in the Wirz trial), and can also give a promise of safe conduct and perhaps a reward, I do not doubt in the least that among those 500 raiders at Andersonville (as they are styled in the testimony) I shall within four weeks find enough testimony to try, condemn, and hang every member of the Wirz military commission on any charge whatever, provided it is done before such a military commission.

Your Excellency knows me. It is unnecessary to state that nothing but a feeling of humanity urges me to ask you for clemency. No remuneration, but labor and vituperation have been the reward of the counsel in this case. God knows that I would not ask you to do anything which was not right. And therefore let the miserable, crippled, half-dying man, at the worst a tool in the hands of superiors, a subaltern officer who had to obey orders, live out the few remaining days of his life, and do not let our hands be tainted with the blood of this miserable and unfortunate being. I know you will believe me if I, with all my heart, declare that he does not deserve that fate. Spare the cripple! Be merciful![9]

Louis Schade.

OR, Ser. 2, Vol. 8: 773–74.

1. Schade (1829–1903), a graduate of the University of Berlin, fled his native Germany after being condemned as a revolutionary, then held a series of federal bureaucratic appointments before establishing himself as an editor and attorney. *NCAB*, 21: 313.

2. Henry Wirz.

3. James Hughes, James W. Denver (1817–1892), and Charles F. Peck (*c*1834-*fl*1884) were partners in a prominent Washington law firm. Denver represented California in Congress (1855–57) before becoming governor of Kansas (1858) and Commissioner of Indian Affairs (1857, 1858–59). *DAB*; N. P. Chipman, *The Tragedy of Andersonville: The Trial of Captain Henry Wirz the Prison Keeper* (San Francisco, 1911), 36; 1870 Census, D.C., Georgetown, 170; Washington, D.C., directories (1863–84).

4. Alexander W. Persons (*c*1837-*fl*1870), who commanded the post at Andersonville during the first half of 1864, became an attorney and pardon broker after the war. His testimony appears in *House Ex. Docs.*, 40 Cong., 2 Sess., No. 23, pp. 99–104, 455–66 (Ser. 1331). CSR, RG109, NA; *OR*, Ser. 2, Vol. 7: 993; 1870 Census, Ga., Bibb, Macon, 31; *Macon Telegraph*, Oct. 4, 1865.

5. John H. Winder (1800–1865) was commissary general of prisoners east of the Mississippi River for the Confederacy. Warner, *Gray*.

6. Wirz's letter of June 6, 1864, can be found in *House Ex. Docs.*, 40 Cong., 2 Sess., No. 23, p. 644 (Ser. 1331).

7. Samuel Hall (1820–1887), an attorney who served as an associate justice of the Georgia Supreme Court from 1882 until his death, had frequently visited the post and prison at Andersonville. Allen D. Candler and Clement A. Evans, eds., *Cyclopedia of Georgia* (4 vols., Spartanburg, S.C., 1972[1906]), 2: 185; *House Ex. Docs.*, 40 Cong., 2 Sess., No. 23, pp. 132–33, 493 (Ser. 1331).

8. After being wounded at Gettysburg, Samuel B. Davis (*c*1845-*c*1915) was assigned to Winder's staff and served briefly as assistant adjutant and inspector general for the post at Andersonville. In January 1865 he was captured in Ohio and condemned as a spy; but his sentence was commuted, and he was released from Fort Warren on December 7, 1865. After a letter to Davis from George W. Bickley was discovered, Johnson ordered Davis rearrested, but this directive was rescinded on December 20. *Con Vet*, 23 (1915): 176; 37 (1929): 450–52; *OR*, Ser. 2, Vol. 7: 377, 518; Vol. 8: 132–33, 181, 191–92, 204, 309, 736, 837; Joseph Holt to Edwin M. Stanton, Dec. 8, 1865; Augustus A. Gibson to Edwin D. Townsend, Dec. 13, 1865, Lets. Recd. (Main Ser.), Files G-953-1865 and G-1001-1865 (M619, Roll 360), RG94, NA; Townsend to Gibson, Dec. 12, 1865, Tels. Sent, Sec. of War (M473, Roll 90), RG107, NA.

9. Upon the recommendation of Holt, the President approved the sentence of the military commission, and Wirz was hanged on November 10, 1865. *House Ex. Docs.*, 40 Cong., 2 Sess., No. 23, pp. 808–15 (Ser. 1331).

From Charles M. Swett[1]

Kennebunk Maine   Oct 26th 1865

Sir:

I have the honor to enclose for your favorable consideration a petition signed by some of the principal commercial men and other leading and influential citizens of this district,[2] also a letter from Enoch Cousens[3] Esq. who has held important offices under the government and now member elect of our Legislature. I beg leave also to call your attention to the fact that two other petitions, having the same object in view were sent to President Lincoln in 1861, one containing a long list of the names of our Republican friends while the other contained the names of nearly all our principal commercial men. When Mr Lincoln was about to take his seat I was promised the office of Collector of the Customs of this district by the leading Republicans of this vicinity including our Representative in Congress Hon John N Goodwin[4] to whose decission Mr Lincoln left the appointments of his district. I may be excused for saying I was cheated out of it and one of the most ultry fanatics appointed[5] who now seeks to be by you reappointed though he has always been directly opposed to you in politics. Full a quarter of a century ago he helped form the first abolition society ever formed in these parts and has always been engaged in firmentating the lamentable strifs that culminated in the terriable war and blood shed of the past four years. Mr Bryant[6] who seeks his place is of precisily the same piece. It is a remarkable coincidence that these two men so much alike, and yet so unlike yourself in their political views should be fighting each other and asking a favor of one whom they have opposed all their life and still opposes him. The most remarkable thing is that these two men are two old superanuated or worn out Freewill or Christian Baptist preachers, neither of whom has been a regular preacher but both of whom have preached occasionally, but both of whom are equally greedy after this little office. And is it right that such men shall be rewarded for life long efforts in disevering that Union you strove so hard before and during the war to hold together against their almost fatal blows and which you are so assiduously striving to cement again now the war is over, though they oppose you still. I trust to your sound sence of justice and right, and feel that our interests are safe in your hands as regards this appointment. Those who recommend my appointment have always been true and loyal men and are your union friends and sincere supporters. May I not hope that you will give their request a favorable consideration and grant their petition.[7]

Charles M Swett

ALS, DNA-RG56, Appts., Customs Service, Collector, Kennebunk, Charles M. Swett.

1. Swett (b. c1817) was a physician and justice of the peace. 1860 Census, Me., York, Kennebunk, 49; *Maine Register* (1856), 73, 256.

2. The petition had thirty-five signatures. George H. Newbegin et al. to Johnson, Oct. 10, 1865, Appts., Customs Service, Collector, Kennebunk, Charles M. Swett, RG56, NA.

3. Cousens (1818–1904), who described Swett as Johnson's "cordial supporter," was a merchant, postmaster, and former deputy collector and inspector of customs at Kennebunkport. Cousens to Johnson, Oct. 24, 1865, ibid.; Harrie B. Coe, ed., *Maine: Resources, Attractions and Its People, A History* (4 vols., New York, 1928), 3: 133; *U.S. Off. Reg.* (1859–61).

4. Following his initial term in Congress (1861–63), Goodwin (1824–1887) had been appointed by Lincoln chief justice and first governor of the Arizona Territory. He later practiced law in New York City. *BDAC.*

5. Commissioner of Customs Nathaniel K. Sargent (c1797-fl1867), a former carriage maker, was again appointed collector at Kennebunk, despite the objections of Swett. 1860 Census, Me., York, Kennebunk, 62; *U.S. Off. Reg.* (1863–67).

6. William M. Bryant (b. *c*1795) had formerly served as inspector under Sargent. 1860 Census, Me., York, Riddleford, 84; *U.S. Off. Reg.* (1863), 60.
7. Swett had written to Johnson about this matter weeks earlier. His first letter, like this one, was routinely referred to the Treasury Department. Swett to Johnson, Sept. 6, 1865, Appts., Customs Service, Collector, Kennebunk, Charles M. Swett, RG56, NA.

From Henry Wikoff

October 26, 1865, Paris, France; ALS, DLC-JP.

Wikoff reminds the President of their conversation on September 4, when "Your Excellency made many interesting and important statements on our domestic affairs, which I conveyed, confidentially, to your very devoted partisan Mr J. G. Bennett." Further, Johnson's "language was so concilliatory," concerning "Mexican matters," that Wikoff "begged permission to repeat it to the French Emperor." Johnson agreed and added that he "was at liberty to say to His Majesty that 'you would do your best to settle all pending difficulties in a friendly and satisfactory manner.'" Wikoff now reports that Napoleon III "expressed his admiration of the ability, prudence & tact by which you were mastering difficulties & dangers that would have overpowered any ordinary man." Protesting that "the force of events" in Mexico had carried him "into a position he had never anticipated," Napoleon III voiced his appreciation at the American government's efforts "to assuage all difficulties in a friendly & satisfactory manner," and indicated that he aimed at "retiring from Mexico at the earliest possible moment" and hoped for "a cordial alliance" with the United States. Wikoff "entreats" Johnson, in his forthcoming message, "to employ phrases of the same forbearing and concilliatory spirit as those which you authorized me in good faith to repeat in your name to His Majesty."

From Benjamin F. Perry

Columbia S C   Oct 27 1865.

President Johnson

The Legislature convened on Wednesday & all the members took the oath to support the Constitution of the United States. My message will be sent you by mail. I have this morning communicated to the Legislature a most admirable code of laws for the protection of the colored persons in their rights of person & property. It was prepared by order of the Convention. I have no doubt it will be adopted.[1] Genl Wade Hampton has been elected Governor of the State.[2] He was not a candidate, and so declared publicly in the Newspapers, but the people took offense at the Nomination of Col Orr by the Convention, & voted for Hampton. There was no political question in the elections. I have just had a full conversation with Genl Hampton & he will sustain your policy of reconstruction as fully & as warmly as any man in South Carolina. He was originally opposed to secession & went for maintaining the rights of the South, in the Union. He was always moderate man. His great personal popularity will enable him to control the disaffected or turbulent, more easily, than Col Orr could have done. He is one of the most admirable & lovable men I ever saw & as honorable, frank & open hearted as can be. I have known him well for 20 years past & will vouch for his loyalty & fidelity. I trust that no difficulty will occur in his getting his pardon by the 4th Monday in November, when he should be inaugurated as Governor.[3] My election to the Senate is pretty certain & I hope my services as Provl Governor will not be needed longer than till the meeting of Congress. I may say that the old union District of Greeneville voted by a large majority for Hampton, although Colonel Orr lives in the adjoining District.

B F Perry   Provl Govr

Tel, DLC-JP.

1. See James L. Orr to Johnson, Oct. 2, Dec. 23, 1865, and Perry to Johnson, Dec. 9, 1865.

2. Perry erred in proclaiming Hampton the victor, for Orr was in fact elected. See Perry to Johnson, Nov. 29, 1865.

3. See Johnson to Perry, Oct. 28, 1865.

From William H. Seward

Washington, 27th Oct. 1865

My dear President:

I see no objection to granting an amnesty and pardon to Mr. Soule.[1]

But his application[2] is very objectionable in containing by way of apology an argument for secession and a detail of hardships neither of which the government could consent to receive. He accepts the true constitutional principles, but only after and because the war settled them against him. Moreover he speaks of this war as fatal to the both parties. I would not consent to receive such a plea.

If you think well of it I will advise him how to draw an unobjectionable paper.[3]

Copy, DNA-RG94, Amnesty Papers (M1003, Roll 29), La., Pierre Soule.

1. Pierre Soule (1801–1870), a senator (1847–53) and minister to Spain (1853–55), served briefly on General Beauregard's staff and attempted in Cuba to recruit a foreign legion for the Confederacy. After the war he returned to Havana and sought to relocate Confederate veterans in Mexico before settling once more in New Orleans. Wakelyn, *BDC*; *DAB*.

2. A copy of Soule's amnesty application cannot be found.

3. Soule's New Orleans home had been confiscated by the federal government, which used it as an "asylum." He subsequently forwarded a letter of explanation to Seward, insisting that he "meant solely to assert" his loyalty to the United States. After Johnson pardoned Soule on October 30, 1865, the property was returned to him despite the protest of the Freedmen's Bureau. Soule to Seward, Oct. 28, 1865, Amnesty Papers (M1003, Roll 29), La., Pierre Soule, RG94, NA; *House Reports*, 40 Cong., 1 Sess., No. 7, p. 25 (Ser. 1314).

From Charles A. Weed & Co.[1]

New Orleans La   Oct 27, 1865

Sir:

Please inform us if your order restoring the plantation of Duncan F. Kenner[2] is intended to set aside the lease made in January 1864 for one year, by Supervising Special Agent. We have invested largely under the lease which was made by authority of Congress, and feel sure you did not intend to veto it.[3]

C A Wood[sic] & Co

Tel, DNA-RG107, Tels. Recd., President, Vol. 4 (1865–66).

1. Weed had been appointed by Gen. Benjamin F. Butler in October 1862 to manage confiscated plantations in south Louisiana for the benefit of the federal government. His name was misspelled by the telegrapher. Marshall, *Butler Correspondence*, 2: 397.

2. At the end of the war Kenner (1813–1887), a Confederate congressman, was in Europe, where he had been sent to negotiate for official recognition of the Confederacy in return for the abolition of slavery. He submitted an amnesty application through the U.S. minister at Paris, but was not pardoned until October 4, after he had returned to Louisiana. Kenner to Robert Schenk, Sept. 14, 1865, Amnesty Papers (M1003, Roll 28), La., Duncan F. Kenner, RG94, NA; *House Ex. Docs.*, 39 Cong., 2 Sess., No. 116, p. 21 (Ser. 1293); Warner and Yearns, *BRCC*.

3. Johnson replied that General Howard had ordered the return of Kenner's Ascension Parish plantation, "subject to the leases on the property," and asked Weed for a "copy of the order under which Kenner makes demand." Kenner soon regained control of "Ashland" and prospered once more in raising sugar cane and racehorses, parlaying his economic status into a successful career in state politics, as he had before the war. Johnson to Weed, Oct. 31, 1865, Tels. Sent, President, Vol. 2 (1865), RG107, NA; Warner and Yearns, *BRCC*.

From Edisto Island Freedmen[1]

Edisto Island S.C.   Oct 28th 1865

To the President of these United States.

We the freedmen of Edisto Island South Carolina have learned from you through Major General O O Howard commissioner of the Freedmans Bureau, with deep sorrow and painful hearts of the possibility of goverment restoring these lands to the former owners.[2] We are well aware of the many perplexing and trying questions that burden your mind and do therefore pray to god (the preserver of all and who has through our Late and beloved President (Lincoln) proclamation and the war made us A free people) that he may guide you in making your decisions and give you that wisdom that cometh from above to settle these great and Important questions for the best interests of the country and the Colored race. Here is where secession was born and nurtured. Here is w[h]ere we have toiled nearly all our lives as slaves and were treated like dumb Driven cattle. This is our home, we have made these lands what they are. We were the only true and Loyal people that were found in posession of these lands. We have been always ready to strike for liberty and humanity yea to fight if needs be to preserve this glorious union. Shall not we who are freedman and have been always true to this Union have the same rights as are enjoyed by others? Have we broken any Law of these United States? Have we forfieted our rights of property in Land? If not then! are not our rights as A free people and good citizens of these United States to be considered before the rights of those who were found in rebellion against this good and just Goverment (and now being conquered) come (as they seem) with penitent hearts and beg forgiveness for past offences and also ask if thier lands cannot be restored to them? Are these rebellious spirits to be reinstated in thier *possessions* and we who have been abused and oppressed for many long years not to be allowed the privilige of purchasing land But be subject to the will of these large Land owners? God fobid. Land monopoly is unjurious to the advancement of the course of freedom, and if Government does not make some provision by which we as freedmen can obtain A Homestead, we have not bettered our condition.

We have been encouraged by Government to take up these lands in small tracts, receiving certificates of the same. We have thus far taken sixteen thousand (16000) acres of Land here on this Island. We are ready to pay for this land when Government calls for it and now after what has been done will the good and just government take from us all this right and make us subject to the will of those who have cheated and oppressed us for many years? God Forbid!

We the freedmen of this Island and of the State of South Carolina—Do therefore petition to you as the President of these United States, that some provisions be made by which every colored man can purchase land, and hold it as his own. We wish to have A home if it be but A few acres. Without some provision is made our future is sad to look upon. Yes our situation is dangerous. We therefore look to you in this trying hour as A true friend of the poor and neglected race, for protection and Equal Rights, with the privilege of purchasing A Homestead—A Homestead right here in the heart of South Carolina.

We pray that God will direct your heart in making such provision for us as freedmen which will tend to unite these states together stronger than ever before. May God bless you in the administration of your duties as the President of these United States is the humble prayer of us all.[3]

ALS (Bram), DNA-RG105, Records of the Commr., Lets. Recd. (M752, Roll 23).

1. The three-man committee writing on behalf of the freedmen was composed of Henry Bram, Ishmael Moultrie, and Yates Sampson, all of whom were signatories to the document.

2. A few days earlier, pursuant to President Johnson's order of October 9, General Howard met with a number of freedmen at the Episcopal church on Edisto Island to announce that the lands would be restored to the planters. In late September the owners

of plantations on the Sea Islands of Edisto, Johns, and Wadmalaw had petitioned Johnson for restoration of the lands that had been reserved for freedmen under terms of
General Sherman's Special Field Orders No. 15. Willie Lee Rose, *Rehearsal for Reconstruction: The Port Royal Experiment* (New York, 1964), 352–55; Charles F. Oubre,
Forty Acres and a Mule: The Freedmen's Bureau and Black Land Ownership (Baton Rouge,
1978), 51–54; *House Ex. Docs.*, 39 Cong., 1 Sess., No. 11, pp. 6–7 (Ser. 1255); South
Carolina Citizens to Johnson, Sept. 23, 1865, Edward M. Stoeber Papers, ScU.
     3. Received at the Executive Mansion on November 9, the Edisto freedmen memorial
was referred to Howard by the President. Howard's reply to these freedmen may be
found in McFeely, *Yankee Stepfather*, 143–44. The controversy over continued possession by the Freedmen's Bureau of Sea Island estates, located within the Sherman reservation, persisted for several years. See William H. Trescot to Johnson, Dec. 1, 1865, for
a follow-up to Howard's visit and decision.

From Joseph S. Fullerton[1]

New Orleans   Oct 28 1865.

Andrew Johnson

By Genl Banks order of March 23d 1865[2] a tax was assessed upon
the people of Louisiania for the support of schools for Freedmen for one
year. It was not Collected at the time. A large sum has been advanced
by the Qr Mrs Dept during the time from the 1st May 1864 to the
30th of September 1865 for the support of such schools. On July
twenty sixth Genl Howard wrote to Genl Canby requesting him to
enforce the order of Genl Banks by which I should obtain means to
repay said advance made by the Qr Mrs Dep't. On August 7th Mr
Conway[3] also requested Genl Canby to enforce said orders. Genl
Canby turned over the matter to the Bureau with the promise to render
Military assistance to collect the tax. 228,000 dollars is the amount of
the tax. This estimate is large. 32,000 dollars had already been collected but this sum was paid out for present schools.[4]

J S Fullerton   Bt BrGenl

Tel, DLC-JP.
     1. Fullerton (1835–1897), who rose to the rank of brigadier general of volunteers,
was sent to Louisiana to investigate complaints regarding the confiscation of property
and the collection of taxes to support schools for freedmen. Brown, *Am. Biographies*, 3:
206; C. Peter Ripley, *Slaves and Freedmen in Civil War Louisiana* (Baton Rouge, 1976),
186–87.
     2. Fullerton refers to Nathaniel P. Banks's General Orders No. 38, March 22, 1864,
which levied a property tax for the support of army-supervised schools for blacks. Howard A. White, *The Freedmen's Bureau in Louisiana* (Baton Rouge, 1970), 167, 174.
     3. Thomas W. Conway.
     4. Upon Johnson's recommendation, Fullerton stopped collecting the tax, admitting
that "further collection was impossible without seizing property by military force." Gen.
Absalom Baird, rather than close the schools, in early 1866 reimposed the tax with Gen.
Oliver O. Howard's approval, but Johnson again intervened after the Louisiana legislature forwarded a petition for relief from the levy. Johnson to Fullerton, Nov. 1, 1865;
Fullerton to Johnson, Nov. 9, 1865, Johnson Papers, LC; White, *Freedmen's Bureau
in La.*, 174; Taylor, *La. Reconstructed*, 457.

To James Johnson

Washington, D.C., October 28 1865.

Your dispatch has been received.[1] The people of Georgia should not hesitate one single moment in repudiating every single Dollar of debt created for the purpose of aiding the rebellion against the Government of the United States. It will not do to levy and collect taxes from a state and people that are loyal and in the Union, to pay a debt that was created to aid in taking them out and thereby subverting the Constitution of the United States.

I do not believe the great mass of the people of the State of Georgia, when left un-influenced, will ever submit to the payment of a debt which was the main cause of bringing on their past and present suffering, the result of the rebellion.

Those who vested their capital in the creation of this debt, must meet their fate and take it as one of the inevitable results of the rebellion, though it may seem hard to them. It should at once be made known, at home and abroad, that no debt contracted for the purpose of dissolving the Union of the States, can, or ever will be paid by taxes levied on the people for such purpose.[2]

Andrew Johnson   President U.S.

Tel, DNA-RG107, Tels. Sent, President, Vol. 2 (1865).

1. The governor had wired the President from Milledgeville on the previous day: "We need some aid to repeal the war debt. Send me word on the Subject. What should the Convention do?" Johnson Papers, LC.

2. After much controversy, the Georgia delegates finally voted to repudiate the state's war debt by a narrow margin of 133 to 117. James Johnson to Johnson, Nov. 7, 1865; Benjamin C. Truman to William A. Browning, Nov. 9, 1865, Johnson Papers, LC.

To Benjamin F. Perry

Washington, D.C., Oct 28th 1865.

Your last two dispatches have been received, and the pardons suggested, have been ordered.[1] I hope that your legislature will have no hesitancy in adopting the amendment to the constitution of the United States abolishing slavery. It will set an example which will no doubt be followed by the other states and place South Carolina in a most favorable attitude before the nation. I trust in God that it will be done. The nation, and state will then be left free and untrameled to take that course which sound policy wisdom and humanity may suggest.[2]

Andrew Johnson   Prest U.S.

Tel, A-Ar, B. F. Perry Papers.

1. The President refers to pardons for Charles M. Furman and Wade Hampton, who were actually pardoned on October 2 and November 13, respectively. Amnesty Papers (M1003, Roll 45), S.C., C. M. Furman and Wade Hampton, RG94, NA. Regarding

Hampton, see Perry to Johnson, Oct. 27, 1865. For Furman, see Perry to Johnson, Oct. 27, 1865, Tels. Recd., President, Vol. 4 (1865–66).

2. See Johnson to Perry, Oct. 31, 1865.

To George Bancroft

Washington D.C.   Oct 29th 1865

Dear Sir

Enclosed please find two extracts—one from Mr Jefferson's Inaugural address[1] which is as much now as it was then the position for this Govenmt to take in reference to our foreign relations & followed with the Statemt or hope that the U.S will not be compelled to abandon it by the policy pursued by other nations: but in the end will not submit to any encroachment that will endanger the nature and character of our institutions as a free Govmt. This is one of the best expositions ever made of democracy *proper*. It is a paper that will to do qoute from and refer to.

The other from Mr Fox[2] is worthy of notice coming from an Enlishmen. In this Speech he Seems to be thoroughly imbued with the spirt of Democracy and a correct understanding of the people. This will give stngth to the fact that a Govnt by the people is the strogest in time of war as well as peace, which will give stability and security for the payment of the public debt. You will see the best use to make of these references if any, and will dispose of them accordingly. Nothing has transpired Since you were here[3] worth of notice more then what you see in the daily papers.

Andrew Johnson

ALS, MHi-George Bancroft Papers.

1. Jefferson listed "essential principles of our Government" in his inaugural address of March 4, 1801, one of which Bancroft inserted for Johnson to quote in his first annual message: "the preservation of the General Government in its whole constitutional vigor as the sheet anchor of our peace at home and safety abroad." Richardson, *Messages*, 1: 311. See Message to Congress, December 4, 1865.

2. Charles J. Fox (1749–1806), a member of the British parliament who variously held the positions of lord of the admiralty, treasury, and foreign secretary, was the long-time leader of the Whig opposition to King George III. The speech was probably his address of October 31, 1776, in which he censured the administration for fostering discontent in America. *DNB*; J. Wright, ed., *The Speeches of The Right Honourable Charles James Fox in the House of Commons* (6 vols., London, 1815), 1: 59–62.

3. Within the last five days Bancroft, at the President's solicitation, had visited Washington. Russel B. Nye, *George Bancroft: Brahmin Rebel* (New York, 1944), 230; Lilian Handlin, *George Bancroft: The Intellectual as Democrat* (New York, 1984), 283.

From John W. Gorham

Clarksville Tenn   Oct 29th 1865

Dr. Friend

You will pleas find enclosed the petition of John W Barker for Pardon.[1] It explains its self. I mentioned his case to *you* while in your city last. You can relye on what he says. He is a plain Farmer and a man of good moral worth. When granted please send it to me as he lives several miles in the country and is quite old and infirm, and I will send to him without delay![2]

I find every thing working well for your administration in this country, the vote of our Legislature to the contrary not withstanding.[3] It dont reflect the will of the People—the People are for you with a will. My word for it.

Dont forget to send me the appointment for I am out of Business.[4]

Jno W Gorham

ALS, DNA-RG94, Amnesty Papers (M1003, Roll 48), Tenn., John W. Barker.

1. Barker (b. c1791) had been a prosperous tobacco farmer in Montgomery County, despite Gorham's depiction of him as "a plain Farmer." In his undated petition Barker asked for pardon under the thirteenth exception. William P. Titus, *Picturesque Clarksville: Past and Present* (Clarksville, 1887), 385–86; 1860 Census, Tenn., Montgomery, N & E of Cumberland River, 41.

2. Endorsements from Cave Johnson and Governor Brownlow are found in the Barker file. On November 14, 1865, Brownlow indicated that he would refer the matter to the Attorney General. President Johnson was evidently in no hurry to pardon Barker, for he did not finally do so until August 18, 1866. Amnesty Papers (M1003, Roll 48), Tenn., John W. Barker, RG94, NA.

3. Although it is not absolutely clear to which vote Gorham is referring, it is probably the tabling by the House of a four-part resolution offered by Representative Cameron on October 11, strongly endorsing President Johnson and his policies. Gorham may have been influenced by the editorial which appeared in his hometown newspaper on October 20. See *Tenn. House Journal, 1865–66*, 44; *Clarksville Chronicle*, Oct. 20, 1865.

4. Gorham was persistent, although unsuccessful, in his attempts to receive a federal appointment from Johnson. See Gorham to Johnson, June 3, 1865, *Johnson Papers*, 8: 172–74; and Gorham to Johnson, Nov. 18, 1865.

From Ladies of Niagara County, New York[1]

South Wilson, Niagara County, N.Y.,
October 29th, 1865.

Honored and Beloved President—

We have viewed with delight your exalted course towards the Southern people, and it has inspired our hearts with courage to address you. In view of the facts that the Southern States are not subjugated, but that they have wisely and opportunely laid down the mistaken policy of the sword for the more effectual, the more consistent and Christian-like weapons of statesmanship; and that they are still contending nobly for the principles dear to every enlightened citizen; and that the contest, still raging, as it unfolds its true character, appers between the great principles of Peace and Union on the one hand and a blood-thirsty fanaticism on the other; and that in this contest you need to summon to your aid all the truly noble—in view of all these facts, we unite our petition with the noble ladies of the South that you would release that pure, though unfortunate statesman, Jefferson Davis, believing that he will co-operate with you in bringing about the results so dear to us all.

Augusta Constitutionalist, Nov. 24, 1865.

1. Among the four signatories, only the first has been conclusively identified. Angeline Gifford (b. *c*1820) was a farmer's wife, New York native, and mother of at least four children. 1860 Census, N.Y., Niagara, Wilson, 43.

From Benjamin F. Perry

Columbia S C   Oct 29 1865.

I thank you most sincerely for your telegram this moment recd informing me that the Pardons of Hampton & Furman[1] have been ordered as I requested in my last two dispatches. I now ask you at the instance of Mrs Pickens[2] once a Tennessee lady for the pardon of her husband Govr Francis W Pickens. Gov Pickens has aided nobly since the fall of the Confederacy in exerting his great personal influence to restore the state to the Union. He was a leading member of the late Convention & advocated all of the Constitutional reforms which you & I had so much at heart. His Conduct towards his Freedmen has been most praiseworthy. He has given his warmest support to your administration & your policy of reconstruction. In every way he has merited his pardon as much so as any one in South Carolina. I trust You will order it & restore him to his full usefulness again. It will also quiet the agonized mind of his affectionate & most estimable wife who has been & now is in deep distress & was going on to Washington till stopped by me.[3]

B F Perry   Pro. Gov.

Tel, DLC-JP.

1. Charles M. Furman (1797–1872) served as an attorney, state legislator (1824–25), secession convention delegate, and president of the Bank of South Carolina at Charleston. *Appleton's Cyclopaedia*.

2. A native of Fayette County, Tenn., Lucy Petway Holcombe (1832–1899), who had become the third wife of Pickens in 1858, took an active interest in Confederate veterans' affairs. Edward T. James et al., eds., *Notable American Women, 1607–1950: A Biographical Dictionary* (3 vols., Cambridge, 1971), 3: 65.

3. There is no evidence that Pickens received an individual pardon.

From Anna Ella Carroll[1]

Private

Monday, Baltimore   October 30th. 65

Mr President:

At the earnest request of Hon Reverdy Johnson, and several other distinguished friends of yourself, the ablest and most important to you of all others in Maryland I would call your attention to the appt yet to be made, of *Collector of Internal Revenue for* the 3d district of Maryland. You said to me, as I understood on Wednesday last,[2] that you wanted the man appointed for whom I was interceding.

On the card addressed to the Secretary, you said you did not know the applicants but the Sec would make the appt.

I understood, of course, that the Secretary was to appt *Fickey*,[3] whom you said to me, you wanted appted if I did. It seems, however that Mr McCulloch construed it to mean that you left it to him, as before.

The Sec has expressed all the time, every disposition to oblige me, in this appt, but expresses himself unable to make the appt, on account of some previous pledge, unless you will intimate that the appt of Fickey will be agreable to you.

The Comm of Internal Revenue[4] has given a letter, in which he says, the interest of the govt, will be best promoted, by the appt of Fickey rather than Finley,[5] the man whose commission you signed.

Mr McCulloch says, he has no doubt *he* is the best qualified, and that he has no personal feeling for Findley whatever and has shown himself not only willing, but *desirous*, that *you* would signify your desire to have Fickey appointed.

Senator Creswell,[6] as I told you, is very much opposed to the appt of *Finley* but for certain reasons, not necessary to explain, desires to take no part.

I have never known Mr Reverdy Johnson to take such a deep interest in any appt, and he says, from his personal interview with you, he felt confident you would give it to Frederick Fickey.

He says, further, that he will tell you if you ask him that, Findley "is not competent."

The case stands now, precisely, where it stood, at my first interview with you, when you told me, to ascertain the facts and come back and report to you: That is to say the Bond is not filed—the Commission is not issued; therefore is yet in a proper condition to receive your favorable action.

I cannot, as one whose whole heart is in the success and glory of yr Administration who is serving you, at all times, in season and out of season, by her pen and by personal influence, I know, that it will strengthen my hands, & as a mark of yr confidence and appreciation, I ask most earnestly, that you will bestow this appt on *Frederick Fickey* of Balt.[7]

A. E. Carroll of Md.

ALS, DNA-RG56, Appts., Internal Revenue Service, Collector, Md., 3rd Dist., Frederick Fickey.

1. Carroll (1815–1894), the daughter of Maryland governor Thomas C. Carroll, was an active political propagandist and journalist. James, *Notable American Women*, 1: 289–92; Janet L. Coryell, *Neither Heroine nor Fool: Anna Ella Carroll of Maryland* (Kent, Ohio, 1990), 109, passim.

2. There is no record of Carroll's interview with the President, though Horace Maynard had earlier written her a note of introduction. Maynard to Carroll, June 21, 1865, A. E. Carroll Papers, MHi.

3. Frederick Fickey, Jr. (c1828–fl1899), a Baltimore "fancy goods" merchant, was later an insurance adjuster. Reverdy Johnson to Johnson, Oct. 12, 1865, Appts., Internal Revenue Service, Collector, Md., 3rd Dist., Frederick Fickey, RG56, NA; 1860 Census, Md., Baltimore, 13th Ward, 395; Baltimore directories (1858–99).

4. William Orton.

5. John V.L. Findlay (1839–1907), wartime state legislator and Baltimore lawyer, served as a Democratic congressman in the 1880s. *BDAC*.

6. John A.J. Creswell.

7. Findlay was nominated for the collectorship but failed to be confirmed by the Senate. On March 31, 1866, William Prescott Smith obtained the appointment. Ser. 6B, Vol. 4: 106, Johnson Papers, LC.

From Joseph E. Davis

Vicksburg Miss   Oct 30th 1865

Sir

On the latter part of September last, before leaving Tuscaloosa Ala., I addressed you informing you of my situation, and asking that your Excellency would restore me the property of which I had been deprived.[1]

On reaching Mississippi, I have seen in various news-papers, notices, that you had done so; for which I am profoundly grateful.[2] This act of your Excellency is the more highly appreciated, as it was done without the aid of influential friends. The greatest evil under which the country now labors, is the "Freedmens Bureau":—demoralizing the negroes, robbing & defrauding them of what little they possess, And the fruits of their toil. I have this day written to Genl. Howard, begging his interposition in their behalf,[3] and hope he will soon apply the proper corrective.

I know nothing of the Freedmens Bureau but from what I have seen here. If Col. Thomas[4] is to be taken as a specimen, there are few evils that can be more intolerable, and he is making every effort to fasten himself upon the country by misrepresenting the facts & circumstances.

Jos. E Davis

ALS, DLC-JP.

1. See Davis to Johnson, Sept. 22, 1865.

2. Reports such as that published in the *Vicksburg Herald* were premature; Davis's plantation was not returned to him until the first day of 1867. *Louisville Democrat*, Oct. 7, 1865; Hermann, *Pursuit of a Dream*, 104. See Davis to Johnson, Nov. 4, 1865.

3. The letter has not been found.

4. Samuel Thomas, who occupied Davis's plantation during the Civil War and afterward became assistant commissioner of the Freedmen's Bureau for Mississippi.

From Hiram Gamage[1]

Tallahassee Fla   Oct 30th 1865

Honored Sir

Having travelled through Georgia and a portion of Florida recently, I deem it necessary (and hope you will excuse the impertenance) to inform you privately of affairs in regard to freedmen that have come under my immediate observation. Being a northern man and of northern principles I write this hoping you will notice it for the benefit of the American Goverment. The freedmen I find and especially where negro troops are stationed lazy idling thievish & impudent. There is really a danger of an insurrection that would surprise you if you were aware of it, caused principally from the secret admonitions of Cold. Troops, which will cause the shedding of a good diel of innocent blood Loyal as well as rebel, and should I be a judge, the rebels are thoroughly conquered and they seem as loyal as could possibly be expected.

The freedman dont pretend to fulfill their contracts but on the contrary are a great expense to the whites, and really in some sections which my business has called me, I have thought that it would have been a blessing for the poor farmer had his effects been confiscated & he banished, rather than be in his present situation. Even if there was no whites here a change would be better in some way as otherwise famine insurrection murder &c will be the go in this country. The freedman are ignorant and instead of having the diabolical principles instilled into them that is, they should be advised by those who are really there friends & the friends of the Union. Hoping that you will excuse this audacity as I write only for my country's good.

Hiram Gamage

ALS, DLC-JP.
    1. Not identified.

To Isaac Murphy[1]

Washington, D.C., October 30th 1865.

There will be no interference with your present organization of state Government. I have learned from E. W. Gantt, Esqr,[2] and other sources, that all is working well, and you will proceed and resume the former relations with the Federal Government, and all the aid in the power of the Government will be given in restoring the state to its former relations.[3]

Andrew Johnson   President U.S.

Tel, DNA-RG107, Tels. Sent, President, Vol. 2 (1865).
    1. The President's telegram was sent to Murphy at Little Rock.
    2. See Gantt to Johnson, June 29, July 4, 1865, *Johnson Papers*, 8: 313–14, 351.
    3. Johnson sent a more succinct version of this telegram to Congressman-elect Anthony A.C. Rogers of Arkansas, who had telegraphed asking him not to appoint Freeman W. Compton as provisional governor of his state. Murphy replied by wire to the President that his support would "give confidence to the timid & wavering but Cannot increase our confidence in your wisdom & patriotism," adding, "you having been tried in the same furnace with ourselves." Rogers to Johnson, Oct. 27, 1865; Johnson to Rogers, Oct. 30, 1865; Murphy to Johnson, Oct. 31, 1865, Johnson Papers, LC.

From Nancy E. Estes

October 31, 1865, Cobb Co., Ga.; ALS, DNA-RG105, Records of the Commr., Lets. Recd. (M752, Roll 23).

Protesting at length her Union loyalty and claiming a friendship with the President, Mrs. Estes paints a heartrending picture of her and her family's plight, having had their property destroyed and provisions carried off by the armies. "I thought I would state to you the Awful condition of my self & famley. . . . My husban has bin afflicted with rheumatism several years. He cant use but one han. Last Winter me & my Daughters had to cut wood all day to make a fier to ceap us from freasing at Night & this Fall we are all so Afflicted with Pains we cant do any thing and the ceces People wount help us without I had Money to Pay them." What do they need? "I haint had any thing But a little corse Bread to eat for the Past three Months & I can't get that now. Our close & Beds and Bedclose torn all to Peices our tabels chairs cubbard furnature cooking vessels all Broak to pieces. I have two oald quilts one Blanket for my Beding." Pleading "for Provision & cloathing," she declares, "we are bearfooted & Naked & starving, & not able to work." [Endorsement: "An Officer has called on Nancy E.Z. Estes, and reports that her husband owns 160 acres of land, on which is a comfortable house, in which the family is living. They have two cows, Six head of hogs, plenty of poultry, a limited supply of provisions, on hand And plenty of cooking utensils for the family, two good beds, and seemingly the family is in good fix for living." The husband was "out chopping wood when the Officer called. . . . The family are by no means objects of humanity."]

From Harris T. Garnett[1]

Brazoria Texas   October 31 1865

Dear Sir

You have doubtless, ere this been advised of the death of your Brother William P. Johnson of Velasco in this county—from a wound in the hand, occasioned by the accidentel discharge of his gun, while hunting.[2] I have known him for the last four years, but have no acquaintence with his family. From the confidence he seemed to repose in me during his life, I feel called on to say a word in behalf of his helpless family. I had a conversation with him at this place a few days before he was wounded in regard to his future prospects and plans; and learned from him that the Sallery he was to receive as collector at Velasco[3] and what little he could make at his trade was his only means for supporting his family; who now after his death are absolutely dependant.[4]

I am informed that Mr. Paine[5] of Velasco and Col. John H. Herndon of this county or his son[6] are now applicants for the place of collector at Velasco. The office is and has been for maney years a sinecure, requiring neither ability industry or risk of any kind. A vessel from a forign Port never enters either the Brazos or San Barnard in peaceful times. Galveston is only about 40 miles distant, and Indianola about 70 miles and besides this the Bars at the mouth of each stream are so shallow as to render it difficult for vessels of any considerable size to enter. All goods and other articles of commerce which come in Ships are landed and received through Galveston & Indianola or Lavacca. The only advantage of a custom officer at Velasco is to prevent smugling. This being the case, a female can attend to the interest of the United States at that point as well as a man of the most consumate business qualities. Col John H Herndon who enjoyed the income of this office for maney years before the war spent most of his time from home attending to his large interests elsewhere, leaving his wife and children to represent him at Velasco.[7] Your brothers widow and her son who I understand is a promising youth of 14 or 15 years of age[8] is as well qualified and suited to protect the interests of the Government in the collection of customs at Velasco as Mr Herndon was in past years.

I see that it is not unfrequently the case that females are appointed to take charge of Post offices. If that be allowable I can see no reason for withholding a collectorship of customs from them, especially when there are no duties to perform. Whatever periodical or other Reports & formal matters may become necessary from time to time, Mrs Johnson will find friends ready to aid her in making them out in proper form. Your brothers son will be old enough in a few years to accept the office himself, the income of which will keep the family in comfortable circumstances. The present applicants Mr. Paine & Col Herndon have no very meritorious claims to the office. Mr. Paine was connected with the commissary and Quarter Master's Office at Velasco during the last two or three years of the War, and in common with his coadjutors accumulated thousands of dollars; it is true that he invested a large share of his gains in negroes but it was not his fault that it did not prove profitable. Col Herndon is a large property holder and in addition is President of the Rail Road from Harrisburg to Allyton[9] with a Sallery (I believe) of $3000.00. During the many years that Col Herndon was collector at Velasco, I do not suppose that he collected customs to the amount of one years sallery. All disinterested just & humane citizens of this county will be rejoiced to see the collectorship at Velasco confered on your brothers widow. If the place is given to her she will find friends to go security in her bond.

If your Excellency shall decline to confer the office on Mrs Johnson, then in preference to either of the applicants named, Col Ruben Brown[10] who resides near Velasco, would have the sympathy and good wishes of the great body of our people. He is a gentleman of the highest character for integrity and uprightness finely qualified for any position of that character and whose pecuniary circumstances are very humble. If Mrs Johnson shall fail it is to be hoped that Col Browns merits may be duly weighed.[11]

In July last I forwarded to your Excellency direct my Petition for Pardon with a duplicate of my amnesty oath on account of my having held and exercised during the war, the office of Confederate states Receiver under the Sequestration Laws of the Confederate States. I have not received a pardon. I presume the mistake in annexing the copy of the oath I ought to have kept instead of the one intended for the Petition will make no material difficulty. When I forwarded my petition to your Excellency I had not seen the order directing applicants for Pardon to present their Petitions to the Governors for their recommendation. In fact Governor Hamilton had not then reached Texas. W. P. Ballinger Esqr.[12] of Galveston who held the same office that I did and who I learn has secured pardon left for Washington City before I had any knowledge of his intending to go. Had I been aware of his visiting Washington in time, I should have gotten him to call your Excellencys attention to my application for pardon.

Governor Hamilton in his proclamation opening the Courts in Texas, directs the Judges to refuse permission to any Lawyers to practice in the Courts who may come under any one of the exceptions of the Amnesty proclamation of your Excellency and who shall not have received special pardon.[13] I have a large family who are entirely dependant on my professional labors for a support; in my present circumstances I can do nothing. I here very respectfully request your Excellency to refer to my Petition which I presume is on file and if not inconsistent with your Excellencys regard for the Public good that a pardon may be granted me at as early a day as practacable.[14] I am not amenable to any other of the exceptions of your Excellencys amnesty proclamation than that of having held & exercised the office named.

H. T. Garnett

ALS, DNA-RG56, Appts., Customs Service, Collector, Saluria, Tex., Mrs. William P. Johnson.

1. Garnett (c1816-fl1877) was a Kentucky-born attorney who emigrated to Texas sometime after being admitted to the bar in Mississippi in 1837. H. L. Bentley and Thomas Pilgrim, *The Texas Legal Directory for 1876–77* (Austin, 1877), 43; 1870 Census, Tex., Brazoria, Brazoria, 12.

2. See John Adriance to Johnson, Oct. 26, 1865.

3. In the summer of 1865 William P. Johnson had travelled to Washington, where on July 5 the President appointed him surveyor, not collector, of customs at Velasco. *Cincinnati Commercial*, Aug. 9, 1865; Ser. 6B, Vol. 1: 184, Johnson Papers, LC.

4. Following orders from Lieut. Col. Jacob C. De Gress, the provost marshal at Columbia, Texas, provided rations to the widow and her four dependent children. De Gress to H. Lofsberg, Nov. 15, 1865, Lofsberg to De Gress, Nov. 22, 1865, Johnson Papers, LC.

5. Possibly William Payne (c1821-fl1870), a merchant. 1870 Census, Tex., Brazoria, Precinct 2, Columbia, 177.

6. Herndon (1813–1878), a Kentucky native who moved to Texas during the Republic period, had been elected colonel of the militia in Fort Bend and Brazoria counties

during the Civil War. His son has not been identified. Webb et al., *Handbook of Texas*, 1: 802.

7. Herndon maintained a summer residence in Velasco before the Civil War as well as a sugar plantation further up the Brazos River. A "Z. Herndon" from Kentucky is listed as surveyor for Velasco in 1859. Abner J. Strobel, *The Old Plantations and Their Owners of Brazoria County, Texas* (Houston, 1926), 20–21; *U.S. Off. Reg.* (1859), 72.

8. Sarah had three sons at home in 1860, the eldest of whom was Nathan (1847–1929). 1860 Census, Texas, Brazoria, Columbia, 40; genealogical material provided by James McDonough, Andrew Johnson Project Files.

9. From 1862 to 1865 Herndon was president of the Buffalo Bayou, Brazos, and Colorado Railway Company. Webb et al., *Handbook of Texas*, 1: 240, 802.

10. Reuben R. Brown (c1808-fl1874), a veteran of the army of the Republic of Texas, had commanded the 35th Tex. Cav. Ibid., 1: 226.

11. W. C. Wayley was appointed surveyor of customs for Velasco in July 1866. Apparently the President's sister-in-law was among the applicants to be collector of customs for Saluria, but Johnson nominated Charles Taylor for the position in July 1866. Ser. 6B, Vol. 4: 211, Johnson Papers, LC.

12. William P. Ballinger.

13. See Samuel Bell Maxey to Johnson, Oct. 24, 1865.

14. Johnson pardoned Garnett on December 2, 1865. Amnesty Papers (M1003, Roll 53), Tex., H. T. Garnett, RG94, NA.

Interview with Alexander K. McClure[1]

[ca. October 31, 1865][2]

However reticent the President may be on some issues, he seems to have no reserve as to the policy he conceives to be the true one to bring back the insurgent States. He discussed the position of those States and their people with great interest and occasional warmth, and with a frankness that left no doubt as to his purpose. He holds that they were never out of the Union; that secession, however accomplished as a fact, cannot be accomplished in law; that the supreme authority of the Government in those States was not overthrown by the rebellion, but simply in abeyance; and of course it logically follows his premises that, *since the rebellion has ceased, the States resume their proper place in the Union, and restoration is accomplished.* This, in brief, was the standpoint from which the President discussed the question of reconstruction for more than an hour, and answered suggestive objections at times with an earnestness that demonstrated how ardently he is working to give success to his policy. I could not but remind him that his theory stripped all traitors of the protection they might claim as public enemies; that it would stamp as guilty of treason within the law every man who aided the rebellion, and of necessity demand at his hands commensurate punishment for what he must hold as unmitigated crime, as appalling murder and desolation, for which there is no extenuation to be plead. "You have," I added, "given us on every hand the nation's monument of Mercy—where will be its monuments of Justice? Davis is a proclaimed assassin, as well as a traitor—his agents have died, another Wirtz will follow[3]—how are the principals to atone to a people doubly bereaved in their homes and in their chief sanctuary of power?"

To this the President answered, with much animation, that the measure of and time for atonement were yet for the future to determine. I shall not soon forget the emphasis with which he declared that the South must come back and be a part of us, "and," he added, "it must come with all its manhood. I don't want it to come eviscerated of its manhood." To this proposition, abstractly, there could be no objection made. We want the South with all its manhood, which I would conceive to be the Southern people with their treason abandoned and their crimes punished—not punished revengefully; not in imitation of the guillotine of France or the Inquisition of Spain; but by making the leaders who conspired to overthrow the Government strangers to its honors and its citizenship, and thus, through life, the monuments of the power, the justice, and the magnanimity of the mightiest nation of the earth. The President said that such may be the measure of punishment; that he had pardoned but few who would come under such a rule; that there are exceptions to all rules, and there were both civil functionaries and army officers who might be pardoned with propriety. He said that he had not yet gone as far in his amnesty, either general or special, as Mr. Lincoln proposed. He explained, what is not generally known, that his pardons are mainly of business men, many of whom were Union men, who must have pardons to enable them to sell or mortgage their lands, or to get credit in their business operations, and added that he had not yet reached the consideration of such cases as Lee, Stephens, Longstreet, Beauregard, and others of that class.

He spoke freely of the proposed trial of Davis, and said that as yet the Government had not taken any steps in the matter. If he is to be tried in Richmond, the trial must necessarily be postponed until the civil authority is fully restored,[4] and then it will be a question of consideration under the condition of affairs which may at that time exist. As Virginia is still practically under martial law—certainly wholly under military rule—I judge that many moons may wax and wane before we can have a great State trial. I do not question the wisdom of this delay, for it is certainly better for the Government to avoid the danger of defeat in attempting to convict of constructive treason in Washington, than to force a trial which might afford a technical escape for Davis, and leave the great question undetermined. If I were going to guess on the subject, I would say that Davis is more likely to be paroled during the next year than to be tried, and if he is ever hanged, he must do it himself.

The President is clearly adverse to confiscation, and that question is practically settled. Whatever might be the views of Congress, confiscation is not possible with an Executive determinedly hostile to it and with the pardoning power in his hands. I infer, however, that on this point Congress will harmonize with the Executive, as a number of even the radical leaders, such as Greeley and Sumner, openly oppose it. If our credit can be sustained otherwise I am content. Five years hence we shall all be wiser on that point than now.

I believe that the President will wield all his power to effect the admission of the Representatives of the rebellious States into Congress during the next session. The Senate being organized, the question cannot come up there until it is brought up in order; but there will be a strong pressure to force the admission of the Southern members, by placing their names on the roll when the House meets. This Mr. McPherson[5] will not do, and on all votes of instructions he will call only those who are returned from States clearly entitled to representation. The law forbids him to do otherwise, and he will be faithful to it. The question of their admission will then agitate the House, and I fear make a sad breach between the President and Congress. The South is encouraged by the position of the Administration to be importunate in its demand for admission, and it is not improbable that it will in the end be admitted. I have seldom seen Congress struggle against power and hold out to the end.

On the future of the freedmen the President talks well. He displays more sense than sentiment on the question, and means to solve the problem fairly, as demanded by civilization and humanity. Of their ability to win a position that will enable them to be incorporated into our system of government as citizens he is not eminently hopeful, but feels that it must be fairly tried, with an open field for the negro. That failing, he looks upon colonization as the only alternative.

It would be foolish to disguise the fact that the President, both by word and deed, disclaims the position of a partisan Executive, and that he is not insensible to the flattering approval of the Administration by the Democratic party. I do not mean by this that he is in sympathy and fellowship with them; but I do mean that he is not wholly in sympathy against them; and he will, I feel warranted in saying, adhere to the political fortunes of the Southern States without regard to political consequences. This may or may not sever him from the party that sustained and cherished him in the darkest days through which he passed, and that won him the highest honors of the nation through a flood of obloquy; but if it does, I infer that he will accept the situation. He evidently means, above all other things, to compass the admission of the Southern members and the complete restoration to power of those States, and if Massachusetts and South Carolina can strike hands over the same Administration, then will we have a faithful President and a harmonious country. If not, I leave the future to tell the story. Where in all this record soon to be made up the nation shall see that "treason is the greatest of crimes and must be punished," is not to my mind apparent.

Washington Morning Chronicle, Nov. 16, 1865.
1. McClure (1828–1909), an active Pennsylvania Republican, published the *Franklin Repository* in Chambersburg. He later recalled that he was accompanied by Gov.

Andrew G. Curtin. *DAB*; Alexander K. McClure, *Colonel Alexander K. McClure's Recollections of Half a Century* (Salem, Mass., 1902), 88.

2. We have assigned this probable date, because the version of this narrative published in the *Picayune* states that McClure gave an account of his interview in a letter dated October 31, 1865, to the *Franklin Repository*. *New Orleans Picayune*, Nov. 23, 1865.

3. Henry Wirz. See Louis Schade to Johnson, Oct. 26, 1865.

4. See Johnson to Salmon P. Chase, Oct. 2, 1865, and Chase to Johnson, Oct. 12, 1865.

5. Edward McPherson (1830–1895), a Pennsylvania newspaperman, served as a Republican in the House (1859–63), then as clerk for that body (1863–75, 1881–83, 1889–91). McClure's prediction proved correct; McPherson omitted the names of representatives from former Confederate states when he called the role in December 1865. *DAB*.

From Charles Mason[1]

Washington   October 31/65

Dear Sir

The difficulty of any other access induces me to take this method of bringing some facts to your attention which are of importance to others & perhaps to yourself.

Several weeks since an order was understood to have been made appointing General Sanders[2] postmaster at Davenport Iowa in place of Mr Russell[3] the editor of the republican newspaper at that place. Notice of this change was long since sent to Gen. Sanders who forwarded his official bonds accordingly but has been disappointed in not receiving his commission. Upon calling at the Post Office Department on yesterday I was informed that the commission had been withheld by order of the President.

The ground on which the removal of Mr Russell had been asked was that he had been foremost among those radicals who were openly endeavouring to thwart the well considered plans of Your Excellency in regard to the early restoration of the federal union. Without resorting to any *ex parte* statements in proof of this accusation Mr Russell himself has been made the witness in the case. An editorial article taken from his own paper has been placed before you for that purpose. And lest this might be supposed to have found its way into the paper by oversight, or lest it might have been misunderstood a second editorial more pointed than the first & written several days afterwards was filed among the papers placed in your hands. These were testified by a petition numerously signed by some of the most substantial men of the city of Davenport asking for the change & giving some of the reasons on which the appointment of General Sanders was asked for.

Understanding that an effort was on foot to induce a reconsideration of the order for the appointment of Gen. Sanders a paper signed by some four hundred names of men doing business with that postoffice was forwarded, strongly remonstrating against any change of that order. This paper & some letters from prominent individuals residing in Davenport were filed in the office of the Post Master General & are probably now with the papers of the case.

Lest it should be supposed that this was a selfish partisan movement on the part of the democrats of that city to place one of their number in a lucrative office I assure Your Excellency that General Sanders never has heretofore been & is not now a member of the democratic party any further than an earnest desire to sustain a course of policy which has now become a cardinal article of democratic faith & practice renders him so.

He has always heretofore been a member of the republican party since its organization. The only tie which unites him with the democrats is the common desire to see all the states restored as soon as practicable to their old positions under the federal constitution.

I am informed that all the federal officers in Iowa are of the same general stamp as Mr Russell. His removal is said to have excited a very general & salutary influence over their conduct. It is the opinion of many intelligent gentlemen that if this change & one or two others had been made a few weeks earlier the conservatives would have been successful in the late election in that state.

I believe that a reconsideration of the order which has been made on this subject would have a pernicious tendency in Iowa & in other western states—especially in Wisconsin where an election is soon to take place.[4]

Chas Mason

ALS, DLC-JP.
1. Mason (1804–1882), who graduated at the head of the West Point class which included Robert E. Lee, resigned from the army and became a noted Iowa jurist. In the 1850s he was U.S. commissioner of patents and later practiced patent law in Washington, D.C. *DAB*.
2. Addison H. Sanders (1823–1912), former editor of the *Davenport Gazette*, served as lieut. col. of the 16th Iowa Inf. (1862–65), earning the brevet of brigadier general of volunteers. In the 1870s he was secretary of the territory and registrar of the U.S. land office for Montana. Harry E. Downer, *History of Davenport and Scott County, Iowa* (2 vols., Chicago, 1910), 2: 966–67; CSR, RG94, NA; Pension Records, Amelia B. Sanders, RG15, NA.
3. British-born Edward Russell (1830-*fl*1887), a newspaper correspondent, was briefly clerk of the local recorder's office before becoming editor of the *Davenport Gazette* in 1862. Postmaster from May 1864 until October 1865, he was, according to one source, "the first official in the United States removed by Johnson on political grounds." Reappointed postmaster by Grant, he served from 1869 until the 1880s. *History of Scott County, Iowa* (Chicago, 1882), 578–82; "Iowa Imprints Before 1861," *IaJHP*, 36 (1938): 120.
4. The Republicans won the governorship and both houses of the legislature in the November 7 Wisconsin election. *American Annual Cyclopaedia* (1865), 823.

To Benjamin F. Perry

Washington   Oct 31 1865.

There is a deep interest felt as to what course the Legislature will take in regard to the adoption of the amendment to the Constitution of the United States abolishing slavery and the assumption of the debt created to aid in the rebellion against the Government of the United States. If the action of the Convention was in good faith why hesitate in making it a part of the constitution of the United States. I trust in God that the restoration of the Union will not be defeated and all that has so far been well done thrown away? I still have faith that all will come out right yet. This opportunity ought to be understood and appreciated by the people of the Southern States. If I know my own heart and every passion which enters it is to restore the blessings of the Union & treat and heal every bleeding wound which has been caused by this fratricidal war.

Let us be guided by love & wisdom from on high & union & peace will once more reign throughout the land.[1]

Andrew Johnson

Tel, A-Ar, B. F. Perry Papers.
1. See Perry to Johnson, Nov. 1, 1865.

From William H. Seward

Washington   Oct 31, 1865

My dear Sir,

It would be practically inconvenient to change the day appointed for Thanksgiving[1] so as to conform to the wishes of this Clergy mentioned in your note,[2] thus I could not advise the attempt. Shall I reply to the Governor of Ohio[3] in this sense?[4]

William H Seward

ALS, John M. Taylor, McLean, Va.
1. On October 28 Johnson had proclaimed the first Thursday in December a national day of thanksgiving. Richardson, *Messages*, 6: 332.
2. Samuel B. Halliday (1812–1897), a Congregational minister, workhouse superintendent, and author, had suggested that the last Thursday in November be designated Thanksgiving Day so as to conform with the date already observed by many states. His letter to the President had been referred by Robert Johnson to Seward on October 14. *NUC*; *New York Times*, July 10, 1897; Halliday to Johnson, Oct. 11, 1865, Misc. Lets., 1789–1906 (M179, Roll 224), RG59, NA.
3. Charles Anderson.
4. The President's endorsement reads: "Let the day Stand as it is."

November 1865

From American Missionary Association Committee

Washington, D.C.   Nov. 1, 1865

The undersigned a Committee from the American Missionary Association,[1] ordered by the last Annual meeting, beg leave to invite your attention to the following.

Early in the rebellion, the escaped or abandoned slaves, called Contrabands, near Fortress Monroe, were located by Military order at Hampton and vicinity, where they have built dwellings, churches & schoolhouses, and which they have repopulated much more densely than before the rebellion. Since then a large number of farms in Eastern Virginia have been occupied by them under military order, and cultivated for their benefit.

In So. Carolina, the Freedmen were first employed in saving the cotton crop, then in an experiment of raising cotton, then in the general cultivation of lands assigned to them; and later were placed by order of Gen. Sherman,[2] or of Government thru him, together with thousands who followed his glorious march, on the Islands of that coast.

In North Carolina a large number of the Freedman were located on Roanoke Island, and an acre of ground given to each family. On these lots they built their houses; and by subduing & cultivating the soil, have multiplied the value of the land, in the estimation of Superintendent James,[3] at least ten fold.

In these and other places, schools have been established for the people, by the American Missionary Association, and others, the pupils in which have given entire satisfaction. From superintendents of schools, from officers appointed by Govt. and others alarming reports relative to the present condition & prospects of the people have reached us, demanding prompt attention.

The restoration of abandoned and confiscated lands, to their former owners, is fast rendering houseless, and homeless and helpless thousands of these families. In one district in Virginia the superintendent says that probably fifteen thousand of them will be turned from their homes, and left with no means of support. On one plantation, called *acre town*, because each family had an acre assigned to it, three hundred families, many of them wives and children, or orphans & widows of coloured soldiers, will lose their homes. Another district in Virginia it is estimated by those best qualified to judge, will have twenty thousand homeless ones; and the Superintendent of schools,[4] under appointment from the Assistant Commissioner,[5] says that at a low estimate not less than seventy thousand are being, or soon to be, ejected from lands re-possessed by late rebel owners, and will be left homeless and without any possible means of support, just at the approach of winter. Disease and death have already commenced their work, and we dare not trust ourselves to stated number of those who must soon perish unless the Government, in an abounding charity bring swift relief.

Like causes are coming into operation elsewhere, and thousands on thousands unless Government interposes will be driven from their homes and left to perish by masters not placated by disaster and defeat.

In behalf of these increasing numbers we entreat your Executive interest. Private or public charity can not reach a case of such magnitude and so widely extended. Government only has the organizations and ability to meet it. Shelter must be supplied, rations, or food, given them, or untold numbers perish, adding to the long account against our people, in relation to this class.

Without any desire to dictate, we would suggest that in some of the following ways help may be afforded.

1. An increased liberality in the supply of Government rations is essential.

2. That rebel owners should be prevented from turning these people off from lands assured to them, until ample provision is otherwise made for locating them. Actual or implied pledges to them should be regarded as no less sacred than those made to whites. Military Governors and Commanders have, in the name of Government made them pledges of protection until they can with proper industry provide for themselves. Congress in the Bureau bill made provision for furnishing them homes, of which the restoration of abandoned lands is depriving them. Until Congress again meets, to make new provision if necessary, the Executive should, we think secure for them every acre of land given them by Congress.

3. If the lands provided for them in the Bureau bill, can not be secured to them, can not the Executive aid in giving them the advantage of the Homestead bill, by furnishing them transportation to lands suitably located, and covered by that bill, and give them temporary supplies of food, till they can begin the cultivation of the soil.[6]

Henry Ward Beecher   Wm. Patton
J. C. Eldredge[7]   Geo. Whipple

ALS (Whipple), DNA-RG105, Records of the Commr., Lets. Recd. (M752, Roll 37).

1. Organized in 1846, the AMA campaigned actively for the abolition of slavery. During the Civil War and Reconstruction, the organization provided economic relief and education for freed slaves in the South. Joe M. Richardson, *Christian Reconstruction: The American Missionary Association and Southern Blacks, 1861–1890* (Athens, Ga., 1986), passim.

2. This is apparently a reference to Gen. William T. Sherman's Special Field Orders No. 15, issued originally in January 1865. See Paul A. Cimbala, "The Freedmen's Bureau, the Freedmen and Sherman's Grant in Reconstruction Georgia, 1865–1867," *JSH*, 55 (1989): 597, 599.

3. Horace James (c1818–1875), a Congregationalist minister, served as chaplain of the 25th Mass. Inf. and superintendent of freedmen in North Carolina before being assigned to the Freedmen's Bureau in that state. He was later discharged for alleged complicity in the murder of a freedman. Richardson, *Christian Reconstruction*, 71; Heitman, *Register*, 1: 570; McFeely, *Yankee Stepfather*, 250–54; Boston directories (1874–75).

4. Ralza M. Manly (c1822-fl1885), former chaplain of the 1st Cav., USCT, served as superintendent of education for the Freedmen's Bureau until 1870. He settled in Richmond, where he worked as a superintendent of schools, a deputy collector of internal revenue taxes, and principal of a black secondary school. 1880 Census, Va., Henrico, Richmond, 84th Enum. Dist., 8; *Senate Ex. Docs.*, 39 Cong., 2 Sess., No. 6, p. 164 (Ser. 1276); *Off. Army Reg.: Vols.*, 1: 90; 8: 141; Richmond directories (1866–85); Virginius Dabney, *Richmond: The Story of a City* (New York, 1976), 229–30.

5. Orlando Brown.

6. Presumably Henry Ward Beecher presented this memorial to the President when he met with him on November 1, 1865. Johnson assured him that no state would be readmitted unless it had ratified the Thirteenth Amendment and provided protection for its freedmen. *New York Tribune*, Nov. 3, 1865.

7. Patton (1798–1879), a Congregationalist minister and author, was a member of the AMA executive committee. Joseph Eldredge (1804–1875) was pastor of a Congregational church in Connecticut. *DAB*; *NUC*.

From Benjamin H. Hill[1]

LaGrange Ga.   Nov. 1st 1865.

Sir:

Having returned from a visit to the Convention of this State now in session, I have thought the time had arrived when I could appropriately call your attention to my application for pardon, and that a few words on the question of public concerns might not be unacceptable.

The prohibition of slavery was inserted in the new Constitution without a known dissenting voice.

A liberal code will be adopted by the Legislature for the protection of the negro in his rights. Indeed, I am satisfied the freedman will find no surer or more liberal protection in any State than in Georgia.

I am pleased also, to say that equal unanimity and yet more heart-earnestness exist among our people in support of your administration.

Our farmers, generally, are preparing to give free negro labor a fair, honest and faithful trial in the production of cotton and other staples in the next year.

Bitterness is subsiding; industry is being encouraged; confidence is growing, and the waste places are being rapidly rebuilt.

All these happy results spring from the conviction, that, while in your policy of re-organization you have required the people to accept continued Union and emancipation as irreversable fruits of the struggle, you have done so with the manly determination to exact nothing and allow nothing which can destroy their sense of manhood and honor, or degrade them to inferiority as a section of our country.

You may trust the Southern people with perfect faith, for you have secured their undoubting confidence; and the more universal your

318 NOVEMBER 1865

clemency, and implicit your trust, the more earnest will be their fidelity until it shall grow into absolute devotion.

If the approaching Congress shall wisely second your efforts, and make available your labors, we may entertain high hopes of an early and permanent return of both harmony and prosperity.

If you are satisfied the act will be in perfect accord with the public weal, and not otherwise, I would be pleased to have favorable action on my application for pardon filed in July last.[2]

Benj. H. Hill

ALS, GU-Brown Family Papers.

1. Hill (1823–1882), a prominent secessionist and Confederate senator, later served in the House (1875–77) and Senate (1877–82). He was not pardoned by Johnson until May 10, 1867. *BDAC*; Warner and Yearns, *BRCC*; Amnesty Papers (M1003, Roll 19), Ga., Benjamin H. Hill, RG94, NA.

2. After having written to Johnson twice in mid-June, Hill wrote to the President on July 4 to repeat his plea for parole. Johnson granted a parole to Hill in July and ordered that transportation to his home in Georgia be provided. On July 24, 1865, Hill took the oath of allegiance in preparation for his pardon request. Hill to Johnson, June 14, 15, 1865, *Johnson Papers*, 8: 240, 244; Hill to Johnson, July 4, 1865, Johnson Papers, LC; Johnson to Commanding Officer, July 20, 1865, Tels. Sent, President, Vol. 2 (1865), RG107, NA. A copy of Hill's oath is in the Amnesty Papers (M1003, Roll 19), Ga., Benjamin H. Hill, RG94, NA.

From Benjamin G. Humphreys

Jackson, Miss., Novr 1st 1865.

Sir

Captain Peck,[1] Sub-Commissioner of Freedmen's Bureau, at Hazelhurst Copiah County, Miss. has been in the habit of charging and collecting from the citizens of that county, three dollars per head for every contract made with Freed-men. Mr D. J. Brown[2] refused to pay the tax and, through Provisional Governor Sharkey, complained to Col Thomas,[3] Assistant Commissioner for this State, at Vicksburg, who promptly responded that the charges made by Capt Peck were unauthorized. Upon the reading of this dispatch a difficulty ensued between Mr Brown and Capt. Peck which resulted in the dragging of Mr Brown by the heels, by colored troops under command of Capt. Peck. Brown made complaint upon affidavit before a magistrate[4] who issued a warrant to the Sheriff[5] on the 18th October, directing him to arrest Capt. Peck for assault and battery on Brown. Capt. Peck, with an armed force, *defied* the Sheriff. The Sheriff called out a posse-Comitatus and succeeded in arresting him. Capt. Peck refused to answer for trial for commitment and the Magistrate required him to give bond for his appearance at next circuit court. The Citizens offered to go his security. He declined to give bond and, in default, was imprisoned in county jail. To day an Armed force under the command of Lt. Col. Gibson[6] of the 58th U.S. Colored Infantry, has released Capt. Peck from the custody of the Sheriff whom I have advised not to resist an armed force but to yield under protest. Capt. Peck has now arrested L. H. Redus, Deputy Sheriff, Col Redus[7] and Henry Cochran[8] for executing the warrant; and holds them in confinement. The civil authority is thus defied and put in subordination to the military, after the case was duly considered by Major general Osterhaus.[9] In pursuance of an order directed by the Convention called by Governor Sharkey, the loyal people of Mississippi have filled all the offices of the state, Executive, Legislative and Judicial, with their most loyal citizens, who are now performing the functions of civil government, under the oath prescribed by the Constitution. The duties of the functionaries of the different departments are so clearly defined and separated by the constitution, that I could find no power to comply with the demand of Gen'l Osterhaus for the release of Capt. Peck. In my reply to him I said, "Capt Peck is in the hands of the Judiciary. His remedy is ample and peaceable if he is disposed to avail himself of it. I have no right to interfere except in the exercise of the pardoning power which I will cheerfully use if it is a case that merits it." My sincere desire and effort was to avoid any collision with the military authorities. The Judiciary has no policy but must administer the law as it is written. The Legislature is now in session and sedulously engaged in adjusting the laws to our altered and anomalous condition—fully purposing to secure to our entire population— the strictest justice and anxiously desirous of reestablishing the most amicable relations with the Federal Authorities. No people have ever manifested in better faith their willingness to abide by the result of their late effort for independence—and no better evidence could be given than the quiet and yielding temper with which they submit to the petty tyranny, wrong and injustice inflicted upon them by many officials connected with the Freedmen's Bureau. Many of the officers connected with that Bureau are gentlemen of honor and integrity; but they appear to be incapable of protecting our citizens from the peculations, frauds and villanies of the vile and vicious.

I forward herewith a letter from the Mayor of Hazelhurst[10] which is a specimen of the complaints daily sent to me.

I respectfully refer the whole matter to you and ask your decision—and I await such action as you may see proper to take.[11]

Benj G Humphreys—Governor of Mississippi

ALS, DLC-JP.

1. Warren Peck (c1840–1907), an enlisted man in the 11th Ill. Inf. before obtaining a commission in the 58th Inf., USCT, was detailed as subassistant commissioner from August until December 1865. CSR, RG94, NA; Pension Records, Louisa Peck, RG15, NA.

2. Drury J. Brown (b. c1813) was a planter and former justice of the peace from North Carolina. 1850 Census, Miss., Hinds, 454; (1860), Copiah, 145.

3. Samuel Thomas.

4. Thomas Jones was a justice of the peace in Copiah County. Joseph Holt to Lorenzo Thomas, Dec. 23, 1865, Lets. Sent (Record Books), Vol. 17, RG153, NA.

5. Humphreys probably refers to deputy sheriff L. H. Redus (b. c1823), a former steamboat captain from Indiana, who actually arrested Peck. Ibid.; 1860 Census, Miss., Copiah, 27.

6. Norman S. Gilson (1839–1914), an attorney from Wisconsin, commanded the garrison at Brookhaven and served periodically as a judge advocate in Mississippi (1865–66). CSR, RG94, NA; Pension Records, Laura B. Gilson, RG15, NA; *Soldiers' and Citizens' Album of Biographical Record . . .* (Chicago, 1888), 164.

7. Probably the Samuel Redus (b. c1797) who is listed in the census as a woodcutter in Copiah County. 1860 Census, Miss., Copiah, 26; Holt to Thomas, Dec. 23, 1865, Lets. Sent (Record Books), Vol. 17, RG153, NA.

8. Henry Cochran (b. c1849) was a Mississippi native who did "stencil work." 1870 Census, Miss., Copiah, Hazlehurst, 2.

9. Peter J. Osterhaus.

10. Henry Hanslow (c1836-fl1870), who served as a Confederate surgeon, moved to Hazlehurst after the war to establish a private practice. He had sent a letter outlining the circumstances surrounding the arrest of Peck and claiming that the whites in Hazlehurst were "living in a state of absolute despotism and terror" owing to outrages committed by black troops. CSR, RG109, NA; 1870 Census, Miss., Copiah, Hazlehurst, 7; Hartwell Cook, ed., *Hazlehurst, Copiah County, Mississippi* (Jackson, Miss., 1985), 362; Hanslow to Humphreys, Oct. 31, 1865, Johnson Papers.

11. Upon receiving Hanslow's letter, Humphreys had immediately wired a summary to Johnson for a decision. Thomas, who had initiated the investigation that led to the release of Peck and the arrest of the Mississippians, also forwarded his findings to Howard. Stanton, by Johnson's order, directed that Redus be freed, that Gilson be relieved of his command until further orders, that there should be no further military interference in the matter, and that Osterhaus should conduct an inquiry. Holt later recommended that the Reduses, Jones, and Cochran be tried by a military commission, but no record of subsequent action has been found. Humphreys to Johnson, Oct. 31, 1865, Johnson Papers, LC; Thomas to Howard, Oct. 31, 1865, Records of the Commr., Lets. Recd. (M752, Roll 22), RG105, NA; Stanton to Osterhaus, Nov. 3, 1865, Tels. Sent, Sec. of War (M473, Roll 90), RG107, NA; Holt to Thomas, Dec. 23, 1865, Lets. Sent (Record Books), Vol. 17, RG153, NA.

From William T. Leacock[1]

Nov. 1 1865

Sir,

I feel, as every southern mind must feel, most grateful for the kindness, which your course of action is daily developing towards us.

You are hewing for yourself, thru the difficulties of your position, a way to our hearts, by your discreet but able efforts for the promotion of our interest, our happiness, & our honour—and from the good, you have already done, we have every confidence that more you have yet in reserve for us—& on this confidence, I feel persuaded, that a return to amicable relations can rapidly & permanently be raised. It is one thing to conquer a people, & another thing to conciliate a people, when conquered—but a more glorious victory cannot be atchieved—& this victory your present course, as far as I am permitted to see, is bound to atchieve.

I am now on my way to New Orleans,[2] to labor for the restoration of peace and harmony—but to accomplish any useful result, we must begin right—& I now appeal to your Excellency to enable me to make this right beginning. Your Excellency must know, that Genl. Butler, when he forced me to retire from New Orleans, threw my church over into the hands of strangers—& those, who built the church, & held this property in the church, were forced, by circumstances, to seek a refuge among other denominations.[3]

Now as Genl. Butler did this, under the plea of a war-necessity, may we not ask you, now that peace has returned to our borders, to undo what he did, as a peace measure—to restore the church to the condition in which he found it, & to restore it to those, from whose hands he wrested it?[4]

We ask this of your excellency as an encouragement, on our part, to return speedily, & as an evidence, on your part, that you wish us thus speedily to return, to all those peaceful relations, which characterized our once happy, but now distracted country.

W. T. Leacock

ALS, DNA-RG94, Amnesty Papers (M1003, Roll 28), La., W. T. Leacock.

1. Leacock (c1810–1884), an Episcopal clergyman from England, was rector of Christ Church in New Orleans from 1852 until his death. Conrad, *La. Biography*, 1: 493–94.

2. In 1862 Leacock had been exiled to New York by Gen. Benjamin F. Butler for refusing to include a prayer for the President of the United States in his church services. Gerald M. Capers, *Occupied City* (Lexington, 1965), 92, 181–82; John S. Kendall, "Christ Church and General Butler," *LHQ*, 23 (1940), 1242, 1253–54.

3. After Leacock's exile, Butler turned Christ Church over to a military chaplain, who later resigned his commission but continued to occupy the church and who supervised the election of a new vestry composed of unionists and Union officers. Taylor, *La. Reconstructed*, 5; Kendall, "Christ Church," 1241–57 passim. See J. P. Sullivan to Johnson, Sept. 14, 1865, Johnson Papers, LC.

4. Johnson referred this application to Gen. Edward R.S. Canby, asking in an endorsement penned by Robert Johnson: "Is there any good reason why this church should not be restored?"

To Oliver P. Morton

Washington, D.C., November 1st 1865.

Your dispatch has been received.[1] Gov Sharkey has been dispatched heretofore on the Same Subject.[2] I will repeat it. I have confidence that all will come out right.

You will accept my thanks for your recent Speech.[3] It has done great good in directing the public minds.

Andrew Johnson.

Tel, DLC-JP.

1. The previous day Morton had wired: "Would not a telegram from you to the Mississippi Legislature in regard to the adoption of the Constitutional amendment abolishing slavery have a good effect. The adoption of the amendment is in Every way important." Morton to Johnson, Oct. 31, 1865, Johnson Papers, LC.

2. See Johnson to Sharkey, Aug. 15, and Sharkey to Johnson, Aug. 28, 1865, *Johnson Papers*, 8: 599–600, 666–67.

3. The President probably refers to Morton's address to a public meeting at Rich-

mond, Ind., on September 29, 1865, which Johnson later praised as "the ablest defense" of presidential Reconstruction policies "yet made public." William D. Foulk, *Life of Oliver P. Morton* (2 vols., Indianapolis, 1899), 1: 446–52.

From Charles O'Conor[1]

New York, Nov. 1st 1865.

Dear Sir,

When it seemed possible that the close of our civil [war] might be signalized by a prosecution of Jefferson Davis for Trea[son I] tendered him my services as Counsel. His reply to my letter [was said] to contain some objectionable matter; and its consequent suppress[ion] caused my tender to remain as yet unanswered. Nevertheless [there is]ground for assuming that it has been accepted and is relied [upon].[2]

Soon after your accession to the Presidential office, it [became] apparent to all who were governed by dispassionate reason that, [when] dealing with the vast interests involved, a most benign and pat[riotic] course had been adopted as the policy of your administration. If to a censorious spirit or even to close critics there seemed to be any occasional deviations, they were found only in occurrences of a minute character which might well be attributed to insurmountable impediments which, for the moment, turned aside from its chosen channel the current of your official action.

The motives which led to my tender of gratuitous services in the defence of Mr. Davis need not be stated. Their nature is sufficiently defined by subsequent circumstances. They induced an abstinence from any step which could by any possibility embarrass you, even in the slightest degree. They dictated to me and enforced upon my part an almost absolute acquiescence. If no other good end was subserved by this, your time and thoughts, necessarily much occupied with progressing arrangements to reinstate public order and general prosperity, were not intruded upon. Such has been my course; if others have acted differently, I feel warranted in saying, as I firmly believe, that they did so without competent authority; and I aver that their acts were without my concurrence.

It is not intended to express any views as to the justice or expediency of prosecuting Mr. Davis. Although I was but slightly acquainted with him and was influenced by no personal considerations whatever in becoming his Counsel; yet, whilst an occupant of that position, I would not presume to advise; neither would it be proper to burden you with the consideration of an elaborate argument.

My aim in addressing you is to mitigate the personal sufferings of Mr. Davis. His physical health has long been precarious. This is well known and needs no proof. To one in his bodily condition, a long imprisonment may become, in effect, an infliction of the death-penalty.

This danger, not slight under any circumstances, must be serious if the precautionary measures prescribed by military forms are of a nature to create disease. I am advised that the loss of sleep, occasioned by a light kept in his room at night and the noise of the sentinels on guard, having created a morbid sensibility, his strength has greatly failed. I venture to assure you that this is the fact.

That large and liberal humanity which is evinced in your public action and that high sense of justice which none but the humane ever possess, will both plead with you in this case. They demand an alleviation, if you can deem it consistent with your duty. I cannot by any force of language address to you an appeal of greater persuasiveness than this bare recital of the facts.

I take the liberty of presenting two distinct proposals, placing them in the order which conforms to my own preference.

In any view of the ultimate course in his case some time may yet elapse before the trial of Mr. Davis. Should a speedy trial be designed, magnanimity would not deny a fair opportunity of arranging his defence. Some relaxation of existing restraints is necessary for this purpose. They are a substantial interdict of aid from Counsel.

I propose that he be withdrawn from his present custody and charged with treason before a committing magistrate. Let bail be then accepted. I will myself enter into a recognizance for his appearance to any amount not exceeding my whole estate. It may be placed at $1 or 200.000, or even at a higher sum, if desired.

Openly, and as a mere voluntary and spontaneous assurance to the public that an escape is not meditated and should not be apprehended, I will pledge myself, at the time of becoming bail, that no indemnity against the hazard exists and that no reimbursement will ever be accepted in any event. On pain of being remanded to close custody, it may be enjoined upon Mr. Davis that he remain within any particular state or other narrower limits that the Government shall think fit to prescribe. A pledge may be required that until his trial he will not pass beyond the bounds of a small farm in the rural part of this Island which is my residence. If desired he shall converse with no persons, except his own family, mine, his Counsel and his medical advisers.

Of course, I set aside without comment, as unworthy of it, one objection which common practice allows to a prosecutor but which a liberal one would not take. I am not a resident of any district which the Government would select for such a prosecution.

If this proposition should be acceptable, then I beg leave to solicit the adoption of such measures as may divest his military imprisonment of the features above mentioned. They render it detrimental to his health and perhaps dangerous to his life. In Aaron Burr's case, even after an indictment for Treason, Chief Justice Marshall, in consideration of similar circumstances, ordered a special custody which took from imprisonment all its rigor, and gave to the accused every desirable facility in preparing for and conducting his defence. Vol. 1. p. 350.[3]

I concede that it is not usual to accept bail on accusations for capital offences; but submit that this case may fairly be considered as peculiar and unprecedented. For this reason some deviation from custom, in respect to mere forms, might be tolerated. This indulgence would be hailed with the approval of all good men; the fidelity of the accused to his pledge, by remaining within the country to abide judgment, would be a peremptory justification, enforcing silence upon all who could claim a right to question your act; and if a violation of the pledge may, for the sake of an illustration, be contemplated as possible, I will add that there would thence result a dishonor to the fugitive and a discredit to his late adherents, constituting the severest infliction upon both that could be desired by the enemies of either.[4]

Ch. O'Conor

LS, DNA-RG60, Office of Atty. Gen., Misc. Papers *re* Imprisonment and Trial of Jefferson Davis.

1. O'Conor (1804–1884) was a New York attorney who, as a Democrat, ardently defended slavery and states' rights. *DAB.*

2. O'Conor had written to Davis on May 31, 1865; but the former Confederate president's response on June 7, though he revised it as instructed, had been retained by Federal authorities. Robert McElroy, *Jefferson Davis: The Unreal and the Real* (2 vols., New York, 1937), 2: 537–39; Strode, *Jefferson Davis*, 3: 241.

3. Actually, upon the insistence of Burr's counsel, Marshall consented to his removal from the public jail to Burr's "former lodgings near the capitol." *Reports of the Trials of Colonel Aaron Burr. . . .* (2 vols., Philadelphia, 1808), 1: 350–51.

4. This letter was referred to Speed, but O'Conor never received a "definite reply." Understanding that bail might be allowed if prominent Unionists pledged their security, O'Conor enlisted the aid of Horace Greeley, who with nine other northerners endorsed Davis's bail bond for $100,000 when it was eventually granted on May 13, 1867. McElroy, *Davis: Unreal and Real*, 2: 542, 584–86; Strode, *Jefferson Davis*, 3: 309.

From Benjamin F. Perry

Columbia S.C.   Nov 1st 1865.

I will send you today the whole proceedings of the state convention properly certified as you requested.[1] The debt contracted by South Carolina during the Rebellion is very inconsiderable. Her Expenditures for War purposes were paid by the confederate Government. She has assumed no debt or any part of any debt of that Government. Her whole state debt at this time is only about six millions 6,000,000 and that is mostly for railroads and building new state House prior to the War. The members of the legislature say they have received no official information of the amendment of the Federal Constitution, abolishing Slavery. They have no objection to adopting the first section of the amendment proposed but they fear that the second section may be construed to give congress power of local legislation over the Negroes and white men, too, after the abolishment of slavery. In good faith South Carolina has abolished slavery and never will wish to restore it again.[2]

The legislature is passing a code of laws providing ample & complete protection for the Negro.[3] There is a sincere desire to do everything necessary to a restoration of the Union and tie up and heal every bleeding wound which has been caused by this fratricidal war. I was elected U.S. Senator by a very flattering vote. The other senator will be elected today.[4]

B. F. Perry

Tel, DLC-JP.
1. See Johnson to Perry, Oct. 30, 1865, Tels. Sent, President, Vol. 2 (1865), RG107, NA.
2. Johnson directed Secretary Seward to "please read this dispatch." Seward informed Perry, on behalf of the President, that Johnson was "not entirely satisfied" with the governor's "explanations" concerning the war debt and the Thirteenth Amendment. Before Perry's term expired, the legislature ratified the amendment but postponed settlement of the war debt question. Kibler, *Perry*, 429–37; Seward to Perry, Nov. 6, 1865, Tels. Sent, Sec. of War (M473, Roll 90), RG107, NA. See James B. Campbell to Johnson, Dec. 31, 1865.
3. See James L. Orr to Johnson, Dec. 23, 1865.
4. John L. Manning.

To William L. Sharkey

Washington, D.C., November 1st 1865.

It is all important that the Legislature adopt the Amendment to the Constitution of the United States, abolishing Slavery. The action of the Legislature of Mississippi is looked to with great interest at this time, and a failure to adopt the Amendment will create the belief that the action of the Convention, abolishing Slavery, will hereafter by the Same body be revoked. The argument is, if the Convention abolished Slavery in good faith, why Should the Legislature hesitate to make it a part of the Constitution of the United States.

I trust in God, that the Legislature will adopt the Amendment, and thereby make the way clear for the admission of Senators and Representatives to their Seats in the present Congress.[1]

I congratulate you and your colleague[2] on your election to the Senate.

Andrew Johnson

Tel, DNA-RG107, Tels. Sent, President, Vol. 2 (1865).
1. The Mississippi House rejected the Thirteenth Amendment by a vote of 45 to 25, and the 39th Congress subsequently refused to admit the state's delegation. Harris, *Presidential Reconstruction*, 142, 144.
2. James Lusk Alcorn.

To J. Madison Wells

Washington, D.C., November 1st 1865.

For the present I would let the cotton go.[1] All cotton transactions cause more difficulty and expense than profit. The Tax levied by Order of March 1865 will not be collected,[2] which will be some relief.

Show this dispatch to Gen'l Canby who will not enforce the collection of the taxes referred to.[3]

Andrew Johnson   President U.S.

Tel, DNA-RG107, Tels. Sent, President, Vol. 2 (1865).

1. See Wells to Johnson, Oct. 9, 1865. In another telegram, Wells repeated his request that Canby be ordered to surrender the 8,000 bales he had confiscated. Wells to Johnson, Oct. 28, 1865, Johnson Papers, LC.

2. See Joseph S. Fullerton to Johnson, Oct. 28, 1865.

3. See Johnson to Wells, Nov. 4, 1865.

To Benjamin F. Butler [1]

Washington D C   November 2nd 1865 [2]

There is no desire to muster officers out of service other than a reduction of the army to the wants of the Govt in time of peace. If you desire any exceptions to be made at this time you will please indicate them.[3]

Andrew Johnson   Prest

Tel, DLC-Benjamin F. Butler Papers.

1. Butler, at this time in Lowell, Mass., retained his appointment as major general, expecting Johnson to ask him to serve on a military commission to try Jefferson Davis; but in late October he was told by Stanton that he would be mustered out. He thereupon wired the President to ask if his dismissal was "desired." Stanton to Butler, Oct. 26, 1865, and Butler to Mrs. M. A. Ware, July 18, 1866, Marshall, *Butler Correspondence*, 5: 677, 684; Butler to Johnson, Oct. 28, 1865, Johnson Papers, LC; Benjamin F. Butler, *Butler's Book: Autobiography and Personal Reminiscences* (Boston, 1892), 915–18.

2. Johnson actually submitted this telegram for transmission on November 1, 1865.

3. The same day that he wired his inquiry to Johnson, Butler also asked Stanton to give the President his resignation, which he had written on October 20 and forwarded by mail. The President accepted Butler's resignation effective November 30. Butler to Stanton, Oct. 28, 1865, Butler Papers, LC; Butler to Johnson, Oct. 20, 1865, ACP Branch, File B-1646-CB-1865, Benjamin F. Butler, RG94, NA; J. C. Kelton to Butler, Dec. 4, 1865, Marshall, *Butler Correspondence*, 5: 684.

From Frank C. Dunnington

Nashville, Nov 2, 1865.

My dear Sir—

Pardon the privilege of this letter. It is based upon an ardent desire for the success of your administration in its conservative policy towards the South, and for the speedy restoration of peace, order and prosperity to the whole country; as well as from a personal solicitude to see a friend relieved from embarrassments that I regard as unnecessarily harsh, if not positively unjust, and which are giving him much trouble. I allude to the case of John Overton.[1] I know Overton well. I was with him in the South. There is nothing peculiar in his case. Friends in their anxiety to serve him may, to some extent, have compromised him with the authorities while you were military Governor of Tennessee; but if so the fault was *theirs*, not *his*. What he did was done in good faith. I have tested him and know him to be a man that can be *relied on*—that he *means* what he says, and *performs his promises*. You once valued such traits of character, and I have no reason to suppose that subsequent experience has taught you to value them less. I know him to be a man of more *intelligence*, more *force of character* and greater capacity for *usefulness* than you thought him when I talked to you concerning him in Washington.

The history of his recent troubles with Gen. Thomas[2] you may but *partially* understand. Overton did not seek a restoration of his property in his first application to the Court at Memphis, but simply to secure additional protection to his property, which he regarded as being improperly managed, by asking that the Federal Court would place it in the hands of a Receiver, by whom it should be rented until final action could be had in his case pending at Washington. This the Court refused to do, but did that which was not sought for, that is, proceeded to try the case upon its merits, maintaining that it was either the property of Overton or of the adverse claimant, and must be determined one way or the other. It thus became a matter of necessity that he should plead his oath of amnesty, taken under President Lincolns proclamation, and which I understand Gen. Thomas to decide as insufficient, and upon which I suppose he bases his action in arresting the determination of the Court.

Pardon me, my dear Sir, for suggesting to you upon so grave a matter that the Courts of the country ought to be upheld by the Executive, and that without it liberty is but a name. An undue exercise of Military power has been regarded as the bane of liberty in all nations. I implore you, therefore, as a recognised champion of free government, to watch it with a jealous eye and restrain it with a firm hand. I submit it to you, if it would not be far better even to consider something of that measure of punishment which policy suggests should be imposed by the government, than to strengthen the presumptions of a power that is always grasping, and to write down precedents in history that can never be bloted out.

The case of Mr. Overton is of trifling importance to the Government in comparason with the magnitude of a great principle. While granting him pardon would relieve the conflict between the Court & the military, the government would be doing nothing more than preserving the harmony of its conservative policy in restoring to the rights of citizenship all who earnestly desire to return to their allegiance and give proof of their willingness to conform to its authority.

I feel bold to say this much from a sense of duty to a valued friend, (and without any suggestion from him or others,)—from a firm conviction that a *vital* principle is in issue—and the belief that however lightly you may value suggestions from so humble a source, you will at least do me the justice to appreciate the motive that has prompted them.

It does not follow because I deemed it best to favor the seperation of the States at a peculiar crisis, and have failed in my desires, that I am not *now* equally interested with every one else in whatever concerns the future of our common country. As a citizen of the United States I have an equal interest with every other citizen in the "general welfare," and shall labor to promote it, and trust that the differences incident to the troubles of the last four years will not make it presumptious in your estimation for me to exercise the same liberty in confering with you that I was in the habit of doing in years past—the happier & better days of the republic.

Frank. C. Dunnington.
Nov. 21, 1865.

N.B I had written the foregoing letter and was in the act of mailing it when I heard that Mr. Overtons pardon had been received by him. I learn to-day that it has been revoked.[3] No one understands better than I do that the Executive may have reasons of public policy, which not being understood by others, will prevent an impartial judgment of the wisdom of his course; at the same time you must pardon me for saying that I believe Mr Overton has been misrepresented and his case improperly prejudiced. He has labored as faithfully as any of us to conform to the requirements of the government and sustain your policy of restoration. I am not warranted in saying, yet I fear, that men less friendly to our future harmony, have sought to have him misunderstood at Washington. We are not always able to divine motives and history is full of examples where the best and wisest of men have been misled by misrepresentations plausibly presented and based upon unworthy motives. God grant that we may have a *substantial* peace and a *substantial* government, but neither will be advanced by the policy of those who seek to dispoil & dishonor those of the South who had the honesty and the manhood to stand by the cause to which they commited themselves in the opening of our recent national troubles.

D.

ALS, DLC-JP.

1. The President had been confronted by the Overton controversy early in his presidency. See, for example, Overton to Johnson, May 6, 1865, *Johnson Papers*, 8: 39–40.

2. Gen. George H. Thomas had objected to Overton's oath, because he had taken it in a state (Kentucky) where he was not a citizen. Writing from Washington in mid-October, Thomas indicated that the President had claimed that Overton had not been pardoned; therefore, he was not entitled to his property. Thomas advised, "Give Genl Fisk instructions to look sharp for these pretended pardoned Rebels." Dorris, *Pardon and Amnesty*, 236–37; Thomas to Robert H. Ramsay, Oct. 16, 1865, Tels. Sent, Sec. of War (M473, Roll 90), RG107, NA.

3. Overton's August 1865 pardon was temporarily revoked. For further developments, see Brownlow to Johnson, Nov. 20, 1865.

From William W. Holden

Raleigh, N.C.   Nov. 2d 1865

My dear Sir:

Mr. Richard C. Badger,[1] who will hand you the Ordinances,[2] and also this, is a son of the Hon. Geo. E. Badger[3] and a young man of intelligent character and superior attainments. He is very well posted in the affairs of this State, and in the operation of my office, being one of my Secretaries; and I would be glad if you could find time to grant him an interview.

The opposition in this State suddenly revealed itself, but it had been maturing for several months. It is the result of the ambition and selfishness of William A. Graham, and the main object is to revive the old Whig party. Effort after effort was made to get leading men to oppose me, but failed, and at length Jonathan Worth was taken up. He, with Graham, Swain, Moore,[4] and others, was very anxious to perpetuate the rebel State government, because the leading officials had been Whigs. But this failed, and at once, from having been bitter opponents or opposers of your plan of restoration, they apparently became earnest advocates. This was because of your great strength with the masses of our people, and to mask their ultimate purposes. When they were forced, to repudiate the rebel debt they did it with gnashing of teeth and much talk of dictation, but they *did it*, for they knew there was no other course. The Convention is to meet again in May. If the State should get back, as I trust it will by that time, a desperate effort will then be made to repeal the Ordinance and assume the debt.

Gov. Graham has raised a great furor in Orange because he has not been pardoned, and he will most probably be elected to the Senate. He is the head and front of all the trouble in this State. I have the most conclusive proof of this. Jo Turner and others are merely the tools he is using. If elected, and he presents himself to take his seat, unpardoned, what course shall I adopt? I am ready to obey your instructions; but I am satisfied that the time has come when such public men should be compelled to respect the national authority. I am too old a campaigner to be unduly excited by a pending election, and therefore I can take a dispassionate view of the whole matter. In many cases the liberality I have shown has not been appreciated; and I fear this will be the case so far as you are concerned with the cotton lords of the cotton States. I fear the day will come when they will "turn and rend you." Our only reliance, after all, is in the great body of the loyal Union people, and in honestly penitent original Secessionists.

In the 1st Congressional District of this State the candidates are Gen. Stubbs, Judge Warren, Dr. R K. Speed, and W. E. Bond.[5] It is impossible to predict the result. Warren and Bond are the best men. Bond can take the oath. Warren is equally loyal, but cannot take the oath.

In the 2d District the candidates are H. E. Lehman and C. C. Clark.[6] The latter is a true destructive, and I fear will be elected, as this is the strongest secession District in the State. Mr. Lehman can take the oath.

In the 3d District the chances are that T. C. Fuller,[7] recently pardoned, will be elected. He was a member of the Confederate Congress, and was at heart a Union man. He will make an acceptable member, but he can not takè the oath.

In the 4th District the candidates are Col. J.P.H. Russ, who visited Washington with me; Col. L. C. Edwards, A. H. Arrington, recently pardoned, and the inevitable, unavoidable Jo Turner.[8] Col. Russ will most probably be elected, though Graham is straining every nerve for Turner, having urged the people over his own name in the newspapers to vote for him. Col. Russ cannot take the oath, but he is true as steel to the cause of the Union.

In the 5th District the candidates are our old friend Bedford Brown and Lewis Hane.[9] Col Brown's election is thought to be certain. He cannot take the oath, but he is true, able, and honest.

In the 6th District the candidates are Dr. William Sloan and Dr. J. G. Ramsay.[10] The chances are that Dr. Sloan will be elected. He is an able man, and can take the oath.

In the 7th District there are several candidates, but the most prominent is Col. Tod R. Caldwell,[11] lately one of my Aids. He is true and able, and can take the oath. I think he will most probably be elected.

So far as the Governor's election is concerned, I have no doubt of the result. The Worth faction, led by Graham, and no doubt secretly encouraged by Vance, are lying, stepping on the verge of treason, and expending money largely in the hope of success, but though the lines of Railroads and most of the towns and villages seem to be against me, yet the great body of *the people* are for me. In the middle Counties, I shall lead him considerably, and in the West my information is I will sweep every thing. I will beat him twelve hundred votes in this County, and a well-informed friend assured me to-day that I would beat him twelve hundred in Chatham. I will beat him in his own County, Randolph, five hundred votes. The palpable effort to revive the old Whig party has induced many of the old secession Democrats to take ground for me, among them Judge Saunders,[12] of this place.

Our friend the Hon. Kenneth Rayner,[13] is a candidate for the Commons in Wake. His chances are good. He is a devoted friend of yours. I trust he may be elected.

W. W. Holden

ALS, DNA-RG59, Misc. Lets., 1789–1906 (M179, Roll 230).

1. A Confederate veteran, Badger (1839–1882) later served as one of Holden's legal advisors during his impeachment hearings. *NUC*; Louis Manarin et al., comps., *North*

Carolina Troops, 1861–1865: A Roster (10 vols., Raleigh, 1966-), 5: 395; Raper, *Holden*, 214.

2. The President later acknowledged receipt of forty "Resolutions, Declarations and Ordinances" passed by the recently adjourned North Carolina convention. Johnson to Holden, Nov. 7, 1865, Johnson Papers, LC.

3. The elder Badger (1795–1866), a former superior court judge, was Secretary of the Navy for six months in 1841, and later served as a Senator (1846–55). *BDAC*.

4. David L. Swain and Bartholomew F. Moore. Swain (1801–1868) was a superior court judge, former governor (1832–35), and longtime president of the University of North Carolina. *DAB*.

5. Worth supporter Jesse R. Stubbs (c1825–1870), a former member of the state legislature and more recently a convention delegate, defeated his opponents. Edward J. Warren (1824–1876) continued serving as a superior court judge. Later, as a state senator, he voted to remove Holden from office. Rufus K. Speed (1812–1891) was an old-line Whig and secession opponent. William E. Bond (c1823-*fl*1867) was a former state legislator. In July 1866 Johnson appointed him internal revenue collector for the first district of North Carolina. 1860 Census, N.C., Martin, Williamston, 4th Dist., 64; (1850), Chowan, Dist. above Edonton, 206; *Wilmington Journal*, Dec. 20, 1865; *Raleigh Standard*, Oct. 30, 1865; *Cyclopedia of the Carolinas*, 2: 131; Susan S. Blosser and Clyde N. Wilson, Jr., *The Southern Historical Collection: A Guide to Manuscripts* (Chapel Hill, 1970); Raper, *Holden*, 65, 218; John E. Wood et al., eds., *Year Book Pasquotank Historical Society* (4 vols., Baltimore, 1956–83), 3: 16; R.D.W. Connor, ed., *A Manual of North Carolina* (Raleigh, 1913), 560; *U.S. Off. Reg.* (1867), 83; Ser. 6B, Vol. 4: 140, Johnson Papers, LC.

6. Charles C. Clark (1829–1911), an ex-Confederate solicitor and a Worth supporter, prevailed in the contest against Robert F. Lehman (c1831–1876), who later served in the state senate and as a federal judge. Johnston, *Vance Papers*, 322n; *Wilmington Journal*, Oct. 25, 1865; 1870 Census, N.C., Craven, New Bern, 1st Ward, 14; Barbara M.H. Thorne, ed., *The Heritage of Craven County North Carolina: Volume I, 1984* (Winston-Salem, 1984), 33; Raper, *Holden*, 209.

7. Elected, but not seated, Thomas C. Fuller (1832–1901), whom Johnson had pardoned in July, served as a federal judge during the last decade of his life. Wakelyn, *BDC*; Fuller to Johnson, June 26, 1865, Amnesty Papers (M1003, Roll 39), N.C., Thomas C. Fuller, RG94, NA.

8. By election day, only John P.H. Russ (c1822-*fl*1870), a prominent Wake County planter and Vance's secretary of state, stood in the way of Josiah Turner's election to Congress. Both Leonidas C. Edwards (c1825-*fl*1871), a Granville County attorney whom Holden had introduced to Johnson as "a gentleman and a true man," and Archibald H. Arrington (1809–1872), a former U.S. and Confederate congressman whom Johnson had pardoned in mid-October, had withdrawn. 1860 Census, N.C., Wake, NW Dist., 35; Granville, Oxford, 2; (1870), Wake, Raleigh Twp., 89; Johnston, *Vance Papers*, 431n; Wakelyn, *BDC*; *Wilmington Journal*, Nov. 9, 1865; Holden to Johnson, Sept. 20, 1865, Misc. Lets., 1789–1906 (M179, Roll 228), RG59, NA; Arrington to Johnson, June 20, 1865, Amnesty Papers (M1003, Roll 37), N.C., Archibald H. Arrington, RG94, NA. See Joseph S. Cannon to Johnson, Nov. 13, 1865.

9. The eventual victor, Brown (1795–1870), a former congressman (1829–40), had "most steadfastly and earnestly" opposed secession, but served in the legislature at the war's outset and was a Confederate commissioner. Lewis C. Hanes (1827–1905) was an ex-Confederate officer and Holden's former private secretary. *BDAC*; Genealogical Society of Davidson County, *The Heritage of Davidson County* (Winston-Salem, 1982), 512–13; Raper, *Holden*, 79; Brown to Johnson, ca. Aug. 19, 1865, Amnesty Papers (M1003, Roll 37), N.C., Bedford Brown, RG94, NA.

10. The election was won by a Holden man, but not by Sloan (c1827-*fl*1870), a physician and iron works operator who succeeded Worth as state treasurer, nor by James G. Ramsay (1823–1903), a former state senator and Confederate congressman. 1860 Census, N.C., Gaston, Dallas, 176; (1870), Mecklenburg, Charlotte, 2nd Ward, 8; Robert F. Cope and Mandy W. Williamson, *The County of Gaston: Two Centuries of a North Carolina Region* (Charlotte, 1961), 77; Wakelyn, *BDC*; Raper, *Holden*, 282; Richard L. Zuber, *Jonathan Worth: A Biography of a Southern Unionist* (Chapel Hill, 1965), 203.

11. Failing in this election bid, Caldwell (1818–1874) later served as the state's lieu-

tenant governor and succeeded Holden upon his ouster from office, before being elected governor in his own right in 1872. Sobel and Raimo, *Governors*, 3: 1140–41.

12. Superior court judge Romulus M. Saunders (1791–1867) was a former member of Congress (1821–27, 1841–45). *BDAC*.

13. Rayner (1808–1884), who had served with Johnson in Congress (1839–45) and later produced a biography of the President, was elected. *BDAC*; Connor, *N.C. Manual*, 832; Rayner to Johnson, Apr. 6, July 2, 1866, Johnson Papers, LC.

From Robert S. Hudson[1]

Yazoo City, Miss.   Nov 2, 1865.

Sir—

Being unknown to you I feel a very great delicacy in addressing you upon any subject and especially the one now prompting me, but as I believe you recognize the right of the citizen to approach you respectfully upon any subject of public interest I will do so, without further apology.

This state has been almost exclusively an agricultural people and are now dependant upon it for employment and support. Our fields are fenceless and one vast waste. Most of the freedmen, and one half the women, boys and girls have left the state, or are dead. One half the white and black labor in this state four years ago, is now invisable, and the remaining half is in idleness and utter demoralization. The freedmen generally refuse to work in the fields on any terms—they have an imperfect idea of contracts and a less regard for them, and being irresponsible pecuniarily for any breach of contract, their contracts and breaches amount to nothing. They prefer to concentrate about the towns in idleness, vice and vagrancy than to live in the country in comfort and on good wages. This country is doomed to perish under this state of things. The "Freedmens Bureau" is a great curse to the freedmen & the country. Their offices are at the Court House, and supported by negro troops. The negroes in the country, if not allowed to do as they please in every respect, run to town to make complaint, and if sent back, several days are lost and the constant repetition and recurrence of this thing renders their labor valueless, even if they would labor well when at home, and that they will not do. They are merely lectured by the Provost, and that they delight to take as the only punishment for going to town and spending several days in town and idleness. In fact it is no punishment or reform, but the effect is just the contrary. Suppose I had 20 freedmen at labor, and lived 20 miles from town. I pledge you any word that I could not get as much as the fair and humane labor of five hands out of the number—and that would not support the 20. I cant go to town every day to report the unfaithful and yet their conduct demands it. When I leave to attend to one such case, the balance are idle and perhaps leave while I am gone, and the fruit of such an experiment is an expense of several dollars, a loss of at least two days, nothing done at home, and a mere lecture to the wayward, that never reformed white or black. The troops give them encouragement in such a course, and the whole affair ends in one grand farce, the destruction of supplies and the return of nothing to the employed but trouble and destitution. It is truly unfortunate for the freedmen that any such Bureau and troops are here. It simply demoralizes them and will end in their complete vagrancy; poverty and distruction. No man of sense or ability will attempt to farm here upon any such management or arrangements, as his crop must be a serious loss, beside sore vexation. The Bureau evidently affords fat employment to many, who seem to enjoy the position and profits, and whose perquisites are not very well defined or understood here. Doubtless many of them are very willing to continue their offices and pay.

There is no more use or necessity for such things here than there is in the State of Maine. He who can question the loyalty of this people now must be the creature of strong prejudices or the victim of false advice and information. If you were to offer them your aid and countenances to put on foot another war, you could not rally for the purpose a corporals guard in this state. There are those who have their opinions about civil and constitutional rights, but support them only in the civil and constitutional forums. The idea of Secession or War is as dead in this country as the sturdy oak of the forest, schathed and sundered by the vivid lightnings of High Heaven.

You, and even those in our own state who stay about the towns, have no full or reasonable conception of the present and still greater early troubles and distress of this people both white and black under existing rules and regulations and their utter impracticability. No man on earth can farm under any such system and no sensible man will attempt it, unless he is a pet and gets special favors and benefits, privileges and aids, and that is said to be the fortune of a few.

I have been a lawyer and planter. I owned over 100 negroes. Not one has ever left me, nor reported me nor have I reported one of them—but with all my aid and efforts they have not made six months support. I have merely boarded them and have done as well as any one around me, except that I am the only man who has not lost the largest half of his old servants. I have called mine up and told them to hunt homes elsewhere. I cannot and will not suffer one to remain about me. I leave my lands and home and return again to the law in my old age as my only hope and chances of living.

I beg you to look into the facts and grant our state relief at the earliest moment.

I refer you to Hon Wm L Sharkey, Hon J. L. Alcorn, Hon Jas T. Harrison,[2] Hon A. M. West,[3] Senators and Congressmen lately elected by this State to the Congress of the United States for my status.

                                                    Ro. S. Hudson

ALS, DLC-JP.

1. State circuit court judge Hudson (1820–1889) chaired the committee on statutory amendments appointed by the Mississippi constitutional convention. The committee's recommendations to the legislature in the fall of 1865 became the basis for oppressive "Black Codes." Hudson also endorsed legislation permitting blacks to testify in court which passed only after the intervention of Governor Humphreys in late November. Irene S. and Norman E. Gillis, comps., *Abstract of Goodspeed's Mississippi* (Baton Rouge, 1962), 290; Harris, *Presidential Reconstruction*, 125–35.

2. James T. Harrison (1811–1879), a Confederate congressman, had attended the Mississippi constitutional convention in 1865. He was elected to the U.S. House in 1867 but was refused his seat. Wakelyn, *BDC*.

3. Absalom M. West (1818-*fl*1872) served as quartermaster general of Mississippi during the Civil War and was president of the Mississippi Central Railroad. He was elected to the U.S. House in the fall of 1865 but was not seated. *OR*, Ser. 1, Vol. 17, Pt. 1: 10; Ser. 4, Vol. 2: 922; Harris, *Presidential Reconstruction*, 45, 114; Gillis, *Goodspeed's Mississippi*, 654; William C. Harris, *The Day of the Carpetbagger: Republican Reconstruction in Mississippi* (Baton Rouge, 1979), 344, 524.

From Andrew H. Kerr[1]

Big Creek Shelby Co Ten.   Nov 2nd, 1865

You will remember that about two months since, in company with our mutual friend Col. Glen[2] of Fayette Co, I had the honor of a brief interview with you, in which amongst other things, I attempted as earnestly and briefly as possible, to impress you with the fact, that the people of this section were undivided and devoted to your policy in the administration of the Government. The substance of this interview, I took the liberty of communicating by letter from Washington to Rev Mr. Cater[3] a thorough friend of the South during her late struggle. Since my return he met me with expressions of the liveliest satisfaction with the contents of my letter; stating that he had showed it to many friends, that it had had the effect of awakening new hopes and feelings in the minds of all who had read it touching the future of the South; and that Gen. Sneed[4] had requested to be permitted to read it at a public meeting last week, to endorse your administration.

Since my return home I have gone repeatedly into the city of Memphis; and having been generally known that I had been in Washington, my acquaintances, (Lawyers, Doctors, Preachers, Merchants, Tradesmen, men of all classes, with whom I have been accustomed to associate) were eager to learn the nature of our interview, and all, all, without an exception, gave to me the fullest, and heartiest expressions of satisfaction, and pleasure. Last week one of our Ecclesiastical judicatures called the Synod of Memphis, after the lapse of four years, met in Covington Tipton County. The jurisdiction of this church Court includes the churches in the whole of the Western District of Tennessee, North Mississippi, North Alabama, and a large part of Arkansas. These numerous and widely scattered churches are equally represented by Preachers, and Elders or laymen. Amongst this latter class, we had with us, amongst other distinguished gentlemen Col. Patton[5] the present candidate for Governor of Alabama. And it gives me sincere satisfaction to say to you that these gentlemen, all grave, thoughtful, Christian gentlemen, like those of whom I have already spoken, gave utterance to but one sentiment; Viz *confidence in*, and *devotion to our Chief Executive.* And you will allow me to add, that on this occasion, were offered the most fervent prayers, for the continued health, life, and usefulness of the President. Having in our interview spoken in such unqualified terms of the revolution in the sentiments of the southern people, especially of the people of this section of the state, I trust you will pardon me for having thought it proper, to confirm those statements, by furnishing you with the foregoing facts.

Mr. President when in Washington I had the pleasure of being introduced to your Son in Law Judge Patterson, who in a casual and brief interview we afterwards had at Willards, asked me the following question. "What do the loyal people in your part of the State say of Gov. Brownlow?["] In reply I answered, substantially as follows: "The relations between Gov. B. and myself so far as I know are perfectly amicable, but *politically, politically,* I do not know *any* Brownlow men." Now that there were a *few* men in this end of the state that did vote for Gov. Brownlow when a candidate for the office he holds, I do not doubt, but I take the liberty of reaffirming to you, what I stated to Judge Patterson, "*politically politically,* I do not *know* any Brownlow men." It is therefore a striking and *remarkable* fact, that whilst there exists such perfect devotion amongst the masses of the people to the President, it should be utterly wanting towards the Governor. I have again and again inquired of my friends since my return from Washington "Do you know any Brownlow men?" And the *invariable* reply has been; "not one". For this difference in the feelings of our people, I know of but one reason, they would, in the present state of the country, (anxious as they are for perfect peace) allow to govern them. You will find that reason embodied in the following statement. It is the *belief* of the people that the President intends that they shall be *freemen* under the *Constitution* of a great and benificent *Government,* in an unbroken *Union.* It is the belief of the people, that the Governor is not actuated by like noble, generous, and patriotic views and feelings. And now Mr. President you will allow me to say, that the most anxious, painfully anxious question with the people is this: When and how are we to be *peaceable freemen?* The sword has been sheathed, the arbitriment of the God of war accepted, and the two great issues in the contest, *secession* and slavery, surrendered; the oath of allegiance to the Federal Goverment, its Constitution and laws, taken in good faith; and yet we are not freemen, we cannot exercise the franchise right; we cannot though strugling ever so earnestly to do so, in the exercise of that franchise, say that our great and good and best earthly friend must and *shall* be our next President. No man lives, and perhaps never lived, unless we except the immortal Washington, who has such a hold upon the confidence, and the affections of Tennesseeans, as their own Tennessee President, and with one heart they look to him and ask when and how shall their political shackles be broken from their limbs?

Mr. President I am no politician. I am an humble Presbyterian preacher, who has always eschewed politicks from the pulpit; but I love my country, and I love and honor those who love my country, and serve it lawfully constitutionally, and in the fullness of my heart, I have sought in this poor communication, to animate and encourage you in your great and arduous work.

Praying God to spair your life, to give you health, to inspire you with needed wisdom. . . .

A. H. Kerr

Should you have leisure or disposition to write me a line it will reach me, by addressing me at Memphis care of Leftwich Cash & Co.[6]

A. H. Kerr

ALS, DLC-JP.

1. Kerr (c1812-fl1877), a prosperous farmer and longtime Presbyterian minister (first in Nashville then in Memphis), had been pardoned by Johnson on August 31. 1860 Census, Tenn., Shelby, 2nd Dist., 129; Memphis directories (1876–77); Thomas C. Barr et al., *The Story of the Presbyteries of Columbia and Nashville* (n.p., 1976), 75; *House Ex. Docs.*, 39 Cong., 2 Sess., No. 116, p. 11 (Ser. 1293).

2. Philip B. Glenn.

3. Edwin Cater (1813–1882), a Presbyterian minister in Oxford, Miss., gained some notoriety in church circles with his attacks upon the Rev. Dr. James Woodrow in the late 1860s and early 1870s. Harold B. Prince, ed., *A Presbyterian Bibliography* (Metuchen, N.J., 1983), 55; Ernest T. Thompson, *Presbyterians in the South* (3 vols., Richmond, 1963–73), 2: 368.

4. John L. T. Sneed.

5. Robert M. Patton (1809–1885) had been an old-line Whig state legislator and vocal opponent of secession. Elected governor of Alabama on November 6, he was inaugurated on December 13, 1865. After his gubernatorial career, Patton was involved with several different railroad ventures. *Northern Alabama: Historical and Biographical* (Birmingham, 1888), 306–9; Sarah W. Wiggins, *The Scalawag in Alabama Politics, 1865–1881* (University, Ala., 1977), 13.

6. This was a prominent cotton brokerage outfit in Memphis, owned and operated by John W. Leftwich and Joseph H. Cash. Leftwich (1826–1870), a graduate of the Philadelphia Medical College, had moved to Memphis in the 1850s. He was elected to Congress in 1865 but was not seated until the summer of 1866. Afterwards he served as mayor of Memphis (1869–70). Cash (c1835-fl1876) continued in the cotton brokerage business in the 1870s and served as city inspector. *BDAC*; Thomas B. Alexander, *Political Reconstruction in Tennessee* (Nashville, 1950), 90; 1870 Census, Tenn., Shelby, Memphis, 9th Ward, 49; Memphis directories (1865–76).

From William Henry Maxwell[1]

Jonesborough Tennessee   November 2nd 1865

Dear Sir—

I wrote a short time ago to David T. Patterson on the subject of the Post Office here. The present incumbent Newton Griffith and his father

Saml E Griffith[2] are avowed enemies of the administration. They are original Whigs and if you received my communication of June last, you know my opinion: that is, that neither they or any of their kind will ever in good faith affiliate with the Democracy. Recent events confirm me in my opinion. In this state we are in the hands of the Philistines and the Democrats are looking to you sir as the "saviour of civil Liberty." The Whig party of this state in my judgment will occupy the same position to the Democracy which they did when Mr. Banks was elected Speaker.[3] This may be true of the entire South. Under the teachings of Brownlow and his sattellite in this place, we have anarchy here. Last week (court week) a man was shot in the street on monday, and is now lying at the point of death—died this morning.[4] On the friday before on the North side of the County, an old man 70 odd years of age was murdered and Rapes committed on Two reputable women (husbands democrats) and an attempt made on a third. The state in short under the present Dynasty (if it is not irreverent to say so) is travelling the same road Ward's Ducks went.[5] Allow me to state a fact to you. There are several Whig enrolling officers (Confed) in this county—Not a single one of whom have been indicted for Treason in a state or Federal court. Not a single Whig in the county to my knowledge has been beat ordered off or driven out of the county. Every Democrat in the county occupying respectable positions in their civil Districts without regard to their conduct in the rebellion, have been sued civilly Indicted in both courts for treason beaten, murdered, and driven out of the country by formal notices given under penalty of death if they remain. There may be an exceptional Whig but it is an exception who has been indicted to keep up appearances. The plan is to rid East Tennessee of Democrats. And now sir your appointees are men (some of them) who approve these things if they are to be judged by their acts. Saml. E. Giffith who has been openly denouncing the administration for pardoning Rebels with one Lieut Douglass[6] are appointed to collect the Revenue for this county (Direct Tax) both Whigs. This is only of a piece with every thing that is going on here-abouts and unless you inform me that I am *boring* you I shall keep you advised of it.

I do think that our relations during the Rebellion and our lives for 20 years entitle me to a hearing. But the matter on which I intended mainly to address you is as to the Post Office. Not wishing to bother you I wrote to Hon D T Patterson, this morning. I understand they have written you and therefore I write. Mr Griffith the present incumbent proposes to resign in favor of Capt. Edgar Grisham, the Editor here.[7] His radicalism and utter disregard of all social interst and welfare has destroyed his influence here not only with Democrats but with the leading Conservative Whigs who are in the majority.

Charles Dawes,[8] is an applicant. He went through the lines in 1863 with his father—and behaved himself well made a little money and after

Knoxville was permanently occupied his mother & family went to Knoxville where they his father & mother both died leaving him the care of 5 brothers & sisters ranging from five to fifteen years old. With a small stock of goods he is keeping them here in comfort & respectability but I think when the present stock of money is exhausted that rescourse will fail. I think I can say that almost any discerning man in this community will be for him. He is a young man of steady habits and he can give any Bond that will be required of him.

I only now state the facts. When the time comes to make the question my opinion is that Mr Grisham & his illustrious prototype will be against this administration.

Wm Henry Maxwell

If there is a pension agency established here I would like to have the appointment of agent.

ALS, DLC-JP.
1. Maxwell was a farmer and lawyer who had served in the state senate. *BDTA*, 2: 613.
2. E. Newton Griffith (*c*1846-*fl*1880) became a lawyer. Samuel E. Griffith (*c*1828–1876) was a member of the state legislature in 1865. Beginning in August 1865, he also served as assistant superintendent of the Freedmen's Bureau for Washington County. Afterwards he was sheriff of that county (1868–74). 1880 Census, Tenn., Washington, 31st Enum. Dist., 2; *BDTA*, 2: 360–61; *Jonesboro Union Flag*, Aug. 25, 1865.
3. Nathaniel P. Banks of Massachusetts had been elected Speaker of the U.S. House on February 2, 1856 (34 Cong.). *BDAC*.
4. Maxwell is probably referring here to the shooting of Moses Pursell by Johnathan Mitler on October 23, 1865. The words "died this morning" were added as an interlineation, evidently after Maxwell completed the text of his letter. For details, see the *Nashville Press and Times*, Nov. 1, 1865.
5. Probably a reference to one of Gen. John Hunt Morgan's regiments, the 9th Tenn. Cav., CSA. Commanded by former Tennessee legislator William W. Ward (1825–1871), this unit was noted for its ability to ford rivers. W.J.L. Hughes, *The Hughes Family and Connections* (Owensboro, Ky., 1911), 30.
6. George W. Douglass (*c*1831-*fl*1900), a former lieutenant in the 8th Tenn. Inf., USA, was briefly Washington County register before several changes of residence led him ultimately to Knoxville. Pension Records (Minor's Certificate), Daisy A. Douglass, RG15, NA; Knoxville directories (1898–1900).
7. George Edgar Grisham (1833–1873), former captain, 8th Tenn. Inf., USA, and editor of the *Jonesboro Union Flag*, attempted to run for the legislative post vacated by the resignation of Samuel E. Griffith in 1865. Grisham served as clerk of the state house of representatives in the 1867–68 session. Bennett and Rae, *Washington County*, 3: 74; Miller, *Political Manual*, 228; *Nashville Press and Times*, Sept. 23, 1865; CSR, RG94, NA.
8. Charles R. Dawes (*c*1848-*fl*1910) for many years was cashier of a Knoxville bank before becoming involved in other business enterprises. His father, William Dawes, is listed as the postmaster at Jonesborough in 1865. 1860 Census, Tenn., Washington, Jonesboro, 147; Knoxville directories (1869–1910); *U.S. Off. Reg.* (1865).

From Albert B. Sloanaker [1]

Whitney Hotel   Washington D.C.   November 2, 1865

My Dear Sir:
I visited Washington once more to call and see you and say that I am very much pained and mortified to hear that you surrendered my claims

to appointment to office, to the caprice of that political sycophant, Jno. W. Forney.[2] I am slow to believe that your Excellency has banished from your memory my personal and unsolicited services in your interest, nor can I believe I have lost your respect, because I feel conscious before high Heaven, that I have in my struggles of life preserved an untarnished reputation.

In my own district, I am proud to say that I enjoy the high confidence and respect of the working classes, even if Jno. W. Forney, who is known to be a political prostitute, sees fit to call such supporters the "lower classes," some 3,600 of whom petitioned your Excellency for my appointment, believing that you still, as in former times, respected their claims and interests.

I beg leave to reiterate the averment that I made you when first in company with our friend Mr. Wm. Flinn,[3] that no matter how the contest might be determined I should always adhere to your Excellency in the kindest and most personal way known to one who is contented with the Forney stigma, of being the favorite of "*the lower classes*."

I consider it due you to state that Jno. W. Forney in the month of March 1865, said to a friend of mine who Masonically informed me that when he inquired as to the truth of the slanders preferred against you on the 4th of March last, replied that "it is all too true, and my God! it was a disgraceful scene to be viewed by the Representatives of Foreign Courts and the assembled loyalty of the Nation." In making this statement, the truth of which I honestly believe, and the responsibility of the assertion, I accept. I denied the aspersion to my friend, as I was on the floor of the Senate, and saw no conduct on your part unbecoming a gentleman and a statesman.

With feelings of high consideration and wishing you every happiness and success. . . .

A B. Sloanaker   late Delegate to the Baltimore
Convention from the 1st Dist Penna.

ALS, DLC-JP.

1. Sloanaker (c1837-fl1883), an attorney and Republican supporter of Johnson, was appointed collector of internal revenue in Pennsylvania after Congress adjourned in 1866, despite being repeatedly rejected by the Senate. 1860 Census, Pa., Philadelphia, Philadelphia, 13th Ward, 317; Philadelphia directories (1861–83); *Nashville Press and Times*, July 31, 1866; *Zanesville Courier* (Ohio), Aug. 1, 1866.

2. Forney had written to Hugh McCulloch that the contemplated appointment of Sloanaker as an internal revenue assessor would be a "*grevious mistake.*" The assignment was consequently not made. Forney to McCulloch, July 30, 1865, Appts., Internal Revenue Service, Assessor, Pa., 1st Dist., RG56, NA; McCulloch to Johnson, March 1, 1866, Johnson Papers, LC.

3. Flinn (c1820-fl1894) was a Washington printer who served in a number of federal bureaucratic offices, but failed in his attempt to be appointed Superintendent of Public Printing by Johnson. 1860 Census, D.C., Washington, 2nd Ward, 159; Washington, D.C., directories (1858–94); *U.S. Off. Reg.* (1877, 1883); S. E. Ancona to Johnson, Jan. 2, 1866, Johnson Papers, LC.

From John Letcher

Lexington Virginia: November 3rd: 1865:

Dear Sir:

In the month of June last, I made application for a pardon, under the provisions of your Proclamation of the 29th May, next preceding. In the interview between us, in the month of July, immediately after my release from the Old Capitol Prison, you called my attention to the fact, that I had not taken the Amnesty oath, and suggested that I should do so, and send you the certificate, to be filed with the petition.[1] The next day I sent the certificate by Mr. Slade[2] your Messenger, and I suppose it was delivered. Subsequently in taking the oath of an Attorney in our re-organized court, I again took that and other oaths, as required by Judge Thompson[3] our Circuit Judge.

I now respectfully ask your attention to my application, and would be gratified if you could give it your early attention, and favorable action. I desire to go regularly to business, and wish to do so, untrammelled by the restraint imposed upon me, by the terms of my parole. Business is frequently tendered to me, in other counties, than my own, requiring immediate attention. All such business I am compelled to decline, as the parties cannot submit to the delay incident to obtaining permission from Washington. Since my return from Washington in July, I have not been out of the county. You were kind enough to grant me permission to go to Bath County,[4] and more recently to visit Richmond, but in both cases, the time had passed before your letters reached this place.

I commenced life a tradesman, and when I obtained license to practice law, in April 1839, the only property I possessed was a few volumes of Law books. Success however, attended my efforts, and I made money rapidly, until my political career commenced in 1850, as a member of the Reform Convention of Virginia.[5] In October 1851, I was elected to the House of Representatives of the U.S. and continued in that body until I was elected Governor of Virginia, in May 1859. I entered upon my duties as Governor January 1st 1860, and retired January 1st, 1864, and resumed the practice of the law—and since have held no office, State or Confederate. When I became Governor, I was in easy circumstances, but during the war I lost almost every thing: by the loss of my property here, and in Washington, and the burning of my tobacco in Richmond. With a large and dependant family, I am now compelled to begin life anew, and by laborious & unremitting effort provide the means for their support, and the education of two sons, and three daughters—all of whom except one are under twelve years of age.

My course as a public man, in the Convention—in Congress—and as Governor, is before the country, and well known to you. Conscientious convictions of duty prompted my acts, in all the positions I have filled, and I can say in truth & sincerity, that I enjoy the confidence and respect of the people of my State without distinction of party, in a higher degree, than ever before. In all my misfortunes, they have manifested their sympathy in every conceivable mode, and have tendered relief most generously, and with a kindness, that will ever be warmly appreciated, and gratefully remembered.

I solicit a pardon, not from a desire to re-enter political life. In my condition, it would be, but little short of madness to think of it. Every obligation of duty, as a husband and as a father, requires me to exert all of energy and talent I possess, to lay up something for the evening of life, now fast approaching. Ten (or twenty years at most,) is all I can reasonably hope for, and it is short enough for the accomplishment of the object. With health and strength, and the favor of Providence, I will achieve it, however.

I have not heretofore, either personally, or by agents, urged action on my case. I have been content to wait until the present time, and trust you will *pardon me*, for calling your attention to it now.[6]

John Letcher

ALS, DNA-RG94, Amnesty Papers (M1003, Roll 64), Va., John Letcher.

1. Letcher's undated petition was referred to the Attorney General and ordered filed on July 17. His "pleasant" half-hour interview with Johnson probably occurred on July 11, when Letcher was released on parole. His amnesty oath, taken at Old Capitol Prison, is dated July 12. See Letcher to Charles W. Purcell, July 20, 1865, Amnesty Papers (M1003, Roll 64), Va., John Letcher, RG94, NA; see also F. N. Boney, *John Letcher of Virginia: The Story of Virginia's Civil War Governor* (University, Ala., 1966), 221.

2. Johnson's steward, William Slade (c1815–1868) had formerly worked as a hotel porter, a hackman, and an assistant messenger of the third auditor's office in Washington. *U.S. Off. Reg.* (1861–63); Washington, D.C., directories (1862–68); *Washington Evening Star*, Mar. 16, 1868.

3. Lucas P. Thompson (c1798–1866) had served as judge of Virginia's eleventh circuit since 1831. *Richmond Dispatch*, Apr. 25, 1866.

4. See Letcher to Johnson, Sept. 21, 1865, Johnson Papers, LC; see also Boney, *John Letcher*, 225.

5. Ibid., 44–50.

6. In November 1865 several Virginia Republicans, including John Minor Botts and John F. Lewis, personally requested Johnson to extend clemency to the former governor; but it was January 15, 1867, before he was pardoned. Ibid., 224, 230.

From Joseph E. Davis

Jackson Mississippi   Nov. 4th 1865

Your Excellency will excuse an other application for the restoration of my property now in the possession of the Freedmens Bureau who are using every device that Fraud *avorice* and *falsehood* can bring to their aid to continue their possessions. I should not even now have ask your attention to the claim of an individual but for the appearance of a notice in the Metropolitan Record of the 28th of Oct to the effect that the assist. "Adjutant Genl. of the Freedmens Bureau in Mississippi[1] had arrived in Washington City and he represents that Mr. Davis had demanded the restoration of the property of Jefferson Davis and that he had declared a determination to possess himself at once of the property even without the consent of the Bureau." No statement could be more [illegible] false and obviously intended to justify the Bureau in holding possession and to enable them to continue their work of Robery Fraud & Pillaige upon the negroes which if not speedily checked will leave them destitute of the means of cultivating the next year. My negroes who occupied the plantation at the time Col. Thomas[2] took possession trying to make a living were Robed of their horses mules oxen & carts, farming tools and implements thus compelled to buy of the Bureau Glandered horses which of course died upon their hands but they made shift to raise some cotton which was taken from them. The present year they have been deprived of the Gin & Mill so as to compell them to sell their cotton for a trifling part of its Value & to deliver it at the Gin now in the hands of the Bureau for which they got noting last year.[3]

Could any thing be more absurd than that an old man entering his 82d year without power, without means without a home, and might almost say without a country, should threaten to expell a Millitary force.

I had two interviews with Col Thomas the first in the street being unable to find him at his office & second at his office. At both persons were present who will testify that at neither of them was the name of Jefferson Davis mentioned or any allusion to his property. If it had I could have informed him that the place he held was not the property of Jefferson Davis.

It is appearant that the Bureau intend to hold possession as they are deriving a large profit from the cotton grown. Said to [be] estimated at three thousand bales this would exceed half a million at the expense of the Goverment.

Now my Dear Sir is there no means by which such fraud robery & pilliage can be exposed and punished & an account of the wanton destruction of private property taken & held for the use of the United States.

Allow me to say in conclusion that I still have an abiding confidence in your Excellencys Justice and hope to add another proof of magnanimity in my own case.

                                                                    J E Davis

ALS, DNA-RG105, Land Div., Lets. Recd.

1. Stuart Eldridge (b. c1842), promoted from sgt., 28th Wis. Inf., to 1st lieut., 64th USCT, was assigned to the Freedmen's Bureau on July 20, 1865. CSR, RG94, NA.

2. Samuel Thomas.

3. These accusations reflect those levelled against Thomas by a group of blacks who wished to be allowed to operate the cotton gin at Davis's Hurricane Plantation as a co-operative venture. Their leader, Benjamin T. Montgomery, a former slave whom Davis had appointed in October 1865 to manage the plantation, appealed to his old master for

aid, prompting a barrage of letters that included this angry missive. Thomas refused to turn over the gin to the blacks; a board of investigation in November 1865 found no evidence for formal charges against him and rebuked Davis and Montgomery for their conduct during the controversy. Johnson declined to take direct action, but allegedly Davis's letters contributed to the removal of Thomas as assistant commissioner for Mississippi in May 1866. Hermann, *Pursuit of a Dream*, 67–95 passim. See Davis to Johnson, Nov. 25, 1865, Land Div., Lets. Recd., RG105, NA; Davis to Johnson, Jan. 17, 1866, Asst. Commr., Miss., Lets. Recd. (M826, Roll 15), RG105, NA; Davis to [Unknown], Jan. 28, 1866, Davis Family Papers, Ms-Ar.

From William W. Holden

Raleigh N.C.   Nov 4th 1865.

Sir,

Dr Powell telegraphs me you were kind enough to authorize him to frame a telegram from you in relation to the Election in this state.[1] If such a telegram should be published, I prefer it directly from you. I am morally certain of my election but I cannot tell what will happen. All the rebel debt interest of the state is against me. The money power is making a last desperate effort to commit the state to the treason of assuming the state rebel debt after the state gets back. A powerful effort is making to rally the old whig party against me and this is succeeding to some extent. Traitors & malcontents have grown bold & insolent because the hand of power has not been placed upon them. If I am beaten a powerful party will at once exist against your administration and what is also to be deplored confiscations arrests & imprisonments would necessarily follow. Vance & Davis[2] & Graham would be the big men of those in power here. Few lines from you would place it beyond all doubt but dont send them if you think it in any respect improper. I would as soon the triumph should be considered Andrew Johnsons as my own. If Mr Badger has arrived He has a letter from me to you giving a detailed account of affairs in this state.[3]

W W Holden

Tel, DLC-JP.

1. Johnson's telegram of the next day was apparently the only response he offered to Holden prior to the election, but the President did later forward a telegram framed by Robert J. Powell. See Johnson to Holden, Nov. 5, 1865, and Powell to Johnson, Nov. 26, 1865.

2. Probably a reference to North Carolina's George Davis (1820–1896), whose determined fervor for the Confederacy as senator and attorney general easily qualified him for inclusion among the "Vance Destructives." Warner and Yearns, *BRCC*. See Davis to Johnson, Nov. 22, 1865.

3. See Holden to Johnson, Nov. 2, 1865.

To J. Madison Wells

Washington, D.C., Nov 4th 1865.

The following dispatch has been Sent to O. H. Burbridge,[1] Treasury Agent, by my direction.

November 4th 1865

O. H. Burbridge, Esqr.
Treasury Agent   New Orleans, La
    Advise with Gov Wells relative to the eight thousand (8000) bales of cotton claimed by the State of Louisiana.[2] Get it to New Orleans as quick as possible, and hold it there subject to my Orders, or the decision of the Courts. Acknowledge receipt of this and report action under it.
                              (Signed) Hugh McCulloch   Secretary of the Treasury

He must confer with you and every Step be taken to prevent fraud and peculation. You will please acknowledge the receipt of this dispatch.
    In reference to the levies and Gen'l Canby I will advise you soon.[3]
                                          Andrew Johnson, Prest U.S.

Tel, DNA-RG107, Tels. Sent, President, Vol. 2 (1865).
    1. Oscar H. Burbridge (1821-*fl*1879), brother of Gen. Stephen G. Burbridge, USA, commanded a Kentucky militia regiment during the war and afterward served as a special agent of the Treasury Department for the District of Louisiana, Arkansas, and Texas. Perrin, *History of Counties*, 561; *U.S. Off. Reg.* (1878-79).
    2. Wells had again telegraphed to ask the President's intervention. Wells to Johnson, Nov. 3, 1865, Johnson Papers, LC. See Wells to Johnson, Oct. 9, 1865, and Johnson to Wells, Nov. 1, 1865.
    3. Wells wired three days later that everything was "satisfactory," except that Canby had not yet been ordered to return $462,000 he had confiscated from the Louisiana State Bank, which was needed to repair the levees. Apparently no further assistance in this matter was given, because Louisiana struggled unsuccessfully to fund levee construction with a series of bond issues. Wells to Johnson, Nov. 7, 1865, Johnson Papers, LC; Taylor, *La. Reconstructed*, 85-86, 193. See Wells to Johnson, Dec. 27, 1865.

From Henderson Crawford[1]

Thomson Columbia co Ga   Nov 5th 1865
Sir
    Mr Andrew Johnson preident of the united States the chief executor of the nation I Henderson Crawford do Herein present of almighty God Appeal to you for the real condition and estate of our rase for the further and the present time. I must now tell you how we live here in the Southern States. Great excitement prevailes throughout the South about the rightes of my racse. They dont want us to have any testimony in court. They say that we have no right to be ruled by any court or government but Be ruled like mules and oxens some thing unto Slavery. If we have no testimony in court how will we Be protected or without will we ever Become a people of the united States with the full rightes and protections of the Government and of the national Council. We can neve Become citizens of the united states without the privilege [of] polical rights of the Constitution of the united States. We done all we could for the union dueing the existing rebellion. We Shed our Blood and gave our lives and aided in restoring the union to its constitutional Rights. Now we live in the South. There is a man By the name of robert Lampkin[2] near appling court house Columbia co ga. He has

killed and wounded at lese 4 colored men. One was killed a week ago and throw into a gulley and his wife was five days hunting for him. Before she found him he was found by the Buzzards. It is reported that gards has been Sent to arrest him. This Bob Lampkin and others are continuely fireing upon our unarmed and unprotected Colored men and women and childern.

Driven off tourn out of doors haff paid for labour tenth of the croup is generaly given $5 per month. Now they say that we are to Bound ourselves to them under harder terms then while in Slavery. In some places whipping and Shooting is the order of the day. Now my prayers is to you and to God for truth and Comfort. I can Say that while Southern people was carring on an awful Rebellion the Colored people was Bleeding and Dieing for the union. While the Southern people was trying to Brake the constitution the colored people was for the union. We have done all we can. We now look to you for help.[3]

H. Crawford

ALS, DNA-RG105, Records of the Commr., Lets. Recd. (M752, Roll 23).

1. By the spring of 1866 Crawford had contracted to work for Alfred Martin of Screven County, Georgia, and complained of ill treatment. Asst. Commr., Ga., Registered Lets. Recd. (M798, Roll 11), RG105, NA.

2. Robert Lamkin (b. c1824) was listed before the war as a planter. 1860 Census, Ga., Columbia, 2nd and 7th Dists., 65.

3. On November 17 Crawford's letter was referred to Gen. O. O. Howard, who forwarded it to Gen. Davis Tillson for investigation. Tillson reported on November 28 that Crawford's statement was "somewhat exagerated" since only one black person had been killed and "a number wounded" by Lamkin and his party. Three attempts had been made to arrest Lamkin, "but he escaped and has left the Country." Records of the Commr., Lets. Recd. (M752, Roll 23), RG105, NA.

To William W. Holden

Washington, D.C., Nov 5th 1865.

Your dispatch has been received. I thank you most sincerely for the deep interest you take and manifest in the administration of the Government. From your dispatch, and information derived from other Sources, I feel well assured that your election is certain. It is doubtful whether further interference would be Sound policy.

I hope all will come out right.[1]

Andrew Johnson   Prest U.S.

Tel, DNA-RG107, Tels. Sent, President, Vol. 2 (1865).

1. Holden's reply read: "I am more than ever convinced of my election by a large majority." Holden to Johnson, Nov. 6, 1865, Johnson Papers, LC. For further comment on the pending North Carolina elections, see Joseph S. Cannon to Johnson, Nov. 13, 1865.

To James Johnson

Washington, D.C., Nov 5th 1865.

The organization of a police force in the Several counties, for the purpose of arresting marauders, suppressing crime, and enforcing the civil authority, as indicated in your preamble and resolutions meets with approbation.[1] It is hoped that your people will as Soon as practicable take upon themselves the responsibility of enforcing and Sustaining all laws, State & Federal, in conformity to the Constitution of the United States.

Andrew Johnson, Prest U.S.

Tel, DNA-RG107, Tels. Sent, President, Vol. 2 (1865).
1. See Hershel V. Johnson to Johnson, Nov. 4, 1865, Johnson Papers, LC.

From George W. Jones

Fayetteville Tennessee   November 5, 1865.

Dear Sir

You have of course, notwithstanding the pressure upon your time, observed that meetings have been held in various parts of our State, approving and endorsing the policy adopted by you in the administration of the government, for the restoration of the late rebel States to their former position in the Union, as coequals in the Sisterhood of States under the constitution. Not seeing anything of the kind from this County, you may in the absence of information infer or suppose that this non-action by the people of Old Lincoln may be caused by, a secret, lingering ill feeling and bitterness cherished in the bosom of your old friends here against you, reasons and causes growing out of the late war, rebellion. I write this to disabuse your mind, if indeed you entertain any such impressions. I have not been about very much since my return home, but, I have seen many of the people of this County and I think I am pretty well posted and informed as to the public feeling and general sentiments of the people of this County. The people of the County are quiet, calm, orderly and hopefull. Really I do not think that there is a County in the State whose people are more loyal than those of Lincoln. And I am sure there is not a County in the State, in which you will be more cordially and unitedly supported than in this. You know the antecedents of these people and what they were before the rebellion. True, they went with the rebellion, and did all in their power to make it a success, but, it failed and when failure was demonstrated by the surrender of the rebel armies, the rebels here surrendered also and returned to their allegiance to the United States. These people had been raised and educated to love the Union and idolize the Stars and

Stripes. They never in their hearts hated the government of the United States, nor regarded the Star Spangled banner as the "emblem of tyranny and oppression." But finally the designs and machinations of certain would be leaders were, unfortunately but too successfull. When the Republicans in 1861 succeeded in electing their candidate upon a purely sectional platform and only by sectional votes, the honest hearted and patriotic people in this immidate locality, devoted as they were to their rights and liberties as defined and guaranteed by the Constitution of our Country were to easily induced to believe that their liberties were lost in the Republican triumph and succession to the Executive Department, which in fact was barely at most, but carrying an out post. The bulwarks of Liberty were still safe under the guardianship of the Legislative and Judicial Departments both of which were in the possession and under the control of the real, true and devoted friends of the Constitution. And had all the Senators and representatives from the states been true men and patriots, continued in their proper places, the rebellion would have been avoided, and all would now be well right with us, as individuals as states and as a Nation. But the past belongs to history. Our duty and interest is with the present and for the future, and I really believe that the people in this part of the Country, have in truth and in fact returned to their allegiance in good faith without any mental reservations, and are determined in the main to devote themselves to the great work of restoration and prosperity individualy and Nationally. All ardently desire peace, harmony, concord, Law and order. And it is wonderfully strange but also most gratifying, to realize with what facility and rapidity these grand and glorious results are being accomplished. This country, which, but, a few short months since was the theatre upon which was being enacted the most gigantic, terrible and bloody war, in the tide of civilization has subsided and passed away and now peace reigns and here we have no soldiers, thanks to you, your will, your patriotism and wisdom. I feel that in this I but express the feelings and sentiments of the people in all the country hereabouts. If this be so, you may very reasonably enquire, why has there been no public meeting or demonstration to give publicity to the sentiments of the people? When at Nashville recently I was spoken to on the subject of a public meeting in this place, for the purpose of approving and sustaining you in your administration of the government, in these difficult times and the many perplexing and embarrasing questions pressing upon you. I thought well of it, and could do so most cordially and so could the people of this county. About that time a meeting was held in Gallatin by which resolutions were adopted, which I thought right and proper, but, in a few days there after I read a communication from Gallatin in one of the Nashville papers making an onslough upon that meeting as being composed entirely of *late* rebels and the writer seemed to think they were still rebels or at most no better than rebels.[1] It was stated that there was not a *Union man* in that meeting and the writer promised in a subsequent communication to make other and further information concerning that meeting and those who composed it. You understand all this and the objects of the writer. Upon reflection and consultation with friends who were liberal and cordial in expressions of sympathy and approval of you and your administration, it was thought, that perhaps under all the circumstances it would be as well not to hold the meeting. You know very well how meetings of the character spoken of are gotten up organized and conducted. However, faithfully the resolutions adopted may reflect the public sentiment, however numerous and respectable the assemblage may be in numbers and in the personel a few individuals' names are all that will every appear in the published proceedings as those who were instrumental in getting up the meeting, organizing it conducting its proceedings. You know us here, what we were and what we are I trust. Now in any meeting of the sort gotten up in this County whose names would figure most prominently and conspicuously? Why the names of those who were more or less conspicuous as rebels during the War and who are not now voters. Whether rightfully or wrongfully this county and its people had rather an unenviable notoriety among Union men all over the Country as the worst and most thorough *Secesh* County in all the state. All these things considered and knowing the tone and temper of the people here I thought that perhaps there might be as much harm as good resulting from a public meeting here at this time. Our mutual friend James B. Lamb as well as others, fully concurred in these views and thought that if I would write to you it would be as satisfactory to you as a public meeting would be. He is as he has ever been your friend and supporter, and fully concurs in what I have written.

I received a long letter from my friend R. R. Bridgers[2] a few days since. He is now President of the Willmington and Weldon Rail Rail. I regretted very much that you could not see more of him when he was in Washington last Summer. I know you would appreciate him if you knew him well. He is the type of a man and politician very much indeed of your school, honest and true.

He like many others who never knew you personally, but only through the newspapers and individuals and these you knew from prejudice or interest frequently represented you as the veriest of demagogues, whose trade was politics and whose ends were selfish. A man named *Martin*[3] who lived at Greenville and represented himself as a *Democrat*, and who said you were the only democrat he had ever voted against met with Bridgers some years ago and by his statements & representations or rather misrepresentations did much to prejudice you in his mind. I did much to disabuse his mind when with him and now not a vistage of it remains with him. He is now one of your sincere admirers and warm supporters. You are his choice for the next President and he believes that by that time, the next election you will be more popular in North Carolina than Andrew Jackson ever was. So be it.

Pardon me, for asking if you have pardoned John Letcher? Everything he had was destroyed by the burning of his house except the lot upon which it was built. He has to rely upon his profession to support his family and his *parol* does not permit him to leave his county.

G. W. Jones

ALS, DLC-JP.
1. Jones refers undoubtedly to the meeting in early October 1865 at Gallatin, at which a number of resolutions were adopted. A. R. Wynne was president of the conclave which among other things urged Johnson to permit each county in the state to establish a militia, much as he had allowed in Mississippi. Such a policy, it was asserted, would enable the President to remove federal troops from the state. The Sumner County group pledged to elect a loyal Union man to head its county militia. Ten days later one of the Nashville newspapers carried a letter from "A Soldier," which took issue with the Sumner County meeting. According to him none of the Union men of Gallatin had been informed of the meeting. *Nashville Union*, Oct. 11, 21, 1865. See Durham, *Rebellion Revisited*, 261–62.
2. Robert R. Bridgers (1819–1888) was a North Carolina lawyer and businessman who had served in the antebellum state legislature and was elected to the Confederate congress in 1861. He became president of the Wilmington and Weldon line in 1865 and remained in that post for twenty years. Supported by Governor Holden, he had applied for and received a presidential pardon in June 1865. Warner and Yearns, *BRCC*; Bridgers to Johnson, ca. June 23, 1865, Amnesty Papers (M1003, Roll 37), N.C., Robert R. Bridgers, RG94, NA.
3. Possibly a reference to James D. Martin.

From Christopher "Kit" Carson[1]

Leavenworth City Kansas   Nov. 6th 1865

I have the honor to state that I have lived in the Rocky Mountains, particularly in New Mexico since my youth. I am familiar with the resources of the County, agricultural and mineral.

The Country is particularly rich in minerals, Platinum, Gold Silver & Copper and I believe Lead.

It would be very gratifying to our people to have Brig: Genl: R. B. Mitchell[2] U.S. Volunteers: appointed Governor of New Mexico,[3] and that authority be granted him to raise ten Regiments of Volunteers to develope, or protect prospectors in developing, the mines of that County.[4]

Should the President grant this request, I believe that a great portion of our National Debt, can in a short time be paid by such development.

C. Carson   Col 1 Cavly N M Vols

ALS, DNA-RG59, Lets. of Appl. and Recomm., 1861–69 (M650, Roll 6), Robert B. Mitchell.
1. Carson (1809–1868), a renowned trapper, army scout, and Indian agent in the Southwest, had been brevetted a brigadier general for his service as commander of the 1st N.M. Vol. Cav., USA. *DAB*.

2. Robert B. Mitchell, commander of the Department of Kansas.

3. Upon the recommendation of several members of Congress and Kansas Gov. Samuel J. Crawford, Johnson did appoint Mitchell, who took office as governor of New Mexico on July 16, 1866. After clashing with Radicals in the territorial legislature, who were supported by Congress, Mitchell eventually resigned and returned to Kansas. Crawford to Johnson, Nov. 13, 1865; P. W. Mitchell to Johnson, Dec. 8, 1865; Edmund Cooper et al. to Johnson, Dec. 8, 1865; James A. Garfield to Johnson, Dec. 9, 1865; Robert C. Schenck to Johnson, Dec. 15, 1865, Lets. of Appl. and Recomm., 1861–69 (M650, Roll 33), Robert B. Mitchell, RG59, NA; J. Francisco Chavez to Johnson, Dec. 29, 1866; Mitchell to Seward, Dec. 31, 1866, Terr. Papers, N.M., 1851–72 (T17, Roll 3), RG59, NA; *DAB*; Eugene H. Berwanger, *The West and Reconstruction* (Urbana, Ill., 1981), 198.

4. Carson's request for volunteers was not approved.

From Mark R. Cockrill[1]

Nashville   Nov 6th 1865

Sir

I desire to claim your especial clemency, calling to mind our mutual efforts to promote the agricultural interest of the country, wishing to be released from any exemption forbidding the exercise of the rights of citizenship, in order that I may devote the few days that may yet remain to me for the benefit of my fellow man.[2]

Mark R Cockrill

ALS, DNA-RG94, Amnesty Papers (M1003, Roll 48), Tenn., Mark R. Cockrill.

1. Cockrill had initially written to Johnson on September 16, the same date on which he took the oath of allegiance; but as Russell Houston indicated, evidently the original pardon request had "been mislaid." Cockrill to Johnson, Sept. 16, 1865; Houston to Johnson, Nov. 8, 1865, Amnesty Papers (M1003, Roll 48), Tenn., Mark R. Cockrill, RG94, NA.

2. Cockrill's plea was successful this time. On November 8, 1865, Brownlow endorsed his pardon application a second time, and it was forwarded to Johnson, who granted a pardon on November 14. Amnesty Papers (M1003, Roll 48), Tenn., Mark R. Cockrill, RG94, NA; *House Ex. Docs.*, 39 Cong., 2 Sess., No. 116, p. 35 (Ser. 1293).

Interview with Baltimore Ladies[1]

[November 6, 1865][2]

Mr. Johnson listened with marked attention and hesitated for some moments before he made reply. Finally he said: That he regretted more than he knew how to express, that he could not grant the petition, and that it would give him far more pleasure to accede to the request of the ladies present than it would give them to have it granted. "If," added he, "it were simply a question, however, between man and man, I would release Mr. Davis at once; but it is a great national question. Mighty issues might be involved, and now is not the time to take such a step. I think," continued the President, "I have the courage, or as you term it, ladies, pluck, to do my duty and have proved it. When the proper time comes for the exercise of magnanimity, I trust that I shall not be found wanting."

In reference to the trial of Mr. Davis, Mr. Johnson said: "Almost every arrangement has been made for the trial of Mr. Davis, but no one can tell what change may be brought about in the course of a few weeks. A hasty and injudicious action in this matter might produce incalculable misery. Mr. Davis has been a great leader in the war against the government, and it is but right he should be tried by the laws of the land. I sympathize with him in his sufferings. His quarters have been changed and his condition ameliorated."

In conclusion Mr. Johnson said: "All men, ladies, are under the influence of woman, and I not less than other men. You are my jewels. I want your help and your prayers."

No knight of old, said one of the ladies, could have been more courtly in his deference nor more gentle in his refusal.[3]

New York Times, Nov. 12, 1865.

1. A committee of twelve presented a petition, signed by 15,000 women, for the pardon of Jefferson Davis. Mary Ann Crittenden Coleman, daughter of the former senator from Kentucky, "addressed the President in feeling and appropriate terms," prompting this response. *National Intelligencer*, Nov. 7, 1865; *Augusta Constitutionalist*, Nov. 16, 1865.

2. Although no date for the interview appears in this *New York Times* account, we are able to supply the November 6 date through the report found in the *National Intelligencer* of November 7, 1865.

3. John Woolley, provost marshal of Baltimore, later wrote to advise Johnson that many of the names on the petition "Represent *negro female servants & children*." Woolley to William Browning, Nov. 12, 1865, Middle Dept., Lets. Sent, Vol. 113, RG393, NA.

From Oliver P. Morton

Indianapolis, Nov 6th 1865

Dear Sir

I trust you will pardon the suggestions I am about to make in reference to the case of Jefferson Davis. Whatever may be said by others I am of the opinion that the pardon of Davis would excite the most intense and lasting indignation in the minds of an overwhelming majority of the people of the North. The pardon of all the other leaders of the rebellion would be esteemed a small matter in comparison. The abiding conviction in the public mind that he knowingly permitted the murder of our prisoners at Andersonville, and other slaughter-pens, even if he did not command it, sends up a cry for vengeance through all the land.

The people will in my opinion, by immense majorities sustain your policy of reconstruction and your views of negro suffrage, and if you will promptly put Davis on his trial for treason your popular triumph will be complete. If he is acquitted let the Court and Jury take the responsibility. If he escapes without a trial the responsibility will be laid at your door, whatever may have been the cause, or whatever may have been your motives, and an indignation aroused which years cannot assuage. If any of the judges of the Supreme Court entertain the opinion that Davis is an alien enemy and must be treated as the head of a *De Facto* government, I would give them a chance to say so, and the world will then understand it. Your enemies throughout the country are endeavouring to excite the people against you by denouncing the pardons you have granted to inferior leaders and criminals in the South and they are ardently praying that you may put a great weapon in their hands by the release of Davis. If you stand firm by the doctrine that rebellion is treason, that treason is a crime, that a state cannot secede or be carried out of the Union by rebels in arms, or be put out by indirection thus standing by the simple theory upon which the war was prosecuted, and which you have so clearly and ably announced, I tell you that even the Supreme Court cannot prevail against you with the Nation. There is a class of men here who are clamoring against you for the pardons you have granted. A part of the same class in the east I am informed are urging the pardon of Davis. In either case they are not your friends, and their judgement or advice cannot be relied on.

The immediate cause of this letter is a despatch which appeared in the papers this morning, and which I enclose.[1] Several of your most intelligent and earnest friends have begged me to write to you, and I do so urging what I beleive is for your benefit and the great advantage of the whole country.

There has been too much blood shed, and treasure wasted, to permit the great leader, and cheif instigator of the Rebellion, to go hence with impunity and walk about in security amidst the graves and desolation he has made.[2]

Beleiving you will not regard as improper these suggestions coming from a political and personal friend, and having the utmost confidence in your wisdom, patriotism, and devotion to the great work of restoring our country I remain. . . .

O. P. Morton

ALS, DLC-JP.

1. Not found. The *Indianapolis Journal* on November 6, 1865, published a report that Davis was to be pardoned and exiled to Europe.

2. Johnson responded: "You will see an explanation in a few days published why Mr. Davis has not been brought to trial which will I trust be satisfactory." Johnson to Morton, Nov. 9, 1865, Tels. Sent, President, Vol. 2 (1865), RG107, NA. See Johnson to Morton, Nov. 14, 1865.

From Cuthbert Bullitt

New Orleans   Nov 7 1865.

We owe to the perfect administration of the government the most orderly election ever known in New Orleans. The Johnson policy as represented by Wells triumphant by overwhelming majority—over Six thousand in the City.[1] The balance of the State will follow in the same

track. The congressional delegation[2] not of the best material but legislature as far as heard from satisfactory.[3]

Cuthbert Bullet[*sic*]   U S Marshal

Tel, DLC-JP.

1. On November 6, 1865, the Democratic ticket, led by J. Madison Wells as the
gubernatorial candidate, swept every office in New Orleans and Algiers except one seat
in the legislature. *New Orleans Picayune*, Nov. 7, 1865. See Hugh Kennedy to Johnson,
Nov. 23, 1865.

2. Former congressman (1851–53, 1885–87) Louis St. Martin (1820–1893),
banker Jacob Barker (1779-*fl*1871), who later lived in Philadelphia, former governor
Robert C. Wickliffe (1819–1895), unionist John E. King (*fl*1870), a New Orleans commission merchant, and Monroe legislator John Ray were refused their seats. *BDAC*;
DAB; *New Orleans Picayune*, Nov. 8, 1865; *Harrisburg Patriot and Union*, Nov. 27,
1865; *Charleston Courier*, May 8, 1871; New Orleans directories (1867–71); King
to Johnson, Aug. 12, 1865, Amnesty Papers (M1003, Roll 28), La., John E. King,
RG94, NA.

3. Many of the newly elected legislators were in fact former Confederates. Taylor, *La.
Reconstructed*, 73.

From Ulysses S. Grant

Washington D.C.   Nov. 7th 1865

Sir:

Knowing that Gen. Longstreet, late of the Army which was in rebellion against the Authority of the United States, is in the City, and
presuming that he intends asking Executive clemency before leaving,[1]
I beg to say a word in his favor.

Gen. Longstreet comes under the 3d 5th & 8th exceptions made in
your Proclamation of the 29th of May 1865. I believe I can safely say
that there is no where among the exceptions a more honorable class of
men than those embraced in the 5th & 8th of these, nor a class who
will more faithfully observe any obligation which they make take upon
themselves. General Longstreet in my opinion stands high among this
class. I have known him well for more than twenty-six years; first as a
Cadet at West Point, and afterwards as an officer of the Army. For five
years from my graduation we served together, a portion of the time in
the same regiment. I speak of him therefore from actual personal
acquaintance.[2]

In the late rebellion I think not one single charge was ever brought
against Gen. Longstreet for persecution of prisoners of War or of persons for their political opinions. If such charges were ever made I never
heard them. I have no hesitation therefore in recommending Gen.
Longstreet to your Excellency for pardon. I will further state that my
opinion of him is such that I shall feel it as a personal favor to myself if
this pardon is granted.[3]

U. S. Grant, Lt. Gen.

ALS, DNA-RG94, Amnesty Papers (M1003, Roll 7), Ala., James Longstreet.
1. James Longstreet personally presented his amnesty petition to the President on
November 7, 1865. James Longstreet, *From Manassas to Appomattox* (Philadelphia,
1896), 633; Longstreet to Johnson, Nov. 7, 1865, Amnesty Papers (M1003, Roll 7),
Ala., James Longstreet, RG94, NA.
2. Both had served in the 4th U.S. Inf. from 1843 to 1844. In addition, they were
related by marriage. Donald B. Sanger and Thomas R. Hay, *James Longstreet* (Baton
Rouge, 1952), 9–10; John Y. Simon, ed., *The Personal Memoirs of Julia Dent Grant*
(New York, 1975), 63–64.
3. At the conclusion of their second interview on November 8, "after a long, pleasant
talk," as Longstreet recalled, Johnson declared: "There are three persons of the South
who can never receive amnesty: Mr. Davis, General Lee, and yourself. You have given
the Union cause too much trouble." Nevertheless, Johnson finally pardoned Longstreet
on June 17, 1867, perhaps owing in part to Grant's continued advocacy. Longstreet,
Manassas, 634; Sanger and Hay, *Longstreet*, 322; *New York Times*, June 20, 21, 1867.

From James M. Tomeny
Personal & confidential

Mobile   Nov. 7. 1865

Dear Sir:

After exhausting all his resources in opposition Mr. Mellen concluded to give me my Commission bearing date Nov. 1st.[1] He is not
your friend and I predict that in less than six months he will be openly,
as he is now covertly, with the "opposition." My opinion is he will
attack you and the Secretary[2] and charge the Administration with the
mismanagement of the cotton business, and thus endeavor to relieve
himself and his friends of the odium for which he should be alone held
responsible, having had the control and general management of the
business for four years. He says he has the facts and may have *to write
a history* of the whole thing. He talks constantly of the *mistakes of the
Administration* or rather of the President, and never utters a word in
vindication of either.

Prior to Mr. Lincoln's renomination, I think he agreed to let Mr.
Chase Keep Mellen, but just before his death determined to remove
him.

I hope, in justice to yourself, your Administration and your friends,
you will force him out of the Department.

When he came here to investigate Dexter's official acts he suspended
him and at first permitted him to sign nothing and perform no official
act and got him *badly scared*.

We arrived here on Wednesday morning Sept 27th. On Thursday I
went into Dexter's office and found him and C. A. Weed of New Orleans, who had come over on the same boat, standing by a desk, with
two rolls of U.S. 7.30 Bonds before them. There could not have been
less than $50,000 in the two rolls. The next morning (Friday) Mellen
said "he was convinced Mr. Dexter was an honest man" and he would
not be removed. No investigation was even attempted. But as Dexter

was incompetent and his business in great confusion "*he and Mellen both desired me to act as Dexter's Deputy*," agreeing to divide the salary and commissions equally with me. I saw through the whole plan. Mellen was paid $50,000 or more, in all probability, for retaining Dexter, and reporting to the Secretary that the "public interests" would be promoted thereby, and the only thing to be done was to satisfy me. I told Mellen I could not relieve the office of the odium attaching to it, I could only share it, and declined to have anything to do with it if Dexter was retained. Geo. A. Fitch[3] of Michigan made charges against Dexter and he offered, for $5,000, to withdraw them, *which same Dexter paid*. This could readily be proven, but this withdrawal gave Mellen a pretext for making no investigation. The frauds perpetrated in Dexter's agency are perfectly *astounding*.

One of his appointees Thos. J. Carver has just been convicted by a Military Commission of frauds upon the Government amounting to over $90,000, and has been sentenced to pay a fine of that sum, and be imprisoned in the penetentiary twelve months and until the fine is paid.[4] I enclose a copy of Genl. Wood's order with the findings and sentence.

This trial was commenced about the time Mellen was here; *yet he could find nothing to investigate*. Carver is only one of a class. Not less than twenty such cases could be exposed.

I shall do all I can to ferret out these frauds recover the property, or its proceeds, and bring the criminals to justice.

Could you not send me special directions and give me full power, to call upon the military authorities for aid, to send for persons and papers, inspect books, and make seizures? With this Authority *direct from you* I could recover a vast amount of property rightfully belonging to the United States and now in the hands of corrupt speculators.[5] I enclose an official communication asking for an enlargement of my agency. It is entirely too small and not at all in accordance with the Geography of the country. Please endorse it favorably and send it to the Secretary.[6] Believe me most truly and faithfully. . . .

J. M. Tomeny

ALS, DLC-Hugh McCulloch Papers.

1. Tomeny had earlier thanked the President for appointing him as a "Supervising Special Agent." Tomeny to Johnson, Nov. 4, 1865, Johnson Papers, LC.

2. Hugh McCulloch.

3. Fitch, probably the mail contractor along the Gulf coast, has not been conclusively identified. *Charleston Courier*, Oct. 6, 1865; *New Orleans Picayune*, Oct. 25, 29, 1865.

4. Carver (d. 1888), a former assistant to treasury agent Duff C. Green, had been appointed in August 1865 a bonded agent for collecting cotton in Choctaw Co., Ala. After paying the fine, Carver obtained his release from prison by agreeing to testify against his coconspirators. Thompson, *Magnolia Cemetery*, 162; *Mobile Register and Advertiser*, Jan. 31, 1865; Joseph Holt to [Edwin Stanton], Apr. 17, 1866, Lets. Sent (Record Books), Vol. 17, RG153, NA.

5. See Tomeny to Johnson, Dec. 20, 1865.

6. The President on November 18 forwarded this letter to McCulloch "for his *per-*

sonal consideration," along with the enclosed application from Tomeny for the enlargement of his district. When Gen. George Thomas later recommended that Tomeny's responsibilities be increased, Johnson wrote: "Referred to the Sec of the Treasury. Genl Thomas would make no recommendation that is not for the best." Ser. 4A, Vol. 3: 336, Johnson Papers, LC; Tomeny to Johnson, Nov. 7, 1865, Second Special Agency, Lets. Sent, Vol. 125, RG366, NA; Thomas to Johnson, Nov. 27, 1865, Misc. Div., Claims for Cotton and Captured and Abandoned Property, RG56, NA.

From Andrew Armstrong[1]

East Donegal Township   Lancaster Co. Pa.
Novr. 8th/65

Dr. Sir

Hoping that an humble farmer may approach you with the same freedom as a Beecher, a Greely, or a Philips, I am induced, in view of the crisis, to intrude for a moment upon your patience. What I have to say is that for some time past, and more especially at the present, I, with hundreds of others, good and true loyal men, who have stood by the Administration through all its trials, not in word only, but by act and deed, stoping at no sacrifice, but giving all that was asked for the salvation of our country, and for the crushing of the Rebellion and the punishment of traitors, have seen with alarm, the tendency of your administration to fritter away very much of what, by our Blood and treasure, has been won. Now Sir, we do most Respectfully, yet most earnestly protest against the wholesale pardon of traitors, and the restoration of Confiscated property by the Chief Executive. We Claim that they have by their act of treason, forfeited all to the Government. The people are the Government, and in them and them only is vested the right to dispose of these questions. We the people have fought the Battles, acheived the victory, and saved the country from the grasp of those vile despoilers, and we claim a right to be heard. I am aware Sir, that a powerful influence is brought to bear upon you in favor of Clemency to all traitors, but who I ask are the parties that are thus profuse with their display of magnanimity? Look around you sir, and see how many of them have made any considerable sacrifice for the Union. On the contrary you will find that their families, their persons, and their pockets are at least as whole as before the Rebellion. Now Sir, I have sacrificed two sons,[2] all that I had. I gave them for my Country, and I am happy to know that by the sacrifice thus made the *phisical* power of treason was broken, but I am not willing that the principal actors in the infamous Rebellion shall go unpunished. The leaders at least, should meet the traitors doom. Now Sir, there is no section which gave you a more hearty support for the Vice Presidency than Lancaster Co. Pa., but we did not then suppose for a moment that we were elevating you to a position to trample on our rights and insult us by restoring to freedom, citizenship, and position, the very fiends who have desolated our fire-

sides and mortgaged our properties. You very well know that the traitor has no rights under the Constitution. He by his own act forfieted
his property to the Government, and to those who remained loyal to
the Government, and I am not aware that we ever vested the right in
any man to dispose of the public property.

We do most respectfully, but most emphatically ask of you that
Justice be done by you, and that neither rank, nor position may be
allowed to screen the guilty.

Relying on your generosity to pardon the freedom and plainness with
which I have written, and hoping that you may be sustained in doing
right, I remain your sincere friend and well wisher.

Andrew Armstrong

N.B. I most sincerely wish I had the same oportunity for an hour's talk
with you, that I had last summer in Nashville Tenn.

A. A.

ALS, DNA-RG94, Amnesty Papers, Jefferson Davis, Pets. to A. Johnson.
1. Armstrong (b. *c*1810) was a native of Pennsylvania. 1860 Census, Pa., Lancaster,
East Donegal Twp., 34.
2. Armstrong had two sons, William F. (*c*1841–1864) and John (b. *c*1844), living
with him in 1860. The former died of gunshot wounds received at Petersburg; no record
of the latter's fate has been found. Ibid.; CSR, RG94, NA.

From James M. Howry [1]

Oxford Mississippi   8 Nov 1865

Dear Sir,

I dispatched you last Monday[2] in relation to the negro garrison at
this place & the students of the University. The facts as I understand
them are, in brief, these. The troops are turned loose, pretty much, on
the town. They assemble on the side walks & in front of the few little
stores we have & will not give the way to white citizens & sometimes,
even ladies. Their general behavior in other respects is as good as could
be expected from negroes who are taught to beleive they are the white
mans equal.

The country is all quiet. The general relation between the whites &
their former slaves is one of peace & generally friendship. Our people
are true to their amnesty vows. They have no other government now
but their state govermt & that of the U.S. They submit to the state of
things that exists, and we can see no possible necessity for garrisons all
over the country. If the government apprehends any oppression on the
negroes lately made free, it might, provide for the contingency by having a guard of a few men sent to any particular locality from some
rendezvous or general post.

The presence of the negro troops is encouraging the negroes in their
idleness. Not one will engage for next year. The preparation for a crop
ought to have commenced a month or two ago.

I am satisfied that the presence of negro garrisons among us is destructive to the general prosperity & our hopes in the future. In our locality we were burnt out—our farms devastated—our houses pillaged by a ruthless army—our slaves turned loose, to eat the little substance left & refusing virtually to labor, presents indeed a gloomy prospect for those of us who have dependent families.

You, Sir, have done many acts of kindness & shown leniency to many of our people. You stated to the South Carolina delegation last Summer that you had no malignity against the southern people to gratify—and that upon evidence of loyalty you would restore their civil rights as fast as you could &c.[3] You have progressed in this good work much to the satisfaction of the people, generally. They award to you the meed of praise for it. You have expressed your intention to not further humiliate us, if I am rightly informed. There is no humiliation more degrading & galling to the southern mind than to be completely under the control of sabres & bayonets in the hands of negroes, & who have daily & hourly intercourse with our former slaves—many of whom are still living with us, and who are generally commanded by illiterate foreigners, who fine our citizens from 25 to $100 if he strikes a negro—even preferring often the testimony of the negro to that of the white man!

Under these circumstances it does appear to me that you can maintain the authority of the govenment, protect the free negroes, with our aid, under our new constitution & laws and be just & generous to a conquered people, and thereby add another chaplet to your wreath of honor.

Our acquaintance began over 30 years ago. You know during your long struggle for eminence I was your friend. I then address you with freedom, and while I may ask nothing for myself, I do ask you in good faith for my fellow citizens & neighbors to remove these negro garrisons from our midst.[4]

The freedman must be *made* to work. They *will not work* unless they are *forced*. Our soil must be tilled. Suffering stares us in the face if it is not done.

I do not think you have been properly advised of the many petty tyrannies which have been practiced upon our people. I have had no personal difficulties with any of them.

I fear I am trespassing on your time by the length of my letter & therefore will close. . . .

James M. Howry
formerly of Hawkins Co. E Ten.

ALS, DNA-RG94, Lets. Recd. (Main Ser.), File H-1556-1865 (M619, Roll 366).

1. Howry (1804–1884) served as secretary to the Tennessee legislature and supreme court, as well as a state circuit court attorney, before moving in 1836 to Mississippi, where he became a state circuit court judge, legislator, and trustee for the University of Mississippi. Brown, *Am. Biographies*, 4: 203; *Historical Catalogue of the University of Mississippi, 1849–1909* (Nashville, 1910), 81; *Chattanooga Times*, Apr. 17, 1884.

2. Howry, along with University of Mississippi chancellor John N. Waddell, had warned the President that "collisions between Negro troops and Students of the University are seriously threatened." Howry and Waddell to Johnson, Nov. 6, 1865, Tels. Recd., President, Vol. 4 (1865–66), RG107, NA.

3. See Interview with South Carolina Delegation, June 24, 1865, *Johnson Papers*, 8: 280–85.

4. In mid-November fifty-five citizens of Oxford, including University faculty and local government officials, also requested the removal of black troops from their town. Citizens of Oxford to Johnson, ca. Nov. 15, 1865, Lets. Recd. (Main Ser.), File C-1565-1865 (M619, Roll 345), RG94, NA. For the President's response, see Johnson to Benjamin G. Humphreys, Nov. 17, 1865.

From Cave Johnson

Clarksville   Nov. 8th, 1865

Dear Sir

Mr. Larkin Harned,[1] a citizen of Christian Co. Kentucky, sends his petition for a pardon. My personal acquaintance with him is but slight but I have long known his character as a plain, straight forward honest man, who may be relied upon in all the statements he makes. I have no doubt, he will be a peacible quiet citizen & will perform his duty as a citizen faithfully as he promises. I therefore unite with him in asking a pardon & the restoration of his land.[2]

C Johnson

ALS, DLC-JP.

1. Harned (c1810-fl1870) was a farmer. 1860 Census, Ky., Christian, 54; (1870), Mt. Vernon Precinct, 3.

2. An application for pardon from Harned with a date coeval with this letter has not been found, but he did apply in June 1866, after confiscation proceedings were initiated against his property. Johnson pardoned him on July 6, 1866. Harned to Johnson, ca. June 13, 1866, Amnesty Papers (M1003, Roll 25), Ky., Larkin Harned, RG94, NA.

From James Johnson

Milledgeville   Nov 8 1865.

The Convention has adjourned in good temper subject to be convened by order of the Gov.[1] I will send you, as soon as possible, the Constitution, ordinances and resolutions adopted, together with the journal of proceedings.[2]

J. Johnson   Governor

Tel, DLC-JP.

1. During the preceding week the governor had kept the President apprised of the convention's progress. James Johnson to Johnson, Oct. 31, Nov. 4, 1865, Johnson Papers, LC.

2. The materials were forwarded to Washington on November 14, 1865. *Senate Ex. Docs.*, 39 Cong., 1 Sess., No. 26, pp. 81–82 (Ser. 1237).

From William A. Lewis and Henry A. Greene[1]

Jersey City, Nov 8th 1865

New Jersey sends greeting. *To day* she stands redeemed,[2] and the work of consecration is still going on in the heart of the people. We are beginning to feel proud of the fact that we are Jersey men & if Jersey will keep on honoring the Lord and working righteousness as she did in yesterdays election, we shall no longer be considered *out* of the Union but one of the Sisterhood of States, fitting to be placed side by side with *loyal New England.* Upwards of fifteen thousand gain over the last gubernatorial election, and this not in this "Rip Van Winkle" State this State of "Camden and Amboy,"[3] this "*Copper-head State of New Jersey!*[4] Some good can come out of Nazareth! Praise be to the Lord, let the people rejoice. The Constitutional Amendment will now be passed. Loyal New Jersey makes haste to place herself *right* on the Constitutional Amendment and the record generally.

The Copperheads have elected just enough *Coroners* to hold an inquest over their defunct and offensive remains. New Jersey supports your administration, and loyal men call for the execution of Jeff Davis as the reward of his *treason.*

Wm. A. Lewis

Joining with Mr Lewis in his congratulations I remain. . . .

H. A. Greene

ALS, DLC-JP.
1. Lewis (c1844-fl1881) was a corporate attorney, and Greene (fl1881) a bookseller, stationer, and insurance agent who served as a postmaster (c1861-c74). 1870 Census, N.J., Hudson, Jersey City, 3rd Ward, 15; Jersey City directories (1861–81).
2. Johnson received similar telegrams, celebrating the election of a Republican governor and a legislature pledged to endorse the Thirteenth Amendment. Charles P. Smith to Johnson; James F. Rusling to Johnson; Alexander G. Cottell to Johnson, Nov. 8, 1865, Johnson Papers, LC.
3. The Camden and Amboy Railroad Company dominated antebellum politics in New Jersey. Howard K. Platt, ed., *Charles Perrin Smith: New Jersey Political Reminiscences, 1828–1882* (New Brunswick, N.J., 1965), 10.
4. In 1864 New Jersey had cast a majority of its votes for George B. McClellan. Ibid., 26.

From Annie Andrews Upshur[1]

New York   Nov 8th 1865

President Johnson

I enclose a letter to my friend Jefferson Davis late President of the Confederate States and ask your permission that it may be forwarded to him.[2] You will please excuse me for trubling but as I know not by what means a letter may reach him I have taken the liberty of writing yourself which I knew would be the only way a letter might reach him and ask your permisin to correspond with him and if he is in need of warm clothing that I may be permited to forward them. I assure you as a lady I shall not abuse the permisn.

Mr Davis has been my frind for years and sometimes in great trials & trubilatns he has befriended me and I cannot forget in this hour of his great sorrow I owe him a life long gratitude for great kindness to me and my child for kindness of years. I know that his health is delicate and I fear that as he is not use to this climate he may need warm clothing for these cold winter.

I know that after all the petitions offed by ladies of influece in behalf of Mr Davis there would be but little use of my writing a word to you in his behalf only that no woman of the South but feels a great interest in his behalf and wishes much for his [illegible] and we as Southerns have much to remember in you for your kindness & forgiving. For my part accept my many thank for all the kindness that you have [and] are constantly Showing the Southern people. I remember of being introduced to you by Mrs John J Crittenden[3] some ten years ago in Washington City. I then was a young lady. Perhaps you may remember me Miss Annie Andrews. I hope that the enclosed letter may meet with your approval and that you will be so kind as to permit my letter to reach Mr Davis and in case I can forward him anything for his comfort I may be permited to do so.

Annie M Upshur
No 223 West 20 st   New York

ALS, DNA-RG94, Amnesty Papers, Jefferson Davis, Pets. to A. Johnson.

1. Andrews (b. 1835) met and married John B. Upshur, II, while she was working as a nurse during the Norfolk yellow fever epidemic of 1855. John A. Upshur, *Upshur Family in Virginia* (Richmond, 1955), 110; H. W. Burton, *The History of Norfolk, Virginia* (Norfolk, 1877), 27; *Appleton's Cyclopaedia*.

2. The letter, dated November 8, 1865, was apparently not forwarded because it can be found in Amnesty Papers, Jefferson Davis, Pets. to A. Johnson, RG94, NA.

3. Elizabeth Moss Ashley (c1807–1873), the wealthy widow of William Henry Ashley, married John J. Crittenden on February 27, 1853. 1860 Census, Ky., Franklin, Frankfort Dist., 83; Albert D. Kirwan, *John J. Crittenden: The Struggle for the Union* (Lexington, Ky., 1962), 282–83; Ann M.C.B. Coleman, ed., *The Life of John J. Crittenden* (2 vols., Philadelphia, 1871), 1: 21; L. U. Reavis, *Saint Louis: The Future Great City of the World* (St. Louis, 1876), 680–83.

From George Bancroft

New York   Nov. 9. '65.

My dear Sir,

My task will be done tomorrow;[1] but as no one knows what I am about, as I am my own secretary, I must ask a day or two more for a careful revision & for making a clean copy which must be done with my own hand. I will send it early, *very early* next week.[2] No pains have been spared to express your ideas with exactness.

Geo. Bancroft

Tel, DLC-JP.
    1. See Johnson to Bancroft, Oct. 29, 1865.
    2. Johnson had telegraphed, "If you are ready I would prefer your coming to Washington at once." The President later instructed Bancroft to "Come in person." Johnson to Bancroft, Nov. 9, 14, 1865, George Bancroft Papers, MHi.

From William S. Groesbeck

Cincinnati   Nov. 9. 1865.

Dear sir:

When I last saw you in Washington, you were kind enough to say, you would be pleased to hear from me upon any of the questions before the country.[1]

I have not, heretofore, supposed, nor do I now suppose, that I am in a condition to say anything upon such questions, which will be of value, but yet I know from my own experience, that suggestions made in a truly friendly spirit, are always acceptable. In this spirit, I venture to call your attention to the subjects of Military Commissions and Finance.

I cannot tell you in a few lines, how much I have been gratified in reading that you were firm in your determination, that Davis should be tried by a jury in a civil court. It seems to me it would be a great mistake to try him, and especially at this time, by a Military Commission. They are a wide departure from the old, familiar ways in which we have been educated and to which we are attached. Trial by jury is esteemed to be a strong bulwark of liberty and, life, and Military commissions are associated with tyranny and despotism. Our people do not wish to get accustomed to them. On the contrary, they want them put away. They did not originate under your administration and you are not responsible for them; and it seems to me it would be well for you to give expression to the general desire, and declare them at an end.

I hope, also, you will announce it, as your fixed policy, to reduce the currency. The wisdom of such a policy is plain, and all the thinking and well-disposed will sustain you in it.

I will not venture to make further suggestions. By your position upon these two alone, you may do much good, and greatly strengthen yourself for trials yet before you.

Allow me, Mr. President, to congratulate you, for I can do so with entire sincerity, upon your extraordinary success, thus far. I am sure, you have abundant cause to be thankful; for your condition has been one of unprecedented difficulty and responsibility.

Hoping that you may be kept in health and strength, and that you may be successful to the end. . . .

W. S. Groesbeck.

ALS, DLC-JP.
    1. It is unclear to which encounter Groesbeck refers.

From Margaret M. Houston[1]

Independence. Texas. Nov. 9th. 1865.

Dear Sir;

I present myself to you Excellency as the widow of Gen. Sam Houston. My object in addressing you is to beseech your clemency in behalf of Mr. Thomas Power[2] an Englishman by birth, who is now in his native country awaiting the result of his application for pardon. Mr. Power married a very dear niece of mine,[3] and she with her children, is now in exile on his account. You can well imagine the distress of her kindred under such circumstances; and I am encouraged from your kindness and magnanimity to our unhappy people, to hope that you will extend your clemency to his case. I plead with you on the score of relationship alone, and if you can grant his pardon and permit him to return, it will fill the hearts of many relatives and friends with joy.[4]

Margaret M. Houston.

ALS, DNA-RG94, Amnesty Papers (M1003, Roll 54), Tex., Thomas B. Power.

1. Margaret M. Lea (1819–1867) had married Sam Houston in 1840. William Seale, *Sam Houston's Wife: A Biography of Margaret Lea Houston* (Norman, Okla., 1970), 5, 6, 257.

2. Power (b. *c*1818), a Galveston merchant, had invested in blockade runners and Confederate privateers. 1860 Census, Tex., Galveston, 4th Ward, 155; Power to Johnson, ca. Sept. 6, 1865, Amnesty Papers (M1003, Roll 54), Tex., Thomas B. Power, RG94, NA.

3. Power married Sarah Ann Royston (b. *c*1828), daughter of Margaret's sister Varilla, on May 21, 1846. Helen S. Swenson, *8800 Texas Marriages, 1824–1850* (2 vols., St. Louis, 1981), 2: 28; Seale, *Sam Houston's Wife*, 6; 1860 Census, Tex., Galveston, 4th Ward, 155.

4. Power wrote on his own behalf to Johnson from Paris, France, asking for a pardon, which he was granted on January 4, 1866. Power to Johnson, ca. Sept. 6, 1865, Amnesty Papers (M1003, Roll 54), Tex., Thomas B. Power, RG94, NA.

From John Marston[1]

Boston   Nov 9th 1865

Sir.

It is with pain & regret that I find myself called upon to write to you in behalf of my Brother, *Col Marston*[2] of the Marine Corps, but the salvation of an entire family from poverty, prompts me to tresspass on you. Colonel Marston has recently been tryed by a Court Martial, for an improper expenditure of money entrusted by the Gov't in his hands; and with Knowing what the sentence of that Court is, yet I venture to palliate his offence in your eyes.

Col Marston has been charged with misusing the public funds, & to this charge he has plead "guilty," acknowledging the truth of it. But are there no mitigating circumstances? He had at one time in his possession *over 60,000 dolls.* which for a long time was laying unemployed; and in an evil hour he was tempted to tresspass on the trust, which had been reposed in him, & entered into a speculation which he thot would be successful, but failing to become so, he extended that tresspass under the hope of retrieving that which had already been expended. This was the rock on which he split. But if we look into the frailty of our own hearts, & see the proneness of our nature to do evil, we shall I am sure be ready to acknowledge, how *almost* natural it was for him to do so.

I do not ask that Col Marston should escape without any punishment, for I am ready to acknowledge that he deserves condemnation; but I intercede with you under the hope that the extreme verdict of the law may be averted; and that a sentence, something like this, may be given him—viz—repremanded by the Honl Secy of the Navy—suspension for three years, and one half of *his retired* pay to be deducted until the whole delinquency is canceled.

In requesting *this leniency* at your hands, I am strengthened in the application by respectfully asking you, whether my brother, has not inherited some claim to it, as the son of one who served throughout the entire revolutionary war with credit to himself, and as we all Know, with success to our Country.[3] And if a farther claim may be proffered in his behalf, whether his own service of forty seven years in the Marine Corps; together with that of a gallant son,[4] who by his bravery and intelligence during the rebellion, raised himself from the ranks to a full Major in the Signal Corps, may not be put into that balance, which I trust will be found preponderating in his favor.

Soliciting a Kind reception of my application[5]. . . .

John Marston   Commodore U S Navy.

ALS, DNA-RG45, Subj. File N, Subsec. NO, Courts-Martial, Box 316, John Marston.

1. Marston (1795–1885), who eventually reached the rank of rear admiral, had served in the Navy since 1813. *Appleton's Cyclopaedia.*

2. Lieut. Col. Ward Marston (c1800–1882) a week earlier had been tried for "scandalous conduct" while commanding the Boston Navy Yard in 1864. He had "received large sums of money from enlisted men . . . and squandered it," leading to a shortage of $8,000. 1870 Census, Mass., Suffolk, Boston, 15th Ward, 333; Callahan, *Navy and Marine List*, 691; Subj. File N, Subsec. NO, Courts-Martial, Box 313, Ward Marston, RG45, NA.

3. Possibly the Boston stockbroker, John Marston (fl1820). Boston directories (1796–1820); *Appleton's Cyclopaedia.*

4. Frank W. Marston (1840–1885), a prewar law student in Philadelphia, served as a lieutenant in the 75th Pa. Inf., before his promotion and transfer to the Signal Corps. ACP Branch, File M-89-CB-1865, Frank W. Marston, RG94, NA; Heitman, *Register*, 1: 691.

5. On November 30, 1865, Johnson modified Ward Marston's sentence exactly the way his brother had suggested. Subj. File N, Subsec. NO, Courts-Martial, Box 313, Ward Marston, RG45, NA.

From Isaac Murphy

Little Rock Ark   Nov 9 1865.

The homestead of Sanford C. Faulkner[1] who has applid for special amnesty and pardon is advertized for sale by the U.S. Mashal[2] of this district under the confiscation[3] and will be sold unless relief is granted before the fifteenth Inst. He has taken the amnesty oath, is an old man and good citizen and I recommend that his pardon be granted & sale of his property stayed. Please answer by telegraph suspending sale.[4]

Isaac Murphy   Gov Ark

Tel, DLC-JP.

1. Faulkner (1803–1874) served as captain of ordnance at the Little Rock arsenal until 1863 when he was ordered to Marshall, Texas. He continued to work there as a military storekeeper until the end of the war. Faulkner to Johnson, ca. Sept. 14, 1865, Amnesty Papers (M1003, Roll 13), Ark., Sanford C. Faulkner, RG94, NA; Dallas T. Herndon, ed., *Centennial History of Arkansas* (3 vols., Chicago, 1922), 1: 755.

2. William O. Stoddard (1835–1925), an Illinois newspaper editor, was one of Lincoln's private secretaries before his appointment as marshal of Arkansas. Later he became an inventor and a prolific writer, his works including seventy-six books for boys. *DAB*.

3. Upon Faulkner's return to Little Rock in September 1865, he learned that his Pulaski County plantation had been seized on March 27, 1865, and consigned for sale by the district court on May 30. Faulkner to Johnson, ca. Sept. 14, 1865, Amnesty Papers (M1003, Roll 13), Ark., Sanford C. Faulkner, RG94, NA.

4. The day after this wire was sent, Johnson replied that Attorney General Speed had ordered the suspension of confiscation proceedings against Faulkner's property and said that his pardon, issued on October 18, would be forwarded. Johnson to Murphy, Nov. 10, 1865, Tels. Sent, President, Vol. 2 (1865), RG107, NA; Amnesty Papers (M1003, Roll 13), Ark., Sanford C. Faulkner, RG94, NA.

From Gideon J. Pillow

St Louis Missouri   Nov 9th 1865

I visited this city for the purpose of getting the mules that were taken from my Plantations in Arkansas[1] restored. As the legal affect of your Pardon of me, I thought the restoration of the mules (171 in number) was a matter of right. Genl. Sherman referred my application, by Telegram, to the secretary of war. I enclose you an official copy of the answer.[2] If the matter was referred to you and the Telegram contains your decision, I shall not complain. But if it is not your decision, then I respectfully ask your attention to my application, which is enclosed herewith.

I gratefully acknowledge your kindness to me Mr President and would have preferred the loss of the mules (reduced as I am in my condition) to giving you either trouble or embarrassment. I was unable to perceive any difference in principal between the restoration of the land and the mules which were taken from it when I was Pardoned.

May I trouble you to have your secretary acknowledge the reception of this communication.[3]

With my best wishes for your health and happiness & with assurances of my full confidence and support of your Administration. . . .

Gid. J. Pillow

ALS, DNA-RG94, Lets. Recd. (Main Ser.), File P-1685-1865 (M619, Roll 400).

1. Pillow's mules had been taken by the troops of Gen. Samuel R. Curtis during his invasion of Arkansas in 1862. Edwin D. Townsend to Pillow, Nov. 23, 1865, Lets. Recd. (Main Ser.), File P-1685-1865 (M619, Roll 400), RG94, NA.

2. In response to a telegram from William T. Sherman, Edwin M. Stanton reported that the matter had been submitted to the President, who declared "that restoration of such property captured during the war, from persons who have been in arms against the Government, cannot be awarded." Furthermore, "the Executive pardon does not contemplate or authorize such restitution." Sherman to Stanton, Nov. 7, 1865; Stanton to Sherman, Nov. 8, 1865, Stanton Papers, LC.

3. Johnson referred this letter to Stanton, instructing him to "please inform the claimant that the mules referred to herein cannot be restored." Edwin D. Townsend did so inform Pillow in November 1865, and again three years later when he sought to renew his application for his mules. Townsend to Pillow, Nov. 23, 1865; Townsend to James A. Hardie, Nov. 2, 1868, Lets. Recd. (Main Ser.), File P-1685-1865 (M619, Roll 400), RG94, NA.

From Mary Jane Wright[1]

Greeneville   Nov 9th/1865

Respected Friend

From my long acquaintance with you and confidence in your humanity, has prompted me to address you in behalf of my unfortunate soninlaw—John T Reynolds, who is now—and has been a prisnor in Knoxville for 18 months.[2]

My health is entirely gone. Emma my daughter—Reynolds wife, has an interesting little daughter two years old. You know Emma has no Father. She has no property, and in feeble health, what I say is to become of her and her little one? How are they to live? Without Father! husband! home! property! Reynolds is pronounced insane by his Physician owing to bad health and long confinement. Emma is now with him, without means. I have no doubt but that you have heard that he has been a desperate man. And perhaps a great many exagerated reports have reached you about him. He has been nothing but a Confederate Soldier, and you shall have the most undoubted proff to your satisfaction. Will you interfere in his behalf and grant his release? For my sake, for his unfortunate wife and infant do I pray have him released, Save O! save his wife and child from an early grave.

I am asking nothing more than I would do for you or yours. You are a parent, none but a parent knows what a parent feels. Be so kind as to answer and let us know our fate.[3]

Mary Jane Wright

ALS, DNA-RG94, Amnesty Papers (M1003, Roll 50), Tenn., John T. Reynolds.

1. Wright (b. c1827) had married William P. Cozart in 1844, and they had two daughters, Emma and Martha. In 1854 she married Charles H. Wright. Burgner, *Greene County Marriages*, 141, 201; 1860 Census, Tenn., Knox, 1st Dist., Knoxville, 9.

2. In mid-August Emma Reynolds visited Washington evidently to press the plea for pardon for her husband. While there she wrote a letter to President Johnson asking for John Reynolds's pardon; this letter was apparently given to Johnson by Sam Milligan and R. A. Crawford of Greeneville, also in Washington at the same time, who expressed sympathy for the Reynolds family and referred the President to "the within letter." Reynolds to Johnson, Aug. 11, 1865; Milligan and Crawford to Johnson, Aug. 11, 1865, Amnesty Papers (M1003, Roll 50), Tenn., John T. Reynolds, RG94, NA.

3. See James W. Harold to Johnson, July 29, 1865, *Johnson Papers*, 8: 498–99.

From William G. Brownlow

Nashville, November 10th, 1865.

President Johnson:

Gen. Thomas and I have just had an interview, and he has kindly shown me two letters addressed to you from East Tennessee. One is from Miss Julia L. Reeve[1] near Jonesborough. Her cousin, the son of Peter M. Reeve,[2] a Unionist, arrived here yesterday. He tells me that the country is very quiet, and that Sheriff Shipley,[3] has his guard of twelve armed men; granted under the new law,[4] armed, and out looking after some rebel horse thieves.

The version given by the other, Maria S Wafford,[5] from Bulls Gap, does not agree with the accounts that two members of the Legislature give, who are just from there. Judge Butler[6] told me, that after a session of two weeks of Court, in Greenville, a great crowd in attendance all the time, they had no fights, nor any disturbances, but perfect quiet and order. It is notoriously quiet throughout East Tennessee. Some few bad Rebels in each county have been driven out, and there friends are very sore under it, and exaggerate all that is done. They have tried me by petitions and memorials, to induce me to make a publication, *censuring*, or *reflecting injuriously*, upon the Union party of East Tenn and I have obstinately refused.

Gen. Thomas named the case of W. C. Kain[7] to me, and exhibited his papers.[8] I have no feeling against Kain, and would be willing to see you turn him out, but the Lawyers tell me that I have no power to release him, as his trial is *pending*, and he has not been *convicted*. There is a copperhead faction in the Legislature, eager to seize upon every thing I do, that smacks of usurping authority.

W. G. Brownlow   Governor &c.

ALS, DLC-JP.

1. Probably Julia L. Reeves (c1834-fl1870), daughter of William P. Reeves, a Washington County farmer. 1850 Census, Tenn., Washington, 4th Subdiv., 272; (1860), Knob Creek Dist., Jonesboro, 27; (1870), 10th Dist., Johnson City, 15.

2. Peter M. Reeves (1807–1891) was a Washington County farmer who had several sons. The one referred to in this letter could be John D. Reeves (1839–1915), also a

farmer in Washington County. Bennett and Rae, *Washington County*, 1: 2; 1850 Census, Tenn., Washington, 4th Subdiv., 245; (1860), Brush Creek Dist., Jonesboro, 1.

3. Shelby T. Shipley.

4. This is doubtless a reference to the law, passed in June 1865 by the Tennessee legislature, which granted authority to the sheriffs to raise posses as county patrols which would enforce "civil law and order." *Tennessee Acts, 1865*, 43–44.

5. Probably a reference to the letter written to Johnson by Wofford on September 11, 1865.

6. Roderick R. Butler.

7. Kain, along with three other men, had been charged with the murder of a fellow East Tennessean in 1861. They were incarcerated for approximately a year before their trial began in Knoxville in June 1866. Eventually they were all acquitted of murder. *Nashville Dispatch*, June 21, 22, 28, 30, July 3, 1866; *Knoxville Whig*, June 20, 1866. See Brownlow to Johnson, May 24, 1865, *Johnson Papers*, 8: 107.

8. In his own behalf, Kain sent a petition to President Johnson in mid-September which Speed subsequently forwarded to General Thomas. This may have been the document referred to here. Kain to Johnson, Sept. 19, 1865, Governors' Papers, TSLA; Speed to Kain, Oct. 18, 1865, Office of Atty. Gen., Lets. Sent, Vol. E (M699, Roll 10), RG60, NA.

From George W. Gregor[1]

Havana   Nov, 10th. 1865.

I the undersigned Geo. W. Gregor, was for many years previous to the breaking out of the rebellion a citizen of New Orleans, La. and upon the formation of the government of the "So called Confederate States" I deemed it my duty to aid said goverment in every honorable way in my power, and did so until the close of the war.

I now find myself (for so doing) exempt from the benefits of Your Excellencys amnesty proclamation of 29th May 1865 Only under the 7th and 11th clauses. 7th in this, that I left New Orleans on the 5th April 1862 and came to this place where I have been engaged in running the blockade to "aid the rebellion."

11th in this, that I aided to equip two privateers in the year 1861, one called the "Calhoun" one, the "J. O. Nixon" to "prey upon the commerce" of the United States. To all the other twelve clauses, I very respectfully answer not guilty.[2]

I learn that I have been accused through the newspaper reports, of having been engaged with Dr. L. P. Blackburn, in a "yellow fever plot." I very solemnly deny any complicity in the affair, and hope the accompanying affidavits upon the subject, will be perfectly satisfactory to Your Excellency upon that point.[3]

I am now sincerely glad that the war, that distracted our country, is at an end, and being anxious to return to my home and become a peaceable and law abiding citizen, I have taken the oath of Allegiance prescribed by Your Excellency, with a firm determination to fulfil the obligations thereof faithfully and conscientiously.[4]

I, therefore, very humbly and respectfully pray Your Excellency to grant me a pardon, under your amnesty proclamation of 29th May last. A copy of my oath of allegiance is enclosed.[5]

George. W. Gregor.

ALS, DNA-RG94, Amnesty Papers (M1003, Roll 28), La., George W. Gregor.

1. Prior to the war Gregor had been a jeweler. New Orleans directories (1856–61).

2. Neither of these lightly-armed vessels was a success. The *Calhoun*, a side-wheel steamer which captured three prizes in May 1861, was abandoned near the mouth of the Mississippi in January 1862. The *J. O. Nixon*, a schooner, was captured in July 1861. *Official Records of the Union and Confederate Navies in the War of the Rebellion* (30 vols., Washington, 1894–1927), Ser. 1, Vol. 1: 818–19; Ser. 2, Vol. 1: 672.

3. Gregor's affidavit swears that he never took part in the yellow fever plot. There is also an affidavit from Blackburn swearing that Gregor had not been involved. Amnesty Papers (M1003, Roll 28), La., George W. Gregor, RG94, NA.

4. Gregor first took the oath on November 9 in Havana; he next took the oath in New York on February 2, 1866. Ibid.

5. Gregor was pardoned on February 10, 1866. *House Ex. Docs.*, 39 Cong., 2 Sess., No. 31, p. 12 (Ser. 1289).

Response to North Carolina Delegation[1]

[November 10, 1865][2]

Hon. Mr. Reade:

I received from you with pleasure, a copy of the proceedings of the Convention of North-Carolina. I reciprocate cordially the conciliatory spirit in which you have addressed me.

The Convention of North-Carolina has done much and well toward restoring the State to her proper natural relations, but something yet remains to be done to render her restoration immediately practicable. An acceptation of the Constitutional amendment abolishing slavery throughout the United States by the Legislature of North-Carolina, is in my judgment practically important to the successful restoration which is so much desired by all.[3]

Without answering specifically the questions you have proposed to me, it will be sufficient to say that my action must depend upon events, and that Mr. Holden will be again instructed to continue the exercise of his functions as Provisional Governor until he shall have been expressly relieved by orders to that effect.[4]

Raleigh Standard, Nov. 28, 1865.

1. Meeting with Johnson were members of the recently adjourned constitutional convention, headed by the former presiding officer and Holden ally Edwin G. Reade (1812–1894), who later joined the Republican party and served as a state supreme court justice. Speaking for the delegation, Reade outlined the convention's accomplishments, praised the President's "ability and impartiality," enlisted his aid in having the test oath repealed, and requested Johnson to declare North Carolina duly reconstructed. Wakelyn, *BDC*.

2. This date is indicated by Reade's letter to Holden, which was printed in the November 28 issue of the *Raleigh Standard*.

3. See Holden to Johnson, Dec. 1, 1865.

4. See Holden to Johnson, Dec. 8, 1865.

From Lafayette C. Baker
Unofficial

Washington City, Nov 11th 1865.

Sir.

I desire to call your attention to a certain class of persons (Male and Female) who are daily visiting the Executive Mansion, known as Pardon Brokers. My attention was sometime since called to these individuals, the means employed in the prosecution of their business; and also a number of persons holding official positions under the Government, &c. I declined however to take any official cognizance of the matter, until quite recently; when I discovered that certain of these Females, of very questionable character and reputation, (to say the least) were almost daily procuring Pardons. They have repeatedly advertised or proclaimed themselves in the public Hotels, and Saloons of the City as Pardon Brokers; asserting that they could procure the pardon of any one applying, in twelve hours. Some days since, an Officer of the U.S. Army, who had been convicted at St Louis, by Military Court Martial; Sentenced to the Penitentiary at Alton Ill's, for two years; but escaped to Canada in 1864; came to Washington to procure his Pardon.[1] He was advised to apply to a Mrs L. L. Cobb,[2] who assured the Officer that she could obtain his pardon in twelve hours, for the sum of Three hundred dollars: remarking at the same time that she Mrs C, would have to pay a portion of said Three hundred dollars, to certain Clerks, and others. The Officer paid Mrs. Cobb, One hundred dollars as retaining fee, taking the following receipt for the same. The original of which is in your Department.

Washington, D.C. No 5th 1865.

For, and in consideration of the Sum of Three hundred dollars, paid to me by Capt. Clarence J. Howell, I hereby agree as follows, to wit. To take from Capt. Howell his statement in regard to his case, and procure for him the full and complete Pardon for his past offences. The money to be paid as follows, one hundred dollars in hand, and the remaining Two hundred on the delivery of his pardon on Monday Evening at Six O'Clock P.M. I further agree that in case I do not succeed in getting the pardon as agreed, I will return to him the one hundred dollars received of him.

("Signed") Mrs L. L. Cobb.

The above contained the following Receipt on the back.

Washington D.C. Nov 5th 1865.

Received on the within, One hundred dollars.

(Signed) Mrs L. L. Cobb.

Mrs. C, informed the officer at their first interview that she had procured, or obtained a great number of Pardons but was always compelled to divide the amount received therefore with certain persons holding positions in different Departments and Bureaus.

Mrs Cobb having failed to procure the Pardon within the time maintained in the above receipt, The Officer became dissatisfied, and complained to me that he feared he should lose the one hundred dollars
advanced.[3]

After hearing his Statement, I found that Mrs. C. might be engaged
with others in Forging the Pardons, and I did not think it possible that
a Woman of her character could procure a Pardon under any circumstances, much less to procure it in the time specified in her agreement
with the Officer. Being desirous and deeming that the ends of justice
would best be subserved I asked the Officer, in case she should succeed
in procuring the Pardon to pay her the remaining Two hundred dollars, in such funds as could be identified: Accordingly I gave the Officer, Four fifty dollar Treasury Notes, and marked them. The same
evening, the Officer went to Mrs. Cobbs, room, No. 20, Avenue House,
paid the Two hundred dollars, taking Mrs. C. receipt. Therefore I then
went to Mrs Cobb's Room, and required her to give me the Two hundred dollars, which she did. I then asked her and her husband[4] to accompany me to my office immediately. The same evening I took the
receipt and Contract of Mrs Cobb's to you.[5] The Pardon was found in
Mrs C's room, and on inquiry I found it had been delivered to her,
before the Oath of Amnesty had been made as required by Law. Mrs
C. remained at my office until nearly eleven O Clock, when I discharged her and her husband, and they returned to the Avenue House
the same evening. During my conversation with her she made a long
statement, claiming that she was not the only Female engaged in procuring Pardons for pay, etc. The Pardon referred to, as procured by
Mrs. Cobb, was in the name of Clarence J. Howell a name assumed for
the occasion. When we take into consideration the notorious bad character and Reputation of this Woman (Mrs Cobb) her conduct while at
the Executive Mansion, which is well known to nearly every Employee
at the White House: her public boastings that she could procure pardons at all times quicker than any other person in Washington. That
she has (if her own Statement can be relied upon) procured a large
number of Pardons, through the assistance of certain Attachees of the
different Departments. I trust I shall be pardoned for calling your attention to the matter, in a written Statement of the facts in regard to Mrs
Ella B. Washington,[6] another Female Pardon Broker, and the person
of whom I spoke at our interview, not long since. I beg leave to say that
she contracted to procure the Pardon of one John Kelly,[7] as appears
from the following Receipt. The original being in my possession.

Washington D.C. Novr 8th 1865.
Received of John Kelley, One hundred dollars, as a retaining fee for obtaining his (Kelleys) pardon from the President.

(Signed) Ella B. Washington

The Pardon was not procured however. I know but little of Mrs W's
previous character. She is however the Wife or Widow of Louis P.

Washington heretofore known as one of the most bitter and uncompromising haters of our government. There are many other very important
facts partially brought to light by this investigation, which go to show
conclusively that a system of Manipulation and Corruption, are being
practiced by persons holding Official positions under the Government
in connection with the procuring of Pardons.[8]

L. C. Baker   Brig Genl & Pro Mar of the War Dept

ALS, DLC-JP.

1. Henry H. Hines (c1830-fl1866) had been a 1st lieutenant in the 2nd Col. Inf. and
the 1st Col. Cav. While serving in St. Louis as assistant provost marshal, he was convicted for false imprisonment, fraud, and granting passes for the removal of slaves from
Missouri. In January 1866 he was arrested again, then paroled at Baker's request to assist
in an "investigation of great importance." He was apparently subsequently acquitted by
a military commission. CSR, RG94, NA; Baker, *Secret Service*, 656, 663.

2. Lucy Livingston Cobb (b. c1839) had operated a cigar stand in Washington and
was briefly a nurse at the Armory Square Hospital. Ibid., 590, 612, 625; *Washington
Evening Star*, May 21, 1867; *Lynchburg Virginian*, Nov. 17, 1865.

3. In his memoirs Baker asserts that from the outset he directed Hines's operations
under the pseudonym Clarence J. Howell. Baker, *Secret Service*, 593–95.

4. Joseph R. Cobb (fl1868), allegedly a former paymaster for the navy, was a clerk in
the Treasury Department. He is misidentified as "John" in Baker's memoirs. Ibid., 590,
609; Washington, D.C., directories (1864–68); *Lynchburg Virginian*, Nov. 17, 1865.

5. For Baker's account of his stormy meeting with Johnson, see Baker, *Secret Service*,
596–98.

6. Washington had become a "*friend*" of the President during the process of securing
a pardon for her husband and the return of their property. See Washington to Johnson,
Aug. 8, 1865, *Johnson Papers*, 8: 546–47.

7. Another assumed name for Hines. Baker, *Secret Service*, 598.

8. Johnson refused to take action against either Cobb or Washington. Indicted in
November 1865 for the false imprisonment of Mrs. Cobb, Baker later testified against
the President during the impeachment investigation. Joseph R. Cobb, who was not allowed to testify before Congress, complained to Johnson in September 1866 that his pay
had been stopped, and, after the conclusion of Baker's trial, asked if Seward or Mc-
Culloch "would give me employment or an asylum in some far removed territory." *Cairo
Democrat*, Nov. 19, 1865; Dorris, *Pardon and Amnesty*, 148–51; Baker, *Secret Service*,
603–91 passim; *House Reports*, 40 Cong., 1 Sess., No. 7, pp. 2–15, 29–33 (Ser. 1314);
Cobb to Johnson, Sept. 26, 1866, May 11, 1867, Johnson Papers, LC.

From Alvan C. Gillem

Chattanooga, Tenn., Nov. 11. 1865.

Dear Sir.

Allow me to return my sincere thanks for my recent Promotion as
Major General of Volunteers, which was the more gratifying as it was
entirely unexpected. I assure you, I shall endeavor to justify, what I fear
is due more to your partiality for me personally, than to any merit I may
possess.

I am certain I have discharged the duties devolving upon me, according to the best of my ability & my honest convictions of right—if my
conduct has met your approbation I am satisfied.

Sometime since Gov Brownlow forwarded to your Excellency a dispatch[1] to the effect that one B. C. Vinson had shot a *negro* & that I was

having said Vinson tried by a commission of officers of negro regiments who were much prejudiced against Vinson, and requesting you to order said Vinson to be turned over to the civil authorities for trial. I regret to say that the Governors dispatch was calculated to mislead you (unintentionally of course). The murdered man, was a *negro* it is true—but he was also a United States *soldier*, and as such was entitled to the protection of the Military Authorities. His murderer was being tried in compliance with orders from Major Generals Thomas & Stoneman. I ordered the court but could not have selected them with any peculiar prejudice against Vinson, as the commission convened several weeks *prior to the murder* for the trial of a Guerrilla from Hawkins County.

To try Vinson by civil law would be equivalent to an acquittal as the evidence of the most material witnesses (negros) would be inadmissable.

No man can be more thoroughly convinced than I am of the incompatibility of Military Courts & those of the Freedmens Bureau with our free institutions—but I am unable to see how either can be dispensed with so long as the great mass of evidence received by them is rejected by the Civil Courts of the State. To obviate this difficulty I have urged the Legislature of Tennessee to legalize negro testimony. I am confident it will be done at an early day—in which case I would respectfully the discontinuance of the Freedmens Bureau in this State.[2]

Under the present system we have officers whose attainments would not compare favorably with our Justices of the Peace deciding cases involving the most intricate legal questions and large amounts of property.

Politically everything is quiet in Tenn. The only point in discussion is which are the better administration men. I have recently seen & conversed much with the people of East Tennessee & am gratified to be able to report that good order & prosperity are rapidly reviving.

In the reorganization of the Regular Army I hope I will not be forgotten—it is my profession. My education & long service probably unfits me for any other.

Requesting your pardon for this intrusion.

                                                    Alvan C Gillem

ALS, DLC-JP.

1. See Brownlow to Johnson, Sept. 19, 1865.

2. A bill to permit blacks to testify in the state's courts was in fact introduced during the fall session of the General Assembly and eventually passed in late January 1866. One of Brownlow's arguments in its behalf was that it would remove the necessity of Freedmen's Bureau courts in the state. Alexander, *Reconstruction*, 100–101.

From Charles Sumner

Boston Nov 11 1865.

As a faithful friend and supporter of your administration I most respectfully petition you to suspend for the present your policy towards the Rebel States. I should not present this prayer if I were not painfully convinced that thus far it has failed to obtain any reasonable guarantees for that security in the future which is essential to peace & reconciliation. To my mind it abandons the freedmen to the control of their ancient Masters & leaves the National debt exposed to repudiation by returning Rebels. The declaration of Independence asserts the equality of all men & the rightful government can be founded only on the consent of the governed. I see small chance of peace unless these great principles are practically established by our Government. Without this, the house will continue divided against itself.

Chas Sumner. Senator of U S.

Tel, DLC-JP.

From J. Madison Wells

New Orleans Nov 11 1865.

Sir,

The Opelousas Rail road has been offered to the Stock holders on terms prescribed by the Secty of War which the Company deem unjust & unreasonable. Can the property be returned to the Company without those Considerations?[1]

J Madison Wells Gov

Tel, DLC-JP.

1. In an endorsement on the Wells document Johnson asked Stanton, "What were the terms &c." Writing just below the Johnson inquiry, the Secretary responded that he "had no knowledge of any terms being required, other than those specified in the orders of *the President.*" See Canby to Johnson, Dec. 9, 1865.

From Absalom A. Kyle

Nashville, 12th Novr. 1865.

Dear Sir,

I have the honor to acknowledge the receipt of your letter of the 9th Inst.[1] in reference to the lands of the two Powels & Orville Rice in Hawkins Co.[2]

C. W. Hall,[3] the U.S. District Atty, has heretofore taken steps to confiscate the lands of the aforesaid parties, in the Federal court at Knoxville & when I last talked to him on the subject, said that he intended to still proceed against the lands of these parties, at the Novr.

court, (4th Monday). If I understand your communication now before me, it is that all parties who have received amnesty, will have their lands restored to them, at the expiration of present leases. Then of course, the Dist. Atty ought to enter a "*Nolle prosequi*" or dismiss proceedings in the Federal court as against the parties herein mentioned, & all others similarly situated. Please reply to this communication, addressing me at Knoxville,[4] and place me in a condition to have all proceedings in the Federal court stopped, against the lands of Orville Rice, George & Saml Powel & Audley Anderson.[5] They are clients of mine.

I wrote to my friend Judge Patterson a day or two since, giving him a list of the names of parties, for whom I am endeavoring to get Pardons.

Application was made for the parties 4 or 5 months ago. They (most of them) are Indicted in the Federal court, & were *Arrested* before receiving Amnesty; hence the urgency of the case. The court comes on two weeks hence, & as yet no Pardon.

Your *early attention*, will place, under increased obligations. . . .

A. A. Kyle

ALS, DLC-JP.

1. At the direction of the President, Robert Morrow wrote to Kyle to acknowledge receipt of Kyle's November 2 letter (which has not been found). Morrow to Kyle, Nov. 9, 1865, Johnson Papers, LC.

2. George R. and Samuel Powel had both written to Johnson earlier asking for pardon. Samuel's was granted on October 23, 1865, but George did not receive his until July 5, 1866. Rice requested a pardon in December 1865, so that his lands could be returned to him. It was granted on January 19, 1866. George R. Powel to Johnson, Aug. 22, 1865, *Johnson Papers*, 8: 643–44; Samuel Powel to Johnson, Aug. 9, 1865, Amnesty Papers (M1003, Roll 50), Tenn., Samuel Powel, RG94, NA; Rice to Johnson, Dec. 2, 1865, Amnesty Papers (M1003, Roll 50), Tenn., Orville Rice, RG94, NA; *House Ex. Docs.*, 39 Cong., 2 Sess., No. 116, p. 48 (Ser. 1293). See also Kyle to Johnson, Dec. 4, 1865, Office of Atty. Gen., Lets. Recd., President, RG60, NA.

3. Crawford W. Hall (*c*1809-*fl*1888), a Lincoln appointee, served as U.S. District Attorney for four years (1865–69). Originally from Kentucky, he had studied in Maryville, Tenn., and years later returned to East Tennessee to live in Rogersville, then in Knoxville. Hall and Kyle were close friends. Crawford W. Hall, *Threescore Years and Ten* (Cincinnati, 1884), 48–49, 79, 201, 203, 210; R. L. Polk & Co., *Knoxville City Directory* (1888), 186; 1860 Census, Tenn., Hawkins, 10th Dist., Rogersville, 11.

4. Once again Robert Morrow wrote on behalf of the President, acknowledging this letter and instructing Kyle that a special pardon was required in order "to restore the lands upon the expiration of the present leases thereon." Morrow to Kyle, Nov. 16, 1865, Johnson Papers, LC.

5. Anderson (b. *c*1822) was a Hawkins County merchant who subsequently moved to Sullivan County. He had held the minor posts of enrolling officer and tax assessor during the Civil War. Anderson wrote to Johnson for pardon in June and took the oath of allegiance in July. His documents were forwarded to Johnson by Kyle in early August, and his pardon request was approved by Brownlow on September 25. His pardon was granted on October 2, 1865. Anderson to Johnson, June 20, 1865; Kyle to Johnson, Aug. 2, 1865, Amnesty Papers (M1003, Roll 48), Tenn., Audley Anderson, RG94, NA; *House Ex. Docs.*, 39 Cong., 2 Sess., No. 116, p. 32 (Ser. 1293); 1860 Census, Tenn., Hawkins, 10th Dist., Rogersville, 4; (1870), Sullivan, 17th Dist., Bristol, 9.

From Joseph S. Cannon[1]

Raleigh, N.C., Novr. 13th, 1865.

Sir.

Governor Holden is confined to his bed from illness, and directs me to write you a few lines.

Only twenty three counties have been heard from, the returns of which leave the election of Governor uncertain. Governor Holden does not despair of his election.

Hon. William A. Graham has been elected to the State Senate from Orange County. Josiah Turner is elected to Congress from this district, and Rufus Y. McAden[2] to the House of Commons from Alamance County.

They are unpardoned and have been reccommended for Suspension by the Governor. It is believed they will soon apply in person to Your Excellency for Pardon.[3]

Governor Graham is the originator and leader of all the disaffection in North Carolina. His great desire is to unite enough of the old whigs, to the Secessionists, the advocates of the payment of the Rebel Debt, and disaffected men, to break down the National Union Party. His opposition to you is as strong as it is to Governor Holden. Jonathan Worth, Josiah Turner and Rufus Y. McAdin were put forward at his instance, against the repeated remonstrances of all the leading union men in the State.

Josiah Turner canvassed the district greatly exciting and increasing the disaffection. The body of his speeches consisted of ridicule and slander of the democratic party. He declared "he would not vote for you to save your life." McAdin has done all he could for the same purposes.

The Union men of the State believe that if Your Excellency will refuse to Pardon these men, disaffection will be struck a death blow in North Carolina, and will not again be able to rise. The Governor greatly desires that these men may not be Pardoned, but may receive a merited rebuke at the hands of Your Excellency.[4]

Jos. S. Cannon, Aid de Camp

ALS, DLC-JP.

1. A secession convention delegate, Cannon (b. c1825) was an attorney, Holden's aide, temporary editor (with Joseph W. Holden) of Holden's *Standard*, and vice-president of the Bank of North Carolina. 1860 Census, N.C., Perquimans, Yeopin Dist., Hertford, 93; Raper, *Holden*, 275–76; Harris, *Holden*, 178; Connor, *N.C. Manual*, 894.

2. Elected to his third of four consecutive terms, McAden (1833–1889) later achieved prominence as a banker, railroad promoter, and cotton mill owner. *Cyclopedia of the Carolinas*, 2: 199–200.

3. See Graham to Johnson, Nov. 14, 1865, Johnson Papers, LC.

4. Although ordered pardoned on December 4, 1865, Graham did not acknowledge receipt of the pardon instrument until some seventeen months later. McAden was pardoned on January 23, 1866. Graham to Johnson, May 2, 1867, Amnesty Papers

(M1003, Roll 39), N.C., William A. Graham, RG94, NA; Amnesty Papers (M1003, Roll 40), N.C., Rufus Y. McAden, RG94, NA. See Francis J. Smith to Johnson, Sept. 28, 1865, Amnesty Papers (M1003, Roll 43), N.C., Josiah Turner, RG94, NA.

From James T. Soutter[1]

New York   13. Novemr. 1865

Mr. President,

Last Monday I had the honor of a personal interview with you for the purpose of urging the release *on parole* of Mr. James A. Seddon,[2] now a prisoner at Fort Pulaski. You were kind enough to hear what I had to say on that subject, and asked me to reduce the same to writing and send it to you for more deliberate Consideration. This I now propose to do.

Mr. Seddon is a man in delicate health and his life is in great jeopardy in such confinement at any season, but, at this time, and during the winter months, I should consider *the risk* in his case *very great*. I visited him in October, and even then I found his appartment any thing but comfortable for a man of his frail constitution.

Mr. Seddon directed me to Say to you that if you would release him *on parole* so that he could discharge his duties to his family he would hold himself subject to the call of the Government in the event of any desire for his rendition of himself for any purpose whatsoever. His word to this effect you know may be relied upon.

Mr. Seddon's family is a large one, some eight or ten children, most of whom are of tender years, and they are suffering bothe want of paternal care and Support. His wife[3] implored me, in the most beseeching manner, to do all in my power to restore their father to the Children.

During my visit to Mr. Seddon in his prison he disclaimed, in the most solemn manner, every feeling of unkindness, much less of cruelty, towards the prisoners who fell into their hands; and, from what I know of his character from an acquaintance of 33 years, I am satisfied he is incapable of any deliberate or wilful act of inhumanity.

Since I returned from the South Mr. Seddon has written me several times imploring his release, on parole if no more, and, in one of his late letters, he made some allusion to his acquaintance with you, and, tho' not intended for your eye, I don't think it will be amiss to hand you an extract which I herein enclose.[4]

I sincerely trust, Mr. President, that you will permit Mr. Seddon to join his family, taking his parole to render himself to your call if at any time the Government shd. require his person.

Your marked courtesy to me has emboldened me to address this letter to you, and I pray that my entreaty in behalf of my friend may meet a favorable response.[5]

Jas. T. Soutter

ALS, DNA-RG107, Lets. Recd., EB12 President 2824 (1865).

1. On the eve of the war Soutter (c1810-fl1874), a Virginia native, was president of the Bank of the Republic in New York. New York City directories (1874–75); Wm. M. Evarts to James Speed, Aug. 3, 1865, Amnesty Papers (M1003, Roll 73), Misc. Northern and Western States, James T. Soutter, RG94, NA.

2. Confederate congressman and secretary of war.

3. Sarah Bruce (1822–1882), who married Seddon in 1845, had herself visited the President and the Secretary of War on her husband's behalf in late October. "The Bruce Family," VMHB, 11 (1904): 442–43; New York Herald, Oct. 27, 1865.

4. Soutter had copied a portion of an October 22 letter in which Seddon had stated that he and Johnson "had some personal, and kindly" conversations when they served together in Congress.

5. Ordered paroled to Virginia on November 21 and granted an enlargement of his parole in May 1866, Seddon finally received a special pardon in November 1867. E. M. Stanton to Commandant of Fort Pulaski, Nov. 21, 1865, Tels. Sent, Sec. of War (M473, Roll 90), RG107, NA; Johnson to Seddon, May 4, 1866, Johnson Papers, LC; Dorris, Pardon and Amnesty, 272.

From George L. Stearns

Boston, Nov. 13, 1865.

My dear Sir

I have received your slip cut from the Washington paper.[1] I sent you in advance of publication, a slip from the "Transcript" office of this city,[2] which, without doubt, was lost on the way. "Reconstruction" was the word in my report, but I have no doubt you used restoration in conversation with me.

Restoration was in your thought, Reconstruction in mine, hence the use of the word. I have made the change in the third line, "he talked for an hour on the process of (Reconstruction) Restoration of Rebel States."

This seems to set *you* right, but the people do not regard it of consequence. They see in that letter a frank expression of your policy which gives them confidence in *you*, and a determination that those states shall not be admitted to the full privileges of loyalty, until they give guarantees for future good behavior, by present good works, even if it takes time to accomplish it.

The return of those states is bound up with our financial condition, the prosperity of which rests entirely on faith in the wisdom of the government. Undue haste in admitting Southern members to seats in Congress, would impair this faith, and many timid persons, although perhaps a small proportion of the holders of Government Debt, would be alarmed at the prospect of indirect repudiation, by refusal to levy taxes, or in some other mode, and these, added to the number who are obliged to sell on account of the rightness of the money market, would, it is feared by many of our leading capitalists, and other sagacious men, produce a panic in stocks.[3]

I do not write this in fear that you will be influenced in favor of hasty measures, but because the papers are full of it, and we understand that great pressure in this direction is made by certain parties.

I send with this the first number of my Newspaper,[4] in which you will find your conversation carefully compared with the original. I do not expect an answer to it or any thing else I may send you, but only ask to be permitted to write a few words occasionally.

George L. Stearns

ALS, DLC-JP.

1. Johnson had probably forwarded a clipping from the *Washington Chronicle* of October 24, 1865, recounting his interview with Stearns. See Interview with George L. Stearns, Oct. 3, 1865.

2. Two days before the publication of Stearns's interview, he mailed another account of it, as well as a copy of his subsequent letter, which would appear in the *Boston Transcript* on October 23, 1865.

3. Stearns later forwarded a proposal for financial stability that included the resumption of specie payments by private banks and the absorption of specie surpluses by the Treasury. Stearns to Johnson, Nov. 21, 1865, Johnson Papers, LC.

4. Not found, but in November 1865 Stearns began publishing the *Right Way*, a radical Republican weekly. *DAB*; *Newspapers in Microform: United States 1948–1983* (2 vols., Washington, 1984), 1: 435.

From Trustees of East Alabama Male College[1]

Auburn Ala.   Novr. 13th 1865

The undersigned "as the executive comittee of the Board of Trustees of the East Alabama Male College" located at Auburn Ala." [*sic*] respectfully represents to your Excellency that the edifice of said Institution is a magnificent structure and has been libelled as property confiscated under the act of Congress, upon the grounds, "as we understand," that it was used pending the rebellion as a Confederate Hospital.

The undersigned further represent that said edifice was impressed and taken from their possession by the Confederate Authorities against their decided remonstrance.

They also state that the college is in a prostrated condition and without funds to embark in Litigation.

Hence they ask that your Excellency will generously order, forthwith, the dismissal of said proceedings without cost to the Institution.

They beg leave to state further that the proceedings aforesaid are pending in the District Court at Montgomery Ala. and will be heard very soon unless promptly dismissed by your order.[2]

P.S. Since the above petition was signed the Committee have ascertained that the Primary Department of the East Ala College has also been libelled and the Committee would respectfully request your Excellency to include it in your order, &c.

John. B. Glenn   Chm.

ALS (Glenn), DNA-RG60, Office of Atty. Gen., Lets. Recd., President.

1. The committee included chairman John B. Glenn (1786–1869), a Methodist minister and Alabama resident since 1837, who co-founded the college, and his neighbors, Isaac Hill (b. c1809), Simeon Perry (b. c1807), James B. Ogletree (1800–1866), and Joshua W. Willis (b. c1815), who were all prosperous farmers. Owen, *History of Ala.*, 3: 667, 811; 1850 Census, Ala., Macon, 21st Dist., 391; (1860), Northern Div., 19, 20, 34, 47; Alexander Nunn, ed., *Lee County and Her Forebears* (Montgomery, 1983), 199.

2. The East Alabama Male College, which opened in 1858 and was a precursor of Auburn University, resumed classes January 8, 1866. Brewer, *Alabama*, 316; *Montgomery Advertiser*, Jan. 7, 1866.

To James Harlan[1]

Washington, November 14th 1865.

I have learned from the Commissioners sent by me to treat with the Indians,[2] whose country borders on the Missouri river and its tributaries, that two of my red children—Nootay-u-hah or Short Gun and the brother of Nootay-u-hah of the Blackfeet tribe of the Sioux, or Dakotah, nation, have rescued two white women from my enemies, and gave their two horses in exchange for them.

I am greatly pleased with this honorable and friendly conduct of Nootay-u-hah and his brother, and direct that one hundred silver dollars be given to him and that one hundred silver dollars be given to his brother, to enable each one to buy for himself another horse.

I also direct that fifty silver dollars be given to each to pay him for his trouble in rescuing these white women and sending them to the white people. And, as a memento of my perpetual friendship for Nootay-u-hah and his brother, so long as they remain friendly with my white children, I direct that a silver medal be given to each of them with a suitable inscription, that all my red children and all my white children, when they look upon it, may know that their Great Father at Washington is greatly pleased with Nootay-u-hah and Nootay-u-hah's brother.

I, also, write my name on this paper, and direct that it be given to Nootay-u-hah, and a duplicate of it to his brother, that they may know that the silver money and the medals have been sent by me to them from Washington.[3]

Andrew Johnson   President U.S.

DS, Ira Goldberg, Beverly Hills, Cal.

1. This document was sent to the Secretary of the Interior for forwarding to Wa Mu de Kta, a Blackfoot chief.

2. In August 1865 Johnson appointed a group of civilians and military officers, led by South Dakota governor Newton Edmunds, to negotiate with various factions of the Sioux. Nine treaties, including one with the Blackfeet, were signed and subsequently ratified by Congress. Herbert S. Schell, *History of South Dakota* (Lincoln, Neb., 1975 [1961]), 86–87; *Washington Evening Star*, Mar. 31, 1866.

3. Another copy of this document, found in the archives of the South Dakota State Historical Society, is endorsed "For Short Gun's son, viz: Chista Tokia."

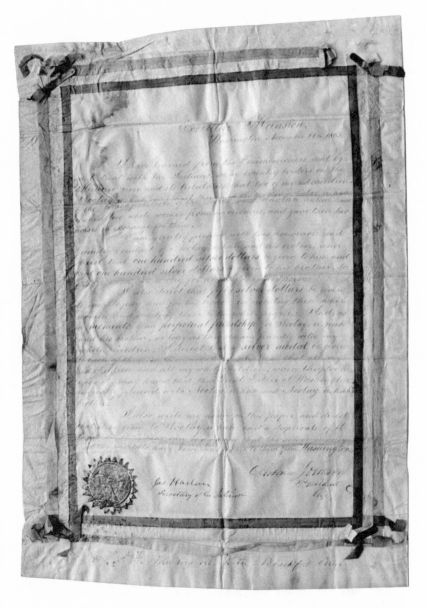

Presidential Letter of Reward to Sioux Brothers
Courtesy Ira Goldberg, Beverly Hills, California

From Benjamin G. Humphreys

Jackson, Miss., Nov 14th 1865.

The pleasing duty has been imposed upon me of transmiting to your excellency, the accompanying "Memorial"[1] with the request that you forward one copy to our friend Jefferson Davis.

In early youth—in schoolboy days I learned to love him for those sterling and manly qualities of head and heart, so prominently displayed throughout his long and illustrious career—A love that has outlived a long life of political opposition and which no misfortune that may befall him, no lapse of time can efface—and now that the holy aspirations of his pure and lofty spirit are blasted, and he pines in gloomy confinement for offences, in which I and thousands of Mississippians participated—every impulse of my heart prompts me to join in the sentiment and prayer of the Memorial.

Let Mississippi be his quiet home. Let Mississippians be his guard and security.

Benjn. G. Humphreys   Governor of Mississippi

ALS, DNA-RG94, Amnesty Papers, Jefferson Davis, Pets. to A. Johnson.

1. Humphreys enclosed a florid memorial, adopted unanimously by the Mississippi legislature, asking for the "liberation" of Jefferson Davis. The legislators asserted that the "attempted revolution was the people's work, and Jefferson Davis was but their chosen instrument." Amnesty Papers, Jefferson Davis, Pets. to A. Johnson, RG94, NA.

To Oliver P. Morton

Washington, D.C., Nov 14th 1865.

Jurisdiction is one of the questions which has been much in our way.[1] The place of trial must be determined hereafter. If the Court and Jury find true Bills against him, it would not interfere with a trial at any other place.

Bills have been found against him at Some two or three places in Tennessee, and in this District.

Andrew Johnson

Tel, DNA-RG107, Tels. Sent, President, Vol. 2 (1865).

1. Morton had wired Johnson that "If there is no question of jurisdiction in the way" Jefferson Davis could be tried in Indiana for the raid by John Hunt Morgan under his authority. Morton to Johnson, Nov. 14, 1865, Tels. Recd., President, Vol. 4 (1865–66), RG107, NA.

From Moses F. Odell

New York, Naval Office, Nov 14" 1865

Dear Sir

Knowing your great personal regard for Hon Preston King, collector it is with great sadness that I assume the duty of informing you that we are under most serious apprehensions as to his welfare.

He has been mentally depressed for some 2 weeks past. His nervous system seemed entirely prostrated. He left a few days since for his Home in Ogdenburg, returned to this city on Saturday last. The young man that came with him told me that on Saturday night & Sunday his bad symtoms all returned, on Monday evening at 7 oclock he left his room to take as he said a short walk. We have heard nothing of him since. We have made use of all the means within our control to find him.[1] So far with no success. We are hoping for the best. He has allowed the responsibility of his office both personal, and to the Govt to have undue influence upon his mind. It produced mental depression. Will advise you at once of the result of our efforts.

M. F. Odell

P.S. Since writing we learn he went to the Hoboken Ferry, and jumped from the Boat. Two children saw him describe him fully. To day his Hat is found and Mr. Terwillager[2] his clk and Mr. Usher[3] my Deputy both identify it as Mr. King's.[4]

M.F.O.

ALS, DLC-JP.
1. Odell also telegraphed Johnson to ask if King was in Washington. Odell to Johnson, Nov. 14, 1865, Johnson Papers, LC.
2. James Terwilliger (*fl*1883), Syracuse resident and longtime clerk of the New York Senate (*c*1855–69), by 1868 became secretary of the Republican State Committee in New York. *U.S. Off. Reg.* (1865), 94; Syracuse directories (1854–83); James A. Garfield to Terwilliger, Sept. 14, 1868, James A. Garfield Papers, LC.
3. William Usher (*fl*1867) was deputy naval officer for New York City. *U.S. Off. Reg.* (1861–67).
4. That same afternoon Odell wired Johnson that King had drowned on the evening of November 13. Odell to Johnson, Nov. 14, 1865, Johnson Papers, LC.

From Joseph C. Bradley

(*Private*)

Huntsville Ala   Novbr 15 1865

Politically our State has gone wild. Our Legislature will be composed 3/4 of officers & privates from the Confederate Army. Every Member of Congress elected Cannot take the oath of office. They become candidates knowing this fact, and were elected by the prejudices of the people aganist the United States Government. The impression

Secretary of the Treasury
Hugh McCulloch
*Courtesy Johnson-Bartlett
Collection, Greeneville*

Preston King,
Collector of New York
*Courtesy Johnson-Bartlett
Collection, Greeneville*

has been made, and reports circulated, that you had stated, that the oath of office would not be required. I have denied that you would make such a declaration to any man, that your known prudence & present position would forbid you saying that much to any man. In every district in our State men of ability & unblemished characters were Candidates who could have taken the Oath,—but they were premeditatedly & overwhelmingly defeated, they were denounced as Traitors to the South—and the prejudices of the people arrayed against them. In this district J M Sheid late of Tennessee who you know well I think was elected to Congress.[1] He was with me at the Charleston Convention in 1860, and with Bob Mathews[2] & other Delegates from Tennessee pretended to be your friend—but when I called on J C Burch Andrew Ewing[3] & others—at the instance of North Western Delegates, to put your name fully before the Convention—none of them would stand up squarely except Genl Millikin[4] of East Tennessee. Now Sheid has made the impression among the "Fire Eaters" in our District, that he had received or seen a letter from you that if he was elected he could take his seat—altho he could not take the oath. Thomas J Foster who you know I believe is elected in the adjoining District. The impression and report has also gone out from him, that you are to obtain his seat in Congress for him. Foster ran against some of the best Union men in the State—and both him and J M Sheid have been elected—by the enemies of the Federal Government. This fact you will ascertain in Decr next. Foster owes me a debt—and I am keeping along as well as I can with him—but let me assure you that I have no political Confidence in him, and neither have I in C C Langdon[5] of the Mobile District, who urged the raising of the "Black Flag" in the rebellion, and the arrest & imprisonment of every Union man in the State. Genl Battle[6] of the Chambers & Barbour District is fresh out of the rebel army & was opposed by as good a union man as ever lived in the U.S. He is a near relative of Eli & J Gill Shorter,[7] who you have pardoned, & of course they done all they could to elect Battle. His opponent was Col George Reese[8] of Chambers an undeviating and uncompromiseing Union Man. All the Secessionists voted for Battle & elected him in the face of the "Test Oath." Major Freeman[9] of the rebel army has defeated Benj Gardner[10] of the Montgomery District one of the best Union men in the State, and I here make the prediction that not a single secessionist round & about Montgomery who you have pardoned voted for Gardner. Columbus W Lee[11] of the Perry District one of the truest Union men in the State, has been defeated by Jos. Taylor[12] a man who has been doing all he could for the Confederate Cause. So you see our State will send a Delegation to Congress—not one of whom can take the oath of office. We have plenty of able men in each District, who can & would if elected take the oath,—and I pray you for the good of the whole Country, & for the benefit of the Union Men, & the Union sentiment, in the South, & particularly in our State, not be beleive any man from Alabama, when he or they will say to you that suitable men for Congress who can take the oath cannot be found in the South or particularly in Alabama. I am excluded therefore as your friend I can & will tell you the truth—and let me assure you that I have changed my mind in regard to men & things since I last wrote you, for not 1/4 of the ["]Fire Eaters" that you have pardoned will prove true to the Government, whenever they get a chance to hit the Government a blow. As a southern man I am truly sorry to have it to Confess to you, that there is a great want of sincerity on the part of our people towards the Government, and if by your influence you obtain the repeal of the test oath,—for the next few sessions of Congress—you may live to see the day that you will regret it. Even if you should not desire to be again elected President of the United States,—your future name & history besides that of your family demands that you be not deceived by protestations from the South of friendship to you politically.

Now My Dear Sir, notice my predictions. If the statement made by Major Stearns [13] of Massts. of a conversation between you & him is true, (which I heartily approve of) you will have but few political friends in the South if our Members of Congress are permited to take their seats in Decr. next. The mere fact of you saying that if you were in Tennessee—that you would be in favor of qualified Negro suffrage, is enough for these Southern people not only to Condemn you while liveing—but will try to blacken your name when dead. The only way to cure these Southern people, is to make them send men to Congress who Can take the oath, & whenever you depart from this Course you will regret it.

I am a native of the south, & I think I fully understand our people. They still have "Nigger" on the brain, and if you give them the least chance, they will try to reestablish slavery, if they have to revolt against the Government. Never allow a State to be restored to the Union until its Legislature accepts of the Constitutional amendment forever abolishing Slavery—repudiates Rebel War debts, and passes such Laws as will allow the Negro to live like a "Freedman." If our States should be restored in Decr. next, you will have trouble in 12 months with Some of the Southern States in regard to the Negro. Make them do right before they get back into the Union,—for if you do not, they will never do it, without more bloodshed. Negros must be heard in our Courts or their Condition will be worse than that of Slavery. Their evidence in our Courts should be on the same footing as that of the white man. If this is not allowed by the differt State Legislatures before our Members of Congress are admited to their seats it will never be done in your day or mine. This County & many others around us have elected men to our Legislature pledged to vote against the Constitutional Amendment. We had a warm Contest for State Senator in this County between D C Humphreys for the admendment & Genl. John N Drake against

it. Drake defeated Humphreys by 413 majority. In the last few days the
friends of Drake, among whom were many men who you have pardoned, have become arlamed—and have held a meeting at our Court
House to endorse your policy. Genl. Drake was present and made a
speech & declared he never would vote for the amendment, & the meeting adjourned without passing any instructions to him to vote for
it—but expect to deceive you by some general or flimsy resolutions. Do
not be deceived by such men for they are not acting sincere & I have
told them so. The proceedings of the meeting will be sent you by the
Chairman [14] one of the bitterest Secessionist in the State & one who is
not the friend of your restoration policy. The same men all voted for
Revd. J R Morris [15] & J M Sheid for Congress—the former declaring
from the public stand, that any man who would take the test oath was
a Black hearted Tory to the South. The latter exulting & exciteing the
prejudices of the people by declaring, that he had to flee from his own
State for the sake of the Confederacy & that he was a true Rebel &
gloried in haveing been so—& would again take the same Course if it
ever become necessary for the South.

It is very strange that the ["]Mail News Paper" at Montgomery
should have all the public printing [16]—when it is out against the Constitutional Amendment, and the Advocate published in this place, the
only paper, that sustains your policy in every respect is debared from
any of the public printing. If Govr. Parsons has any thing to do with
this printing business—he is not acting in good faith to the Union
element of Ala.

The United States Districy Atty J Q Smith is here preparing for his
Court. You made a good selection in appointing him to the important
office he holds. He is your friend, & the friend of the Federal Government. I have only seen him for a few minutes as he is very much engaged with the U S Marshal & the Clerk of his Court. [17] I learned before
he reached here that perhaps you had received complaints against him [18]
from South Ala. Do not beleive a word against him—until you know
the facts. He is doing his duty & as long as he continues to stand up for
the Government, they the "Sore Heads" & fire Eaters' will try to destroy him in your estimation. Smith is an efficient officer of the Government & he is the man for the place, and will do his duty regardless of
Consequences. I give Hon P M Dox of this place a letter to you [19]—and
I hope you read it. It explains itself. Dox is not reliable. He is courting
& affiliateing with the Secessionists to be elected U S Senator. If he
should be elected and goes to Washington you will be able to read him
at once.

"The Freedmens" Bureau are doing well in this part of Ala. I have
been called in very often, and I can assure you that the Superintendent
here Major Goodfellow [20] is trying to do strict justice to both whites &
Blacks. No more suitable or more Competent man could be found to

fill this office than Majr Goodfellow, & I hope he will be retained here for the benefit of all classes. I do not care if Ala is restored to her proper place in the Union it will be necessary for the protection of the Colored people that this Bureau should be continued for 1 or 2 years. For my own satisfaction & to learn the truth, I frequently visit Majr Goodfellows Court Room to listen to trials between whites & Blacks, *and in every* instance he has decided according to Justice & Equity, & none of the parties had any right to Complain.

For the protection of union men in North it will be necessary to keep some U S troops in this part of the state for their protection. Threats are continuely made that as soon as Troops are removed that union men shall also leave the Country. If Judge Dox has said differently to you—he has made wrong statements—he will be safe for he is doing every thing possible to make himself personally acceptable to the Secessionist & disaffected—but you never hear him open his mouth in favor of the Government or your policy but is continuely finding fault with the Government to please his secession friends.

A very strange & remarkable occurence has taken place in our State under the administration of Govr. Parsons, and if it is allowed to stand great injustice will have been done to us union men who have in good faith come forward & took the Amnasty Oath, to make ourselves citizens of the United States. In the late election for Govr. Members of Congress, State Legislature, & State officers the amnasty oath has been laid aside or dispensed with, and any man & every man has been allowed to vote. Do you intend for men who are not Citizens of the U S—and men who have declared they never would take your Amnasty Oath, come forward to the polls & vote for Members of Congress & elect them to seats in the National Congress, in defiance to your known restoration policy? Why Sir Thousands of men have voted in this State who have defiantly stated that they would never take the amnasty oath, and these same men have elected State Senators & Representatives to our Legislature who will assemble next Monday in Montgomery to elect United States Senators. Is this according to your policy—or is the State Government in the hands of the friends of the Federal Government? There is hardly a friend of the National Government returned to our Legislature, and if I were the Provisional Govr. of Ala at this time with your sanction, I would revolve every thing back into the Condition it was, when you appointed Govr. Parsons & take a fresh start, and so shape a course as would place our state in the keeping of the friends of the Federal government, & in accordance with the policy you have laid down for the rebellious States.

Our State has hid from the Government and you a large war debt, in which great injustice has been done unprotected woman & children. There was a Law passed by our Legislature, authoriseing Exr. Admr. Guardians & Trustees to invest the funds of their Estates & Wards in

Confederate Treasury Notes or Bonds or in State Treasury Notes or Bonds. This was done to aid the rebellion by appreciateing these Securities,—and our Convention revived this Law—& by its action have robed a large number of our woman & children, and destroyed or rendered insolvent a large number of Estates. This is a part of the war debt of Ala & other Southern States & should be declared null & void,— before any State is restored. Now My Dear Sir, I have wrote you this long letter—because I beleived it my duty to do so. I feel more than common interest in your success. I want no office, at your hands,—but must frankly say that I have never heard you utter a word politically nor have I ever read any thing from you—but what I sincerely approved of, which makes me feel more than passing respect & hope for your success. This letter for you individually & not as President.

Joseph C Bradley

ALS, DLC-JP.

1. James M. Sheid (c1814-fl1880), who had represented Coffee Co., Tenn., in the state senate during Johnson's tenure as governor, actually lost the 1865 congressional race. *BDTA*, 1: 665–66; 1880 Census, Ala., Calhoun, Beat 2, 6th Enum. Dist., 64. See Bradley's retraction in Bradley to Johnson, Nov. 27, 1865.

2. Shelbyville merchant Robert Mathews.

3. Burch, a Nashville editor, and Ewing, an attorney.

4. Sam Milligan. For an alternate assessment of the roles played by Mathews and Sheid during the Charleston convention, see William E. B. Jones to Johnson, May 15, 1860, *Johnson Papers*, 3: 599.

5. Charles C. Langdon (1805–1889) had been a Whig editor, Mobile mayor, state legislator, and member of the constitutional convention of 1865. Owen, *History of Ala.*, 4: 1008–9.

6. Cullen A. Battle (1829–1905) later removed to New Bern, N.C., where he edited a newspaper and served as mayor. Warner, *Gray*.

7. Barbour County secessionists Eli S. Shorter (1823–1879), formerly an aide to his brother and a Conservative Democrat in Congress (1855–59), and John G. Shorter (1818–1872), Alabama's governor (1861–63), were pardoned by Johnson on September 5 and November 4, 1865, respectively. Warner and Yearns, *BRCC*; Owen, *History of Ala.*, 4: 1551–52; Benjamin Fitzpatrick to Johnson, July 20, 1865; John G. Shorter to Johnson, July 8, 1865, Amnesty Papers (M1003, Roll 10), Ala., Eli S. Shorter and John Gill Shorter, RG94, NA; *House Ex. Docs.*, 40 Cong., 2 Sess., No. 15, p. 34 (Ser. 1330).

8. Reese (c1796–1877) formerly sat in the legislatures of South Carolina, Georgia, and Alabama. Owen, *History of Ala.*, 4: 1420–21; 1860 Census, Ala., Chambers, So. Div., West Point, 23.

9. George C. Freeman (1825–1866), a Lowndes Co., Ala., planter, attorney, and delegate to the constitutional convention of 1865. Owen, *History of Ala.*, 3: 614–15.

10. Gardner (1814–1902), a former journalist who resigned his Confederate commission early in the war, was elected state attorney general on the Republican ticket in 1872. Ibid., 632.

11. Lea (1800–1869), a former Douglas Democrat who stood "decidedly" against secession, had been pardoned by Johnson on August 11, 1865. Brewer, *Alabama*, 491–92; Lea to Johnson, July 27, 1865, Amnesty Papers (M1003, Roll 7), Ala., Columbus W. Lee, RG94, NA.

12. Joseph W. Taylor (1820-fl1872) had represented Greene County in both houses of the Alabama legislature in the 1840s and 1850s and was later a newspaper editor in Tuscaloosa. Brewer, *Alabama*, 267–68.

13. See Interview with George L. Stearns, Oct. 3, 1865.

14. Edwin L. Anthony [Antony] (c1815–1876), a Huntsville physician, forwarded a copy of the resolutions to the President. 1860 Census, Ala., Madison, Huntsville, 48;

Gandrud, *Alabama Records*, 71: 85; 161: 99; Madison County, Ala., Citizens to Johnson, Nov. 18, 1865, Johnson Papers, LC.
    15. Joseph R. Morris (1826-*fl*1876) was a Cumberland Presbyterian minister and the uncle of one of Frank B. Gurley's men. Gandrud, *Alabama Records*, 48: 47; 54: 69; 124: 88; 1860 Census, Ala., Madison, SE Div., New Hope, 24; (1870), Twp. No. 2, Range No. 1 W., 28. See Joseph Holt to Johnson, Jan. 5, 1866.
    16. See Parsons to Johnson, Oct. 4, 1865.
    17. Edward E. Douglass (1822–1881), who had formerly served as sheriff under the Confederate regime, was the marshal, and John H. King was the clerk. Gandrud, *Alabama Records*, 131: 63; 161: 57; Bradley et al. to Johnson, Nov. 30, 1865, Court-Martial Records, MM-1326, RG153, NA.
    18. See Smith to Johnson, Oct. 23, 1865.
    19. See Bradley to Johnson, Oct. 13, 1865, Johnson Papers, LC.
    20. Thomas M. Goodfellow (*c*1822-*fl*1868), a Methodist Episcopal clergyman who had been a U.S. Army chaplain (1861–65), later served in the Alabama legislature. 1860 Census, Iowa, Pottawattomie, 4th Ward, Council Bluff City, 45; Goodfellow to O. O. Howard, June 1, 1865, Records of the Commr., Lets. Recd. (M752, Roll 15), RG105, NA; *Huntsville Advocate*, July 17, 1868.

From Pleasant M. and John H. Craigmiles[1]

Griffin Ga   Nov 15 1865.
We have stored a lot of Cotton here. Have paid the Revenue & got permit to ship. The military refuse to let it go. Please give them proper instructions by telegh.[2]

H M Craigmills[*sic*]

J Craigmills[*sic*]

Tel, DLC-JP.
    1. The Craigmiles brothers formerly resided near Greeneville, Tenn. Pleasant M. was a merchant in Dalton, Ga., before moving to Cleveland, Tenn., in the 1850s. John H. (1825–1899) owned a San Francisco shipping business prior to relocating in Cleveland in 1857. A Confederate commissary agent, he later worked as a banker and real estate developer. Penelope J. Allen, *Leaves From the Family Tree* (Easley, S.C., 1982), 50–51; *Chattanooga Times*, Jan. 8, 1899; Earnest L. Ross, comp., *Historical Cemetery Records of Bradley County, Tennessee* (2 vols., Cleveland, Tenn., 1973), 1: 76.
    2. Within a few hours after receiving this dispatch, the President inquired directly of the commanding officer at Griffin: "By what authority do you detain" the Craigmiles' cotton? Lt. Col. Charles F. Springer, of the 150th Ill. Inf., replied that the order originated from his superior officer, as well as a treasury agent in Atlanta. On November 23 Johnson asked the elder Craigmiles if his cotton had been "delivered up," to which the latter and his brother responded in the affirmative and expressed their "renewed obligations." Johnson to [Springer], Nov. 17, 1865; Johnson to P. M. Craigmiles, Nov. 23, 1865, Tels. Sent, President, Vol. 2 (1865), RG107, NA; Springer to Johnson, Nov. 20; P. M. Craigmiles & Bros. to Johnson, Nov. 25, 1865, Johnson Papers, LC.

From John A. Dix[1]
Private.

New York   15. Nov. 1865.
My dear sir:
    The custom-house in this City has for years been a sink of corruption. Mr. King began a vigorous system of reform, which his deplorable death has unhappily interrupted. I do not often intrude suggestions

upon you. But I cannot forbear to express the earnest hope that no hacknied politician or subservient follower of any political clique may be appointed to this office.[2] He should be an independent and a fearless man, who is not trameled by associations, which will disqualify him for carying out to completion what Mr. King commenced. Under any other than such a person there will be great danger that existing abuses, instead of being corrected, will be aggravated to the serious prejudice of the public interests and the honor of your administration. This consideration is my only motive in writing, and I trust it will need no apology.

John A. Dix

ALS, DNA-RG56, Appts., Customs Service, Collector, New York, John A. Dix.
1. The former general was now a candidate for the New York collectorship. Among other recommendations, see Edwards Pierrepont to Johnson, Nov. 15, 1865, Appts., Customs Service, Collector, New York, John A. Dix, RG56, NA.
2. See Henry A. Smythe to Johnson, Dec. 18, 1865.

From John K. Brady[1]

Balto Md   Nov 16 1865

Dear Sir

I have for sale a very rare & important Autograph note of Gen And Jackson written by him in 1797 to Gov Savier with whom he was to fight a duel or perhaps *did* fight one.[2] This note relates in some measure to the duel and what makes it more interesting is that it was carried by hand from Gen Jackson to Gov Savier therefore the world is ignorant of its contents. It is dated Nashville May 13 1797. I will send it for your examination if you should so desire. The price is $20.00.[3]

John Brady

ALS, DLC-JP.
1. Brady (c1818-c1883) was an "antiquarian book seller." 1860 Census, Md., Baltimore, Baltimore, 3rd Ward, 249; Baltimore directories (1858–84).
2. John Sevier (1745–1815) was the first governor of Tennessee and subsequently a member of Congress. He and Jackson clashed several times, but they never fought a formal duel. BDAC; Robert V. Remini, *Andrew Jackson and the Course of American Empire, 1767–1821* (New York, 1977), 100–102, 117–23.
3. Johnson apparently did not purchase the document, which is probably that now in the Henry M. Breckenridge Collection, University of Pittsburgh Library. See Sam B. Smith et al., eds., *The Papers of Andrew Jackson* (2 vols., Knoxville, 1980–   ), 1: 145.

From John Cochrane

Albany   Nov 16th 1865

Dear Sir

The struggle which unquestionably is now proceeding between rival political interests, for the Collectorship of the Port of New York induces me to trouble you with a few lines. I would not do so, were it not that

I am quite confident that upon this appointment will men and politicians in this State begin to arrange their action for the future.

While the democratic party in the late election took an unexceptionable platform, the people saw in its leading supporters their old enemies—the Copperheads. The honest democrats, therefore suspecting a trick, refused their support and the whole concern, hypocritical, loyal democrat, and honestly loyal democrat, Copperhead, and War Generals were ploughed under together.

This defeat, effectually winnows the wheat from the tares. The Copperheads have been excised from the democrats, and these last are ready for a coalition with those of the successful party, with whom they can assimilate and are willing to join.

The successful party is rent by two factions—the one in the interest of Mr Seward—the other in opposition to him. The purified democracy can unite with the last. They will not with the former. And those opposed to Mr Seward within the ranks of the present Union party are willing to unite with the purged democracy. These opponents of Mr Seward Comprise the Secret loyal leagues of New York, having enrolled a numerical preponderance of their (the Union) party, and with the democrats referred to, can sweep the State easily. Now these two classes of politicians are desirous of sustainig you and of organisig under your auspices. They will do so, if permitted, but will oppose you eventually if not permitted. They will construe the appointment to be made of collector at New York, whether freindly or unfriendly to them, as determinative of their attitude of coherence or opposition.

I am not Mr President projecting speculations upon your attention. I write what I know unqualifiedly from gentlemen who are authorized to speak posetively and unconditionally on these subjects.

My conversation has been free and unreserved with Dean Richmond and also with Waldo Hutchins[1] of New York City upon this Matter. Others of equal weight give their entire assent.

If these are facts, you will therefore percieve, that upon your action depends grave interests. Would it not be wise to await somewhat the developement of events before making the appointment. The customs will not suffer, as during the interval, Mr Clinch,[2] the Asst Collector, is, by law, the Collector of the port with full power; and he is excellently well qualified. The political parties will have more distinctly signified their course and you will, the more satisfactorily, be able to determine who are truly your friends.

I repeat what I have said to you, that a more important personage to you, does not exist in the political world, than the Collector of New York. And on him above all men, should you be able to rely. The rumour that the radical (so called) men in the Union Convention in this State, were opposed to your policy is false. I saw the resolutions subsequently, which they proposed to report to the Convention. They were more decisively in favour of you, & your policy, than those actually adopted. But they contained no endorsement of Mr Seward. If, as I think, these radicles, constituted of the young men of the Union Party, and of the loyal leagues, are your Supporters, then their approaching coalition with the loyal democrats who favour your policy, would establish your position impeccably in New York. There is *no possibility* of a union between the democrats proper and Mr Sewards friends. You may rest securely assured of this.

I had engaged with Mr Hutchins to go on and see you. Dean Richmond also has desired me to go on, and say thus much to you. But, as I am now actually engaged in our Courts, I must be, for the present, at least, contented with writing to you. Mr Richmond desired me to say also, that he would signify to you (if desirable) in writing that my appointment to the vacancy would gratify his friends. I introduce the fact, not to subserve his personal end but to denote to you his disposition to continue with his political associates, among your friends. He says also, that *you* may abandon your policy but that *they will not.*

My opinion, (diffidently expressed) is that the Selection Should fall on no active partisan, but on one, who, without being, in that respect, distinctively marked, embraces the qualities of Unionism, loyalty and freedom of objection to both Union men and the pacified democracy. There are so many of men, that I feel no apprehension, when saying thus much, that: I will be misunderstood as soliciting for myself—*I am no office seeker.*

Permit me also to suggest for your consideration whether you would not materially strengthen your position in coming conflicts by referring courteously to Mr Bennett[3] for the expression of an opinion as to the selection. I have neither seen nor consulted him regarding it, nor should I: but I think the attention would attach him cordially to you throughout.

I have written rapidly and as thoughts have arisen and with no other view, Mr President, than of, perhaps, suggesting something of use to you at this crisis.

As to the event of our late election I am rejoiced. I could not act with the democrats as their lead. I was afraid of Copperheadism which I think, at last, has been effectually paralysed. Doubtless Mr Hutchins, will shortly see you. I should say here that I agree with what he designs to propose.

John Cochrane

ALS, DNA-RG56, Appts., Customs Service, Collector, New York, John Cochrane.

1. Hutchins (1822–1891) was a park commissioner (1857–69, 1887–91) who was later elected to Congress (1879–85). *BDAC.*

2. Despite the opposition of Thurlow Weed and others, Johnson appointed Charles P. Clinch (1797–1880), a longtime employee of the Customs Service (1838–76), as acting collector. *DAB; New York Times,* Nov. 21, 1865.

3. James Gordon Bennett.

From Thomas J. Devine[1]

New Orleans   November 16th 1865

The petition of Thomas J Devine, who resides in San Antonio Texas, respectfully represents:

That petitioner was Confederate States Judge of the District Court of Texas, and is one of those who are excepted from the provisions of the Amnesty proclamation of your Excellency of the 29th May 1865; he was one of the Commissioners of the State of Texas, who took possession of the property of the United States Government, after the Secession Ordinance was passed by the State of Texas[2] & he is worth over twenty thousand D'll'rs.

That petitioner prepared at San Antonio, an application for pardon which he forwarded to Governor Hamilton at Austin; that shortly after doing so petitioner was arrested at his residence, and he did not receive the same:[3] that he is now in New Orleans, en route for Fort Jackson, on the Mississippi, where he is to be confined by order of Major General P. H. Sheridan,[4] hence this petition is prepared at this place.

Petitioner yields and has yielded since the war terminated willing allegiance to the United States Government, and pledges himself to observe the Oath of allegiance that he has taken a copy of which accompanies this petition. He, therefore asks at the hands of your Excellency a special pardon, and an order for his release from imprisonment.[5]

Thos. J. Devine

LS, DNA-RG94, Amnesty Papers (M1003, Roll 52), Tex., Thomas Devine.

1. Devine (1820–1890), a native of Canada, emigrated in 1843 to Texas, where he served as a state district judge (1851–61) and presided over the Confederate court for the western district of Texas. He later returned to railroad development, was appointed to the Texas Supreme Court (1874–75), and became a regent for the University of Texas (1881–82). Webb et al., *Handbook of Texas*, 1: 495; Davis and Grobe, *New Encyclopedia of Texas*, 3: 1513; Mary O. Meredith, "The Life and Work of Thomas Jefferson Devine" (M.A. thesis, University of Texas at Austin, 1930), passim.

2. Devine, together with Samuel A. Maverick and others, negotiated the surrender of all U.S. troops and property in Texas in February 1861, before the secession ordinance had been approved in a public referendum and officially adopted. Ibid., 40–52. See Hamilton to Johnson, Sept. 12, 1865.

3. Fearing arrest, Devine fled to Mexico in June 1865, but three months later returned to San Antonio, where he was arrested. He was released on parole after posting bond and signing a loyalty oath. Devine subsequently applied for pardon, but his petition was not forwarded until after James W. Throckmorton took office as governor in August 1866. Devine to Johnson, Oct. 21, 1865, with endorsement of Throckmorton, Aug. 28, 1866; Loyalty Oath of Thomas J. Devine, Oct. 6, 1865, Amnesty Papers (M1003, Roll 52), Tex., Thomas Devine, RG94, NA; Meredith, "Devine," 74–76, "Appendix": 47–48, 54–55.

4. In November 1865 federal authorities arrested Devine again in San Antonio and attempted to expedite him to New Orleans but "by accident" left him in Houston. He reported on his own to officials in Galveston and was incarcerated in Jackson Barracks in New Orleans. Meredith, "Devine," 76–77, "Appendix": 50.

5. Sheridan's endorsement on this letter recommended that Devine "be among the last recipients of the Presidents clemency." Those who petitioned in favor of pardoning

Devine included Gov. J. Madison Wells, who asserted that "clemency in this case could be exercised without detriment to the State or good morals." Devine was released in June 1866 but not pardoned until May 1867. Endorsement of Sheridan, Nov. 20, 1865; Wells to Johnson, Nov. 17, 1865; Lemuel D. Evans to Johnson, May 1, 1867, Amnesty Papers (M1003, Roll 52), Tex., Thomas Devine, RG94, NA; Meredith, "Devine," 71–73, 77–78, "Appendix": 29–44, 59–60.

From Horace Greeley

New York, Nov. 16, 1865.

Dear Sir:

Hitherto, I have resisted every entreaty to address you on the subject of Pardons, not only because of the detestable brokerage in pardons which has sprung up, but because I think your course has been eminently generous and merciful. But, learning that Mr. S. R. Mallory of Florida is still in prison, I write to express a hope that he may at least be set at liberty and thus allowed to rejoin his family. I am very sure no public good is subserved by his imprisonment.[1]

Horace Greeley.

ALS, NHi-Andrew Johnson Papers.

1. Mallory received a "partial parole" on March 10, 1866. Durkin, *Stephen R. Mallory*, 379–80.

From Benjamin G. Humphreys

Jackson Miss   Nov 16 1865.

Dispatch from President Mobile & Ohio RR[1] says Passenger train of cars was attacked on evening of fourteenth & Possession taken by garrison of Colored troops at Lauderdale Springs.[2] Ladies insulted & abused. Officers in Command unable to Control them. The Legislature has memoralized for removal of US Troops from the State[3] & appear willing to extend to Freedmen the right to testify in Courts, if assured that the troops would be withdrawn. Members fear that one Concession will only lead to others. What assurances Can I give on the subject?[4]

Benj Humphreys   Govr of Miss

Tel, DLC-JP.

1. Milton Brown also reported the incident to the President. See Brown to Johnson, Nov. 15, 1865, Lets. Recd., Executive (M494, Roll 75), RG107, NA.

2. A detachment from the 59th Inf., USCT, under orders from Col. George M. Ziegler, commanding the post at Meridian, Miss., stopped the train to remove confiscated cotton being shipped to Mobile. Brown to McCulloch, Nov. 20, 1865; O. S. Holland to J. P. Fresenis, Nov. 15, 1865, Johnson Papers, LC; *Off. Army Reg.: Vols.*, 8: 225.

3. The memorial, adopted by the Mississippi legislature on November 8, 1865, did not reach the President's office until the end of the month. Johnson Papers, LC.

4. See Johnson to Humphreys, Nov. 17, 1865.

From Memphis Citizens[1]

Memphis   Nov 16 1865.

On behalf of the citizens of Memphis & the planters of the County we petition that for the present at least the Freedmens Bureau will be kept under military authority. We regard placing it under civil rule as impolitic & neither to the interest of the Freedmen or planter. In Gen Dudley[2] we recognize the able & judicious officer, one that has given satisfaction to all parties concerned. Under present orders his functions will cease this week & the community at large will be grateful to have him retained.[3] Send an answer through Gen Smith.[4]

Tel, DLC-JP.

1. Nine names were given at the conclusion of the telegram, including William M. Farrington, John W. Leftwich, Samuel Tate, and Samuel P. Walker.

2. Nathan A.M. Dudley.

3. The Freedmen's Bureau commissioner, Gen. O. O. Howard, was in Memphis, while Gen. Clinton B. Fisk, the assistant commissioner for Tennessee, was in Washington during the time of this controversy over the retention of Dudley. Upon receipt of this telegram, Johnson instructed that it "be shown to the Sec of War & Genl Fisk." Having already received a copy of the dispatch, Fisk replied that Dudley would remain in office until he, Fisk, had a chance to conduct a personal investigation. A Memphis paper, which earlier in the week claimed that Dudley had been removed from office, reported on the 18th that Dudley had been ordered retained by General Fisk. A few days later, Fisk had an interview with the President. *Memphis Appeal*, Nov. 14, 16, 18, 1865; *Cincinnati Commercial*, Nov. 24, 1865; Fisk to Johnson, Nov. 17, 1865, attached to the Memphis Citizens document.

4. John E. Smith endorsed the telegram, stating that the Bureau should remain under military authority until the rights of freedmen were fully protected by state law.

From Joseph C. Bradley

Huntsville Alabama   Novbr 17 1865

Mrs Margaret McClung[1] of Madison Co Ala. will send you through Miss Mary White,[2] her relative in Nashville Tennessee, a petition for pardon. Mrs McClung is the widow of the late Col James W Mc-Clung[3] of this place. He was a native of Knoxville Tennessee & you doubtless recollect the high character he attained before his death.

I have known Mrs McClung for many years and can willingly say to you that there is not a more high toned & honorable Lady than her that belongs to our State. She was very much opposed to the late rebellion & was among the few union Ladies in our place. When the war commenced—her sons[4] had to engage in it & as a kind mother she had to feel for them. I have told Mrs McClung that you would grant her a pardon[5] without the recommendation of Govr. Parsons. If not asking too much you will please return O H Bynums[6] pardon thro Miss White.

Joseph C Bradley

ALS, DNA-RG94, Amnesty Papers (M1003, Roll 7), Ala., Margaret McClung.

1. Margaret Patrick (b. 1819), whose estate on the eve of the war amounted to more than $100,000, was the third wife of James W. McClung. 1860 Census, Ala., Madison, Huntsville, 231; William McClung, *The McClung Genealogy* (Pittsburgh, 1904), 32.

2. Not further identified.

3. A native of Knoxville, Tenn., and nephew of Hugh Lawson White, McClung (1798–1848) was an Alabama legislator and presiding officer in both houses. Ibid., 30–32; Brewer, *Alabama*, 359–60.

4. William P. (1840-*fl*1904) and Frank A. McClung (1843-*fl*1904) had served the Confederacy as a 2nd lieutenant, Co. K, 49th Ala. Inf., and a private, Co. C, 4th (Russell's) Ala. Cav., respectively. McClung, *McClung Genealogy*, 32; CSR, RG109, NA.

5. Mrs. McClung obtained a pardon on the date Bradley's letter was received and filed, December 9, 1865. Amnesty Papers (M1003, Roll 7), Ala., Margaret McClung, RG94, NA.

6. Cotton planter Oakley H. Bynum (b. *c*1820), a prewar state representative and senator who currently served as a Freedmen's Bureau agent in Lawrence County, was granted his amnesty on November 28, 1865. James E. Saunders et al., *Early Settlers of Alabama* (New Orleans, 1899), 15; Owen, *History of Ala.*, 3: 276; 1860 Census, Ala., Lawrence, Northern Div., Courtland, 64; Bynum to Johnson, Nov. 9, 1865; Bradley to Johnson, Nov. 17, 1865, Amnesty Papers (M1003, Roll 2), Ala., Oakley H. Bynum, RG94, NA.

To Benjamin G. Humphreys

Washington, D.C., Nov 17th 1865.

The troops will be withdrawn from Mississippi, when in the opinion of the Government, that peace and order, and the Civil Authority has been restored and can be maintained, without them.[1] Every step will be taken while they are there, to enforce strict discipline and subordination to the Civil Authority.

There can be no other or greater assurance given, than has heretofore been on the part of the Federal Government. There is no concession required on the part of the people of Mississippi, or the Legislature, other than a loyal Compliance with the laws and Constitution of the United States, and the adoption of such measures, giving protection to all freedmen, or freemen, in person and property, without regard to Color, as will entitle them to resume all their Constitutional relations in the Federal Union.

The people of Mississippi may feel well assured that there is no disposition, arbitrarily, on the part of the Government, to dictate what their action should be, but on the Contrary, simply and kindly advise a policy that is believed will result in restoring all the relations which should exist between the States composing the Federal Union.

It is hoped that they will feel and appreciate the suggestions *herein* made for they are done in that spirit which should pervade the bosom of all who desire peace, harmony and a thorough restoration of the Union.

There must be confidence between the Government and the States. While the Government confides in the people—the people must have faith in the Government. This must be mutual and reciprocal, or all that has been done will be thrown away.

Andrew Johnson   President U.S.

Tel, DNA-RG107, Tels. Sent, President, Vol. 2 (1865).

1. Beginning in January 1866, all black regiments in Mississippi were mustered out over a four-month period, leaving only a small battalion of regular infantry in the state. Harris, *Presidential Reconstruction*, 77; James W. Garner, *Reconstruction in Mississippi* (Baton Rouge, 1968[1901]), 106–7.

To James Johnson[1]

Washington, D.C., Nov. 17th 1865.

I transmit by this days mail to you the order of the Qr. Mr. Gen'l. to Maj. Gen'l. Donaldson,[2] Chf. Q.M at Nashville, directing him to furnish transportation for you from Nashville, Tenn to Velasco Texas and from Velasco back to Nashville Tenn for yourself and four (4) other persons upon your application to him.[3]

Andrew Johnson.

Tel, DNA-RG107, Tels. Sent, President, Vol. 2 (1865).

1. Johnson (1838–1919), a "deputy keeper" at the Tennessee Penitentiary, was the son of the President's brother, William P. Johnson, who had died in Texas on October 24. About a week later the President had notified his nephews of their father's death. Hugh B. Johnston, *"William Patterson Johnson*: The Only Brother of President Andrew Johnson" (typescript, n.d., Andrew Johnson Project Files), 5; *Tenn. Senate Journal Appendix, Oct. 2, 1865-May 28, 1866*, 112; Johnson to Andrew Johnson, Jr., Nov. 1, 1865, Tels. Sent, President, Vol. 2 (1865), RG107, NA.

2. James L. Donaldson.

3. See Andrew Johnson, Jr. to Johnson, Dec. 23, 1865.

From Granville Moody[1]

Piqua Ohio   Novr. 17th 1865

Sir:

I take pleasure in sending you an Editoral[2] in our City paper from the pen of Mr. D M Fleming[3] the Gentleman who has the honor of nominating you for Vice President in advance of any Editor in the United States.

He is the Gentleman whom you appointed "Assessor of the 4th Congressional District in Ohio["] on my recommendation. He is more than meeting the expectations of his friends in the discharge of his Official duties.[4]

He has been very vigilant in bringing large amounts on the Tax list which have greatly increased the resources of the Government— amounts that have not hitherto been brought on said lists.

I presumed that you would like to hear from the appointment of Mr. Fleming and I am happy to assure you that he makes a most vigilant and reliable public Officer.

Your wise, firm and successful administration commands the commendation of Union men in this section of the country. You are making hosts of friends here and if an election for President should come off next week you would be elected President by an overwhelming majority.

The miserable Copperheads now think you are as bad as any Union man, and they would not toss a copper between you and Abraham Lincoln.

We rejoice in the wisdom given you from on high. Your just discriminations in the exercise of executive clemency command respect.

We remember that "That Mercy is above the sceptered sway. It is an attribute of God himself! And earthly power doth then show likest God's When Mercy seasons Justice."[5]

Still there are sins and *sinners*, who cannot be pardoned with safety to the Government; and whilst we do not advocate *vindictive* Justice in God or Man; Yet we do advocate a vindication of the majesty of the Laws; by which citizens of this Great Republic, shall know for all coming time; that *Treason is the highest crime* by receiving in the persons of its Chief actor, or actors, the startling telling penalty that shall make the ears of him that heareth it to tingle, viz Death—or everlasting banishment from our land, and her institutions; and the glory of their power—as God scored[6] *Satan* the Jeff Davis of his own immediate presence.

Hoping that you a Southern man with *National Principles*, will be a willing instrument in bringing about that glorious crisis

> "When all men's good shall be each man's rule
> And Universal peace be like a shaft of light
> Across the land
> And like a lane of beams athwart the sea
> Through all the circle of the golden year."[7]

Granville Moody

ALS, DNA-RG94, Amnesty Papers, Jefferson Davis, Pets. to A. Johnson.

1. Moody (1812–1887) commanded the 74th Ohio Vol. Inf. until he was severely wounded at Murfreesboro. After the war he resumed his work as a Methodist minister. Boatner, *CWD*.

2. Not found.

3. David M. Fleming (1827-*fl*1880) edited the *Piqua Enquirer*, which he renamed the *Journal* in 1860 when he switched from the Democratic to the Republican party. *The History of Miami County, Ohio* (Chicago, 1880), 587.

4. Fleming was removed in November 1866 but was reappointed by Johnson in July 1868 and served until February 1870. Ibid.; Appt. Bk. 4: 262, Ser. 6B, Johnson Papers, LC.

5. Slightly inaccurate rendering of Shakespeare's *Merchant of Venice*, Act IV, scene 1, line 184.

6. Scourged.

7. A slightly flawed version of lines from Alfred Lord Tennyson's *The Golden Year*.

From Thomas J. Noble

November 17, 1865, Powhatan Court House, Va.; ALS, DNA-RG56, Appts., Internal Revenue Service, Collector, Va., 4th Dist., Thomas J. Noble.

Strongly opposed to secession, Noble nonetheless went into the war with his volunteer company, serving as regimental quartermaster, and "did my whole duty to the So called Confederacy." He now asks a place in government so that he may support his family, "having been reduced to poverty by our late troubles." Noble observes that he, "while with Genl. Longstreet in E. Tennes at Greenville took particular care of your library & would not allow a book to be carried off or interrupted as long as I remained." [John H. Anderson received the appointment as collector.]

To William L. Sharkey

Washington, D.C., Nov 17th 1865.

Gov Sharkey has heretofore been notified, will continue to exercise any and all the functions of Provisional Governor of Mississippi. He will please report from time to time, what progress is being made in the restoration of the functions of the State, and make such suggestions, as he may deem proper, and calculated to accomplish the great work in which he is engaged.[1]

It is earnestly hoped that your Legislature will without delay place the State in an attitude which will enable her to resume all Constitutional relations between her and the Federal Government.

Let the Amendment to the Constitution of the United States, abolishing Slavery be adopted.[2] Let such laws be passed for the protection of freedmen, in person and property, as Justice and equity demand. The admission of negro testimony, they all being free, will be as much for the protection of the white man, as the Colored.[3]

I do hope that the Southern people will see the position that they now occupy, and avail themselves of the favorable opportunity of once more resuming all their former relations to the Government of the United States, and in so doing restore peace, prosperity, happiness, and fraternal love.

Governor Sharkey will please show this dispatch to B. G. Humphreys, Governor elect.

Andrew Johnson   President U.S.

Tel, DNA-RG107, Tels. Sent, President, Vol. 2 (1865).

1. Johnson's telegram was prompted by the recent experience of Gen. George H. Thomas, who had been sent to discover the intentions of the newly-elected legislature with respect to freedmen. Sharkey, assuming that Benjamin G. Humphreys, chosen governor in the October 2 election, was the state's executive, referred Thomas to Humphreys. When Thomas reported this response to Stanton, the President reassured Thomas that Sharkey had "not been relieved as Provisional Governor. . . . He will continue to act as such until he is relieved and his Successor acknowledged by the Authority

of the United States." On the other hand, at his "own discretion," Thomas might "confer with the Governor Elect, upon matters relating to, and promotive of restoration and the well being of the State." Harris, *Presidential Reconstruction*, 117, 133; Johnson to Thomas, Nov. 17, 1865, Tels. Sent, President, Vol. 2 (1865), RG107, NA; Stanton to Thomas, Nov. 17, 1865, Tels. Sent, Sec. of War (M473, Roll 90), RG107, NA.

2. See Johnson to Sharkey, Nov. 1, 1865.

3. See Robert S. Hudson to Johnson, Nov. 2, 1865.

From Robert J. Brent[1]

Baltimore   Nov 18/65

Dear Sir

This will be handed to you by Thos O. Moore ex Governor of Louisiana in whose behalf I had the honor of speaking to you some time ago. He now reports his presence in the country to you & does not press his application for Pardon at present, but asks that he may be allowed to return to his home & family upon his parol. No one in Louisiana can exercise more influence than Gov. Moore for the restoration of peace & good will.[2]

Robt J. Brent

ALS, DNA-RG94, Amnesty Papers (M1003, Roll 28), La., Thomas O. Moore.

1. A son of a former Louisiana congressman, Brent (1811–1872), a Baltimore lawyer, had served as Maryland's attorney general (1851–52). J. Alexis Shriver, "A Maryland Tour in 1844: Diary of Isaac Van Bibler," *MdHM*, 39 (1944): 245n; Baltimore directories (1864–72); *BDAC*.

2. Johnson granted Moore a parole, provided he take the oath of allegiance and remain available to answer any charges that might be placed against him. Parole of Thomas O. Moore, Nov. 18, 1865, Johnson Papers, LC.

From Jesse J. Finley[1]

Lake City East Florida   Nov 18th 1865.

Sir.

As a citizen of Florida, who, notwithstanding his participation in the late war against the United States, sincerely desires a restoration of the Union, I cannot but cherish the earnest hope, that the recent action of the Convention of this State, will fully meet your Excellency's views on the subject of reconstruction.[2]

I think your Excellency will agree, that in the abolition of Slavery;—and in the adjustment of the Status of the negro; and in the repudiation of the war debt, the Convention came fully up to the duties and necessities of the hour; and I do not doubt, but that it will greatly add to your gratification, when you are assured, that in their disposition of these important subjects, they are heartily sustained, by the almost universal approval of the people of this State.

The suspicion which prevailed to some extent, among the members of that body when it first convened, that there was an attempt at executive dictation, was soon removed, by a better understanding of the motives and policy of your Excellency. It was in the light of this new conviction, that what you had urged upon the States lately in insurrection, as necessary to ensure an early restoration of former political relations, was received as the friendly recommendation of one who, from the kindest motives, was anxious to do all in his power, to facilitate and secure so desirable a result. When this corrected impression of your Excellency's motives was accepted, the Convention had no difficulty in arriving at the conclusion, that what your Excellency advised, was not only just and proper in itself, but was also in harmony and agreement with the soundest views of expediency;—and the result was, that involuntary Servitude except for crime &c was forever abolished;—the negro allowed to testify in all cases affecting his rights of person and property, and the repudiation of the whole of the public debt of the State, created for the support and prosecution of the war. Thus it was, that the Convention of Florida, raised itself above all irritation and prejudice, into the clear and calm atmosphere of statesmanlike deliberation and action—just as your Excellency has done, in adopting so generous and benign a policy towards the lately revolted States.

If you could but know the deep and earnest devotion with which the southern people turn to a restored union, in which, your Excellency's policy has encouraged them to hope for security against future oppression; and if you could but see, with what grateful confidence, the whole South looks to your Excellency for a just and paternal administration of the government, you could not but experience the deepest gratification. Indeed, not to do so, when a brave and confiding people, so recently the armed enemies of government of which you are the head, are now, almost without an individual exception, your friends; would argue that your Excellency had attained to that superhuman perfection, which would render you alike indifferent to love or hate, to praise or censure.

It is seriously apprehended by many in the South, that the radical majority in the two houses of Congress will object to the admission of the Southern members, on the ground, that the States from which they come, have denied the negro the right of suffrage, and excluded him from the jury box. I must confess, that I am not prepared to beleive this. I cannot but think, that the leading and reflecting men among the radicals, must see and know, that if they adopt a harsh and unjust policy towards the South upon such an issue, it must and will lead to a political combination against them, which will diminish their power and influence, if it does not annihilate their party. Your Excellency need not be pointed to the sections and the elements which would enter into, and form this combination.

If the radicals should, however, be restrained by the wholesome appeal to their fears, may it not be probable, that they will be inclined to the opposite and more liberal policy, of admitting the Southern members, without even the show of resistance?

With grateful recollection of the civility and kindness extended to me, in the very brief interview I had with your Excellency last summer when in Washington,[3] I beg to subscribe myself, with the highest consideration and respect. . . .

J. J. Finley.

ALS, DLC-JP.

1. A native Tennessean and former Memphis mayor (1845), Finley (1812–1904) commanded a Florida brigade during the Battle of Chattanooga and the Atlanta Campaign. He later served three partial terms in Congress. *BDAC*; Warner, *Gray*.

2. See William Marvin to Johnson, Nov. 18, 1865.

3. The interview was probably in reference to Finley's pardon, which was ordered issued on November 27, 1866. See Finley to Johnson, June 14, 1865, Amnesty Papers (M1003, Roll 15), Fla., Jesse Johnson Finley, RG94, NA; see also Finley to Johnson, Jan. 24, 1867, Johnson Papers, LC.

From John W. Gorham

Clarksville Tenn   Nov. 18th 1865

I am highly pleased to see it announced that you have sent Genl. John A. Logan & Col. Browning[1] as our Representatives to the *Republic* of Mexico, and not to Maximilian's *assumed Government*. This is a step in my opinion calculated to strengthen our Government, and to sustain *your Liberal* administration. May you never make a wrong step is my most ardent wish. I am equally well pleased to learn that you have appointed your son, Col. Robert, the successor to Col. Browning. Bob is a good hearted man, and quite popular, with the People. Of this I have a better opertunity of knowing than you can have. Give him my kindest regards, and my thanks for his many courtesies while in your city last. I hope he will doe well, and can see nothing to hinder him from so doing. Munford And Whitehead[2] are both at Home and feel verry greatfull to you, for your great clemmency to them, and pledge me their honors you shall never regret pardoning them. Every day adds to your strength with the People of this Country. I know what I say, for you know I mix with them.

We Are having conciderable trouble with bands of Robbers threw the country. Woodlawn a small town 9 miles below hear was robbed last night.[3] The citizens are after them, but losses are so frequent with me that I scarcely look for any thing else. Since I saw you last I have lost my Land in consequence of defective title, and all the parties are broke. Consequently *Money Land* and all are *gone* and if *you* dont help me and that soon I am *gone* to a certainty. Give me something to do and send me some whare to do it and I will work for you as faithfully as any man ever worked for another. Excuse me for being so urgent for necessity drives me too it. My Family are all well.

Jno W. Gorham

P.S. Let me hear from you soon.

ALS, DLC-JP.

1. Logan was appointed minister but declined; William A. Browning was appointed secretary of the legation but died in early 1866 before he was confirmed. *Boston Evening Transcript*, Nov. 15, 1865; *New York Tribune*, Nov. 21, 1865; *A Biography of Gen. John A. Logan* (New York and Chicago, 1884), 529; *Johnson Papers*, 4: 422n.

2. William E. Munford and George H. Whitehead had recently been paroled by the President. The former (b. *c*1837), a Clarksville clerk and adjutant, 14th Tenn. Inf., CSA, had been captured at Sullivan, Ind., September 30, 1864, and charged with being a spy. *Augusta Constitutionalist*, Sept. 1, 1865; Ser. 8A, p. 214, Johnson Papers, LC; 1860 Census, Tenn., Montgomery, N & E of Cumberland River, 19; CSR, RG109, NA.

3. Accounts of the robbery at Woodlawn may be found in the *Clarksville Chronicle*, Nov. 17, 24, 1865.

From William Marvin

Tallahassee Fla   Nov 18 1865.

The Convention has annulled the ordinance of secession abolished slavery & declared that all the inhabitants of the State without distinction of color are free & that no person shall be incompetent to testify as a witness on account of Color in any matter wherein a Colored person is concerned. It has repudiated the State debt contracted in support of the rebellion, amended the Constitution in other respects & adjourned.[1]

Wm Marvin   Prvl Gov

Tel, DLC-JP.

1. See Johnson to Marvin, Nov. 20, 1865.

From Christopher G. Memminger

Flat Rock [N.C.]   November 18, 1865.

The Memorial of C. G. Memminger of South Carolina respectfully showeth:

That your Memorialist is excluded from the benefit of the Amnesty Proclamation of the President of the United States under two of the Exceptions made therein: namely that which excepts persons who held office under the late Confederate Government and that which excludes persons whose property exceeded Twenty Thousand Dollars in value.

Your Memorialist engaged in the late War with the United States under the conviction that his duty to the State of South Carolina of which he was a citizen, required him to do so. That State in the year 1834 by a Convention of her people asserted the doctrine that paramount allegiance was due to her, and by an Amendment of her Constitution required a corresponding oath from her citizens, which Oath your Memorialist has been repeatedly required to take as a public officer. In 1851 another Convention asserted the right to secede from the

Union, and in 1860 that assertion was practically put in operation by an Ordinance of Secession. In 1865 the State by another Convention has repealed this Ordinance, resumed her place in the Union; and by a change of the State Constitution has receded from the positions taken in 1834 and in 1851, and thereby relieved her citizens from the conflicting duties of obedience to the Federal and State authorities.

Under these circumstances, your Memorialist with the same sincerity and conviction of duty which has hitherto governed him, respectfully proffers his submission to the authorities of the United States and hereby declares his readiness to discharge the duties of a citizen of the said United States. He has accordingly taken the Oath required by the Amnesty Proclamation, a Copy whereof is hereunto annexed, and respectfully prays that the benefits of the said Amnesty may be extended to him, and that he may be admitted to all the privileges of a citizen of the United States: and your Memorialist as in duty bound will every pray &c.[1]

C G Memminger.

LS, DNA-RG94, Amnesty Papers (M1003, Roll 46), S.C., C. G. Memminger.
1. The petition was filed December 4, 1865. With recommendations from William H. Seward, David Dudley Field of New York, and Gov. Joel Parker of New Jersey, among others, Memminger was finally ordered pardoned on December 19, 1866. Amnesty Papers (M1003, Roll 46), S.C., C. G. Memminger, RG94, NA.

From William E. Bond

November 20, 1865, Edenton, N.C.; ALS, DNA-RG56, Appts., Internal Revenue Service, Collector, N.C., 1st Dist., William E. Bond.

Describing himself as "*a quiet, conscientious Constitutional Union-man,*" but with the evasive qualification, "except under such circumstances of Military or Mobocratic coercion, as rightfully to absolve me from all moral & political responsibility therefor," Bond makes his bid for appointment as collector for the 1st North Carolina District. Having recently run unsuccessfully for Congress in a three-way race in which both other candidates received a large number of votes (2,783 and 2,013, as against his 450), despite their inability to take the oath, he concludes "that it is useless for any one to come before the people for office yet awhile, whose feelings & proclivities have been known to be Unionistic:—the people have not yet lost their dread of the Secession tyrants:—are not yet able to shake off their rule and influence." [Bond was commissioned collector in July 1866.]

From William G. Brownlow

Nashville, Nov. 20th 1865.

Sir;

Enclosed I send the pardon of John Overton, recalled in compliance with your telegram of the 16th.[1] It came, with eighty (80) others, some weeks since and was delivered to Mr. O. on its arrival. It is understood that Judge Trigg acted on it immediately, so far as to release all proceedings in the U.S. Courts against Overton's property. I enclose, also, the accompanying protest from Mr. Overton.[2]

W. G. Brownlow   Gov of Tenn.

LS, DLC-JP.

1. The President had telegraphed Brownlow to request that Overton's pardon be returned to Johnson's office. This action had evidently been prompted by Overton's dispute with the Freedmen's Bureau over some of his lands which the agency had leased. Johnson to Brownlow, Nov. 16, 1865, Tels. Sent, President, Vol. 2 (1865), RG107, NA; *Clarksville Chronicle*, Nov. 24, 1865; *Zanesville Courier* (Ohio), Nov. 20, 1865; Dorris, *Pardon and Amnesty*, 237. See John H. Almond to Johnson, Oct. 15, 1865, and Frank C. Dunnington to Johnson, Nov. 2, 1865.

2. In his letter to Brownlow, Overton reluctantly agreed to hand over his pardon, expressing confidence that the President, "upon learning the true state of the facts," would return it. In mid-December the Freedmen's Bureau top leadership discussed Overton's case, and a Memphis newspaper reported that Johnson had decided to return Overton's pardon. Yet not until late January 1866 was Overton's property restored by order of General Howard. Overton to Brownlow, Nov. 20, 1865; Howard to Johnson, Jan. 25, 1866; Howard to Fisk, Jan 25, 1866, Johnson Papers, LC; Fisk to Howard, Dec. 13, 1865; Howard to Stanton, Dec. 14, 1865, Records of the Commr., Lets. Recd. (M752, Roll 21), RG105, NA; *Memphis Appeal*, Dec. 16, 1865. See Johnson to George H. Thomas, Jan. 19, 1866.

From Lewis D. Campbell

Hamilton O.   Nov 20, 1865.

My Dear Sir—

A mutual friend of ours who casually called to see me yesterday informed me that our friend Galloway[1] wrote to me whilst I was in Washington enclosing an original letter from Mr Lincoln, written in 1859, which I was to exhibit to you.[2] I know nothing about its contents, or, of what importance it may be, except as our friend has explained. I desire that you have your son Robert procure the letter. You may then open, read and retain it. If it be of any importance, all right. If not no harm will be done except in consumption of your time, so valuable just now.

I learn vaguely that Lincoln's letter indorses the decision of Judge Swan,[3] Chief Justice of the Ohio Supreme Court, made in May 1859, in which the principles of State Sovereignty and the right of Ohio to nullify a law of Congress was involved. The case is an interesting one under the Fugitive Slave law. I will attempt to state briefly the main facts and points in the case.

A Slave named *John*[4] escaping from his master in Kentucky was sent by the "*underground rail road*" to its terminus at Oberlin, Ohio. There he was reclaimed under the Fugitive Slave law. After a hearing the U.S. Commissioner ordered John restored to his master according to the act. Some two or three hundred *Oberlinites*, headed by *Bushnell* and *Langston*,[5] assembled and forcibly rescued the slave John and set him at liberty. At the Nov. Term 1858 of the U.S. Circuit Court, Bushnell and Langston were indicted, tried convicted and sent to prison. A writ of habeas corpus was sued out and the case brought before the Supreme Court of the State—all five Judges being present. It was elaborately argued by the U.S. District Attorney[6] for the Government and by Wolcott[7] (brother in-law of Secy. of War *Stanton*) Attorney General of the State of Ohio. Wolcott's argument is full of the State Sovereignty and nullification doctrine from beginning to end. Wolcott was then of the *Abby Kelly* school of politicians[8] and a *pet* of Mr. Chase then Governor of the State. It was then and still is understood by both Judges and members of the bar that the Governor Chase and perhaps Mr. Stanton assisted Wolcott in the preparation of this argument. The Governor was present giving him aid and countenance during its delivery in Court. Judge Swan delivered the opinion of a majority of the Court in which this *Chase-Wolcott-Stanton-Oberlin-State Sovereignty-nullification doctrine* was upset, and wholly repudiated. Judges *Sutliff* and *Brinkerhoff*,[9] now two of the "earnest men" of Ohio, who are for "crushing out" all men who sustain your policy, *dissented*, and indorsed the abominable heresies. Gov. Chase was quite indignant at the majority's decision. The whole case which is an interesting one, will be found in Critchfields 9th Ohio Reports p. 77.[10] If you have time you ought to read it. The volume I presume can be found in your libraries at Washington. If not I will at any time you desire, take or send it to you. The pertinacy of Mr. Lincoln's letter, sent to me by Galloway, for your inspection, as I understand, is that he fully *indorsed* Swans decision whilst Chase *condemned* it.

Judge Swans term of office expired soon after. I went to our State Convention in June 1859 with a view to re-nominate him and give his decision the indorsement of our state. But "Oberlin" and the Western Reserve sent down their hordes of "earnest men" headed by Joshua R. Giddings and his Brigadiers who, backed by the influence of Gov. Chase then in Office, after a long struggle, proved too strong for us, and Judge Swan was defeated.

Now, my dear Sir, the point of the whole matter is this. It has a direct and important bearing on the trial of Jeff Davis—a subject of National and world-wide interest. These same "earnest men" are swearing that you ought to try him by *military Commission* and hang him, and I doubt not Chief Justice Chase would like to put that responsibility wholly on your shoulders.

Since my return home, and since the publication of the points of your correspondence with him about that matter,[11] I find his *particular* friends are *nervous*. They know about these antecedents. They know that the Oberlin affair of "earnest men" headed by Bushnell and Langston was just as much a *rebellion* and just as much *treason*, (morally at least) in a small way, as that of the "Fire-eaters" of the South, headed by Jeff Davis, *was*, in more powerful proportions. They know, too, that Chief Justice Chase their intended candidate for the next presidency fully indorsed the idea that those engaged in the *Oberlin rebellion* were but exercising a lawful right. He knows too that if he has to try Jeff. Davis he must either *acquit him* or *back down* from his former positions—either of which horns of the dilemma would greatly interfere with his aspirations.

Excuse me for again writing so lengthily.[12] I can but give you in a letter an outline of this interesting Chapter in Ohio jurisprudence and politics—bearing as it now does an important relation to National affairs. I intended talking with you about it when in Washington; but my mind did not happen to strike the subject at any time whilst I was with you. I am satisfied that when you look into the whole matter, in all its bearings, you will see a beautiful opportunity of making a *flank movement* on Mr. Chief Justice and his "earnest men" who have embarked so eagerly in the business of *crushing*.

Lewis D. Campbell

ALS, DLC-JP.

1. Samuel Galloway, a former Republican congressman.

2. Campbell had left Washington before receiving the Lincoln letter which, at his request, was forwarded to the President. R.P.L. Baber to Johnson, Nov. 20, 1865, Johnson Papers, LC.

3. Joseph R. Swan (1802–1884), a Columbus attorney and legal writer, served one term (1854–59) on the Ohio supreme court. *DAB*.

4. John Price (b. *c*1838) formerly belonged to John G. Bacon, of Mason County, Ky. Charles B. Galbreath, *History of Ohio* (5 vols., Chicago and New York, 1925), 2: 224.

5. Both Simeon M. Bushnell (*c*1830–1861) and Charles H. Langston (d. 1890), a brother of black Republican partisan John M. Langston, had formerly attended Oberlin College. 1860 Census, Ohio, Lorain, Oberlin, 47; *Oberlin College Alumni Register: Graduates and Former Students, Teaching and Administrative Staff 1833–1960* (Oberlin, Ohio, 1960), 335, 353.

6. George W. Belden (*c*1803-*c*1869), of Canton, Ohio, had served as state district and common pleas judge before his appointment in 1857 as U.S. district attorney. *Portrait and Biographical Record of Stark County* (Chicago, 1892), 508–9; Herbert T.O. Blue, *History of Stark County* (3 vols., Chicago, 1928), 1: 875.

7. Christopher P. Wolcott (1820–1863), an Akron lawyer, was later assistant secretary of war (1862–63). Samuel A. Lane, *Fifty Years and Over of Akron and Summit County* (Akron, Ohio, 1892), 553.

8. Abigail Kelley Foster (1810–1887), popularly known as Abby Kelley, was a radical abolitionist and also a noted woman's rights advocate. As an outspoken crusader, she attracted considerable criticism from various quarters. Campbell's allusion in his letter was evidently intended to paint Wolcott with the brush of radicalism. *DAB*; James, *Notable American Women*, 1: 647–50.

9. Noted Ohio abolitionists Milton Sutliff and Jacob Brinkerhoff. The former (1806–1878) served in the legislature as a Free Soiler before his election in 1857 to the state supreme court. In 1872 Sutliff was defeated as a Democratic congressional candidate, losing to James A. Garfield. Henry Howe, *Historical Collection of Ohio* (2 vols., Norwalk, Ohio, 1896), 1: 676–77; *BDAC*.

10. Leander J. Critchfield (1827–1896), a reporter of Ohio's supreme court decisions for five consecutive terms, prepared and published seventeen volumes of "Ohio State Reports." *NUC*; *Biographical Cyclopaedia of Ohio*, 2: 449.

11. References to an exchange of correspondence between Johnson and Chase appeared in Ohio newspapers in early November. See, for example, the *Cincinnati Enquirer*, Nov. 8, 10, 1865, and the *Cleveland Plain Dealer*, Nov. 11, 1865.

12. Campbell's most recent letter had included nearly three pages outlining his "thoughts" on states' rights and black suffrage. Campbell to Johnson, Nov. 16, 1865, Johnson Papers, LC.

From Edward Clark[1]

City of Washington D.C.   November 20th 1865.

Your Petitioner, Edward Clark, of the State of Texas, would respectfully represent unto your Excellency, That he desires to obtain the benefits of the Proclamation of the 29th day of May 1865, "offering amnesty and pardon to certain persons who had directly or by implication, engaged in the rebellion." His case comes under the 9th exception of said proclamation and none other.

He respectfully represents that he held, and performed the duties of the office of Governor of said state of Texas, from the   day of April until the   day of November 1861.

That upon the expiration of his term of service as Governor of said state, he entered the military service of the Confederacy, with the rank of Colonel, which position he continued to hold until the surrender of Genl Jos. E. Johnson, and the dissolution of the army of the Trans-Mississippi Department of said Confederacy.

That, as Governor of the state of Texas, he endeavored to be equally just Towards all of her citizens without regard to their political opinions, and that no one was molested or persecuted, or, in any way, hindered in the enjoyment and exercise of his rights and privileges, because of his attachment to the Union or opposition to Secession.

That as Colonel in the Confederate army, he always endeavored to maintain the rules and usages of honorable warfare, never encouraging or permitting the abuse or mistreatment, in any way, of prisoners that came under his control, or the improper distruction of the enemy's property.

That he has returned to his loyalty to the government of the United States, by taking the oath prescribed by the Proclamation aforesaid, and which said oath accompanies this petition.[2]

All of which is respectfully submitted.

Edward Clark

ALS, DNA-RG94, Amnesty Papers (M1003, Roll 52), Tex., Edward Clark.

1. Clark (1815–1880) served as a Texas legislator, army officer, and secretary of state before being elected lieutenant governor in 1859. He succeeded Sam Houston as governor on March 16, 1861, after the latter refused to take an oath of allegiance to the Confederacy and, when defeated for reelection, organized the 14th Tex. Inf., CSA. Fleeing to Mexico at the close of the war, he returned to submit this application. Webb et al., *Handbook of Texas*, 1: 354.

2. No individual pardon for Clark has been found.

From Howell Cobb

Macon Ga   20th Nov 1865

Dear Sir

My friend Judge H R Jackson has just handed me your autograph permission to report to the Hon Secretary of State at Washington. I beg to express to you my high appreciation of this additional evidence of your kind personal feeling. I should be most happy to avail myself of the opportunity, which your generous kindness has extended to me of visiting Washington, if I were not restrained from doing so, by considerations both of a private and public character. I must say frankly that the main object of such a visit would be to present to you in a personal interview, such considerations as would induce your early—and I trust—favorable action on my application under your amnesty proclamation. When I remember however, the fact, that at this particular juncture, you are overwhelmed with the most important public business—I hesitate to thrust my merely personal affairs upon you, to the extent of occupying your time with personal interviews. This in connection with the fact that much I would say—has already been laid before you through the kindness of my friend Judge Jackson, and that you have intimated, that my position was well understood by yourself, induces me to forego, for the present at least, the opportunity of visiting Washington. All I have ever desired was that you might know the truth, in reference to my course and action;—and being satisfied that the gross misrepresentations, which have been made of me—especially in reference to prisoners—are not credited by you—I am content to abide your decision in my case,[1] in full confidence that you will, at the proper time, respond favorably to my application.

Howell Cobb

ALS, DLC-JP.
    1. Apparently Cobb did not receive an individual pardon.

From Viola M. Cundiff[1]

Urbana Ohio   Nov 20th 1865.

Sir:

I am a loyal Southern woman—the wife of a disabled *soldier*—a Yankee soldier at that.[2] I have incured the displeasure of all my friends at the South for adhereance to my sentiments and also my prophecys that they would certainly fail. The Government was said to be strong, but it is stronger now. It has triumphed over all its assailants. And to-day you are among its *victors*—cast out as unworthy, villefied—and pronounced a plebian—Now President—and those gallant chivalrous sons

of Mars have to pay you homage—good! good! I am no flatterer as the
above may sugest—but a plain-spoken. I am a pardon-seeker—not for
Jefferson Davis as I will be the only exception of a Southern lady. My
father is a Tailor and I a decendent of a Knight of *board* and *scicsors*
and have claims on you for this—if nothing more.[3] He was a United
States Postmaster—was a rebel Postmaster—and is now nothing—not
even an enfranchised citizen of the land that gave him birth. All he has
forfeited for violating the law of the land. But you *must* pardon him.
You pardoned Reagan of Texas,[4]—and you must pardon Samuel D.
Pace of Purdy Tenn. He knows that he made a "leap in the dark." He
is humbled blasted in his hopes—in the sacrifice of his son—the hope
of declining years—and in the autumn of life—all have perished. He
was always a Johnson advocate—and sustained you in your last election. He is my father—is likewise deserving—and you must grant his
pardon. He knows nothing of my intentions of trying to procure the
same. I want to surprise him. This will be the first favor I ever asked of
the Government. If I succeed—I may make application for an embas-
sadorship—to the Court of St James or some other country. I am importunate in this. You dread being bored—and will grant on the grond
of the unjust Judge who complied—"Lest she weary me."

Dont stop—if you are engaged on Your Message—I will wait a few
days to *accommodate you.*

(Mrs) Viola M. Cundiff   Urbana. O.

ALS, DNA-RG94, Amnesty Papers (M1003, Roll 50), Tenn., Samuel D. Pace.

1. Cundiff (b. *c*1830) was a native Tennessean. 1860 Census, Ohio, Champaign,
Urbana, 1.

2. John M. Cundiff (b. *c*1830) had been a recruit in Co. D, 13th Ohio Inf. Ibid.;
Evan P. Middleton, *History of Champaign County Ohio* (2 vols., Indianapolis, 1917), 1:
693.

3. A native of Georgia, Samuel D. Pace (*c*1804-*fl*1870) was an early settler of Purdy.
We are unable to find any record of a pardon date for him. Marcus J. Wright, *Reminiscences of the Early Settlement and Early Settlers of McNairy County, Tennessee* (Washington, D.C., 1882), 41; 1850 Census, Tenn., McNairy, Purdy, 1; (1870), 7th Civil Dist.,
Purdy, 7.

4. Cundiff is confused about Reagan, for he was *paroled* on October 11, 1865, but
was not *pardoned* until April 29, 1867. See Order *re* Release of Prominent Confederate
Prisoners, Oct. 11, 1865. See also Reagan to Johnson, May 28, 1865, *Johnson Papers*,
8: 127.

From Andrew J. Fletcher

Nashville, Nov 20 1865.

Dear Sir

The Bill to allow colored persons to testify in the Courts will not
pass the House unless they believe that its failure to pass may prevent
the admission of our delegation to Congress. Nor can any other legislation favorable to the negro pass without a *reaction.*

If it is your opinion that the defeat of the "Negro Testimony Bill" will prevent our delegation from admittance I would be very glad if you would Telegraph that opinion to me.[1]

A. J. Fletcher   Sec. of State

ALS, DLC-JP.
1. See Johnson to Fletcher, Dec. 9, 1865.

To William Marvin

Washington, D.C., Nov 20th 1865.

Your dispatch of 18th inst received, for which accept my thanks. I congratulate you on the action of your State Convention, and hope your Legislature will, without hesitation adopt the Amendment to the Constitution of the United States abolishing Slavery.[1] South Carolina has already adopted the Amendment, and it is believed that the other States will.

Andrew Johnson   President U.S.

Tel, DNA-RG107, Tels. Sent, President, Vol. 2 (1865).
1. See Marvin to Johnson, Dec. 29, 1865.

From Montgomery Blair

Washn.   21. Nov. 1865

My dear Mr. President,

I submit the enclosed letter from Mr. Cochrane[1] in accordance with what seems to be his wishes. If you wish to know my views on this or any subject I shall be happy to give them, & I will call whenever it suits your convenience.

The revelations of Mr. Hutchings[2] as to the means by which a platform antagonistic to your policy was carried in the Union Convention at Syracuse is in keeping with Mr. Sewards course towards Mr. Lincoln, of which I have informed you. The same influences will I doubt not succeed in consolidating the Union party in Congress against you.

But my faith is unshaken that you will baffle all intrigues and intriguers by your Steadfast adherence to the Constitution & the Union. Parties must soon reform on the fundamental principls announced in your inaugural on the 4th of March,[3] for a more full & formal exposition of which the Country looks in your forth coming message.

M Blair

ALS, DLC-JP.
1. John Cochrane's letter to Blair consisted primarily of the same information that he had forwarded earlier to Johnson. Cochrane to Blair, Nov. 19, 1865, Johnson Papers, LC. See Cochrane to Johnson, Nov. 16, 1865.
2. Blair's reference to Waldo Hutchins is unclear.
3. See Remarks at Vice-Presidential Swearing-In, Mar. 4, 1865, *Johnson Papers*, 7: 502–7.

From Henry S. Randall[1]

Cortland Village N.Y.   Nov. 21, 1865.

Sir,

Some time after the completion of my Life of President Jefferson, I was urged by friends to write the "Life & Times" of President Polk. The Rebellion interrupted the correspondence on the subject. Mrs. Polk[2] through a distinguished gentleman recently proposed to me to undertake the work. Before adopting any final conclusion, I asked her if *you* ought not to be consulted & your aid invoked. I made these enquiries for two reasons. First, I felt that I would not attempt to write the history of Mr Polks *Times*—the history of Tennessee politics &c, &c., without the friendly countenance of one who in addition to acting so prominent a part as you did in the proceedings to be described, was the neighbor, friend & political coactor of the subject of my work. Second, I wished to gather incidentally, but decisively, whether Mrs. Polk, or her friends, entertained feelings which would lead her, or them, to expect the work in question to be tinged by any prejudices against those who have been instrumental in putting down the Rebellion.

Mrs. Polk's reply was not, it is to be presumed, intended for any eye but mine. But I do not feel that I violate the spirit of any confidence in making use of her expressions to promote her own views, & when I only carry them to an ear which she regards as a friendly one. And it is absolutely due to you that you know her attitude in the matter, before you form any conclusions. She wrote to me October 21st:

> In reply to your letter now before me, relative to President Johnson's being consulted & his aid invoked in the anticipated undertaking, I will say that it meets with my entire approbation. The propriety of it had presented itself to my mind. The personal relations that existed between Mr Polk & Mr Johnson were friendly. x x x My personal relations with President Johnson have been of an agreeable character. During his term as Govr. of the State, Senator in Congress & Military Governor, I received from him marked attention. I believe that he will be disposed to extend to me any favor that will be consistent.

In meeting Mrs Polk's & my own wishes in this matter, it would not be my desire to have you, either publicly or privately, make yourself responsible for a word which is to appear in the work. But to fill my canvas properly, it will be necessary for me to have liberal facilities for consulting official papers in the Departments at Washington; & though I should be entirely content to leave each case subject to your discretion as it arises, I should *hope* at times, if you approve of my *attempt*, for intimations which would enable me to take the true *standpoint* in respect to some of those important & mooted questions in President Polk's career on which you were a prominent actor, or an observer having the advantage of standing behind the scenes.

Not having the honor of a personal acquaintance with you, I had thought of bringing this subject before you through some common friend, but I did not feel at liberty to express Mrs. Polk's wishes, & especially to quote her language, for any eye but yours; and this fact, I trust, will serve as my apology for addressing you.[3]

Henry S. Randall

ALS, DLC-JP.

1. Randall (1811–1876), Democratic legislator and secretary of state for New York, wrote primarily agricultural works but did pen *The Life of Thomas Jefferson* (1858). *DAB.*

2. Sarah C. Polk.

3. Although Mrs. Polk later asked Johnson to devote his "kind attention" to Randall's request (because the President's "approbation & concurrence" was desired before the work would commence) there is no record of a response, and Randall did not publish a biography of Polk. Polk to Johnson, Mar. 16, 1866, Johnson Papers, LC.

From Louis Schade

Washington D.C.   Novbr. 21. 1865.

Sir:

It is eleven o'clock at night. The reading of the N.Y. papers of to-day, just finished, has again called to my mind your difficult position.[1] Not being able to talk to you, I will write, hoping that you may have a few moments leisure time, to read these few lines, which, I dare say, come from the heart of one that is attached to you as any man can possibly be, not merely on personal grounds, but because he loves his adopted country and wishes to see it happy and its liberties secured. It is unnecessary to assure you that I am not guided by any personal motives—your friendship I have,—and offices I do not want. That is enough for me.

You will recollect that I handed to you, some time ago, a statistical table, showing the ratio of the negro and white population in the different states.[2] Knowing that you are preparing your message, I respectfully call your attention upon the same. It has never been published in any paper, and I vouch for the correctness of the same. In my humble opinion, I do not know anything stronger against the insidious policy of the radicals than this table. Figures always tell. There is no way of contradicting them. This table will prove more than anything else the wisdom of your policy of restoration and the foolishness on the part of the radicals, and particularly their injustice and wrong in trying to compel the Southern people to surrender their rights to an ignorant mass of negroes. For that table will show that in four or five States the negro population numerically predominates over the white, whilst in the North, particularly in the radical States, there are very few negroes. The policy of the radicals carried out will lead to a war of extermination between the two races. If the white race succeeds the poor negroes will be the innocent sufferers; succeed the latter the fairest portion of the Republic will be Africanised. There can be no doubt (vide the British colonies and Hayti) that the negro is not fit for self-government. His own welfare requires that he must be guided by the Caucasian. And here let me say that at least in my opinion it would be much better for our Southern negroes, if the Freedmans Bureau were abolished. Instead of assisting them it puts only notions into the heads of the negroes, which makes them unwilling to work. And work they must. The Southern people, who know the negro character best, should certainly be the better judges. And slavery having been abolished, it is the interest of those people to treat the negroes well and induce them to work. In the end you will have anyhow to fall back on their good will, as it is impossible that any Government can regulate the laborer question. Napoleon III has tried it and has failed.[3]

Our radicals maintain that the negroes must vote, if the Republic shall continue. The negroes themselves (except out of 4 millions perhaps 10,000) do not ask it. They do not want to vote. They want bread instead of votes. And if those radicals were indeed philanthropists they would assist the Southern people in building up the South so that both whites and blacks may be saved from starvation.

Mr. President: Yours is a great task. Your acts are perhaps to shape the fate of the country for centuries. Think always, when the clamors of the radicals become too vehement, that you live for the whole country and for posterity. If you make a mistake now, it will perhaps be impossible for your successors, if there will be any, to remedy that mistake. Take history as your guide. Look at the consequences of Emancipation in other countries and profit through and by the blunders of others. History is the only grave, just and impartial judge of human affairs, and as Mr Lincoln says "we cannot escape history."

Place yourself above all parties. Let the whole country be your motto. You do not owe your present high position to party but to the Will of God. The republicans would never have elected you Vice President, if they had known the untimely fate of Mr. Lincoln. Be firm! The country will sustain you, if by order of party-dictates you will not allow the country to be ruined.

Now, I am almost afraid, after reading this over, that my heart has run away again with my head. But this letter is only between you and me, and therefore I talk as in "olden times."

Please think of that table. Begging most respectfully to be excused for this long letter, and assuring you of my undying attachment. . . .

                                                                Louis Schade

ALS, DLC-JP.
   1. Probably a reference to a *New York Times* editorial of November 21, 1865, which discussed the opposition of Thaddeus Stevens and Charles Sumner to Johnson's reconstruction policies.
   2. Not found.

3. Schade refers to the French emperor's labor reform efforts, whose success was limited by the relatively small number of industrial workers in France and by the instability of the French economy. W.H.C. Smith, *Napoleon III* (London, 1972), 109–15.

From James M. Tomeny

Mobile Ala   Nov 21 1865.

Gen Woods has arrested Dexter & is trying him by Military Commission. The frauds perpetrated upon the Govt. are astounding & many of them will be exposed by this trial.[1] Judge Busted has issued a writ to take the case out of Gen Woods hands.[2] He has declined to obey the writ, as he is acting directly under telegram orders from you.[3] Gen Woods should be sustained. It is the only way to expose this unprecedented corruption. Please answer by telegraph.[4]

J M Tomeny   Supt Spl Agent

Tel, DLC-JP.

1. Tomeny himself was later implicated in the scandal. See Tomeny to Johnson, Dec. 20, 1865.

2. Federal district judge Richard Busteed, ruling that Thomas C.A. Dexter had been unlawfully detained, issued a writ of habeas corpus requiring Gen. Charles R. Woods to deliver the accused to the district court. *Mobile Register and Advertiser*, Nov. 24, 25, Dec. 12, 1865.

3. Woods explained that he ignored Busteed's directive on the basis of Lincoln's suspension of the writ and by later orders from Johnson and Gen. George H. Thomas. Ibid., Dec. 20, 1865; *New Orleans Picayune*, Nov. 25, 1865. See Johnson to Thomas, Aug. 13, 1865, *Johnson Papers*, 8: 582.

4. Upon receipt of this dispatch, Johnson had his son Robert inquire of Stanton whether he had authorized Woods's actions. The Secretary answered that he had not, and the President wired Tomeny, asking, "When, and by whom were the orders given to have Dexter tried by Military Court?" Both Tomeny and Thomas reminded Johnson of his August directive asking Thomas for an investigation of cotton frauds. With Johnson's subsequent permission, the military commission convicted Dexter of fraud and malfeasance, pending the President's approval. Johnson to Tomeny, Nov. 23, 27, 1865, Tels. Sent, President, Vol. 2 (1865), RG107, NA; Tomeny to Johnson, Nov. 25, 1865; Thomas to Johnson, Nov. 25, 1865, Johnson Papers, LC; Joseph Holt to Johnson, Apr. 12, 1866, Lets. Sent (Record Books), Vol. 17, RG153, NA.

From George Davis

In prison, Fort LaFayette   Nov 22d 1865

Sir,

Desiring and intending, in good faith, to accept and abide by all the results of the late unhappy contest, I respectfully tender to you my honest and loyal submission to the authority and laws of the United States.

Such was my intention before my arrest, and when arrested at Key West, I was only awaiting the arrival of a ship in which I might take passage to New York for that purpose.[1]

My antecedents are well known to Gov. Holden, of No. Carolina, to whom I respectfully refer your Excellency for information. He can attest that I never advocated secession, but strenuously opposed it, until the adjournment of the Peace Congress in February 1861, when it became apparent to me that I must choose whether to sustain the South against the Union, or the Union against the South. Having chosen my part with upright motives, I abided in it faithfully to the end.

Permit me to indulge the hope that you will generously accept a submission which is as honest and true as the faith I formerly pledged to the Confederate States.

I desire nothing now but to devote myself, in private life, to a quiet obedience to the laws of my country, and to providing for the necessities of my children.

I respectfully appeal to your Excellency for the exercise of your clemency in my behalf; and humbly pray that I may be pardoned for my offences committed against the peace and dignity of the United States.[2]

Geo. Davis   Late Attorney General
of the Confederate States.

ALS, DNA-RG94, Amnesty Papers (M1003, Roll 38), N.C., George Davis.

1. Following his resignation in late April 1865, Davis had eluded Federal authorities by travelling incognito through South Carolina and Georgia to Florida, where he surrendered in October and was subsequently transported under armed guard to Fort Lafayette. Burke Davis, *The Long Surrender* (New York, 1985), 94, 167–69.

2. Recommended for pardon by Gov. Jonathan Worth and many Wilmington, N.C., citizens, Davis was paroled on January 1 but was not pardoned until July 23, 1866. Daniel B. Baker et al. to Johnson, Nov. 27, 1865; Parole of George Davis, Jan. 1, 1866, Lets. Recd. (Main Ser.), File P-1765-1865, George Davis, RG94, NA; Jonathan Worth to Johnson, Apr. 20, 1866, Amnesty Papers (M1003, Roll 38), N.C., George Davis, RG94, NA.

From Samuel R. Rodgers
(Copy)

Knoxville Tennessee   Nov. 22nd 1865.

Sir

I hope you will pardon me for addressing you upon a subject of great importance to this community. I mean that of keeping the negro soldiers in this place. The conduct of said soldiers are such that it is almost impossible to restrain our people from violence. They assault our citizens coming to and going from this place: some three or four days since they attacked John Roberts Esq.[1] a sober and peaceable Justice of the peace and beat him and followed him for one half mile threatening to kill him. A few days since I am informed they attacked Lieut Parham[2] and a gentleman with him, said Parham had to draw his pistol to release himself from them. On Sunday last Capt. W. C. Coker[3] who has served his tour in the U S. Army was standing on the pavement in this place, when a negro guard came along and ordered him off. Coker refused to go and the guard drew his gun and threatened to run the bayonet through him, and a sergeant (negro) came up and told the guard that he ought to use his gun when he was not obeyed. On yesterday the Freedmen's Bureau under the control of Col. John R. Henry (citizin) on some information of a negro, sent a detachment of negro soldiers, to the house of Mr Bridwell[4] Chief of Police, to arrest Bridwell and did arrest him, for disarming some negro (not a soldier) by taking from him his pistol, and said soldiers without provocation, shot at Bridwell hitting his clothes. The Police had been ordered by the corporation authorities to disarm the colored men of Knoxville (who are not soldiers). Said negro soldiers are committing depredations upon the neighborhood in every manner possible. They are killing the milch cows around town, taking the hind quarters and leaving the balance for the hogs, such as they dont want. The conduct of these negro soldiers is such that while they remain we cannot expect to have good order.

I am perfectly satisfied that if they could be removed, we would have peace and good order at once and thereby put down much prejudice against the negro. Especially if the Freedmen Bureau could be removed also. *Then our people would* take care of the negroes. But everything is working to beget hostility towards that class of our people. I trust you who know us and our position, will do something to relieve us. I think I can pledge that this community in the event we can be relieved, will be all you can ask, that is loyal and peaceable. Our Courts are in full operation and but for Military interference everything would be just as it was befor the *War*. If there is any use for a Military force here, I confess I cannot see it. We would most willingly volunteer to guard the Military Officers free of charge if they think they need it. It does seem to me that we deserve something from the Government for the course we took in this *War*.

I think we ought not to be so vexed and annoyed with a useless force to destroy the little that has been left after the conflict of arms.

I am satisfied that if you can, you will give us relief for you know us to have been truly loyal.

(Signed) S. R. Rodgers   Chancellor

Copy, DNA-RG105, Subasst. Commr., Knoxville, Tenn., Lets. Recd.

1. Not otherwise identified.

2. Thomas W. Parham (c1830–1872) served in the 6th Tenn. Inf., USA, and after the war operated a Knoxville livery stable and was a barkeeper. Pension Records, Henry C. Parham, RG15, NA; 1870 Census, Tenn., Knox, 11th Civil Dist., Knoxville, 30.

3. Probably Charles W. Coker (1830–1907), who had served with Co. E, 3rd Tenn. Cav., USA, until his discharge in May 1864. Pension Records, Sarah V. Coker, RG15, NA.

4. Martin B. Bridwell (b. c1835) was formerly the city marshal. 1860 Census, Tenn., Knox, 1st Dist., 98; *Williams' Knoxville Directory* (1859–60), 41.

From Carl Schurz

Washington D.C.   Nov. 22d. 1865

Dear Sir,

I asked your permission to substitute a general report for my occasional despatches from the South for the reason that the latter were mostly written on the spur on the moment with a view to give you information about local circumstances and particular persons. It was my intention from the beginning to arrange their contents in such a form as to present a comprehensive view of the condition of things in the States I have visited. You will therefore find in the general report I have the honor to present today, most of the statements contained in my dispatches, but in new connections and some of them modified according to new lights shed upon facts by information subsequently received and a generally enlarged experience. You will find also many additions and amplifications which I undertake to present to you only after having surveyed the whole field subject to my observation.

I would now respectfully ask your permission to publish this report.[1] Its contents are interesting to the people at large and I should be glad to lay them before the country in the same form in which I presented them to you. In order to avoid misunderstandings, and in order to assume for myself the whole responsibility for the views I express, I would, if it so please you, preface the report with an introductory notice to this effect: "This report is published by permission of the President, it being however understood that, as the President before giving that permission, had not time to subject the report to a close examination, the permission thus given does not involve an Endorsement on his part of all the views and opinions expressed therein"—or something like this.

I should be greatly obliged to you, if you would give me your reply to this request at your earliest convenience,—if possible today. As the documents which accompanied my despatches, are also referred to in the general report, I would respectfully request to have them returned to me for an hour, for the purpose of arranging and numbering them in order.

I have the honor to deliver to you also a letter from Genl. Woods comanding the Department of Alabama.[2] This letter was intended to reach me and to be brought to your notice immediately after my return from the South, but owing to some mistake it went to the War Department and came to my hands only yesterday. The delay is, therefore, not my fault.

C. Schurz.

ALS, DLC-JP.

1. Schurz repeated his request a few days later, but no response from Johnson has

been found. On December 18, 1865, the President forwarded Schurz's lengthy report to Congress, along with a letter summarizing its contents for those senators unwilling to endure a reading of the entire document. Schurz to Johnson, Nov. 25, 1865, Johnson Papers, LC; *Senate Ex. Docs.*, 39 Cong., 1 Sess., No. 2, pp. 2–46 (Ser. 1237); *Advice*, 241–43.

2. Dated September 29, Gen. Charles R. Woods's letter asked Schurz to convey to the President the facts in his current dispute with Bishop Richard H. Wilmer. Enclosing copies of Wilmer's June 20 pastoral letter, his September 22 letter of protest, and Woods's own reply of the same date, the general alleged that "the clergymen of this State, especially the Protestant Episcopal Church, are the most disloyal and mischievous of all the citizens." Johnson Papers, LC.

From Clement C. Clay, Jr.

Fortress Monroe, Nov. 23d 1865

Mr. President.

I have now been during nearly seven months a prisoner in close confinement & under guard—for such was my condition *en route* to this place.

By letters, dated 30" June, 19th Augt. & 1st Oct.,[1] I asked a trial for my imputed complicity in the murder of Mr. Lincoln; to neither of which have I had any answer.

Had your Proclamation[2] charged me with the very act of Booth, I should not have been more surprised & amazed than I was at being charged with concerting the crime. I had then been absent from Canada nearly six months; had never known or heard of Booth or either of those charged as immediate accomplices; & had not, to my knowledge or belief, ever seen him or either of them.[3] Conscious of my innocence of either concerting, consenting to, conceiving or being privy to this crime, or anything base, cowardly or dishonorable or unwarranted by the laws of war & the example of the United States; confident that no act or word of mine could be tortured into complicity in any such crime; & trusting & expecting that I would ere long be allowed means & opportunity of removing from my name a stain more painful than any would you could have inflicted on my body; I parted from those who have escaped arrest (despite their dissuasions & admonitions that I would be made to suffer severely,) travelled back to Macon, Ga., 170 miles distant, & surrendered myself to Maj. Genl. Wilson.[4] I felt & feel that neither liberty nor life is valuable with a dishonored name. I knew that my own people would not credit my guilt, but I was unwilling that the great world—who did not know me—should doubt my innocence. I flattered myself that neither you, nor Mr Seward, would yield credence to this accusation without strong evidence of it. I had shared his hospitality, & according to the morals of barbarians—Arabs or Indians—could not assassinate him. I had been tendered yours & was indebted to you for relief when in distress at your own town.[5] Besides, I thought you accorded me at least courage & integrity; which are utterly irreconcilable with the crime imputed to me. I, therefore, surrendered myself with the expectation that I would long since have been relieved from a disgraceful charge that has weighed like an incubus upon my spirits. But I am still in prison, as ignorant of the grounds of accusation as when I came here: for I have been allowed to see no paper that alluded to it & have heard nothing implicating me from my wardens. My condition has been not unlike that of one whose wife or daughter was forced from him into outer darkness—to death or dishonor—while he was lying bound gagged & blind—folded within his honor. I have borne such anguish of soul while enduring the pains of physical disorders & infirmity greatly aggravated by my prison discipline. I have suffered long and severely—enough, I think, to satisfy the vengeance of my worst enemy.

Now I submit to you whether public justice requires that I should longer endure such punishment. If there be no evidence to warrant this imputation, should not my family, if not I, be relieved from the reproach of it? If there be any, should not I be allowed means to rebut it & vindicate myself? The long delay of my trial persuades me that the evidence of my complicity—if any—is insufficient to warrant a prosecution. But the greater rigor with which I am treated—if I may credit newspaper reports of privileges accorded political prisoners elsewhere—impresses me with the belief that I am regarded as more criminal than they are.

Of those professing my faith in the sovereignty of the states & the right of secession, & acting with me—some with more power & efficiency & in higher positions—it appears that many have suffered no imprisonment or arrest, no confiscation or seizure of their property; while others have undergone shorter & less rigorous imprisonment & are now at liberty. I was educated in that faith; held it religiously; maintained it honestly & unselfishly; gave it both my hands & all my heart; sacrificed to it an ample fortune & a seat in the U.S. Senate, which I could have held during my life. I still think the States did not surrender that right in adopting the U.S. Constitution; & I know that the power of coercing them is not granted in that instrument & was refused when asked. I have ever regarded the States rights dogma as conservative of popular liberty & personal rights.

But the subordination of the States & supremacy of the General Government has been established in the Court of last resort—the field of battle—& its judgment is conclusive & final. The established theory now is, that the citizen owes his highest & first allegiance to the Genl. Govt. Such is the fact & none should dispute it. I should deprecate any effort to revive defunct principles & obsolete ideas, that can never prevail but may irritate the wounds & aggravate the sufferings of the conquered states.

No rebellion insurrection or resistance to the U.S. Govt. could be excited, in my opinion, in either of the Southern States. They have not only been overcome & subjugated, but quite disabled for self protection. Emancipation has paralyzed their mutilated limbs. They are not only powerless to resist the will of the majority of States, but, I fear, to preserve domestic peace, tranquillity, order, law & justice within her own limits. It will at all events require all their moral & physical resources, with the aid of the Genl. Govt., to do so. They have not only to reorganize governments in new forms, but to recast society & create strange & hitherto repugnant relations between blacks & whites, conceding to the former rights heretofore denied & maintaining them, & restraining the latter from exercising accustomed rights, by prohibiting & punishing them as wrongs. A revolution so radical can scarcely be effected without great distress, serious difficulties, anxious disquietude & common distrust. It will demand almost superhuman wisdom & virtue to mature the new social & political system & preserve harmony & respect for each others rights between the two races. Both have not only to learn new lessons of political & social rights & duties, but to unlearn old ones; & it is easier to teach ignorance than to correct error. Any wrong, real or imaginary, even a blunder or erronious suggestion of over-zealous friends in Northern States, may cause scenes of bloodshed such as have lately been exhibited in Jamaica.[6] To borrow Mr. Jefferson's figure, the South no longer holds the wolf by the ears—he is loose & she must keep even on the watch. Hence the Genl. Govt. will be necessary as a guardian of the people of the Southern States, especially where there is a large negro population. If such is not the prevailing sentiment now, it will be of necessity ere long.

Entertaining these opinions, I would not, if I could, countervail yr. efforts to reconstruct the Union on the new basis. You offer the best remedy in yr. judgment (I doubt not) for the present disorganization & disorders of the South. It is bitter to me, I confess, but, emancipation being achieved, it is necessary to prevent continual convulsions & preserve what is left.

Now I donot think these views would disturb the peace & order of Southern Society, if I should publish them. If not, in yr. judgment, why should I be kept in close confinement? I am sure I should not break my parol, if my prison bounds were enlarged to the limits of Ala. The release of other prisoners & yr. treatment of leading secessionists throughout the South, assures me that yr. official conduct is not controlled by any vindictiveness of spirit. I know no cause of personal bitterness to me, & do not attribute to such feelings my continued close confinement, but to yr. sense of public duty, under unfavorable impressions created by false accusations. If such be the fact, I think I should be given opportunity to admit or deny them & sustain my answer. I have done nothing that I would deny or conceal.

If in yr. judgment the public interest requires my longer imprisonment, I conced that I should not be released. But, in that case, I hope, in consideration of my asthmatic habit, you will have me removed to some fortress further South, where I will suffer less bodily pain because I can enjoy more fresh air. The approaching cold weather will make it necessary in this latitude to keep the doors & windows closed, & consequently, the confined air, impregnated with gas from coal & coal oil, will cause me great distress from oppression of my chest & difficult respiration, if it do not bring on the agonizing spasms—terrible as death—under which I so long suffered.

I have written this under severe & unremitting pain & may not have expressed myself as I would have done, if well, but I submit it, confiding in yr. disposition to do me justice, & trusting that you will take some action on my application ere winter begins.[7]

C C. Clay Jr.

Copy, DNA-RG153, Lets. Recd. (1854–94), File 1891.

1. Only Clay's letter of June 30 to Stanton has been found. Nuermberger, *Clays*, 289–90, 291n.

2. See Proclamation of Rewards for Arrest of Sundry Confederates, May 2, 1865, *Johnson Papers*, 8: 15–16.

3. Based upon his examination of the records, Judge Advocate General Holt charged that Clay's claims were "*utterly false.*" Holt to Stanton, Dec. 6, 1865, Lets. Sent (Record Books), Vol. 17, RG153, NA.

4. Benjamin H. Hill later claimed that Clay was visiting at his home in La Grange, Georgia, at the time of Johnson's proclamation, and left from there to surrender to Gen. James H. Wilson. Hill to Johnson, Nov. 26, 1865, Johnson Papers, LC.

5. The specific occurrence to which Clay alludes is unknown.

6. A reference to the Morant Bay rebellion by discontented blacks in October 1865. *New York Times*, Nov. 17, 1865.

7. The President referred Clay's letter to Stanton to be read and returned. Stanton in turn sent the letter to Holt. Despite subsequent pleas by Clay and others, including General Grant, Johnson did not authorize Clay's release from prison until the spring of 1866. Ser. 4A, Vol. 3: 69; Grant to Johnson, Nov. 26, 1865, Johnson Papers, LC; Nuermberger, *Clays*, 281, 293.

From Joshua Hill

Madison. Ga.   Nov. 23d. 1865.

Sir,

I take occasion to ask of you the appointment of Marshal, of the U.S. for Georgia, for my personal friend, Mathew B. Peters,[1] now of Macon. Judge Lochrane, of Macon, has written you on the same subject.[2] I beg leave to say, that Mr. Peters, was really & sincerely one of the most earnest and devoted friends of the Union, I knew in this State. He affected no sentiment, that he did not feel. His capacity as a man of superior business character, is rarely equalled. He is a superior accountant, correspondent and active, energetic businessman. I shall feel personally much indebted for his appointment. If consistent with your sense of public duty—I will hope for his success. Do not consider me importunate, if I insist, on your bearing this application in mind.[3]

(*Confidential.*) While the action of the State Convention, was not all I desired, and endeavored to make it—I trust it may not have proven offensive to you. As for the members elect to Congress, I am inclined to think, not one of them, can take the official oath. The true Union men of the State, desire me to be a candidate for the Senate. I think it doubtful, whether I could be chosen. My denunciation of secessionists, unrepentant still of their errors, and of Union men, or cooperationists as they styled themselves in 1860 (though I was never a cooperationist & refused the name and principle,) such as Jenkins[4] & the like—who are now more bitter towards men of my mode of thinking and feeling, than are the original secessionists; I presume, make me unavailable. Brown[5] & his immediate friends, are well disposed towards me. *The friends of Mr. Davis, are not my friends.* I made opposition to the action of the Convention, in annoying you with an unmeaning application, asking for pardon for Davis, Stephens, Genl. Mercer, (charged with a terrible crime)[6] *and all other prisoners*—on the ground of inappropriateness of duty—on the part of such a body. All this, with my open, avowed rejoicing at the overthrow of the tyranny, under which the South had suffered so long—coupled with my associations with Provl. Gov. Johnson & the Army officers, especially Genl. Steedman, create strong opposition to me. I do not desire the place—but think I shall stand a canvass, in order to test the tone of the Legislature. *I am one of the very few men in the State, who can take the oath.* Men generally, know this. By reference to my application for pardon[7]—I am sure in strictness, this will appear. If the Legislature, reject me—they will elect some one over me, who will make it matter of boasting, that he can not take the oath.[8] In this event, it will not cost much trouble to determine the actual state of feeling in Georgia.

I take it for granted, that the Govr. keeps you advised of our true condition & progress. He is not well satisfied, but hopeful. He and I are good friends. I would have advised his running as the Union candidate for Govr. but knew he could not possibly be elected—with the forestalling of public opinion in favor of Mr. Jenkins. Of course, events here, as in other States, will determine your future action as to the policy for Georgia.

Once for all, I desire it understood, at home and abroad, that I am the enemy of agitators and malcontents in general, and particularly in Georgia.

Excuse this unintended and cursory glance at home affairs, on the ground, that I thought, it might in some degree assist you, in forming a Judgment in regard to them. If mistaken in this, however, I beg you to pardon an intrusion, free from any selfish design.

Joshua Hill

ALS, DNA-RG60, Appt. Files for Judicial Dists., Ga., Mathew B. Peters.

1. Peters "of New York," who two years prior to the war had married a Georgian, was a U.S. Treasury agent at Macon. Willard R. Rocker, comp., *Marriages and Obituaries From the Macon Messenger, 1818–1865* (Easley, S.C., 1988), 511; [Hugh McCulloch] to E. M. Bruce, Jan. 23, 1866, Lets. Sent *re* Restricted Commercial Intercourse (BE Ser.), Vol. 12, RG56, NA.

2. See Osborne A. Lochrane to Johnson, Nov. 11, 1865, Appt. Files for Judicial Dists., Ga., Mathew B. Peters, RG60, NA.

3. Peters did not obtain the appointment, although he wrote on his own behalf, and Hill again petitioned the President. Peters to Johnson, Nov. 11, 1865; Hill to Johnson, Nov. 26, 1865, ibid.

4. Charles J. Jenkins (1805–1883), an Augusta lawyer, legislator, and state supreme court judge, replaced James Johnson as governor in December 1865. *DAB*.

5. Joseph E. Brown.

6. Hugh W. Mercer (1808–1877), a West Point graduate and Savannah banker, had served as a Confederate brigadier general. In late January 1866 a U.S. military court acquitted him of murdering seven Federal soldiers who had "been induced to enlist in the Confederate army." Warner, *Gray*; *Augusta Constitutionalist*, Jan. 30, 1866; *Mobile Register and Advertiser*, Feb. 6, 1866.

7. Hill had applied for pardon solely because he was worth over $20,000. His pardon was ordered by Johnson three days later. Hill to Johnson, June 19, 1865, Amnesty Papers (M1003, Roll 19), Ga., Joshua Hill, RG94, NA.

8. See Alexander H. Stephens to Johnson, Jan. 31, 1866.

From James Johnson

Milledgeville   No 23rd 1865

Dr Sir

I have this day had an interview with Dr Wm. C Daniel[1] and since our conversation & his assurances I am fully satisfied that he will conform to and advise others also to conform to the demands and requirements of the Government in its reconstruction policy.

I therefore state that I think he will make a good citizen and ask for him the Amnesty he seeks.[2]

J Johnson

ALS, DNA-RG94, Amnesty Papers (M1003, Roll 17), Ga., William C. Daniell.

1. A physician, rice planter, former state representative, and onetime mayor of Savannah, Daniell (1793–1868) had served as Confederate sequestration receiver for the southern district of Georgia. Myers, *Children of Pride*, 1504; Daniell to Johnson, Aug. 15, 1865, Amnesty Papers (M1003, Roll 17), Ga., William C. Daniell, RG94, NA.

2. Johnson endorsed Daniell's file, which contained two applications, "Let the pardon issue in its proper order." Daniell was pardoned on December 4, 1865. Daniell to Johnson, July 14, Aug. 15, 1865; Andrew K. Long to Speed, Dec. 4, 1865, ibid.

From Hugh Kennedy

[New Orleans] City Hall, Novbr; 23'rd 1865

Sir,

The Governor has requested me to transmit for your perusal copy of his forthcoming message,[1] which, altho' the General Assembly was to meet & organize this day, is not likely to be delivered before next Monday, the 27th inst. The tardy arrival of representatives from the North-Western part of the State will cause some little delay in proceeding to active business. Meantime we are not idle in pushing investigations as to the probable strength and the plan of the campaign contemplated by your opponents, and providing to frustrate them.

We are as yet without full returns of the election from Northern parishes being yet to hear from, but I think it is safe to state, that the entire vote will be about twenty-eight thousand, of which Allen will probably have five thousand.[2]

In my letters to Senator Patterson,[3] which I suppose he communicated for your perusal, I undertook to explain the character of the combination to elect Allen, whose vote has exceeded considerably the number I had supposed he could possibly obtain.

I suggested to Senator Patterson whether it might not be advisable to quarter a negro regiment in each of the parishes which had given Allen a majority.

The leaven of dissafection seems to have infused itself among parties whom the Govr. and myself had taken unusual pains to commend for your clemency, and otherwise to win over to common sense & loyalty. Perhaps it is as well to allow a fermentation to exist and manifest itself, so that the true intentions of those who meditate opposition & mischief can be ascertained.

I took the liberty, some months ago, to mention the existence of secret political associations, and the danger of their ramification in the country.

The Governor has pointedly drawn the attention of the legislature to this danger, and asked for power to deal with it. If the legislature fails to comply, my opinion is the power of the national government will be sapped.

An attempt will soon be made to force a City election. The Governor expresses anxiety about the matter, and would like to hear from you whether it is to be permitted, and how soon.[4]

The happiest effects have followed the brief official visit of Genl. Fullerton,[5] and all parties interested in the welfare of the State now breathe more freely. He did all that was desirable, and his successor[6] follows in his footsteps.

Marshal Bullitt will telegraph from time to time such occurrences as may be worthy,[7] and the Governor's office and mine will always furnish him with such information as they have which is reliable.

Govr. Wells desires to have his most respectful remembrances presented to the President, and I have the honor to be. . . .

                                                    Hu. Kennedy   Mayor

ALS, DLC-JP.
1. Not found, but J. Madison Wells's address was published in the *New Orleans Picayune* of November 30, 1865.

2. Former Confederate governor Henry Watkins Allen, exiled in Mexico, received 5,497 votes, while Wells garnered 22,312. Willie M. Caskey, *The Secession and Restoration of Louisiana* (Baton Rouge, 1938), 178.

3. Not found.

4. The growing menace of the "Southern Cross Association" and other secret political societies prompted the legislature to postpone municipal elections. Ted Tunnell, *Crucible of Reconstruction: War, Radicalism, and Race in Louisiana, 1862–1877* (Baton Rouge, 1984), 101–2. See Wells to Johnson, Jan. 29, 1866.

5. See Joseph S. Fullerton to Johnson, Oct. 28, 1865.

6. Absalom Baird.

7. See, for example, Cuthbert Bullitt to Johnson, Nov. 7, 1865.

From Hugh McCulloch

Treasury Department, November 23d, 1865.

Sir:

I have the honor to acknowledge the receipt, with your endorsement thereon, of the application of Mrs. Emily Miller,[1] with enclosures as stated, asking for the return to her of certain seventy two (72) bales of cotton.

It appears from her statement that the cotton in question was "seized by Capt. John W. Jack,[2] of the 9th Inda. Cavy., by order of Col. Geo. W. Jackson,[3] com'g. said regiment, and turned over to the Agents of the Treasury Department;" and it is stated in the record of the lot claimed by her, that "a Mrs. Miller claims this lot of cotton on the ground that she purchased it from the C.S.A. government, previous to the surrender, paying therefor stock, provisions etc."

I am desirous of carrying out your wishes, as expressed in the endorsement, but in view of the admitted fact that the cotton comes to this Department through the military authorities, and that it is alleged she acquired title thereto from the late so called confederate states government, and under the Attorney Generals opinion concerning captured property, and in view of the policy understood to be adopted by Government in regard to property, the title to which has been derived from the late so called confederate states government, I do not feel authorized to pay the proceeds arising from the sale of this cotton, particularly, when the probable eventual results of such a precedent being set by me is taken into consideration.

I am satisfied, however, that in many cases, small in the amounts involved, and meritorious in their character, some relief should be afforded; and it occurs to me that any difficulty in such cases may be obviated by an order issued by you, in virtue of your position as commander-in-chief, which would be regarded as setting aside the action of the military authorities in taking possession of and turning over the property, or the proceeds arising therefrom, which it is desired shall be released, thus making as it were, each an exceptional case, and not establishing a general precedent, to be taken advantage of by persons presenting larger and less meritorious claims. If, therefore, you will make such an order in this case as would seem to leave me no discretion in the premises, the desired relief can, in my opinion, be afforded without coming in conflict with the understood policy of the Government on the subject.[4]

H McCulloch   Secretary of the Treas.

LS, DNA-RG56, Misc. Div., Claims for Cotton and Captured and Abandoned Property.

1. Miller (b. c1826), the Mississippi widow of planter Samuel Miller, had asked Johnson to help her obtain the proceeds from her cotton, which had been seized by the federal government and sold. The President had endorsed her petition, "From the examination I have given this case, it seems to be meritorious and should be adjusted, if the funds have not passed beyond the control of the Secretary of the Treasury." 1860 Census, Miss., Claiborne, 4th Police Dist., Port Gibson, 82; Miller to Johnson, n.d. (with endorsement of Nov. 23, 1865), Misc. Div., Claims for Cotton and Captured and Abandoned Property, RG56, NA.

2. Probably Sgt. John W. Jackson (1842–1927), who was a farmer before the war but afterward became a Methodist minister. Pension Records, John W. Jackson, RG15, NA.

3. George W. Jackson (c1833–1912) was a carriage builder before the war. Pension Records, George W. Jackson, RG15, NA.

4. In a subsequent endorsement Johnson ordered an exception made for Miller in the "rigid application" of regulations concerning captured property. She was "allowed" the net proceeds from the sale of her cotton in January 1866 but later wrote that a portion was still being held "unjustly" for taxes. *Senate Ex. Docs.*, 40 Cong., 2 Sess., No. 22, p. 12 (Ser. 1316); Miller to Johnson, n.d. (with endorsement of Dec. 1, 1865); Miller to McCulloch, Sept. 15, 1866, Misc. Div., Claims for Cotton and Captured and Abandoned Property, RG56, NA.

From R. Weakley Brown

Nashville   Nov 24, 1865

My Dear Friend,

Enclosed please find a recommendation of a number of the Nashville Bar for the appointment of Hon Connally F Trigg as the successor of the late Judge Catron.[1] I am reliably informed that my friend Hon Russell Houston does not desire the position and have been told that he intends writing you a letter recommending the appointment of Judge Trigg.[2]

Judge T possesses many of the high traits of character which so preeminently distinguish Gen Jackson and yourself. He has integrity—a strong will and true personal and moral courage. He is a good lawyer and his appointment would receive the approbation of an overwhelming majority of the people of Tennessee. He more than any other public man in the state is using his influence to sustain your policy. I could have obtained many more signatures but had not time to call on them, and some of the radicals were not applied to at all.

Of course all these matters are respectfully referred to your favorable consideration. And Judge Trigg and his friends will be satisfied with your decision whatever that may be.[3] We all have full confidence in your determination to do all in your power for the good of the people of Tennessee and other States. I wrote you some time since a letter in regard to my uncle Doct John M Watson.[4] He has received partial possession of his property—but many freedmen have their shanties on his lot extending nearly to his dwelling. He has had an unusually hard time of it. I would be glad if he could have an order for the Freedmen's Bureau to restore his entire property. Mr. East told me he had left his papers with you and requested me to write you on the subject. I also enclosed you a letter from my father[5]—and one from Gen Granville P Smith—and others.[6] I hope they will secure an early and favorable consideration.[7]

R. W. Brown

ALS, DNA-RG60, Appt. Files for Judicial Dists., S.C., Connally F. Trigg.

1. The enclosed petition was signed by thirty attorneys. Also in the appointment files is a petition from forty-seven Memphis and West Tennessee lawyers, received in Washington on October 16, 1865, recommending Trigg's appointment. Appt. Files for Judicial Dists., S.C., Connally F. Trigg, RG60, NA.

2. We have been unable to locate such a letter from Houston.

3. Johnson was not permitted to replace Catron, for Congress reduced the number of justices.

4. See Brown to Johnson, Oct. 20, 1865.

5. Probably a reference to John L. Brown to Johnson, Oct. 19, 1865, Amnesty Papers (M1003, Roll 48), Tenn., John L. Brown, RG94, NA.

6. Brown perhaps refers here to Smith's letter of October 19, 1865. It is not clear to what other letters Brown makes reference. See Smith to Johnson, Oct. 19, 1865, Amnesty Papers (M1003, Roll 51), Tenn., Granville P. Smith, RG94, NA.

7. Brown evidently did not realize that by this time his father, uncle, and Smith had all been pardoned by the President. There was extreme delay in sending Smith's pardon to him, for he did not acknowledge receipt of it until late December. See Smith to Johnson, Dec. 26, 1865, Johnson Papers, LC.

From Benjamin Perley Poore[1]

Washington, November 24, 1865.

The subscriber, a loyal citizen, who has endeavored to defend the flag of our Union with his sword, and to support its Rulers with his pen, Respectfully Represents.

That he has an engagement to send short daily telegraphic dispatches to the New Orleans Daily Times, a loyal paper, edited by W.H.C. King, who has the honor of President Johnson's acquaintance.

That after sending some four or five of these dispatches, hereto annexed,[2] he was told at the Telegraph Office that he could not send any more, by order of the War Department.

That he endeavored to have this edict set aside, ascertaining that the wires between this city and New Orleans are open to the public, and are daily used by Cotton Speculators, rebels, and any one else who will pay the tolls.

That he would not of course expect even his brief dispatches to be sent if Government desired to use the wires, and the fact that everything sent is subjected to a censorship would be a guarantee against the transmission of any thing improper.

That it has been represented to the subscriber that L. C. Baker endeavored to have the restrictions on the telegraph removed, but that the subject was discussed in Cabinet Meeting, and unanimously decided in the negative.[3]

This, the subscriber beleives, can only have been done upon a misstatement of the above *facts*, which can be fully substantiated.

Therefore the Subscriber respectfully requests permission to send brief dispatches to the New Orleans Times, that the people of Louisiana may be informed by a *free press* of what is being done to restore the Union, and that he may earn his livelihood by the legitimate exercise of his profession as a journalist.

Ben: Perley Poore

ALS, DLC-JP.

1. Poore (1822–1887), eminent antebellum newspaperman and erstwhile senatorial clerk, served in the 8th Mass. Inf. during the war and afterward became noted for his historical publications. *Appleton's Cyclopaedia.*

2. Poore enclosed undated clippings of his telegrams published in the *New Orleans Times.*

3. Nothing further regarding Poore's allegations has been found.

From Horace H. Harrison

Nashville, Tenn   Nov 25th 1865.

In response to your telegram to me of this date, I have the honor to Enclose a transcript of the decree of the United States District Court for this district, dismissing the Proceeding in Confiscation against John Overton, upon his plea of the Amnesty of the 8, Decr. 1863.[1]

I recd. your dispatch late this afternoon, and sent an order to the Clerk of the District Court[2] to make a transcript as Called for in the dispatch; intending to have him make a Copy of Overtons plea in the cause, which was sworn to, and in which plea he averred on oath, that he had taken the oath exhibited, on the 15 Febry 1865, in good faith, and with an intention to faithfully observe & Keep the same, and that he had Kept the same inviolate, and stating further that he did not come within any of the exceptions in said proclamation of 8, Dec 1863. But I failed to get the Copy in time to send it with this by to nights mail. The record sent shows that I declined to traverse the facts stated in the plea, and I did so because the fact that he had taken the oath, was shown by the highest Evidence of that fact, the Certificate of the Clk of the U.S. Dist Court at Louisville, under the seal of that Court, and I was further satisfied that he was not excepted out of the benefits of the Amnesty of 1863: and lastly because so far as the motives with

which he took the Oath, and his intentions in reference to its observance were Concerned, I could not successfully traverse his sworn
statements in relation thereto, because his motives and intentions were
Known only to him and to his God.

Horace H. Harrison   U S. Dist Atty &c

ALS, DLC-JP.

1. Having a few days earlier revoked Overton's pardon temporarily, Johnson apparently wanted to review the controversy over Overton's Nashville property before reaching
a definite conclusion about the matter. Johnson to Harrison, Nov. 25, 1865, Johnson
Papers, LC. Enclosed transcript is also found in Johnson Papers, LC.

2. Robert M. Smith (1837–1897), a Nashville lawyer, later became a U.S. district
attorney and a Vanderbilt professor. *Nashville Banner*, Dec. 14, 1897.

From Alexander N. Wilson

Savannah, Geo.   No. 25th, 1865

My Dear Sir.

No doubt you are posted from various Sources on matters in Geo.
but having reported to you, after a short visit to this State in June last,
that the people were loyal,[1] I feel it my duty to amend a little after three
months residence. In June it was seeing a bad boy just after a terrible
thrashing by the old gentleman; now the smart is gone, and amiable
manifestations on the part of the old one, have given the subdued Devil
courage to show itself.

You have treated the Southern people right, by saying to them, "The
war has settled certain points, reconstruct your State Governments
accordingly."

They have attempted reconstruction, *cunningly* throwing the *odium*
of every distasteful measure upon you; and still not coming up to the
requisitions.

In the Congressional delegation, only one Union man, viz: Wm. T.
Wofford has been elected,[2] and he was a Confederate Brig. General.

The Convention in its organic law, making two years residence necessary to vote, instead of the Statute, heretofore requiring six months
residence, intended a direct insult to the Government, at the same time
putting the iron clamps of Secession upon the Union men.[3]

Open hostility to the Government exists in every section of the State,
by those who have taken the amnesty oath, and even by Some who
have Pardons in their pockets. Let the military be removed, and not
one emphatic Union man can remain in the State and live.

Pledges of honor disipate as the morning mist. From my stand point,
to restore the State to all her privileges, would be ruin to the Govern-
ment-loving and law-abiding people. The Hydrophobia is more malignant than it was five years ago. I now think the immediate trial,
conviction and execution of Jeff. Davis, followed by the trials, convictions and execution of Lee, Johnston, Bragg & that concentration of all

lies and bragadocio, G. T. Beauregard would have the effect of restoring a hearty respect for the Government. It would teach these fellows,
who think Heaven, Hell and all the earth must bow to them, that there
is a power above them.

Personally, I have been treated with a great deal of respect and
courtesy.

Alex. N. Wilson

ALS, DLC-JP.
    1. See Wilson to Johnson, June 16, 1865, *Johnson Papers*, 8: 248–49.
    2. Wofford (1824–1884), a planter, attorney, and former editor whom Johnson had
pardoned on July 24, 1865, was never seated in Congress. Wakelyn, *BDC*; *House Ex.
Docs.*, 40 Cong., 2 Sess., No. 16, p. 143 (Ser. 1330).
    3. See Finlay Y. Clark to Johnson, Dec. 4, 1865.

To James Johnson

Washington, D.C., Nov 26th 1865.
    You will continue to act as Provisional Governor of Georgia, until
relieved, and your successor recognized by the Government.[1]
    At present, as Provisional Governor, I would issue no certificates of
election to members of Congress elect. If I understand your dispatch,[2]
none of the members elect to Congress from Georgia can take the Oath
of Office as it now stands. Please advise me of their real status as to
loyalty and qualification in regard to disability under the law and the
Constitution.
    I regret to hear that you have apprehensions as to the action of your
Legislature, and hope that all will come out right. You will accept the
approbation of the Government for the loyal and efficient manner in
which you have discharged your duty as Provisional Governor.[3]

Andrew Johnson   President U.S.

Tel, DNA-RG107, Tels. Sent, President, Vol. 2 (1865).
    1. On November 24 the governor had inquired, "Will the inauguration of the Gov-
ernor elect [Charles Jenkins] releive me of duty?" Johnson Papers, LC.
    2. Governor Johnson had asked whether he should certify the elections of Georgia
congressmen and added that the legislature would "probably be to some extent impracticable & refactory." He advised that a "suspension of pardons might have a salutary
effect." Too, "I shall be a candidate for the Senate & of course will be defeated." James
Johnson to Johnson, Nov. 21, 1865, Johnson Papers, LC.
    3. See Johnson to James Johnson, Dec. 11, 1865.

From Robert J. Powell

Raleigh N.C.   Novr 26 1865
Dear Sir:
    Since my arrival here, I find the rebelous element aided by the aris-
tocracy much stronger and more bitter than I had supposed before I
left Washington and they seem to have full power in their hands. Govr
Holden is improving but is still confined to his bed. All profess a desire

to carry out your wishes. Yet Graham, Vance and other leaders are industriously deceiving the masses as to your views.

Our leading friends are of opinion that it is of the greatest importance that your wishes be made known in such manner that they can't be misunderstood by any one. I think that if you can send or telegraph something as follows it will do great good.

The results of the recent elections in N. Carolina have greatly damaged the prospects of the state in the restoration of its Governmental relations. Should the action and the spirit of the Legislature be in the same direction, it will greatly increase the mischief already done, and might be fatal. It is hoped the action and spirit manifested by the Legislature will be so directed as rather to repair than to increase the difficulties under which the state has already placed itself.[1]

Our friends are very confident that such a message from you would do great good, hence I have taken the liberty to suggest it. Please let me hear from you immediately.[2]

R. J. Powell

Tel, DLC-JP.

1. The President transmitted Powell's suggested paragraph to Holden, accompanied by the preface: "Accept my thanks for the noble and efficient manner in which you have discharged your duty as Provisional Governor. You will be sustained by the Government." Johnson to Holden, Nov. 27, 1865, Johnson Papers, LC. See Powell to Johnson, and Johnson to Powell, Nov. 27, 1865, Johnson Papers, LC.

2. On December 2 Powell notified the President that the Thirteenth Amendment had been ratified by the legislature, owing largely "to your timely Telegram." Johnson Papers, LC. See Holden to Johnson, Dec. 1, 1865.

From Philip H. Sheridan

Personal.

New Orleans, La., Novr. 26th 1865.

My dear Sir:

I saw Mr. Hendrick day before yesterday and will with great pleasure use all the influence which I may have in promoting the objects he mentioned to me.[1]

There are without doubt many malcontents in the State of Louisiana and much bitterness, but this bitterness is all that is left for these people, there is no power of resistance left, the Country is impoverished and the probability is that in two or three years there will be almost a total transfer of landed property, the North will own every Railroad, every Steamboat, every large mercantile establishment and everything which requires capital to carry it on; in fact Mr. President I consider the South now Northernized. The slave is free and the whole world cannot again enslave him, and with all these facts staring us in the face we can well afford to be lenient to this last annoyance, impotent ill feeling.

Then it is so hard by any species of legislation to correct this feeling, magnanimity is the safest and most manly course. How hard it would

be to change the opinions of Mr. Wendell Phillips and make him a
Vallandigham democrat by any species of legislation. I have the most
abiding faith in the solution of the question of a restored Union, if we
can only wait and trust to a little time and the working of natural
causes.

P. H. Sheridan   Maj Genl

ALS, DLC-JP.

1. Sheridan later recalled that, although Sen. Thomas A. Hendricks tried to persuade
him to support Johnson's Reconstruction policy, he "was powerless to convince me of its
beneficence." Philip H. Sheridan, *Personal Memoirs of P. H. Sheridan* (2 vols., New York,
1888), 2: 278–79.

To James B. Steedman

Private & Confidential

Washington, D.C., Nov 24th[26][1] 1865.

I am free to say that it would be exceedingly impolitic for Mr A. H.
Stephens' name to be used in connection with the Senatorial election.
If elected he would not be permitted to take his seat, or in other words
he could not take the Oath required, other difficulties being out of the
way. He stands charged with Treason, and no disposition has been
made of his case. His present position will enable him to do far more
good, than any other.

Mr Stephens knows that there is no one whose personal feelings are
more kind than mine, and have been so since we first met in Congress.
The information we have here is that all the members elect to Congress
from Georgia, will not be able to take the Oath of Office. A modification
of the Oath by the present Congress is exceedingly doubtful. I hope
you will Confer with Mr Stephens on this subject freely, not as coming
from me.

There seems in many of the elections Something like defiance, which
is all out of place at this time.[2]

Andrew Johnson

Tel, DNA-RG107, Tels. Sent, President, Vol. 2 (1865).

1. Although clearly dated "Nov 24th," this dispatch probably was not sent until two
days later, after Steedman had inquired from Augusta whether the President considered
Stephens's nomination a violation of his parole. Steedman to Johnson, Nov. 25, 1865,
Johnson Papers, LC.

2. See Stephens to Johnson, Jan. 31, 1866.

From Joseph C. Bradley

Huntsville Alabama   Novbr 27 1865

Frank M Gurley[1] who was sentenced for execution in Nashville Tennessee for killing Genl McCook, & afterwards released or exchanged
last spring, was rearrested here last Friday by Military authority & sent
to Nashville, was this evening returned here to be executed next Friday

1st Decr.[2] I do not know on what grounds he was taken up so suddenly, and to be executed so rapidly. Since his return home there has not been in our State any man who has Conducted himself more loyally to the Federal Government than Gurley,—indeed his Conduct has been exemplary as a good & loyal Citizen of our Government. He to my own knowledge, has advised our people, to be obedient to the mandates of the Civil & Military authorities of the United States Government. Now I hope you will make all due allowance for my writeing to you in behalf of Gurley[3]—when I will say to you that when a Company of Rebel Soldiers reached Huntsville after the evacuation of Huntsville in 1862 by the Federal Troops, that an order had been issued to arrest the Hon D C Humphreys Nick Davis & myself as disloyal men to the Confederate Government, Gurley arrived with his Company, and stated to the other Rebel officer who had orders to arrest us, that he should not do it without the loss of his life, & by this course we were releived. Hon D C Humphreys has been hunted down by men who are not the friends of you or the United States Government, and of all the men in Ala, I say to you as your friend that you can implicitly rely on him in every respect. He will be able to give you a better insight into Southern feelings than all the members of Congress from the South—beleive what he says in preference to every Senator & Representative in Congress from Ala. not excepting my friend Govr. Parsons if he should be one of our Senators. When you talk freely with Humphreys,[4] you will soon find that he more nearly accords with your political feelings & views than any other public man in our State, and is willing an able at all times to defend you & your administration. Give him your Confidence & kindness, for he is one of the few men you will have to depend on in Ala. among our public men in the future.

D C Humphreys is accompanied by an out & out Union Man P L Harrison[5] who has never been connected in any shape or form with the Rebellion. He is now & has always been the friend of the Government, & has met with much persecution for his union sentiments. He is a near relative of Genl John A Logan, & if Logan is right politically so is Harrison—this man is worthy of the respect & Confidence of the Government. Mr B T Pope a good union man was elected in our Congressional District over J M Sheid by 32 votes[6]—he is the only Conservative Member of Congress from Ala. You may beleive me wrong when I say to you, that if the Test Oath for Members of Congress is altered—and it will allow the present members elect from the South, to take seats in that body that it will be one of the worst days work that ever happened for the future wellfare of the Union.

Joseph C Bradley

ALS, DLC-JP.
1. Before the war Gurley (1836–1920) was a farmer in his native Madison County, Ala. O. Edward Cunningham, "Captain Frank B. Gurly, Fourth Alabama Cavalry, C.S.A.: Murderer or Victim," *AR*, 28 (1975): 84, 103.

2. Although Gurley had received no pardon for the alleged murder of Robert L. McCook, he had been released in an exchange of prisoners held "in close confinement or in irons" in the spring of 1865. He had subsequently been elected sheriff, but Johnson, on August 29, had ordered his execution, a sentence the President had originally approved as military governor. Ibid., 98, 100. See Holt to Johnson, Jan. 5, 1866.

3. That same day Bradley and others also telegraphed the President on Gurley's behalf. Bradley et al. to Johnson, Nov. 27, 1865, Johnson Papers, LC.

4. Humphreys was to present to Johnson a petition signed by Bradley and more than seventy others requesting that Gurley be "spared." Bradley et al. to Johnson, Nov. 30, 1865; Bradley to Johnson, Dec. 2, 1865, Court-Martial Records, MM-1326, Frank Gurley, RG153, NA. For a discussion of a similar petition from Tennessee, see Holt to Johnson, Jan. 29, 1866.

5. Perry L. Harrison (1829–1885), a farmer, later served as a Madison County commissioner and tax collector. 1860 Census, Ala., Jackson, 4th Div., Paint Rock, 1; Gandrud, *Alabama Records*, 42: 55; 157: 2, 99; 173: 10–11.

6. Although successful, Burwell T. Pope (1813–1868) was not seated in Congress. He later obtained an appointment as a state circuit court judge the year preceding his death. Owen, *History of Ala.*, 4: 1374.

From Andrew J. Hamilton

Austin Texas, Novr 27. 1865.

Mr President:

I have already advised you, by telegram, that I had by Proclamation ordered an election, on the 8th of January, for delegates, to assemble in Convention, on the 7th of February next.[1] I can well conceive, that you have thought me slow to move in this matter, and that you may have felt some impatience, at Texas, being so far behind the other Southern States, in this necessary work.[2] I believe, I have in former communications, given you the reasons, why it could not be done earlier—and I could also give reasons, why it might have been better for Texas, to have delayed the call still longer.[3] The great body of the people are quiet and orderly. They seem disposed to obey the laws, and are doubtless, glad to be once more under the protection of the government of the United States, and anxious to accept every benefit it confers. Still it must be confessed, that a great many, even of this class, have had their minds and hearts so perverted by past teachings, that they accept the favor of Government, as a matter of course, without feeling any corresponding obligation on their part, to make the slightest sacrifice to sustain the Government, or its policy. Even Union men throughout the war, never doubted but the emancipation of slavery would be the result, now that it has come, are some of them, sore and complaining. The sacred negro, (sacred only when a slave) could not be yielded up, without a struggle. Now all sensible men admit, that slavery is dead, but still, there seems to be a desire, and a hope, that some plan will be adopted, which will keep the negro, practically, in bondage. This, it must not be supposed, is either the expectation or wish of *all* of the late slave owners; but certainly of many of them. And even those who do not desire this, have not for the most part, progressed far enough in the lessons taught by the rebellion, to accord to the negro, equal rights, under the law. I speak, not of suffrage; but protection of life, liberty, and property. There is an evident improvement in the public mind upon this subject, steadily going forward: but the public press of the State, and the political teachers became, so utterly depraved during the rebellion, and committed themselves and the people to such extravagances, that they cannot, thus early, embrace and declare the truth; hence, the public mind is working slowly, but I believe steadily, in the right direction. Six months would bring it right. And I even hope, that Congress when it meets, will give such early indications of what is expected of the people of the South, that our Convention will be inclined to act, with more deliberation, and better matured judgment, than would control them, under other circumstances. I can only form my own opinion of what will be expected of the Convention. I have determined in my own mind what it ought to do.

1st To declare the ordinance of Secession null and void from the beginning.

2nd That there is no such Thing as a legal or Constitutional right in a State, to secede, or otherwise attempt, a disruption of the Union.

3rd That slavery is extinguished by the Proclamation of the President, and the acts of Congress.

4th That slavery shall never again exist, in the State.

5th The ratification of the amendments to the U.S. Constitution, prohibiting slavery in all the States and Territories.

6th That the freedom of the late slaves, shall be protected, by guarantees to life liberty and property, by equal laws, allowing to them, the benefit of their oaths, in the courts of the country, upon the same rules of admissability and credability that apply to others.

7th That the debt of the State, created for the purpose of upholding the rebellion, and destroying the Government of the United States; is not, and cannot be binding upon the people of Texas; and cannot be paid, or recognized, without an implied endorsement, of the rebellion, not only unjust to the people of the State; but contumacious and insulting to the Government: and that the same, is not, and can never be, a charge upon the people of Texas. These, I think, are necessary, as Constitutional provisions, to put us in proper position, to assume our former relations to the Union. Less than this, I confess, I would not, myself, be satisfied with; and something like this, in my judgment, will be expected and demanded by the American people, through their representatives in Congress. The influences to be contended against in bringing about this desirable action, are manifold. It would be nearly impossible to enumerate them all: but among the most prominent are: 1st, The wounded pride, resulting from the failure of the rebellion, and the consequent exposure of the false prophesies of its leaders. 2nd The indulgence of that spirit, which causes men, to refuse to be reconciled, to those, whom they have deeply injured, without cause.

3rd The false pride, of not acknowledging an error—together with the want of correct information: soreness at the loss of property—the desire to be again considered political oracles—envy and hatred of Union men—and last and worst; even Union men, who, in order to obtain present preferment, are willing to pander to all of the prejudices of the past—and are full of cant about the tyranny of Govt. &c. &c. To meet all these, I have but little help, from any quarter. The best men of the State, feel very much disinclined, to throw themselves into the breach, and give their active exertions to sweep away all of these hindrances, to right action. I have done what I could, and shall continue to labor to the last. I contemplate making a tour through the most populous portions of the State, before the election, to address the people. I shall plainly and frankly present the views I entertain, of their situation and their duty. This is much needed. The people want to know the truth, and seem to feel instinctively that their former teachers are not the men from whom they can learn it. I have every day calls upon me to go out and talk to them, but up to this time, I have not been able to leave here, even for one day, or an hour. But having organized the State, and got it to running smoothly, I think, I can better employ my time, for two or three weeks, by mingling with the people and giving them good advice, than by attending to the mere details of business in my office, which can be as well done, by my Secretary of State.[4] It is a labor necessary to be performed, and if I dont perform it, so far as I can see, no one will. I could say to you, much more, as to the temper of the people, touching political questions; but it would be tedious. There have been, as was to be expected, many outrages committed upon the freedmen. I have done all in my power to prevent such, and to bring to punishment the guilty parties. But in sections of the State, remote from any Military force, I have not been able to accomplish much. You will perceive, that I felt it my duty, to issue an address to the freedmen, with a view of disabusing their minds of false notions, as to what the Government would do for them. There is no doubt, but that many of them, really believed, that about Christmas, they would be furnished with homes, and whatever else they might need.[5] This was calculated to disincline them to hire, to labor for fair wages, and I had reason to fear that mid winter, would find them without homes or food, and that they would be compelled to go stealing, to preserve life, and then the whites, would have something more than a pretext, for killing them: and with a view, to prevent such a state of things, I issued the address to the freedmen: also, an authority to the Chief Justices of the Counties, to organize a Police force,[6] to preserve order, and prevent violence—copies of which, I herewith enclose; as also a copy of my

Proclamation for a Convention.[7] I feel confident, that they will have the desired effect, and that the public peace will be maintained.

You will permit me now, Mr. President, to say a word, upon the subject of diminishing the Military force in Texas. I will not present you the reasons, at this time, for what I urge; beyond the statement which I deliberately make; that it will not be safe, to reduce it lower, than it now is. I do not mean that the United States would have anything to fear in a military point of view; but it would have much to lose, in the way of deferring the restoration of Society and Civil Government in Texas. There is no fear, of an organized force to openly defy the power of the Government, but there would, beyond doubt, be thousands of individual acts of insult and injury, to loyal citizens, by that class of men, who are bitter in their feelings towards the Government and its friends. They are not the majority, but there is so large a percentum of such men, as to enable them; in many localities, in the present demoralized condition of society, to defy the local civil law. The largest portion of the forces, now in the State, are on the Rio Grande, and this, I suppose, for obvious reasons, will continue to be the case; so that there is left for the whole of the immense territory of the State, where our people actually reside, not more than six or eight thousand troops. If this number should be distributed between such points in the State, as will afford reasonable aid to the Civil authorities, in keeping the public peace, they will be found hardly adequate to the task. As it now is, very much the largest portion of the State, in territory; and very much the largest portion of our people, have no such protection. Besides, the people on our Indian border, are suffering terribly, from the constant depredations of the Indians. So far, no permanent Posts, have been established on this border. If it is not soon done, the whole Northern frontier will be compelled to recede. It is now, in fact, daily receding. Our people have been patient. They know that they have not been blameless in producing this state of things. But it is sad, that the innocent, must suffer, for the wrongs of the guilty. I most respectfully urge upon your Excellency, that a force, be directed to occupy the Indian frontier and I at the same time, for the reasons given, would strongly recommend that no further diminution of the forces in Texas, be made.

They are needed, and will be, for many months to some, if we are to have order and security to life and property.[8]

A J Hamilton   Provl. Govr. of Texas

ALS, DLC-JP.

1. See Hamilton to Johnson, Nov. 17, 1865, Johnson Papers, LC.

2. By the time Congress met in December 1865, Texas was the only former Confederate state that had neither held a constitutional convention nor conducted congressional and legislative elections. Johnson later expressed his pleasure at Hamilton's call for a convention, assuring him that "Nothing shall be left undone by the Government which will give you aid in the work of restoration." Johnson to Hamilton, Dec. 1, 1865, Tels. Sent, President, Vol. 2 (1865), RG107, NA.

3. See Hamilton to Johnson, Sept. 23, Oct. 21, 1865.

4. James H. Bell.

5. On November 17, 1865, Hamilton pointed out to blacks that the Federal government owned no land in Texas and that the state would not take land from whites to give to freedmen. "Address to the Freedmen of Texas," Nov. 17, 1865, Executive Record Book 281: 129–31, Tx-Ar.

6. These local units would consist of "not less than ten, nor more than fifty men" who, "in conjunction with . . . the United States military authorities," would safeguard the "peace and quiet of the country." "Proclamation by the Governor," Nov. 18, 1865, ibid., 132–33.

7. Not found. A copy of the latter proclamation, dated November 15, 1865, can be found in ibid., 124–28.

8. Despite Johnson's assurances, demobilization of volunteer units in Texas proceeded apace, leading to a marked decrease in the number of troops in the state by mid-1866. William L. Richter, *The Army in Texas During Reconstruction, 1865–1870* (College Station, Tex., 1987), 27.

From William W. Holden

Raleigh   Nov 27 1865.

Sir.

Your dispatch has been received.[1] I am very grateful to you for this additional proof of your confidence & friendship. My health has much improved. Hope to be able in a few days to attend actively to my duties. I trust your dispatch will have a good effect upon the Legislature but the indications thus far are not satisfactory.

There is a tie in the Senate between Settle unionist and Ferebee secessionist for the Speakership[2]—tomorrow or next day will decide. Mr Phillips[3] elected Speaker of Commons not satisfactory to the Unionist. Two of the clerks of the Commons Secessionists. McAden of Alamance unpardoned rebell has taken his seat and votes.

I will oust him by force if necessary as soon as the Houses are organized. Gov Graham presented his credentials in the Senate but did not claim his seat. He requested me to inform you that He had been elected to the senate from the County of Orange & He desires to know your determination in regard to his pardon.[4] I do this as a matter of form. I do not advise His pardon.

He ought not to be pardoned at this time. He is the head & front of the present opposition to the administration & his friends are retarding the work of reconstruction. The Worth or Graham faction are said to be alarmed & may offer a compromise—but on the other hand it is the current talk that Graham & Vance are to be the senators.

Rest assured Sir, I will do all in my power to prevent bad men from ruining our poor old state.

W W Holden   Pro Gov

Tel, DLC-JP.

1. Johnson to Holden, Nov. 27, 1865, Johnson Papers, LC. See Robert J. Powell to Johnson, Nov. 26, 1865.

2. Thomas Settle, Jr. (1831–1888), was a Confederate officer whom Grant later appointed minister to Peru and a district judge in Florida. Dennis D. Ferebee

(1815–1884) was a former legislator who had been among a handful of convention delegates who opposed declaring the secession ordinance null and void. Settle, Holden's choice, defeated Worth's candidate, Ferebee. *DAB*; Johnston, *Vance Papers*, 1: 341; Robert J. Powell to Johnson, Nov. 27, 1865, Johnson Papers, LC.

3. According to Powell, Samuel F. Phillips (1824–1903), who during the war had represented Orange County in the Assembly, was elected speaker "without opposition." Ibid.; *NUC*; Connor, *N.C. Manual*, 742.

4. See Joseph S. Cannon to Johnson, Nov. 13, 1865.

From Benjamin F. Perry

Columbia S.C. Nov 27. 1865.

Will you please inform me whether the South Carolina members of Congress should be in Washington at the organization of the House? Will the clerk of the House,[1] call their names? If their credentials are presented to him, will the test oath be required or will it be refused by Congress? If the members are not allowed to take their seats they do not wish to incur the trouble & expense of going on and the mortification of being rejected. Do give your views and wishes.

B W[*sic*] Perry   Prov Gov S.C.

Tel, DLC-JP.
1. Edward McPherson.

To Benjamin F. Perry

Washington   Nov 27th 1865.

I do not think it necessary for the members elect for S.C. to be present, at the organization of congress. On the contrary it will be better policy to present their certificates of election after the two houses are organized which will then be a simple question, under the constitution, of the members taking their seats. Each house must judge for itself the election returns & qualification of its own members. As to what the two houses will do, in reference to the oath, now required to be taken, before the members can take their seats, is unknown to me; & I do not like to predict. But upon the whole I am of opinion that it would be better for the question to come up & be disposed of after the two houses have been organized. I hope that your legislature will adopt a code in reference to free persons of color that will be acceptable to the country at the same time doing justice to the white & colored population.[1]

Andrew Johnson   Presdt

Tel, A-AR, B. F. Perry Papers.
1. See Perry to Johnson, Dec. 9, 1865. See also James L. Orr to Johnson, Dec. 23, 1865.

From Lucy E.W. Polk[1]

Warrenton   Nov 27th [1865][2]

Mr President

I believe I am indebted by promise a letter but, have hesitated to comply, knowing your public duties are such as to monopolize so entirely your time as to allow you but little leisure for social or private correspondence. But I act on your suggestion that "I was as much entitled to a part of your time as any one else." After leaving Washington City in June I went directly to Nashville & Columbia, found our friends quite well, & I believe generally disposed to act in concert with the government for the best interest of the Country. All seemed anxious to be employed & I trust will be wiser & better from the four years of sad experience. I did not remain but a few days with Mrs James K. Polk heard her speak of Mrs Patterson who report says will do the honors of "The White House." I hope to have the pleasure of seeing her this winter unless prevented from going to Washington. I left Tennessee about the last of September came to Carolina hoping to collect the fragments of a scattered fortune but thus far without success. My only reliance now, is that the Government will attend to the necessities of its loyal citizens & your kind promise to aid me, as far as in your power. At all events, I have the "clerkship["] to fall back on. I wrote Mr. Hughes[3] to say to you, that if the Government needed my services, I hoped you would command them. I have not the vanity to presume that I can convey any items of Political news. Our State elections passed off very quietly. Our Freedmen, but few will make any contracts until after Christmas. They are thoroughly impressed with the idea that the Government intends giving them the lands. Our mails but imperfectly managed, yet much better than we could expect. What paper is the organ of the "Presidents" Party? I would like to get it. I suppose there are quite a number of Tennesseans now in Washington. I hope Mrs. J. has recovered her health. If in the multitude of your cares & joys, a stray thought should wander to friends in Carolina is it requesting too much to ask you to commit it to Paper? We all are interested in your wellfare. The prayers of a Nation are offered for your prosperity & happiness.

Mrs. William H. Polk   Warrenton N.C.

ALS, DLC-JP.

1. The third wife of William H. Polk, brother of the late President, Lucy E. Williams (b. c1831) was a native of Warren County, N.C. Her husband had died in 1862. Mrs. Frank M. Angellotti, *The Polks of North Carolina and Tennessee* (Easley, S.C., 1984), 65–66; 1860 Census, Tenn., Maury, 9th Dist., Columbia, 71.

2. Internal evidence contained in the letter confirms that this document was written in 1865.

3. Not identified.

From Lewis E. Parsons

Montgomery Ala   Nov 28 1865.

Sir

I am informed by several loyal citizens of Madison County that Frank Gurley is to be returned to that place on Friday the 1st December. They earnestly desire Execution of sentence, may be suspended till the loyal men of Alabama Can be heard from. I join in their request, in a most earnest & respectfull manner. I trust you will grant it. I know nothing of the facts except from the paper reports, but am sure no harm Can result from a suspension of the sentence. Please answer to me & telegraph Genl Grierson.[1] All is progressing favorably in regard to Construction.

L E Parsons   Pro Gov

Tel, DLC-JP.

1. Later that afternoon Johnson ordered Gen. Benjamin H. Grierson (1826–1911), the cavalry officer who as district commander had custody of Gurley, to suspend the Alabamian's sentence. Subsequently, the President directed that the judge advocate general review the case against Gurley. Warner, *Blue*; Johnson to Parsons, Nov. 28, 1865; Johnson to Grierson, Nov. 28, 1865, Tels. Sent, President, Vol. 2 (1865), RG107, NA. See Holt to Johnson, Jan. 5, 29, 1866.

From John T. Pickett[1]

Washington, November 28th 1865.

Mr President,

I am a paroled officer of the late Confederate army. Having come to this place (where I had resided before the war), some months ago meditating an application for the benefit of your amnesty proclamation, I was given to understand, by what I deemed to be competent authority, that, inasmuch as I had been Commissioner of the Confederate Government to a foreign state (Mexico) my petition would be rejected. I therefore resolved to await patiently a more favorable opportunity for the restoration of my political rights. It is not my intention now to molest you with any such application, but I do most respectfully request such indulgence as will ensure me protection in person and property (not recently molested, it is true), until the dawn of an era of better feeling, in which you may be able to carry out fully your magnanimous policy.[2]

Jno: T. Pickett

ALS, DLC-JP.

1. After the war Pickett (1822–1884), a former U.S. diplomat and expansionist, practiced law in the District of Columbia. Wakelyn, *BDC*; *NUC*.

2. Pickett's parole, which permitted him to remain in Washington undisturbed, was signed by Johnson on December 9, 1865. A subsequent pardon request by Pickett has not been found. Causten-Pickett Papers, LC.

From Adrian V.S. Lindsley

Nashville   Nov. 29th 1865

Dear Sir

Dr John D. Kelly formerly of this City,[1] but since the first of this year a citizen of Paducah Kentucky, is an applicant for the Collectorship of Internal Revenue for the District in Kentucky embracing Paducah.

It affords me great pleasure to state that Dr Kelly during the whole of this rebellion has been a firm, consistant & devoted Union man. He is well qualified for the situation he is seeking. He is also an old resident of Paducah & represented the County in which Paducah is situated in the Kentucky Legislature, before he removed to Nashville.

The Dr. enjoys the confidence of the Union men of Nashville & Davidson County,[2] and his appointment to the place asked for would be a great gratification to all of them.[3]

A.V.S. Lindsley

ALS, DNA-RG56, Appts., Internal Revenue Service, Collector, Ky., 1st Dist., John D. Kelly.

1. Kelly (c1810–1870) had practiced medicine in Nashville for almost thirty years. John Wooldridge, ed., *History of Nashville* (Nashville, 1890), 529; 1860 Census, Tenn., Davidson, Nashville, 2nd Ward, 37.

2. The files contain several letters in support of the appointment of Kelly from notable Nashville residents. See, for example, Russell Houston to Johnson, Dec. 1, 1865; Edward H. East to Johnson, Dec. 2, 1865; John Trimble to Johnson, Nov. 29, 1865, Appts., Internal Revenue Service, Collector, Ky., 1st Dist., John D. Kelly, RG56, NA.

3. Members of Johnson's family also became involved in this matter. In 1866 Kelly was appointed collector of internal revenue for the 1st district of Kentucky, located at Paducah. Robert Johnson to William E. Chandler, Dec. 21, 1865; Kelly to David T. Patterson, Nov. 30, 1865, ibid.; Wooldridge, *Nashville*, 529; *U.S. Off. Reg.* (1867), 81.

From Elizabeth R. Milligan

Greenville   Nov 29th 1865.

I trust your Excellency will pardon the liberty I take, of thus intruding upon your time. And the only apology I can offer is, that I feel some manifestation of gratitude is due you, for your kindness in extending pardon, to my unfortunate and *misled* brother.[1]

My husband reached home safely, and another object of my letter is to thank you, for the kindness and hospitality, shown him, by yourself and family, during his sojourn in Washington.[2] We feel that our obligations to you, are named *Legion*, and if we can never repay you, in a more *substantial* way, you will at any rate, *always* have the confidence and esteem of two honest hearts.

I feel the deepest interest, in the success of your Administration, and if you can get the machinery of our beloved Government to working as harmoniously, as it did, before the outbreak of the late accursed rebellion, the nation's thanks, will be due you, and from no heart, will go out, a louder, warmer, or more sincere response, than yours. . . .

E. R. Milligan.

ALS, DLC-JP.
1. George A. Howard had on June 1 applied for pardon, which was granted on November 16. Amnesty Papers (M1003, Roll 49), Tenn., George A. Howard, RG94, NA.
2. Johnson had been attempting for some weeks to entice Sam Milligan to visit him at Washington. Johnson to Milligan, Oct. 27, Nov. 2, 1865, Tels. Sent, President, Vol. 2 (1865), RG107, NA; Milligan to Johnson, Nov. 4, 1865, Johnson Papers, LC.

From Benjamin F. Perry

Columbia   Nov 29 1865

On Counting the votes yesterday it was ascertained that Jas L Orr was elected Govr by a small majority.[1] He was inaugurated today & made a most admirable address. By our new Constitution all bills must be presented to the Govr for his approval. This required his immediate inauguration in order to pass the law for protection of the Freedmen. I hope you will permit me to turn over the Govt of the State to him.[2] There is the most loyal feeling possible in the legislature.

B F Perry   Pro Gov

Tel, DLC-JP.
1. Orr defeated Wade Hampton, who refused to be a candidate, by fewer than eight hundred votes. Roger P. Leemhuis, *James L. Orr and the Sectional Conflict* (Washington, D.C., 1979), 102.
2. See Perry to Johnson, Dec. 9, 1865.

From Zebulon B. Vance

Statesville N.C.   Novr. 29th 1865

I respectfully ask permission to visit Washington City for the purpose of obtaining an interview with you.

Should you not see proper to grant this request, I would be greatly obliged if your Excellency would order my enlargement so far as to permit me to enter into some business by which to support my family.[1]

Zebulon B. Vance

ALS, DNA-RG94, Amnesty Papers (M1003, Roll 43), N.C., Zebulon B. Vance.
1. In mid-December the President permitted Vance to travel freely throughout the state of North Carolina. However, Johnson ignored this and other requests for an interview and refused to pardon Vance until March 1867. Dowd, *Life of Vance*, 100–101; Dorris, *Pardon and Amnesty*, 217–18.

From William O. Bartlett[1]

Metropolitan Hotel [New York][2], Nov. 30, 1865.

Dear Sir:

My great anxiety is that the message should relieve you of all responsibility for the financial crime of Mr. Chase,[3] which has cost the country not less than a thousand millions of dollars. Then, when the crash comes, which is now as certain as the law of gravitation, your supporters can say to the public: "President Johnson warned you of this in his very first Message. It is Mr. Chase's doing, not his."

If the language in which your antagonism to his policy is stated be as mild as that of the enclosed paper[4] it seems to me that it should be no less clear and unambiguous to make your position universally understood. This is necessary from the circumstance that you were elected on the same ticket with Mr. Lincoln, upon whose administration Mr. Chase had saddled his disastrous blunder; and the necessity for it is heightened by your inheriting from Mr. Lincoln a Secretary of the Treasury and a Comptroller of the Currency,[5] both strong Chase men, original supporters of his policy, and even now, to say the least, its apologists and whitewashers. Without such disclaimer they give a degree of Chase odor to your administration, which will be fatal to its popularity, when the unavoidable financial collapse comes; even if, on all other subjects your policy were dictated by super human wisdom.

The brief and simple statement of the saving to be made by the substitution of Government currency, for that of the banks, once spread before the people in the President's Message, they will take care—prompted by self-interest—to compel Congress to provide some practical measure to carry it into effect.

This could easily be done by taxing the banks, say ten per cent, on every re-issue of their notes, and providing that such notes as were not redeemed by the banks, after a certain date, should be redeemed by the U.S. Treasurer; in which case, by the terms of the law, the bonds deposited with him as security become forfeit to the Government, and could be cancelled.

W. O. Bartlett

ALS, DLC-JP.

1. Bartlett (c1820–1881) was an attorney who later became a writer for several prominent New York newspapers. *New York Times*, Sept. 24, 1881.

2. The Metropolitan Hotel from which Bartlett wrote was presumably the one in New York City where he had his office. *Trow's New York City Directory* (1866), 62.

3. Salmon P. Chase.

4. Bartlett enclosed his proposal for a passage in Johnson's upcoming annual message to Congress. Beginning with a statement that the issue of paper currency was to be "regretted" as a "violation of a fixed and inflexible principle of finance," the draft called for the substitution of notes issued by the national government for "those of the national banks." This plan, it concluded, would retire the public debt in thirty-eight years.

5. Hugh McCulloch and probably Robert W. Taylor (*c*1813-*fl*1875), a former Ohio state auditor who by 1863 had been appointed to the 1st comptroller position. 1860 Census, Ohio, Franklin, Columbus, 3rd Ward, 215; *U.S. Off. Reg.* (1863–75).

From Henry S. Fitch[1]

New York   Nov 30, 1865

Sir

I sail with my family this week for Savannah and as my professional arrangements will depend greatly upon the success or failure of my application for U S Dist Attorney for Georgia, your early decision is to me a matter of great importance. I have been so deeply impressed by the unexampled responsibilities demanding every moment of your time that I have not written even this brief letter without hessitation—but my necessities must plead my excuse. That my appointment would prove acceptable, I think, the influential names upon my petition including the endorsement of the Provisional Governor will abundantly show and as to my legal qualifications I would respectfully refer to Hon O H Browning Hon James Hughes, Judge E Peck, Genl Farnsworth[2] and Hon Thurlow Weed.

Assuring your, Excellency that whether I shall be the recipient of your kindness or among the many who must be necessarially disappointed I will ever remain a sincere admirer of your firm but generous policy towards a people with whom I have cast my fortunes.[3]

Henry S. Fitch

ALS, DNA-RG60, Appt. Files for Judicial Dists., Ga., Henry S. Fitch.

1. A son of Graham N. Fitch, Johnson's former congressional colleague from Indiana, Fitch (1834–1871) served previously as U.S. district attorney at Chicago and as staff officer under Generals Fremont, Pope, and William T. Sherman. Roscoe C. Fitch, comp., *History of the Fitch Family* (2 vols., Haverhill, Mass., 1930), 2: 65–66; *Logansport Journal* (Ind.), Nov. 30, 1892.

2. Ebenezer Peck (1805–1881) was judge of the court of claims in Washington, D.C. John F. Farnsworth (1820–1897) was a former brigadier and a Republican congressman (1856–60, 1863–73) from Illinois. *BDAC*; *Appleton's Cyclopaedia.*

3. Recommended by the mayor and other residents of Savannah, Fitch received the appointment and began work on May 9, 1866. Richard D. Arnold et al. to Johnson, Aug. 16, 1865, Appt. Files for Judicial Dists., Ga., Henry S. Fitch, RG60, NA; Avery, *Georgia*, 360.

December 1865

From Douglas H. Cooper

[ca. December 1865, Indian Territory]; ALS, DNA-RG94, Amnesty Papers (M1003, Roll 13), Ark., Douglas Hancock Cooper.

A Mississippian who served as agent to the Choctaws and Chickasaws until May 1861 applies for pardon. Following his adoption by the Chickasaws, he organized "*a force for the defence of the Indian Country, and the preservation of order*," inasmuch as the withdrawal of United States forces "had *left* them, 'free and independent' to adopt Such measures as in their judgment were necessary and proper *for self preservation and defence*." For the Confederacy he acted as Indian agent, though he never received a commission, and as colonel of a mounted regiment. As soon as Kirby Smith surrendered the Trans-Mississippi Department, Cooper urged the Grand Council of the Nations and Tribes "to renew treaties, and restore ancient relations of Peace and Friendship with the United States." He continues "his efforts to reconcile the Indians to the new order of things." His petition for pardon may not conform to the prescribed regulations because "he does not reside within any State or organized territory of the United States," but he "hopes that he will not be held to a strict compliance." [He was pardoned on April 27, 1866.]

From George Bancroft[1]

New York, 1 Dec, '65.

My dear Sir,

Mr. Sumner was here yesterday, & spent two or three hours with me. I did all in my power to calm him down on the suffrage question, & he admitted fully that *the President* could not have granted the suffrage.

I believe he left me, bent on making in the Senate certain speeches, which he has prepared elaborately, but resolved to cultivate friendly relations with you. He told me he should call on you tomorrow night.[2] I take leave to hint, that on *foreign relations* he agrees with you exactly; & that, as he is chairman of the Committee of foreign relations, a *little freedom of conversation* on your part on our foreign affairs would conciliate him amazingly. He goes in the main well-disposed.

Public opinion is all with you.

Geo. B

ALS, DLC-JP.
1. Bancroft marked the front of the envelope of his letter, "For the President alone"; on the back he wrote, "Private."
2. An account of Charles Sumner's stormy meeting with the President can be found in David Donald, *Charles Sumner and the Rights of Man* (New York, 1970), 237–38.

From Jennie Brice[1]

Raleigh N. Carolina, December 1st, 1865.

President Johnson:

Ladies, I believe are at all times recognized as privileged characters; exercising my perogative as such, I address *you*, believing that you will at least peruse these lines. If I *seem* to lack respect attribute it to the *head*, not the *heart*. *I mean* to address you with the respect due the man whose actions show that his soul expands with magnanimity, & that he is truly great & noble.

I embrace this method of asking a favor. Do not turn away. It is not for "an office for a friend" nor the "pardon of myself or friends." *I* do not feel that any crime lies at my door, unless hating the yankees with an intensity that defies expression be such—but it is to ask that you visit your native state and this your native city. Come as a private individual, so disguised as that none will know you. Mingle among the people, hear their sentiments towards yourself—see the people *as they are*—in short come, use *your* own eyes and ears instead of Gov. Holden's.

You know that this state was slow to secede—slow to enter a war that she vainly, but bravely tried to ward off. When it came, she could but enter it, and *nobly* did she do her part in fighting, as she then felt, for liberty. The old North state may be wrong in many ways, but hypocritical *never*!

Being known as a rebel, I have been thrown much among those who *have been* the most rebellious; I have conversed with Carolina's best & noblest sons—and I have never yet heard one word spoken against you, or the course you have pursued. They assert their willingness to support you, but like myself they cannot believe that *you* and *W. W. Holden are one and the same person*. It is generally believed that Holden was appointed provisional governor from *necessity* not choice. We believe you to be consistent while *we know*, as does all the reading world that Holden has no idea what that word means. *Office* is his god and he would sell his soul for it. (Is it treason to speak thus of a provisional governor? If so—I am a traitoress.) The people of N.C. look upon you as a generous, kind and noble man—who is willing to forgive those who swear allegiance to the government you represent, and while yankee soldiers and Holden are not *beloved*, you are. We do not, can not, *will not* believe that you are such a man as Holden, and while you see abusive articles refering to him, you find nothing of the kind in connection with your name. Pray tell me what confidence we can put in a man who is first a "methodist"—then an "Episcopalian"—One year a Democrat next a Whig—then a "know nothing"—a ranting secessionist then a Unionist? Can such a "turn coat" have the confidence of the people? Never, never!! Yet Holden would lead you to believe that we are working against *you* & the government, while he knows as well as we do it is not you or the government, but W. W. Holden, whom we would work against. We know him too well to love him!—too well to trust him, and if you would have N.C. love her governor give her another whom she can *trust*. Take him from us!

The man elected by the voice of the people to the gubernatorial chair,[2] has never been a secessionist, has ever been for the Union. He is the people's choice; Holden never was and never can be—he is too much of a demagogue.

Come to Carolina, learn for yourself that we have been grossly misrepresented, learn, what you may never learn in Washington that the old north state can and will submit to the powers that be. We have been called a people of common sense, at least—and does not *that* teach us that we are powerless? We are tired of military law, and N.C. is willing to go back to her old place in the Union, not merely willing but anxious. We know as well as you do that we were over-powered and that to-day as Poland, we lie as powerless—helpless—worn, weary, wounded, crushed and ruined at the feet of a mighty conquerer. *Unlike* Poland, we are in the hand of a "generous foe"—(no I must call you *friend*, if you will allow a little rebel girl to do so—) one whose heart yearns over us, and while that one is beloved, and reverenced he is not a terror to the erring asses. Come and see that N. Carolina has lost none of her nobleness, and that she feels that you are her truest friend.

I believe that God in his infinite love gave us into *your* hands—(I mean to cast no reproach on him, whose sad death gave you the presidential chair) and that He is watching over us, and that He moves your heart to feel for the poor downtrodden children of the South. May He *guide guard*, protect and eternally preserve you!

Forgive me for thus tresspassing on your time, but if I could only believe that these lines would vindicate the cause of our state, I think that *you would* freely forgive. Will you not make an effort to see North Carolina as it is? If I could only be instrumental in bringing about a better understanding between you and this state, I would feel that my life had not been spent in vain,—feel that I had accomplished that, of which the greatest might be proud.

I know not whither came the *courage* to address the chief ruler of this nation. Alone in my room miles and miles from those I love, in the midst of strangers I sit night after night and think of my dearly loved country and of the misunderstanding between the government and the people, and tears course down my cheeks. Tonight suddenly I thought that I, little and unknown, tho' I am, might perhaps reach your ear, and I have written *just* as I *feel*—written what I know to be true and I am hoping that you will at least read these lines.

The door is open for you to add fresh laurels to those that already adorn your brow. See—know, and *trust* the people. Make to yourself a name in the South and the homeless widow and orphan—the generous & brave men will "rise up and call you blessed."

                    Jennie Brice   At L. Branson's[3]   Raleigh N.C.

Permit me to ask that this be burned, lest it fall into the hands of your subordinates and this rebel girl be ridiculed.

ALS, DLC-JP.
   1. Not identified.
   2. Jonathan Worth.
   3. Levi Branson (1832–1903) was variously an instructor, a publisher, and a Methodist minister. 1860 Census, N.C., Lenoir, Bear Creek Dist., Lenoir Institute, 71; Murray, *Wake County N.C.*, 565, 567; *NUC*; *Atlanta Constitution*, Dec. 7, 1903.

From William W. Holden

                                    Raleigh   Dec 1st 1865.
Sir

The legislature has ratified with but six dissenting voices The congressional amendment abolishing slavery. Five Judges have been elected all good selections. Three of my provisional appointments have been confirmed. Your dispatch[1] has had a good effect but I cannot predict the result as to the senatorships. Senators will be elected on monday. It is believed that gov Graham will be elected. There appears to be a clear anti administion or secession majority on Joint ballot. I have not changed my opinion in regard to gov Graham. He is more subdued however & may take occasion in a day or two to define his position. There are all kinds of combinations here but I still hope for the best.[2]

                                    W W Holden   Pro Gov

Tel, DLC-JP.
   1. See Robert J. Powell to Johnson, Nov. 26, 1865.
   2. See Powell to Johnson, Dec. 2, 1865 and Holden to Johnson, Dec. 6, 1865.

From A.O.P. Nicholson
(Private)

                                    Columbia Tenn.   Dec. 1, 1865.
Dear Sir:

For several months past I have been indulging the hope that I would be able to make a visit to Washington, which would enable me to tender to you in person my sincere thanks for your kindness in extending to me a special Pardon,[1] but week after week, I have found myself so pressed for means to supply the wants of my family, that I have been utterly unable to command either the time or the means to make the contemplated visit. As I can now see no reasonable prospect of being able soon to tender to you in person my acknowledgments I beg of you now to accept of them and to be assured that I am deeply grateful not only for your kindness in granting me a pardon but for your kindness to me whilst I was in prison. I would much prefer to make these acknowledgments in person but I am compelled to admit that I am not able to command either the time or the means to do so. When I was imprisoned my family had been stripped of evey necessary of life— when I was released, by your kind interference, it became necessary for me to work without intermission, to procure the necessaries of subsistence. Such has been my situation ever since and such, I fear, is to be my situation indefinitely hereafter.

But I have been blessed with good health and on that account I can submit without complaint to all my privations.

After waiting some months and becoming satisfied that I could do so with safety, I resumed the practice of the Law. I have not found it so easy, as I hoped, to procure a living business, but by close attention I still hope to be able to live, unless the Legislature should take away my license, as they propose to do. If the pending bill, rendering lawyers incapable of practicing, should become a law, I shall have either to migrate to some other state, or take the chance between starving or making a living by manual labor. I hope, however, that the Legislature may not do so absurd a thing as they now propose.[2]

I have observed your course as President with much interest and have had much occasion, in so doing, to approve your policy and to feel hopeful of the future. I have all the time had misgivings as to the success of your policy, because my faith was weak in the patriotism of the extreme radicals. My hope and that of our people has been centered in you, and I think I can safely say, that at no time of your life have you enjoyed so much of the confidence of our people as since your policy as President has been developed. I wish it were in my power to give to your administration some more substantial support than my hearty approval. But I have learned patience and resignation under all circumstances, and hence, as I can do no more, I give you my constant prayers for your safe deliverance from all your trials and responsibilities, and a successful solution of all the difficulties which surround your position. I hope it is not necessary for me to add, that it would give me happiness at any time to serve you either as an individual or as an official in any capacity in which you might choose to command my services.

A.O.P. Nicholson

ALS, DLC-JP.

1. Nicholson had been pardoned by Johnson on August 28, 1865. See Nicholson to Johnson, June 4, 1865, *Johnson Papers*, 8: 178–79.

2. Although the legislature did not pass such a measure, Nicholson's fears may have been raised by a bill introduced on October 27, "Declaring certain persons ineligible to hold certain offices." *Tenn. House Journal, 1865–66*, 96.

From William Henry Trescot

Columbia [S.C.]   Dec 1st 1865.

Genl Howard in pursuance of your instructions ordered the restoration of the Island lands where the owners Consented to make Contracts with the Freedmen. He appointed a Supervising Board of Contracts.[1] His representative, Capt Ketchum[2] decided that a Negro should be one of the Board. Gen Howard while I was in Washington Telegraphed that he meant the Board to be Composed of whites one Selected by the Freedmen.[3] In defiance of this instruction a negro has been placed upon the Board. He has declared that no Contracts will be made that nothing but the ownership of the lands will satisfy the Freedmen. Capt Ketchum has through him submitted to the Freedmen of Edisto Certain questions. One is whether the Freedmen will buy the lands of the former owners if assisted by the U.S. I earnestly urged upon you when in Washington the removal of Gen Saxton. Here is the proof of the utter impossibility of doing anything as long as he Controls this Dept of the Bureau.

I have just received reliable intelligence that Gen Syckles has been obliged to order a Compy to Edisto.[4] I again most earnestly appeal for the immediate removal of Gen Saxton.[5]

Wm. Henry Trescott[sic]   Ex agt of the State of S C.

Tel, DLC-JP.

1. Issued on October 19, 1865, Howard's Special Field Orders No. 1 had directed that the board consist of a Freedmen's Bureau agent and "two other citizens—one to be selected by the land-owners or their agents, the second by the resident freedmen or their agents." *House Ex. Docs.*, 39 Cong., 1 Sess., No. 11, p. 7 (Ser. 1255).

2. Alexander P. Ketchum (1839-*fl*1901), a former aide to Gen. Rufus Saxton, was later appointed by Grant to fill several Treasury Department posts in New York. *NCAB*, 2: 351; *Trow's New York City Directory* (1902), 713.

3. Ketchum had replied that, unless a black board member was allowed to serve, an agreement with the freedmen could not be reached. See Howard to William Whaley, Nov. 23; Howard to Ketchum, Nov. 25; Max Woodhull to Ketchum, Dec. 4, 1865, Records of the Commr., Lets. Sent (M742, Roll 1), RG105, NA.

4. Although Howard had authorized the formation of a military "police force" to keep the peace between the freedmen and former owners, such an order by Gen. Daniel E. Sickles, commander of the district of South Carolina at Charleston, has not been found.

5. This telegram was endorsed by Benjamin F. Perry and James L. Orr. After an official investigation prompted by a petition signed by former governor William Aiken and others, Saxton was removed by Johnson's order on January 15, 1866. By late February Ketchum had been transferred to Washington, D.C. *House Reports*, 39 Cong., 1 Sess., No. 30, "Joint Committee on Reconstruction," pt. 2: 216 (Ser. 1273); Oubre, *Forty Acres and A Mule*, 61; Henry E. Tremain, *Two Days of War: A Gettysburg Narrative and Other Excursions* (New York, 1905), 247–83.

From Gideon Welles

December 1, 1865, Washington, D.C.; LS, NN-Gideon Welles Papers.

In response to the President's referral of a complaint from the working men of New York "on the subject chiefly of wages in the Navy Yards," the Secretary of the Navy encloses a copy of Rear Admiral Joseph Smith's report on the matter. According to law, Navy Yard employees' salaries "shall conform, as nearly as is consistent with the public interest, with those of private establishments in the immediate vicinity of the respective yards." Welles confesses to the Department's embarrassment that "it has been found almost impossible . . . to comply with the law . . . and give satisfaction at the same time to all classes of mechanics." Indirectly, he suggests that current discontent may reflect the recent war's-end reduction in the number of workmen in the yards.

From Lewis E. Parsons

Montgomery   Dec 2d 1865.

Tis done. The amendment as adopted by Alabama by more than 2/3d vote in the House & by 4/5 in the Senate.[1] When the act is passed giving the same protection to the persons & property of Freedmen as our non-voting white population enjoy[2] shall I be permitted to turn over the Government to the Governor elect? He is perfectly reliable. Please answer.[3]

L E Parsons

Tel, DLC-JP.

1. On this same date Parsons telegraphed Stanton, asking if Johnson would "allude to the fact that Alabama is the twenty seventh state" to ratify the Thirteenth Amendment. Stanton's reply was noncommittal, but Seward later conveyed the congratulations of the President on Alabama's completing the requisite two-thirds for ratification. Parsons to Stanton, Dec. 2, 1865, Johnson Papers, LC; Stanton to Parsons, Dec. 4, 1865; Seward to Parsons, Dec. 5, 1865, Tels. Sent, Sec. of War (M473, Roll 90), RG107, NA.

2. See Parsons to Johnson, Dec. 9, 1865, Johnson Papers, LC.

3. Johnson replied on December 6 that he would send "full instructions" the next day, but it was not until after a second inquiry from Parsons that the President authorized Robert M. Patton's inauguration, which took place on December 13. Pursuant to instructions from Seward, Parsons officially transferred the government of Alabama to Patton on December 20. Johnson to Parsons, Dec. 6, 10, 1865, Tels. Sent, President, Vol. 2 (1865), RG107, NA; *Senate Ex. Docs.*, 39 Cong., 1 Sess., No. 26, pp. 110–12 (Ser. 1237).

From Benjamin F. Perry

Columbia S.C   Dec 2nd. 1865

My Dear Sir

The enclosed state[ment] is from a gentleman of the strictest veracity,[1] and exhibits the Deplorable condition of our State.

The Treasury agents are practicing great frauds & in many instances robbing individuals of private cotton, horses, saddles, &c without the possibility of redress. Let me entreat your Exellency, to organize a District Court of the United States, in South Carolina,[2] to hear and try all cases in which the Government claims property in possession of individuals. Do not let these Treasury agents take & robb at will any longer. I feel assured that they are doing so in many instances for their own exclusive gain & that no returns are made to the government. I have known them to claim a horse & sell it to the owner for fifty dollars, & in a few days an other agent would come, take the horse, & sell it again to the owner for fifty dollars more!

The State Government is now perfectly organized, & the people every where disposed to be faithful & loyal. But they wish to be governed by law once more. They have been disposed to do every thing required of them, & now they ask to be relieved of military rule. There is no necessity for any military force, out of Charleston, GeorgeTown & Beaufort. To keep troops any longer in the country is mischievous & vexatious. I would not advise as I have, if I were not entirely satisfied of its propriety.

Ben. F. Perry   Pro: Gov, S.C

ALS, DNA-RG60, Office of Atty. Gen., Lets. Recd., President.

1. Perry enclosed an extended disquisition from Dr. John Wallace (b. c1815), a planter from the Fairfield District, who complained not only about the continued seizures by the U.S. military of all horses and mules bearing the government's brand, but also of the general idleness on the part of freedmen who had contracted to work for their former masters. Wallace to Perry, Nov. 30, 1865, Johnson Papers, LC; 1860 Census, S.C., Fairfield, Winnsboro, 37.

2. A district court for South Carolina was finally organized by April 1866 with the appointments of George S. Bryan, judge, J.P.M. Epping, marshal, John Phillips, attorney, and Daniel Horlbeck, clerk. Ser. 6B, Vol. 4: 152–53, Johnson Papers, LC; Reynolds, *Reconstruction in S.C.*, 34.

From Robert J. Powell

Raleigh   Dec 2 1865.

Twelve Oclock Monday is the time fixed for the election of the U.S. Senators. Grahams friends have proposed to me that if his pardon can be obtained they will elect him & Holden or Bedford Brown or any one I may name.[1] I have said that without a public declaration from him of his unqualified approval of your plan of restoration & of his determination to give a cordial & hearty support to the National & State administrations his pardon cannot be asked for. They say he is ready & willing to make such declarations. Again I have suggested that the election to the U S Senate of any man who had been in the Rebel Senate might weaken us & strengthen the radicals. Is this opinion correct? He & his friends say not. They have the power & will elect him unless I can have your authority for saying that it would be imprudent. Your reply will not, of course, be published or made known to only a few reliable persons hence it had better be directed to me rather than to Gov Holden.

R. J. Powell

Tel, DLC-JP.
1. At stake was not only a full term in the Senate but also an unexpired term created in 1861 when Thomas L. Clingman resigned. William A. Graham won the long term. Although privately offered to him, Holden declined an appointment to the short term. Raper, *Holden*, 83–84; Holden to Johnson, Dec. 4, 1865, Johnson Papers, LC. See Joseph S. Cannon to Johnson, Nov. 13, 1865; Holden to Johnson, Dec. 6, 1865; Clingman to Johnson, Jan. 3, 1866.

From Settlers in Cherokee Neutral Lands [1]

Shanee Ford [Kansas]   Decr. 2 65

Dear Sir

About three months ago a report went a flote that the strip of land lying west of the west line of the state of Missouria and runing parelel from fort scott along the Missouria line south to baxter springs known as the nutrel land,[2] had ben treeted for and was open for settlement.

Consequentley a grate rush of Emegration from Iowa Ills, and Missouria has fluded this countery. Some two thousand families have taken clames many of which have made Quite considerble improovements and seem to be delighted with the new country ready and willing at any time to Enter their selected home and become tax payers, which would add no little to the goverment revenew.

Many of these families have spent Every thing they had geting hear and have underwent a good [deal?] of hardships befor they could poseble fix themselves in comfortable quorters for the Winter.

Yet they ware so delighted with the countery they Endured it with pleasure. But alas a report becomes curent that all the nutrel land was about to be donated to a Rail Road compeny. Meny of these men well knew how the settlers ware treeted along the line of the Centerel Road in Ills, and also in Missouria. Of corse it struck them with harer and improoving Seecest. Now they know not what to do, nor who to apeal too for protection. But thinking you would if made acquanted with the use your influence in favour of those pioners who, have settled this countery. And if Congress dos donate this land to any compeny we as a body of petetioners pray to the honerble body of Congress to do it in such away that the clames of the actual settlers shall be respected.[3] We also wish a publication in a St Louis paper that we may understand our situation.

Sence the above was writen we called a little meeting, and the cetements above was sanctioned by us. And out of the number of signers below 27 ware solgers who have served in the union armey and I understand it is a generel thing all over this countery that 3/4 of the inhabetence of this new countery is those who have recently returned frome the armey.

Pet, DNA-RG75, Lets. Recd., Cherokee.

1. There are thirty-six signatures appended.

2. Under a treaty signed in 1836 the Cherokees had bought 800,000 acres in southeast Kansas, though they never settled in the area. Before the Civil War the federal government repeatedly refused to repurchase this "Neutral Tract," but over 2,000 white squatters moved in anyway. Despite violent clashes with hostile Cherokees, federal authorities, and Confederate raiders, rumors that the region would be officially opened to settlement prompted a second rush of homesteaders after the war. Paul W. Gates, *Fifty Million Acres: Conflicts Over Kansas Land Policy, 1854–1890* (Ithaca, N.Y., 1954), 153–55; Gary E. Moulton, *John Ross, Cherokee Chief* (Athens, Ga., 1978), 157–59.

3. On July 19, 1866, the Cherokees ceded the Neutral Tract to the United States in a treaty that guaranteed squatters the right to buy their claims, but Secretary of the Interior Harlan sold the entire parcel to the American Emigrant Company. Johnson ordered the removal of all settlers but, distressed by public condemnation of the transaction, subsequently cancelled the sale. He later recommended selling the land to the Atlantic & Pacific Railroad, but the Senate rejected this proposal on April 17, 1867. A supplemental treaty with the Cherokees signed by the President in 1868 permitted sale of the tract to the Missouri River, Fort Scott, & Gulf Railroad; allegedly some of the sponsors of this company were congressmen who opposed impeachment. Angry at the terms of the sale, which restricted their claims, settlers in the Neutral Tract initiated both a violent guerrilla war against the railroad and a campaign in Washington to get the agreement invalidated. Johnson refused to intervene further, leaving the matter to his successor, Ulysses S. Grant, who sent troops to restore order. Although its title was confirmed, the railroad was forced by the turmoil into receivership by 1878. Gates, *Fifty Million Acres*, 155–93 passim; H. Craig Miner and William E. Unrau, *The End of Indian Kansas: A Study of Cultural Revolution, 1854–1871* (Lawrence, Kan., 1978), 116–20; Edward D. Townsend to William J. Hancock, Sept. 26, 1866, Lets. Sent (Main Ser.), Vol. 43 (M565, Roll 30), RG94, NA.

From Abel Alderson[1]

Jackson Miss. Dec. 3rd, 1865—

The importance of removing the troops from the different states late in rebellion is daily being pressed upon your consideration for immediate action to that end. The great confidence I have in your Excellency's ability to manage this matter when in possession of all the facts has induced me to write you a few lines on the subject.

I have put myself to much trouble to learn the real condition of things in this state, and elsewhere in the South, and I find that many systems of servitude, are, even now, being matured to send the negro back to his former master, and to make it a penal offence to attempt, or in any way induce him to leave that master, even by offering him higher wages, or otherwise. They will not allow him to *own* real estate, and propose to punish the white man that would dare to rent or lease him real estate for farming purposes. Forbidden to own real estate, and the white man not allowed to rent or lease it to him, the poor negro stands trembling between starvation and death upon one hand, and a condition of bondage on the other hand worce than the condition of slavery from which he has just escaped. One of the two conditions, as things now stand, is his inevitable fate—a system of bitter servitude, without a master to protect him, or death by starvation.

If the troops are removed the Freedman's Bureau falls as a matter of course, and the negro goes back into a state of bondage worce than the one from which he has just escaped. If it be the policy of the government to give the negro back to his former owner then the troops should be removed at once. But if it is the policy of the government, as I understand it to be, to stand by, and protect those who have nowhere else to look for protection, then the troops should *not* be removed until the FACT, that the negro is free, is recognised and respected. For rest assured that this truth stands fast—*Slavery* is not yet broken up. The hold of the master has only been loosened, and not severed from his slave. Remove the troops and the master will tighten his grasp, and the negro—the bleeding victim of many wrongs, is again a slave just as certain as the sun rises and sets. But would it be safe, even forgetting the condition of the negro, to remove the troops at this time? Many *Union* men, who are what they profess to be, truly loyal to their country, have told me that it would be fraught with the greatest danger, and I, from what I have seen, would tremble at the consequences that would certainly follow the untimely removal of the troops from the states late in rebellion. Those who remained true to the union, and those who came back to their loyalty in *good faith*, are not the ones who are making the loudest demands for their removal, but they are such men as C. K. Marshall of Vicksburg, who, I am told, but resantly received a pardon at the hands of your Excellency,[2] and who but a few nights ago, in the Representative's Hall in the Capital, made one of the most inflamatory and revolutionary speeches I ever heard even in the days of the rebellion.[3] And said that when HE died, if he had a friend living, he wished him to have written upon his tombstone "*Here lies a rebel.*" This speech was loudly applauded by members of the Legislature and others present on the occasion. These are the kind of men who are so clamerous about the removal of the troops and the abolition of the Freedman's Bureau. I find no difficulty in getting along with the military here, and other Union men have told me the same thing. Nine tenths of the outrages as published committed by Negro troops are either false, or greatly exagerated. The most of them are utterly false.

I have written this letter at the request of General Howard, and with a desire that your Excellency may be in possion of facts in making up your mind on this delicate subject.

                                                                    A. Alderson

N.B. The cry that the execution of Jeff Davis would make a martyr of him is false. He is as little tho't of by the people South as he is by the people north. Outside of the Legislature I have heard but one man speak in his behalf. And he said that the government had as much right to hang him as it had to hang Davis. And I believe he was right, for he was a notorious Rebel.

A. A.

ALS, DLC-JP.

1. Alderson (b. *c*1815), a Maryland-born attorney, served as a Radical Republican delegate to the Mississippi constitutional convention in 1868. 1860 Census, Miss., Jefferson, Fayette, 5; Harris, *Day of the Carpetbagger*, 116.

2. Charles K. Marshall (1811–1891), a Methodist minister and philanthropist, had been pardoned on August 15, 1865. James B. Lloyd, ed., *Lives of Mississippi Authors, 1817–1967* (Jackson, Miss., 1981), 325; John K. Bettersworth, *Confederate Mississippi* (Baton Rouge, 1943), 290; Amnesty Papers (M1003, Roll 33), Miss., C. K. Marshall, RG94, NA.

3. Probably a reference to Marshall's speech on November 14, 1865, in which he advocated the importation of Northern and European laborers to replace blacks. This address included "impolitic" remarks in its "political phases." *Jackson Clarion*, Nov. 15, 1865.

To Edwin H. East

Washington, D.C.   Decr. 3d. 1865.

You will receive, by Express on Tuesday morning, a package addressed to you at Nashville. Please do not break the Seal until you receive a despatch from the Acting Assistant Secretary of War, when you will deliver the contents of the package for publication.

Andrew Johnson

Tel, DNA-RG107, Tels. Sent, President, Vol. 2 (1865).

From "The Voice of the People"

Columbus Mississippi   Lowndes Co   Dec. 3rd 1865

Mr President

As an humble citizen I wish, respectfully to call the earnest attention of the head of this great Nation to the following stubborn facts.

It would be utterly useless to address Military Officers who are blind to the acts of their own soldiers on all occasions. I would cheerfully give you my name in confidence but fear to trust it through the mails for if it was known here that I addressed you on this subject your entire force could not, *if they would*, protect me or this place from certain destruction by secret means.

Let it be enough for you—that I am a warm friend of your friend Levi W. Reeves[1] formerly of Tennessee, now residing in Alabama— that I knew you when a citizen of Tennessee have heard you often on the stump, and am now a supporter of your policy. This place has about three thousand inhabitants, loyal intelligent moral and well disposed towards the Government. There has not been one act of disloyalty here since the surrender. About four weeks ago Brevet Gen'l G.M.L Johnson[2] was in command of this Post nominally with his 13th Indiana

Cavalry. The last week that command staid here—there was a perfect reign of terror—citizens were brutally knocked down daily by the soldiers without the slightest provocation—and in one instance, when Col Wm B. Wade[3] a citizen of this place whose gallant service in the Mexican War shines brightly on the page of history—attempted to defend himself—he was mortally wounded, taken by guards to the Federal Hospital and whilst there under guard that night was killed.

A few of the Federal Officers pronounced it a most shocking murder. No arrests were ever made for these outrages—theft was a nightly occurrence—and a *private* by the name of Scott[4] was the *real* commandant of the Post. That command left to the joy of every one. The 26th Indiana Regiment commanded by Col Logan[5] arrived, and for the first week behaved themselves like soldiers and gentlemen. I believe the most of them are gallant men, and under different circumstances would have continued their good conduct. The citizens treat them kindly, as they do every person who comes here. The second Saturday night after the arrival of the 26th Indiana—a two story home not far from their quarters was burned down—it was a current report that they had said they would burn it.

Saturday night last week the large two story brick building, entirely isolated and enclosed with a high fence, was burnt down with 3,600 bales of Government cotton which it contained. It was guarded by Federal soldiers—and it was a moonlight night. The front of the building was occupied by the Quarters Masters Department. The building was evidently fired in some ten or twenty places. It is useless to say who set it on fire—it is too evident. That night, many of the soldiers were heard to say they were "glad the cotton was burnt" they "would not guard the Government Cotton when the Officials were daily stealing it.["] "This was not the only cotton which would be burnt"—"The work of burning would not stop with cotton either" &c. The following Monday & Tuesday after the fire, soldiers were selling the cotton saved, at from $75 to $100 per bale in open market. Ware house keepers were afraid to refuse storage for it and buyers were afraid not to buy—for fear their property would be destroyed. The Military officials towards the *latter part* of the week, commenced collecting the cotton up from the buyers—who of course lose their money. The troops say all the other Indiana regiments have been mustered out, and they would have been also, but for their Officers—who want to make all they can—and that they want to go home. They are generally dissatisfied and the very greatest demoralization exists among them. Last Friday morning, another dwelling was burned down.

The foregoing three fires are the only ones that had occurred here for five years previous.

Last night the *word was general* that the troops with a few mean negroes were going to burn the town. Rumors are rife again this morning of it. There could be no cause for such threats or acts except to plunder. The negroes were tried in the ordeal of the past four years—they are not in the least dreaded—except when soldiers are near to aid—and incite them. Saturday night several of the cotton ware houses were visited by squads of soldiers as they have been often before, and cotton demanded—stating they wanted Government cotton—but knowing there was none—and only intent upon committing theft, or arson. Horrid terror reigns again supreme. How long Mr President shall such things last? The troops say there is *no need* for them here & they tell *the truth*! All the Government stock & stores have been sold—and what little Government cotton is left here about 200 bales will not be here—if they stay a week longer.

Our Courts are established. Militia companies organized our people fully able to take care of the town & will never have any peace or quiet until the troops leave. I have written nothing in malice—have aimed to give you facts as I know them. If the whole story of theft, knavery & bribery from the highest officer, to the lowest private, was told, you would not believe it. In conclusion I beseech you in the name of the women & children of this place, to rely upon what I have written & telegraph the Commander here to remove his troops at once—and that you will hold them *responsible* for their conduct whilst here. It is very important they should leave before the Christmas holidays. Hoping you will respect this statement thus made for the good of all—for men are afraid to open their mouths here—and that you will remove the troops—the source of all evil, and apprehension, *at once*.

The Voice of the People Here

Please destroy this.

L, DLC-JP.

1. After serving as an aide-de-camp to Johnson during his second term as governor of Tennessee, Reeves (b. 1832) moved in 1857 to Alabama where he invested heavily in slaves and cotton. Reeves to Johnson, Aug. 3, 1865, Amnesty Papers (M1003, Roll 9), Ala., Levi W. Reeves, RG94, NA.

2. Gilbert M.L. Johnson (c1840–1871) was mustered out of the service on November 18, 1865, and subsequently worked as a "tobacco commission merchant" in Cincinnati. Pension File, Sue B. Johnson, RG15, NA.

3. Wade (c1826–1865), a 2nd lieutenant in the 1st Miss. Rifles during the Mexican war, served as sheriff of Lowndes County before commanding the 8th Confed. Cav. His death is recounted in the *Augusta Constitutionalist* of November 26, 1865. 1860 Census, Miss., Lowndes, Columbus, 133; Heitman, *Register*, 2: 71; CSR, RG109, NA.

4. Not identified.

5. Lt. Col. Newton A. Logan (1836–1919) assumed command of the post at Columbus on October 30, 1865. After he was mustered out on January 15, 1866, he worked as a farmer, miller, and house painter in Indiana. CSR, RG94, NA; Pension Files, Newton A. Logan, RG15, NA.

From Finlay Y. Clark[1]

Savannah   Dec 4th 1865

Honorable Sir

We hope your Excellency will excuse the liberty we take in addressing you this letter & attribute it to no desire of notoriety or publicity
on our part, but to a heart felt wish to serve the country by drawing
your attention to the true condition of affairs as they now exist in this
State.

When in your prescence in last June in connection with the Georgia
Delegation, & that from Texas[2] we did not fail to observe the effort you
made to impress every man with his duty Promising that if the leaders
of the Rebellion would return & do their whole duty to the country that
they would not find you negligent in yours to them. How this duty has
been performed in other states we do not profess to know but in this
State we do know we have lived in Georgia for about twenty years; was
here during the war & as we have traveled over the State not long since
& have closely observed men & things we believe we are well prepared
to express an honest opinion. The State of Georgia is in almost as *rebellious a condition at heart to day as she has been any time during the
war.* This condition has we believe been brought about first by Pardons Secondly by allowing those who held high possitions in the rebel
service to hold office, & Thirdly by Military Commanders, & others
currying favor with rebels in order to live peacefully & profitably
among them.

Before Pardons were granted the political instigators of the Rebellion
were held in check; they were all endeavoring to see which could do
most for the Union & magnifying little acts of courtseys to Union men
during the war into great deeds. Now that they all have their Pardons
they are on the other track; all trying to see which done the most for
the rebel cause, & counciling the people to weigh every man accordingly. From the Congressman elect down to the lowest officer this is
perfectly apparent. For the truth of this we would call your attention to
the election for Members for the state convention: to the action of that
convention, & then again to the last election for Governor—Members
of Congress & Members of the State Legislator. Almost in every town,
& county in the state the men most obnoctious to the government were
elected. Union men, & their supporters were directly or indirectly insulted intimidated or driven from the election. In this City Solomon
Cohen,[3] & Col E. C. Anderson[4] two of the strongest secessionests in
the county were elected by a very large majority. The first of these men
was Post Master under the Federal Government & then held the same
place under the Rebel government & was well known for his bitterness
towards the U.S. Government. He is now member elect from this dis-

trict to Congress. The other E C Anderson about the commencement of the war brought over a cargo of arm by the British steamer Fingal & afterwards Col in the Rebel service & for about three years in command of the Watter Battries around Savannah. Col E C Anderson is now up for Mayor of this city & as he was brought out for the great help he gave the Rebel cause & this is published in the news papers over his name he is therefore sure of election. We have no other object in aluding to these two men than to give you a fair specimen of others elected throughout the State. Now with such men in council what better could have been expected of them than what they have done? Before the war a man had to be in the state six months before he was allowed to vote. The new constitution of this convention says he must be here two years. Is not this an insult to the goverment & the true men who have been fighting under its flag? For it was done for no other object than to keep those men from northern states who choose to cast their lots among us from voting. We could name many other acts such as the state debt &c equally insulting were it not for the fear of beeing tedious. Most of these men with Pardons in their pockets on which the ink is barely dry & the oath of allegiance fresh on their lips violete their solom pledge every hour of the day & thus set an example to lesser minds to do the same. While we see them thus act we cannot but regret that they were not kept a little longer on the stool of repentance. Had this been done we believe more honest & humble men would have long ere this placed Georgia in an inviable possition. But as it is now the truely loyal men who might lead the controllable class in the right path are now power-less for good & so they will be so so long as the old political instigators of the rebellion can make the people believe their treason was more an honor than a crime. It is now a disgrase to be a Union man here. Such men are persecuted insulted & avoided in divers ways & if things go on at the same rate it will not be long before it will be very unsafe to be known as such. You have persued a humane & concilatory course with prominent rebels in this state but your motives have not been appreci-ated & those men never will appreciate them until they understand they must. *The Rebellion must be looked on as a disgrace.*

In conclusion I would say that in writing this letter I am actuated by no other motive than a heart felt desire to see the state of Georgia once more prosperous & happy under the old flag. You have my record in Washington. I do not believe I have atal exagerated in any statement that I have made.

F. Y. Clark

ALS, DLC-JP.

1. Clark (c1820-fl1877) was a Scottish-born dentist. 1860 Census, Ga., Chatham, Savannah, 3rd Dist., 187; Savannah directories (1858–77).

2. Clark probably refers to an interview on June 16, when he and other Georgia Unionists met with the President. There is no record of a joint meeting with delegations from Georgia and Texas, though Andrew J. Hamilton did meet with the President in

mid-June prior to his appointment as provisional governor of the latter state. *National Intelligencer*, June 17, 1865; *New York World*, June 15, 1865. See Osborne A. Lochrane to Johnson, June 16, 1865, Johnson Papers, LC.

3. Upon the recommendation of Montgomery Blair, Cohen (1802–1875), a former legislator for both South Carolina and Georgia who claimed that he opposed secession, was pardoned on July 13, 1865. Cohen to Johnson, July 1, 1865, Amnesty Papers (M1003, Roll 17), Ga., Solomon Cohen, RG94, NA; *House Ex. Docs.*, 40 Cong., 2 Sess., No. 16, p. 109 (Ser. 1330); *NUC Manuscript Collections* (1979), 68.

4. Edward C. Anderson (1815–1883) was a planter who served as mayor of Savannah (1855–56, 1865–69, 1873–76) and director of several railroad and banking firms. Myers, *Children of Pride*, 1452; 1860 Census, Ga., Chatham, Savannah, 3rd Dist., 224.

From Lizinka C. Ewell

Springhill [Tenn.]   4th Dec. 1865

My dear Friend

A day or two since I received a letter from Messrs Nelson & Murfree,[1] Real Estate Agents in Nashville enquiring whether I would sell my house & lot to the State for One-hundred-thousand dollars ($100,000) as they think it can be sold for that price. I have given no decided answer because I prefer waiting to know your views on the subject. If you have any wish to purchase, I would prefer selling to you to selling to any one else. I would be willing to sell either the whole or a part of the lot with the house. Please let me know your wishes on this subject as soon as convenient as I will do nothing until I hear from you.[2]

I enclose Maj. Hubbard's[3] application for pardon. He & my Aunt[4] are living with us for the present. He has lost all his property his health seems quite feeble—his children are scattered & his sources of enjoyment very few. I cannot believe you will refuse to grant his application *at once* as it will yield him the assuranse he desires that the remnant of his days will be undisturbed.

Please present me kindly to Mrs. Patterson & my young friend Belle.[5]

L. C. Ewell

ALS, DLC-JP.

1. Anson Nelson and William L. Murfree. Circumstances surrounding the property in Nashville had engaged the attention of President Johnson for several months. Ewell to Johnson, June 30, 1865, *Johnson Papers*, 8: 320; Helena W. Knox to Johnson, Sept. 4, 1865; Ewell to Johnson, Sept. 5, 1865.

2. See Johnson to Ewell, Dec. 9, 1865.

3. David Hubbard (1792–1874) was a U.S. and C.S. congressman and a Confederate Commissioner of Indian Affairs. His application, dated August 26, 1865, was recommended by Lewis E. Parsons and was granted on December 8, 1865. *DAB*; Amnesty Papers (M1003, Roll 6), Ala., David Hubbard, RG94, NA.

4. Rebecca Stoddert (1797–1872), the daughter of the first Secretary of the Navy, was Hubbard's second wife. Acklen, *Tenn. Records*, 1: 27.

5. Mrs. Martha Johnson Patterson and her six-year-old daughter, Mary Belle.

Message to Congress

WASHINGTON, *December* 4, 1865.

MESSAGE OF THE PRESIDENT OF THE UNITED STATES TO THE TWO HOUSES OF CONGRESS AT THE COMMENCEMENT OF THE FIRST SESSION OF THE THIRTY-NINTH CONGRESS.

FELLOW-CITIZENS OF THE SENATE AND HOUSE OF REPRESENTATIVES:

To express gratitude to God, in the name of the People, for the preservation of the United States, is my first duty in addressing you. Our thoughts next revert to the death of the late President by an act of parricidal treason. The grief of the nation is still fresh; it finds some solace in the consideration that he lived to enjoy the highest proof of its confidence by entering on the renewed term of the Chief Magistracy, to which he had been elected; that he brought the civil war substantially to a close; that his loss was deplored in all parts of the Union; and that foreign nations have rendered justice to his memory. His removal cast upon me a heavier weight of cares than ever devolved upon any one of his predecessors. To fulfil my trust I need the support and confidence of all who are associated with me in the various departments of Government, and the support and confidence of the people. There is but one way in which I can hope to gain their necessary aid; it is, to state with frankness the principles which guide my conduct, and their application to the present state of affairs, well aware that the efficiency of my labors will, in a great measure, depend on your and their undivided approbation.

The Union of the United States of America was intended by its authors to last as long as the States themselves shall last. "THE UNION SHALL BE PERPETUAL" are the words of the Confederation. "TO FORM A MORE PERFECT UNION," by an ordinance of the people of the United States, is the declared purpose of the Constitution. The hand of Divine Providence was never more plainly visible in the affairs of men than in the framing and the adopting of that instrument. It is, beyond comparison, the greatest event in American history; and indeed is it not, of all events in modern times, the most pregnant with consequences for every people of the earth? The members of the Convention which prepared it, brought to their work the experience of the Confederation, of their several States, and of other Republican Governments, old and new; but they needed and they obtained a wisdom superior to experience. And when for its validity it required the approval of a people that occupied a large part of a continent and acted separately in many distinct conventions, what is more wonderful than that, after earnest contention and long discussion, all feelings and all opinions were ultimately drawn in one way to its support?

The President in 1865
By William Sartain
Courtesy National Portrait Gallery

The Constitution to which life was thus imparted contains within itself ample resources for its own preservation. It has power to enforce the laws, punish treason, and ensure domestic tranquillity. In case of the usurpation of the Government of a State by one man, or an oligarchy, it becomes a duty of the United States to make good the guarantee to that State of a republican form of government, and so to maintain the homogeneousness of all. Does the lapse of time reveal defects? A simple mode of amendment is provided in the Constitution itself, so that its conditions can always be made to conform to the requirements of advancing civilization. No room is allowed even for the thought of a possibility of its coming to an end. And these powers of self-preservation have always been asserted in their complete integrity by every patriotic Chief Magistrate—by Jefferson and Jackson, not less than by Washington and Madison. The parting advice of the Father of his Country, while yet President, to the people of the United States, was, that "the free Constitution, which was the work of their hands, might be sacredly maintained;" and the inaugural words of President Jefferson held up "the preservation of the General Government, in its constitutional vigor, as the sheet anchor of our peace at home and safety abroad." The Constitution is the work of "the People of the United States," and it should be as indestructible as the people.

It is not strange that the framers of the Constitution, which had no model in the past, should not have fully comprehended the excellence of their own work. Fresh from a struggle against arbitrary power, many patriots suffered from harassing fears of an absorption of the State Governments by the General Government, and many from a dread that the States would break away from their orbits. But the very greatness of our country should allay the apprehension of encroachments by the General Government. The subjects that come unquestionably within its jurisdiction are so numerous, that it must ever naturally refuse to be embarrassed by questions that lie beyond it. Were it otherwise, the Executive would sink beneath the burden; the channels of justice would be choked; legislation would be obstructed by excess; so that there is a greater temptation to exercise some of the functions of the General Government through the States than to trespass on their rightful sphere. "The absolute acquiescence in the decisions of the majority" was, at the beginning of the century, enforced by Jefferson "as the vital principle of republics," and the events of the last four years have established, we will hope forever, that there lies no appeal to force.

The maintenance of the Union brings with it "the support of the State Governments in all their rights;" but it is not one of the rights of any State Government to renounce its own place in the Union, or to nullify the laws of the Union. The largest liberty is to be maintained in the discussion of the acts of the Federal Government; but there is no appeal from its laws, except to the various branches of that Government itself, or to the people, who grant to the members of the Legislative and of the Executive Departments no tenure but a limited one, and in that manner always retain the powers of redress.

"The sovereignty of the States" is the language of the Confederacy, and not the language of the Constitution. The latter contains the emphatic words: "The Constitution, and the laws of the United States which shall be made in pursuance thereof, and all treaties made or which shall be made under the authority of the United States, shall be the supreme law of the land; and the judges in every State shall be bound thereby, anything in the constitution or laws of any State to the contrary notwithstanding."

Certainly the Government of the United States is a limited government; and so is every State government a limited government. With us, this idea of limitation spreads through every form of administration, general, State, and municipal, and rests on the great distinguishing principle of the recognition of the rights of man. The ancient republics absorbed the individual in the State, prescribed his religion, and controlled his activity. The American system rests on the assertion of the equal right of every man to life, liberty, and the pursuit of happiness; to freedom of conscience, to the culture and exercise of all his faculties. As a consequence, the State Government is limited, as to the General Government in the interest of Union, as to the individual citizen in the interest of freedom.

States, with proper limitations of power, are essential to the existence of the Constitution of the United States. At the very commencement, when we assumed a place among the Powers of the earth, the Declaration of Independence was adopted by States; so also were the Articles of Confederation; and when "the People of the United States" ordained and established the Constitution, it was the assent of the States, one by one, which gave it vitality. In the event, too, of any amendment to the Constitution, the proposition of Congress needs the confirmation of States. Without States, one great branch of the legislative government would be wanting. And, if we look beyond the letter of the Constitution to the character of our country, its capacity for comprehending within its jurisdiction a vast continental empire is due to the system of States. The best security for the perpetual existence of the States is the "supreme authority" of the Constitution of the United States. The perpetuity of the Constitution brings with it the perpetuity of the States; their mutual relation makes us what we are, and in our political system their connexion is indissoluble. The whole cannot exist without the parts, nor the parts without the whole. So long as the Constitution of the United States endures, the States will endure; the destruction of the one is the destruction of the other; the preservation of the one is the preservation of the other.

I have thus explained my views of the mutual relations of the Constitution and the States, because they unfold the principles on which I have sought to solve the momentous questions and overcome the appalling difficulties that met me at the very commencement of my administration. It has been my steadfast object to escape from the sway of momentary passions, and to derive a healing policy from the fundamental and unchanging principles of the Constitution.

I found the States suffering from the effects of a civil war. Resistance to the General Government appeared to have exhausted itself. The United States had recovered possession of their forts and arsenals; and their armies were in the occupation of every State which had attempted to secede. Whether the territory within the limits of those States should be held as conquered territory, under military authority emanating from the President as the head of the army, was the first question that presented itself for decision.

Now, military governments, established for an indefinite period, would have offered no security for the early suppression of discontent; would have divided the people into the vanquishers and the vanquished; and would have envenomed hatred, rather than have restored affection. Once established, no precise limit to their continuance was conceivable. They would have occasioned an incalculable and exhausting expense. Peaceful emigration to and from that portion of the country is one of the best means that can be thought of for the restoration of harmony; and that emigration would have been prevented; for what emigrant from abroad, what industrious citizen at home, would place himself willingly under military rule? The chief persons who would have followed in the train of the army would have been dependents on the General Government, or men who expected profit from the miseries of their erring fellow-citizens. The powers of patronage and rule which would have been exercised, under the President, over a vast, and populous, and naturally wealthy region, are greater than, unless under extreme necessity, I should be willing to entrust to any one man; they are such as, for myself, I could never, unless on occasions of great emergency, consent to exercise. The wilful use of such powers, if continued through a period of years, would have endangered the purity of the general administration and the liberties of the States which remained loyal.

Besides, the policy of military rule over a conquered territory would have implied that the States whose inhabitants may have taken part in the rebellion had, by the act of those inhabitants, ceased to exist. But the true theory is, that all pretended acts of secession were, from the beginning, null and void. The States cannot commit treason, nor screen the individual citizens who may have committed treason, any more than they can make valid treaties or engage in lawful commerce with any foreign Power. The States attempting to secede placed themselves in a

condition where their vitality was impaired, but not extinguished—
their functions suspended, but not destroyed.

But if any State neglects or refuses to perform its offices, there is the
more need that the General Government should maintain all its authority, and, as soon as practicable, resume the exercise of all its functions.
On this principle I have acted, and have gradually and quietly, and by
almost imperceptible steps, sought to restore the rightful energy of the
General Government and of the States. To that end, Provisional Governors have been appointed for the States, Conventions called, Governors elected, Legislatures assembled, and Senators and Representatives
chosen to the Congress of the United States. At the same time, the
Courts of the United States, as far as could be done, have been reopened, so that the laws of the United States may be enforced through
their agency. The blockade has been removed and the custom-houses
re-established in ports of entry, so that the revenue of the United States
may be collected. The Post Office Department renews its ceaseless activity, and the General Government is thereby enabled to communicate
promptly with its officers and agents. The courts bring security to persons and property; the opening of the ports invites the restoration of
industry and commerce; the post office renews the facilities of social
intercourse and of business. And is it not happy for us all, that the
restoration of each one of these functions of the General Government
brings with it a blessing to the States over which they are extended? Is
it not a sure promise of harmony and renewed attachment to the Union
that, after all that has happened, the return of the General Government
is known only as a beneficence?

I know very well that this policy is attended with some risk; that for
its success it requires at least the acquiescence of the States which it
concerns; that it implies an invitation to those States, by renewing their
allegiance to the United States, to resume their functions as States of
the Union. But it is a risk that must be taken; in the choice of difficulties, it is the smallest risk; and to diminish, and, if possible, to remove
all danger, I have felt it incumbent on me to assert one other power of
the General Government—the power of pardon. As no State can throw
a defence over the crime of treason, the power of pardon is exclusively
vested in the Executive Government of the United States. In exercising
that power, I have taken every precaution to connect it with the clearest
recognition of the binding force of the laws of the United States, and
an unqualified acknowledgment of the great social change of condition
in regard to slavery which has grown out of the war.

The next step which I have taken to restore the constitutional relations of the States, has been an invitation to them to participate in the
high office of amending the Constitution. Every patriot must wish for
a general amnesty at the earliest epoch consistent with public safety.

For this great end there is need of a concurrence of all opinions, and the spirit of mutual conciliation. All parties in the late terrible conflict must work together in harmony. It is not too much to ask, in the name of the whole people, that, on the one side, the plan of restoration shall proceed in conformity with a willingness to cast the disorders of the past into oblivion; and that, on the other, the evidence of sincerity in the future maintenance of the Union shall be put beyond any doubt by the ratification of the proposed amendment to the Constitution, which provides for the abolition of slavery forever within the limits of our country. So long as the adoption of this amendment is delayed, so long will doubt, and jealousy, and uncertainty prevail. This is the measure which will efface the sad memory of the past; this is the measure which will most certainly call population, and capital, and security to those parts of the Union that need them most. Indeed, it is not too much to ask of the States which are now resuming their places in the family of the Union to give this pledge of perpetual loyalty and peace. Until it is done, the past, however much we may desire it, will not be forgotten. The adoption of the amendment reunites us beyond all power of disruption. It heals the wound that is still imperfectly closed; it removes slavery, the element which has so long perplexed and divided the country; it makes of us once more a united people, renewed and strengthened, bound more than ever to mutual affection and support.

The amendment to the Constitution being adopted, it would remain for the States, whose powers have been so long in abeyance, to resume their places in the two branches of the National Legislature, and thereby complete the work of restoration. Here it is for you, fellow-citizens of the Senate, and for you, fellow-citizens of the House of Representatives, to judge, each of you for yourselves, of the elections, returns, and qualifications of your own members.

The full assertion of the powers of the General Government requires the holding of Circuit Courts of the United States within the districts where their authority has been interrupted. In the present posture of our public affairs, strong objections have been urged to holding those courts in any of the States where the rebellion has existed; and it was ascertained, by inquiry, that the Circuit Court of the United States would not be held within the District of Virginia during the autumn or early winter, nor until Congress should have "an opportunity to consider and act on the whole subject." To your deliberations the restoration of this branch of the civil authority of the United States is therefore necessarily referred, with the hope that early provision will be made for the resumption of all its functions. It is manifest that treason, most flagrant in character, has been committed. Persons who are charged with its commission should have fair and impartial trials in the highest civil tribunals of the country, in order that the Constitution and the laws may be fully vindicated; the truth clearly established and affirmed that treason is a crime, that traitors should be punished and the offence made infamous; and, at the same time, that the question may be judicially settled, finally and forever, that no State of its own will has the right to renounce its place in the Union.

The relations of the General Government towards the four millions of inhabitants whom the war has called into freedom, have engaged my most serious consideration. On the propriety of attempting to make the freedmen electors by the proclamation of the Executive, I took for my counsel the Constitution itself, the interpretations of that instrument by its authors and their contemporaries, and recent legislation by Congress. When, at the first movement towards independence, the Congress of the United States instructed the several States to institute governments of their own, they left each State to decide for itself the conditions for the enjoyment of the elective franchise. During the period of the Confederacy, there continued to exist a very great diversity in the qualifications of electors in the several States; and even within a State a distinction of qualifications prevailed with regard to the officers who were to be chosen. The Constitution of the United States recognises these diversities when it enjoins that, in the choice of members of the House of Representatives of the United States, "the electors in each State shall have the qualifications requisite for electors of the most numerous branch of the State Legislature." After the formation of the Constitution, it remained, as before, the uniform usage for each State to enlarge the body of its electors, according to its own judgment; and, under this system, one State after another has proceeded to increase the number of its electors, until now universal suffrage, or something very near it, is the general rule. So fixed was this reservation of power in the habits of the people, and so unquestioned has been the interpretation of the Constitution, that during the civil war the late President never harbored the purpose—certainly never avowed the purpose—of disregarding it; and in the acts of Congress, during that period, nothing can be found which, during the continuance of hostilities, much less after their close, would have sanctioned any departure by the Executive from a policy which has so uniformly obtained. Moreover, a concession of the elective franchise to the freedmen, by act of the President of the United States, must have been extended to all colored men, wherever found, and so must have established a change of suffrage in the Northern, Middle, and Western States, not less than in the Southern and Southwestern. Such an act would have created a new class of voters, and would have been an assumption of power by the President which nothing in the Constitution or laws of the United States would have warranted.

On the other hand, every danger of conflict is avoided when the settlement of the question is referred to the several States. They can, each for itself, decide on the measure, and whether it is to be adopted at once and absolutely, or introduced gradually and with conditions. In my judgment, the freedmen, if they show patience and manly virtues, will sooner obtain a participation in the elective franchise through the States than through the General Government, even if it had power to intervene. When the tumult of emotions that have been raised by the suddenness of the social change shall have subsided, it may prove that they will receive the kindliest usage from some of those on whom they have heretofore most closely depended.

But while I have no doubt that now, after the close of the war, it is not competent for the General Government to extend the elective franchise in the several States, it is equally clear that good faith requires the security of the freedmen in their liberty and their property, their right to labor, and their right to claim the just return of their labor. I cannot too strongly urge a dispassionate treatment of this subject, which should be carefully kept aloof from all party strife. We must equally avoid hasty assumptions of any natural impossibility for the two races to live side by side, in a state of mutual benefit and good will. The experiment involves us in no inconsistency; let us then, go on and make that experiment in good faith, and not be too easily disheartened. The country is in need of labor, and the freedmen are in need of employment, culture, and protection. While their right of voluntary migration and expatriation is not to be questioned, I would not advise their forced removal and colonization. Let us rather encourage them to honorable and useful industry, where it may be beneficial to themselves and to the country; and, instead of hasty anticipations of the certainty of failure, let there be nothing wanting to the fair trial of the experiment. The change in their condition is the substitution of labor by contract for the status of slavery. The freedman cannot fairly be accused of unwillingness to work, so long as a doubt remains about his freedom of choice in his pursuits, and the certainty of his recovering his stipulated wages. In this the interests of the employer and the employed coincide. The employer desires in his workmen spirit and alacrity, and these can be permanently secured in no other way. And if the one ought to be able to enforce the contract, so ought the other. The public interest will be best promoted, if the several States will provide adequate protection and remedies for the freedmen. Until this is in some way accomplished, there is no chance for the advantageous use of their labor; and the blame of ill-success will not rest on them.

I know that sincere philanthropy is earnest for the immediate realization of its remotest aims; but time is always an element in reform. It is one of the greatest acts on record to have brought four millions of people into freedom. The career of free industry must be fairly opened to them; and then their future prosperity and condition must, after all, rest mainly on themselves. If they fail, and so perish away, let us be careful that the failure shall not be attributable to any denial of justice.

In all that relates to the destiny of the freedmen, we need not be too anxious to read the future; many incidents which, from a speculative point of view, might raise alarm, will quietly settle themselves.

Now that slavery is at an end or near its end, the greatness of its evil, in the point of view of public economy, becomes more and more apparent. Slavery was essentially a monopoly of labor, and as such locked the States where it prevailed against the incoming of free industry. Where labor was the property of the capitalist, the white man was excluded from employment, or had but the second best chance of finding it; and the foreign emigrant turned away from the region where his condition would be so precarious. With the destruction of the monopoly, free labor will hasten from all parts of the civilized world to assist in developing various and immeasurable resources which have hitherto lain dormant. The eight or nine States nearest the Gulf of Mexico have a soil of exuberant fertility, a climate friendly to long life, and can sustain a denser population than is found as yet in any part of our country. And the future influx of population to them will be mainly from the North, or from the most cultivated nations in Europe. From the sufferings that have attended them during our late struggle, let us look away to the future, which is sure to be laden for them with greater prosperity than has ever before been known. The removal of the monopoly of slave labor is a pledge that those regions will be peopled by a numerous and enterprising population, which will vie with any in the Union in compactness, inventive genius, wealth, and industry.

Our Government springs from and was made for the people—not the people for the Government. To them it owes allegiance; from them it must derive its courage, strength, and wisdom. But, while the Government is thus bound to defer to the people, from whom it derives its existence, it should, from the very consideration of its origin, be strong in its power of resistance to the establishment of inequalities. Monopolies, perpetuities, and class legislation, are contrary to the genius of free government, and ought not to be allowed. Here, there is no room for favored classes or monopolies[;] the principle of our Government is that of equal laws and freedom of industry. Wherever monopoly attains a foothold, it is sure to be a source of danger, discord, and trouble. We shall but fulfil our duties as legislators by according "equal and exact justice to all men," special privileges to none. The Government is subordinate to the people; but, as the agent and representative of the people, it must be held superior to monopolies, which, in themselves, ought never to be granted, and which, where they exist, must be subordinate and yield to the Government.

The Constitution confers on Congress the right to regulate commerce among the several States. It is of the first necessity, for the maintenance of the Union, that that commerce should be free and unobstructed. No State can be justified in any device to tax the transit of travel and commerce between States. The position of many States is such that, if they were allowed to take advantage of it for purposes of local revenue, the commerce between States might be injuriously burdened, or even virtually prohibited. It is best, while the country is still young, and while the tendency to dangerous monopolies of this kind is still feeble, to use the power of Congress so as to prevent any selfish impediment to the free circulation of men and merchandise. A tax on travel and merchandise, in their transit, constitutes one of the worst forms of monopoly, and the evil is increased if coupled with a denial of the choice of route. When the vast extent of our country is considered, it is plain that every obstacle to the free circulation of commerce between the States ought to be sternly guarded against by appropriate legislation, within the limits of the Constitution.

The report of the Secretary of the Interior explains the condition of the public lands, the transactions of the Patent Office and the Pension Bureau, the management of our Indian affairs, the progress made in the construction of the Pacific railroad, and furnishes information in reference to matters of local interest in the District of Columbia. It also presents evidence of the successful operation of the Homestead Act, under the provisions of which 1,160,533 acres of the public lands were entered during the last fiscal year—more than one-fourth of the whole number of acres sold or otherwise disposed of during that period. It is estimated that the receipts derived from this source are sufficient to cover the expenses incident to the survey and disposal of the lands entered under this Act, and that payments in cash to the extent of from forty to fifty per cent. will be made by settlers, who may thus at any time acquire title before the expiration of the period at which it would otherwise vest. The homestead policy was established only after long and earnest resistance; experience proves its wisdom. The lands, in the hands of industrious settlers, whose labor creates wealth and contributes to the public resources, are worth more to the United States than if they had been reserved as a solitude for future purchasers.

The lamentable events of the last four years, and the sacrifices made by the gallant men of our Army and Navy, have swelled the records of the Pension Bureau to an unprecedented extent. On the 30th day of June last, the total number of pensioners was 85,986, requiring for their annual pay, exclusive of expenses, the sum of $8,023,445. The number of applications that have been allowed since that date will require a large increase of this amount for the next fiscal year. The means for the payment of the stipends due, under existing laws, to our disabled soldiers and sailors, and to the families of such as have perished in the service of the country, will no doubt be cheerfully and promptly granted. A grateful people will not hesitate to sanction any measures having for their object the relief of soldiers mutilated and families made fatherless in the efforts to preserve our national existence.

The report of the Postmaster General presents an encouraging exhibit of the operations of the Post Office Department during the year. The revenues of the past year from the loyal States alone exceeded the maximum annual receipts from all the States previous to the rebellion, in the sum of $6,038,091; and the annual average increase of revenue during the last four years, compared with the revenues of the four years immediately preceding the rebellion, was $3,533,845. The revenues of the last fiscal year amounted to $14,556,158, and the expenditures to $13,694,728, leaving a surplus of receipts over expenditures of $861,430. Progress has been made in restoring the postal service in the Southern States. The views presented by the Postmaster General against the policy of granting subsidies to ocean mail steamship lines upon estabished routes, and in favor of continuing the present system, which limits the compensation for ocean service to the postage earnings, are recommended to the careful consideration of Congress.

It appears, from the report of the Secretary of the Navy, that while, at the commencement of the present year, there were in commission 530 vessels of all classes and descriptions, armed with 3,000 guns and manned by 51,000 men, the number of vessels at present in commission is 117, with 830 guns and 12,128 men. By this prompt reduction of the naval forces the expenses of the Government have been largely diminished, and a number of vessels, purchased for naval purposes from the merchant marine, have been returned to the peaceful pursuits of commerce. Since the suppression of active hostilities our foreign squadrons have been re-established, and consist of vessels much more efficient than those employed on similar service previous to the rebellion. The suggestion for the enlargement of the navy-yards, and especially for the establishment of one in fresh water for iron-clad vessels, is deserving of consideration, as is also the recommendation for a different location and more ample grounds for the Naval Academy.

In the report of the Secretary of War, a general summary is given of the military campaigns of 1864 and 1865, ending in the suppression of armed resistance to the national authority in the insurgent States. The operations of the general administrative Bureaus of the War Department during the past year are detailed, and an estimate made of the appropriations that will be required for military purposes in the fiscal year commencing the 30th day of June, 1866. The national military force on the 1st of May, 1865, numbered 1,000,516 men. It is proposed to reduce the military establishment to a peace footing, comprehending fifty thousand troops of all arms, organized so as to admit of an enlargement by filling up the ranks to eighty-two thousand six hundred, if the circumstances of the country should require an augmentation of the army. The volunteer force has already been reduced by the discharge from service of over eight hundred thousand troops, and the Department is proceeding rapidly in the work of further reduction. The war estimates are reduced from $516,240,131 to $33,814,461, which amount, in the opinion of the Department, is adequate for a peace establishment. The measures of retrenchment in each Bureau and branch of the service exhibit a diligent economy worthy of commendation. Reference is also made in the report to the necessity of providing for a uniform militia system, and to the propriety of making suitable provision for wounded and disabled officers and soldiers.

The revenue system of the country is a subject of vital interest to its honor and prosperity, and should command the earnest consideration of Congress. The Secretary of the Treasury will lay before you a full and detailed report of the receipts and disbursements of the last fiscal year, of the first quarter of the present fiscal year, of the probable receipts and expenditures for the other three quarters, and the estimates for the year following the 30th of June, 1866. I might content myself with a reference to that report, in which you will find all the information required for your deliberations and decision. But the paramount importance of the subject so presses itself on my own mind, that I cannot but lay before you my views of the measures which are required for the good character, and, I might almost say, for the existence of this people. The life of a republic lies certainly in the energy, virtue, and intelligence of its citizens; but it is equally true that a good revenue system is the life of an organized government. I meet you at a time when the nation has voluntarily burdened itself with a debt unprecedented in our annals. Vast as is its amount, it fades away into nothing when compared with the countless blessings that will be conferred upon our country and upon man by the preservation of the nation's life. Now, on the first occasion of the meeting of Congress since the return of peace, it is of the utmost importance to inaugurate a just policy, which shall at once be put in motion, and which shall commend itself to those who come after us for its continuance. We must aim at nothing less than the complete effacement of the financial evils that necessarily followed a state of civil war. We must endeavor to apply the earliest remedy to the deranged state of the currency, and not shrink from devising a policy which, without being oppressive to the people, shall immediately begin to effect a reduction of the debt, and, if persisted in, discharge it fully within a definitely fixed number of years.

It is our first duty to prepare in earnest for our recovery from the ever-increasing evils of an irredeemable currency, without a sudden revulsion, and yet without untimely procrastination. For that end, we must, each in our respective positions, prepare the way. I hold it the duty of the Executive to insist upon frugality in the expenditures; and a sparing economy is itself a great national resource. Of the banks to which authority has been given to issue notes secured by bonds of the United States, we may require the greatest moderation and prudence, and the law must be rigidly enforced when its limits are exceeded. We may, each one of us, counsel our active and enterprising countrymen to be constantly on their guard, to liquidate debts contracted in a paper currency, and, by conducting business as nearly as possible on a system of cash payments or short credits, to hold themselves prepared to return to the standard of gold and silver. To aid our fellow-citizens in the prudent management of their monetary affairs, the duty devolves on us to diminish by law the amount of paper money now in circulation. Five years ago the bank-note circulation of the country amounted to not much more than two hundred millions; now the circulation, bank and national, exceeds seven hundred millions. The simple statement of the fact recommends more strongly than any words of mine could do, the necessity of our restraining this expansion. The gradual reduction of the currency is the only measure that can save the business of the country from disastrous calamities; and this can be almost imperceptibly accomplished by gradually funding the national circulation in securities that may be made redeemable at the pleasure of the Government.

Our debt is doubly secure—first in the actual wealth and still greater undeveloped resources of the country; and next in the character of our institutions. The most intelligent observers among political economists have not failed to remark, that the public debt of a country is safe in proportion as its people are free; that the debt of a republic is the safest of all. Our history confirms and establishes the theory, and is, I firmly believe, destined to give it a still more signal illustration. The secret of this superiority springs not merely from the fact that in a republic the national obligations are distributed more widely through countless numbers in all classes of society; it has its root in the character of our laws. Here all men contribute to the public welfare, and bear their fair share of the public burdens. During the war, under the impulses of patriotism, the men of the great body of the people, without regard to their own comparative want of wealth, thronged to our armies and filled our fleets of war, and held themselves ready to offer their lives for the public good. Now, in their turn, the property and income of the country should bear their just proportion of the burden of taxation, while in our impost system, through means of which increased vitality is incidentally imparted to all the industrial interests of the nation, the duties should be so adjusted as to fall most heavily on articles of luxury, leaving the necessaries of life as free from taxation as the absolute wants of the Government, economically administered, will justify. No favored class should demand freedom from assessment, and the taxes should be so distributed as not to fall unduly on the poor, but rather on the accumulated wealth of the country. We should look at the national debt just as it is—not as a national blessing, but as a heavy burden on the industry of the country, to be discharged without unnecessary delay.

It is estimated by the Secretary of the Treasury that the expenditures for the fiscal year ending the 30th of June, 1866, will exceed the receipts $112,194,947. It is gratifying, however, to state that it is also estimated that the revenue for the year ending the 30th of June, 1867, will exceed the expenditures in the sum of $111,682,818. This amount, or so much as may be deemed sufficient for the purpose, may be applied to the reduction of the public debt, which, on the 31st day of October, 1865, was $2,740,854,750. Every reduction will diminish the total amount of interest to be paid, and so enlarge the means of still further reductions, until the whole shall be liquidated; and this, as will be seen from the estimates of the Secretary of the Treasury, may be accomplished by annual payments even within a period not exceeding thirty years. I have faith that we shall do all this within a reasonable time; that, as we have amazed the world by the suppression of a civil war which was thought to be beyond the control of any Government, so we shall equally show the superiority of our institutions by the prompt and faithful discharge of our national obligations.

The Department of Agriculture, under its present direction, is accomplishing much in developing and utilizing the vast agricultural capabilities of the country, and for information respecting the details of its management reference is made to the annual report of the Commissioner.

I have dwelt thus fully on our domestic affairs because of their transcendent importance. Under any circumstances, our great extent of territory and variety of climate, producing almost every thing that is necessary for the wants, and even the comforts of man, make us singularly independent of the varying policy of foreign Powers, and protect us against every temptation to "entangling alliances," while at the present moment the re-establishment of harmony, and the strength that comes from harmony, will be our best security against "nations who feel power and forget right." For myself, it has been and it will be my constant aim to promote peace and amity with all foreign nations and Powers; and I have every reason to believe that they all, without exception, are animated by the same disposition. Our relations with the Emperor of China, so recent in their origin, are most friendly. Our commerce with his dominions is receiving new developments; and it is very pleasing to find that the Government of that great Empire manifests satisfaction with our policy, and reposes just confidence in the fairness which marks our intercourse. The unbroken harmony between the United States and the Emperor of Russia is receiving a new support from an enterprise designed to carry telegraphic lines across the continent of Asia, through his dominions, and so to connect us with all Europe by a new channel of intercourse. Our commerce with South America is about to receive encouragement by a direct line of mail steamships to the rising Empire of Brazil. The distinguished party of men of science who have recently left our country to make a scientific exploration of the natural history and rivers and mountain ranges of that region, have received from the Emperor that generous welcome which was to have been expected from his constant friendship for the United States, and his well-known zeal in promoting the advancement of knowledge. A hope is entertained that our commerce with the rich and populous countries that border the Mediterranean sea may be largely increased. Nothing will be wanting, on the part of this Government, to extend the protection of our flag over the enterprise of our fellow-citizens. We receive from the Powers in that region assurances of good will; and it is worthy of note that a special envoy has brought us messages of condolence on the death of our late Chief Magistrate from the Bey of Tunis, whose rule includes the old dominions of Carthage, on the African coast.

Our domestic contest, now happily ended, has left some traces in our relations with one at least of the great maritime Powers. The formal accordance of belligerent rights to the insurgent States was unprecedented, and has not been justified by the issue. But in the systems of neutrality pursued by the Powers which made that concession, there was a marked difference. The materials of war for the insurgent States were furnished, in a great measure, from the workshops of Great Britain; and British ships, manned by British subjects, and prepared for receiving British armaments, sallied from the ports of Great Britain to make war on American commerce, under the shelter of a commission from the insurgent States. These ships, having once escaped from British ports, ever afterwards entered them in every part of the world, to refit, and so to renew their depredations. The consequences of this conduct were most disastrous to the States then in rebellion, increasing their desolation and misery by the prolongation of our civil contest. It had, moreover, the effect, to a great extent, to drive the American flag from the sea, and to transfer much of our shipping and our commerce to the very Power whose subjects had created the necessity for such a change. These events took place before I was called to the administration of the Government. The sincere desire for peace by which I am animated led me to approve the proposal, already made, to submit the questions which had thus arisen between the countries to arbitration. These questions are of such moment that they must have commanded the attention of the great Powers, and are so interwoven with the peace and interests of every one of them as to have ensured an impartial decision. I regret to inform you that Great Britain declined the arbitrament, but, on the other hand, invited us to the formation of a joint commission to settle mutual claims between the two countries, from which those for the depredations before mentioned should be excluded. The proposition, in that very unsatisfactory form, has been declined.

The United States did not present the subject as an impeachment of the good faith of a Power which was professing the most friendly dispositions, but as involving questions of public law, of which the settlement is essential to the peace of nations; and, though pecuniary reparation to their injured citizens would have followed incidentally on a decision against Great Britain, such compensation was not their primary object. They had a higher motive, and it was in the interests of peace and justice to establish important principles of international law. The correspondence will be placed before you. The ground on which the British Minister rests his justification is, substantially, that the municipal law of a nation, and the domestic interpretations of that law, are the measure of its duty as a neutral; and I feel bound to declare my opinion, before you and before the world, that that justification cannot be sustained before the tribunal of nations. At the same time I do not advise to any present attempt at redress by acts of legislation. For the future, friendship between the two countries must rest on the basis of mutual justice.

From the moment of the establishment of our free Constitution, the civilized world has been convulsed by revolutions in the interests of democracy or of monarchy; but through all those revolutions the United States have wisely and firmly refused to become propagandists of republicanism. It is the only government suited to our condition; but we have never sought to impose it on others; and we have consistently followed the advice of Washington to recommend it only by the careful preservation and prudent use of the blessing. During all the intervening period the policy of European Powers and of the United States has, on the whole, been harmonious. Twice, indeed, rumors of the invasion of some parts of America, in the interest of monarchy, have prevailed; twice my predecessors have had occasion to announce the views of this nation in respect to such interference. On both occasions the remonstrance of the United States was respected, from a deep conviction, on the part of European Governments, that the system of non-interference and mutual abstinence from propagandism was the true rule for the two hemispheres. Since those times we have advanced in wealth and power; but we retain the same purpose to leave the nations of Europe to choose their own dynasties and form their own systems of government. This consistent moderation may justly demand a corresponding moderation. We should regard it as a great calamity to ourselves, to the cause of good government, and to the peace of the world, should any European Power challenge the American people, as it were, to the defence of republicanism against foreign interference. We cannot foresee and are unwilling to consider what opportunities might present themselves, what combinations might offer to protect ourselves against designs inimical to our form of government. The United States desire to act in the future as they have ever acted heretofore; they never will be driven from that course but by the aggression of European Powers; and we rely on the wisdom and justice of those Powers to respect the system of non-interference which has so long been sanctioned by time, and which, by its good results, has approved itself to both continents.

The correspondence between the United States and France, in reference to questions which have become subjects of discussion between the two Governments, will, at a proper time, be laid before Congress.

When, on the organization of our Government, under the Constitution, the President of the United States delivered his inaugural address to the two Houses of Congress, he said to them, and through them to the country and to mankind, that "the preservation of the sacred fire of liberty and the destiny of the republican model of government are justly considered as deeply, perhaps as finally staked on the experiment intrusted to the American people." And the House of Representatives answered Washington by the voice of Madison: "We adore the invisible hand which has led the American people, through so many difficulties, to cherish a conscious responsibility for the destiny of republican liberty." More than seventy-six years have glided away since these words were spoken; the United States have passed through severer trials than were foreseen; and now, at this new epoch in our existence as one nation, with our Union purified by sorrows, and strengthened by conflict, and established by the virtue of the people, the greatness of the occasion invites us once more to repeat, with solemnity, the pledges of our fathers to hold ourselves answerable before our fellow-men for the success of the republican form of government. Experience has proved its sufficiency in peace and in war; it has vindicated its authority through dangers, and afflictions, and sudden and terrible emergencies, which would have crushed any system that had been less firmly fixed in the heart of the people. At the inauguration of Washington the foreign relations of the country were few, and its trade was repressed by hostile regulations; now all the civilized nations of the globe welcome our commerce, and their Governments profess towards us amity. Then our country felt its way hesitatingly along an untried path, with States so little bound together by rapid means of communication as to be hardly known to one another, and with historic traditions extending over very few years; now intercourse between the States is swift and intimate; the experience of centuries has been crowded into a few generations, and has created an intense, indestructible nationality. Then our jurisdiction did not reach beyond the inconvenient boundaries of the territory which had achieved independence; now, through cessions of lands, first colonized by Spain and France, the country has acquired a more complex character, and has for its natural limits the chain of Lakes, the Gulf of Mexico, and on the east and the west the two great oceans. Other nations were wasted by civil wars for ages before they could establish for themselves the necessary degree of unity; the latent conviction that our form of government is the best ever known to the world, has enabled us to emerge from civil war within four years, with a complete vindication of the constitutional authority of the General Government, and with our local liberties and State institutions unimpaired. The throngs of emigrants that crowd to our shores are witnesses of the confidence of all peoples in our permanence. Here is the great land of free labor, where industry is blessed with unexampled rewards, and the bread of the workingman is sweetened by the consciousness that the cause of the country "is his own cause, his own safety, his own dignity." Here every one enjoys the free use of his faculties and the choice of activity as a natural right. Here, under the combined influence of a fruitful soil, genial climes, and happy institutions, population has increased fifteen-fold within a century. Here, through the easy development of boundless resources, wealth has increased with two-fold greater rapidity than numbers, so that we have become secure against the financial vicissitudes of other countries, and, alike in business and in opinion, are self-centered and truly independent. Here more and more care is given to provide education for every one born on our soil. Here religion, released from political connection with the civil government, refuses to subserve the craft of statesmen, and becomes, in its independence, the spiritual life of the people. Here toleration is extended to every opinion, in the quiet certainty that truth needs only a fair field to secure the victory. Here the human mind goes forth unshackled in the pursuit of science, to collect stores of knowledge and acquire an ever-increasing mastery over the forces of nature. Here the national domain is offered and held in millions of separate freeholds, so that our fellow-citizens, beyond the occupants of any other part of the earth, constitute in reality a people. Here exists the democratic form of government; and that form of government, by the confession of European statesmen, "gives a power of which no other form is capable, because it incorporates every man with the State, and arouses every thing that belongs to the soul."

Where, in past history, does a parallel exist to the public happiness which is within the reach of the people of the United States? Where, in any part of the globe, can institutions be found so suited to their habits or so entitled to their love as their own free Constitution? Every one of them, then, in whatever part of the land he has his home, must wish its perpetuity. Who of them will not now acknowledge, in the words of Washington, that "every step by which the people of the United States have advanced to the character of an independent nation, seems to have been distinguished by some token of Providential agency?" Who will not join with me in the prayer, that the invisible hand which has led us through the clouds that gloomed around our path, will so guide us onward to a perfect restoration of fraternal affection, that we of this day may be able to transmit our great inheritance, of State Governments in all their rights, of the General Government in its whole constitutional vigor, to our posterity, and they to theirs through countless generations?

ANDREW JOHNSON.

PD, Johnson-Bartlett Col.

From John Woodard

December 5, 1865, Springfield, Tenn.; ALS, DNA-RG105, Records of the Commr., Lets. Recd. (M752, Roll 23).

The son of Johnson's friend Thomas Woodard asks the President's consideration of a dispute with Gen. Clinton B. Fisk of the Freedmen's Bureau. In February 1864 the elder Woodard agreed to sell a slave to the slave's father, Miles Childress, a free black. Arrangement was made for payment over time, but Childress paid only a portion of the total amount and then demanded its return. He was supported by Fisk, even to the extent of levying a fine of $50 on Woodard without a hearing. The elder Woodard "insists that it is an outrage upon all the principles of Justice to permit any man, no matter how exalted he may be, much less a free negro, to go before some military officer to make complaint against some Citizen for some alledged offence, and upon that statement, without the person complained of having any notice of the proceeding, or any opportunity of making any defence, deprive him of his property and mulct him with a fine." [This letter was referred to General Howard's office and in turn to General Fisk, who responded that "Mr Woodards statements are not altogether true" since the slave in question "was a *free man*, made so by the act of Congress approved July 17th 1862." Woodard "could appeal direct . . . with any evidence he might have," which he has not yet done, and Fisk would "cheerfully hear him at any time and insure *justice*." On December 27 Howard ordered the letter returned to the President.]

From George Bancroft

New York, 17, West 21st St.
Dec. 6, 1865. 8, P.M.

My dear Sir,

Many thanks for your thoughtful goodness in sending me a copy of your message. I have spent the day among all sorts of people, & hear but one opinion of the position you have taken. In less than twenty days the extreme radical opposition will be over. *All* of all parties applaud the ground you have taken. The extreme friends of the South are gratified at the total want of *asperity* and passion: the Union men are perfectly satisfied: the radicals are compelled to approve. I have clipped from all sorts of papers their editorials: several written with very little talent or insight, but all approving.[1]

Geo. Bancroft

ALS, DLC-JP.
1. Not found, though Bancroft noted that one of the extracts was from "A German Daily."

From William W. Holden

Raleigh, N.C., Dec. 6th, 1865.

My dear Sir:

I received your Message on Tuesday night about ten o'clock, and you may be sure I read it with interest and avidity. As long as I have been in public life I do not remember to have seen any document which I so entirely approve as I do this; and I venture the assertion that it will command the hearty assent of a vast majority of the American people. The theory of the government, as maintained by the Fathers, and as settled for all time by the result of the late rebellion, is stated with clearness and accuracy. Your plan of restoration, which was the only feasible one under the circumstances, is explained, vindicated, and commended to the Congress; yet, after all, it is left to that body to say whether the States shall be restored and the work completed by the admission of the members from the insurgent States. The representatives of the insurgent States, having broken away from the Congress to engage in the rebellion, the question is how representatives from these States can again obtain seats, and this is a matter for the Congress itself. You have done your duty in so re-establishing the machinery of self-government in these States as to render them presentable through their representatives to the common Congress. Whether they shall be admitted or excluded, and the work of restoration commenced *de novo*, your skirts are clear. In a spirit of patriotism, and out of intense love of the Union, you have ventured a great deal; and I regret that in some instances your liberality and self-sacrificing disposition have not been responded to as they should have been.

Allow me also to congratulate you on your foreign policy. We cannot afford to engage in war now, except in a clear case of insult to the national honor. We need at least ten years of profound peace. Believe me, Sir, a foreign war would develop elements in these Southern States little thought of by the superficial observer, and which might seriously embarrass and cloud the national arms.

But I need not dwell on special points in the Message. I repeat, it is what I for the most part expected, and cannot fail to strengthen your hold on the confidence and affections of your countrymen.

Dr. Powell will communicate to you much information in relation to the condition of things in this State;[1] but there are some points to which I wish to call your attention.

The late election in this State was shaped by secession votes and the rebel debt. More than half of those who voted for Mr. Worth are original secessionists and Vance men, still more or less unsubdued, and who are disposed to return to the Union only under their chosen leaders. Mr. Worth himself was in favor of continuing the rebel State government, and he fled with Vance on the approach of Gen. Sherman. Up to a period somewhat subsequent to the committal of Gov. Graham and other former Union leaders to the Davis policy of "fighting it out," Mr. Worth had been a devoted Union man. I appointed him Provisional Treasurer in the liberal spirit which characterized your policy, in the hope that I might thereby obliterate lines of difference and make our people a unit. Still, I do not think he would have been a candidate but for the influence of Ex. Governors Vance and Graham. Indeed, it is known that he had agreed to disentangle himself from the secessionists and retire, but another letter from Gov. Graham determined him to be a candidate. These are facts of which I am well convinced.

I regret to say that there is much of a rebellious spirit still in this State. In this respect I admit I have been deceived. In May and June last these rebellious spirits would not have dared to show their heads even for the office of constable; but leniency has emboldened them, and the copperhead now shows his fangs. If these men had supreme power in this State the condition of the real Union men and of the freedmen would be exceedingly disagreeable. They vaunt themselves on their devotion to the Confederacy; they make that a test of fidelity, declaring that as they were true to Davis, so they will be true to you. Yet every word that wounds true hearts, and every measure calculated to obstruct the work of restoration, proceeds from them. And strange to say, the true Union men were so oppressed under Confederate rule, and so cowed by the charge incessantly made that they were traitors, that they seem not to have entirely recovered their manhood, and hence it is that these malcontents are not denounced and exposed as they should be.

I communicate these convictions with regret. It may be that the policy of the government has been too lenient; or it may be that I have seriously erred in the discharge of duty, or that I was not the proper person for Provisional Governor. You may recollect that when in Washington I sought an interview with you at your private residence. My purpose then was to ask you to appoint some one else to this position, but I perceived that you were pressed for time, as the moment for the review of the troops had arrived, and I told you, in reply to a question, that I had nothing more to say.[2] My friends subsequently urged me in the most earnest terms not to decline the appointment, and I did not, therefore, mention to you what I intended to say on the morning I made the visit referred to. I am ready and willing at any moment to retire from this position; and if you have the shadow of a wish that I should do so, I pray you as a friend to let me know it.[3] My chief wish is to be of benefit to my afflicted State, and to see your administration successful.

The election of Mr. Pool to the Senate[4] is highly gratifying to the true Union men of the State. His record is as good as it was possible it could be under the circumstances. He is a gentleman of very high character and marked ability; and he has the cordial confidences of our friends in all parts of the State. In this connection it may not be improper for me to say that I was offered a Senatorship "by authority" with Ex-Governor Graham, but I emphatically declared that I felt I owed it to you to remain where I am, and that in no event could I accept it.

If this Provisional Government is to be continued it will be indispensable that the Courts of the State shall be put in full operation. Thefts, robberies, and murders are increasing, and the strong arm of the law is indispensable to preserve life and property. Please give me instructions on this subject. I will have sufficient means to support a Provisional Government, and to put the entire machinery in full operation. A Supreme Court will be necessary as a Court of Appeals, and the Court elected by the Legislature might be appointed a Provisional Court. I am glad to be able to inform you that nearly all my Provisional appointments have been confirmed by the Legislature.

I have thus taxed your patience at much length, but my situation and the importance of the subjects must be my apology. Our friend Dr. Powell, who has borne himself here with much discretion, and who has made friends by his visit, can give you all the details.

W. W. Holden.

ALS, DLC-JP.
1. See, for example, Powell to Johnson, Jan. 17, 1866.
2. The interview Holden refers to here probably occurred on either May 23 or 24, the dates of the "Grand Review."
3. In a dispatch dated December 4, Secretary Seward notified Holden that the President would relieve him of his duties as soon as Worth had "become qualified" to serve as governor. *Senate Ex. Docs.*, 39 Cong., 1 Sess., No. 26, p. 47 (Ser. 1237). See Holden to Johnson, Dec. 8, 1865.
4. A former peace advocate, John Pool (1826–1884) was elected to fill the state's unexpired term, though he was not seated until his election as a Republican Senator in 1868. *BDAC*.

From Anna H.J. Saunders[1]

Raleigh   Decr. 6 1865

I herewith enclose to your Excellency the recommendation[2] of the members of both branches of the Legislature of our General Assembly in favour of the Pardon of Bradley T. Johnson[3] late a Brigadier Genl. in the service of the so called Confederate States. This testimonial in favour of the applicant, in addition to the recommendation of Gov. Holden,[4] and that of Judge Read[5] as President of our State Convention, will I trust satisfy your Excellency, of the deep interest felt by our people in favour of the applicant, and that he is to be considered in some degree as a citizen of this State. Whatever may have been the zeal of Mr. Johnson in that discharge of his Military duty he cannot be accused of practising undue severity to the soldiers of either army—so far from it, that when the prisons of the Federal Soldiers were broken up in Salisbury a deputation of their officers waited upon him to thank him on their behalf for what he had done for them. Of one thing I can with truth assure your excellency that no female in the country has manifested greater zeal in favour of the wounded than has his wife[6] in her getting up & attending to the hospitals in the country.

As early as the year 1851 Mr. Johnson was married to our daughter, and then obtained his Law license with the view of locating in this State. He gave up the idea at the time, but did not abandon his purpose at some future day, Hence his sympathy for the South in the unfortunate contest between the North and South which followed. He is now an exile from his native State, having lost his home and the rest of his fortune, with the exception of a few thousand dollars for which proceedings are now pending in the District Courts for the United States in Baltimore—and which is likely to be taken from him unless thro' the interference of your Excellency. He has now been nearly twelve months absent from his wife & child. His wife has been forced to go North for medical aid[7] her ill health no doubt being aggrevated by her anxiety for the fate of her Husband.

You Mr. President are a Husband and Father and cannot but feel for those so deeply concerned in the fate of our Son in Law, so necessary to our assistance. He is now at the South endeavouring to recover the fortune left by my father (Judge Johnson of the Supreme Court of the United States) for my family, the recovery of which is so all important to our necessary support.[8]

I beg you to consider Mr. President that my Husband is now more than three score and ten years of age, and confined to his chamber, unable to render any assistance to his family—so as to render the aid of his Son in Law so important to save us from absolute want. Your Excellency will I hope excuse me for adverting to the misfortunes of our family.

The Gentleman who married my eldest daughter[9] was for five years a Surgeon in the United States service and by his skill as a Physician saved the lives of many of the soldiers both in Key West and Fort Moultrie from that scurge the yellow fever, finally lost his life in Pensacola, leaving three small children, who with his wife, are all dependent upon us. Your Excellency will thus see how much we are dependent upon your humane interference. Allow me therefore to throw myself on the mercy of Your Excellency, and to entreat your merciful intervention, and I shall ever pray that every blessing may attend you.[10]

A H Saunders

ALS, DNA-RG94, Amnesty Papers (M1003, Roll 40), N.C., Bradley T. Johnson.

1. Saunders (c1801-fl1870) was the wife of Judge Romulus M. Saunders. 1860 Census, N.C., Wake, Raleigh, 48; (1870), 214.

2. Thomas Settle et al. to Johnson, Amnesty Papers (M1003, Roll 40), N.C., Bradley T. Johnson, RG94, NA.

3. Johnson (1829–1903), who had already submitted an application for pardon, was an active Democratic partisan before the war and afterward practiced law in Richmond for nearly fifteen years before relocating in his native Maryland. *DAB*; Bradley T. Johnson to Johnson, July 8, 1865, *Johnson Papers*, 8: 372.

4. In three previous communications Holden had asked the President to pardon Johnson as a favor to Judge Saunders. Holden to Johnson, n.d., Sept. 25, Dec. 1, 1865, Amnesty Papers (M1003, Rolls 30, 40), Md. and N.C., Bradley T. Johnson, RG94, NA.

5. Edwin G. Reade's letter had been forwarded to Robert J. Powell by Judge Saunders, who asked that it be given to the President. Reade to Johnson, Oct. 18, 1865; Saunders to Powell, Oct. 20, 1865, Amnesty Papers (M1003, Roll 40), N.C., Bradley T. Johnson, RG94, NA. See Saunders to Powell, Oct. 25, 1865, Johnson Papers, LC.

6. Jane Claudia Saunders Johnson (1832–1899), whose involvement in charitable work continued long after the war. "Work of a Confederate Woman," *Con Vet*, 9 (1901): 321–25.

7. Mrs. Johnson was currently residing with her sister-in-law in Milwaukee, Wis. Mrs. Johnson to Johnson, Feb. 27, 1866; Mrs. H. Johnson Schley to Johnson, Feb. 26, 1866, Amnesty Papers (M1003, Roll 40), N.C., Bradley T. Johnson, RG94, NA.

8. William Johnson (1771–1834), an attorney and author, was a Jefferson appointee to the Supreme Court. *DAB*. For a synopsis of the legal wrangles attending his estate, see Romulus M. Saunders to Holden, Sept. 20, 1865, Amnesty Papers (M1003, Roll 30), Md., Bradley T. Johnson, RG94, NA.

9. William J. L'Engle (b. *c*1828), who resided with the Saunders family while he attended medical school, married Margaret M. Saunders (b. *c*1831) in 1854, two years before he joined the army. 1850 Census, N.C., Wake, Raleigh, 572; Brent H. Holcomb, comp., *Marriages of Wake County, North Carolina 1770–1868* (Baltimore, 1983), 82; Powell, *Army List*, 432.

10. There is some confusion about the date of Johnson's pardon. One apparently was authorized for him "by Executive order" on November 1, 1865. There was a delay in his reception of it, perhaps due to accusations of "atrocities" committed by his troops during Gen. Jubal Early's campaign in the summer of 1864, as well as Johnson's command of the prison at Salisbury, N.C. Johnson was arrested for the former offenses in Maryland but, upon the recommendation of General Grant, all charges were dismissed by order of the President. A presidential directive for the issue of Johnson's pardon was sent to Speed on May 11, 1866. Amnesty Papers (M1003, Rolls 30, 40), Md. and N.C., Bradley T. Johnson, RG94, NA; Tucker, *Zeb Vance*, 424–25; *Augusta Constitutionalist*, Apr. 8, 1866.

From Aaron A. Bradley[1]

Savannah Ga   7 Dec 1865.

Prest Johnson

My private School of three hundred pupils was ordered to be discontinued and the pitition because I was called on to speak at a mass meeting for the suffrage and spoke against your reconstruction.[2] Sir, will you please open my School?[3]

A. Braudley[*sic*]   Colored

Tel, DLC-JP.

1. A runaway slave, Bradley (*c*1815–1882) had practiced law in Boston before returning to Georgia during or immediately after the war. Although elected to the Georgia constitutional convention (1867–68) and the state senate (1868, 1870), he was expelled from both bodies. E. Merton Coulter, "Aaron Alpeoria Bradley, Georgia Negro Politician During Reconstruction Times," *GHQ*, 51 (1967): 15–16, 24–25, 37, 156–64, 302.

2. In his speech on December 5, Bradley had urged blacks to defy Johnson's order

that restored the Sea Island plantations to their former owners. He had also circulated a petition demanding black suffrage as well as other civil rights. Ibid., 18; Joseph P. Reidy, "Aaron A. Bradley: A Voice of Black Labor in the Georgia Lowcountry," in *Southern Black Leaders of the Reconstruction Era*, ed., Howard N. Rabinowitz (Urbana, Ill., 1982), 286.

3. For having used "seditious and insurrectionary language," Bradley was sentenced by a military commission to one year at hard labor in Fort Pulaski. In December 1865 Stanton ordered him paroled until Johnson reviewed the case but, in February 1866, exiled the contentious black from Georgia for his disruptive remarks at a freedmen's convention. Bradley made his way to Washington, where he appealed to Johnson for a reversal of the commission's ruling. It was not until December 1866, after the Supreme Court invalidated his conviction by its ruling in *Ex Parte Milligan*, that Bradley returned to Georgia. Ibid.; Coulter, "Bradley," 18–21; Bradley to Johnson, Dec. 27, 1865, Lets. Recd. (Main Ser.), S-42-1866, RG94, NA; Townsend to John M. Brannan, Dec. 27, 1865; Townsend to Steedman, Feb. 7, 1866, Tels. Sent, Sec. of War (M473, Roll 90), RG107, NA; Bradley to Johnson, Apr. 27, 1866, Amnesty Papers (M1003, Roll 16), Ga., Aaron A. Bradley, RG94, NA.

From Howell E. Jackson [1]

Memphis Tenn   Dec 7th 1865

Sir

I am a native of Tennessee—a young man and a Lawyer by profession—having but recently commenced the practice of Law, at the outbreak of the late unfortunate Rebellion. Like the great mass of the young men of the South, I was carried along with the tide of Secession & Rebellion, without being a Leader in the movement or an active participator in bringing it about. In the fall of 1861 after war had commenced I accepted the position of "*Receiver*" for the District of West Tennessee, under the *Sequestration Act* passed by the Rebel Congress and held the office until June 1862 when the U S Forces occupied West Tenn. I do not come within any of the Excepted classes enumerated in Your Excellency's Proclamation of the 29th May 1865, who are denied the benefits of Amnesty except on Special application, other than that of having been a civil officer as Stated.[2]

In the discharge of the duties of the office of *Receiver*, nothing of any value or consequence came into my hands or was received by me, except *Notes, bills bonds* & *Stocks* belonging to *Northern* parties—all of which were carefully preserved and have since the close of the war, been returned by me to their lawful & respective owners.

I have in good faith and with the "bonafide" intent of keeping & observing the same, both in letter & Spirit, taken and Subscribed to the oath of Amnesty, which accompanies this application to your Excellency. And wishing most Sincerely to be restored to the rights and privileges of citizenship—which will never again be violated or abused by me—but will be honestly kept and observed, with true allegiance to the Government of which Your Excellency is the Honored Head—I most earnestly and respectfully petition Your Excellency to extend to me the Executive pardon & amnesty, already granted to the great mass of our people.[3] All of which is very Respectfully Submitted by

Howell E Jackson

ALS, DNA-RG94, Amnesty Papers (M1003, Roll 49), Tenn., Howell E. Jackson.
    1. Jackson (1832–1895) enjoyed an illustrious political and judicial career after the war, serving as a U.S. Senator, circuit judge, and Supreme Court Justice. *BDAC*.
    2. Jackson first sought a pardon from the President in June. Amnesty Papers (M1003, Roll 49), Tenn., Howell E. Jackson, RG94, NA.
    3. The President pardoned Jackson on January 26, 1866. *House Ex. Docs.*, 39 Cong., 2 Sess., No. 116, p. 42 (Ser. 1293).

From Oliver P. Morton

New York   Dec 7th 1865.

Dear Sir,

Since the publication of your message I have conversed with a number of the first men in New York, in the financial and commercial departments of business, and have found all to heartily approve it. I cannot be mistaken in the opinion that the great body of the people in the North will endorse your doctrines and policy, and this the members of Congress will find out before they are ninety days older. The firmness with which you may stand to them will make you friends and conquer opposition. It is as I expected, and I believe told you, that Congress would begin with a majority against your policy; but there should be nothing disheartening in this, for it will surely melt away or break to pieces in a short time.

Were I in your place I would not fail to employ every power and instrumentality in my hands to sustain my policy, and the friends who sustain it. While it is understood that members of Congress can oppose you, and in breaking down your policy break down your administration and yet control your patronage, you may expect to have opposition and to fail. The resolute wielding of your patronage in favor of your friends, *inside the Union party*, cannot fail to build you up with the people and disarm the Opposition in Congress.

Believing you to be right and guided solely by the desire to rebuild permanently our broken and disordered country, besides feeling great interest in your personal success, I trust you will excuse the freedom of these suggestions.

The joint resolution which has passed the house[1] to which is to be referred the question of the admission of Southern members is cunningly devised and is intended to entrap your friends in such a manner they cannot escape. How can either house make the question of admitting members depend upon the action of the other? "Each house shall be the judge of the qualifications of its members" says the Constitution and the power can neither be abdicated or delegated to the other.

I am sorry to say my health is no better. My arrangements are made to sail next week on Wednesday.[2]

With earnest wishes for your health and success I remain. . . .

O. P Morton

ALS, DLC-JP.
1. Morton refers to the resolution creating the Joint Committee on Reconstruction, which passed the House on December 4, 1865. *Congressional Globe*, 39 Cong., 1 Sess., p. 6.
2. Morton travelled to France in a futile quest for a remedy for the stroke that had left him paralyzed in the summer of 1865. *DAB*. See Morton to Johnson, Dec. 29, 1865.

From Reuben D. Mussey

Washington D.C.   Dec 7th 1865.

Mr President,

I have the honor herewith to present my resignation of my commissions as captain in the 19th U.S. Infty and colonel in the 100th U.S.C.I. and to very respectfully and urgently request that it be accepted by you.[1]

I have been more or less identified with the Colored Troops and as the services of my Regiment are no longer required I should like to end my military service with theirs.

I wish to get into Civil Life and do my humble part, while sustaining my family, towards developing the resources of our Country[2] and helping to make it what you so clearly and forcibly point it out to be in the future in your message.

I appeal to you directly in this matter because of your great, continued and warm friendship—I hope I may be allowed to write—to me, and because I fear that the unsettled state of my accounts would make an appeal forwarded through the regular channels unsuccessful.[3]

You are familiar with the state of my affairs in that regard. I do not seek to avoid the responsibilities it devolves upon me nor to sneak away. But my pay is stopped[4] and I have barely enough money to support me through the month and I want to get the means of support till they are settled. As an officer I cannot. As a civilian I believe I can in an enterprise which I think will be of service to the country but which I think I have good reasons for not mentioning to you more in detail.

If my resignation Could be accepted to take effect at once, but I to have no honorable discharge nor final settlements till my accounts were satisfactorily adjusted it would be a *very* great favor to me.

In your recent message you have achieved a great triumph. May I not ask you to crown this success with an act of kindness to one, who, whatever your decision will not cease to pray for your personal and political welfare and success?

R. D. Mussey   Col 100th USCI   Capt 19th U.S. Infy

ALS, DLC-JP.

1. See Mussey to Johnson, Dec. 18, 1865.

2. By 1866 Mussey had become a partner in the Cumberland Land Company of Tennessee. Frank R. Levstik, "A View from Within: Reuben D. Mussey on Andrew Johnson and Reconstruction," *Historical New Hampshire*, 27 (1972), 168; *Tennessee Acts, 1865–66*, 331–32.

3. Mussey resigned not only because of personal matters but also because he differed with Johnson's policies. He confided to a friend in mid-October: "A struggle (political at least) is inevitable I fear. In that struggle my sympathies would be one way and my loyalty and allegiance another." Levstik, "A View from Within," 168–69, 171.

4. See Mussey to Johnson, Oct. 16, 1865.

From Robert C. Schenck

Washington   Dec. 7, 1865

Sir,

I have the honor to state that since the adjournment of the Senate, in April or May, John C. Dunlevy[1] was appointed Assesor of Internal Revenue for the 3rd Congl. Dist. of Ohio, in place of William Miner[2] removed.

I had nothing to do with the removal or the new appointment, further than to recommend Dunlevy in case of a vacancy; but protesting that, without any reference to my expressed wishes as Representative of the District, Miner ought not to be removed if he was a good officer, & on the contrary ought not to be retained if he were incompetent. I put the case, solely on the ground of his fitness or unfitness, as the records of the Treasury Department might furnish evidence of the one or the other. He was thereupon removed for alleged cause. It is claimed by Mr. Miner that this was a wrong decision brought about by sinister means, & intrigue, & that no cause of complaint justifying such treatment can be found, or exists.

I beg leave to request that before Mr Dunlevy's name is sent to the Senate for confirmation an investigation may be made into these allegations. If there has been an unwarranted injury done it should be rectified. It will be due also to Mr Dunlevy that it shall be ascertained & reported in what manner, & with what results, he has performed the duties of the office since his appointment.

While I want the government well served, I desire also that no wrong shall be done to a good man.[3]

Robt. C. Schenck

LS, DNA-RG56, Appts., Internal Revenue Service, Collector, Ohio, 3rd Dist., William Miner.

1. Dunlevy (1823–1897) was an attorney who served as probate judge of Warren County (1852–55, 1860–64). *History of Warren County, Ohio* (Chicago, 1882), 424; *American Ancestry* (12 vols., Baltimore, 1968[1887–99]), 12: 141.

2. Miner (b. *c*1798) was a former circuit court clerk appointed by Lincoln at the inception of the internal revenue system. 1860 Census, Ohio, Warren, Union Twp., 35;

Noah H. Swayne to Johnson, Oct. 26, 1865, Appts., Internal Revenue Service, Assessor, Ohio, 3rd Dist., William Miner, RG56, NA.

3. Despite the remonstrances of Schenck, Supreme Court Justice Noah H. Swayne, and Ohio legislator A. G. McBurney, neither Dunlevy nor Miner received the appointment. Obadiah C. Maxwell was nominated and confirmed as assessor for the 3rd District in July 1866, serving at least through September 1867. Swayne to Johnson, Oct. 26, 1865; McBurney to Johnson, Oct. 28, 1865, ibid.; Ser. 6B, Vol. 4: 256, Johnson Papers, LC; *U.S. Off. Reg.* (1867), 77.

From Henry Watterson

Nashville   Dec 7th 1865

My Dear Sir;

I enclose you a brief notice of your message.[1] It is my candid opinion, and embodies the general expression of intelligent men throughout the community.

On arriving in Nashville after I left you, I began work in earnest and have labored ceaselessly ever since. How far my work may have proven of value in a political point of view, I am of course unprepared to decide; but it has been pecuniarily profitable and the "Banner," is now, I think, assured of the future. Its patronage is already more extensive than any other of the city papers; it issues nearly two thousand dailies and fifteen hundred weeklies, and increases every day; so that I feel very confident of making a comfortable livelihood and founding a permanent and paying business. With this prospect I shall seteled down into a house of my own, and a wife, on the 15th of the present month.[2]

I wish to repeat what I said to you at Washington, that my object is to support your policy and to strengthen your hands. I wish to join, as far as one of such poor capacity can do, in the construction of that national administration party, on which reposes the sole hope of the country. With this constantly before me, I have endeavored to impress upon the people a sense of their true condition; & to urge the necessity for a liberal spirit toward men and measures; to counsel an abandonment of the old cant about abolitionism, and a recognition of the new and future relations of the sections; of consigning the war and its passions to a common grave; and of looking to no party in the North, but to the discretion and sound impulses of the whole people for relief. But for Brownlow and his madmen—who are your personal and political enemies as well as the enemies of the country—the task would be half again as light. Yet I do not despair, and am looking ahead cheerfully.

Excuse this long letter. You have little leisure I know for such visits as mine; but I felt bound to let you know how I feel and think. I have nothing to ask of you but your confidence and counsel. I don't need any patronage, and am already indebted more than I can repay, for your kindness to me and mine.

Henry Watterson.

ALS, DLC-JP.

1. Watterson probably refers here to the laudatory editorial which appeared in the *Nashville Republican Banner* on December 7, 1865. A clipping of the editorial, presumably the one enclosed by Watterson, is found in Vol. 11, Ser. 11, Johnson Papers, LC.

2. On December 20 Watterson married Rebecca Ewing, daughter of Andrew Ewing. *Nashville Republican Banner*, Dec. 21, 1865.

From William W. Holden

Raleigh   Dec 8th 1865.

Sir.

The Legislature of the State today passed the following resolution. Resolved The house of commons concurring that the committee appointed to count the votes polled for Governor in November last be instructed to make arrangements for the administration of the Oath of Office to the Governor elect at the same time the returns are opened and the vote counted. Is their authority to administer this oath. I am not informed of the views of the General assembly on this subject. The oath proposed to be administered may be intended to be administered only prospective; what course shall I adopt? Please let me hear from you soon.[1] Dr. Powell left for Washington this morning. I have written you by him at length in relation to affairs in this state.[2]

W W Holden   Prov Govr

Tel, DLC-JP.

1. In a follow-up dispatch Holden informed the President that the legislature had rescinded the "joint agreement to administer the oaths of office" and that Worth would be declared governor "at the close of the Provisional Government." On December 15, and again seven days later, Worth was sworn into office; on December 28 Holden's term officially ended. Holden to Johnson, Dec. 9, 1865, Johnson Papers, LC; Raper, *Holden*, 85; Zuber, *Worth*, 210.

2. See Holden to Johnson, Dec. 6, 1865.

To James Johnson

Washington, D.C., Dec 8th 1865.

Your dispatches received.[1] The first last. Permit me to congratulate you and the Legislature on their action in adopting and ratifying the Amendment to the Constitution of the United States, abolishing Slavery.

Andrew Johnson   Pres't U.S.

Tel, DNA-RG107, Tels. Sent, President, Vol. 3 (1865–68).

1. On December 5 the governor had notified Johnson that the Georgia legislature would "probably" ratify the Thirteenth Amendment. In a dispatch sent on the following day, he announced that the legislature had adopted the Amendment, as well as a resolution protecting freedmen's rights, including that of testifying in court. Johnson Papers, LC. See Joseph E. Brown to Johnson, Dec. 6, 1865, Johnson Papers, LC.

From John M. Lea

Nashville, Dec 8 1865.

Dear Sir,

The people of Tennessee awaited with most anxious solicitude the delivery of your first Message to Congress. The suspense is over and it has doubtless by thousands been read and re-read. The paper in manner and tone is just what I supposed it would be; but it is not my purpose, as you know it is not my habit, to deal in the language of compliment. My aim is more useful. As a practical statesman, called to preside in times more trying than ever before occurred in the history of our country, it is right that you should know the temper and feeling of the people. Nineteen twentieths of the people of Tennessee cordially approve of your policy, and, tho.' you may be thwarted by politicians for a time, success will crown your efforts in the end.

The people of Tennessee are fast returning to their loyalty. If a few radicals on either side were out of the way, public sentiment would be eminently sound and wholesome. The idea of re-establishing slavery *in any form* is no where entertained—it could not and would not be re-established, if there were no constraint operating upon us.

The State Government is going ahead as successfully as could be expected under the circumstances. The Legislature will I think yet admit the testimony of colored persons in all suits where a colored man is plaintiff or defendant.[1] It is also hoped, the Legislature will *not* do some things which are insisted upon by a few well-meaning but unthoughtful men.

Trusting that health may be granted to you—and your wise policy successfully carried out I remain,

John M. Lea.

ALS, DLC-JP.
1. Numerous references to this legislation appear in letters from Tennesseans to Johnson in the fall of 1865. The bill did not pass both houses of the legislature until late January 1866. Alexander, *Reconstruction*, 100–101.

To Hugh McCulloch

Washington, D.C., Decr. 8th, 1865.

Sir:

You will please designate Mr. F. Smith[1] to search for and to seize such cotton in the Southern States as is claimed by Alexander Collie & Co. of London, who it is alleged were in league with the insurgent States during the recent rebellion.[2] All cotton claimed by the said firm will be held by the Treasury Department until all the facts can be ascertained and reported by Mr. Smith, when the case will be submitted to me for decision.

You will prepare and deliver to Mr. Smith the necessary instructions, and allow such compensation for his services as you may deem just and proper.[3]

Andrew Johnson

LS, DNA-RG56, Misc. Div., Claims for Cotton and Captured and Abandoned Property.

1. Frank Smith (fl1870) was after the war a commission merchant and securities broker. New York City directories (1867–71).

2. The British firm had supplied ordnance and commissary items, as well as ships, to the Confederacy in exchange for cotton and tobacco. In a separate memo Johnson authorized Smith to investigate and report to him all information concerning the "fitting out and equiping of" the Confederate raider *Shenandoah*. Apparently Smith had earlier requested such authorization from McCulloch, but he was reluctant to sanction the investigation. *OR*, Ser. 4, Vol. 2: 630; Vol. 3: 10, 529–30; Smith to Johnson, ca. Dec. 7, 1865; Johnson to Smith, Dec. 8, 1865, Johnson Papers, LC.

3. On December 9 McCulloch appointed Smith to confiscate all cotton claimed by Collie & Co. Smith subsequently seized several thousand bales which had been claimed by another British firm. After Johnson ordered the cotton to be sold by the Treasury Department, many months of litigation ensued. Smith repeatedly sought the President's intervention in settling his claim for compensation before receiving $33,000 in 1867. Caleb Cushing to Stanbery, Oct. 30, 1867; Smith to Johnson, Apr. 2, 1867; Executive Order, Mar. 21, 1866, Misc. Div., Claims for Cotton and Captured and Abandoned Property, RG56, NA; *Senate Ex. Docs.*, 40 Cong., 2 Sess., No. 32, passim (Ser. 1316); Smith to Johnson, Mar. 5, May 16, June 17, Aug. 23, Oct. 11, 15, 30, Dec. 26, 1867, Johnson Papers, LC.

From William B. Phillips [1]

Private.

100 East 28th. Street New York   De' 8h/65

Dear Sir,

I enclose my "leader" in yesterday's Herald on "The proceedings in Congress and the president's position."[2] I hope you may consider it as "right to the point." I shall follow it up in to-morrow's or Sunday's issue, and afterwards.[3] If you think proper, as I said to you when I had the honor of a conversation, to suggest any views or your wishes through your son or otherwise I shall be happy to attend to them.

I hope you are well and that God may preserve you.

W. B. Phillips.

ALS, DLC-JP.

1. An editor and novelist, Phillips (fl1889) a few months later applied unsuccessfully to serve as Johnson's private secretary. *NUC*; New York City directories (1872–73); Phillips to Johnson, Mar. 5, 1866, Johnson Papers, LC.

2. Not found, but an unsigned article was published in the *New York Herald* of December 7, 1865. The writer was incensed that, while several Republican members of Congress had triumphed in 1864 by "carrying the banner" of Lincoln and "Andy Johnson," those same men were now making a disrespectful "assault" upon the latter's reconstruction policy.

3. Perhaps a reference to "The Charter Election and the Republicans in Congress," "The Republicans in Congress Repudiating Their Own Pledges," and "The Meeting of Congress To-day—The Stevens Resolutions." *New York Herald*, Dec. 9, 10, 11, 1865.

From James Thompson

December 8, 1865, Philadelphia, Pa.; ALS, DLC-JP.

A former congressman from Erie, Penn., writes with the sole object of expressing "how much I am gratified by a perusal of your Message." He has always "been anxious for the suppression of the rebellion & the punishment of rebels, but not for the suppression of the states wherein they lived & just here is the difference between you & the fanatics or radicals of the North." In order to achieve "'Death to the South' . . . they would change the characteristics of the whole government." The people look to Johnson to restore "the natural functions, without disturbing any of them."

From Edward R.S. Canby

New Orleans   Dec 9 1865.

His Ex The President

The Opelousas road has repeatedly been tendered the directors but has been refused by them.[1]

The city of New Orleans own a controlling interest & I have been informed that the acting mayor[2] has forbidden the directors to receive the road unless their extravagant & unjust claims against the gov't are admitted.[3] These have been declined because it involved, first, an usurpation of executive authority, second, the admission of a principle that requires the gov't to defray the cost of suppressing the rebellion, and at the same time that of maintaining the war that has been carried on against it. Full reports have been made on this subject the last of which have probably reached the War Dep't by this date. By instructions from the Quartermaster Genl[4] of August eighteenth—the road is now under the charge of the division commanders.[5]

E R S Canby   Maj Gen Comdg

Tel, DLC-JP.

1. In response to a second inquiry from Governor Wells, Johnson had telegraphed Canby to ask, "What difficulties are in the way of turning over the Opelousas Railroad to the President and Directors of the Company?" Wells to Johnson, Dec. 6, 1865, Johnson Papers, LC; Johnson to Canby, Dec. 8, 1865, Tels. Sent, President, Vol. 3 (1865–68), RG107, NA. See Wells to Johnson, Nov. 11, 1865.

2. Hugh Kennedy.

3. Under guidelines established by Johnson in an order issued to Gen. George H. Thomas on August 8, 1865, companies were required to pay for equipment furnished by the government and for all repairs except those necessitated by the operations of the army. The directors of the New Orleans, Opelousas, and Great Western Railroad refused to pay the costs of any repairs by the government and demanded that federal authorities give to them all earnings of the line while under military control. *OR*, Ser. 3, Vol. 5: 355–56; *House Reports*, 39 Cong., 2 Sess., No. 34, pp. 168, 248 (Ser. 1306).

4. Montgomery C. Meigs.

5. Canby turned this matter over to Gen. Philip H. Sheridan, who surrendered the railroad to its directors on January 31, 1866. The company agreed to pay for the new rolling stock but not for any repairs made on the road. *House Reports*, 39 Cong., 2 Sess., No. 34, pp. 168–69, 248 (Ser. 1306); *House Ex. Docs.*, 39 Cong., 2 Sess., No. 1, pp. 166, 171 (Ser. 1285).

To Lizinka C. Ewell

Washington, D.C.   Decr. 9th 1865.

Dear Madam:

Your letter of 4th instant has been received. The pardon for which Major Hubbard applies will be granted and forwarded to you as soon as issued.

In reference to the proposed sale of your property at Nashville, I am very much obliged to you for the opportunity you offer me of becoming its purchaser. I am unable, however, to avail myself of your kindness, for the very good and substantial reason that I am too poor to command the necessary means. I would like to own the property for the purpose indicated to you many years ago, when I first expressed the desire to become its possessor. This, however, can never be, at the price specified in your letter, and I therefore advise you to sell the building and grounds upon the best terms that can be obtained. In my judgment, the price offered by the State is just, fair, and reasonable. Most of my life has been spent in toiling for others; and, as a consequence, I am deprived of the means that others have obtained who devoted all of their time and labor to the advancement of their own interests.

Trusting that you are well and in good spirits. . . .

Andrew Johnson

Copy, DLC-JP.

To Andrew J. Fletcher

Washington, D.C., Dec 9th 1865.

Your dispatch was received,[1] and would have been answered before now, but thought my message, which was about being sent in, would indicate my views upon the subject of Negro, testimony, in all cases where they are parties, would be conclusive.

It is to be regretted that our Legislature failed to make some advance at its present session upon this question, indicating that the public judgement was moving in the right direction.[2]

I have forwarded to you some copies of my message.

Andrew Johnson

Tel, DNA-RG107, Tels. Sent, President, Vol. 3 (1865–68).

1. See Fletcher to Johnson, Nov. 20, 1865.

2. Fletcher's response indicated his optimism about passage of the testimony bill. Later in the week William B. Lewis forwarded to the President a newspaper excerpt of Lewis's speech given before the Tennessee legislature in behalf of the bill. Fletcher to Johnson, Dec. 11, 1865; Lewis to Johnson, Dec. 13, 1865, Johnson Papers, LC.

From Benjamin F. Perry

Columbia S C.   Dec 9 1865.

His Ex Prest Johnson

Your message was received here this morning[1] by the members of
the Legislature with unmingled Satisfaction and approval. It has inspired every one with a Confident hope that we shall soon be fully
restored to the union and once more happy and prosperous. The State
is fully organized and the Code for the protection of the Freedmen has
passed both Houses on its Second reading.[2] I am waiting your Excellencys orders in regard to my duties as Provisional Governor. When is
it likely I shall be allowed to take my Seat in the Senate? How long will
the provisional Governorship of this State be Continued?

I wish to return to Greenville next week and should like to hear from
you before leaving Columbia. The Legislature will probably adjourn
next week.[3]

B. F. Perry   Prov Gov S C

Tel, DLC-JP.
   1. A "telegraphic Synopsis" of Johnson's message to Congress had been received by
Perry on the night of December 6. Perry to Johnson, Dec. 7, Johnson Papers, LC.
   2. See James L. Orr to Johnson, Dec. 23, 1865.
   3. Thanking him for his dispatch, Johnson promised Perry that "in a few days" he
would "receive full instructions as to being relieved as Provisional Governor." Seward's
wire discharging Perry finally reached him on Christmas Eve, three days after the legislature had adjourned. Johnson to Perry, Dec. 11, 1865, Tels. Sent, President, Vol. 2
(1865), RG107, NA; Perry to Johnson, Dec. 25, 1865, Johnson Papers, LC; Kibler,
Perry, 437.

From Davidson M. Leatherman

Memphis Tenn   10th December 1865

I have the honor and pleasure of saying to you—that your message
is here complete, has been read by all with great interest. The universal
expression is that which Major Donaldson[1] has expressed in his letter
to you of this date. It meets the approbation and gratifies all as being
the ablest paper ever sent to the American Congress, one that will live
forever in the history of the Government, as will the Declaration of
independence. I send you a printed review—also paper from Genl.
Sherman.[2]

In addition to letters here enclosed in connection with the mission to
Brussells there are letters in the hands of Judge Hughes,[3] Charles T.
Sherman and Col Perryman[4]—from General Buckland,[5] during the
War Commanding here—now a member of Congress from Ohio, one
from Genl. Roberts,[6] one from the prominent men of Shelby County,

also Fayette & Lauderdale & letters from others that will be presented to you by them.[7]

I regret not being able to speak of the workings of the freedmans Bureau so favourable as heretofore.[8] Nothing would be so gratifying to the minds and hearts of the people here as the immediate disbanding of the Negro Troops, their arms taken from them and placed in the hands of such number of White Troops as may be thought necessary[9] until the Wisdom of all the States can meet in Constitution and legal Council together—and until the several states can do the same—and provide by-laws of the several states for the new condition of the colored man, growing out of and being the result of the rebellion—and our great National trouble and the war that has just ended—the freedmans Bureau then being turned over to the several states.

This suggestion is induced by the impression that there is nothing more certain than that the Rebellion is over and that peace exists in place of War.

Hoping to be able to serve you in some way in carrying out your great Policy. . . .

D. M. Leatherman

ALS, DNA-RG59, Lets. of Appl. and Recomm., 1861–69 (M650, Roll 29), Davidson M. Leatherman.

1. Probably Andrew J. Donelson, though we have not located a letter from him to Johnson for December 10.

2. These items have not been located.

3. James Hughes.

4. Probably John D. Perryman (*fl*1875), a temporary Memphis resident and 1864 Democratic electoral candidate, who in mid-1866 applied for the West Tennessee collectorship. He wrote Johnson from many different locales, seemingly as a transient. Roy P. Basler, ed., *The Collected Works of Abraham Lincoln* (9 vols., New Brunswick, N.J., 1953–55), 8: 58–65; Perryman to Johnson, Aug. 20, 1866, Feb. 26, 1867, July 10, Dec. 5, 1868, Jan. 29, 1875, Johnson Papers, LC.

5. See Ralph P. Buckland to Johnson, Nov. 11, 1865, Lets. of Appl. and Recomm., 1861–69 (M650, Roll 29), Davidson M. Leatherman, RG59, NA.

6. Benjamin S. Roberts (1810–1875), a graduate of West Point and veteran of the Mexican War, served as John Pope's inspector general and chief of his cavalry during the Civil War. He later went to Yale as a professor of military science. Warner, *Blue*. See Roberts to Johnson, Nov. 16, 1865, Lets. of Appl. and Recomm., 1861–69 (M650, Roll 29), Davidson M. Leatherman, RG59, NA.

7. Leatherman was nominated for the consular position at Hamburg, Germany, on August 4, 1866, but declined the appointment. Ser. 6B, 3: 424, Johnson Papers, LC. See George B. Hoge to Johnson, Nov. 28, 1865; Rolfe S. Saunders et al. to Johnson, Nov. 1865; N. B. Glenn to Johnson, Dec. 10, 1865; Petition from Ripley, Tenn., Dec. 8, 1865, Lets. of Appl. and Recomm., 1861–69 (M650, Roll 29), Davidson M. Leatherman, RG59, NA. See also Fayette County, Tenn., Citizens to Johnson, Sept. 21, 1865, Johnson Papers, LC.

8. See Leatherman to Johnson, Sept. 8, 1865. See also Leatherman to Johnson, Oct. 6, 1865, Lets. of Appl. and Recomm., 1861–69 (M650, Roll 29), Davidson M. Leatherman, RG59, NA.

9. For virtually identical views, see Memphis Citizens to Johnson, Dec. 10, 1865, *Philadelphia Press*, Feb. 8, 1866.

To James Johnson

Washington, D.C., Dec 11th 1865.

The Governor elect will be inaugurated, which will not interfere with you as Provisional Governor. You will receive instructions in a few days in regard to being relieved as Provisional Governor.[1]

Why can't you be elected as Senator?[2] I would issue no commissions for Members to Congress—leave that for the incoming Governor.

We are under many obligations to you for the noble efficient and patriotic manner in which you have discharged the duties of Provisional Governor, and will be sustained by the Government.[3]

Andrew Johnson   President U.S.

Tel, DNA-RG107, Tels. Sent, President, Vol. 3 (1865–68).

1. The President is responding to two previous inquiries from Governor Johnson about this subject. James Johnson to Johnson, Nov. 24, Dec. 10, 1865, Johnson Papers, LC.

2. Here the President is addressing Governor Johnson's dispatch of November 21. The Governor released the following version of this interrogatory to both the legislature and the press: "Why can you not elect a Senator?" *Augusta Constitutionalist*, Dec. 14, 1865. See Johnson to James Johnson, Nov. 26, 1865.

3. See James Johnson to Johnson, Dec. 15, 1865.

From William S. Winder[1]

[Canada][2]   Dec 11th/65

Much to my supprise I found my name included in the charge of conspiracy which was brought against Capt Wirz;[3] I was living at the time in Baltimore, and remained there till September when I went to New York, while there was informed that I would be arrested, and reluctantly consented to remove to Canada not wishing to be placed in Prison.

So far as I am concerned and so far as I know of the others embraced in the charge of conspiracy, I will say that it is unjust and untrue.

I was paroled with Gen Jos E Johnstons army, and have taken the amnesty oath prescribed by your Excellency.

I would respectfully refer your Excellency to your Private Secretary Mr Wm. H. Browning, who went to college with me and can tell you who I am, and what I was.

I am very anxious to return to the United States, and go to work and make a support for those who are now dependant upon me. I will be under many obligations, if your Excellency will give me a permit to return not to be molested.[4]

W S Winder

ALS, DNA-RG107, Lets. Recd., Executive (M494, Roll 85).

1. Winder (d. 1905), a Confederate captain, practiced law in Baltimore after the

war. Baltimore directories (1875–1901); "Frank L. Byrne to Editor," *MdHM*, 64 (1969): 370.

2. According to the file sheet, attached by Johnson's clerks, Winder's letter had been sent from Canada.

3. Winder, as assistant adjutant general for his father, Gen. John H. Winder, selected the site for Andersonville prison camp. For his work in developing and administering the camp, he was named as a codefendant in the first charge against commandant Henry Wirz: conspiring "to injure the health and destroy the lives" of federal prisoners. Hesseltine, *Civil War Prisons*, 131, 240; *House Ex. Docs.*, 40 Cong., 2 Sess., No. 23, pp. 3, 23, 100, 222, 234, 359, 421–22, 620 (Ser. 1331).

4. No direct action or response by Johnson has been discovered.

From John W. Leftwich and William B. Campbell

Washington, D.C.   Dec 12th 1865

Sir

For the following brief reasons we respectfully ask the appointment of Thos W Keesee[1] of Columbia Tenn as Internal Revenue Tax Assessor for that (the [5]th) Disct.[2]

He has at *all* times been openly earnestly and actively Loyal to the U.S. Govt.

He is equally so towards you and the Policy of your Administration.

He commenced life as a poor Mechanic and remained such for years but by dint of energy and industry afterwards became wealthy in the property peculiar to our state all of which he lost (without a murmur towards the Federal Govt) as a result of the War.[3]

His decided ability and unbounded personal popularity will make his appointment very acceptable to his people and give him an influence for good second to no one in the state.[4]

Jno W Leftwich

W B Campbell

ALS (Leftwich), DNA-RG56, Appts., Internal Revenue Service, Assessor, Tenn., 5th Dist., Thomas W. Keesee.

1. Keesee (*c*1817-*fl*1880) was a longtime resident of Columbia who had been in the coach-making business. Johnson nominated him as collector of internal revenue for the 6th district of Tennessee on October 16, 1866, and again on January 14, 1867. The second nomination was rejected a month later. 1880 Census, Tenn., Maury, 163rd Enum. Dist., 15; Jill K. Garrett, *Maury County, Tennessee Historical Sketches* (Columbia, 1967), 192; Ser. 6B, 3: 424, 4: 228, Johnson Papers, LC.

2. The writers of this letter left the district number blank. We have inserted "5" because that is the district for which Keesee applied. Since that particular post was filled by someone else, the Johnson administration evidently decided later to shift Keesee's nomination to the 6th district.

3. During the Civil War Keesee was victimized by guerrillas who stole bales of cotton from him. After the war he submitted claims in the amount of $2,100 to the U.S. government; he was paid $1,400. *Nashville Union*, June 10, 1864; *House Misc. Docs.*, 44 Cong., 2 Sess., No. 4, p. 19 (Ser. 1762).

4. One of the intriguing facets of this letter is that Keesee was also endorsed, in attached statements, by Isaac R. Hawkins, William B. Stokes, and Nathaniel G. Taylor, all of whom, along with Leftwich and Campbell, had been elected to Congress but were not seated until the summer of 1866. Appts., Internal Revenue Service, Assessor, Tenn., 5th Dist., Thomas W. Keesee, RG56, NA.

From Alexander H. Stephens

Crawfordville Ga   12 Decr. 1865

Dear Sir

Hon Garnett Andrews[1] of this state informs me that he expects soon to visit Washington on business that may require a personal interview with you.[2] In that event I take pleasure in his behalf in making him known to you by these lines. He is emphatically one of the first men in Georgia. His position for many years upon the Bench in this state kept him from figuring on the national boards. But for talents ability integrity and all that gives nobility to character he has but few superiors in this or any other state. I have known him personally and intimately for thirty years and I mean all I say.

He was ever a strong union man—[earlier?] life a Jackson union man—opposed with great ability & that zeal which strong conviction can alone inspire the doctrine of nullification. He was one of the ablest and most efficient advocates of the cause of the union in 1850 & 51. With equal zeal & determination he opposed secession in 1860. He has had nothing to do with the war I think. He is an able lawyer, a learned Judge and an upright honest man if ever one lived. I take great pleasure in commending him to your special attention in any matter that he may have to present to you.

Alexander Stephens

P.S. If the U.S District attorneyship for this State is not yet filled and Judge Andrews could be induced to accept it I do not think a better appointment could be made.[3]

A. H. S.

Copy, DLC-JP.

1. Andrews (1798–1873) served as judge of the northern circuit of Georgia (1836–55, 1868–73). Kenneth Coleman and Charles S. Gurr, eds., *Dictionary of Georgia Biography* (2 vols., Athens, 1983), 1: 31.

2. In a subsequent letter to Horace Maynard, Andrews wrote that he was "unable to go to Washington, as expected." He therefore forwarded this copy, retaining the original in anticipation of a later visit to the capital to press for an appointment as federal district attorney. Johnson received this copy on February 5, 1866. Ser. 4A, 4: 670; Andrew to Maynard, Jan. 26, 1866, Johnson Papers, LC.

3. Henry S. Fitch received the appointment. See Fitch to Johnson, Nov. 30, 1865.

Interview with James F. Wilson and Hiram Price[1]

[December 14, 1865][2]

The passage of Mr. WILSON's resolution[3] by a vote thoroughly testing the sense of the great majority of the House upon the President's Southern policy, on Thursday last, furnished a proper occasion for the mutual explanation he desired, and hence he sought the White House, in company with his colleague, Mr. PRICE, on the evening of the same day. The President received his visitors very cordially, and, upon an introductory remark of Mr. WILSON, announcing the object of their call, invited them to an unreserved expression of opinions and suggestions. Thereupon Mr. WILSON proceeded to say substantially as follows:

"Mr. President, you have, no doubt, been informed of the resolution I offered to-day in the House, and of the vote upon it. In explanation of it, I wish to say, that *neither myself nor the rest of the majority voting for it, are disposed to make any distinction between Tennessee and the other States lately engaged in rebellion*[4] in our preliminary examination into their respective claims to representation in Congress. At the same time the joint Committee of Fifteen may, and probably will, extend to the former State *priority of consideration* by taking up and disposing of its case first, and to this the majority will not oppose." Passing from this special, to the general subject of reconstruction at large, Mr. WILSON continued: "I am aware that there are men in Congress, styling themselves 'Conservatives,' that claim to be your friends par excellence. Now, I do not hesitate to avow that I am what is commonly called a 'Radical.' I contributed, in my humble way, all I could to the success of the party that placed you in power. Hence I claim the right to call myself the friend of your administration. Myself and those acting with me in Congress are all friendly to it, and desire its entire success. But we think, and with us our constituencies, that by your plan of reconstruction that result is not likely to be attained. We hold, at the same time, that there is one way in which it could be reached. In our opinion, your efforts to reorganize the rebel States, and restore them to the Union, after an uninterrupted trial of some seven months, *have not proved successful to the extent required to insure the future peace, safety and prosperity of the country.* Congress, in pursuance of what it considers its solemn duty, now proposes, after due investigation of the whole subject, *to devise, if possible, some better plan of reorganization and restoration.* The plan Congress will probably adopt will be *to submit such amendments to the constitution as will, if accepted by the State Legislatures, furnish ample guarantees for the future.* The majority of Congress expect and ask that, while engaged in investigating the whole subject of reconstruction, and devising some new plan it may be left free to act as it may deem best, and that *no attempt be made by the Executive to interfere with and influence its action by the distribution of patronage or in any other way. If thus left free by you, there can be no possible difficulty between the executive and legislative branches of the government. But if you are disposed to interfere with Congress, by patronage or otherwise, and force your peculiar ideas and plans upon Congress and the country, you will meet with serious opposition by those that are now the friends of your administration, and desire sincerely to make it successful.* The plan

Congress will probably adopt will not render it necessary for you to surrender any of your own views in relation to reconstruction. Inasmuch as under the constitution of the United States you cannot be asked to approve the resolutions of Congress submitting certain amendments to the constitution. You will not be responsible for our action, but we will be responsible for it to our constituents, who called upon to determine upon the merits of our plan of reconstruction. Hence there will be no occasion for serious differences between the Executive and Congress, if each branch of the government simply leaves the other to do what it consider its duty. And let me add this: *the so-called conservatives of Congress, the men that claim to be your exclusive friends, go with you to-day because they think it is to their advantage to do so; but they will oppose you to-morrow if they shall find that it is to their disadvantage to support you. You will find in the end that the men who differ from you to-day from sincere convictions, and honest patriotic motives, are much more reliable and trustworthy friends than these timeservers."*

The President, in reply, stated that he was anxious to avoid a division among the friends of his administration in Congress; that he would regret to see any difficulties arise between them and the executive. He then proceeded to review at length his policy of reconstruction, reiterating the points in support of it made in his published speeches, and more lately in his message; *but said nothing that could be construed into an admission of its failure.* On the contrary, he seemed to be fully persuaded of its present and future success. *Nor did he say a word indicating an intention to abstain from interference with Congress in its legislation upon reconstruction.* He did not say that he would interfere; but neither did he commit himself to the opposite line of action. However pressed by Mr. WILSON in this direction, *he would not give the assurances desired of him.* That he would have made a formal disclaimer of a purpose to meddle with Congress, if he did not entertain it, may be fully presumed. And this was the impression left by the tone and tenor of his remarks upon the minds of his visitors.

New York Times, Dec. 29, 1865.

1. Hiram Price (1814–1901), a native of Pennsylvania, was president of the State Bank of Iowa and served five terms in Congress (1863–69, 1877–81). *BDAC*.

2. Internal evidence indicates that the interview actually took place on this date, although the *Chicago Tribune* report, found in the *New York Times*, was dated December 19.

3. On December 14, 1865, the Iowa representative had successfully introduced a resolution restoring key passages deleted by the Senate from the legislation creating the Joint Committee on Reconstruction. These passages required that all materials pertaining to the admission of the former Confederate states be submitted without debate to the Joint Committee and stipulated that no member from such states would be admitted before Congress declared them to be entitled to representation. *Congressional Globe*, 39 Cong., 2 Sess., pp. 61–62.

4. Wilson had refused to exempt Tennessee from the provisions of his resolution. *Congressional Globe*, 39 Cong., 2 Sess., p. 61.

From George L. Stearns

Boston, Dec 14th 1865.

Dear Sir

You will perhaps recollect, that I asked permission to send you the opinion of Prof. Parsons of the Harvard Law School,[1] on the Duty of Congress to guarantee to each State of the Union a Republican form of government.

What he had previously given me in conversation, is now clearly stated in the enclosed article in the "Boston Daily Advertiser" of the 9th inst. "What can Congress do."[2] I should have forwarded it earlier, if severe illness had not compelled me to suspend all mental as well as physical labor.

My private correspondence from the rebel states, as well as that coming from other sources I know to be reliable, compels me to believe, that as yet, the mass of the Southern people do not at all appreciate their new position.

They still adhere to their aristocratic prejudices, desiring to return as nearly as possible to the old order of affairs, and to subjugate the laboring classes, both white and black to their rule as in former times.

In this antagonism of aristocratic and Democratic ideas, I have no fear for the ultimate success of the Negro. Many thousands of them will die from want, and ignorance of the means of self preservation, but the more intelligent and strong will live through their trials, making them, as a race, more compact and efficient.

It is the white man who will suffer the most, through the indulgence of bad passions and depraved appetites, from which the Negro is comparatively free. The thirty years of misrule of Jamaica is not possible in the United States. Our people will not tolerate it. This spirit of caste will be fatal to the prosperity of the late ruling class at the South, and if fostered will gradually exterminate them through poverty, sickness and disappointment, and introduce in their stead an enterprising population who are not ashamed to lay the foundation of a lasting prosperity by manual labor. How can we remedy this?

In legislating for a territory so extensive as these states, specialities should be avoided, and general laws passed, that will apply to the whole country.

For indeed we need the same changes in the Constitution and laws, for the North as for the South; if we would base our action on principle, not on Caste and Prejudice.

You, Mr President, are from your antecedents and present position, better fitted to *lead* in this reformation of our legislation, than any man in the country.

Your opposition to the Aristocracy of Tennessee in former times, the sacrifices you made for the Union in the first years of the rebellion, the broad and progressive tendency of your whole being, eminently fit you for a *leader in this great work,* in which you would have the almost undivided support of Congress and the Northern States. What we need is a return to the principles that underlie our National Constitution.

In the formation and adoption of that noble instrument of self government, Negroes voted in all the States except New Jersey and South Carolina, and the condition of those states to day tells the tale of fearful demoralization, consequent on their ignorance of the true policy of Nations.

Let us then, restore as far as possible to the Negro the Rights of which we have unjustly deprived him, and repealing in all our laws the distinction of race and color, substitute that of intellectual qualification to apply equally to all voters.

All men stand before Divine Justice on terms of perfect equality. Should not Justice on Earth seek to imitate the Justice of Heaven?

Abrogating then all artificial distinctions, let each man stand in our Courts on terms of perfect equality.

This cannot be done in a moment. The weak and ignorant must be protected and encouraged, and the strong, but wilful man, be made to bow to the majesty of just laws, until the tone of society at the South corrects the evils arising from their past condition. Industry and Education must be encouraged as the antidotes of Vice and Misrule.

No person, Mr President, has to day so much power for good or evil as you have, and in proportion to your acceptance of the true policy of Reconstruction, will be your reward.

If, looking with a single eye to the welfare of the whole country, you give the weight of your influence in favor of absolute Justice, whether that is attained or not, Your name will descend to posterity as one of the distinguished benefactors of mankind.

That God will give you wisdom and strength, in proportion to the responsibility he has laid on you, is the daily prayer of

George L Stearns

ALS, DLC-JP.

1. Theophilus Parsons (1797–1882), a prolific author, taught law at his alma mater from 1848 until 1869. In August 1865 Stearns had forwarded an address on Reconstruction written by Parsons to which was appended a long list of endorsements. *DAB;* Stearns to Johnson, Aug. 16, 1865, Johnson Papers, LC.

2. Not found, but the *Boston Advertiser* of December 9, 1865, contained a lengthy essay on the constitutional powers of Congress penned by Parsons.

From James B. Campbell

Columbia, So. Ca.   Decr 15/65

My Dear Sir/.

I write for the purpose of rendering my reccommendation of Mr W. J. Gayer[1] for the appointment of U.S. Marshal of this judicial district.

During the war Mr Gayer was detailed to act as Provost Marshal of Charleston and in the discharge of his duties had the care of the Union Prisoners and to his determined sense of propriety and humanity and the liberality of Messrs Trenholm, Wagner, Nelson,[2] and others who supplied money for him to apply, it happened that the Union prisoners were better treated at Charleston than any other place South. This brought upon him some obloquy and abuse from violent and evil minded persons, but the sober people of Charleston during the war and since have signified their opinion of him by electing him to our legislature, of which he is still a very useful member. Besides the considerations which I have named and which I think every Union officer or soldier who was a prisoner in Charleston will confirm, Mr Gayer is admirably fitted for the performance of the duty of the office.[3]

In my opinion there could not be a better selection mad in this state.[4]

Jas. B. Campbell

ALS, DNA-RG60, Appt. Files for Judicial Dists., S.C., William J. Gayer.

1. William J. Gayer (c1832-fl1881), an attorney, was a delegate to the secession convention. John F. Poppenheim to Johnson, June 18, 1865, Johnson Papers, LC; 1870 Census, S.C., Charleston, 3rd Ward, Charleston, 20; Charleston directories (1874–81).

2. George A. Trenholm and probably Theodore D. Wagner (1819–1880), a secession convention delegate who operated a blockade-running business. Nelson has not been identified. May and Faunt, *South Carolina Secedes*, 221.

3. Another correspondent denounced Gayer as a "Villian" who, after having "inflicted all the punishment he could on Union Citizens and Soldiers, has now the arrogant audacity to ask to be rewarded for such brutality." D. W. Wayne to James Speed, Oct. 4, 1865, Appt. Files for Judicial Dists., S.C., William J. Gayer, RG60, NA.

4. Governor Perry also endorsed Gayer as "eminently qualified." Nevertheless, Johnson did not appoint him. Perry to Johnson, Dec. 15, 1865, ibid.

From James Johnson

Milledgeville   Dec 15 1865.

The Legislature takes a recess until the fifteenth (15) of January without Electing Senators. Gov Jenkins was inaugurated on yesterday. You will be pleased with his address. I feel Confident that there will be entire harmony between him and yourself.

J Johnson   Provl Gov

Tel, DLC-JP.

From Jesse Smith[1]

Reedsburg Wis   Dec 15th 1865

Sir

I see by the Cairo papers that Wm. C. Quantrell[2] the notorious Missouri guerilla has passed through there enroute for Washington to obtain a pardon from you for the part he has taken in the late rebellion.

You have doubtless reliable information of the inhuman massacre committed by his orders at Lawrence Kansas.[3]

On the sixth of Oct 1863 he surprised Gen. J. G. Blunts[4] body guard and captured seventy five men of which I was one.

After we were captured we were shot in obedience to his orders Quantrell setting his men the example by himself shooting one who was disarmed and severely wounded.

Five of us lived and seventy were killed.[5]

Such conduct on the part of an officer needs no comment, and I hope your excellency will elect that such men can receive no pardon.[6]

Jesse Smith   late of Co. "J" 3d Wis Cav

ALS, DNA-RG94, Amnesty Papers (M1003, Roll 36), Mo., William C. Quantrell.

1. Not further identified.

2. Quantrill (1837–1865), the guerrilla commander who allegedly held a Confederate commission, had been killed the previous summer during a raid in Kentucky. *DAB.*

3. In August 1863 guerrillas under Quantrill's command killed about 150 men and boys at Lawrence. Boatner, *CWD.*

4. James G. Blunt (1826–1881), a former Kansas Jayhawker, commanded the Army of the Frontier in the West. Warner, *Blue.*

5. Blunt's column dispersed when it was attacked by Quantrill's raiders near Baxter Springs, Kansas, in October 1863. Many of the Union troopers were shot as they fled from the guerrillas. Albert Castel, *A Frontier State at War: Kansas, 1861–1865* (Ithaca, N.Y., 1958), 158–61.

6. Concern that Quantrill was not actually dead occasionally surfaced during the first year after the war. Apparently Johnson did not respond to this missive, but, at his direction, earlier in December orders had been sent to Cairo for Quantrill's arrest. In March 1866 Stanton wired orders to New York for Quantrill's arrest. Edwin D. Townsend to Lewis C. Skinner, Dec. 2, 1865; Stanton to John A. Kennedy, Mar. 10, 1866, Tels. Sent, Sec. of War (M473, Roll 90), RG107, NA.

From John Binny[1]

New York   16th Decr 1865.

Dear Sir

I hope you will excuse my writing you a few additional lines in reference to the work of reconstruction.[2]

Now that the constitutional amendment is virtually if not legally passed by the requisite majority of States, and that slavery is for ever annihilated in this grand republic, it is a very solemn question for your consideration whether it is not the duty of the Government to have the capestone put on the work of reconstruction by enfranchising the coloured people. I propose that it should be done twenty five years hence so that due time might be given for the heated passions of the Southern people to subside and also a sufficient time might be allowed for the coloured people to be trained and educated to an intelligent exercise of the franchise. As it is proposed to clear off the war debt of the nation in the course of the next thirty years[3]—a most wise & judicious step; so it would be a just & noble action to introduce a measure by constitutional amendment or otherwise—by which the coloured people may have the franchise similar to the whites in the southern states in the course of the next twenty five years.

Unless this is adopted the work of reconstruction is certainly incomplete & unsatisfactory. Not only should the coloured people in the Southern states be legally put in full possession of their civil rights[4] but they should as soon as possible receive the same political rights as the whites in the South.

I am aware that Mr Seward is of opinion that the individual states alone have the right to arrange as to the franchise within their own territories—the rebel states being regarded by him as Constitutional states, and thereby trammeled with constitutional restrictions—but I would humbly submit that by their criminal act of secession they ceased to be *constitutional* and came under the *law of war*. I send you a copy of the Tribune of today in which you will find an able speech of Gerrit Smith on this very point.[5] You would be wise to advise solemnly with Mr Seward, Mr Stanton and other members of the cabinet on this question which is pregnant with mighty consequences to the peace & safety of the nation in the future.

Were you to contemplate the duty & expediency of introducing an additional measure to secure the franchise to the blacks similar to the whites in the south at the expirg of the next twenty five years, two questions arise.

Shall you confine this measure to the blacks in the south or shall you extend it to all the states of the Union? If you do not think it is wise to extend this enfranchisement to the loyal states—there are serious considerations which ought to determine you, if possible to secure their political rights to the coloured people in the south. They are a very numerous class in the southern states & may become very dangerous from a deep sense of being wronged. Then the southern states are under the war power & are not yet to be recognized as constitutional states, so that you have it in your power to adopt a substantial method of reconstruction and not leave a root of bitterness to rankle in the south which will inevitably burst into agitation & quarrelling and bloodshed in the future.

I do not see how you are to have a solid guarantee that those coloured people shall be protected in their civil rights without a measure of enfranchisement. You place them greatly in the power & under the mercy of their late rebel masters.

I suggest these hints for your serious Consideration—as essential toward a substantial & permanent reconstruction.

John Binny

ALS, DLC-JP.
1. Binny (*fl*1897), a New York Republican who corresponded with subsequent presidents, later moved to London. Binny to James A. Garfield, Feb. 3, 1875, June 22, 1880,

June 21, 1881, Garfield Papers, LC; Binny to Benjamin Harrison, Dec. 1, 1897, Harrison Papers, LC.

2. Binny had written the President a week earlier that "The franchise could be given immediately to the coloured soldiers who fought in the late war." Binny to Johnson, Dec. 9, 1865, Johnson Papers, LC.

3. See Message to Congress, Dec. 4, 1865.

4. The next month Binny wrote again to urge the President to take action against the "Black codes of the ex-rebel states." Binny to Johnson, Jan. 10, 1866, Johnson Papers, LC.

5. The *New York Tribune* of December 16, 1865, published Smith's November 28, 1865, speech, in which he advocated black suffrage.

From Duff Green

Washington   December 16th 1865

To the President

I have just read what purports to be a letter from W S Oldham[1] of Texas, given in evidence before the late Military Commission,[2] and which it appears led to the arrest and imprisonment of Professor McCullough.[3] It says

The combustable material consists of several preparations and not one alone, and can be used without exposing the party using them to the least danger of detection whatever. The preparations are not in the hands of McDaniel[4] but are in the hands of professor McCullough and are known but to him and one other party as I understand.[5]

It will be seen that there is nothing here stated which charges Professor McCullough with being the inventor or with having manufactured or used the material here referred to. His knowledge of it may have been given to him by the inventor. This letter was written in February 1865 and it so happens that I was living in Montgomery, Alabama, in the summer of 1864 with my son who was the Quarter Master General of that State,[6] and there saw a person who called at our residence and exhibited to him specimens of a material of which he claimed to be the inventor.[7] It was in appearance like coal, and the properties and use of it he then described to be much the same as stated by Mr. Oldham in the letter from which the above extract is made. He then said that he had applied to Mr. Seddon,[8] as Secretary of War, and that he had refused to use it because he did not approve of that mode of conducting the War.[9]

When I came to Richmond in the fall of 1864 I found Professor McCullough there. I had known him for many years. His father[10] and I were intimate personal friends and he was confidential in his communications to me. He said that he came to Richmond to tender his services to the Confederate Government and had been assigned to duty in the Nitre and mining Bureau, but that being dissatisfied with St John,[11] the chief of that Bureau, he had resigned and had determined to go to France. He said further that he had been requested to take charge of some chemical experiments or preparations which he had refused to do. He did leave Richmond intending to go to France and was arrested, as I am told, in his attempt to run the blockade.[12]

I respectfully submit that the facts in this case, within my own knowledge are such as to make it my duty earnestly to solicit Professor McCullough's release from imprisonment and as I intend going immediately to Richmond you will confer a great, a very great favor, if you will permit me to announce to him that you have released him.[13]

Duff Green

ALS, DNA-RG107, Lets. Recd., EB12 President 2961 (1865).

1. A Confederate Senator, Williamson S. Oldham (1813–1868) served in the Arkansas legislature before moving to Texas. Webb et al., *Handbook of Texas*, 2: 311.

2. The commission that tried the Lincoln conspirators also reviewed evidence concerning other clandestine Confederate activities, including the Oldham letter. Benn Pitman, *The Assassination of President Lincoln and the Trial of the Conspirators* (Cincinnati, 1865), 47–49.

3. Richard S. McCulloh (1818–1894) was a professor of chemistry and physics at Princeton and Columbia universities before becoming a chemist for the Confederate Nitre and Mining Bureau. After the war he returned to teaching. Clark A. Elliott, *Biographical Dictionary of American Science: The Seventeenth Through the Nineteenth Centuries* (Westport, Conn., 1979), 165.

4. Capt. Zedekiah McDaniel (b. *c*1822) commanded a "torpedo company" in the Confederate Secret Service. Noted for sinking the USS *Cairo* with a submarine mine, he also issued the orders for the explosion of a bomb at City Point, Va., which reportedly killed over a hundred people and caused extensive damage. 1860 Census, Ky., Barren, 2nd Dist., Glasgow, 162; *OR*, Ser. 4, Vol. 3: 177; Ser. 1, Vol. 42: 954–56; Milton F. Perry, *Infernal Machines: The Story of Confederate Submarine and Mine Warfare* (Baton Rouge, 1965), 32–34.

5. The complete text of the Oldham letter can be found in *OR*, Ser. 4, Vol. 3: 1078–79.

6. Duff C. Green. See Hugh McCulloch to Johnson, Sept. 14, 1865.

7. Probably Capt. Thomas E. Courtenay (b. *c*1822), a former cotton broker from St. Louis. Perry, *Infernal Machines*, 135.

8. James A. Seddon.

9. The Confederate Secret Service, at the request of President Davis, may have used these bombs, which consisted of a cast iron casing serrated and painted to resemble coal and containing a fuse and explosive. Courtenay and others, including McCulloh, were authorized to raise small companies to use these and similar devices against military targets in the North. Perry, *Infernal Machines*, 135–38; *OR*, Ser. 4, Vol. 3: 37–38.

10. James W. McCulloh (*c*1789–*fl*1858) was a bank official who was the focus of a pivotal Supreme Court case, *McCulloh* v. *Maryland*. In 1842 he was appointed a comptroller for the U.S. Treasury. 1850 Census, D.C., 1st Ward, Washington, 60; *Boyd's Washington and Georgetown Directory* (1858), 206; Margaret G. Myers, *A Financial History of the United States* (New York, 1970), 85; *Senate Ex. Journal*, 6: 43, 47.

11. Isaac Monroe St. John (1827–1880) was a civil engineer for several railroad companies prior to the Civil War. He commanded the Confederate Nitre and Mining Bureau from April 1862 to February 1865 when he was appointed commissary general of the army. Wakelyn, *BDC*.

12. McCulloh was captured on May 17, 1865, as he, along with seven companions, tried to escape from Florida to Cuba. *Cincinnati Enquirer*, May 29, 1865.

13. Johnson forwarded this request, as he had earlier petitions from McCulloh's family in New York, to Stanton for a "report of the reasons why the prayer of the petitioners may not be granted." Judge Advocate General Holt opposed releasing McCulloh, noting the "strange and revolting insensibility to the criminality of this man, on the part of his brother." McCulloh was paroled to New York on March 25, 1866. Ser. 4A, Vol. 3: 248; Grace McCulloh to Johnson, Dec. 11, 1865; John MacLean to Johnson,

Dec. 12, 1865, Johnson Papers, LC; James W. McCulloh to Johnson, Nov. 4, 1865, Lets. Recd., EB12 President 2718 (1865), RG107, NA; James W. McCulloh to Johnson, Nov. 20, 1865, Robert Garrett Family Papers, LC; Holt to Stanton, Nov. 10, 1865, Lets. Sent (Record Books), Vol. 16, RG153, NA; E. D. Townsend to Alfred H. Terry, Mar. 25, 1866, Tels. Sent, Sec. of War (M473, Roll 90), RG107, NA.

From Joseph Holt

Washington, D.C.   Dec. 16, 1865.

In reply to the communication of His Excellency of the 15th. inst.,[1] by which I am requested to furnish him with a "report of all facts that I may have in my possession concerning one Porterfield,[2] a banker in Canada, who, it is alleged, was engaged in financial transactions with the rebel agents in that Province during the progress of the rebellion"—I have the honor to submit that the only facts within the knowledge of this bureau in regard to this party are derived from the testimony adduced upon the trial of the Assassins of President Lincoln and their accomplices.

The principal witness at this trial upon the point of the complicity of the leaders of the rebellion in the assassination,—after stating that he was well acquainted with Porterfield and knew him as constantly associated with Thompson, Clay, Sanders, Tucker, Cleary and other agents of Davis in Canada, as well as with Blackburn the party principally engaged in introducing yellow fever into the country by means of infected clothing—goes on to depose as follows.[3]

I saw *John H. Surratt*[4] in Canada three or four days after the assassination of the President. I saw him in the street with a Mr. Porterfield. I learned immediately after that Surratt was suspected; that officers were on his track; and that he had decamped. Mr. Porterfield is a Southern gentleman, now a British subject, having been made so, I believe, by a special act of the Canadian Parliament. He has been for some time a broker or banker there. He is the agent who took charge of the St. Albans plunder for the Ontario bank, when prematurely given up by Judge Coursol.[5] Porterfield is on very intimate terms with Thompson and Sanders.

It would thus seem to be most clear that Porterfield was an important and influential member of that clique of traitors in Canada, who, as the representatives of the Richmond government in that country, were for so long a period occupied in devising and maturing treasonable enterprizes in aid of the rebellion and in violation of the laws of war, which at length culminated in the monstrous crime in which they were adjudged by the late Military Commission to have been implicated.

It is with such traitors as these that Porterfield appears in the character of fellow conspirator and ally, as well as banker and financier; and there can be no doubt that in the latter capacity, as well as the former, he rendered valuable service to the rebel cause.

It is to be added that the witness referred to—a man of unusual intelligence and observation and regarded by this bureau as entirely reliable and trustworthy—is not now in Washington but is expected to arrive here in a few days. Upon his return he will be more particularly inquired of as to the antecedents of Porterfield and his transactions in Canada; and such additional facts as may be elicited upon such inquiry will be forthwith communicated to His Excellency the President.[6]

J. Holt. Judge Advocate General.

LS, DLC-JP.

1. See Johnson to Holt, Dec. 15, 1865, Johnson Papers, LC.

2. John Porterfield (1819–1874), former president of the Trader's Bank in Nashville, fled to Canada during the war. In October 1865 General Thomas ordered his arrest if he returned to Tennessee. *Nashville Union and American*, Dec. 29, 1874; George H. Thomas to Robert H. Ramsay, Oct. 13, 1865, Tels. Sent, Sec. of War (M473, Roll 90), RG107, NA.

3. The testimony quoted by Holt was that of Charles Dunham (alias Sanford Conover, and also James W. Wallace). Pitman, *Assassination of Lincoln*, 28–34. See Thomas R. Turner, *Beware the People Weeping: Public Opinion and the Assassination of Abraham Lincoln* (Baton Rouge, 1982), 208–9.

4. Surratt (1844–1916), a son of Mary E. Surratt who was suspected of being involved in the assassination of Lincoln, escaped to Canada and then to Rome, Italy. Finally captured, he was brought back to the United States where in 1867 he was acquitted, although he was not released from prison for nearly another year. Boatner, *CWD*.

5. Charles-Joseph Coursol (1819–1888), Montreal lawyer and district judge, in December 1864 discharged the St. Albans raiders, who had been arrested by Canadian authorities, because he did not think the British Parliament had recognized the Canadian extradition act of 1861. *Dictionary of Canadian Biography* (11 vols., Toronto, 1966–   ), 11: 206–7.

6. Subsequent investigations revealed that Dunham had "coached witnesses in perjury and manufactured evidence." In May 1866 Johnson ordered the release of Porterfield, who had returned to Nashville with the permission of Governor Brownlow, but did not pardon him despite the entreaties of numerous petitioners. The President also did not pardon Dunham, who was convicted of perjury. James Taylor, Jr., to Johnson, ca. Feb. 1866, Amnesty Papers (M1003, Roll 50), Tenn., John Porterfield, RG94, NA; E. D. Townsend to Thomas, May 23, 1866, Tels. Sent, Sec. of War (M473, Roll 90), RG107, NA; Turner, *Beware the People Weeping*, 215–23.

From Reuben D. Mussey

New York   Dec 18 1865.

My dear Mr. President.

You must not think me ungrateful nor neglectful of duty and courtesy that I have not called on you to thank you for your great kindness in accepting my conditional resignation.[1] I could not trust myself to express in person my thanks and I understood from my friend Judge Hood[2] that he had an appointment with you and I asked him to say what I felt and also to inform you that immediately upon General Grant's arrival he approved my resignation. I trust I may be able some time, my dear Sir, to show you my gratitude in some substantial and active method—and in any event and under all circumstances you have my warmest affection and esteem.

When I left Washington on Thursday my papers had not come from Nashville.[3] I hope to find them on my return. I shall then work at them vigorously for a month or so and then Providence permitting go Westward.

I am here trying to make arrangements for my living while at work on them and provision for my family while I am away. I have not been so successful as I hoped but shall probably get something to do. Having now no personal favors to ask of you I should like upon my return to call upon you occasionally *socially* now that I can do so without obtruding my personal wishes and needs upon you.

Since I have been here (two days) I have heard a good deal said about Mexico and the N.Y. Collectorship.

As to the first the Loan Agents feel hopeful and the general sentiment that the French have no business there gains ground. A disinclination to further War is as prevalent as the former sentiment but the conviction grows that Mr Seward's temporizing policy will *drift* us into War, and that the best way to avoid it is to guarantee, in some way, the Mexican Loan, taking of course sufficient pledge for that guarantee. To straighten the southern boundary line of Arizona so as to give the United States a port on the Gulf of Mexico; to obtain Naval Stations in Lower California; or more to get the whole of Lower California—these are propositions that attract capitalists and seem to favor a peaceable solution of the Mexican Question.

Considerable talk is being made about a large meeting during the holidays to exemplify and inculcate a moral support of American Republics by the United States.

The papers have a "Rumor" that Marshall O. Roberts[4] has been offered the N.Y. Collectorship. He is an excellent business man and one of character. But he is committed to Maximilian being President of a silver company whose charter comes from him and the friends of Mexico fear that he would use, if appointed, his vast official influence against the Republic.

A Mr Haight I have heard mentioned as a candidate for the Collectorship.[5] I do not know him nor do I know his politics.

He is said to have been the first man to aid our Government, early in the War, financially being President of the Commonwealth Bank of this City.

Let me bring this gossippy letter to a close with a "good story" they tell of Mr Seward. The other day after dinner he said "Mr Johnson is a better President in many respects and in especially this very important respects—that *he don't tell one Cabinet Minister what another one says about him*![")]

I see by the papers that poor Tom Corwin is dying. He was the salaried Agent in Washington of Maximilian and the French Government. A prominent Mexican speaking to me of his death said—"The Lord understands His business!"

R D Mussey

ALS, DLC-JP.
1. See Mussey to Johnson, Dec. 7, 1865.
2. Thomas Hood.
3. Mussey had asked in October for his books and papers to be sent from Nashville. Mussey to John D. Cochrane, Oct. 24, 1865, Tels. Sent, President, Vol. 2 (1865), RG107, NA.
4. Roberts (1814–1880), a New York City native, was a developer of steamship lines and an active Republican who profitted greatly from questionable government contracts during the Civil War. *DAB*.
5. New York City native Edward Haight (1817–1885) had served a term in Congress (1861–63) as a Republican. *BDAC*. For a letter in support of Haight's appointment, see James E. English to Johnson, Feb. 12, 1866, Appts., Customs Service, Naval Officer, New York, Edward Haight, RG56, NA.

From Thomas J. Sizer[1]
(*About the N.Y. Collectorship*)

Buffalo   December 18, 1865.

Dear Sir:

There are only two respects in which I claim an interest in this subject, to justify me in writing to you about it. One is, my high regard for the late Preston King—whose confidence and regard I am proud to have had—and the other is the thought which I have given to it, in connection with the interests of the Democratic Republican cause.

I am not an applicant for this place, and do not write in the interest of any one who is.

I casually, but quite directly, heard of its being said, of Mr. King (since his death) by a member of our (Union) State Committee, and in allusion to Mr. King's rumored resignation, that he ought to have resigned, because he refused to assess his Clerks for political purposes, or to allow politicians to come to the Custom House to collect assessments from them.

To me this is suggestive of many things; but I will not trouble you with details, for I have confidence in your political knowledge and wisdom. You doubtless know, and fully appreciate, that; with the present rate of duties, the privilege of directing and controlling the patronage of the N.Y. Custom House, may be worth millions monthly, to a combination of importers and politicians.

Some things, however, you may not know, especially about this state, and more especially, about this end of it, so well as I. Always a Democratic Republican, and therefore a supporter of Jackson & Van Buren, I came here, from Oneida County, and studied law in the office of Messrs Fillmore, Hall and Haven;[2] and, being disposed to the further study, have thus had the opportunity, and have made myself thoroughly acquainted with the real political character of the people of Western New York. You know that they were Antimasonic, and that thus they became Whig—this was one of Mr. Weed's[3] bargains—and *they* gave success for a time to the Whigs in the State, and advanced Mr. Seward. But success cured them; and I assure you that they are really and reliably, *Democratic Republican.*

Preston King fairly represented the political character of a decided majority of the people of this state, *including Western New York*; and the superior prestige of Messrs. Seward and Weed is due to adroit management, and especially to a misconception, out of the State, of the real sentiments of the people of New York. In our changing organizations these men have largely controlled the wires, but not the sentiments nor the judgments of the people. They have not even represented them, even when their own political salvation seemed almost to depend on their doing so; and I think it is because they do not believe in the people so much as they do in management and in politicians: that is, because they are "Whigs" and can't forget it. Through their management, and through the acquiescence of Democratic Republicans for the sake of the cause in such times as we have lately passed through, an apparent character has been given to the party in this state, supporting your and Mr. Lincoln's Administrations, that the facts and the real condition of political opinion in the State, do not warrant. Hence the character of our Senators in Congress; and hence, also, our small relative majorities; and, also, many other facts which might be specified.

Of course, many Democratic Republicans, finding, especially, that Federal patronage came largely through Mr. Weed, have worked in that line; as was, naturally to be expected; but the great underlying fact, to which I would now call attention, is, the real, substantial, and (I think) right, political character of the State. I am sure that, with less "Whig" management, such as of Weed, Greeley, Raymond, &c. and with more real Republicanism, Mr. Seymour[4] and his set, could not have so nearly divided the political strength of the state.

Now my object is accomplished if I have laid this fact before you.

From it, if properly possessed, you will, I am confident, draw the proper inferences—and, among others,

That, for the support of a Democratic Republican organization in this state, it is not necessary to have *any body* in the N.Y. Custom House and its patronage, as a leading financial means; and,

That, on the contrary, a simple, straight-forward, strict, legal management of its affairs, as a natural incident of a like administration at Washington, and such as I know Mr. King meant his should be, will do more—even if it shall offend the managing politicians—to sustain the Republican cause in this State, and to bring honor on your Administration.

Please excuse any seeming officiousness in my writing this to you; in consideration, partly, that we, of this Congressional District, have not a Republican Representative at Washington: the cause of which is, in my opinion, the same bad management here, in trying to be "Whig" when the voters are Democratic Republican.

Thomas J. Sizer

ALS, DLC-JP.

1. Sizer (c1812-fl1892) was an attorney and war pamphleteer. 1880 Census, N.Y., Erie, Buffalo, 160 Enum. Dist., 52; Buffalo directories (1848–92); *NUC*.

2. Solomon G. Haven (1810–1861) and Nathan K. Hall were law partners with Millard Fillmore during the 1830s. Haven later served as a Whig in Congress (1851–57). Buffalo directories (1835–36); *BDAC*.

3. Thurlow Weed.

4. Horatio Seymour.

From Henry A. Smythe[1]

New York   18th Decr 1865

My dear Sir

Having been so Kindly received by you & so impressed with the interview, I cannot resist addressing you informally, trusting you will pardon me for doing so.

I confess, my desire for the office of Collector of this port has increased. I do not intend however to urge my appointment, nor would I obtrude myself upon your time in any way.

After I had the pleasure of an interview with you I unexpectedly met with some obstacles to my appointment, among your immediate surroundings.[2] I believe they have been entirely removed however, & I doubt if an objection would now be raised to me. How *far*, or how *strongly*, some of the leading politicians would *advocate* me, I am unable to tell. I am more strongly urged here than ever. Encouraging letters come to me from every quarter. At the same time, I am strongly pressed by many to give up the matter altogether. So in point of fact, I *must* do one thing or the other ere long. My many responsibilities & duties require, that I either give them up transferring them to the care of others, or that I give up all idea of the *Collectorship*.

Should I be appointed, I shall enter upon the duties of the office with entire confidence & will discharge the same according to the best of my ability, never loosing sight of the welfare of the Administration, or of your wishes & interest personally. And whether appointed, or not, I shall always take both pride & pleasure in serving your Excellency.[3]

H. A. Smythe.

ALS, DNA-RG56, Appts., Customs Service, Collector, New York, Henry A. Smythe.

1. Smythe (c1818-fl1882), a New York City merchant, banker, and conservative Union Republican, had visited with Johnson four days earlier. 1850 Census, New York, New York, 15th Ward, Western Half, 104; New York City directories (1849–82); Robert J. Walker to Hugh McCulloch, Nov. 21, 1865; William K. Strong to Johnson, Nov. 24, 1865, Appts., Customs Service, Collector, New York, Henry A. Smythe, RG56, NA; *New York Times*, Dec. 15, 1865.

2. The reference here is unclear, but Gideon Welles expressed reservations about appointing Smythe as collector and later opposed Johnson's appointment of Smythe as

Henry A. Smythe, Applicant
for the New York Collectorship
*Courtesy Johnson-Bartlett
Collection, Greeneville*

Robert Morrow, One of
the President's Secretaries
*Courtesy Johnson-Bartlett
Collection, Greeneville*

minister to Austria. Howard K. Beale, ed., *Diary of Gideon Welles* (3 vols., New York, 1960), 2: 484, 558; 3: 391.

3. After receiving many recommendations from New York factions, Johnson did appoint Smythe as collector in April 1866. Jerome Mushkat, *The Reconstruction of New York Democracy, 1861–1874* (East Brunswick, N.J., 1981), 94–95. See Harry C. Page to Johnson, Dec. 22, 1865, and Abiel A. Low to Johnson, Dec. 29, 1865.

From Benjamin B. Dykes[1]

Americus Ga   Decr. 19th 1865

Mr President

I have resided at and own the lands at Andersonville Sumter County Ga. Upon the 25th of Sept. last I recd a pardon from your Excellency and I therefore most respectfully petition your Excellency for an order to have my lands and tenements delivered up to me.

I am willing to sell or grant to the Government the grave yard or sell all my premises to them.

Benjamin B. Dykes

P.S The so called Confederate Government never bought leased or rented any of my land and what they did was done without my consent or disire.

B.B.D

N.B If your Excellincy believe me to be worthy I will take charge of the graveyard.[2]

B B D

ALS, DNA-RG105, Land Div., Lets. Recd.

1. Dykes (*c*1813–*fl*1875) was a farmer who served as a Confederate postmaster and an agent for the Southern Express Company at Anderson Station, Ga. Dykes to Johnson, Aug. 17, 1865, Amnesty Papers (M1003, Roll 18), Ga., Benjamin B. Dykes, RG94, NA; Confederate Papers *re* Citizens or Business Firms (M346, Roll 269), RG109, NA.

2. Although the U.S. Army took possession of the burial grounds at Andersonville Prison in the summer of 1865 and erected a sign designating it as a National Cemetery, Dykes was not compensated until 1875 when he received $3,300. Peggy Sheppard, *Andersonville Georgia U.S.A.* (Andersonville, 1987[1973]), 13; *House Ex. Docs.*, 39 Cong., 1 Sess., No. 1, pp. 263–65 (Ser. 1249).

From Lewis D. Campbell

Washington D.C.   Decr 20, 1865.

My Dear Sir—

I must leave for home this afternoon at 7 o'clock, and as I may not have an opportunity of seeing you, I write this note to assure you that I have a very high appreciation of the friendship you have evinced for me. Your proposition in regard to the mission to the Republic of Mexico is a high, unexpected and unmerited compliment and one that I shall ever hold in grateful remembrance.[1]

I cannot leave without again repeating that I sympathize with you most fully in the arduous, vexatious and responsible labors with which

Clara Barton Raising the U.S. Flag at Andersonville National Cemetery
Harper's Weekly, October 7, 1865

you are overwhelmed, and deeply regret that there are those here who seem desirous rather of embarrassing you than of giving you aid and support in your trying position.

I am ambitious only to help you in whatever way I may be of most practical service in your great work of restoring and strengthening our Nationality. It is not for me to be the judge of the position in which I can best carry out this desire to help. That I am entirely willing to leave to you, and I must assure you that I shall not be chagrined if it is deemed best to allow me to remain a private in the ranks. Whether in public or private life I shall never forget your many kindnesses, and shall give the policy you have enunciated my cordial and undivided support.

I sincerely believe that there are other positions better suited to my abilities than that of Minister to Mexico, *in which I could be of more advantage to your administration.* Besides in the event of my having to go upon such a mission it would be scarcely possible for me to take with me my wife and three daughters whom I love too much to think of a very long separation from them.

I leave my case wholly in your hands. Should you be disposed to call on me for any service however humble, you have only to let me know the fact by telegraph and I will promptly respond.[1]

I trust in God that your health may be spared and that your earnest labors for our common Country may be crowned with success.

Lewis D Campbell

ALS, DLC-JP.
1. Campbell later accepted Johnson's appointment as minister to Mexico but, though he did travel to that country, he resigned in June 1867 without ever presenting his credentials to the Benito Juarez government. *DAB.*

From William C. Loftin [1]

Custom House New Bern N.C.   Decr 20th 1865.

Sir:

From a Telegram which I received, I learned that I have been removed, and my successor reccommended to the Senate.[2]

As a matter of justice to myself, I respectfully beg leave to submit the following facts—*on the square.*[3]

First— My commission was received direct from you as Collector of this Port with the approbation of Gov Holden and many other Eminent loyal Citizens of my acquaintance. My removal (in the way I have heard it) I know does me very great injustice and looks to me is a very cool reflection on my friends that reccommended me. I know that I can establish in North Carolina a clean record as to my Union principles or intigrity. I have been pecniarily ruined by the Rebel Government, and now, not to be properly protected by the Government of our Fathers looks a little hard.

When I entered upon my duties as Collector I complied strictly with all the requisitions of the law, gave a good bond &c. I was inexperienced with regard to the duties of the office, and I found no office, or any thing else to direct me. I employed the best Clerk I could get at my own expense. I entered upon my duties on the 30th day of July since which time have collected and deposited about Eighty Six thousand dollars, and have a large amount on hand now to be deposited. One thing is very certain I have collected the money for the Government and with our present instructions I profess to understand the science of the business.

Secondly— I understand that my removal was Effected by a young man by the name of Hartley,[4] who visited the office as a Treasury Agent; and who I treated kindly—opened all of my books to him, and received his hearty approval of all that he reviewed. He reccommended nothing only a little alteration in a Hospital report. I have lately learned also, that he was made a dupe of by a secret clique of my enemies (as I believe) who, for personal and political purposes have meditated my destruction. I have had heretofore the approbation of Col Heaton[5] with whom I have made my deposits, and I believe if he was privately consulted would give his approval now.

I pray you in conclusion to give me a fair and impartial hearing before I am sacrificed.

W. C. Loftin   Collector

LS, DNA-RG56, Appts., Customs Service, Collector, New Bern, William C. Loftin.

1. Loftin (c1802–1866), a merchant, farmer, and former clerk of the local court of common pleas, had been briefly incarcerated during the war for his unionist sympathies. 1850 Census, N.C., Lenoir, Kinston, 369; (1860), Craven, Russel's Dist., 60; *Raleigh Standard*, Mar. 31, 1866; P. Hardee et al. to Johnson, Dec. 21, 1865, Appts., Customs Service, Collector, New Bern, William C. Loftin, RG56, NA.

2. Francis A. Fuller (fl1866), a Boston native, had fled from Charleston at the outbreak of the war, then worked in the quartermaster's department in New York City. Upon the recommendation of many prominent Massachusetts officials, Johnson had appointed him as surveyor of customs at Wilmington, but Fuller later asked for a more lucrative post. In December 1865 he was commissioned as collector at New Bern. Fuller to Johnson, Aug. 7, Oct. 9, 1865; Henry J. Gardner to "whom it may concern," June 24, 1865; Charles E. Fuller to John A. Andrew, June 24, 1865, ibid.; Ser. 6A, Vol. 4: 140, Johnson Papers, LC.

3. From Miguel Cervantes, *Don Quixote*, pt. 2, bk. 3, chap. 5, p. 475; the phrase "on the square" implies honesty.

4. Possibly Edward Hartley (fl1867), who in 1865 was incorrectly listed as assistant special agent "E. Hubbs" at New Bern, and two years later was stationed in Baltimore. *U.S. Off. Reg.* (1865–67).

5. David Heaton, supervising special agent for the Treasury Department.

From James M. Tomeny

Mobile   Dec 20 1865.

Your dispatch received.[1] One of the same tenor from the Sec'y came to Millan yesterday.[2] Some one is making false representation to you and to the Dep't concerning my official action.[3] I am doing all I can to protect public interests confided with as little Embarrassment to private interests as possible.

Representations to you relative to my releasing cotton are maliciously false. I do hope you will have confidence enough in me to believe that I am doing right till you know I have done wrong. Perfect harmony & cooperation exists between the military authorities & myself.[4]

J. M. Tomeny   Supt Special Agt

Tel, DLC-JP.

1. The previous day Johnson had wired Tomeny: "While you respect private rights, be sure that no cotton is released that properly belongs to the Government." Johnson to Tomeny, Dec. 19, 1865, Tels. Sent, President, Vol. 3 (1865–68), RG107, NA.

2. William P. Mellen. The document has not been found.

3. The President may have referred this telegram to the Treasury Department, because two days later William E. Chandler wrote that his department's actions were "not based upon any charges against Mr. T. or any other person by name, but upon general complaints of fraudulent transactions in cotton at and near Mobile." Chandler to Johnson, Dec. 22, 1865, Johnson Papers, LC.

4. In response to a request from Mellen, Johnson authorized Gen. Charles R. Woods to arrest all persons in his department who had "defrauded" the government. Tomeny was indicted by the federal district court of Alabama in April 1866 for conspiring to defraud the government, forcing his resignation as acting collector of customs at Mobile; the charges were later dismissed. Tomeny to Johnson, May 14, 1866, ibid.; Johnson to Wood, Dec. 20, 1865; Hugh McCulloch to Mellen, Dec. 20, 1865, General Agent, Tels. Recd., RG366, NA; Tomeny to Johnson, Apr. 16, 1867, Appt. Files for Judicial Dists., Ky., James M. Tomeny, RG60, NA.

From William E. Chandler

Treasury Department   December 21, 1865.

The President.

Relative to the telegram from Mr. Lamar[1] which you submit, I have the honor to state that this Department did not request his arrest, and knows nothing of it, except that his sister represents that he was arrested for attempting to bribe an Agent of the Treasury Department.

I see no good reason why he should come to Washington in regard to his examination, inasmuch as all evidence can be procured and facts ascertained with more facility in Georgia than here; but I beg to respectfully suggest that the military authorities under whose charge he is to be directed to afford him every reasonable opportunity in the procurement and presentation of papers, testimony, etc., to make good his defence.

The telegram is herewith respectfully returned, for such action as you may think proper.[2]

Wm. E. Chandler, Act'g Secretary of the Treasury.

LBcopy, DNA-RG56, Lets. Sent *re* Restricted Commercial Intercourse (BE Ser.), Vol. 12.

1. Gazaway B. Lamar had requested a "passport" to Washington and an order for the return of his financial records, confiscated by the Treasury Department, so that he could secure the release of his cotton. Lamar to Johnson, Dec. 18, 1865, Tels. Recd., President, Vol. 4 (1865–66), RG107, NA. See Lamar to Johnson, Nov. 15, 1865, Fifth Special Agency, Lets. Recd., RG366, NA.

2. Johnson subsequently wired Gen. John M. Brannan in Savannah, seeking an explanation for Lamar's arrest and the "facts in his case." Brannan's reply confirmed that Lamar had been arrested for attempting to bribe government officials and that he would soon be tried by a military commission. Johnson to Brannan, Dec. 21, 1865; Brannan to Johnson, Dec. 22, 1865, Johnson Papers, LC. See Charles J. Jenkins to Johnson, Jan. 1, 1866.

From James L. Orr

Columbia   21st December 1865.

Sir:

It is made my pleasing duty to communicate to you the enclosed resolutions, passed yesterday, with great unanimity by the general assembly of this state.[1]

I am very confident if the wise and liberal policy of reconstruction which you have inaugurated is carried into execution by the other departments of the government no doubt in the future need be cherished of the unreserved loyalty of South Carolina at least, to the Federal union.

When civil rule is fully restored (and I trust it will at an early day) no other force than our own citizens will be needed to maintain the supremacy of the constitution and laws of the United States within her limits.

I avail myself of this occasion to express to you my hearty approval of the resolutions.

James. L. Orr

ALS, DLC-JP.

1. The resolutions declared that it was Johnson's policies that had brought the "restoration of harmony between the people of this state and the General Government." South Carolina General Assembly to Johnson, Dec. 20, 1865, Johnson Papers, LC.

From Hannibal Hamlin

Boston   Dec 22 1865

My Dear Sir

I have learned that it is probable that Secy Harlan may be again returned to the Senate and his place become vacant. In that event I desire cordially and earnestly to commend to your favorable consideration Ex Gov Randall of Wisconsin. He is eminently fitted for the place, and there are, as it seems to me substantial reasons why such an appointment, can, most appropriately be conceded to that State.[1]

H Hamlin

ALS, DLC-JP.
1. Orville H. Browning became Secretary of the Interior after James Harlan resigned to return to the Senate; Alexander W. Randall became Johnson's postmaster general (1866–69). *DAB*.

From J. Glancy Jones [1]
Confidential

Washington   22 Dec '65

My Dear Sir

In order to impress on your mind the few points referred to by me I drop a note: 1st Judge Black,[2] & Senator Buckaleu[3] both proposed yesterday to meet me in Phila. the last of Jany. or first of Feby. to consult on the Gubernatorial nomination in Penna. Buckaleu would naturally prefer Clymer[4]—Black would prefer Cass.[5] They both assured me they would yield all preferences to policy & expedience.

My own private judgment is to have all withdraw & nominate *Hancock*[6] provided he is right with you; & stands on your policy & will accept. I can say to you: if you desire to have him, that I think I can bring about his nomination with perfect unanimity or any other good democrat you may name—but, will he *resign* his commission for a Governorship. If he is wanted, I think he will, with assurance, that his friends will take care of him in future. Let me have your views on this point in any way you may choose but in perfect confidence. There is not much time to lose. Hancocks antecends are democratic.

The 2d point is that you will send to the Treasury Depart: for all the papers in relation to the appointment of Assessor in the 8th Revenue Dist. of Penna. (Buks County). You will find Col Alexander;[7] a soldier backed by all the soldiers, & a majority of the Republicans. Col A. is & always was a republican; Tutton[8] the present incumbent is a radical; & has had the office, for four years. I will send leading republicans to Washington & if you yield to interfere it will be to *them* & they must have all the credit. It should be unknown to any one, save yourself & Alexander, that I had any agency in it.[9]

J. Glancy Jones

P.S. I was pleased to find Mrs Senator clay[10] of Alabama, an enthusiastic friend of yours. I told her to write to all our friends South, to do every thing *you required*, & trust to luck; & stand by you not only now but in all future time. She said she had & would now add that after, *my interview* I had assured her that President Johnson was entitled to our unreserved confidence & support.

J G.J.

ALS, DLC-JP.

1. Jones (1811–1878) had served as a Democrat in Congress (1851–53, 1854–58) and as minister to Austria (1858–61). *BDAC*.

2. Jeremiah S. Black.

3. Charles R. Buckalew (1821–1899), former minister to Ecuador (1858–61), was a Democrat who served in the Senate (1863–69) and in the House (1887–91). *BDAC*.

4. Hiester Clymer (1827–1884), an attorney serving in the Pennsylvania senate, was the Democratic nominee for the governorship of that state in 1866. He was defeated but was later elected to Congress (1873–81). *BDAC*.

5. George W. Cass (1810–1888), a West Point graduate and nephew of Lewis Cass, was president of the Pittsburgh, Ft. Wayne, & Chicago Railway Company. An active Democratic partisan, he was passed over in favor of Clymer in 1866 but was nominated for an equally unsuccessful bid for the governorship in 1869. *History of Alleghany County, Pennsylvania* (2 vols., Chicago, 1889), 2: 292; Bradley, *Militant Republicanism*, 203, 260–61, 346–47.

6. Winfield S. Hancock.

7. George W. Alexander (1829–1903), who had manufactured cotton laps before the war, served as lt. col. of the 47th Penn. Inf. Afterward he returned to his previous vocation, then later produced fur hats. *New York Times*, May 6, 1903; Reading directories (1856, 1860, 1869–71).

8. Alexander P. Tutton (1823–*fl*1893), a former schoolmaster, had become assessor of internal revenue for the 8th District in Pennsylvania in 1862. Late in life he became a partner in a plant that manufactured paper mill machinery. Samuel T. Wiley, *Biographical and Portrait Cyclopedia of Chester County, Pennsylvania*, ed., Winfield S. Garner (Philadelphia, 1893), 581–82.

9. Nathaniel P. Banks also endorsed Alexander, who replaced Tutton after he was removed in 1866. Three years later, President Grant appointed Tutton as a supervisor of internal revenue in Pennsylvania, a position he retained until Grant chose him to be collector of customs for Philadelphia (1876–80). Banks to Johnson, Feb. 16, 1866, Johnson Papers, LC; Wiley, *Chester County*, 581.

10. Virginia C. Clay.

From Sarah F. Mudd[1]

Bryantown Md   Dec 22ond 1865

Dear Sir,

I hesitate to address you—but love is stronger than fear—timidity must yield. I must petition for him who is so very very dear to me.

Mr President after many weeks anxious waiting for news from my innocent suffering husband, Dr Samuel Mudd last nights mail brought the sad tidings he with others—"by order from the War department were heavily ironed and obliged to perform hard work."[2] The plea for this cruel treatment is that the Government is in possession of news of a plot orriginating in Havana or New Orleans for the rescue of the said Prisoners. Besides the food furnished is of such miserable quality, he finds it impossible to eat it. Health and strength is fast yielding. To my poor intellect it seems an ineffectual plan to put down a plot by avenging upon the prisoners the acts of others. I suppose Sct Stanton knows better.

It strikes me very forcibly your Excellency is ignorant of this order. I saw you in Septr. and although I felt I was not as kindly treated as others, I looked into your face and if it is true the face is an index to the heart[3] I read a good kind heart that can sympathise with the sufferings of others. I marked the courteous manner you addressed ladies particularly the aged. These things encourages me to pray you to interpose your higher authority. I ask you to pardon my husband although the setting of a leg is no crime that calls for forgiveness. I aske you to release him. I believe you will do it. But above all I beg you in the name of humanity, by all that is dear to you, in the name of his aged and suffering Parents[4] his wife and four baies[5] to immediately put a stop to this inhuman treatment. By a stroke of your pen you can cause those irons to fall and food to be supplyed. By that same pen you can give him liberty. Think how much depends upon you. You were elected the Father of this People, then their welfare is your welfare. Then in the name of high Heaven if you let him die under this treatment, he an American Citizen, who has never raised his arm or his voice against his Country, Can those People love you? Forgive me I speak planely, but my heart is so sore. You say women are your jewels "you hope for much from their prayers."[6] I do not love you yet, neither will I ask the Almighty to bless you. But give back my husband to me to his parents who are miserable. The wealth of my love and gratitude will be yours. My prayers shall ascend in union with my little Children who are in happy ignorance daily looking for the return of their "Pa." To him who has said suffer little children to come unto me,[7] God of mercy I pray you tuch the heart of thy servant. Make him give back my husband. Could you look into our once happy house holds it would give you a subject for meditation. In Doctors childhood home there is his Father who is old and infirm. When he hears the name of his boy his lips trembels, but he thinks it not manly to yield to tears, besides he has confidence in you. His Mother has scarcely left her sick room since his first arrest. She waits she says to see him. Then like holy Simeon she is willing to die.[8] Pass from this to my poor little household. I a wife drag out life in entire dispondency. I who was shielded from every care by him who is now suffering a liveing death am miserable to battle with this overwhelming trouble. I am the mother of four babeys, the oldest but seven years the youngest but one. The third a delicate boy requiring constant medical attention. Myself and children are in poverty. All the money accumulated has been spent in Lawyers fees and expences. The crop of last year was distroyed, and eaten by the soldiers who also caried off the farm servants consequently there was but a very slight crop planted not enough to give my children bread another year. I have never known poverty until now, and how I am to take care of the children I do not know. Doctors Father owns much poor land—to pay the taxes will impovish him so you see it is out of his power to render much assistance. Think of this. Judge Holt says I am asking the release of my Husband two soon that publick opinion is not yet satisfyed, and that the petition which I presented to him in Sept.—In my simplicity written by myself—cast an odium upon the Court.[9] But he (Judge Holt) said it was as well done as a woman could do, but a Lawyer could have done better. I enclose the petition with this to you. I believe you will receive the best a woman can do. I cannot believe you will permit him to be offered a victim to satisfy public opinion. The spirit of President Lincoln if it is in eternal rest does not demand the unjust offering—and I believe the publick favour is on the side of Dr Mudd and you would make friends by setting him at liberty. Eight months punishment is enough for the setting a mans leg and the court knew and God knows that was his only connection with that horrible crime. Mr President when you and your loved ones are enjoying the coming festivities cast one thought on me, and as an offering to that Infant Savior who was born to suffer and die to save us all give back my husband. Then will prayers assend to Heaven for you such as can only come from the heart of a sorrowing wife and Mother. I hope to be pardoned for trespassing so long upon your time. But in Gods name act upon my petition.[10] My trust and confidence is in President Johnson who has the "spirit to do the right thing in the right time."

Sarah F. Mudd

ALS, DNA-RG204, Pardon Case File B-596, Samuel A. Mudd.

1. Sarah F. Dyer (1835–1911) had married Samuel A. Mudd in 1857. Richard D. Mudd, *The Mudd Family of the United States* (Ann Arbor, Mich., 1951), 529.

2. In September 1865 Mudd tried to escape from Fort Jefferson, where he was imprisoned, by having himself hidden in the hold of a steamer. He was discovered and "immediately placed in the dungeon in irons." Ibid., 538–39; George C. Wentworth to Lorenzo Thomas, Sept. 25, 1865, Lets. Recd. (Main Ser.), File M-1919-1865 (M619, Roll 385), RG94, NA.

3. A common epigram of obscure origin, a variation of which appears in the popular temperance tract by T. S. Arthur, *Ten Nights in a Bar-room* (1854). Burton Stevenson, comp., *The Macmillan Book of Proverbs, Maxims, and Famous Phrases* (New York, 1948), 739.

4. Henry L. Mudd (1798–1877), a planter, and his wife, Sarah Ann Reeves Mudd (1811–1868), lived near their son's home in Maryland. Mudd, *Mudd Family*, 520–22.

5. Andrew J. (1858–1882), Lillian A. (1860–1940), Thomas D. (1861–1929), and Samuel A., Jr. (1864–1930). Ibid., 529, 544, 554.

6. See Interview with Baltimore Ladies, Nov. 6, 1865.

7. Luke 18: 16.

8. Luke 2: 25–32.

9. See Mudd to Johnson, Sept. 23, 1865, Pardon Case File B-596, Samuel A. Mudd, RG204, NA. For a synopsis of a deposition submitted by Sarah Mudd on behalf of her husband, see Thomas Ewing, Jr., to Johnson, July 10, 1865, *Johnson Papers*, 8: 380–81.

10. Upon receipt of this Johnson allegedly ordered the irons removed from Mudd and other prisoners at Fort Jefferson, and they were given better quarters. Despite yet another entreaty from Sarah Mudd, however, the President did not pardon her husband until February 1869, and Mudd was released the following month. Nettie Mudd, ed., *The Life of Dr. Samuel A. Mudd* (New York, 1906), 163, 219; Sarah F. Mudd to Johnson, June 28, 1866, Pardon Case File B-596, Samuel A. Mudd, RG204, NA; pardon of Samuel A. Mudd, Feb. 8, 1869, IHi.

From Harry C. Page
Important.

Office of the Daily Era,
New York, Dec. 22/65.

To the President:

Myself and the Era have been your firm and true friends, ever since you first stepped foot into the Senate of the United States.

My columns have frequently borne testimony of my devotion to you, and from the masthead of the Era we have flung the flag of our country with your name inscribed thereon there to remain until the People shall have decided, in 1868, who is to be the next President of the United States. Heartily and without reserve we have committed ourselves to your advocacy & vindication, and we have done so because we believe you to be a *good man* and a *patriot*. Now, having taken this decided stand, it naturally follows that we feel some anxiety in regard to your appointments, because these have an important bearing in the *future*. We do not feel this anxiety because we expect or desire any official position. Far from it; for, instead, *the servants of the general government who hold official position at your hands, and who have advertising to hire out, always neglect and proscribe the Era*; therefore, if *that* can't be done for the Era,—if a *recognition* so *legitimate & proper in its character* can't be done for a journal that flies your flag—there is but little hope that any official position, for which there is so much scramble and contest, will ever be awarded us.[1]

In view of this fact you will give us credit for disinterestedness, and appreciate our friendship accordingly.

Mr. President, it is undoubtedly true that you must have a *party* as well as a *policy*, and when we talk of parties, we have to come down to *men*, for it has got to be in this country, that men are almost coequal with principles. You are the standard-bearer of the party of the Administration, and as such it is due to *all your friends* that you should recognize them, to such an extent as may be proper. Here are the two great parties—the Union party and the Democratic party. And then there is the *War Democracy*, men after *your own heart*, who have followed in *your footsteps*. They are naturally your best friends. The Era is a War Democratic journal, or rather was, for now it is an *Andrew Johnson journal*, the war being over. What status are the War Democrats to have in the party of the administration? That is a question for you to decide. No class of men have been more devoted to their country, none have more strength *with* THE PEOPLE. Today in all this broad state & great city, *none of their number*, hold any official position. Take the City of New York, for instance: In the Naval officer, (and a gentleman he is, indeed,) we have a McClellan Democrat.[2] He is a good friend of the

President, and I am glad he was appointed. In the United States sub-treasurer we have a Republican;[3] also in the Surveyor of the Port,[4] Naval store-keeper,[5] and, in fact, *all the other numerous positions* of power under the general government, there are gentlemen alone of Republican antecedents. And in the political organization or machinery of the Union party, the War Democrats have been assigned no position whatever. In fact we have always acted auxillary to that party that we thought was nearest right in sustaining the government—have always supported their candidates altho' we had no voice in their nomination.

So much for the record, and so much for the facts, as they at present exist.

Thus *all* the *elements* which now support the administration are recognized except the War Democrats, and the question arises ought they to be longer proscribed or neglected? Do they deserve fair and equitable treatment? If so it is alone from your hands that they can expect to receive it.

Looking at matters in a political light, it is not alone necessary, in our opinion, that men should sustain your policy, but they should also sustain you at the polls. Men, in this world, are actuated by different motives. Some sustain your policy because it is *right*, and because they have *always*, now and in the past, been your firm friends, & had and have, confidence in your patriotism & statesmanship. Such are the War Democrats. Others sustain your policy for various reasons: some because it is popular with the people, and they are sagacious enough not run counter to the popular current; some because they hope for power; some because they hope to become vested with that power, or its concomitants, in order that one of these days it may be wielded for their own purposes.

Human nature is still human nature; and now, as ever the politicians protest, but their protestations may fail in the future as they have in the past. In all experience we have seen that *the politicians are not to be trusted too much*.

It is not enough that the men who receive your executive approval should support your policy NOW; but they should also, *without any doubt whatever*, support YOU AND YOUR POLICY IN 1868. At least your *true friends* are not willing to leave your cause in the hands alone of the mere politicians whose conventions, so long yet in the future as 1868, are SUSCEPTIBLE OF BEING MANIPULATED AT THE LAST HOUR, and to this end they do not like to see weapons put in the hands of those except they may be your *true and reliable friends*.

The great trouble with men who have been long in politics is, that they have so many "friends to reward and enemies to punish," that *they are not capable of being of service to the hand that appoints and makes them*.

Take, for instance, the position of Collector of this Port. I do not allude to this matter because there is now a vacancy here to be filled, but because it is an apt illustration, and because the appointment about to be made is pregnant with the *utmost importance* as regards the political future. Following up the ideas I have herein elucidated, and coming down to men as representing the points I have made, I take it upon myself to say emphatically and in solemn earnest that *Henry H. Van Dyck is not the man who should be appointed.*

Neither is my nephew, Robert Denniston,[6] Simeon Draper, Charles A. Dana,[7] Mr. Bailey,[8] or any gentleman of that interest. I know these gentlemen personally, & cheerfully bear tribute to their personal worth, but no one of them is the man who should be collector. And, really, if I were called upon to suggest a man, I could not say now to whom so important a trust should be assigned. And yet there are in *this State* and city many good men who have no "friends to reward or enemies to punish," but who desire to serve you faithfully and truly, whose appointment would be popular with the people.

But if Mr. Van Dyck be appointed, your true friends will live to see the day that it will be *bitterly regretted—mark the prediction.*

And it would seem nothing more than right or just that now, that there is an opportunity, that the element that is sustaining you which has hitherto not been recognized—the War Democrats—should be remembered. And yet I would not have a War Democrat appointed unless he was a true friend, now—in 1866, 1867 AND 1868—an active, true and zealous friend of Andrew Johnson.

There are other matters I should like to suggest to you, but this note has already been extended more than I had intended at the outset.[9]

H. C. Page.

ALS, DLC-JP.

1. Although Democratic legislator Charles Reed of Vermont later wrote that Page had "fairly earned" the patronage of the federal government and should be rewarded "in any practical way," there is no record of a response from Johnson. Reed to Johnson, Jan. 29, 1866, Johnson Papers, LC.

2. Moses F. Odell.

3. Henry H. Van Dyck (c1810-fl1882), former bank superintendent for New York, served as assistant subtreasurer in New York City until his resignation in 1869. 1880 Census, N.Y., Kings, Brooklyn, 198th Enum. Dist., 12; *U.S. Off. Reg.* (1865–67); Van Dyck to Grant, Apr. 10, 1869, Appls. *re* Asst. Treasurers and Mint Officers, RG56, NA; New York City directories (1870–82).

4. Abram Wakeman (1824–1889) had also served as a legislator, congressman (1855–57), and postmaster of New York City (1857–64). *BDAC.*

5. Daniel D.T. Marshall (c1817–1888), a merchant, later became president of the "Homeopathic Life Assurance Company." *U.S. Off. Reg.* (1861–65); New York City directories (1860–88); *New York Tribune,* Aug. 14, 1888.

6. Denniston (1800–1867) was a former legislator and comptroller for the state of New York. Cuyler Reynolds, ed., *Genealogical and Family History of Southern New York and the Hudson River Valley* (2 vols., New York, 1914), 2: 896.

7. Dana (1819–1897) was an editor for the *New York Tribune* until his resignation in 1862, after which he became an assistant secretary of war (1862–65) and later proprietor of the *New York Sun. DAB.* For his application, see Dana to Johnson, Jan. 20, 1866.

8. Joshua F. Bailey (*fl*1874) served as collector of internal revenue in New York City until 1870, when he moved to Argentina. Alfred H. Pratt, a former clerk in the customs house and himself an applicant for the collectorship, wrote that Bailey's appointment would be a "great misfortune to the Community" and a "source of mortification & regret." *U.S. Off. Reg.* (1863–69); Pratt to Johnson, Dec. 30, 1865, Mar. 18, 1866, Appts., Customs Service, Collector, New York, Alfred H. Pratt, RG56, NA; *New York Times*, Apr. 11, 1874.

9. Johnson responded by stating that Page's "suggestion" had "been considered" and "duly appreciated." Johnson to Page, Dec. 26, 1865, Johnson Papers, LC.

From Andrew T. Stone[1]

Strictly Private.

Custom House, New Orleans.
Surveyor's Office, Dec. 22" 1865

Sir,

I trust I shall be pardoned for the following. Of late some two or three of the bitterest radicals—men holding by your appointment, or rather by appointment of the President, not *rebel* but *southern* haters, men of more bitterness than wisdom, have seen fit to charge my Deputy,[2] a worthy gentleman, a union man, and a creole of this city, though not a radical, and through him myself, with reporting and causing to be dismissed some two or three officers of the customs, on account, *as they allege*, of their being union men.

It is true I suspended and caused to be dismissed, among others some two or three good union men, but who happened to be a disgrace to the government, whatever their politics. They were absolutely incompetent and worthless, and I know of no authority by which I am empowered to keep men in office who have no other qualifications than that they have not fought against *the flag*.

There are at this port a large number of worthless *hangers-on*, who were appointed only as a necessity, and then by the most radical of the Republican party, to positions in the Custom House, and who have no qualifications for their respective positions except that have not been in the *rebel army*—unfortunately they have not been in *any army*. It is the delight of some gentlemen here to attempt to embarrass the government by insisting that these men shall be provided for, and retained in office, or the "powers that be" in Washington will be prevailed upon to "put somebody in office who will." The latter clause of the foregoing sentence contains the exact words of a government official in the Custom House.

Now I do not propose to vary from my determined line of duty which is that no man who is incompetent shall hold a government office under my administration. Further than this I intend to be governed by what *I believe* to be the best interest of the government and of the Administration under whose appointment I hold, and not be men who I know oppose the Presidents course in respect to the South, and particularly in respect to his attempt to conciliate, and, what is much more important, though it is not every man who has sense enough to see it, to commit the Southern people, and particularly leading secessionists on the side of the Government.

Did I not know how contemptable in the eyes of the executive a man must appear for so doing, I would ask to be informed if it is intended that the Customhouse at this Port shall be a hospital or an asylum for thieves and vagabonds whose only qualifications are that they have not been in the rebel army.

Some of our *best officers* and I may say, *most reliable union men*, are those who have been in the rebel army, and who do not believe that either wisdom or justice demand that negroes should generally be permitted to take part in our civil government.

A. T. Stone   Surveyor of Customs, Port of N.O.

ALS, DLC-JP.

1. Stone (c1835-fl1871), a Louisiana unionist who had been forced into the Confederate army, was appointed surveyor of customs at New Orleans in August 1865 upon the recommendations of several federal appointees and state officials from Louisiana and Illinois. He resigned in late December 1865, then worked for the Treasury Department in the national capital. 1870 Census, D.C., 2nd Ward, Washington, 174; *Boyd's Directory of Washington* . . . (1871), 332; *New Orleans Picayune*, Aug. 31, 1865; Thomas M. Wells et al. to Johnson, May 8, 1865; Stone to Hugh McCulloch, Dec. 27, 1865, Appts., Customs Service, Surveyor, New Orleans, Andrew T. Stone, RG56, NA. See J. Madison Wells to Johnson, Aug. 11, 1865, *Johnson Papers*, 8: 569.

2. Jules Cassard (c1810-c1885) later became a bank president. 1870 Census, La., Orleans, New Orleans, 4th Ward, 42; New Orleans directories (1861–85); *New Orleans Picayune*, Oct. 29, 1865.

To Richard Vaux[1]

Washington, D.C.   Decr. 22d 1865.

Dear Sir:

I thank you for the words of encouragement and the kind wishes expressed in your letter of yesterday's date.[2] Having at heart nothing but the interests of the entire country, all of my efforts will be directed towards the preservation of the Union, the maintenance of the Constitution, the enforcement of the laws, and an early, complete, and cordial restoration of the relations of the States to the Federal Government, and of the people to each other. Knowing that in this great work I shall have the cooperation of yourself and of all truly patriotic citizens. . . .

Andrew Johnson.

Copy, DLC-JP.

1. Vaux (1816–1895), former Democratic mayor of Philadelphia, was president of the board of city trusts. He later served a partial term in Congress (1890–91). *BDAC*.

2. Praising Johnson's first message to Congress as "worthy of that order of true Statesmanship which had become extinct in the Executive department," Vaux urged the President "to save the Country" from the "Puritan destructiveness" of "New England politics." Vaux to Johnson, Dec. 21, 1865, Johnson Papers, LC.

From Andrew Johnson, Jr.

Office Tenne. Penitentiary
Nashville   Dec 23rd 1865

Dear Uncle

I write you this to inform you that Brother James left here a month ago for Texas.[1] I heard from him on his arrival at Galveston but have heard nothing more, and wish to inquire if you have heard any thing.

On our Books I find an a/c against you for $22.70 which please find inclosed.[2]

If you have heard anything from Brother James please inform me.[3]

Col James Dowdy Representative of Anderson County informs me that it has been reported that he was not a candide for Tax Assessor or Tax collector for his District, and request me to Say to you that the report is not correct, and that he is a candidate and would be pleased to get the position. Mr Dowdy will be hear on the 8th January, and would like for you to drop me a line in regard to the matter So that I may be able to give him Some information.[4]

This leaves myself and family well, hoping to hear from you Soon.

Andrew Johnson Jr   Agent

ALS, DLC-JP.

1. See Johnson to James Johnson, Nov. 17, 1865.

2. The enclosed document itemized Johnson's purchases of prison-made shoes and other articles during the 1863–65 period.

3. The President did not hear from James until about three weeks later. See James Johnson to Johnson, Jan. 10, 1866.

4. James A. Doughty was not among those whose names were presented by Johnson to the Senate on May 21, 1866. Ser. 6B, Vol. 4: 227, Johnson Papers, LC.

From Sam Milligan

private

Nashville Ten.   Dember 23, 1865

Dear Sir:

I have now been here three weeks.[1] I have worked, day & night, like a galley-slave; and I feel, I have reasonably sustained myself. All the *magnates* have been before the Court—such as Judge R L Caruthers—Gov Neil S Brown—and the Nashville bar generally, including lots of Rebel Generals &c. We make them all swear over, before they can practice in *our Court.* They comply with the rule of the Court, and I think, it has had a good effect. The docket is very heavy, nearly 600. causes. We will get through, I hope, by the last of January. We take recess for Christmas. Hawkins & *Shack*[2] have gone home. I will stay here and work. Already I am 5 or 6 heavy records a head of them, and in their absence, I will put myself out of their reach this Court.

I have read your message with care, and without flattery, it is emphatically the paper of the age. You need fear no attack upon it, or the policy it inculcates. It will tryumph, in the end, over evey man that assails it: and God grant it may, because it contains the doctrines of an enlightened Statesman, and a Christain philanthopist! All here—every man—so far as I have heard, heartily subscribe to it, except one or two, who still desire military rule.

Sam Milligan

ALS, DLC-JP.

    1. His duties as a member of the state supreme court took Milligan to Nashville.

    2. Alvin Hawkins and James O. Shackelford, Milligan's colleagues on the bench.

From James L. Orr

Executive Dept S.C.   Columbia   23. Decr. 1865

Sir:

I have this day enclosed to you two newspapers containing all the acts passed at the late session of the legislature with references to the freedmen.[1] They have not yet been printed in pamphlet form.

Some of the provisions are objectionable but as a whole I think ample & complete protection is given to the present property of the negro.

He is allowed to testify in court where the rights of a freedman are in any way involved. Their children are legitimized. They can sue and be sued can hold property real & personal—can sell give or devise it. They can contract for themselves.

The vagrant Laws are stringent but necessary but they will only be enforced against the idle & dissolute and many of them you know will not work without the compulsion of law.

Things are progressing here smoothly—some little irregularities but they are small. Kind feelings are rapidly taking the place of hate and revenge.

I hope that our legislation with reference to the freedmen may be satisfactory to you[2] and that it will suit your views at an early day to remove the troops and turn over all our people to our state laws.

I hope to be able to come on to Washington in Febrey when I can learn more fully your views and policy.

The extreme radicals from appearances seem a little irresolute about making war upon your re-construction policy.

If in any way I can serve or strengthen you in your great undertaking you can command me at your pleasure.

James L Orr

ALS, DLC-JP.

    1. Not found, but for a partial list of acts passed by the South Carolina legislature, see the *Charleston Courier* of December 23, 1865.

2. Orr had signed the "Black Codes" into law but soon realized that such laws were impolitic. Therefore, at Orr's request, Gen. Daniel E. Sickles in January 1866 ordered a suspension of their enforcement. Leemhuis, *James L. Orr*, 105.

From Charles Hegamin[1]

Troy N Y   Monday Dec 25th 1865

Dear Sir

I Charles Hegamin Has a Son Samuel Incarserated at fort Jefferson.[2] Pray your Hon. Cant you Have Him Released? It is for a trivel offence. He followed the Patomack army under Gen G B McClennen and then he enlisted in the 14th Heavy artilery of R I. exposed himself to the Perrils of a camp life at Plaquem LA. The war we may Consider at an end and Cant you cause his release? You have children and you can feel for a father. We are a poor and abused Rase. If god is Just you must try and Be so to. The Judgment of a just god will fall on this grate Republic for there injustice to the Poor Black man. We are the Loyal Portion of this grate nation and we feel the Interest of it. For god sake respond to me.[3]

Charles Hegamin

Mannin House on 125 Terry st   Troy N Y

Do hear my entreaty to you. Remember your [illegible].

ALS, DNA-RG94, USCT Div., Lets. Recd., File P-646-1865.
1. Hegamin (c1823–1894) was a waiter and housepainter. 1860 Census, N.Y., Rensselaer, Troy, 3rd Ward, 299; Troy directories (1861–94).
2. Samuel H. Hegamin (c1843-fl1877), a private in the 11th Hvy. Arty., USCT, formerly the 14th R.I. Hvy. Arty., had been sentenced in March 1865 to two years of hard labor at Fort Jefferson, Fla., for striking an officer and disobeying orders. CSR, RG94, NA; Troy directories (1870–77); *Off. Army Reg.: Vols.*, 8: 159; Court-Martial Records, MM-1720, RG153, NA.
3. At the President's direction, the unexecuted portion of Hegamin's sentence was remitted; he was released in March 1866. Endorsement of Johnson, Feb. 16, 1866, USCT Div., Lets. Recd., File P-646-1865, RG94, NA; CSR, RG94, NA.

From William S. Rosecrans

New York   Dec 25 1865

I asked and you gave me leave of absence for six months.[1] My intention was to make arrangements to quit the service where I am not needed.

That injustice which removed me from active command where I dare say I have always rendered honest faithful and not unimportant services to my country and while conferring brevets on others for even administrative services has failed to give me any *recognition* for Iuka Corinth Stone River Tullahoma Chicamauga and the over throw of Price[2] and the conspirators in Missouri, compels me on the advice of friends, who are your friends, to make a personal application to you.

I have not been able to complete my arrangements for business on the Pacific Coast, so that with justice to my family I can resign immediately. But my intention is to do so as early as possible.

If under these circumstances you deem my past services to have deserved so much, and you do not consider it inconsistent with the interests of the country, I ask as a favor that you will excuse the personal application and order an extension of my leave until the first of July next.[3]

Should this be accorded I will not burden the service any longer than may be necessary to make the arrangements to which I have alluded, and you will add another to my personal obligations to you.

W. S. Rosecrans   Maj Gen Vols

P.S. I should have been pleased to see you personally on this matter and others but the existence of an order preventing officers on leave from visiting Washington without special permission and the apprehension of being treated as was General Granger deterred of making an application.[4]

W.S.R

ALS, DNA-RG94, Lets. Recd. (Main Ser.), File R-1010-1865 (M619, Roll 406).

1. Rosecrans had been awaiting orders since his removal as commander of the Department of Missouri in December 1864. William M. Lamers, *The Edge of Glory: A Biography of William S. Rosecrans, U.S.A.* (New York, 1961), 437–38, 440.

2. Sterling Price.

3. On January 9, 1866, Johnson granted Rosecrans's request for leave. He was mustered out of volunteer service that same month but retained his regular army commission until March 1867. Ser. 7C, Vol. 1: 2; Rosecrans to Johnson, Jan. 15, 1866, Johnson Papers, LC; Heitman, *Register*, 1: 846.

4. Apparently, orders issued in August 1862 that leaves of absence would not include Washington, D.C., had not been rescinded. Gordon Granger, who like his former commander was in New York, had applied for permission to visit the capital in early December, but had evidently been denied. *OR*, Ser. 3, Vol. 2: 423; Granger to Lorenzo Thomas, Dec. 6, 26, 1865, Lets. Recd. (Main Ser.), File G-986-1865 (M619, Roll 360), RG94, NA.

From William M. Fishback

December 26, 1865, Little Rock, Ark.; ALS, DLC-JP.

A senator-elect from Arkansas, who had been refused his seat, writes Johnson about the "coming contest between the Congress and yourself" over the course of reconstruction. Asserting that "the sympathies, as will be the cooperation, of the entire South, Loyal and disloyal alike, are with yourself and your policy," Fishback assures the President that, whatever "exaggerated Newspaper Articles may indicate, I think I hazzard nothing in stating . . . that the great '*public*,' outside of those having selfish and partisan objects in view, appreciate your motives and your task and will lend you an earnest and patriotic support."

From Brown Cozzens[1]

Natchez Mi   Decr. 27/65

Dear Sir,

Will you pardon a humbel individual for presuming to address you? Be assured my dear Sir, that it is the love I have for our common Country, that induces me to take this liberty.

I *regret, deepley regret*, to see by the reported proceedings, of Congress that Mr Sumner, of Mass (and others) are doing all they can to arouse a new hostile, spirit in the Southern States. He states, that there still exhists much dissatisfaction, and revolting—Spirit, in the seeceding States, and professes to sustain his statment by Letters &c.[2]

Now Sir, I have just returned from a tour, threw most of these States and I do assure you, I have witnessed no hostile spirit manifested, nor dissattisfaction, excepting at the *unrelenting disposition manifested by the radicals of the North*. But all expriss that confidence, and willingniss and entire approval of your plan, for reconstruction, and to chearfully submit to the *Constitutional Govirment* of *the United States*.

In every part where I have been, I am known, as a Southern Man (but no Sessionist) and I am sure if such spirit as represented by Mr Sumner exhisted I should have seen it.

B Cozzens   Natchez Mi

ALS, DLC-JP.

1. Cozzens (b. c1796), a Rhode Island native, had resided in Missouri before locating in Mississippi. 1860 Census, Miss., Adams, Natchez, 91.

2. On December 20, 1865, Sumner presented a number of petitions and memorials to illustrate "that the people in the rebellious districts . . . by their own acts vacated their rights as citizens and as state organizations." *Congressional Globe*, 39 Cong., 1 Sess., 88–96.

From Joseph Holt

Bureau of Military Justice   Dec. 27. 1865.

The accompanying petitions and letters in behalf of C. C. Reese,[1] under sentence of death for the murder of Nellie West,[2] freedwoman, are respectfully returned.

The three petitions are nearly identical in language, and are signed by some six hundred names of persons residing in Georgia.[3] They base their prayer for clemency on the youth and inexperience of the condemned. Many of the appended names present the appearance of being signed by the same hand.

The letters accompanying these petitions, are appeals to the Executive clemency from individual citizens of Georgia, one of them from Alexander H. Stephens.[4] They present no facts or arguments which were not known to and carefully considered by this Bureau at the time of the preparation of its report upon the record. Enclosed in the letter of Mr. Stephens, is a petition that clemency may be shown to Reese, signed by sixteen of the murdered woman's relatives, and certified as signed without persuasion or intimidation, by one L. M. Acree, J.P.[5] for whose integrity Mr. Stephens vouches.

The opinions expressed by this Bureau,[6] touching the correctness of the judgment of the Court, and the necessity for the execution of the sentence of death upon both Brown[7] and Reese, remains unchanged. The fiendish barbarity of the murder, committed by Reese with his own hand; his cruel and unprovoked threats of death to the aged, feeble, and despairing woman on the morning of the homicide; his perjury, almost in the presence of the Almighty, whom he impiously calls upon to witness his falsehoods in behalf of his fellow-miscreant, Brown, are all circumstances which aggravate immensely his original crime, and should be regarded as justly taking from him every ground on which to base a hope of Executive favor. His attempt to deceive the government into a belief in his confederates innocence, by an affidavit sworn to by him when on the very threshold of death, and replete with falsehoods from beginning to end, has already been exposed. It is believed his present efforts to escape the penalty of his fearful guilt, should meet with a like defeat. That the sons, daughters, and other relatives of his defenceless victim should have, voluntarily and without solicitation or threat, joined in these groundless prayers for the pardon of their mother's murderer, is so wholly unnatural and incredible, that the effect of this unworthy pretence on the part of the assassin's sympathizers, is solely to cast, if that were possible, a deeper shade over the enormity of his guilt.

It is recommended that these petitions be disregarded, and that both Brown and Reese be suffered by the Executive to atone with their lives for the life of the poor, crushed woman, whom they so deliberately slew without a cause.[8]

J. Holt.   Judge Advocate General.

LBcopy, DNA-RG153, Lets. Sent (Record Books), Vol. 17.

1. Christopher C. Reese (c1845-fl1870), a Georgia farmer's son and a Confederate veteran, had been sentenced by a military commission to be executed on January 5, 1866, for the brutal slaying of Nellie West. 1870 Census, Ga., Taliaferro, Crawfordville, 23; Senate Ex. Docs., 39 Cong., 1 Sess., No. 11, pp. 54, 57, 61, 101–2 (Ser. 1237).

2. West (d. 1865) had worked as a slave on a plantation owned by Thomas B. West. Ibid., 46; 1860 Census, Ga., Columbia, Eubanks, 8th and 10th Dists., 15.

3. Petitions and accompanying letters on behalf of Reese can be found in Senate Ex. Docs., 39 Cong., 1 Sess., No. 11, pp. 130–38, 143–50 (Ser. 1237).

4. Stephens had written letters of introduction for Reese's mother to both Johnson and David T. Patterson. Ibid., 148–49.

5. Seaborn N. Acree (c1821–1898), a farmer and former Confederate cavalryman, was misidentified as "Graham" N. Acree in official reports. Ibid., 149; 1860 Census, Ga., Taliaferro, Crawfordville, 34; Alvin M. Lunceford, Jr., Taliaferro County, Georgia, Rec-

ords and Notes (Spartanburg, S.C., 1988), 361, 470; Wiley B. Jones, comp., *Rest in Peace: A Cemetery Census of Taliaferro County, Georgia* (Washington, Ga., 1984), 14.

6. See Holt to Johnson, Nov. 15, Dec. 23, 1865, in *Senate Ex. Docs.*, 39 Cong., 1 Sess., No. 11, pp. 124–27, 129–30 (Ser. 1237).

7. John M. Brown (b. c1827) was Nellie West's former overseer and the stepfather of a girl toward whom Reese "was partial." Ibid., 50, 111, 131–32; 1860 Census, Ga., Wilkes, Washington, 72.

8. Although Johnson had approved the original sentences, he issued an order suspending the executions of both Reese and Brown. Several years later Reese shot and killed a man during a barroom brawl in Crawfordville, Ga. *Senate Ex. Docs.*, 39 Cong., 1 Sess., No. 11, p. 102 (Ser. 1237); Johnson to [John M. Brannan], Dec. 27, 1865; Brannan to Johnson, Dec. 29, 1865, Johnson Papers, LC; *Augusta Constitutionalist*, July 27, 1869.

From Stewart Van Vliet[1]

New York   Dec 27/65

Sir:

I appeal to you most respectfully on behalf of my sister-in-law Mrs Mary A. Moore.[2]

She is the wife of an officer in the late rebel Army & the daughter of the late Major Jacob Brown of the U.S. Army who was killed in the Mexican war while defending Fort Brown on the Rio Grande[3] against an attack made on it by the Mexicans.

Mrs Moore is a Northern & truly loyal woman but remained South during the rebellion to be with her husband & children.

Her property left her by her Father, & in Little Rock, Arkansas, has been seized & sold & I appeal to you most respectfully & earnestly for her pardon & the restoration of her property.[4]

Stewart Van Vliet   Bvt Major Genl, & Qr. Master.

ALS, DNA-RG94, Amnesty Papers (M1003, Roll 14), Ark., Mary A. Moore.

1. Van Vliet (1815–1901), a West Point graduate and a veteran of the Mexican War, served in the quartermaster's department for twenty years, until his retirement in 1881. Warner, *Blue*.

2. Mary Augusta Brown (c1827–1912), whose sister married Van Vliet, was married in 1845 to Samuel P. Moore (1813–1889), a U.S. Army surgeon who became surgeon general of the Confederacy. *DAB*; *New York Times*, Jan. 3, 1912.

3. The post that was renamed for Brown (d. 1846), a career soldier who had served in the War of 1812, is located at present-day Brownsville, Texas. Webb et al., *Handbook of Texas*, 1: 224.

4. Van Vliet forwarded this application through Stanton, to whom he explained that the property in question belonged exclusively to Mary. She was pardoned on March 6, 1867, and recovered 1,500 acres in Desha County left to her by her father, but it is unclear whether her real estate in Little Rock was restored. Van Vliet to Stanton, Dec. 27, 1865, Amnesty Papers (M1003, Roll 14), Ark., Mary A. Moore, RG94, NA; John W. Payne, "Samuel Preston Moore's Letters to William E. Woodruff," *ArHQ*, 15 (1956): 246.

From J. Madison Wells

New Orleans   Dec 27' 65

W. P. Melone[1] Treasy Agent is interfering with Mr Burbridge[2] & myself in the securing of the cottons belonging to the state as authorized in your dispatch of Novr. 4th.[3] I request he be instructed that his interference is unauthorized and contrary to your orders.[4]

J Madison Wells   Gov La

Tel, DNA-RG107, Tels. Recd., President, Vol. 4 (1865–66).
  1. William P. Mellen.
  2. Oscar H. Burbridge.
  3. See Johnson to Wells, Nov. 4, 1865.
  4. The President referred this telegram to McCulloch, who wired Wells that Burbridge "should not operate outside of his own agency." McCulloch to Wells, Jan. 2, 1866, Tels. Sent, Sec. of War (M473, Roll 90), RG107, NA.

From Simon Cameron, Morton McMichael, and Alexander G. Cattell[1]

Philadelphia, Decr 28th 1865.

Having learned that an effort has been or is likely to be made to induce you to remove the Hon. Isaac Newton[2] from the charge of the Bureau of Agriculture, we beg leave to respectfully and earnestly request that your Excellency will be pleased to continue him in that position.

Mr N. is a *practical* farmer—has long taken a deep interest in agriculture as a science—and from his early training as a member of the Society of Friends, as well as from what we know to have been his uniform character through life, we feel perfectly assured, that if continued, he would continue to administer the affairs of his department with ability, economy, and fidelity.

As your Excellency is probably aware, Mr Newton represents a class of people, in the great state of Pennsylvania, who have never been distinguished as *place seekers*, and yet, as one of their communion, they would justly feel aggrieved at his removal. They bore a noble share in the late struggle, and we would, with all deference, suggest whether they are not entitled to such a mark of respect as would be paid to their wishes in the continuance of Mr Newton.[3]

With best wishes for your Excellency's personal welfare, and for the success of your efforts to restore and bless our common country, we are. . . .

Simon Cameron
Morton McMichael
Alexr. G. Cattell

LS, DLC-JP.

1. McMichael (1807–1879), a newspaper and magazine editor, served as sheriff and mayor of Philadelphia. Cattell (1816–1894), a Philadelphia businessman and banker, was appointed to the U.S. Senate from his native New Jersey (1866–71). *DAB; BDAC.*

2. Newton (1800–1867), noted for his profitable management of several farms in Pennsylvania, was appointed by Abraham Lincoln as the first federal commissioner of agriculture. *DAB.*

3. Upon the recommendation of these and other prominent persons—including eleven congressmen, the governor of Kansas, and Methodist bishop Matthew Simpson—Johnson did not remove Newton. See letters to Johnson from Garrett Davis, Ebon C. Ingersoll, Daniel Morris, John H. Hubbard, Lazarus W. Powell, Rufus P. Spalding, John F. Starr, James S. Rollins, Charles R. Buckalew, Alexander Ramsey, Sidney Clark, and Samuel J. Crawford, as well as Simpson to James Harlan, Dec. 27, 1865, in Johnson Papers, LC.

From Ulysses S. Grant

Washington   Dec. 28" 1865

Sir:

Application having been made to me for an extension of the limits to which Mrs. Jefferson Davis is now confined, so as to permit her to go where she pleases in the United States, or Canada, without forfeiting her present privilege of corresponding with her husband, I would respectfully recommend the following: That Mrs. Davis and her family be put precisely on the same footing as the families of other State prisoners only excluding her from visiting the Capital or her husband except with special permission.[1]

U. S. Grant   Lt. Gen'l[2]

Copy, DLC-JP.

1. This inquiry, which was prompted by an appeal from Varina Davis to Grant, was not forwarded to Johnson until December 30. On January 23, 1866, Attorney General Speed wired Mrs. Davis that, by the direction of the President, she could go to her children in Canada "whenever it may suit your convenience." Simon, *Grant Papers*, 15: 445–46; Grant to Johnson, Dec. 30, 1865, Johnson Papers, LC; *OR*, Ser. 2, Vol. 8: 870.

2. Grant signed the notation that this was an "Official Copy."

From J. George Harris[1]

Boston   Paymaster's Office, Dec. 28th 1865

My Dear Friend—

I know how vast and weighty are your responsibilities, how entirely you are absorbed in the great work of Reconstruction and Re-Union, and I pray that God will give you health and strength to accomplish it. It seems to me that the path you have chosen is the *only* path to a perfect restoration of peace and prosperity. You are doing Right—and how often I have heard Gen. Jackson say if statesmen in high places will do right they need never fear the consequences. I know the waves of faction will lash you on either side as the waves of the sea in stormy times beat against the high rocks of the ocean—and I know you will stand as firmly and unmoved amid the tempest as they stand, while your enemies rapidly become your friends. The principles and policy of your administration, as reflected in your message, show to the country that you are determined to re-unite these States and restore their harmonious nationality, according to the governing ideas of those who declared our Independence and gave us a liberal Constitution as Supreme Law. You will do it. And your great reward will be commensurate with the magnitude of the achievement.

We have an opportunity here in the New England metropolis of knowing something of the state of public sentiment and feeling, and of marking its changes. You may rest assured that the masses here in these eastern states are daily becoming more and more convinced that our only hope of a speedy, solid, and satisfactory *Reunion* of hearts and hands, is in the prevalence of your just and generous Reconstruction Policy.

In and about Boston, at this time, the popular tide is setting deeply and strongly in that direction. These people do not see the "Whitewash" on your late message, which Mr Sumner with his over-keen optics, supposed he had discovered.[2] That classical gentleman, whose late lecture on Scylla and Charybdis in the Atlantic Monthly was evidently written especially for your perusal,[3] should now give us a treatise on the Roman youth who hurled a missile at the statue of Cesar the rebound of which knocked him down.

I have thus taken the liberty to write you on the score of our old and undisturbed friendship, and because I have really wanted to do so. I am stationed here, as I suppose for two or three years, unless the emergencies of service should require me at another post—and when you visit Boston, as I hope you will, I should feel highly honored by a call from you here at my humble little home within the yard.

J. Geo: Harris.

ALS, DLC-JP.

1. Former editor of the *Nashville Union* and since 1845 a naval disbursing officer.

2. During the Senatorial debate over reading aloud in its entirety Carl Schurz's lengthy report on the South, Sumner compared Johnson's summary to the "whitewashing message of Franklin Pierce with regard to the enormities in Kansas." *Congressional Globe*, 39 Cong., 1 Sess., p. 79.

3. Sumner's article, which he described as a "long whip with a snapper to it," ostensibly discussed the origin of two common proverbs but concluded with a warning against hastily pardoning "belligerent traitors." *At Mon*, 16 (1865): 745–60; Donald, *Sumner and the Rights of Man*, 228.

From Jane H. Todd

December 28, 1865, Louisville, Ky.; ALS, DLC-JP.

A widowed "soldiers Mother," who "buckled the armor of war on my two boys bidding them go fight in defense of their bleeding country," complains: "Our soldiers have returned home. Some ... have saved Money but the Majority have not." They "Have been trying for Months to get into some employment to support their widowed mothers and wifes," but to no avail. "Every Honorable means of gaining a livelihood have been taken up by those who have been Braggarts in time of Peace and skulking Cowards in the time of their Countrys peril." "If Congress will for one hour drop the eternal negro question and devote that time to the interest of the suffering Soldiers," Todd and others will be grateful. Asks for "the speedy passage of the equalization of bounty and appropriation of land" law. "It will prevent thousands from starvation."

From Abiel A. Low[1]

New York   Dec 29 1865

Sir.

I venture to address you a few lines in regard to the Collectorship of this port, and Professor Davies,[2] who has consented to be the bearer of this, will explain that, in doing so, I am not actuated by a desire to urge myself on your attention. Nor will I weary you with many words.

The appointment of a Collector for the Port of New York is a matter of much concern to our Commercial Community as it is a matter of great importance to the Government of the United States. I am disposed to think that our Merchants, generally would regard the selection of a Man trained to Mercantile pursuits with more favor than any other.[3] It is probable that this consideration has had full weight enough in the recommendation of particular men who have been presented by memorial or petition to the Executive as Candidates for the office. I am perfectly aware, at the same time, how few of our merchants are available—possessing the necessary qualifications for the discharge of its various duties.

If political considerations must enter in, and to some extent govern this appointment; if the Candidate for this high office, must not only be qualified to interpret justly, and administer honestly, the laws, but at the same time, to control with an equitable and discriminating judgement the large patronage that appertains to it, let me express the hope that when a choice is finally made, it will fall upon a Gentleman of intelligence, ability and sterling character. For however much I may feel to be due to the Merchants of this City for their loyal support of the Government of the United States during the four past years, in the Selection of an Officer with whom they are so often brought in contact—I am persuaded it will chiefly interest them to know that the Collection of the Revenue and the administration of the laws connected therewith, have been committed to a faithful man assuring public confidence, of whatever Profession. Such an one will not unwisely disturb the successful working of forces trained by long experience, or needlessly embarrass the business of those who are engaged in the pursuit of an honorable calling; nor overlook the malpractices of any who defy alike the laws of God & man. Holding these views, may I not be permitted to say, then, with how much pleasure I have learned that Judge Henry E. Davies[4] of this City is understood to be willing to accept an appointment to the office in question full of care and large responsibility as it is. It will be grateful, I am sure, to our Community to behold the upright Judge whose decisions have proved the fairness of his mind and the clearness of his head—enter thus into the Service of his Country, blending with the discharge of his onerous duties, the graces of a courteous Gentleman.

If on the other hand anything be due from the Government of the Country to one of its most loyal citizens—whose generous nature is capable of contemplating the interests of the whole land and of all our people, whether white or black (and of *white* as well as black); where some have been distinguished for faithful and valiant service throughout the recent war—with what propriety may an appointment so honorable in itself be conferred on one so worthy!

If the thoughts thus presented seem to merit, and command attention, and the President of the United States is thereby inclined favorably to regard Judge Davies—already so widely known & so much esteemed, I shall feel it to be a privilege to be permitted to speak these few words for a true patriot—an honored friend.

A. A. Low

ALS, DNA-RG56, Appts., Customs Service, Collector, New York, Henry Davies.

1. Low (1811–1893), chairman of the New York chamber of commerce, had prospered in the clipper ship trade with Asia before the Civil War and invested in railroads and other enterprises. John N. Ingham, *Biographical Dictionary of American Business Leaders* (4 vols., Westport, Conn., 1983), 2: 824.

2. Charles Davies (1798–1876), a West Point graduate, retired in 1865 from a teaching career that included positions at the Academy and Columbia College in New York. *NCAB.*

3. Low had been among eighty-seven New York "merchants and Importers" who signed a petition nominating Henry A. Smythe to be collector. George Griswold et al. to Johnson, Nov. 20, 1865, Appts., Customs Service, Collector, New York, Henry A. Smythe, RG56, NA. See Smythe to Johnson, Dec. 18, 1865.

4. Davies (1805–1881), brother of Charles, was a former justice of the New York supreme court of appeals. *NCAB.*

From William Marvin

Tallahasse Florida   Dec 29, 1865

Sir

I attempted to send you a telegram a few days since but I am informed that the wires are down or working badly on a portion of the line. I take occasion to report the substance by letter.

An election for Governor members of the General Assembly and other state officers under the new constitution, and for member to congress, was held on the 29th day of November. David S. Walker[1] was elected Governor and Ferdinand McLeod,[2] member to congress. The

General Assembly met at the capital in this city on the 18th of December and Gov Walker was inaugurated in the presence of both houses on the 21st.[3] The General Assembly ratified in due form the proposed Amendment to the Constitution of the United States on the 29th and on the same day elected Wilkinson Call[4] and William Marvin Senators.

The objects of my appointment having been accomplished, I shall leave here in a day or two to report in person at Washington.

Wm Marvin

ALS, DLC-JP.

1. Prior to the war Walker (1815–1891) had been register of public lands and superintendent of public schools. Appointed to the state supreme court in 1858, he opposed secession but retained his seat throughout the war. Sobel and Raimo, *Governors*, 1: 255–56.

2. McLeod (*c*1825-*fl*1870), a former Whig who had seen service in the Confederate army, was denied his congressional seat when he presented himself. 1870 Census, Fla., Columbia, Lake City, 100; Jerrell H. Shofner, *Nor Is It Over Yet: Florida in the Era of Reconstruction* (Gainesville, 1974), 46, 57.

3. Considerable confusion seems to surround the exact dates of Marvin's relinquishment of office and Walker's assumption of power. Customary sources are not in agreement about the date of Walker's inauguration, although the discrepancy is merely between December 20 and December 21. Evidently Marvin shortly thereafter left the state for Washington and other places. But on January 18, 1866, the State Department sent a letter to him formally relieving him of his duties as governor; on that same date a letter was also sent to Walker informing him of the Marvin letter and offering the cooperation of the U.S. government in his new duties as governor of Florida. Sobel and Raimo, *Governors*, 1: 254–56; William W. Davis, *Civil War and Reconstruction in Florida* (Gainesville, 1964[1913]), 408–9; *National Intelligencer*, Jan. 5, 19, 1866.

4. Call (1834–1910), a former adjutant general in the Confederate army "who advocated acceptance of the president's plan only as a necessity" was, along with Marvin, denied his seat but did later serve in the Senate (1879–97). Ibid., 57; *BDAC*.

From Oliver P. Morton[1]

Paris Dec 29 1865.

Dear Sir

I arrived at Liverpool on Sunday, and being anxious to take medical advice without delay, made a very breif stay in England and reached here last night. The benefit anticipated from the voyage has not thus far been realized, and my limbs are perceptibly weaker than when I left New York. Today I have consulted an eminent physician who encourages me to beleive that I shall soon be better, though he ominously bids me have patience.

The general tone of the English press is highly favorable to your message, but not so much so as the French.[2] Both nations take very kindly what you have said which may touch their policy and position, and it is easy to see that the French people detest the whole Mexican business and are impatient for the time when France shall be well rid of it.

From what I have read and heard here it is manifest that the French people are almost unanimous in favor of evacuating Mexico and leaving

Maximillian to his fate but they do not want to do it under a menace, or under circumstances of humiliation further than such as now exist. Sooner than submit to this, I am advised, and believe from my knowledge of the French character the whole nation would clamor for war.[3]

You have asserted in your message the traditional doctrine of our country in a manner which commands respect but does not give offense, and should our government now stand still for a time, no advantage can be taken of her silence, and Louis Napoleon will avail himself of the opportunity to withdraw from a country, in regard to the temper and desires of whose people he will say he was mistaken. So it is said here, and so I beleive. But he cannot without losing prestige before all Europe and especially having regard for the sensitive character of the French people as revealed in the Army, retire from Mexico under a threat. In a war with France we could hardly come off without adding another thousand millions to our public debt, and with a navy so powerful as that of France, and with the number of privateers she could equip and send out, our commerce would be swept from the ocean; we cannot doubt this when we consider the damage done by the Alabama and two or three other Confederate cruisers. It is true we can destroy French Commerce, but that will not pay us back our losses; and during this time the carrying trade of the world would be thrown almost entirely into the hands of England, and her position as a commercial and naval power be made far stronger than ever before. Whether we can stand any great addition to our public debt, and especially when the means of paying the interest should be crippled by the existence of a foreign war, is a question which has undoubtedly occurred to your mind. The French people say that the interference in Mexican affairs on their part is without reasonable motive, and that if it were successful they cannot see how they are to profit by it. Might not the same thing be said of us at the end of a bloody and expensive war? Maximillian would be gone, the empire at an end, and Mexico resolved back to anarchy—to repeat her past history for thirty years. Unless indeed we should annex her territory which would be an abandonment of the principle upon which we set out, saying nothing of the fact that we do not want her people or should establish a protectorate over her which would be expensive, dangerous, and at variance with the theory of our Government.

We have had war enough to last us for a good while, and we have debt enough and to spare, and successful reconstruction is far more important to us than the most successful war could be.

I should be glad to see Louis Napoleon while here and have a plain talk with him. I could tell him some things about our Government and people and I think make him beleive them, for which nobody would be responsible but myself, and I intend to ask Mr Bigelow[4] if it can be incidentally brought about.

I shall remain here, most likely all winter, and should be very glad to hear from you if you have leisure from your most arduous and responsible duties to write.[5]

Ever praying for your success as President of the United States, and for your personal prosperity. . . .

O. P. Morton

ALS, DLC-JP.

1. The governor travelled ostensibly to study military administration in Europe and to seek a cure for his paralysis, but apparently Johnson had also asked him "to intimate informally" to Napoleon III that a voluntary withdrawal by France from Mexico would be expedient. Foulke, *Life of Morton*, 1: 457–59.

2. See George Bancroft to Johnson, Jan. 14, 1866.

3. See Johnson to Napoleon III, Jan. 25, 1866.

4. John Bigelow (1817–1911), a newspaper editor and prolific author, had been appointed minister to France in April 1865. *DAB.*

5. Here, at the top of a page, Morton wrote "and in conflict with the theory of our Government." This is an obvious false start to a line that appears at the top of the preceding page: "and at variance with the theory of our Government."

To Jonathan Worth

Washington, D.C., Dec 29th 1865.

We would prefer having your endorsement, for or against all pardons forwarded by you.[1] Your knowledge of the parties is of great worth to us here in issuing of pardons.

(sgd) Andrew Johnson   President U.S.

Tel, DNA-RG107, Tels. Sent, President, Vol. 3 (1865–68).

1. Worth had inquired whether Johnson wanted pardon petitions to "be forwarded through my hands with my views endorsed as to merits or demerits of applicant." Worth to Johnson, Dec. 28, 1865, Johnson Papers, LC.

From James B. Campbell

Columbia So. Ca.   Dec. 31, 1865.

My Dear Sir,

I have been weather bound and health bound here, ever since our Legislature adjourned. We did nothing about repudiation of the war debt. The subject went to Committee without debate and never was reported back. There was therefore no public discussion. In private, it was the subject of much anxious consideration, and the prevalent opinion seemed to be, that as the Legislature, in consequence of the action of the Convention, could do nothing binding it was better to do nothing than to do an act, which being *notoriously* void, our enemies might charge against us as delusive or an attempt to deceive. My mind settled into this opinion and that if Repudiation becomes a fixed necessity, then, that a Convention be called for the purpose.

The confidence in yourself is full and universal. Sensible, considerate, good men, *all* now rise beyond the limited but natural first impression of *mere gratitude* for a timely friend in our greatest need, and see that all you have done and are doing is entirely consistent with your life-long principles, with your responsible guardianship of the interests and welfare and honour of the *whole, undivided* country and with a wise statesmanship, which regardful of the past, comprehends within its horizon also, the long *future*, as well as the *present*.

Nothing could be more gratifying than the reception *every where* given to your Message. Even, a bigoted but clever British official, to whom, on my journey, I gave a copy, declared it the only real, statesmanlike, American State paper he had seen for a long time.

In the main, every thing is getting on here pretty well. Of course, the complaints of the Freedman's Bureau and the cotton agents continue. The *former* are, I fear *frequently* well founded, and the latter I am quite sure are *generally* so. It would be a very curious Treasury Exhibit showing a true comparison between the quantity of cotton *seized* by Treasury Agents and that which finds its way to the Treasury. These Agents irritate and impoverish the country by their seizures of cotton. They claim *Black Mail* or every bag as prize of War, and their machinery works altogether against a fair trial and the honest, rightful, individual owner. Indeed, his case is hopeless unless by the aid of *ransom* money.

Governor Orr has gone to his home in the mountains, for a time.

I go to Charleston in the morning. I am in excellent spirits at the state of things at Washington. Your opponents in congress will surely put themselves on one side, and you and the People on the other. They have made the issue just in the way of all others the surest to produce that result. I think it great good fortune that the Southern members are not admitted or present to embarrass you, as they would be sure to do, by foolish sayings and doings. It is to be the old fight renewed of Gen. Jackson and the People on one side—Bloated, Arrogant Politicians on the other. No fear of the result.

I am induced to ask of you to oblige me, as you have often done before. The following persons are my friends, and are in trouble about their property, for want of their Pardons. Their applications are on file approved. They are all under the 13th Exception only. All are proper subjects for your favour and clemency. I desire not to miss any opportunity to be instrumental in serving them and if you will order their warrants to be sent to me at Charleston I shall be very grateful Viz: *Mitchell C. King, Allan McFarlan, James K. Robinson, Arthur M. Huger.*[1]

In this connection, I desire to repeat that in these cases, as in every other case where I have applied, I receive and have received no compensation whatever. I have never yet, received *one dollar* or *its value* for my services in obtaining *pardons*. I have the voluntary promise (yet unperformed) in one instance of two or three dozen *old wine*, hidden and saved from Genl. Sherman, and in another, of a *similar* Treat. Of course, however, it is indirectly, as you must know, a great advantage to be the instrument in rendering such service, and as I said, I shall be very grateful for your kindness.[2]

The case of the owners of the Steamer *James Adger* (Gov. Aikin and others) whose petition I presented to you,[3] is professional business for which I am paid. They have two other Steamships *seized* by *individuals* in New York and in that behalf, I shall go North in January. On my way, I hope to see you.[4] With my earnest wishes that you may find in your full success and in the approbation of all good men the just reward of your labours and anxieties.

Jas. B. Campbell

LS, DLC-JP.

1. King (c1810-fl1879) was a Charleston physician and planter who resided periodically in North Carolina; McFarlan (b. c1820) was a railroad president and former legislator; Robinson (b. c1810) was a retired merchant; and Huger (c1822–1870) was a merchant who served as a militia officer during the war. King to Johnson, ca. Sept. 13, Dec. 4, 1865, Amnesty Papers (M1003, Rolls 40 and 45), N.C. and S.C., Mitchell C. King, RG94, NA; Asst. Commr., Ga., Reg. of Lets. Recd. (M798, Roll 11), RG105, NA; Elise Pinkney, tr., "Register of St. John-in-the-Wilderness, Flat Rock," *SCHM*, 63 (1962): 176; 1850 Census, S.C., Chesterfield, 269; (1860), Charleston, 5th Ward, 74; 1st Ward, 3; *Charleston Courier*, May 8, 1866, May 17, 1870; Walter B. Edgar et al., eds., *Biographical Directory of the South Carolina House of Representatives Volume 1: Session Lists, 1692–1973* (Columbia, 1974), 378, 382; *OR*, Ser. 1, Vol. 1: 45, 58; Vol. 6: 13–17, 423.

2. Campbell later repeated his requests and added the name of Joseph A. Huger, brother of Arthur M. Huger, to the list. Pardons for the Hugers and Robinson had previously been granted and were forwarded on January 11. A pardon for McFarlan was sent on the same date, but Campbell was subsequently asked to "recover" it; there is no record of a pardon date for or an application from McFarlan. King's pardon was allegedly forwarded on January 13, but official reports indicate that he was not pardoned until April 23, 1866. Campbell to Johnson, Jan. 8, 1866, Johnson Papers, LC; Andrew K. Long to Campbell, Jan. 11, 13, Feb. 3, 15, 1866, Tels. Sent, President, Vol. 3 (1865–68), RG107, NA; *House Ex. Docs.*, 40 Cong., 1 Sess., No. 32, pp. 51, 54, 59 (Ser. 1331).

3. Not found. The *James Adger*, a wooden sidewheeler acquired by the U.S. Navy at New York in 1861, was removed from service in May 1866 and sold to Campbell the following October for $32,000, which was less than a third of what had been spent to repair the vessel during the war. *OR-Navy*, Ser. 2, Vol. 1: 112.

4. No report of an interview between Campbell and the President during January 1866 has been found.

January 1866

From Thomas J. Greenwood[1]

[Malden, Mass., ca. 1866][2]

I pray you have patience to read this letter. I am a Clergyman, 67 years of age, and nearly the only one in New England who has not prostituted the *Pulpit* to political harrangues. My failure to do this has ostracised me in my profession.

I have been a life-long Democrat, having twice served in the *Senate* of this state. I *opposed* your election as Vice President, on the supposition that you would be expected to advocate the measures now pressed by a fraction of Congress which I knew if successful would be ruinous to the Country.

Your course has undeceived me. I heartily endorse your plan for the restoration of the Union, and of Peace, because I do not wish to see my Country ruined as it must be if the Radicals succeed. And desiring to be placed where I can live and advocate your course, I ask some official appointment suited to my age where I can use my pen, and tongue in freedom.

Gen. N. P. Banks is my sister's[3] son, and perhaps it will be sufficient recommendation to your confidence to say, that at the last election, I was run as candidate for Congress in opposition to him, as I was also, the term previous, in opposition to Mr Gooch.[4]

I will furnish any vouchers for my character which may be required, from members of all parties.

It would be convenient for my present residence if my appointment could be in Boston or vicinity.[5]

Thos. J Greenwood

P.S. I have never before applied for any office, in the gift of Government; nor should I now, but for reasons already indicated.

ALS, DNA-RG56, Appts., Customs Service, Sub-Officer, Boston, Thomas J. Greenwood.

1. Greenwood (1799–1874) had published several sermons and discourses. *NUC*.
2. Greenwood resided in Malden, Mass., at about the time that internal evidence indicates this letter was written.
3. Rebecca Greenwood Banks is not further identified.
4. Daniel W. Gooch.
5. Greenwood failed to secure an appointment.

From Charles J. Jenkins

Augusta, Ga.   January 1st. 1866

Sir.

I had the honor of addressing to you to day a telegram,[1] requesting the suspension of a trial, now progressing in Savannah, against G. B. Lamar, a citizen of Georgia, before a military tribunal, upon charges of larceny, and bribery, until the reception of this fuller communication. The property, of which the larceny is charged to have been committed, is alleged to be cotton in the possession of an officer of the U.S.A. as the property of the Government; and the bribery is charged to have been attempted with an officer of the U.S.A.

Mr. Lamar neither is nor ever has been in any way connected with the army; consequently the jurisdiction of a military tribunal, does not attach to his person. He is not charged with a violation of any rule, article or regulation of war, extending to citizens; hence it seems to me the jurisdiction of the military Court does not result from the nature of the offences. Larceny and bribery are made penal offences by the laws of the United states, and of the several States, and it would seem that the jurisdiction of the Courts, appertaining to the civil establishment, of the one or the other governments, attaches. I am aware that, upon the cessation of hostilities, and the armed occupation of Georgia, the functions of the State Courts were suspended, and that the Federal Circuit, and district Courts have not yet been fully reorganized and put in operation. But by your kind Exutive permission, our State Courts are again in full operation, and the government proper, of the State, fully restored to her functionaries, legislative, executive, and judicial.

The crimes charged against Mr. Lamar, having been committed within the state, and the Laws of the United States, being laws of Georgia, our Courts (if it were the pleasure of the Government to institute prosecutions in them) would have jurisdiction. At all events the Federal Court, where opened, would have jurisdiction, if the State Courts have not; and, I thought, if it be not, in accordance with the design of your Excellency to open it immediately, Mr. Lamar and others similarly situated, might be recognised to appear, when it shall be opened, which I trust will be ere long.[2]

If my memory of Mr. Atty. Genl. Speed's opinion, in relation to the proper tribunal for the trial of persons charged with the assassination of the late President (of which I have no copy at hand) be not at fault, it would not sustain the jurisdiction in this case. But I refer to this hesitatingly.

Allow me to say, Honored Sir, from a very thorough knowledge of them, and from continuous intercourse of an official, or quasi-official character with leading men from all parts of the State, during the past

two months, our People, have the right spirit, and are intent upon doing their duty to the whole Country, and to the Federal Government.
They look as anxiously to the restoration, in all its amplitude, of their
ancient status, as citizens of the United States, as did the Hebrews in
the Wilderness, to an entrance into the promised land. Their hearts are
full of gratitude to you, Sir, for all you have done and are doing, to the
accomplishment of that end. But permit me to say, with no less of respectful kindness than of frankness, that when they saw their Courts
reopened—a legislature and a Governor of their own choice, with your
approbation and consent, in the discharge of their proper functions, and
the provisional Governor of your appointment, relieved by your order,
they indulged the hope, that military trials, for offences not military,
were over. Like all American citizens they look upon trial by jury as
one of the strongest bulwarks of Liberty, and, without it, they cannot
feel the security which, I am sure it would be your pleasure to give
them. For this reason, not that I have aught to allege against the fairness, and justice exhibited, heretofore, by those Courts, in Georgia, I
earnestly entreat your Excellency, so far as, in your judgment, may
consist with public safety, to dispense with such trials, and remit us to
the ancient, and coveted order of things. It would be very gratifying to
myself and to our people generally, if, as the initiative, your Excellency
would dissolve the military Court in Savannah, already referred to, and
order all of the accused, recognised to appear before a civil tribunal.

One other request, I would respectfully, but earnestly prefer, viz, that
the colored troops among us may be removed, as speedily as the convenience of the Government may permit. They certainly do exert an
unhappy influence over their own race, not in the army. Frequent
scenes of violence occur from their disorders. Not long since one of our
City police felt constrained, to take the life of one of them, who was
disturbing the public peace, and resisting his authority. The policeman
has been tried by a military Court, and acquitted, but there is reason to
fear, the temper of the surviving colored troops is not improved by the
result.[3] Three evenings since, in this immediate neighborhood, a party
of them, with others of their own color, drawn in by them, attacked, a
private residence, without provocation, but in execution of a threat.
Three or four of the assailants were killed and several others wounded,
I learn.[4] No injury was done to the persons of the family assailed,
though their property suffered considerably. But for the timely interposition of Col. Ruth,[5] their commander, and his energetic and noble
conduct, there is no knowing where the affair would have ended. Believe me, Sir, if they were removed public peace, and good order would
be promoted.[6]

I trust you will not consider this communication intrusive. I regret
to feel constrained to trouble you at all, but my People, who confide in
you, have also honored me with their confidence, and expect me to

represent their interest to you. I think, also that this appeal does not transcend the limits of the cooperation of your Government towards complete restoration, so kindly tendered through Mr. Seward.

It is not intended to ask any departure from a settled programme, but a simple extension (if it be not premature) of a policy already instituted.

At all events, I but make requests, not doubting, that if deemed reasonable, they will be complied with; but if otherwise I shall cheerfully acquiesce and indulge the hope that they have not been the cause of offence.

Charles J. Jenkins

ALS, DNA-RG153, Court-Martial Records, MM-3469.

1. Jenkins's dispatch, which actually bore the date of January 2, 1866, can be found in the Johnson Papers, LC.

2. Upon receiving Jenkins's telegram, Johnson replied that the military commission would proceed, adding that upon its conclusion the "whole case" would be "reviewed" and might "be transferred to a civil tribunal" if Lamar had not received a "fair trial." In 1869 Johnson did disapprove the commission's proceedings. Johnson to Jenkins, Jan. 4, 1866, Tels. Sent, President, Vol. 3 (1865–68), RG107, NA; Ser. 8A, Vol. 2: 122, Johnson Papers, LC.

3. Augusta policeman Thomas Olive, tried before a military commission for murdering a black soldier, was acquitted on December 23, 1865. Local newspapers are silent regarding the reaction of black troops. *Augusta Constitutionalist*, Dec. 24, 1865.

4. As many as thirty black soldiers and "desperadoes" had attacked the home of a widow after midnight on December 29, seeking vengeance for the killing of a black soldier by her son during the previous afternoon. Ibid., Dec. 30, 1865.

5. Richard Root (1834–1903), a veteran of two Iowa regiments, commanded the 136th Inf., USCT. After the unit was mustered out in January 1866, he returned to Iowa, where he became a hotelkeeper, U.S. marshal, sheriff, and postmaster. *Off. Army Reg.: Vols.*, 8: 310; *Portrait and Biographical Album of Lee County, Iowa* (Chicago, 1887), 535–36; Pension File, Angeline P. Root, RG15, NA.

6. On behalf of Johnson, Stanton replied: "Your letter has been received and the matters mentioned have been considered by the President." By April 1866 all black regiments had been removed from Georgia. Stanton to Jenkins, Jan. 12, 1866, Tels. Sent, Sec. of War (M473, Roll 90), RG107, NA; James E. Sefton, *The United States Army and Reconstruction, 1865–1877* (Baton Rouge, 1967), 261. For subsequent correspondence regarding federal troops in Georgia, see Jenkins to Johnson, Jan. 25, 1866. See also Jenkins to Johnson, Feb. 15, 1866, Lets. Recd. *re* Military Discipline, RG108, NA.

From William T. Weaver[1]

Macon Ga   Jany. 1st 1865[6]

When Genl Wilson passed through our country some Government stock was abandoned which fell into the hands of such as had lost their stock. Shortly afterwards Genl Steedman issued an order, to wit: those who had taken up such stock were entitled to it on faith of said order. The stock was carefully nursed and is now fat. Army officers are now taking up such stock thereby entailing great suffering upon the part of the community. On behalf of the citizens of Upson County Georgia I send you this dispatch, hoping that you will stay the execution of said order until the matter can be properly investigated.[2]

W. T. Weaver   Thomaston Ga

Tel, DNA-RG107, Tels. Recd., President, Vol. 4 (1865–66).

1. Weaver (1840–1912), a Confederate veteran, served as a justice of the state inferior court (1866–68), then taught school and later worked as a county surveyor. Carolyn W. Nottingham and Evelyn Hannah, *History of Upson County, Georgia* (Vidalia, Ga., 1969[1930]), 40, 46, 1019–20.

2. Johnson responded by directing the "suspension of proceedings under the order" requiring "the citizens of Upson County Georgia to give up the stock left in the country by General Sherman on his march—until the matter can be investigated." Edwin D. Townsend to Steedman, Jan. 4, 1866, Tels. Sent, Sec. of War (M473, Roll 90), RG107, NA.

From Ransom Balcom[1]

Binghamton N.Y.   Jany. 2, 1866.

Dear Sir

I am a stranger to you, but I am your sincere friend and a member of the Union Party that elected you.

I address you as a friend. I think I know the sentiments of the people of the state of Newyork. I go from County to County holding courts as Justice of the Supreme Court and I have the opportunity of learning the sentiments of the people.

I find Democratic politicians are jubilant & praising you wherever I go; and their course makes the masses of the Union party feel as members of a Christian Church do when Sabbath breakers, whoremasters and gamblers praise their preacher.

The men who sustained the Administration of President Lincoln & supported the war for the Union feel bad and distrust you when such enemies of the Union as Horatio Seymour & Fernando Wood praise you & profess to be your especial friends & admirers—and predict that you will soon turn out Seward, Dickinson[2] & all other appointees of Lincoln whom they hate as much as they would hate you, did they not think they can win you over to their embraces by pretended support & flattery and thus divide & weaken the Union Party?

The fate of Tyler & Fillmore is before you. And should your administration be such as to be heartily supported by the Democratic Party only a portion of Union office holders and office seekers would follow you. And should you continue Union men in office the Democratic Party would not support you and you would then only have the support of office holders and office seekers. No President can serve two political parties—any easier than a christian can serve God & Mammon. The thing is impossible.

If you should alienate the masses of the Union Party from you, as they now fear you will, you would be as helpless as a child. The Democratic Party could give you no substantial support. It is disgraced & damded for all coming time. Its treason stinks in the nostrils of the people. The young men of the country are against it, & no body now boasts of belonging to it. It is in as bad a condition as the Federal Party was at the close of our last war with England.

Union men who have lost sons in the war for the Union & pay taxes for interest on the National debt, have vacant chairs in their houses draped in black with labels on them as follows. "This chair is made vacant by the treason of the Democratic Party." And such fathers curse the Democratic Party & all its leaders morning noon & night—and whenever they pay a national tax they lay it, as they justly should, to the treason of the Democratic Party.

General Slocom[3] was a good Union General; but he joined the Democratic Party last fall & was the candidate of that party for secretary of State of this State; he was repudiated by all our Union Soldiers—hardly one of them voted for him; & he was justly defeated.

The Union Party is composed of enlightened men, who are as determined as the followers of Cromwell were. They will not follow any man where conscience & a sense of duty do not lead them. They are unlike the Demoralised democracy, who will say anything and profess anything, to regain political ascendency.

I hope it is not too late for you to save yourself. But you can only do it, by taking such a course as will satisfy men of all parties that you will remain with the party that elected you & sink or swim with it.

The Union Party will distrust you until Voorhies & Salsbury[4] stop endorsing your Administration.

I do not think the Union Party believes the Rebellious States should be governed as territories—or that such states have ever been out of the Union. But they do believe, (& no power on earth can convince them to the contrary,) that the Union should be so reconstructed that such Rebels as Mason & Hunter[5] of Virginia—Tombs[6] of Georgia, Wade Hampton of South Carolina and Breckenridge[7] of Kentucky can never come back into Congress. All Republicans & moderate democrats say this; and no congressman could be reelected from this State out of the City of N.Y. who should vote to let such men into Congress. The masses of the Union Party also believe the Rebels still hate the Union, & that they will vote for Horatio Seymour or General Lee for President in 1868 if they shall think they can elect either of them—and that none of them nor any northern democrat really loves you. The masses of the Union party believe the freedmen of the South are cruelly & barbourously treated by their old masters, and that their rights must be secured and they protected in some way before any Rebellious state should be represented in Congress.

The masses of the Union Party are for justice to all friends of the Union & they think justice & mercy should go hand in hand.

I sincerely pitty you. You are surrounded & talked to by Rebels & Copperheads, who are as hypocritical as Satan himself—and I fear members of Congress & office holders & office seekers, who belong to the Union Party, misjudge or fear to tell you the whole truth. And this is my apology for writing to you.

I shall hope & pray that you may not share the fate of Fillmore or Tyler; and that you may have the wisdom to follow public sentiment and be governed by the logic of events as Lincoln was. His differences with Congress never weakened his administration, because no man ever suspected or believed he would abandon the party that elected him.

I hope you will pardon me for inflicting this long letter upon you. I have written it with the best of motives.

Ransom Balcom

ALS, DLC-JP.
1. Balcom (1818–1879) served twenty-two years on the New York supreme court (1855–77). H. P. Smith, ed., *History of Broome County* (Syracuse, N.Y., 1885), 125–26.
2. Daniel S. Dickinson, U.S. district attorney for New York.
3. Henry W. Slocum.
4. Daniel W. Voorhees and Willard Saulsbury. Voorhees (1827–1897), a Democrat from Indiana, served in both the U.S. House (1861–66, 1869–73) and Senate (1877–97). *BDAC*.
5. James M. Mason and Robert M.T. Hunter.
6. Robert Toombs.
7. John C. Breckinridge.

From Moses Bates

Office of Democratic State Committee, 4 Lindall Street,
Boston, January 2 1866.

Dear Sir

As one of the conservative men of New England, who afford an unconditional support to your Administration simply because we believe it is *right*, and honest, and patriotic, I have deemed it my duty to transmit for your inspection the enclosed copy of a newspaper printed and published in Old Plymouth, and owned in part by *Charles G. Davis*[1] the Assessor of Internal Revenue for the First District of Massachusetts. This article[2] (like others of a similar nature) was written by this public officer, was set by the compositor from his manuscript, and he corrected the proof in his office as Assessor, and it is enclosed only for information as to what manner a support to the Administration is maintained by this disciple of Charles Sumner. The democratic conservatives of this State have no favors to ask, but they do wish to know, what constitutes a support of your administration, now *generally* conceded to be an able and honest one.

Moses Bates

ALS, DLC-JP.

1. Davis (1820–1903), an attorney born in Plymouth, served seven years as an assessor of internal revenue (1862–69) then was a state district court judge from 1874 until his death. D. Hamilton Hurd, comp., *History of Plymouth County, Massachusetts* (Philadelphia, 1884), 48–49; *New York Times*, July 4, 1903.

2. Not found.

From John W. Forney

New York, Jany 2, 1866.

My dear Mr. President—

I have been in this city for two days, and now write under an impulse which I can not restrain, because I feel it to be for your own good and that of the country. I take it for granted you are resolved not to be unmindful of your own fame, and that you will not allow your friends, who heartily sustain your policy, to feel that they are without your aid and encouragement. Whether you are a candidate for President or not, and if you are not, I shall be greatly surprised with the wonderful favor that has crowned your restoration policy. You should not allow the great offices go to indifferent men, or those clearly in the interests of your foes. I need not repeat to you that I am now, as ever, for twenty years shown in my writings, and since your great act of patriotism in 1860 especially, your open and avowed friend. Where I am to-day my two newspapers[1] both daily show to the world. Hence, in what I now say, I speak no idle words, but mean all I say. The Collector's office at New York City is a post that you should dispose of outside of all the politicians, not I mean to defy them, but to select your own man, who should be free only to help you and serve the Government—one they could neither attack nor use. Such a man is (Henry G. Stebbins)[2] of this city. He was elected to Congress in (1860) as a Democrat, but *like you* refused to follow the party into treason. He served a short time with great distinction, and resigned on account of ill health. He was a member of the Committee of Ways and Means and won great applause. He is a very able man, educated to finance, intensely national, honest and independent, and could furnish millions of Security. He has an organizing mind, would make you a party or fight your battles single handed. He is an Andrew Johnson Democrat in short. I write in the knowledge that he would accept, and that his appointment would be hailed with joy by this whole community.

J. W. Forney

ALS, DLC-JP.

1. *Philadelphia Press* and *Washington Morning Chronicle*.

2. Stebbins (1811–1881), financier and sometime president of the New York Stock Exchange, had served briefly in Congress (1863–64). *BDAC*.

From Taliaferro P. Shaffner

Washington, January 2, 1866.

Dear Sir:

Since my arrival in this city I have read with much interest the official report of Lieutenant General Grant,[1] giving an account of the condition of affairs in the Southern States, so far as came under his observation on the route leading through Richmond, Virginia; Raleigh, North Carolina; Charleston, South Carolina; and Augusta, Georgia.

I have recently returned from a journey through Southern Virginia, North Carolina, South Carolina, Georgia, Alabama, Tennessee, Kentucky, and Missouri. I made this journey for my own personal information, having a solicitude to see those countries under the present circumstances, depleted of population, and during the general desolation. I had no political consideration to move me in the formation of conclusions or to warp my judgment either for or against the people, my sole object being to realize the condition of things that my pen might be guided in after years, should I continue my history of America beyond the epoch embraced in the heretofore published volumes.[2]

I travelled by railway, coach, wagon, on horse, and occasionally on foot, and during my stay at the different places along the route I mingled with the people, white and colored, of every grade of society, and I did not spare any pains to get their views in regard to the future of the South, and their individual aspirations, State and national. Having in former years travelled over most of the civilized world with attentive ears and watchful eyes, ever searching for knowledge, I felt prepared and qualified by experience to refrain from forming hasty conclusions respecting the Southern States, so recently emerged from the passions of war. Besides my experience as a traveller through many foreign countries, I had gone through foreign wars, and traversed regions invaded by large armies, and I was exceedingly anxious to see with my own eyes the result of a civil war in my own country, waged by my own people, many of whom, too, were my kin.

The report of Lieutenant General Grant gives a very correct account of affairs, as I observed them, in the regions traversed by me, and nothing gave me more satisfaction than his remarks upon the conduct of the subordinates of the Freedmen's Bureau, who are, perhaps, the most responsible for disturbances and contentions between the white and colored people of the South. I never heard of any complaint against the military throughout the whole of my journey, but nearly everywhere I learned that the agents of the Freedmen's Bureau had been more energetic to disturb the peace of society than to promote the welfare of the poor wandering colored people.

The colored people had been informed by some of those agents that, after the 1st of January, the lands belonging to the whites who had been slaveholders were to be divided among the colored people; that after that date the "bottom rail was to be on top," and that after Christmas the Union railroads were to carry all colored people free of expense. These representations were confidently believed by the colored people, and in this manner they have been deluded and enticed from industry to idleness. I saw many thousands tented by the roadside, many living under shelters made with the boughs of trees, and many had no other canopy than the canopy of heaven. I saw many hardy men wandering about, with bundle and stick, and when asked whither they were travelling, I received in answer that they were searching after rich lands, or, in other words, they were prospecting ere the day of general division. At night they quartered with some colored persons, and it does not require much guessing to determine from whence they drew their rations.

I addressed a very large assembly of colored people in Georgia, and advised them to make up their minds to believe that freedom consisted in the right to labor, to earn their bread by the sweat of their brow, and to enjoy at will the gains of their toil. I told them that freedom meant the right to be industrious, under the protection of the civil laws, which would be accorded to them as fairly as administered to the white people. I also told them that on assuming the privileges of freemen they became responsible to society at large to be useful in the affairs of this world, and that they had not the right to stand in the vineyard all the day idle. The assembly listened to my remarks with much attention, and many of the elder persons present urged me to address another and a larger meeting which they proposed to hold. They told me that I spoke differently from what others had, and that they wanted advice. I think, Mr. President, that the colored people of the South ought to have information respecting their duties. Some capable persons might prepare a lecture to be read by the whole clergy of the South to the people, white and colored, as advice, by authority of the Government.

In some districts societies have been formed, each member contributing one dollar, and the funds thus raised are to be employed in defraying the expenses of immigration to that part of the country where the lands might be found the most valuable at the time of the general division.

I was very much pained to learn that there were a few wicked and low white people who occasionally plundered the poor colored people, but the spite seemed to be against those who were free before the war. I was unable to comprehend why this class of people should be subjected to malignity. Respectable white people seemed to regret these robberies, but they had no power to punish the guilty. It is proper, however, to state that many robberies were committed by the colored people, and such acts will continue until order is fully restored.

The people with whom I conversed were anxious to establish by law a labor code, and in South Carolina an attempt had been made to enact one, which, in the judgment of legislators, was considered eminently favorable to the colored people. I read the bill, which had passed to the third reading, and dissented respecting the equity of the principles it recognized; for example, a colored man was required to obtain a license from a court to learn an artisan's trade, which formality in practice would be equivalent to a prohibition. I expressed this opinion to several eminent gentlemen, and urged them to establish by law equalization in all matters of labor and capital; but if any special law be made upon the subject, it would be just to award to the colored man a premium on becoming a master workman in any of the mechanical branches. On reflection it was conceded by every gentleman present that there should not be any distinction between races on questions of labor, although white laborers were strongly opposed to allowing the colored man equal rights. At that time farming hands were in demand, and none could be hired, except until New Year. Mechanics were full of engagements, and unable to execute the work of reconstruction of the many houses destroyed by the war, and yet they were generally unwilling to see their special labor interfered with by the colored man. The demand for labor by the planters, and the opposition of the white mechanics to competition, gives an explanation to the legislative enactment.

I occasionally met persons who perhaps had never owned a slave decidedly opposed to any elevation of the colored people, and they shuddered at the thought of even a probability of educating the African race; but those who thus manifested so much horror respecting the equalization of the races were generally regarded as persons of inordinate self-importance.

I was much surprised to observe an indifference for the old and infirm colored people manifested by the younger and healthy of that race. Sons and daughters seemed only to care for themselves, not appreciating any responsibility for their own parents. This class of people, Mr. President, should receive special consideration by the Freedmen's Bureau, and supplies should be withdrawn from those able to work. The propriety of establishing "work farms," consisting of some two hundred or more acres of land, with suitable workhouses for old and infirm colored people, might be gravely considered. The establishments might be located in different parts of each State, under fixed regulations, and if properly conducted would be a great blessing to many thousands who are now thrown upon their own resources for bread and raiment. If the Freedmen's Bureau cannot carry out a scheme of sufficient magnitude to meet the necessities of the case, it seems to me the whole nation might be called upon to render aid. Perhaps some may think the former masters should support the aged and infirm freedmen until the end of life, but what can those masters do, with their farms desolated, where houses lay in ashes, fences gone, and no sound of the hoof heard?

The people generally seemed to be infused with a desire to make the best of the condition of things in which peace had placed them. Nationality with them now was a matter of pride—the certainty that there would never be another war originating from attempt to divide the Union, and the prospect of peace throughout the country, with a restoration of fraternal relations, were subjects of general felicitation.

The policy you have inaugurated for the re-establishment of tranquillity, and the enforcement of the laws of the United States in the regions lately at war with the Federal authority, is universally commended with expressions of gratitude. I never heard a dissent. On all occasions I observed a real desire to conform to the laws of the Federal Government, as interpreted by you, and many expressed sentiments gratefully recognizing in you a degree of patriotism and good feeling for the present and future welfare of the people, which confounded them so extremely that they felt incapable of reciprocating, commensurately, in efforts to sustain the honor and integrity of the Federal Union and all the sequences of nationality. They realize the fact that they have committed a great crime in attempting to destroy the greatest political structure ever conceived by man, and that their atonement should be full and unreserved. To be treated with kindness, and be recognized in the same degree of fellowship that had existed before the war, were manifestations of grace that demanded from them their greatest effort to recognize, by substantial acts of integrity, full and unqualified obedience.

I am quite sure, Mr. President, you were fortunate in the organization of a policy best calculated to perfect a restoration of Federal authority, nationality of sentiment, and a general desire for a fraternal reciprocity regardless of sectionalism. As a grateful people, who have suffered much, living in the midst of evidences of desolation, the severest that any war has ever produced, they will, I opine, demonstrate by example that they are worthy of the confidence you have reposed in them.

They have had enough of war, and judging from what I saw and heard when in their midst, when those with whom I associated were free from any embarrassment and spoke without reserve, I am of opinion that they will, for all time, revere the symbol of their nationality, and behold it with emotions of joy and gratitude, whether at home or abroad, upon land or at sea.

Tal. P. Shaffner.

National Intelligencer, Jan. 8, 1866.

　1. See Grant to Johnson, Dec. 18, 1865, *Advice*, 212–14.

2. Shaffner had published *The Secession War in America* (1862) and *History of America* (1863) but did not produce any other histories of the United States. *NCAB.*

To John Van Buren

Washington, D.C.   Jan. 2d. 1866.

Sir.

I take pleasure in acknowledging the receipt, from the Ancient Society of Tammany, of an invitation to attend their semi-centennial celebration of the anniversary of the Battle of New Orleans.[1] It would afford me sincere gratification to join you in commemorating the eminent Services of the hero of that great victory, who, in field & in council, ever signalized his devotion to the Union of the States & won for himself enduring national renown. My engagements, however, will not permit me to be present, and I regret this the more, as the occasion is in honor of an event to which, as you justly remark, reunited brethren, in every portion of the Republic, can recur with equal gratification & pride. The inspirations derived from the contemplation of common trials, common victories, and national traditions, sacredly cherished by every American, cannot fail to exert an important influence in healing the irritation of sectional wounds & strengthening the feeling of devotion to the Federal Union—the maintenance & preservation of which, in all its dignity & purity, was the sole aim of the intrepid & incorruptible patriot, Andrew Jackson.

Andrew Johnson.

Copy, DLC-JP.
  1. On December 18, 1865, Van Buren, as chairman of the Tammany Society's "Committee of Arrangements," invited the President to "a grand dinner" on January 8 to commemorate what they referred to as "their semi-centennial celebration of the great victory of a Southern hero, who . . . devoted his subsequent life to the establishment and security of constitutional liberty." *New York Herald*, Feb. 7, 1866.

From J. Madison Wells

New Orleans   January 2d 1866

I had the honor in a former paper[1] to recommend to your Excellencys favorable consideration, Governor Sharkey, as a candidate for the Circuit Judgeship of the Sixth Judicial District.

I wish in addition to say that should circumstances be such that his name will not be pressed the appointment of Honorable E H. Durell to that position would be highly satisfactory to the friends of Your Excellency, and of the Government in this State.[2]

J Madison Wells   Gov. La.

LS, DNA-RG60, Appt. Files for Judicial Dists., La., E. H. Durell.
  1. Not found.
  2. At issue was the vacancy caused by the May 1865 death of Associate Justice John

Catron, who had presided over the sixth district. Neither Sharkey nor Durell received the appointment because Congress eliminated this position in July 1866. See R. Weakley Brown to Johnson, Nov. 24, 1865.

From Jonathan Worth

Raleigh N.C.   Jany 2nd 1866.

Sir:

It is represented through the newspapers that you have ordered the Sheriffs of this state to abstain from executing some of the enactments of the ordinance of our Convention for raising revenue. Govr. Holden informs me he has received no instructions on the subject.

I would be glad to have a copy of any order you may have made on the subject.[1]

Jonathan Worth   Gov'r

Tel, DNA-RG107, Tels. Recd., President, Vol. 4 (1865–66).

1. The President replied that "No orders in reference to the Sheriffs in North Carolina have been issued by me." At issue was the October 1865 ordinance which authorized retrospective income, sales, and property taxes, as well as business licensing fees. Johnson to Worth, Jan. 2, 1866, Tels. Sent, President, Vol. 3 (1865–68), RG107, NA; *Senate Ex. Docs.*, 39 Cong., 1 Sess., No. 26, pp. 31–33 (Ser. 1237). See James T. Hough to Johnson, Jan. 10, 1866.

From R. Weakley Brown

Nashville   Jan'y 3d 1866,

My Dear Friend

I enclose you a letter from my friend Genl John L.T. Sneed whom I have long known.[1] I hope you can find time to read it, for I know it will cheer you in this dark hour.

My friend be of *good cheer*, though the political horizon is dark, there is a silver to the clouds.

I hope and pray the God of Washington and Jackson will be with you to the end.

You are doing your duty nobly and will come out right. Your message *begins right*, is *right* all the *way through*, and *ends right*. The *message displays* the iron will and fixed purpose of Andrew Jackson, coupled with the moderation, and wisdom of the *Great* and *good Washington* and with Washington's farewell Address and circular letter and Jefferson's first Inaugural Address, it will be read and treasured while Constitutional liberty, and a white-man's Republican government, has a *votary* upon *Earth*.

You are standing by the Constitution, and the rights of the people, and God and the *people* will *stand* by *you*. The southern people now know who is "there *real* and *best friend*." As you have no time to read long letters I will close with the hope and prayer that God will guide and direct you in your efforts to preserve the *Constitution*, and to deal justly, kindly and mercifully with the southern people.

R. W. Brown

N.B. I hope you received my father's letter and his amnesty oath accompanying it, and that his pardon may be forwarded as early as practicable.[2] My friend Ex Gov Neil S. Brown is nobly sustaining you. I wrote you that he remarked to me sometime since that as long as you stood by the principles announced in your address of Sept '65 to the southern delegation "he would sustain you as *ardently* as he ever supported Henry Clay."[3]

Judge Caruthers is very sanguine. You will finally overcome the radical. Many leading men in the *South* now discover that you were 4 years ago much wiser—and more far seeing—*than themselves*.

R.W.B.

ALS, DLC-JP.
  1. Not found.
  2. See R. Weakley Brown to Johnson, Oct. 20, 1865. The elder Brown had been pardoned on October 25, 1865; obviously by January the family had not learned of this.
  3. See Brown to Johnson, Oct. 16, 1865, for the first reference to Neill S. Brown's statement.

From Thomas L. Clingman

City of Washington   Jan 3, 1866

Sir

I respectfully ask your Excellencys favourable consideration of my application for a pardon for my conduct during the late civil war. I have been excluded from the benefits of the General Amnesty upon two grounds. In the first place I was a senator of the United States having commenced a six years term on the 4th of March 1861. Secondly I was a Brig General in service of the Confederate Armies.

During the extra session of March 1861 I served as a senator to its close but after the passage of the Ordinance of Secession by North Carolina on the 20th of May 1861 I regarded my seat as vacated. During the month of August following I was in my absence and without seeking it, elected a Colonel of one of the North Carolina regiments (the 25th) and entered the military service. In the next year I was commissioned as a Brig General and except when disabled by the casualties of battle I served to the close of the war, and was surrendered and paroled with the command of Gen. Joseph E. Johnston.

As I originally represented a district in Congress adjoining that of your Excellency and as we passed many years in the two Houses of Congress together I presume you are acquainted with my general course. I respectfully refer your Excellency however to the accompanying letter should further information be desired as to my action and views. It is my purpose to support faithfully the constitution and obey the laws of the United States and I respectfully ask your Excellency to extend to me your clemency and that I may be restored to such rights as belong to the other citizens of my state and the United States.[1]

T. L. Clingman

ALS, DNA-RG94, Amnesty Papers (M1003, Roll 38), N.C., Thomas L. Clingman.

1. Although recommended by Jonathan Worth and William W. Holden, Clingman was not pardoned until June 14, 1867. Worth to Johnson, Jan. 30, 1866; Holden to Johnson, Feb. 1, 1866, Amnesty Papers (M1003, Roll 38), N.C., Thomas L. Clingman, RG94, NA.

To George H. Thomas

January 3d, 1866.

General:

I enclose a newspaper statement relative to a conflict of authority between the civil and military authorities at Dandridge, East Tennessee.[1] Will you be kind enough to furnish me with a report upon the subject, in order that I may be fully informed respecting the occurrences referred to?[2]

Andrew Johnson

Tel, DLC-JP.

1. The incident to which Johnson refers is obviously the one that occurred when Gen. Alvan C. Gillem sent a subordinate and a few troops to Dandridge in order to free two soldiers believed to be improperly jailed there. Gillem's troops were met with such a show of force by the sheriff of Jefferson County and his posse that they retreated, whereupon Gillem sent a detachment of some 200 troops who successfully liberated the two jailed soldiers. *Nashville Union*, Jan. 3, 1866.

2. See Gillem to Johnson, Feb. 13, 1866, Johnson Papers, LC, for a brief recounting of the affair.

From James Speed

Attorney-General's Office, January 4, 1866.

Sir:

I have the honor to acknowledge the receipt from you of a copy of the resolution of the Senate of the United States of date the 21st of December, 1865.[1] In that resolution the Senate respectfully requests to be informed upon what charges and for what reasons Jefferson Davis is still held in confinement, and why he has not been put upon his trial.

When the war was at its crisis Jefferson Davis, the commander-in-chief of the army of the insurgents, was taken prisoner, with other prominent rebels, by the military forces of the United States. It was the duty of the military so to take them. They have been heretofore and are yet held as prisoners of war. Though active hostilities have ceased a state of war still exists over the territory in rebellion. Until peace shall come in fact and in law they can rightfully be held as prisoners of war.

I have ever thought that trials for high treason cannot be had before a military tribunal. The civil courts have alone jurisdiction of that crime. The question then arises: Where and when must the trials thereof be held?

In that clause of the Constitution mentioned in the resolution of the Senate[2] it is plainly written that they must be held in the State and district "wherein the crime shall have been committed." I know that many persons (of learning and ability) entertain the opinion that the commander-in-chief of the rebel armies should be regarded as constructively present with all the insurgents who prosecuted hostilities and made raids upon the northern and southern borders of the loyal States.

This doctrine of constructive presence, carried out to its logical consequences, would make all who had been connected with the rebel armies liable to trial in any State and district into which any portion of those armies had made the slightest incursion.[3] Not being persuaded of the correctness of that opinion, but regarding the doctrine mentioned as of doubtful constitutionality, I have thought it not proper to advise you to cause criminal proceedings to be instituted against Jefferson Davis, or any other insurgent, in States or districts in which they were not actually present during the prosecution of hostilities.

Some prominent rebels were personally present at the invasions of Maryland and Pennsylvania; but all or nearly all of them received military paroles upon the surrender of the rebel armies. Whilst I think that those paroles are not ultimate protection for prosecutions for high treason, I have thought that it would be a violation of the paroles to prosecute those persons for crimes before the political power of the Government has proclaimed that the rebellion has been suppressed.[4]

It follows from what I have said that I am of the opinion that Jefferson Davis and others of the insurgents ought to be tried in some one of the States or districts in which they in person respectively committed the crimes with which they may be charged. Though active hostilities and flagrant war have not for some time existed between the United States and the insurgents, peaceful relations between the Government and the people in the States and districts in rebellion have not yet been fully restored. None of the justices of the Supreme Court have held circuit courts in those States and districts since actual hostilities ceased.[5]

When the courts are open and the laws can be peacefully administered and enforced in those States whose people rebelled against the Government—when thus peace shall have come, in fact and in law, the persons now held in military custody as prisoners of war, and who may not have been tried and convicted for offenses against the laws of war, should be transferred into the custody of the civil authorities of the proper districts to be tried for such high crimes and misdemeanors as may be alleged against them.

I think that it is the plain duty of the President to cause criminal prosecutions to be instituted before the proper tribunals and at the proper times against some of those who were mainly instrumental inaugurating and most conspicuous in conducting the late hostilities.

I should regard it as a direful calamity if many whom the sword has spared the law should spare also; but I would deem it a more direful calamity still if the Executive, in performing his constitutional duty of bringing those persons before the bar of justice to answer for their crimes, should violate the plain meaning of the Constitution, or infringe in the least particular the living spirit of that instrument.[6]

James Speed, Attorney-General.

Senate Ex. Docs., 39 Cong., 1 Sess., No. 7, pp. 3–4 (Ser. 1237).

1. See *Senate Ex. Docs.*, 39 Cong., 1 Sess., No. 7, pp. 2–3 (Ser. 1237).

2. The resolution included an excerpt from the Sixth Amendment to the Constitution.

3. See, for example, Johnson to Oliver P. Morton, Nov. 14, 1865.

4. See Anna H.J. Saunders to Johnson, Dec. 6, 1865.

5. For the Chief Justice's opinion on opening the federal courts in the South, see Salmon P. Chase to Johnson, Oct. 12, 1865.

6. The President forwarded to the Senate statements from both Speed and Stanton, who concurred with the Attorney General, and also advised the Senate to consult his December 4 message. Johnson to Senate, Jan. 5, 1866, *Senate Ex. Docs.*, 39 Cong., 1 Sess., No. 7, pp. 1–2 (Ser. 1237).

From Joseph Holt

Bureau of Military Justice.
January 5. 1866.

To the President.

In compliance with your directions,[1] time has been allowed for filing additional affidavits, and the same having now been received, the record and papers relating to the case of *Frank B. Gurley*, are respectfully submitted with the following remarks.

(1) The full report of the Judge Adv. General, dated March 11, 1864, setting forth with minute particularity, the facts and circumstances of the murder of Genl. Robt. McCook by the prisoner, as detailed in the testimony, and earnestly advising the execution of the sentence of death adjudged by the Military Commission, before which the accused was tried, is herewith enclosed, and attention invited thereto.

The late President on May 11, 1864, approved the sentence.

(2) The execution of the sentence not having taken place, a communication in behalf of Gurley and others, from Judge Brien,[2] was forwarded January 23, 1865, by Your Excellency, then Military Governor of Tennessee, with these remarks.

I must be permitted to say that the within statements, coming as they do, have no influence with me, believing that the parties ought to be punished, and the sentence of the Court executed in a reasonable time. They deserve death without regard to their having at one time constituted part of the rebel army, which does not palliate in the slightest degree, the enormity of their offence.

Upon reference to this Bureau, a further report was prepared, reviewing the case, & re-affirming the previous conclusion. This report, dated March 21, 1865, is also enclosed for the more complete information of the President.

(3) On the 29th of August 1865, the President directed that Gurley—who, under some misapprehension, had been exchanged—should be executed whenever he could be secured.

(4) A petition is now presented signed by many citizens of Alabama, fortified by a letter from J. C. Bradley[3] of Huntsville, and urged by Messrs. Humphreys & Harrison in person, praying Executive interposition in behalf of the criminal, the warrant for whose execution the late President and your Excellency have issued, and repeatedly confirmed after renewed examination of the case.

The claim is now set up that Gurley did not in fact commit the murder proved. It is asserted, and three of the band commanded by the prisoner make affidavit, that many shots were indiscriminately fired, and that by no possibility can it be ascertained who discharged the fatal one; while J. M. Hambrick,[4] who was an officer of the same party, deposes that no signal of surrender was made by the persons in the wagon in which Genl. McCook rode. To confute these pretences, this Bureau invites the attention of The President to the testimony of Capt. Brook,[5] set forth in the report first above mentioned. This staff-officer—the aide and attendant of General McCook—not only states as an eye-witness, that Gurley shot the deceased, but also mentions that the murderer subsequently boasted of his exploit.[6] It is respectfully submitted, that to reject the evidence of this respectable and loyal United States officer, whose means of knowledge were of the best, and to accept as entitled to superior credit a newly invented version on the oaths of two or three traitors, whose story shows them participants in the crime—would violate all principles that should govern the weighing of conflicting testimony.

Moreover, it deserves to be noticed that the defence at the trial did not hint any doubts as to the truth of the allegation, that the prisoner was the person who killed Genl. McCook. The elaborate printed argument read in his behalf nowhere denies this, but, on the contrary, justifies the shooting as a legitimate act of war;—and, on p. 8. thereof, it is stated that—"The facts and circumstances attending the fatal shot, as detailed in the testimony of Capt. Brook, do not conflict with the statements of the prisoner."

It is represented—"that the said Gurley since the surrender has been at his home in this county; and that his demeanor and avowed sentiments have all been loyal, and exhibit entire good faith in abiding by his amnesty oath."[7] But this Bureau cannot consider these acts of negative merit as absolving him from liability to suffer the punishment due to his cowardly and infamous offence.

The petition may now be dismissed from consideration, with the following extract from its contents:

"They" (the signers) "of course know nothing and make no representations as to the facts proved on the trial of said matter."

The other new affidavits are those of men named Gibson, Scroggs, Hopkins, Moore, and Street,[8] which merely go to establish the claim that Gurley's command, in which they were enlisted, was authorized to be raised as "Partizan Rangers," so-called, and was organized, clothed and paid by the insurgent government styled the Confederate States; and those of J. C. Bradley, D. B. Turner, & C. H. Patton,[9] citizens of Alabama, and well acquainted in the vicinity where Gurley has resided, who state that "he has always borne the character of a quiet, orderly, peaceable man, remarkable for his kindness, amiability and generosity."

Upon these it may be remarked—first—that the character of the organization to which he belonged cannot palliate nor alter in any manner, the liability of the accused for the crime with which he stands convicted,—namely, the murder of a helpless captive; second—that the uniform experience of this Bureau teaches that certificates of moral character are readily procured in behalf of traitors, guerrillas, and conspirators to assassinate the executive heads of the government; and that the beautiful traits ascribed to this convict, Gurley, have in scores of cases, been depicted as the shining virtues of adherents of the rebellion, arraigned for offences, and whom these qualities have failed to restrain from butchering unionists at every opportunity.

This was a murder, which by its almost unexampled atrocity, called forth at the time of its perpetration the execrations of all right-thinking men. A Major General of the United States service, not the least distinguished of a family of heroes whose conspicuous ability and ardent patriotism have illustrated the annals of the war—a prisoner, unarmed, sick, with hands uplifted in supplication, was, in violation of the laws of civilized warfare and of the maxims even of savage magnanimity—shot down like a dog. A hecatomb of Gurleys would not atone for such an infernal deed. But to pardon the convicted felon would, it is confidently believed, repudiate the demands of justice by action disrespectful to the claims of the living and to the memory of the dead.[10]

J. Holt. Judge Advocate General.

LS, DNA-RG153, Court-Martial Records, MM-1326.

1. Upon a written plea from David C. Humphreys, dated December 14, 1865, Johnson had endorsed: "Time will be given for the arrival of the papers in F Gurleys case." This letter and endorsement, as well as other "papers" listed herein, can be found in Court-Martial Records, MM-1326, RG153, NA.

2. Former state circuit judge John S. Brien of Nashville.

3. See Joseph C. Bradley to Johnson, Nov. 27, 1865.

4. James M. Hambrick (1831–1881), a prosperous Madison County, Ala., farmer, had been Gurley's commanding officer. 1860 Census, Ala., Madison, 1st Dist., Hayes Store, 69; Dorothy S. Johnson, *Cemeteries of Madison County, Alabama* (2 vols., Huntsville, 1971–78), 2: 181; Cunningham, "Murderer or Victim," 86.

5. Hunter Brooke currently served as provost marshal general for the Department of Alabama. *New Orleans Picayune*, Nov. 25, 1865.

6. Soon after McCook's death in August 1862, Brooke had also reportedly stated that the "attack" had been made by "regular Confederate States cavalry," not guerrillas. *OR*, Ser. 1, Vol. 16, Pt. 1: 839.

7. This extract, as well as others that Holt furnishes below, are taken from Joseph C. Bradley et al. to Johnson, Nov. 30, 1865, Court-Martial Records, MM-1326, RG153, NA.

8. Lt. John A. Gibson (1838–1870), Corp. William J. Street (d. 1883), and Pvts. Benjamin P. Scruggs (*c*1843-*fl*1868) and Thomas B. Hopkins (*fl*1872) had served under Gurley in Company C, 4th Ala. Cav. Pvt. George A. Morris (1842-*fl*1907) had been a member of another company in the same regiment. CSR, RG109, NA; Johnson, *Cemeteries*, 2: 91; Pauline J. Gandrud, comp., *Marriage, Death and Legal Notices from Early Alabama Newspapers, 1819–1893* (Easley, S.C., 1981), 242, 261; 1860 Census, Ala., Madison, N.W. Div., Madison Station, 25; S.E. Div., 91; Gandrud, *Alabama Records*, 124: 88; 173: 70; 191: 23; Dorothy S. Johnson, comp., *1907 Confederate Census: Limestone, Morgan, & Madison Counties, Alabama* (Huntsville, 1981), 17.

9. Daniel B. Turner and Charles H. Patton had, along with Bradley, signed the petition to Johnson of November 30, 1865.

10. See Holt to Johnson, Jan. 29, 1866.

From George Bancroft

New York Monday   8th January '65 [1866][1]

My dear Sir,

The joint committee of Congress have invited me to deliver the address on the life & character of Mr. Lincoln.[2] I wish I were near you, & could run in upon you & take your advice. Are you willing to send me word by *telegram* or letter, What I had better do?[3] The request of a joint committee is a great honor, not to be lightly put aside; but I am fully occupied.

Geo. Bancroft

ALS, DLC-JP.

1. The content of this letter makes it obvious that it was written in 1866.

2. The previous day Bancroft, apparently unaware that he would be asked to be the principal speaker after Stanton declined the honor, had accepted Johnson's invitation to attend the commemoration. Bancroft to Johnson, Jan. 7, 1866, Johnson Papers, LC.

3. See Johnson to Bancroft, Jan. 10, 1866.

To James Hughes

Washington, D.C.   January 8th, 1866,

The Honorable James Hughes has been specially designated by me to proceed to Kentucky, Tennessee, Alabama, Georgia, North Carolina, Virginia, and such others of the Southern States as he may deem it necessary to visit for the purpose herein expressed, with instructions to obtain and report full and accurate information respecting the condition of affairs in said States.[1]

All officers in the civil and military service of the United States are requested to afford him such facilities and courtesies as may aid him in the discharge of the duties with which he is entrusted.

Andrew Johnson.

Copy, DLC-JP.

1. Within a few days Hughes did go to Frankfort, Kentucky, but, because he was back in Washington by late January, it is uncertain whether he actually completed his assigned itinerary. *Nashville Union and American*, Feb. 1, 1866. See Johnson to Hughes, Jan. 19, 1866.

From Mary Evans Jennings[1]

Nashville   Jan 8th 1866

You will doubtless wonder what has prompted one personally so little known to the great men of the day as the writer of this epistle to think of addressing Your Excellency, nevertheless "stranger things have happened," and hoping you will pardon my audacity in thus intruding upon your time and attention I will now inform you why I have thus ventured. You doubtless remember the house in which you resided during the time you were Military Governor of this State & perhaps you also remember the house next it on Vine St. The latter was owned by Mr. T. W. Evans[2] (my Father) to whom your Excellency has already extended your pardon & protection at the request of Mr. Hugh Douglas. My Father gave me the house & furniture about six months afer my marriage to Mr. R. W. Jennings[3] of this city. In the month of June 1864, it was taken (under the plea of Military necessity) by Gen. John F. Miller then Commanding Post—since which time it has been occupied by different officers for quarters. Now the favor which I wish to ask of your Excellency is one which although it may appear trifling to you is let me assure you of no light moment to us—and I pray you do not hastily refuse my request. After Several interviews with Major Wills[4] A.Q.M. in this city my husband had almost despaired of getting possession of the house which was once our happy home. I told him however to cheer up—adding that I believed if I could see our President & state the case to him he would restore to us our property; and it is in accordance with this belief that I have presumed to address your Excellency being at present unable to go to Washington City. We have two little children, a sister in delicate health, & a nurse, a faithful old family Servant whose hair is white with age & who has always refused to leave us, although perfectly free to do so, if she wished, having been emancipated by my Father eight or nine years ago. So we have a family of six and being unable to procure a house to live in we are compelled to board at an enormous price, for very inferior accommodations. Now while there was actual necessity for the occupation of our home by the Military I did not complain nor even wonder that it was thus held and occupied, for I did not deem myself better or more entitled to favor than those around me whose houses were also held in a like manner. But I *do* think it very strange that though almost every one of those whose property was used for the same purposes, have been reinstated in their homes, we are still kept out of ours without the shadow of an excuse. I say without excuse, because it was promised us once, but for *some* reason (or rather *none*) Major Wills refused to comply with that promise. Now that the war is over and Military necessity no longer exists to the extent of depriving people of their homes, I must say that I cannot see any right or justice in such action as the military authorities here have taken in regard to this matter. Once when your Excellency was Governor of this State you promised a little friend & warm admirer of yours' that should she ever need assistance, if she would call upon Gov. Johnson he would surely give it, if in his power. That little friend now calls upon you with the hope that you will not *now refuse* to grant that assistance which was promised years ago. Perhaps I can recall the circumstances which amid the many troubles and cares which have crowded your mind since that time you have doubtless forgotten, together with her to whom the promise was made. In the year 1857 you were a boarder at the Commercial Hotel on Cedar St. in this city. Mr Jas. W. Manier[5] (perhaps you remember him), boarded with his family at the hotel at the same time. He was a strong democrat in politics; a personal acquaintance of yours and one of your warmest friends. Being an Uncle of mine I was very often there in his rooms and it was during one of my visits to his family that I met & was introduced to your Excellency *at that time Gov. Johnson*. The conversation turned upon the poor of the city, and several compliments were paid you, upon you liberality. After a few moments cheerful conversation you arose to leave and after shaking each one cordially by the hand you turned to me & still holding my hand you said—"Remember, my little friend, should it so happen in future years, that you ever need the advice & assistance of a friend call upon Andrew Johnson and he will not fail to render it if in his power to do so." The time has come! The power to render that assistance is yours! Oh will not Your Excellency give it? Will you not add another to your many acts of kindness & restore to us our much loved home! Do this and your name will rise to Heaven in our prayers for those we love, not only as the ruler of a great & powerful nation but as the true, the tried & faithful friend.[6]

Mrs R. W. Jennings   Daughter of T. W Evans.

ALS, DNA-RG107, Lets. Recd., EB14 President 60 (1866).

1. Jennings (1842–1871) was a Nashville resident throughout her short life. By the time of the 1870 census, she and her husband had three sons and two daughters. Acklen, *Tenn. Records*, 1: 92; 1870 Census, Tenn., Davidson, Nashville, 5th Ward, 9.

2. Thomas W. Evans (c1818-fl1901), a longtime Nashville merchant, was a whole-

sale dealer in staple and dry goods through the firm Evans, Porter & Co., then Evans & Co., and finally as Evans, Fite & Co. . He sought a pardon from President Johnson in June and received it in August 1865. By the late 1860s he was a resident of New York City. Nashville directories (1855–71); New York City directories (1867–1901); 1860 Census, Tenn., Davidson, Nashville, 5th Ward, 159; Evans to Johnson, June 7, 1865; Hu Douglas to Johnson, June 7, 1865, Amnesty Papers (M1003, Roll 49), Tenn., Thomas W. Evans, RG94, NA.

3. Robert W. Jennings (1838–fl1913) was a Nashville merchant who for a time worked in his father-in-law's business but subsequently began his own firm, R. W. Jennings & Co. By the turn of the century he had begun the Jennings Business College in Nashville. He remarried after the death of his first wife. 1900 Census, Tenn., Davidson, Nashville, Enum. Dist. 94, Sheet 3A; Nashville directories (1860–1913).

4. Andrew W. Wills (1841–1918) became a captain and assistant quartermaster in December 1863 and was assigned to duty in Nashville. He was in charge of public and private buildings and therefore dealt with the Jennings family. Later he served for twenty years as Nashville postmaster. ACP Branch, File W-0973-1867, A. W. Wills, RG94, NA; *Nashville Banner*, Jan. 14, 1914, July 15, 1918.

5. Manier (1825–1913) was for a number of years a merchant affiliated with the firm of Evans, Porter & Co., then Evans & Co., and finally with Pique, Manier & Co., all of which were Nashville merchandise businesses. 1860 Census, Tenn., Davidson, Nashville, 4th Ward, 131; (1870), 62; Nashville directories (1855–84); *Nashville Tennessean*, Aug. 3, 1913.

6. Exactly one month after Mary Jennings's letter, Secretary Stanton informed Johnson that the Jennings house was occupied by General Fisk and therefore could not be returned to the family. Stanton to Johnson, Feb. 8, 1866, Lets. Sent to President, Vol. 6 (M421, Roll 3), RG107, NA.

From Ann H. Kincheloe[1]

Livermore [Ky.]   January 8th 1866

Sir

I am informed that the Slaves of this State are all set free in our midst. I have had no other means of support but their wages. Now they are not under my control, and I am in advanced life, a widow of three score years. I have not yet received pay for my black man that was pressed in the Federal Service the first of December 1865.[2] I have the certificate to show that He was taken to the Army, but that certificate will not buy my meat nor bread. I have no income now for a sufficient support, and I am two old to engague in any business. Now I respectfully ask your advice what I must do, as the Government has cut off all my Revenue of support. To you I most earnestly appeal for aid by council and means for my Slave that was pressed in the Army.[3] I was offered $1300 for Him before He was pressed in the service but He was a favourite Slave and I was unwilling to part with Him. That amount was offered in my hand for Him. As I am able to certify, I had six, three Females and three males, but our servant over twenty five years all young Likely and valuable, being well trained. Col. McHenry has proffered to collect the money for my Man Burr that was pressed in the Army by the Federals but says that it will be some time before I get it. I enclose you his letter containing his proposition.[4] I do assure you that I need the money now. You can better imagine my necessity than I can express it.

Burrs services brought me two hundred dollars a year besides the hire of the others. That gave a very genteel support for myself and school some of my Orphan Grand Children that looks up to me for Aid.[5]

Ann H Kincheloe

ALS, DNA-RG94, USCT Div., Lets. Recd., File P-48-1866.

1. Kincheloe (b. c1798) was the widow of William Kincheloe of Muhlenberg County. 1850 Census, Ky., Muhlenberg, 2nd Subdiv., 460.

2. As early as the fall of 1862 those slaveowners who were proven to be loyal were promised compensation for slaves who were impressed by the military. In February 1864 a new conscription act was passed providing that "all able-bodied blacks between the ages of twenty and forty-five . . . were liable to the draft," but loyal owners would be compensated. Howard, *Black Liberation*, 45–46, 56–57.

3. For similar examples of Kentuckians seeking compensation, see M. Hughes to Johnson, Nov. 2, 1865, and Richard Harcourt to Johnson, Nov. 11, 1865, USCT Div., Lets. Recd., Files P-577-1865 and P-614-1865, RG94, NA.

4. John H. McHenry, Jr., an Owensboro, Ky., attorney who had commanded a Union regiment during the war, had offered to present Kincheloe's claims to the "proper officers" in return for "ten percent in the amount collected." McHenry to Kincheloe, Nov. 29, 1865, USCT Div., Lets. Recd., File P-48-1866, RG94, NA.

5. This letter was referred to Stanton. An assistant adjutant general replied, informing Kincheloe that her claim could not be investigated until a special commission was appointed in her state. Eventually Kentucky did establish procedures to review claims, but very few former slaveowners were ever compensated. George Foster to Kincheloe, Jan. 27, 1866, ibid.; Coulter, *Civil War Kentucky*, 385–86.

From John S. Morgan[1]

Tuscumbia Ala   Jany 8/66

Dear Sir

Some months since I wrote you asking appointment in your gift,[2] designated none in particular. Your secretary answered, telling me that my letter had been referred to the Provisional Gov of Ala. I supposed this refference had been made to assertain my loyalty. This was done, and understand the application was recommended by Gov. Parsons. Since then I have heard nothing from the application. Now I desire verry much to have an appointment in the Custom House at Mobile Ala and I prefer the appointment of Inspector of Cloths, the duties of which appointment I think I am fully qualified to discharge, as I have worked in cloths many years a calling you once adorned your self. Should your sense of duty allow you, to confer the appointment, or some other one I will ever remember it with grateful pleasure.[3]

John. S. Morgan.

ALS, DNA-RG56, Appts., Customs Service, Inspector of Cloths, Mobile, John S. Morgan.

1. Morgan (b. c1808) was allegedly a partner with Johnson in the tailor shop at Greeneville, and his wife was the daughter of John Johnson, the President's uncle. He had served as a justice of the peace for "many years" but in April 1866 was not reelected because of his "Union proclivities." 1860 Census, Ala., Franklin, E. Subdiv., Tuscumbia, 35; *Augusta Constitutionalist*, Apr. 26, 1866; Hugh B. Johnston, "President Andrew Johnson's Uncle John Johnson" (typescript, n.d., Andrew Johnson Project Files); Mor-

gan to George S. Houston, Feb. 5, 1866, Appts., Customs Service, Inspector of Cloths, Mobile, RG56, NA; Morgan to Robert Johnson, Jan. 31, 1867, Johnson Papers, LC.

2. Not found.

3. Morgan's application was supported by letters of endorsement from Gov. Robert M. Patton, former Congressman George S. Houston, and former Alabama legislator Sidney C. Posey. Although Patton spoke with the President, and Morgan wrote again in March 1866 asking for any office "that would make me a support," he did not receive a federal appointment until May 1867, when Robert Johnson forwarded a commission as mail agent for the Memphis & Charleston Railroad. Posey to Johnson, Dec. 12, 1865; Patton to Johnson, Jan. 15, 1866; Houston to Johnson, Feb. 22, 1866; Morgan to Johnson, Mar. 5, 1866, Appts., Customs Service, Inspector of Cloths, Mobile, RG56, NA; Morgan to Robert Johnson, Jan. 31, May 10, 1867, Johnson Papers, LC.

From J. Maxwell Pringle[1]

Columbia So Ca   Jan 8th 1866

May it please your excellency, I would most respectfully refer to the accompanying letter for such particulars, as may be necessary in presenting the following application.[2] I am informed that the office of General visitor and Supervisor of Schools for the Freedmen has been only in part, and temporarily filled by the Revd. Mr. French.[3] May I venture to offer myself to your Excellency to serve the Govt. in this capacity, and to solicit this appointment under your hand.

Permit me with sincere defference to your superior judgment to add, that if, by your timely and wise control, the work of elevating and improving our former slaves should be separated from those allusions and statements, which, unconsciously to the official speakers and agents themselves, are even now silently exerting an incendiary influence, then would the piety of the South at once throw all its weight into the scale of cordial return and adhesion to our common Govt., and in the retrospect of our late unhappy struggle we shall be able to accept the result with a sentiment not merely of conviction but of acquiescence, such as by a slight alteration of the words of an ancient celebrated line, I may most concisely express as follows, "victrix causa hominibus placuit; victa Deo."

Hoping to be favoured with your confidence and patronage in the important duties to which I desire to devote myself, I am. . . .[4]

J. Maxwell Pringle

ALS, DNA-RG105, Records of the Commr., Lets. Recd. (M752, Roll 23).

1. Pringle (1838–1906) was an Episcopal clergyman. *NUC Manuscript Collections* (1982), 219.

2. Pringle may refer to the endorsements of Benjamin F. Perry and William W. Boyce, as well as a cover letter provided by the latter, which accompanied this application. Boyce to Johnson, Jan. 25, 1866; Endorsements by Perry and Boyce, Jan. 12, 24, 1866, Records of the Commr., Lets. Recd. (M752, Roll 23), RG105, NA.

3. Mansfield French (1810–1876) headed several colleges in Ohio prior to publishing an antislavery religious monthly in New York City. During the war he organized the National Freedmen's Relief Association and began educating former slaves in Port Royal, S.C. Brown, *Am. Biographies*, 3: 192.

4. Pringle's application was referred to General Howard who forwarded it to the

assistant commissioner of the Freedmen's Bureau in South Carolina, Gen. Robert K. Scott. On February 2, 1866, Scott replied: "Revd. Mr. French and Mr. R. Tomlinson fill the post applied for by Mr Pringle to my Entire satisfaction." Records of the Commr., Lets. Recd. (M752, Roll 23), RG105, NA.

From William H. Rohrer[1]

Washington   Jany 8 /65[66][2]

I have the honor to present to you my application, addressed to the Secretary of War, for the position of "Post Sutler" at or near Brownsville, Texas. If it meets with your approbation, may I once more trouble you for your friendly intercession in behalf of one who already owes so much to your extreme kindness.

I desire to add that it is my intention to build up a trade in Texas, and this appointment will very materially assist me in that intention; and, as it is my sole object to conduct the business in an honorable and conscientious manner, and being determined not to associate myself with any one not holding the same views, I hardly think that my appointment will in any way be distasteful to the army now quarted there, or that may hereafter be sent to that point.[3]

Wm H. Rohrer

ALS, DNA-RG94, ACP Branch, File R-37-CB-1866, William H. Rohrer.

1. Formerly a Senate messenger during Johnson's tenure as senator, Rohrer now served as clerk of that body.

2. Endorsements indicate that 1866 is the correct date.

3. In forwarding this letter to Stanton on January 25, 1866, Johnson wrote, "It is hoped that this appointment will be made." Later annotations indicate that Rohrer received his "warrant" on February 2, 1866.

From E. George Squier[1]

105 East 39th St.
New York, Jan. 8, 1866.

Sir:

I have the honor to enclose to you herewith slips from several of the newspapers of this city, containing the proceedings of a public meeting of the citizens of New York, held in the Cooper Institute on the evening of the 6th inst., in favor of the vindication of the "Monroe Doctrine."[2]

It was believed by the promoters of this meeting that such a gathering made up of all parties, would contribute towards strengthening the hands of the government, inasmuch as it would enable it, in its relations with foreign and aggressive nations, of whose conduct we have cause to complain, to represent that the sentiment of the American people in their primary, as well as representative capacity, is in open and uncompromising hostility to their conduct and purposes, and that, as the government of the United States is truly representative, it must sooner or later reflect and carry out the popular sentiment and will. We believe that the Monroe Doctrine is not one of these "glittering generalities" of which we have heard, but a radical and vital principle of American policy, and our intention has been to assure the President and his advisers, as well as the coordinate branches of the Government, in our humble way and in exercise of our rights as a fraction of the people, that we are ready to support them in the assertion and vindication of that principle, in whatever way their superior judgment and more direct responsibility may dictate or approve.

We have to regret that one or two gentlemen in Washington,[3] aspiring to high and it is understood even to Cabinet appointments, and who came on to New York, to speak at the meeting, discovering that commerce is always cowardly and seldom patriotic, and distrusting the people, "Struck their tents like the Arabs, and as quietly stole away."[4] They will not be forgotten by the thousands of thorough Americans who filled the Cooper Inst. on the night of the 6th of January.

I enclose these proceedings to you as Chairman of the Committee organizing the Meeting referred to, and on their behalf and my own, have only to reiterate the expressions of regard and confidence embodied in one of the resolutions adopted by the Meeting, referring to yourself.[5]

E. Geo. Squier—Chm—

ALS, DLC-JP.

1. Squier (1821–1888), author and amateur archaeologist of some note, had been U.S. commissioner to Peru (1863–65) and later served as consul general for Honduras in New York City. *DAB*.

2. Not found, but accounts of the rally were published in the *New York Herald* and *New York Times* on January 7, 1866, and in the *New York Tribune* on January 8, 1866.

3. Not further identified.

4. A variant of Henry Wadsworth Longfellow, "The Day is Done," Stanza 11.

5. The resolution praised Johnson as a "noble illustration of the fostering influence of republican institutions" who would "dedicate himself to the vindication of those great national principles enunciated by our fathers as essential to our peace and safety, and among which the Monroe doctrine is one of the most vital." *New York Herald*, Jan. 7, 1866.

From the Central Committee of the Union Party of Tennessee

ca. January 9, 1866, Nashville, Tenn.; Mem., DLC-JP.

The thirteen signers delineate the eclipse of Union men and the alarming ascendancy of rebels in Tennessee. They paint a grim picture of what has happened to loyal people in Tennessee under the restored government. The Franchise Law of 1865 has produced a situation in which "the loyal people of the State have now little hope that its enforcement can prevent the political organization of the State from passing at no distant day, into the hands of those who have been in active sympathy with the rebellion." In fact, "Service in the rebel army is, in many parts of the State the best passport to position and power, while to have been connected with the Union Army is regarded as afflicting a stigma 'deeper and more indelible, than the brand upon the brow of Cain.'" Although pleased that there is now a loyal judiciary, thanks to Governor Brownlow's appointing power, the memorialists fear that "rebel Juries" will practice "the grossest injustice towards loyal men." Furthermore, "In a social and business point of view, Union men, and Union families are proscribed and insulted." As for the masses "who were misled and betrayed by demagogues into rebellion," they are still under the influence of their "false teachers"—rebel lawyers, rebel preachers, rebel physicians, rebel teachers, rebel presses. Finally, while acknowledging emancipation as "an *accomplished fact*," the former rebels do not regard it as "a *fact legally accomplished*," and aim through legislation to "reduce them to a bondage more abject than that from which they have escaped." The memorialists urge admission of the Tennesseans elected to the two houses of congress.

From Green T. Henderson

Murfreesboro, Tennessee   January the 9th 1866.

Dear Sir.

Application has been made to the government, by those most interrested, for aid to rebuild the Presbyterian Church in this city, which was destroyed by a part of the Federal army during the late war.

I desire to call your attention to the subject, to inform you that the object is a worthy one, and to ask the aid of your influence in obtaining the compensation sought. The house was a large, well finished, and well furnished brick edifice. It was torn down to its foundation, and all its furniture destroyed.

The congregation, a worthy portion of our community, is not able to rebuild the house. It asks aid of the government; and I am convinced that an object of the kind, more entitled to compensation can not be presented.

Any assistance you may give in this matter, a matter of importance to us, by endorsing our petition to the proper department, or in any manner that your good judgment and kind feelings may suggest, will be thankfully received, and kindly remembered by a large portion of this community; and by your old friend, and humble servant.[1]

G. T. Henderson

ALS, DLC-JP.

1. A plea from the members of the church was forwarded to Johnson by Tennessee Representative Edmund Cooper in the fall of 1866. It too was not acted upon after it was reported that the destruction was not entirely the fault of the army, that many members were "bitter and active rebels of influence," and that there were no funds available to pay such claims without a special act of Congress. A new church building was constructed in 1867 at a cost to the congregation of $18,000. Cooper to Johnson, Oct. 8, 1866; E. B. Whitman to Thomas Swords, Jan. 8, 1867; Daniel H. Rucker to Stanton, Jan. 21, 1867, Lets. Recd., Executive (M494, Roll 96), RG107, NA; Carlton C. Sims, ed., *A History of Rutherford County* (Murfreesboro, Tenn., 1947), 195.

From Asa W. Messenger [1]

Tuscumbia Ala   Jany 9th 1866

Dear Sir,

The undersigned an old citizen of this place, without any pretentions to notoriety or high sounding title, takes the liberty to address you, on a subject which he deems of deep interest in the public welfare. Without any exceptions, so far as has come to his knowledge, the people of this place, & vicinity have been orderly, & well satisfied with the efforts made by you for the reconstruction of the National Government; but within the last three days they have been greatly humiliated by the appearance, in our town, of a garrison of *colored* troops quartered among us. Those of us especially, who like yourself, have uniformly condemned the secession movement & have zealously labored for a restoration of the Union, see or think we see, in this measure, an unnecessary aggravation which will tend greatly to imbitter the feelings of those whom it should be our principal aim to conciliate.

Are there not still in the service of the United State *white* troops enough to garrison such towns as may need their presents? If there are, for the sake of harmony & a due regard for the feelings of our people let us have them. Elsewhere collisions are daily occurring betwen citizens & colored soldiers, often with the most fatal results. We wish, if possible to be spared of like calamities & of the bad state of feeling towards the government which they proclaim. This can only be done by removing from our mids our *black masters*. Is not the South already sufficieny humiliated?

We wish not to paliate the great wrong of secession; Alabama has sinned, deeply & most foolishly; but she is now repentant, and is humbeled to the very dust. She has made every consission that could honorably be required of her. Then why longer aggravate her wounded sensibilities by suffering her to be subjected to *black* military rule? [2]

Excuse this liberty on the part of old man who wishes well to his country & who has suffered much proscription for his unyielding support of the Union.

A. W Messenger   former editor of the North Alabamian

ALS, DNA-RG108, Lets. Recd. *re* Military Discipline.

1. Messenger (c1799–1866), a New Englander who in 1830 founded the *North Alabamian*, had more recently owned a steam saw mill. 1860 Census, Ala., Franklin, E. Subdiv., 106; *Montgomery Advertiser*, Mar. 24, 1866.

2. This letter was forwarded to Grant, but there is no record of a reply. Gen. George H. Thomas in January 1866 told Robert M. Patton that troops would be withdrawn from Alabama "whenever he, the Governor, should say the word." In April all volunteers, white and black, were ordered mustered out in the military division of Tennessee, and after the summer "few soldiers" remained in Alabama. *Nashville Union and American*, Jan. 18, 1866; Fleming, *Alabama*, 417, 420; John Hope Franklin, *Reconstruction: After the Civil War* (Chicago, 1961), 36. See Alabama Legislature to Johnson, Jan. 16, 1866.

From Nathan Ranney

January 9, 1866, St. Louis, Mo.; ALS, DLC-JP.

Believing that commerce is king and that it will soon "make our country the greatest nation . . . on the face of the Earth," Ranney, a freight agent, informs the President that, despite the bitter cold, a "Verry large and Enthusiastic" meeting was held on the night of January 8 to support Johnson's "just and wise" reconstruction plans. He adds that, as a resident of Missouri for forty-seven years, he is "well acquainted all over the State—and can say I am shure that a vast majority of the people most cordially approve the Presidents policy."

From William F.M. Arny[1]

Santa Fe, New Mexico, January 10th 1866

Sir

In compliance with the instructions of the Legislative assembly of the Territory of New Mexico I have the honor to send herewith a trans-lated Copy of Joint Resolutions of thanks to your Excellency[2] which I hope will be received by you in due time.

W.F.M. Arny, Secretary Territory New Mexico

ALS, DLC-JP.

1. Affiliated with both Alexander Campbell and Bethany College as business manager and secretary, Arny (1813–1881), an Illinois agrarian promoter and Kansas land and relief agent, was several times agent to the Utes, Pueblos, and Navajos, and twice (1862–67, 1872–73) secretary of New Mexico Territory. Lawrence R. Murphy, *Frontier Crusader—William F.M. Arny* (Tucson, Ariz., 1972), passim.

2. The legislature's resolutions, originally written in Spanish, thanked Johnson for the appointment of Julius K. Graves as a "special agent, to investigate the Indian Affairs of our Territory." A joint legislative committee was to give Graves "such information as he may require" and "prepare such laws, resolutions or memorials, as may be deemed necessary for the action of the Legislative Assembly." Johnson Papers, LC.

To George Bancroft

Washington, D.C.   Jany 10th 1866.

My dear Sir:

I have received your note,[1] and hardly know how to advise you in the premises. The Joint Committee of Congress, in selecting you to deliver the eulogy on the life and character of President Lincoln, have unques-tionably conferred upon you a high honor; and in my estimation, there is no one in the United States more competent to perform the task. Not knowing the nature of your engagements, however, I am at a loss what advice to give, and therefore can only say that if you accept the invita-tion, I will take great pleasure in making any suggestions that may in the least aid you in the preparation of the eulogy, and shall insist that when you come to Washington, you do me the favor of becoming my guest.[2]

Andrew Johnson

LS, MHi-George Bancroft Papers.
1. See Bancroft to Johnson, Jan. 8, 1866.
2. Bancroft accepted both invitations. For a synopsis of his speech, see the *Washington Evening Star*, Feb. 12, 1866.

From David Davis[1]

Washington, DC, Jany. 10, 1866.

My Dear Sir,

I am advised, that an effort is being made, to remove the Hon Kirby Benedict,[2] the present Chief Justice of New Mexico.

I should regret this exceedingly, for I know Judge Benedict, intimately, & advised to his re-appointment. He is an honorable man & upright judge, & thoroughly loyal. His course in New Mexico has been overwhelmingly sustained by the people of New Mexico in the election of Col. Chavis,[3] the present member.

I believe all opposition to him is factious. I practised Law with Judge Benedict for many years, & know him to be pure & above reproach.

Although a Whig in politics, I recommended his appnt. to Genl. Pierce.[4] Mr. Benedict was a democrat until this war broke out, & immediately devoted himself to the Govt.

I do most earnestly request, that he be not removed, & would with equal earnestness recommend his reappointment, when his present term expires.[5]

David Davis

ALS, DNA-RG60, Appt. Files for Judicial Dists., N.M., Kirby Benedict.
1. Davis (1815–1886) served as an associate justice of the Supreme Court from 1862 until his election as a Senator (1877–83). *BDAC*.
2. Benedict (1810–1874) had been a legal associate of both Davis and Abraham Lincoln in Illinois and had served in the legislature with the former. He was appointed associate justice of New Mexico in 1852 and chief justice of that territory in 1858. Aurora Hunt, *Kirby Benedict, Frontier Federal Judge* (Glendale, Cal., 1961), passim.
3. Jose Francisco Chaves (1833–1904), a former president of the New Mexico Territorial Council and lt. col. of the 1st N.M. Inf., served as a delegate to Congress for three consecutive terms (1865–71). Four days earlier he had written a letter in support of Benedict, whom he characterized as a "faithful and indefatigable" judge who had "discharged his duties with the most commendable promptitude and efficiency." Chaves to Speed, Jan. 6, 1866, Appt. Files for Judicial Dists., N.M., Kirby Benedict, RG60, NA.
4. Franklin Pierce.
5. Attempts to remove Benedict originated with his opposition to the heavy-handed rule of Gen. James H. Carleton. Lincoln, disregarding charges of drunkenness and corruption levelled against Benedict, reappointed him in 1862. Johnson was besieged by petitioners from both sides. Davis, Gov. Richard Yates, Lyman Trumbull, and the New Mexico legislature supported Benedict, while James R. Doolittle called for his removal and Francisco Perea, Chaves's predecessor as territorial delegate, alleged that Lincoln had agreed to remove Benedict. Johnson followed the advice of H. B. Denman and replaced Benedict with John P. Slough. When Benedict later applied for another judge-

ship, Chaves wrote a letter denigrating him as a "confirmed inebriate." Diego Archuleta et al. to Johnson, Jan. 22, 1865; Thomas D. Wheaton et al. to Speed, May 8, 1865; Perea to Johnson, July 1, 1865; J. L. Collins et al. to Johnson, Jan. 13, 1866; Denman to Johnson, Jan. 15, 1866, Appt. Files, Judicial Dists., N.M., Kirby Benedict, RG60, NA; Hunt, *Kirby Benedict*, 170; Arie W. Poldervaart, *Black-Robed Justice* (New York, 1976[1948]), 58–66. See Doolittle to Johnson, Sept. 23, 1865.

From Andrew J. Hamilton

Houston Texas   Jany 10 1866

The election for delegates to a Convention for this State took place on the 8th inst. There was not as much interest manifested among the people generally as ought to have been felt. The vote of the State I fear will not amount to more than half the registered voting population if so much from what little I have heard of the result of the election & from what I know of the candidates generally. Few of original union men will be returned.[1] The election went off so far as heard from very quietly. The body of the people are quiet yet, There is in Section of the State many Lawless and many acts of violence & wrongs Committed and especially towards the Freedmen.[2] When the Convention meets seventh (7) prox I will keep you Constantly advised of its actions.[3]

A J Hamilton   Gov Texas

Tel, DLC-JP.
1. During the election of delegates "only a small vote" was cast "because of the inclemency of the weather." Unionists comprised a small minority of those elected. Charles W. Ramsdell, *Reconstruction in Texas* (New York, 1910), 89.
2. See Hamilton to Johnson, Oct. 21, 1865.
3. See Hamilton to Johnson, Feb. 11, 16, 28, Mar. 1, 17, 29, 1866, Johnson Papers, LC.

From James T. Hough[1]

Newberne N C   Jany 10 1866

It was the Hon B. F. Moore who gave decision that the State Convention had no power to impose retrospective Taxes.[2]

Am informed that the atty General[3] has given no decision. Instructions from Gov Worth to Sheriff is that the Tax must & shall be collected.

Myself with other business men have been arrested under Provisions of the law. Enforcement is causing great distress among us. Please answer immediately.[4]

J. T. Hough

Tel, DLC-JP.
1. Mayor Hough, who was also a wholesale grocer, had complained two days earlier about attempts by Craven County Sheriff Harper to collect the taxes imposed by the convention, and had asked the President to "interfere." Johnson responded that he had "been advised that the Attorney General of the State has given an opinion that settled this matter," and asked "what is the difficulty?" Hough to Johnson, Jan. 9, 1866,

Johnson Papers, LC; Johnson to Hough, Jan. 9, 1866, Tels. Sent, President, Vol. 3 (1865–68), RG107, NA.

2. Moore had actually given a "written opinion" that "merchants trading in insurrectionary districts under license from the Secretary of Treasury, are not liable to the convention tax." Worth to George Stronach, Feb. 5, 1866, in J. G. de Roulhac Hamilton, ed., *The Correspondence of Jonathan Worth* (2 vols., Raleigh, 1909), 1: 496.

3. Sion H. Rogers (1825–1874), a Confederate colonel and U.S. congressman (1853–55, 1871–73), had also served as attorney general under both Vance and Holden. *BDAC*.

4. The President telegraphed Governor Worth, directing that steps be taken to resolve this matter. Johnson to Worth, Jan. 13, 1866, Johnson Papers, LC. See Worth to Johnson, Jan. 14, 1866.

From James Johnson

Nashville   Jan 10th/66

Dear Uncle

On behalf of Mother, Sister, Brothers & myself allow me to express to you the gratitude we all feel for the kindness you have ever shown us and especially under our late affliction.[1] It would be unnecessary for me to enter into a detail of Fathers affairs as I am aware you know his circumstances. It now devolves upon myself & Bro Andrew to support Mother & family and as I am not in a condition in my present situation, I ask you to help me in this respect, feeling that I can fill any position that you may be kind enough to assign me, with honesty & credit, both to myself & you.

Whilst in Galveston I was informed that the present Collector of that Port was to be removed[2] and if so I would respectfully ask to be appointed to fill the vacancy. Should there be no change made there, I would submit my case to your discretion as I am ignorant what positions are open. I have writen to Cousin Robert[3] and refered to my case in the letter to him. I would make the application in person, were it not from a lack of funds, and I therefore hope this letter may meet your approval.[4]

James Johnson

ALS, DLC-JP.

1. The reference here is to the late October death of William P. Johnson, the President's brother and James's father. See Andrew Johnson to Andrew Johnson, Jr., Nov. 1, 1865, Tels. Sent, President, Vol. 2 (1865), RG107, NA. See also John Adriance to Johnson, Oct. 26, 1865.

2. Richard R. Peebles had been appointed collector but was unable to assume his duties.

3. The letter to Robert Johnson has not been found.

4. In March 1866 former brevet brig. gen. Loren Kent was appointed collector at Galveston, replacing Peebles. Subsequently in July 1866, the President appointed James Johnson assessor of taxes at Galveston. He served briefly in that post before returning to Davidson County, Tennessee, to operate a farm. Ser. 6B, Vol. 4: 211, Johnson Papers, LC; Simon, *Grant Papers*, 16: 4–5; *U.S. Off. Reg.* (1867), 78; Galveston directories (1868); 1870 Census, Tenn., Davidson, 20th Dist., Goodlettsville, 23.

From Sam Milligan
Private

Nashville Ten   Jan. 10, 1866

Dear Sir:

I am still here. During the Christmas hollidays, while my associates were at play, I administered on the *late* Confederate States. I hope you have found time to read two of my opinions delivered the week after Christmas. One is relation to Confederate money, and a *de facto* government; and the other had reference to the unlawful sale of a gun, and *bellegerent* rights.[1] Right or wrong they produced a commotion in the Camp when they were delivered. The Court room was almost full of rebel lawyers, but all appear now to acquiese in them. Several of the older lawyers here—such as Houston, Fogg[2] and others have told me they had advocated a different doctrine before Trigg, but they did not believe it was the law when they were advocating it. Fogg is sincere, Houston isent. At all events the two opinions broke up a very well laid scheme to justify every thing under a *de facto* government, and *belleger-ent* rights, in which he was involved. On the whole, I believe I have done some good here, both for the State, and I hope for myself. At all events, whatever I have found to do, I have done it *the best I could*, without stint in labor or pains.

We will not get through before early in February. I am really worn out. I hope you will have a pleasant winter, but I fear you may have trouble.

Sam Milligan

ALS, DLC-JP.

1. One of the cases heard on appeal by the state supreme court found Judge Milligan ruling that the Confederate government was not a legal entity and therefore its money could not be recognized as legal. In the second case Milligan declared that an individual who had sold a gun to Confederate officers could not recover its cost, since the gun had been furnished for an unlawful purpose. Brief details of both decisions are found in the *Nashville Dispatch* of January 4 and 5, 1866.

2. Russell Houston and Francis B. Fogg.

From Jonathan Worth

Raleigh, Jan. 10 1866

Sir

The pressure of other duties has hitherto prevented me from assuring you of the Universal joy of the people of this State at the almost complete restoration of civil government to us. We think the generosity & magnanimity you have exhibited towards the South were at the same time conducive to the best interests of the whole nation: and hence the people of this State, as well those lately in arms against the United

States, as those who were not, support your administration with equal cordiality.

In these feelings & sentiments I fully concur; and I invite your confidence, assuring you of my readiness and desire to co-operate with you in all your plans tending to the complete restoration of the Union on terms compatible with the honor & prosperity of all its parts—and in all other measures looking to the common good of our Country.

The Genl. Assembly of this State will meet on the 18th instant.

Jonathan Worth—Govr. of N C

ALS, Nc-Ar, Andrew Johnson Papers.

From George C. Abbott

January 11, 1866, Hempstead, Tex.; DNA-RG105, Records of the Commr., Lets. Recd. (M752, Roll 23).

The sub-assistant commissioner at Hempstead asks to be relieved from duty with the Freedmen's Bureau because "I do not feel that I can do impartial justice in my present office under the existing circumstances." The Texans are "truly penitent" and "peaceably disposed," but "I have observed a spirit manifested in some of [the Bureau's] officers here which if persisted in will give rise to more bitterness of feeling amongst the citizens." Gen. Edward M. Gregory, commander of the Bureau in Texas, has required whites, "under pain of imprisonment," to pay blacks only in specie because the "poor ignorant creatures" expect it. Abbott points out that he is paid in "Greenbacks," adding, "I do not think it right that Ignorance should command such a heavy premium." Too, when he refused to surrender a black youth to a freedwoman who claimed to be his mother, preferring instead to submit the case to a civil court, Gregory overruled him and sent the youth to his son's plantation. When confronted, Gregory insisted that the woman was the youth's mother, despite the denial of the latter and the "sworn evidence of respectable citizens" that she was not. Abbott also reports that when he asked Gregory what to do if a black refused to honor his labor agreement, the General replied, "Break the contract." But when he inquired about recalcitrant whites he was told to use "soldiers to force them to it." In conclusion, he avers, "I and my kin have been hunted Refugees, so you can Judge whether I would be likely to be oversensitive in regard to the treatment of Rebels." [This letter was forwarded to General Gregory, whose March 19, 1866, endorsement defended his decisions and concluded, "The writer of this communication made an application on the 16th day of January last to be relieved from duty in this Dept., pleading his incompetency as an excuse. Agreeing with his judgment of himself I relieved him as soon as possible."]

From Washington Barrow

Nashville   January 11" 1866

Sir:

I hope I may be excused for trespassing briefly on your valuable time. If the matter were of a purely personal nature I should not do so.

I learn, through my friend General Dix[1] of New York, and also from the Hon Mr. Colyar[2] of this State who was lately in Washington city, that my application for pardon forwarded to the proper officer last fall, was duly received, and has been favorably acted on.[3] From the latter, I also learn that it has been deemed proper by you, for reasons of a public character to withold its issuance for the present.[4]

I am frank to say, Mr President, that the condition of my private affairs demanding my attention, would be not little promoted, if I were placed again in proper relationship with the government; and this fact, in my present debilitated state of health, has made me solicitous to regain, at as early a day as was possible, such an attitude; but the object of this letter is to assure you that I am grateful for the favorable view you have taken of my application; and, that relying upon your judgment, and sympathizing with you in your arduous labor of restoring peace and permanency to the government, I desire to say, that I am content to bide the time when you may think proper to confer it, and am willing to make any personal sacrifice, which will contribute in the least to give you support and encouragement in the great task you have been called to fulfill.

May I be permitted to say, Sir, that it has been our fortune to differ on matters of public policy all through our lives—alike in the political contests preceding the late unfortunate strife, and perhaps still more widely in that issue—but that every consideration of duty to the country and to posterity, requires that I should yield my support to the liberal, comprehensive, and truly statesmanlike policy of your Administration. I feel it to be proper to say this much to you, and that I shall so act, without desire of favor, fee or reward, and whatever may be the fate which awaits me.

Sincerely wishing you health, and success which shall redound to your own honor, and the prosperity of the country, I subscribe myself. . . .

Washington Barrow

LS, DNA-RG94, Amnesty Papers (M1003, Roll 48), Tenn., Washington Barrow.

1. John A. Dix wrote to Johnson on two different occasions in behalf of Barrow's pardon. In the second communication Dix enclosed this letter. Dix to Johnson, Oct. 2, 1865, Jan. 17, 1866, Amnesty Papers (M1003, Roll 48), Tenn., Washington Barrow, RG94, NA.

2. Arthur S. Colyar, a former Confederate congressman.

3. Barrow first petitioned for a presidential pardon on September 15, 1865; his request was supported by letters from a number of prominent persons, including William G. Brownlow, Edward H. East, and Neill S. Brown. He was pardoned by Johnson on October 6, 1865. Amnesty Papers (M1003, Roll 48), Tenn., Washington Barrow, RG94, NA; *House Ex. Docs.*, 39 Cong., 2 Sess., No. 116, p. 33 (Ser. 1293).

4. We have been unable to determine the reasons why Johnson delayed forwarding Barrow's pardon or when it was eventually sent to him.

From Henry Bergh[1]

New York   January 11, 1866

Sir

A subject which has long engaged my attention: namely the founding of a Society for the *Prevention of Cruelty to Animals* is now about to be realized, through the co-operation of some of the leading men and women of our great city of new York.

During nearly 40 years, the parent Society, as it may be called, located in London[2] has accomplished an amount of moral good for its citizens, as well as physical exemption from suffering and torture on the part of the lower Animals, that is not susceptible of human computation.

The Queen of Great Britain is at the head of that Institution, and the most distinguished of the Aristocracy, male and female constitute its patrons and patronesses.

We desire to create a similar Society and make it National.

My object in addressing your Excellency is to solicit the influence and support which your honored name—so identified with the peace and prosperity of our common country, would impart to this merciful design.

May we not also count upon the patronage of the ladies of your Excellency's household?[3]

Your Excellency will perceive by the inclosed card, that I have been invited by one of our most enlightened Institutions to deliver an address before it, upon this subject.[4]

A letter from your Excellency, expressive of your sympathy with this cause, which might serve as an example to our citizens generally, would be of incalculable advantage.[5]

Henry Bergh   late U.S. Secretary of Legation in Russia

ALS, DNA-RG59, Misc. Lets., 1789–1906 (M179, Roll 232).

1. Bergh (1823–1888), a persistent advocate for the humane treatment of animals, also founded a society for the prevention of cruelty to children. *NCAB*, 3: 106.

2. The Royal Society for the Prevention of Cruelty to Animals.

3. No participation in Bergh's proposed society by the ladies of the White House is known.

4. The card indicated that on February 8, 1866, Bergh was to read a paper in New York City before the American Geographical and Statistical Society with the view of creating a society for the protection of animals. Misc. Lets., 1789–1906 (M179, Roll 232), RG59, NA. For a synopsis of his address see *New York Tribune*, Feb. 9, 1866.

5. Johnson referred Bergh's letter to the Secretary of State.

From Burton C. Cook[1]

Washington, D.C.   Jany 11th 1866

Dear Sir

I have the honor to transmit to you a memorial adopted by a very large and respectable convention of farmers of Illinois assembled at Bloomington Dec 15th 1865.[2]

Permit me to say that the prosperity of the State and its ability to bear its share of the public burdens depends to a great extent upon the ability of the farmers to send their surplus products to the seaboard. The avenues of transportation are now so limited that the price of freight is fixed by the dearest route, and it costs the price of three bushels of corn to send one bushel to the market.

B. C. Cook

ALS, DNA-RG59, Misc. Lets., 1789–1906 (M179, Roll 232).

1. Cook (1819–1894), an attorney, state senator, and Republican congressman (1865–71), had nominated Lincoln for president in 1864. *BDAC*.

2. The memorial asked that "negotiations may be opened with the British Government to acquire the free use of the St. Lawrence River and also the use—at a moderate rate of toll—of such canals in the Canadian Provinces as may facilitate the transportation of produce to the ocean." When the reciprocity treaty guaranteeing free trade on the St. Lawrence expired in March 1866, however, Seward did not support its renewal. A subsequent agreement was not negotiated during Johnson's presidency, perhaps because the Canadian government permitted free use of the river without a formal agreement. Arthur Bryant to Johnson, n.d., Misc. Lets., 1789–1906 (M179, Roll 232), RG59, NA; *House Ex. Docs.*, 40 Cong., 2 Sess., No. 240, pp. 2, 4, 9–10 (Ser. 1341); Glyndon G. Van Deusen, *William Henry Seward* (New York, 1967), 536.

From Henry Addison[1]

Grgeton D.C.   January 12th 1866

Sir

I have been instructed by the Alderman and Common Council of this Town to respectfully inform you that our voters were requested to attend the Polls at the Election Precincts on the 28th of December last and to express by their ballots their sentiments upon the subject of the proposed extension of the right of suffrage to our colored population.

The Election was duly held on that day, and the Judges reported that Eight hundred and thirteen votes had been cast—that Eight hundred and twelve were in opposition to the proposed extension and one in favor of it.

I am, also, directed to state that the average vote at the four preceding annual elections for members of our City Government was five hundred and forty one being two hundred and seventy less votes than were polled on the 28th ultimo.[2]

Henry Addissen[*sic*]   Mayor

ALS, DLC-JP.

1. Addison (1798–1870), a merchant born in Maryland, served as mayor of Georgetown for twenty-two years. *NUC*; *Washington Evening Star*, Jan. 4, 1870.

2. The turnout was also unusually large in Washington, where 6,556 voters opposed
black suffrage and only thirty-five favored it. *Senate Journal*, 39 Cong., 2 Sess., p. 64
(Ser. 1275). For further developments regarding black suffrage in the District of Columbia, see Lewis D. Campbell to Johnson, Jan. 19, 1866.

From James W. Bradbury

January 12, 1866, Augusta, Me.; ALS, DLC-JP.

An old "Congressional acquaintance," a former senator, writes to extend his
"warm congratulations, and *hearty thanks* for your *excellent message,"* adding
that "Whatever may be the *apparent* sentiment, as coming from mere politicians, the vast majority of the people, the thinking masses are *with you* in your
policy of restoration." He concludes that war, "the highest human tribunal,"
has pronounced secession treasonous, and that now "the land yearns for peace,
and quiet, and a return of business relations."

To Mary Todd Lincoln

Washington, January 12, 1866.

Madam,

Pursuant to the request of CONGRESS therein contained, I have the
honor to transmit a copy of the Resolutions of that Body, of the 18th of
last month, passed upon the occasion of the violent and tragic death of
ABRAHAM LINCOLN, late President of the United States.[1]

In accordance with the further request contained in the Resolutions,
I also have the honor to assure you of the profound sympathy of the two
Houses of Congress, for your deep personal affliction, and of their sin-
cere condolence for the late national bereavement.

Andrew Johnson

LS, ICU.

1. The joint resolution announced that on February 12, 1866, both houses of Congress, the President, members of the cabinet, representatives of foreign governments, and
various army and navy officers would assemble to hear "an address upon the life and
character of Abraham Lincoln." *Congressional Globe*, 39 Cong., 1 Sess., pp. 67, 71.

Message re Admission of Colorado

Washington, January 12, 1866.

To the Senate and House of Representatives:

I transmit herewith a communication addressed to me by Messrs.
John Evans[1] and J. B. Chaffee,[2] as "United States senators elected from
the State of Colorado," together with the accompanying documents.

Under authority of the act of Congress approved the 21st day of

March, 1864, the people of Colorado, through a convention, formed a constitution making provision for a State government, which, when submitted to the qualified voters of the Territory, was rejected. In the summer of 1865, a second convention was called by the executive committees of the several political parties in the Territory, which assembled at Denver on the 8th of August, 1865. On the 12th of that month this convention adopted a State constitution, which was submitted to the people on the 5th of September, 1865, and ratified by a majority of 155 of the qualified voters. The proceedings in the second instance for the formation of a State government having differed in time and mode from those specified in the act of March 21, 1864, I have declined to issue the proclamation for which provision is made in the fifth section of the law, and therefore submit the question for the consideration and further action of Congress.[3]

Andrew Johnson.

Senate Ex. Docs., 39 Cong., 1 Sess., No. 10, p. 1 (Ser. 1237).

1. A physician, reformer, and railroad developer who helped establish two universities, Evans (1814–1897) had served as territorial governor of Colorado (1862–65). *DAB.*

2. Jerome B. Chaffee (1825–1886), a prosperous mine operator and president of a Denver bank, had been elected to the Colorado legislature in 1861 and 1863. *History of Colorado* (5 vols., Denver, 1927), 5: 419–20.

3. Congress approved the Colorado statehood bill in May 1866, but Johnson promptly vetoed it, objecting to the territory's small population, the lack of strong support for admission, and the irregularity of holding a second referendum on the issue. Allegedly Johnson was also angry that Evans and Chaffee would not sign an agreement to support his policies if allowed to take their seats as senators. Chaffee did later serve as Colorado's congressional delegate (1871–75) and senator (1876–79). Berwanger, *West and Reconstruction*, 66–68; *BDAC*; *Senate Ex. Docs.*, 39 Cong., 1 Sess., No. 45, pp. 1–4 (Ser. 1238).

From Benjamin Rawls[1]
Private

Columbia So. Ca.   Jany. 12th 1866.

Dear Sir

I address this second letter[2] to your Excellency, to inform you that, in reply to my first, I received answer from the War department, by your order (as I suppose) that Congress alone could give me relief for my property which was destroyed by the U.S. Army under General Sherman in this City.[3] The petition and Memmorial herewith transmitted to you was intended to be sent to the two senators elected for this state, viz, Honl. B. F. Perry & Honl. John L. Manning, Both of whom know me personally. But I learn from the News papers, that there is so much opposition to their admission in Congress, that it is uncertain whether they will be let in this session or not. I am now in the ninety-fourth year of my age and out of House, or Home, or Money to get either. Some of my freinds are in the same state of destitution, but are young and able to work. If I was only fifty, or even sixty years old, I could reinstate myself. But my time can not be very much longer in this world and if I am to get any help I wish to know it as early as possible, and also if I am to get none, as a state of susspence is very disagreeable to the mind, and especially, to a person of my age. The so called Radical party in Congress appear to be trying to make themselves a Root of bitterness to the people of the south who desire to return to the fold of the union again, from which they, either foolishly, or wickedly, straggled, by the act of secession. But thanks be to Almighty God, who by His Wisom and inscrutible providence placed your Excellency over the United States to check the evil designs of the destroying spirit of those puritanical fanatics who are not satisfied with the destruction of all that the south possessed, but like Satan said about Job, "all that a man has will he give for his life."[4] Surely those people never say "Forgive us our trespasses as we forgive them that trespass against us."

At all events however, I feel confident that God will enable you to carry out your plan of restoring the refractory states their original standing in the union, and establish peace, Harmony and Freindship, throughout the United States.

In the absence of our Senators elect in their places, I humbly request you to have the enclosed papers sent to the Senate and House of Representatives,[5] And you will confer a great favor on an old helpless Freind to the union of United States.

Benj Rawls

ALS, DNA-RG107, Lets. Recd., Executive (M494, Roll 74).

1. Rawls (1772–1866), a longtime Columbia resident and watchmaker, had been postmaster in the 1830s. Rawls to Johnson, Aug. 24, 1865, Lets. Recd., Executive (M494, Roll 74), NA; 1860 Census, S.C., Richland, Columbia, 61; *Augusta Constitutionalist*, May 13, 1866.

2. An earlier letter outlined Rawls's unionism from the nullification crisis forward and his losses at Columbia. Rawls to Johnson, Aug. 24, 1865, Lets. Recd., Executive (M494, Roll 74), RG107, NA.

3. Acting War Department head Thomas T. Eckert had so informed Rawls on September 20, 1865. Ibid.

4. Job 2: 4.

5. Rawls's appeal to Congress again alluded to his unionism and enumerated his losses: a "good Brick-House" and other property worth altogether $10,000. On March 12, 1866, after reading a letter from Gen. William T. Sherman denying responsibility for burning Columbia, Senator John Sherman presented Rawls's petition, declaring he did not think it should be granted but should "receive a respectful hearing." On March 30, Rawls wrote a sharp rejoinder to General Sherman, continuing to hold him responsible for the destruction of Columbia. The case ended when Rawls died early in May. Rawls to the U.S. Senate and House of Representatives, Dec. 1865, Lets. Recd., Executive (M494, Roll 74), RG107, NA; *Congressional Globe*, 39 Cong., 1 Sess., p. 1320; *Augusta Constitutionalist*, Apr. 11, May 13, 1866.

From Albert Q. Withers

January 12, 1866, Holly Springs, Miss.; ALS, DNA-RG56, Appts., Internal
Revenue Service, Collector, Miss., 3rd Dist., A. Q. Withers.

A former state representative, "reduced from affluance to Want by the ravages
of the late War," applies for a federal appointment. Although he was of the
"moderate Whig school" and "Reprobated Sesession," after the "Voice of the
People decided" the issue, "no one did more in aid of the South for their means
& ability." Living at a strategic crossroad, he suffered from the depredations of
both armies. Confederates burned 365 bales of his cotton, "besides many other
damages only known to me." On March 22, 1864, in retaliation for a Confederate raid, Union troops killed or took all of his livestock, destroyed his crops,
and burned his and his late father's residences along with the furnishings and
outbuildings. He believes he has committed "no wrongs to my government"
but finds it "truly humbling & humiliating" to be reduced to begging for a
position when "men doubly Traitors" who led the South into war are "Now
millionars by theft artifice & corruption." [He received no appointment.]

From Davidson M. Leatherman

Memphis Tenn.   Jany 13", 1866

In this region—above & below this point capital & labor are begining to develope their true relation—and I am happy to inform you,
since the hollidays are passed, and the New Year has opened upon our
land, with its coming Events, Negroes & the Freedmens Bureau are
promising in the future more than heretofore.[1] The many false & su-
perstitious impressions of Negroes not being realized they are becoming willing to go with the planter who owns the lands, and labor for
wages. These facts are confirmed by planters & farmers in this portion
of the South, whom I have seen.

If the policy of the Freedmens Bureau would inaugurate a degree of
force necessary to compel the Negro to keep his contract in good faith
this year, the next year in my judgement would be an easy going
thing—and the Freedmens Bureau would be a success & a self-sustain-
ing institution, to the End & extent of taking care & providing, for the
old, the infirm & children.

We have Elected Mr Saml. P. Walker to the Legislature from this
county, because of his known position in connection with your policy.
He desired me to say to you on the day he left for Nashville, that he
was your unyeilding friend, and would stand by & labor upon principle
for the success of your policy.

All here now are feeling happy at the success at the same over all
efforts of radicals to the contrary.

May health & life be yours until you witness the final & complete
success of the principles of your great message.

D M Leatherman

ALS, DLC-JP.
1. See Leatherman to Johnson, Dec. 10, 1865, for other observations about blacks and the Freedmen's Bureau.

From Representatives of "Disloyal" Indians [1]

Washington D.C.   Jan. 13. 1866

The undersigned, representatives of those Indians called, "disloyal," not wishing to shelter themselves and their people from the consequences of their participation in the late rebellion, under the paltry and untrue excuse of undue influence, of officers or citizens of the United States, respecfully represent.

That the treaties made by the several Nations they represent, with the so-called Confederate States, were made in good faith, freely, voluntarily and with a full and deliberate conviction that their best interests demanded such treaties; and that they were not induced by the machinations of any persons whatever to ally themselves with the rebellion.

We may have acted "*perfidiously*" towards the United States, as we are charged to have done; we are too weak and impotent to argue that question with any prospect of benefit, but we are manly enough to scorn the miserable plea of compulsion, or undue influence on the part of any of the officers or agents of the so-called Confederate States.

We deem the above statement due several gentlemen, who now suffer under the unjust imputation of having led us astray from our "allegiance" to the U.S.

We repudiated publicly at the Grand Council at Fort Smith last September,[2] the declaration in the preamble of the preliminary treaty made there, that we were induced by the evil counsel and machinations of designing men to form treaties with the so-called Confederate States.

We respectfully request your Excellency to grant a speedy pardon to Genl Albert Pike, Genl. Douglas H. Cooper and Elias Rector[3]—all of whom in their relations with the Indians before, and since the war, have manifested a kind, and attentive consideration for our wants and interests, which we duly appreciate, and shall never forget.

Elias Rector, so far as we know, had no office under the rebellion, connected with Indian affairs, and is not responsible in any respect for the course our several Nations have taken; we take pleasure in testifying that in his connection with our affairs he has always borne himself as a faithful and just officer, and a kind and generous friend of the Indian.

We again ask your Excellency to grant him a speedy pardon.

ALS (Boudinot), DNA-RG94, Amnesty Papers (M1003, Roll 14), Ark., Elias Rector.
1. This document was signed by twelve delegates, from the pro-Confederate factions of the southern tribes, to a peace conference held in the capital: Elias C. Boudinot and William P. Adair for the Cherokee; John F. Brown for the Seminole; John Page, Robert

M. Jones, James Riley, and Alfred Wade for the Choctaw; and Holmes Colbert, Colbert Carter, Winchester Colbert, and Edmund Pickens for the Chickasaw. Annie H. Abel, *The American Indian Under Reconstruction* (Cleveland, Oh., 1925), 301–63 passim.

2. United States commissioners had met with delegates from the southern tribes who had signed treaties with the Confederacy. Although most of the Indians present represented factions that had not supported the Confederates, all were compelled to sign new declarations of allegiance to the United States. Ibid., 173–218.

3. Pike was pardoned on April 23, 1866, and Cooper four days later. Rector (1802–1878), a former U.S. marshal and superintendent of Indian affairs for the southern tribes, submitted on his own behalf a petition accompanied by a letter of recommendation from Gov. Isaac Murphy of Arkansas. He was pardoned on Jan. 29, 1866. Goodspeed's *History of Benton, Washington, Carroll, Madison, Crawford, Franklin, and Sebastian Counties, Arkansas* (Chicago, 1889), 735–36; Rector to Johnson, n.d.; Murphy to Johnson, Dec. 28, 1865, Amnesty Papers (M1003, Roll 14), Ark., Elias Rector, RG94, NA. See Pike to Johnson, June 24, 1865, *Johnson Papers*, 8: 287. See also Cooper to Johnson, ca. Dec. 1865.

From David S. Walker

January 13, 1866, Tallahassee, Fla.; LS, DLC-JP.

Walker forwards resolutions adopted by the Florida General Assembly expressing concern that the Freedmen's Bureau has "not been conducted with good judgment or economy" and alarm that its agents have led freedmen to believe that "the lands of their former owners, will, at least in part be divided among them," the latter expectation having "seriously" interfered with making contracts. The resolutions recommend the adoption of the plan submitted by Lt. Gen. Grant to Johnson on December 18, 1865, calling for U.S. Army officers to act as Bureau agents, thereby eliminating duplication between army and Bureau personnel, and relieving "from duty and pay a large number of employees of the Government."

From George Bancroft

New York   Jan' 14, 1866.

My dear Sir,

The London Saturday Review is one of the ablest papers in England. The enclosed extract from it is, if you have time, worth perusal.[1] It shows that you in your message, made exactly the point, which the English cannot answer.

You may have seen the extract which I enclose from La Presse, one of the chief papers of Paris.[2] What is said of the influence of the Message in favor of democracy in Europe is undoubtedly true. Your enunciation of our success in restoring the republic gives immense strength to the cause of liberty in the Old World.[3]

Geo. Bancroft

ALS, DLC-JP.
1. Not found; but *The London Review of Politics, Society, Literature, Art, & Science* of December 23, 1865, referred to Johnson's message as "calm, moderate, and statesmanlike."

2. Not found. *La Presse* editorialized that Johnson explained "with great logical force, that the late events . . . have only added new guarantees of preservation and of progress to the Republic of the United States." The message was called "a chef d'oeuvre of intelligence, of moderation, of wisdom. We do not believe that there is in Europe a statesman capable of writing a more complete or more remarkable programme of governmental science, or who could give a more elevated lesson to the governing and the governed." Clipping, n.d., Ser. 11, Vol. 1: 26, Johnson Papers, LC.

3. Six days earlier Bancroft had forwarded clippings from "three very leading journals" published in France, asserting that "All the liberal press in France will sustain & second your wish for the evacuation of Mexico by the French." Bancroft to Johnson, Jan. 8, 1866, Johnson Papers, LC.

From Virginia C. Clay

4 1/2 & G. streets
Washington   Jany 14th/66.

Dear Mr Johnson,

Mental distress has made me almost ill.[1] I am so nervous & unhappy I cannot leave the house for Church & fear I may not be able to see you this evening. I will however beg to avail myself of the proffered privilege of an interview *tomorrow* evening at 7 o'clk when I trust in God you will have resolved for Mercy's sake the sake of Justice & Right my husband's sake, his father's, *yours*, & lastly, not leastly *mine*, to yield the *Parole*, & send Mr. Clay to his unhappy Parent![2] *I* will bring him to you, & then return with him to you, whenever ordered. I trust you will really enjoy a *rest day* this Sabbath, & even under all the fearfully responsible cares & duties of President, feel a lighter & happier heart in yr. bosom then.

V. C. Clay

I will bring you some interesting letters of *yourself* to read, an eloquently approving voice from the "Far West."

V.C.C.

Tomorrow will be my birth-day. Will you not memorize by the precious gift of *Parole*? I know you will![3]

ALS, DLC-JP.

1. A few days earlier Mrs. Clay had been grief-stricken after word reached her concerning the death of her mother-in-law and had subsequently written an appeal for her husband's release from prison. Virginia C. Clay to Johnson, Jan. 11, 1866, Johnson Papers, LC.

2. Clement Comer Clay (1789–1866), former governor of Alabama and U.S. Senator, had himself been arrested by federal authorities. *DAB*.

3. Although Mrs. Clay had several interviews with Johnson, she did not obtain the objective she so fervently desired until April 1866. Nuermberger, *Clays*, 280, 281, 290, 292–93.

From Jonathan Worth

Raleigh N C   Jany 14th 1866

We have no law authorizing the Attorney General[1] to give opinions to executive officers. He has given no opinion on the convention revenue law so far as I know. B. F. Moore a distinguished lawyer on application of State Treasurer[2] gave an opinion that some of the provisions of the ordinance are unconstitutional. This opinion will not protect the Treasurer or sheriffs in stopping collections. Our Judges now qualified can protect tax payers by injunctions, or tax payers can pay under protest to bring action in the civil courts. Can relieve if the ordinance be unconstitutional.[3]

Jonathan Worth   Govr of N C

Tel, DLC-JP.
1. Sion H. Rogers.
2. Either William B. Sloan, the provisional treasurer, or Kemp P. Battle, the state's treasurer as of January 1, 1866. Battle (1831–1919) later served as university president and professor of history at the University of North Carolina. Battle, *Old-Time Tar Heel*, 163, 204, 281–96.
3. Responding to several protests, Gen. Thomas H. Ruger, commander of the Department of North Carolina, ordered the sheriff of Craven County to refrain from enforcing the convention's ordinance, which in turn led Governor Worth to complain of military interference. In its spring term the Craven superior court convicted several merchants for refusing to pay their taxes but their convictions were eventually overturned upon appeal to the state supreme court. Hamilton, *Worth Correspondence*, 1: 489–91; *Raleigh Standard*, Jan. 29, 1866; *North Carolina Reports*, 61: 24–26.

From the Alabama Legislature

January 16, 1866, Montgomery, Ala.; Mem, DLC-JP.

Asserting the "manifested" loyalty of the people of Alabama, their "determination to preserve peace, maintain order, and to enforce the execution of the laws," and the assembly's "like determination to provide for the wants of the freedmen . . . and to protect them in the enjoyment of their constitutional rights," the legislature argues that "Alabama can be entrusted with the execution of the laws, the protection of her population and the management of her own internal affairs." Therefore, they request the withdrawal of Federal troops, whose "continued presence . . . is a constant source of irritation to the people." They point out the problem of subsisting the troops "in consequence of an unprecedented scarcity of provisions," and the adverse influence of the troops, especially "the colored portions of them" on the freedmen, leading them to "cherish the belief that their idleness, violation of contracts and insubordination" will be condoned. Under the circumstances "the evils and horrors of domestic insurrection may be resonably anticipated." Moreover, there are now militia companies in each county to aid the civil authorities in preserving peace and order. Such companies would be available to the Freedmen's Bureau "to enforce their rules and orders when necessary."

From Caleb Lyon

Boise City   Idaho Territory.
January 16th 1866.

I have the honor to transmit the enclosed Resolutions passed unanimously by the Legislature of the Territory of Idaho,[1] and it gives me great pleasure to assure you that, not only the Legislature, but the people of Idaho, sincerely endorse the principles of your "reconstruction policy" and entire administration.[2]

Caleb Lyon of Lyonsdale   The Governor of Idaho.

LS, DLC-JP.

1. On January 12, 1866, the legislators had not only commended Johnson for "his efforts to restore the Union of our Fathers," but also added that they were "well satisfied" with Lyon and had "full reliance in his integrity, ability, and energy." Several years earlier Lyon had clashed often with the Democratic majority in the legislature and in December 1864 had fled the territory for eleven months. Johnson replaced Lyon with David W. Ballard on April 10, 1866. Johnson Papers, LC; McMullin and Walker, *Territorial Governors*, 127–29.

2. The last three words of this sentence are written in Lyon's hand.

From Sam Milligan

Nashville Ten   January 16, 1865[1866][1]

Sir:

Before this reaches you, you will have seen a memorial addressed to you, and one to the re-construction committee.[2] They were, I have no doubt, prepaired by Andrew Jackson Fletcher Esq., and may be looked upon, not as his eminations, but as the higher authority in the State—W.G.B.,[3] who I fear has been moved and instigated by the Hon H. M.[4] I have but little leisure to mix with any part of the population, except the lawyers; and unless they grossly misrepresent the facts, these memorials do not represent the true state of things in Tennessee. As a rule the people are quiet, and disposed to attend to their domestic affairs, and to obey the laws. Here & there, and now & then, a disperado, or a drunken man, says an improper thing, or does an evil deed, but these things are the exception to the rule, rather than the rule itself.

The fact is, there are a few men in the State, in order to perpetuate their own power, are anxious to see military rule continued for the balance of their days in Tennessee; and they are under false professions, doing all in their power, to defeat the admission of the Tennessee delegation to their seats.

The people of the State do not sympathise with them, and they will manifest that want of sympathy whenever they get a chance.

I do not want to get mixed up with politics, and therefore ask you to regard this as confidential; but you may feel assured, your support by the men I have referred to, is hollow, and unreliable.

I am getting a long in court as well as a man could expect, with a dead snake hanging around his neck. We will not adjourn before early in February. I am worked down, but well.

Sam Milligan

P.S. I think the Legislature will pass the negro testimony Bill. I have done all I could to secure its passage.

ALS, DLC-JP.
1. Internal evidence clearly indicates that Milligan misdated his letter; it is in fact an 1866 document.
2. See Central Committee of the Union Party of Tennessee to Johnson, ca. Jan. 9, 1866.
3. William G. Brownlow.
4. Horace Maynard.

From Robert J. Powell

Washington, D.C.   17th of Jany. 1866.

To the President:

In accordance with your request of Monday, I copy below that portion of Gov. Holden's letter which I read to you on that occasion.

Please say to the President that the representations by citizens of Beaufort of outrages by negro troops, are no doubt true.[1] The memorialists are persons for the most part known to me. They are incapable of misstating the facts. As a rule the policy of confining colored troops to their Forts is a good one but Fort Macon is an exception. We think it is within two miles of Beaufort and Moreland City and comes near to both places. One company of white regulars would be ample for both places.[2]

R. J. Powell

ALS, DNA-RG108, Lets. Recd. *re* Military Discipline.
1. For a synopsis of these depredations, see *Raleigh Standard*, Jan. 5, 1866.
2. Under Gen. Thomas H. Ruger's direction the number of black troops was reduced until, by March 1866, only a single black regiment remained in the Carolinas. Roberta S. Alexander, *North Carolina Faces the Freedmen* (Durham, N.C., 1985), 9.

From Edwin R. Meade[1]

63 Wall Street   New York
January 18, 1866

Honored Sir,

I beg you will pardon my presumption in making the suggestions I do in regard to the important matter of the appointment of Collector for this port. If they shall be found to contain merit it is on that account alone that I expect they will receive your consideration.

Of the names I have observed mentioned in connection with this appointment, that of Hon. Daniel S. Dickinson[2] strikes me as most appropriate and my reasons for the preference are:

In the first place his freedom from local factions.

The great bane in New York politics has always been the prevalence of factions which have had their origin in individual ambition or else been controlled to that purpose. These factions have for the most part arisen in this city and have existed to a greater or less extent in all parties but have been for the time being more strongly developed in the dominant one. It cannot have escaped your observation that such factions now exist here in the Union party which threaten to destroy its efficiency in this State and which are characterised by so much acrimony that an appointment from either would result very much in retarding if not wholly staying the wholesome influence which the important office in question should exert over the general interests of the country. Mr. Dickinson has never been identified with either of these factions. In the Democratic party he was regarded as belonging to the Hard Shell organization but his connection with it was rather of accident than design, indeed his influence was ever exerted for harmony and was always sought as a rallying point when unity of action was desired.

In the second place, I regard that Mr. Dickinson's past and present political standing eminently fit him for the position. Your knowledge of him renders it I presume superfluous to speak of him as a National Democrat. In this State, he was regarded the foremost man among us though it is true combinations of less able though more unscrupulous men of the party were sometimes able to defeat the wishes of its masses to honor him. His frankness and consistency always gained him the respect of all parties. When the secession movement commenced he never doubted his course or hesitated in it. When both Republican and Democratic parties waited he boldly struck out and organised the Union movement which in six weeks from its inception carried the State with him at the head of its ticket by a majority unparalleled, being nearly 110000.[2] The questionable conduct of the Democratic organization caused his separation from it for while he went onward in the path of duty, those who sought and succeeded in misrepresenting that party fell off to the right and left to bring defeat and disgrace upon its time honored character but he never lost the confidence of his old friends and associates while he gained largely in the esteem of those with whom he was now for the first time brought in friendly contact. He maintains his position without abatement and I fully believe if a vote of confidence were to be taken upon him he would receive four fifths of all the suffrages in the State. The signs of the times point to a new organization composed of the conservative strength of the country. It appears to me therefore that the political history and character of the individual to receive the appointment of collector should be in harmony with the manifest sentiment of the country in respect to the new order of things.

A further reason for Mr. Dickinson's appointment is his extensive acquaintance and intimate knowledge of men and interests of the State. So long as the policy of change in appointments continues, an essential qualification in the office of collector here will be his ability to make judicious selection of subordinates which must naturally depend upon the extent and nature of his acquaintance. The area and diversity of interests of the State add force to this suggestion. A New York city man always fails at this point. Municipal politics are so absorbing that he seldom sees beyond; then, too, he has his ward or district preferences and prejudices which he carries into the collector's office and which prove his destruction. I do not believe it possible to find one with so extended an acquaintance with the men of the State and local interests therein as Mr. Dickinson, besides, he has always lived in the country, far enough to be aloof from local differences and near enough on account of his position in society and politics to be well known to the people here.

Again, Mr. Dickinson possesses the respect and confidence of the commercial classes of this city. As chairman of the Senate committee on Finance and from his professional and general business connections he is well known to our merchants and business men and it is doubtful if an appointment could be made which would be more universally popular with this large and influential body of our citizens.

It cannot be necessary to speak of Mr. Dickinson's great ability or his integrity which must be well known to you and to mention in fitting terms might give me the character of an eulogist. His industrious habits and physical capacity to endure the fatiguing duties of the office are considerations of a considerable account.

I will not trouble you with a further mention of my reasons for judging Mr. Dickinson the proper person to secure your warrant of confidence. I deem it my duty to add that this writing is without his knowledge or assent nor is he in any wise responsible for what may be my indiscretion. What I have done has been inspired by the best of motives and with the best wishes for the success of your administration and also from a friendly appreciation of the many virtues I find in the gentleman I have alluded to.

E. R. Meade

ALS, DNA-RG56, Appts., Customs Service, Collector, New York, Daniel S. Dickinson.

1. Edwin R. Meade (1836–1889), a New York City attorney, served as a Democrat in Congress (1875–77). New York City directories (1865–90); *BDAC*.

2. Dickinson was elected attorney general of New York on a "Union" ticket in 1861. *DAB*.

From John F. Miller
Private

San Francisco   Jan 18th 1866

Honoured Sir

Nothing of great moment has transpired on this Coast since my last to you[1] and knowing that your time is very greatly occupied I have refrained from writing you for some Weeks.

The political condition of this State has improved greatly in the last two months. The asperites of party cliques have in a great degree passed away. The result of the late Senatorial contest has been fortunate for the friends of the National administration and has done much to harmonise the conflicting elements of the Union party. Mr. Cole[2] is I believe a true friend to your policy of reconstruction and I think he fully and cordially endorses all the measures of your administration; at all events the people give you almost universally an earnest and cordial support. If it be true as reported by telegraph here that the California delegation in Congress have cast their fortunes with the opponents of your policy, they are unquestionably misrepresenting their constituency.[3] I have lately seen a letter however from Mr. Conness[4] in which he states that he gives your administration a cordial support. He moreover expresses perfect satisfaction with my appointment. Your message to Congress has been received here with great favor and both press and people have given it the warmest commendation. Distinguished men of all parties have declared it the ablest and most admirable State paper which has emanated from the Executive Department for very many years. As a friend you will pardon me for speaking plainly this important truth to you and at the same time I trust you will allow me to offer my heartfelt congratulations.

That part of your message relating to Mexican affairs was especially gratifying to the people of this Coast, whom you may have heard are very strongly in favor of the liberal party in that distracted Country.[5] Only one consideration permits the people from openly declaring themselves in favor of War against Maximillian whom they regard as an usurper, and that is the present condition of the National finances.

Your Excellency may have observed that expression has frequently been given to a growing sentiment amongst this people in favor of the appointment of a Cabinet Minister from their State or the Pacific Slope. Recently this project has been revived and I think from present indications that it may be pressed upon you with some vigor should there be a prospect of a change in your Cabinet. It would unquestionably be very gratifying to this people to have in the Cabinet a representative of their interests the greatest of which may be reckoned the Pacific Rail Way and the mining interest. I mention this matter more to acquaint your Excellency with the fact that such a sentiment exists than to give any opinion as to the policy or feasibility of such a recognition of the interests of the Pacific States and in this connection I deem it proper to say that some difficulty might be experienced in making a judicious selection from among the aspirants to so high a position.

With many thanks for the kindness which your Excellency has ever been pleased to show towards me and with the kindest wishes for your prosperity & happiness—and the success of your administration of public affairs. . . .

Jno. F. Miller

ALS, DLC-JP.
1. Following his arrival in San Francisco to assume the office of collector of customs, Miller had written two brief confidential reports on opposition in California to Johnson's administration. Miller to Johnson, Nov. 11, 17, 1865, Johnson Papers, LC.
2. Cornelius Cole (1822–1924), a New York native, emigrated to California in 1849. After mining gold for a year, he resumed his law practice and became an active Republican partisan, serving in the U.S. House (1863–65) and Senate (1867–73). *BDAC*.
3. If the California delegation was indeed ambivalent toward Johnson, many of their constituents became inflamed against him by his veto of the Freedmen's Bureau bill. Among his bitterest opponents was Cole, who wrote, "He is stopping the car of progress & trampling upon humanity." Miller recounted a speech by Cole against Johnson, adding, "I thought better of Cole than this." Berwanger, *West and Reconstruction*, 55, 59, 60, 69–70; Miller to McCulloch, Mar. 6, 1866, Johnson Papers, LC.
4. Senator John Conness of California.
5. In his address to Congress in December 1865, Johnson had admonished France, then supporting the regime of Ferdinand Maximilian in Mexico, to adhere to the doctrine of reciprocal "noninterference" between the European and American nations. See Message to Congress, Dec. 4, 1865.

From New Haven, Connecticut, Citizens

January 18, 1865, New Haven, Conn.; Mem, DLC-JP.

Declaring their support of Johnson and using the current deliberations of the *"Joint Committee of the two Houses on the Restoration of the insurgent States"* as the occasion for their memorial, twenty-five citizens set forth their views. While they "believe in the justice of impartial suffrage," of the whole free population, they concede that there are problems in applying this to the South and that "some appropriate change of the basis of Representation" may be necessary. They ask for measures "to protect the freedmen *in their civil rights and their equality before the law with other freemen*." They approve Johnson's contention that the Confederate debt be rejected, that the doctrine of secession be disavowed, and that "'Treason must be treated as a crime." Expressing concern that Congress and the President not "allow the nation's *credit*, or *faith*, or *life* to be imperrilled," they propose that the returning states be obliged to make "an unalterable compact with the Union." They regard as "the most critical of all" topics the *"stability of the national finances"* on which the President "has not yet found occasion to make any specific recommendation to Congress." They fear a minority in Congress may be successful in inducing "the concession of enormous and inequitable War claims, or failing in that, may break up financial quiet just when the return to a specie basis, and the transmutation or liquidation of accruing amounts of the Public Debt will make confidence, both abroad and at home, a prime necessity." Seeing such efforts as equivalent to treason, they urge Johnson to support a move in the Joint Committee to require meeting current expenses and retiring of the debt "by an equable taxation . . . in all States and Territories."

From Lewis D. Campbell
(*Private*)

Hamilton, O.   January 19th 1866.

My Dear Sir—

The heavy vote in the House of Reps. yesterday to impose *unrestricted negro suffrage* on the people of the District,[1] portends, in my opinion, the breaking up of the Union party, as at present organized. I am well satisfied that if such a proposition for Ohio were submitted to a vote of our people, it would be defeated *by a majority of at least one hundred thousand*. And our people will not approve a measure which fastens upon others a system which they will not themselves adopt. I predict therefore that not more than one or two of the members from this State who voted for that bill will be re-elected next fall.[2]

I regard the vote in the House as certain evidence that, whatever the professions of the members of your Cabinet, most of them have been lending their countenance to the support of this radical measure. If, on the contrary, they are zealous friends of your policy, is it not passing strange that you have not more outspoken and fearless advocates in the House? When I was in Washington, I had very satisfactory evidence that some members of your Cabinet were lending their influence to schemes that would greatly embarrass you in carrying out your policy of restoration. It was a delicate subject for me to mention to you *then*, and I feel that it is so *now*; and I do it only because I feel deeply interested in your success and the speedy return of an harmonious Union. If the question were now put to a vote of our people in Ohio, without identifying it with parties, *four fifths of them at least* would approve your policy. But if things go along as they have since Congress opened, and you retain the same council you have around you, controlling the Executive patronage to promote *their* views and not *yours*, I greatly fear the radicals will rapidly increase in power and strength. The developments that are now being made by *your radical opponents* are just those that I predicted in my letter to you last August. The Chase Sumner, Stanton radical influence will never heartily co-operate in the support of your policy, and the sooner you cut yourself loose from them the better for you and for the Country. To this complexion it must come at last and the longer your action is delayed the stronger will be their power to embarrass you. I venture these plain words as suggestive merely, and delicate as the subject is I give them to you for your consideration satisfied that you will at least regard me as sincere.

I should have visited you again ere this, but I see the Senate still holds that Mexican nomination under advisement.[3] As you certainly made it without any "coercion" on my part, and are responsible for it, I am too proud to go to Washington whilst it is pending and subject myself to the suspicion of desiring to *electioneer with the Senate*. Whenever they act on it, *pro* or *con*, I will go on and see you. If you wish me sooner, you will of course telegraph me. I have some suspicion that some of my radical friends(?) such as Mr. Sumner and others to whom I expressed myself very strongly and freely on the subject of their breaking ground against you, may have a design to degrade me by a refusal to confirm the nomination. I hope there may be no grounds for this suspicion; but I am satisfied they mean *war* with you sooner or later, and I shall not be disappointed if they evince a desire *to take my scalp*, as I have had some distinction for my activity in supporting you as well as in condemning their impracticable and suicidal policy.

Lewis D Campbell

P.S. All your real friends with whom I have conversed express the opinion that your policy of reconstructing the *Union* will never prove a success, until you reconstruct our Cabinet and make it a *unit*.

L D C.

ALS, DLC-JP.

1. In January 1866 the House passed a bill to permit blacks to vote in the District of Columbia despite the opposition of a majority of the voters there, but the Senate delayed consideration until after the fall elections. Johnson opposed the measure but it was eventually adopted over his veto in January 1867. Patrick W. Riddleberger, *1866: The Critical Year Revisited* (Carbondale, Ill., 1979), 168, 248–49. See Interview with James Dixon, Jan. 28, 1866.

2. Of sixteen Ohio Representatives who voted in favor of the bill, only Hezekia A. Bundy, who declined to be a candidate, failed to be reelected to Congress. *Congressional Globe*, 39 Cong., 1 Sess., p. 310; *BDAC*.

3. A reference to Johnson's appointment of Campbell as minister to the Benito Juarez government in Mexico. See Campbell to Johnson, Dec. 20, 1865.

To James Hughes

Washington, D.C., January 19th 1866

It is hoped that the necessity for the suspension of the writ of Habeas Corpus and the continuance of the troops in Kentucky will soon cease.[1]

It is believed that this will soon be the case and therepon the troops will be removed and the suspension of the writ of Habeas Corpus revoked.[2]

It is the earnest desire of the Goverment to take that course, that will be most satisfactory to the loyal people of Kentucky, and which will restore peace, harmony and good order throughout the state.

(sgd) Andrew Johnson

Tel, DNA-RG107, Tels. Sent, President, Vol. 3 (1865–68).

1. Two days earlier Hughes had wired the President that if troops were removed and the writ restored "the Conservative members of the Legislature & people of Kentucky will cheerfully endorse and support your administration." Hughes to Johnson, Jan. 17, 1866, Johnson Papers, LC. See also Lovell H. Rousseau to Johnson, Jan. 17, 1866, ibid.

2. After Johnson's April 2 proclamation declaring the rebellion over, and the Supreme Court's decision in *Ex Parte Milligan* the next day, several Kentuckians sent unanswered inquiries regarding the writ. It was not until May 1 that an executive order officially restored habeas corpus in the states where it was suspended. Meanwhile, in April, all volunteers in the Division of Tennessee, which included Kentucky, had been ordered to be mustered out. Fairman, *Reconstruction and Reunion*, 143–46; Edward McPherson, *The Political History of the United States of America During the Period of Reconstruction* (Washington, D.C., 1880), 17; Franklin, *Reconstruction*, 36; D. L. Price to Johnson, Apr. 3, 1866; J. D. Osborn et al. to Johnson, Apr. 25, 1866, Johnson Papers, LC.

To George H. Thomas

Washington, D.C.   Jan'y 19" 1866.

General:

The amnesty oath taken by Mr. John Overton, of Nashville, Tennessee, has been pleaded in Court, and all suits brought against his property, in consequence of his participation in the rebellion, have been dismissed. A pardon has also been issued in his case, which places him upon a footing with all other persons to whom pardons have been granted. I do not see how, under these circumstances, his property can be longer held by the United States, and therefore request that you will consider this communication as setting aside any special order which may have been given by the War Department in reference to Mr. Overton's property.[1]

Andrew Johnson.

LB copy, DLC-JP.

1. For a discussion of the controversy surrounding Overton's pardon, see Brownlow to Johnson, Nov. 20, 1865.

From Francis P. Blair, Jr.

St Louis   Jany 20, 1866

Sir:

I observe by the dispatches in the public Journals that Genl. John McNeil of St. Louis has been appointed surveyor of this Port.[1]

Genl. McNeil is one of those officers of the type of Ben Butler & Fremont,[2] who has sought to make character with the country by his extreme Radicalism and to cover his incapacity as a military man, by advocating measures which fall in with the excited passions of the multitude. He has generally had some station in Missouri where there was no organized force of the enemy to oppose him and made himself notorious by ordering a dozen men to be shot in cold blood & without trial or proof, because they lived in the neighborhood where some Bushwhackers had torn up the Railroad.[3] I understand that he gave the order for the execution of these persons upon the recommendation of one Strachan his Provost Marshall[4] who was subsequently convicted by a court martial upon the charge of having released one of the Prisoners who had been designated to be shot upon the intercession of his wife & on the condition that she prostituted herself to his brutal lusts.[5] Strachan was also found guilty at the same time of having swindled the Government and robbed the people of the District.[6] His conduct was notorious and well known to McNeil who nevertheless sustained him and carried out by his orders his murderous recommendations.

While these transactions were taking place in the North Eastern part of Missouri at a safe distance from any organized force of the enemy, our armies were pressing the rebel forces at the south and many of our brave soldiers on picket & scouting duty and many others by the fortunes of war were made prisoners while exposing themselves for the safety of our great armies and aiding to crush the rebellion. Many of these men were shot by the enemy in retaliation for the murder of these men by McNeil. I believe on my conscience that the perpetrators of the dastardly act of murder, are responsible for the killing of our prisoners in retaliation for these acts. You will recollect that the surrender of McNeil was demanded by the Confederate authorities (so called) and retribution threatened.[7] McNeils act was the beginning of those acts of atrocious murder which afterwards became so common, which embittered the war & disgraced my country.

This man is not a representative of your wise humane & enlightened policy, nor is he a representative of that lofty spirit of patriotism which characterizes the body of our officers & which induced them to expose their lives to maintain our Government and not to indulge in acts of barbarism. I hope that the report is untrue that you have given such a man a position which ought to be filled by some one among the thousands who have rendered real & substantial service to the Government.[8]

Frank P Blair

ALS, DNA-RG56, Appts., Customs Service, Collector, St. Louis, John McNeil.

1. Upon the recommendation of Secretary McCulloch, who wrote that McNeil was "strongly recommended by the Missouri delegation," Johnson had nominated McNeil to be surveyor of customs at St. Louis on January 15. McCulloch to Johnson, Jan. 9, 1866, Lets. Sent *re* Customs Service Employees (QC Ser.), Vol. 3, RG56, NA; Ser. 6B, Vol. 4: 315, Johnson Papers, LC.

2. Benjamin F. Butler and John C. Fremont.

3. After a Confederate detachment kidnapped a member of the provost guard at Palmyra, Mo., McNeil had ten prisoners executed there on October 18, 1862. Carl W. Breihan, *Quantrill and His Civil War Guerrillas* (Denver, 1959), 62–70; *OR*, Ser. 1, Vol. 22, Pt. 1: 816–18.

4. William R. Strachan (b. *c*1822), a farmer, legislator, and former U.S. deputy marshal, was a volunteer member of McNeil's staff who served as provost marshal at Palmyra.

1860 Census, Mo., Shelby, Clay Twp., 92; *OR*, Ser. 1, Vol. 22, Pt. 1: 260; Ser. 2, Vol. 1: 207; *St. Louis Missouri Democrat*, Aug. 3, 1864.

5. William T. Humphrey was spared after his wife Mary appealed to McNeil. Believing that her husband might be shot at a later date, Mary submitted to Strachan's demands in an effort to win his release. Breihan, *Quantrill*, 67–68, 70–71.

6. Strachan in 1864 was tried by a court martial on more than thirty charges but was convicted only on a single count of embezzlement, which was later dismissed by Gen. William S. Rosecrans. *St. Louis Missouri Democrat*, July 29, Aug. 3, 1864.

7. Jefferson Davis, upon receiving a newspaper report of the Palmyra affair, ordered Gen. Theophilus S. Holmes to execute the "first ten United States officers" he captured if McNeil were not turned over to him. After Gen. Samuel R. Curtis, commanding the Federal troops in Missouri, refused to surrender McNeil, Gen. E. Kirby Smith recommended to Richmond authorities in June 1863 that because so much time had elapsed since the "murders," plans for retaliation should be dropped. *OR*, Ser. 1, Vol. 22, Pt. 1: 816–19, 860–61, 879–80; Pt. 2: 307, 852.

8. Blair wrote to David T. Patterson as well, asking him to intercede against McNeil. Missouri congressmen John Hogan and Thomas E. Noell also protested the nomination of McNeil, who they both characterized as an ally of the Missouri Radicals opposed to Johnson. At the President's suggestion Noell asked Sen. John B. Henderson of Missouri to move for a postponement of McNeil's confirmation by the Senate so that Johnson could "take the matter under further advisement," but Henderson "peremptorily refused." The Senate confirmed McNeil as surveyor on January 26, 1866, but he was never commissioned in that office. Blair to "Judge," n.d. and Jan. 18, 1866; Hogan to Johnson, Jan. 22, 1866; Noell to Johnson, Jan. 25, 1866 (two letters), Appts., Customs Service, Collector, St. Louis, John McNeil, RG56, NA; Ser. 6B, Vol. 4: 315, Johnson Papers, LC.

From Charles A. Dana

Chicago   Jan. 20th 1866.

Dear Sir.

Some of my friends in the New York delegation in Congress want me to be Collector of New-York. I should be glad to have that office, and accordingly I address myself to you.

I have been a resident of New-York City for nearly twenty years, till a few months since, I came here on leaving the War Department. I know New-York, its merchants and its politicians. But, by reason of my connection with the War Department, I have been absent so as to be free from all identification with the political factions or personal controversies by which the Union party there has been much divided.

I believe there is no person of any prominence in the party whose appointment would give greater general satisfaction than mine. Should you be disposed so far to entertain the idea as to wish for information concerning my capacity to administer the office, there is no one who can judge better as to that than Mr Stanton. Let me add that I am myself confident of performing the duties, should they be entrusted to me, to the advantage of the public service, and to your entire satisfaction.[1]

Charles A. Dana.

Copy, Johnson-Bartlett Col.

1. After his application was rejected Dana, editor of the *Chicago Republican*, published several editorials excoriating Johnson. *Washington National Republican*, Mar. 16, 1866.

From Kitty G. Hill [1]

[Lexington, Ky., January 20, 1866] [2]

Your Petitioner Kitty G. Hill, respectfully representeth that she is the widow and administratrix of Ambrose P. Hill [3] a Lieutenant General in the Confederate Army, and natural guardian of three little children [4] of her deceased husband: that the estate of her husband was very nearly destroyed by the war, and the greater part of the available means he left for the support of her-self and their children is in such a condition as renders it perhaps impossible for her to obtain possession of it with-out a pardon from your Excellency—being in the form of notes owed by persons who refuse to pay them until she is pardoned. She files with this a copy of the Amnesty Oath contained in the proclamation of Your Excellency issued May 29th, 1865. While it would be untrue to deny that she deeply sympathized with her husband in his support of the Confederate Cause, she has taken the amnesty oath in good faith, and respectfully and earnestly petitions Your Excellency for a special pardon. [5]

Kitty G. Hill

LS, DNA-RG94, Amnesty Papers (M1003, Roll 25), Ky., Kitty G. Hill.

1. The sister of John Hunt Morgan, Hill (1834–1920) remarried in 1870. James I. Robertson, Jr., *General A. P. Hill: The Story of a Confederate Warrior* (New York, 1987), 30, 324–25.

2. In the absence of other indication, the date and place of the attached oath of allegiance are assigned to this letter. Amnesty Papers (M1003, Roll 25), Ky., Kitty G. Hill, RG94, NA.

3. Hill (1825–1865), a West Point graduate who had served in Mexico and against the Seminoles, had commanded a corps in the Army of Northern Virginia. Warner, *Gray.*

4. Hill refers to their three surviving daughters: Frances Russell (1861–1917), Lucy Lee (1863–1931), and Ann Powell (1865–1868). Robertson, *General A. P. Hill*, 43, 242, 321–22, 325.

5. Hill's petition was witnessed by her brothers, Calvin C. and Richard C. Morgan. She was pardoned on May 4, 1866. Amnesty Papers (M1003, Roll 25), Ky., Kitty G. Hill, RG94, NA.

From Albert G. Hodges [1]

Frankfort, Kentucky, January 20, 1866.

Sir:

A day or two ago I transmitted to you a series of Resolutions adopted by the Union members of the Legislature of Kentucky. [2] At the request of many of those gentlemen I address you now to ask that, should you deem it proper to grant the requests contained in those resolutions, in whole or in part, you will be kind enough to say, it was in deference to their request. We believe this will give us a good deal of additional strength with people of our State.

Furthermore, I warn you not to give too much credence to those who control the Copperhead Conservative element in our Legislature. If they are honest in their professions of friendship towards you, and their approval of your administration, let them come out like men and adopt the principles laid down in our Resolutions, and unite with us in the enactment of such laws as will give complete protection to the Freedmen, in person and property.

Another reason why you should be careful about putting too much reliance in the professions of this Conservative Party—or rather its leaders—is this: They were the most bitter of all your opponents for the Vice Presidency. And my word for it, there is but little reliance to be placed in their professions, unless it enures to the advancement of their schemes and purposes. I know them well, and have known them long. But few of them have deceived me during the late Rebellion.

I have more confidence now in those who shouldered their muskets and went into the rebellion, and of those who remained at home and sympathised with the rebellious, than I have in this Copperhead faction. Some of both of these classes of Southern Sympathisers are coming out on our side, and many more will do so, when they shall have read our resolutions and find that we are sustained by the President of the United States.

In addressing you upon this subject I have no other purpose to subserve than that of complying with the wishes of many of the members of the Legislature who are *truly* and *sincerely* your friends, and who desire nothing more ardently than the good of their whole Country.

I had the pleasure of an introduction to you a short time before President Lincoln's death, in the ante-room adjoining the President's reception room. In the great number of persons to whom you have been introduced, I do not, for a moment, suppose you could recollect me. I am intimately acquainted with your worthy Attorney General, and have been for years. I am also personally known to all the members of your Cabinet except Secretary McCulloch—to whom I refer for any information I may communicate to you.

A. G. Hodges

ALS, DLC-JP.

1. A newspaperman and state printer, Hodges (1802–1881) edited the *Frankfort Commonwealth* until 1872. Perrin et al., *Kentucky*, 493; G. Glenn Clift, "Civil War Letters of Brothers William T. and Joseph L. McClure," *KHSR*, 60 (1962): 216.

2. Among the resolutions forwarded by Hodges, the secretary of the meeting, were those calling for the restoration of the writ of habeas corpus and the removal of the Freedmen's Bureau from Kentucky, as well as protesting against "granting the right of Suffrage in the States to persons of African descent." Hodges to Johnson, Jan. 18, 1865, Johnson Papers, LC.

From John Howard[1]

Prescott Arizona Terry.   January 20th 1866.

Sir—

The Loyal and National Administration portion of the population of this far-off, and somewhat benighted territory (Arizona) have watched with *deep interest your course since you became the honored head of the Genl. Government*, and especially have they noted with much pleasure your plans, and patriotic course with regard to the Re-Construction of the States lately in Rebellion against the National Government. It is in this connection then I wish to call your attention to the sad condition of this (Arizona) Territory, and to ask you to re-construct it, so far at least as to give us a new Governor, and Secretary, for if there ever was any portion of the country under the jurisdiction of the Government of the United States, that needed "re-constructing," and Re-organizing, it is this (Arizona) territory. For it is now more than two years, since these men, with the other appointees, reached the Territory,[2] and at a time too when the Genl. Government was contending for its very exhistance, and when it was expected that every true and loyal man, and more especially those holding commissions under, and drawing their subsistance, from that Government, would do all in their power, to uphold and sustain it, and discoutenance every enemy of the government, and as it was well known by these officials, that this territory at that time, was peopled by persons of known hostility, and hatred to the Government, it was especially the duty of these men, to announce to this people, that they had been sent here, to extend the laws of the U.S. Government over this territory, and that a strict obediance to those laws would be required, and that the laws would be enforced. These Gentlemen could easily have done all this without any danger of trouble, either to themselves or danger to the Government, for at the same time—the military authorities, had placed a large number of Troops, at the command of the Governor, and a post ordered to be established where the Gov. should establish his head quarters, or locate temporarily his Capital, so that he had all the necessary means at hand to have enforced these declarations, and at the same time have convinced the disloyal element of the territory that he was in earnest, and in this way would have either closed the mouthes of these Dis-loyal Railers against the Government, or obliged them to quit the territory. But in stead of taking this course, both the Gov. & Secy, took this disloyal element, into their confidence, and placed in their hands all the patronage they had to distribute, and saying to these men—they did not care what their sentiments were &c. The consequence has been, that a man of known—and professed Union sentiments, has received but little or no countenance from these men, and have at times been greatly abused, and even their lives have been threatened, by some of these very men sustained by this Gov. & Secy. on account of their known and professed Sympathy with the U.S. Government.

Of course the magnitude of events transpiring in the States to this time—have been such as to have rendered it, almost impossible for the authorities at Washington to have listened to our complaints, or to have found the time necessary to investigate into their truth, alth'o these things have been before represented to the late Prest. but now that the War is over, and peace once more pervades the Atlantic states, we wish Very Respectfully Mr President, to call your serious attention to the state of things here, for in stead of our territory advancing it is really retrograding! and all owing to the want of the Re-constructing herein refered to—for our people have lost confidence in these men—well knowing that they are not worthy of the slightest confidence, either in a political, or moral point of view, for their only course has been ever since they reached the territory, to monopolize everything for them selves and a few of their adherants, and to throw every embarrassment in the way, of all those that would not, or could not be made their Tools. Thus they have controlled the Legislation of the Territory, using their personal, and official influance—to prevent the election of any, and every man—they thought could not be used to promote their sordid, and selfish end's, and by this means, they have procured the passage of laws and acts giving them special privileges, and a perfect monopoly of all the Rail Road, & Telegraph, lines of our Territory, also most ruinous, laws governing the mining, and landed intrests of the Territory, and by which they are enabled to monopolize, under what is known as the Posessory act,[3] very large tracts of land, which they hold for purposes of speculation, and to the exclusion of Bona fide Settlers, also a large quantity of mining ledges, or lodes, which they hold in the same way, and for the same purposes, by which actual settlers—who might come here and work these mines, and cultivate these lands are debarred, and the country thereby retarded in its progress, and as long as these men remain in power here—it is impossible for the people to remedy these evils.

It is for these, and very many other good and valid reasons that I will not urge here—that these men ought to be superseded, and their places filled by good, Honest, Loyal, and Competant men, such as will act in good faith, and are known friends of the National Administration, and who will do all in their power to advance the intrest of the territory.

And in view of our Indian troubles the kind of man best suited for Governor of this territory at this time, would be one who has had some Military expearance during the late war, and who posesses good Executive abilities, and energy of Character, and a Secretary that embodies the same elements, to some extent.

And in the selection by you of men to fill any of the offices, to be filled by you for this territory, I will respectfully suggest, that you thoroughly, scrutonize—the political antecedants of any man urged for such appointment, by John N. Goodwin, who claims to be the Delegate elect from this territory to Congress,[4] for it is a well known fact here, that he has promised men positions, or to use his influence to obtain them, that are now, and ever have been during the dark days of the Government, the most determined opponants of its success, for it was this class of men that supported him at the late election for Delegate, and who claimed his election as a Democratic or Anti-National Administration Victory.

The present Secretary and Acting Governor of the territory is pledged to the support of Goodwin & his friends, and has ever been the warm friend of the class of men above refered to—and the strong opponant of the true union element of the Territory, and his little Newspaper (the only one in the Territory) owned and edited solely by himself,[5] has been made the medium of abuse of every man that had both—the independance and patriotism to expose the abuses of this man McCormick, and his friend Goodwin, and their Tools, and to Puff himself, and misrepresent his standing with the people here, all of which is intended for a foreign market, and to deceave the authorities at Washington of his true standing with the Loyal people of this territory. The other officials of the territory, to wit: The U.S. Judges Marshall &c, I beleave to be good, loyal, and competant men, and against whom, I hear but little or no complaint, except, by this man Secy. McCormick, and his Colaborers, Jno N. Goodwin, and their Disloyal friends and supporters.

Now Mr President, I have thus written you frankly, at the earnest request of many of the leading and best men of our territory, those who have ever been true to the "Old Flag" and the Union, during its dark days, firmly beleaving that you will do all in your power to remedy the evils herein spoken of, and place this territory in the hands of men, that are, and ever have been true to the Union, and the National administration.[6]

Should not this brief statemt of the facts herein narated be satisfactory to accomplish the object desired, we will at some future time forward a long petition, embodying the within statemts, and signed by the leading men of our territory; not having a Representative in Washington in whom we can rely to lay these facts fairly before you for the one now there claiming to be the Representative, does not enjoy the confidence of the Loyal people of this territory, and all we expect to do, should he get his seat in Congress, is to prevent him from doing us, and the Territory serious harm.

As I am not personally known to you, I will respectfully refer you for my credability, and Unionism, to the following named Gentlemen.

Hon Allen A. Bradford Delegate from Colorado,
" J. Francisco Chavez, "   " New Mexico,
" Chs. D. Poston late "   " Arizona,
" G. M. Chilcott, Representative Elect from Colorado, under the state organization.[7]

Jno. Howard.

ALS, DLC-JP.

1. Howard (c1820-fl1870), a former territorial judge in Colorado, emigrated to Prescott in 1863 with several members of Arizona's first territorial administration. 1870 Census, Ariz., Yavapai, Prescott, 6; John Nicolson, ed., *The Arizona of Joseph Pratt Allyn, Letters from a Pioneer Judge: Observations and Travels, 1863–1866* (Tucson, 1974), 139.

2. Appointees to Arizona's first territorial government, formally organized in December 1863, included governor John N. Goodwin; secretary Richard C. McCormick (1832–1901), a war correspondent and active Republican partisan; judges William F. Turner (1816–1899), a Republican attorney from Iowa, Joseph P. Allyn (1833–1869), a newspaper reporter and erstwhile congressional clerk, and William T. Howell (1811–1870), a Michigan legislator; attorney Almon P. Gage (1817–1895), a Universalist minister; and marshal Milton H. Duffield (1810–1874), an itinerant miner and alleged member of Gen. John C. Fremont's staff. *DAB*; Nicolson, *Letters from a Pioneer Judge*, 3–41, 251–60, passim; John S. Goff, "William F. Turner, First Chief Justice of Arizona," *JAzH*, 19 (1978): 189–210, passim; Gilbert J. Pederson, "The Founding First," *JAzH*, 7 (1966): 47–58, passim; B. Sacks, "Arizona's Angry Man: United States Marshal Milton B. Duffield," *JAzH*, 8 (1967): 1–29, 99–113, passim; *U.S. Off. Reg.* (1863–65).

3. Not identified. The first territorial legislature of Arizona did adopt "some well-digested mining laws that would secure the rights of mine developers." Among the beneficiaries of legislative "boons" were Goodwin and McCormick, who were among a group given an exclusive charter to build a railroad from Guaymas, Mexico, to La Paz on the Colorado River. This "Arizona Railway Company" never constructed its proposed line. Jay J. Wagoner, *Arizona Territory, 1863–1912: A Political History* (Tucson, 1970), 53.

4. Goodwin did serve as Arizona's delegate to the 39th Congress (1865–67). *BDAC*.

5. McCormick, who became acting governor upon Goodwin's departure for Washington, D.C., in the fall of 1865, published the *Arizona Weekly Miner* in Prescott. *DAB*.

6. Despite the opposition of Howard and others, including Chief Justice Turner, Johnson appointed McCormick governor of Arizona. He proved to be quite popular and in 1869 was elected to the first of three consecutive terms as Arizona's delegate in Congress (1869–75). *DAB*; Wagoner, *Arizona Territory*, 66–67.

7. Bradford (1815–1888), a former territorial judge in Colorado, served twice in Congress (1865–67, 1869–71). Poston (1825–1902) had been a delegate to the 38th Congress (1864–65). George M. Chilcott (1828–1892), Republican legislator (1861–62, 1872–74) and register of the land office (1863–67) in Colorado, attended the 40th Congress as a delegate (1867–69) and the 47th Congress as a senator (1882–83). *BDAC*. See David Davis to Johnson, Jan. 10, 1866, for more information on Chavez.

From William G. McAdoo

Milledgeville, Ga.   Jan'y. 20. 1866.

Sir:

I beg leave respectfully to solicit the appointment of District Attorney of the United States Court for *either* of the two Districts of the State of Georgia.

My residence in Georgia is permanent; but within a few months, I shall probably remove to the sea-coast near Savannah, or return to my former residence at Marietta. I *prefer* the latter; and would, in the first place, respectfully ask the appointment for the *Northern* District, the Court of which is held at Marietta; but I would very cheerfully accept the appointment for the *Southern* District if I could not get the other.

I believe I am *qualified* to discharge the duties of the office I solicit. I was for about nine years the Attorney General of the state courts in Tennessee, in the Knoxville circuit. I beg to refer you for information respecting my qualifications and powers to the Hon. D. T. Patterson, U.S. Senator from Tennessee, who is acquainted with the manner in which I discharged the duties of that office.[1]

Wm. G. McAdoo

ALS, DNA-RG60, Appt. Files for Judicial Dists., Ga., William G. McAdoo.

1. Although highly recommended by Joseph E. Brown in an attached endorsement, McAdoo received neither appointment.

From Thomas F. Meagher

Territory of Montana,
Virginia City, January 20th 1866.

My Dear Sir,

With the hope that I commit no impropriety in addressing you a private communication, which to a great extent must relate to public matters and the official position I have now the honour to occupy, I presume upon the friendly regard you have satisfied me you entertain for me, to give you, in a familiar way, a frank account of myself since I reached this Territory, and had to assume the duties of the Governorship in addition to those of the Secretaryship, which in so complimentary a manner you devolved upon me.[1]

After a very tedious, and somewhat precarious, journey of several weeks over the plains from Atchison, Kansas, by Denver and Salt Lake City, I arrived at Bannock, the former Capital of Montana, the last of September. I there found Governor Edgerton,[2] who was eagerly awaiting me, as he had made arrangements and was fully prepared to start with his family for the States—as all that portion of the Union, east of the Missouri, is called out here. Having given me a sketch of the position of affairs in Montana, he told me that it was possible he might not return, in which event, should I desire it, he would cheerfully and cordially recommend me to you as his successor. Thanking him for his friendly disposition, I replied that, in case it was agreeable to you, I would accept the appointment of Governor, feeling, as I did, that my views and purposes were in perfect harmony with the generous policy of the Administration, and that my services, naturally and freely rendered as they would be in support of that policy, might serve here to subdue the asperities that had sprung out from the war, and reconcile sincerely even the most disaffected to the victory the Nation had achieved.

That evening, Governor Edgerton introduced me to a number of the citizens of the little town of Bannock and the neighbourhood, who had assembled to welcome me to the Territory. In acknowledging their friendly greetings, I took occasion to announce emphatically, that, in the discharge of my duties, as Secretary and acting-Governor, all parties would be alike to me, and that my official action would be governed and animated by the liberal and conciliatory spirit which you had not only counseled, but to which you had, in your relations and transactions with the South, given an assured testimony and a practical effect. This declaration was cordially received, and I felt I had taken the first step to ensure in Montana that healthier and nobler condition of the public mind upon which the fruits of the National triumph must depend for their soundness and abundance.

Virginia City having been made the Capital by Legislative enactment, I left Bannock the day after Governor Edgerton started on his journey, and reached here the first week of October. My arrival was most pleasantly welcomed. Men of all parties came to congratulate and greet me and in the presence of many hundreds who honoured me with a serenade, I repeated the declaration I had made at Bannock, and my determination to administer the affairs of the Territory, as long as I was responsible for its good-order and well-being, in an impartial and generous manner.

The day after this Serenade, I opened the Executive office, and proceeded to business. The first thing I had to do, was to direct the United-States District Attorney, Mr. Nealley,[3] to proceed without delay to New York, and, taking them with him, have the Territorial laws as expeditiously published, and as carefully and economically, as his personal direction in the matter, would ensure it. No step had been previously taken in this business, and, in the absence of printed laws, the Territory, was all adrift—so much so, that the laws of Idaho were by common consent accepted and used in all legal transactions—these being the only laws, applicable to the concerns of Montana, which, being printed and partially distributed, could afford any guidance and authority to our people in the pursuit of their several callings, and the interests eventuating from them.

The second duty I found it imperative to discharge, was to make a requisition on Major-General Wheaton,[4] commanding at Fort Laramie the Military District of Nebraska in which Montana is included, for a cavalry force of not less than five hundred men. The interests of the Territory, as well as the situation of the Federal officers, representing the several branches and departments of the Government, dictated to me this requisition, and urged its necessity. There was not a soldier within three hundred miles of the Territory. The pioneers, developing the resources of the Territory, farmers as well as miners, were, in the most favoured and promising regions of it, exposed to the depredations and brutality of the Indians. These brave and persistent adventurers were extending the out-posts of our civilization at a desperate hazard, and, in many instances, at a fearful cost. Within the more settled portion of the Territory, the civil magistracy and lawfully-constituted tribunals were powerless to suppress the devilish outrages perpetrated by an organized conspiracy, the members of which were known and designated as "Road Agents."[5] Robberies and murders, of the most desperate character, were committed by these miscreants with impunity, the civil authorities, Federal as well as local, having no power to curb and paralize them; and juries, where the ruffians were brought into Courts of justice, (being afraid to convict) serving rather to embolden than deter them. This being the state of things, several of the best citizens of the Territory—men of substance as well as excellent reputation—organized themselves here, in Virginia, in Bannock, in Helena, and other parts, into a "Vigilance Committee," and proceeded to capture, summarily try, and quickly dispatch, by hanging, some of the more notorious and daring of the ruffians.[6] I should be falsifying the record and doing violence to my positive convictions, were I not to admit, frankly and boldly, that this "Vigilance Committee" rendered eminent and vital good service to the community, and that it is owing to their intrepid and vigorous proceedings we now enjoy almost perfect exemption from such ruffians and brigands as I have referred to. Yet the "Vigilance Committee" remains organized, and prepared to act in such cases as demand their attention, up to the present moment; and will continue to do so until the regularly-constituted authorities posess, and are enabled effectively to exercise, the power to protect the lives and properties of the people, and bring to due punishment the cut-purses and cut-throats who are banded for the destruction of the one and the spoliation and plunder of the other.

This, of course, cannot be sanctioned, but, to the contrary, it must be completely overcome and set aside, the legitimate magistracy and tribunals reinstated in their just and wholesome supremacy and in their undivided and unimpaired jurisdiction, and the community placed, in accordance with the laws and their prescribed and proper operation, in a condition of reliable safety and strength. To this end I saw that a military force was essential, and for such a force there, in the proper quarters, renewed and urgently pressed the application I made, in the first instance, to General Wheaton.

A fortnight or so after my arrival in Virginia, I had to proceed on horseback to Fort Benton, a distance of nearly three hundred miles from this point, to assist Major Upson,[7] the Indian Agent, in his negotiation of a Treaty he had been instructed by the Department of the

Interior to conclude with the Black Feet and other Indians—the Su-
perintendency of Indian Affairs in Montana having devolved upon me
as acting-Governor of the Territory. We experienced no difficulty whatever in obtaining the consent of the Indians to the Treaty in question,
which, when ratified at Washington, will cede to the United States all
that portion of the Territory embraced by the British Line, the Missouri from Fort Union to a point on that river which may be considered
the central point of the Territory, thence by a line running due west to
the great range of the Rocky Mountains, and up that range back to the
British line—comprehending something like 300,000 square miles,
with the exception of a [illegible] reservation to the Contracting Indians, north of the Missouri to the British line, and defined by the Teton
and Marias rivers in the West, and Milk river in the east.[8]

The irregularity and tardiness with which the different Tribes—
essential parties to the Treaty—assembled at Fort Benton, detained me
at that place some four or five weeks longer than was otherwise necessary, and, I was, in consequence, compelled to abandon, until Spring
my intention of visiting the greater part of the Territory—that part
especially lying West of the Great Devide and fringing the Territory of
Idaho. Nevertheless, my rides to Fort Benton afforded me an opportunity of seeing a considerable segment of the Territory, and acquiring,
from personal intercourse and observation, much useful and very serviceable information in relation to the mineral and agricultural resources of Montana, the operations of the farmers and miners, their
wants as well as their prospects and achievements.

Returning here, and resuming the business of the Executive office, I
was presented with a petition, requesting me to convoke a Legislature;
or, in the event of my being legally disabled from doing that, requesting
me to call a Convention, which would so far supply the place of a Legislature, as to bring in a formal and somewhat authoritative manner
before Congress, the capabilities, the successes, the requirements, and
the condition generally, of the Territory. In reply to this petition or
memorial, I was obliged to send a letter, a copy of which I enclose,[9]
from which you will perceive that we are most inconveniently and per-
plexingly situated, as far as the Legislative functions of the Territory
are concerned; and you will, perhaps, see fit to agree with me that an
Enabling Act, reviving those functions, has now become absolutely
necessary. Unwilling, however, to keep the Territory dumb and inac-
tive, in relation to its interests, when it was in my power to bid it speak
and act, I have called a Convention, from which, it is very probable, an
application for immediate admission into the Union as a State, will
emanate from the people of the Territory.[10]

For my part, Jacksonian Democrat as I am, I shall, with all due deference to your wishes and instructions (should I be favoured with

them) heartily support any and every well-considered and loyal movement that has for its object the elevation of the Territory to the responsibilities and self-reliant position of a State. I fear we are too great a
distance from Washington, and communication between there and the
Territory is too much subject to interruption, for us to benefit by our
present relations with Congress and the National Government, to the
extent that our necessities and interests, present and prospective, require. Once a State, I am strongly of opinion, that the activity and
enterprize of our miners, farmers, merchants, and all others doing business in Montana, would acquire a fresh life, and prove more eager to
give the natural endowments of the country, which are wonderful indeed, a broader and bolder development. Once a State, if I do not great
miscalculate, capital and immigration would experience a quicker and
more courageous impulse than either the one or the other now
obeys—even the ordinary guarantees of a State encouraging and assuming both in a more decisive measure than our dependence upon the
protection of the National Government and the generosity of Congress
can possibly do. And here I beg respectfully to inform you, that up to
the present time not a dollar of the Appropriations (voted two years
ago) for the Legislative expenses of the Territory has reached us, nor
has there been a single dollar forwarded in payment of the Salaries of
the Federal Officers. We are, in the midst of gold and silver, abounding
in our streams and mountains to an exorbitant excess, in a downright
destitute condition. We are living upon air, and the hope of some
wholesome manna refreshingly visiting us, one of these days, in the
enchanted wilderness through which we are passing.

I have now to state, that the Territory has proved to my experience
to be all that I conjectured and desired. It is, indeed, a singularly favoured portion of our great common country. It's mineral wealth is
incalculable. It's agricultural resources are hardly less so. Were every
grain of gold—were every speck of silver—by some violent effort of
nature wrested from it, it would still posess all the necessary elements
of substantial prosperity and happiness that a republican people, enlightened and energetic as our's are, need aspire to and labour for. I
know of no part of the country where the provisions of your noble
Homestead Act can be so propitiously reduced to practice. Take away
the months of December, January, February, and March, and the year
round is most delightfully genial and fructifying. Timber abounds—
water abounds—the soil yields in profusion all the grain and vegetables
of the temperate latitudes. Planted in the beautiful and prolific vallies
of the huge mountains of our Continent, an industrious and active
community have command of two of the grandest high-roads of the
Nation—the Missouri to the East—the Columbia to the West. A
few miles of railroad, through Minnesota, across the upper plains of

Dakotah, thence through our Territory South of the Missouri and the Yellowstone, will make the Great Lakes our base of commerce with New England, and the more Northern states on the Atlantic slope.

To have the power of helping the development of Montana to the utmost, and its organization as a free, loyal, and influential State of the Union, I desire to be, and now frankly but respectfully ask you to retain me, acting Governor of Montana.[11]

I am well aware that the radicals and extremists of the Republican party of the Territory, who, animated by the same malevolent and bitter spirit that confronts your grand policy of reconciliation, and would inflict an eternal proscription upon the South, regard no Federal officer with favour, or with ordinary fairness even, who refuses to be a mean tool or a mischevious firebrand in their hands. I am well aware that, as I have adhered steadily and firmly to the declaration with which I entered upon my duties, the malice of these men has found an active embodiment in a cowardly conspiracy, which, as I refuse to bend, or swerve, or compromise from the high and patriotic line of conduct you have pointed out, and in which you have resolved to travel, is sworn to *disable me by slander*, or overthrow me in Washington *by scandalous misrepresentations*, to be submitted to you, perhaps, by their deluded or their deliberate accomplices.[12]

Should these wicked partizans of faction and fanaticism, who still would ride the whirlwind and revel in the storm, submit any case to you, in derrogation of my title to the Governorship, should Mr Edgerton conclude not to return, *all I ask is that you appoint no one else until you afford me a full opportunity to meet, contradict, and utterly refute the base calumnies which these disturbers of the public peace may have, through their agents at Washington, the dastardly spite or the reckless audacity to submit to your consideration*, with the view of stripping me of the little ability I now command, by virtue of my position, to carry out in this glorious and most promising New Territory, the healthful and benignant work you have devoted yourself to, and of which a reconciled, united, and indissoluable nation will be, for generations and generations to come, the sacred as well as the magnificent result.

Sincerely and warmly wishing you the happiest and highest success in your great care and labours—the brightest hours for your family and household all through the grave term of your Magistracy, and for many years after it shall have honorably and triumphantly closed. . . .

Thomas Francis Meagher
Acting-Governor Territory of Montana

ALS, DLC-JP.
  1. See Meagher to Johnson, July 25, 1865, *Johnson Papers*, 8: 487.
  2. Sidney Edgerton (1818–1900), a former Republican congressman (1859–63), had been appointed in 1864 as the first territorial governor of Montana. *DAB*.
  3. Edward B. Neally (1837–1905), a former Navy Department clerk in Washington,

D.C., was later a Maine legislator and a Bangor businessman. Louis C. Hatch, ed., *Maine: A History* (5 vols., New York, 1919), 4: 127–29.

4. Frank Wheaton (1833–1903) served in the army on the western frontier prior to the Civil War, and had been brevetted a major general for his service during that conflict. Warner, *Blue.*

5. An organized group of thieves, murderers, and other undesirables led by Henry Plummer, the sheriff of Bannock City. Michael P. Malone and Richard B. Roeder, *Montana: A History of Two Centuries* (Seattle, 1976), 61–62.

6. In December 1863 a Montana vigilante association was formed. It ranged widely, hanging thirty-two men by April 1, 1864. Although within six months Plummer's gang was destroyed, the association remained active until the 1880s. Michael P. Malone and Richard B. Roeder, eds., *The Montana Past: An Anthology* (Missoula, Mont., 1969), 83–84; Richard M. Brown, *Strain of Violence: Historical Studies of American Violence and Vigilantism* (New York, 1975), 101.

7. Gad E. Upson (1823–1866), a former pension clerk in Washington, D.C., was agent to the Blackfeet from 1863 until his death. *Sacramento Bee*, Mar. 29, 1866; *U.S. Off. Reg.* (1863), 116; Upson to William P. Dole, Nov. 10, 1863, Lets. Recd., Blackfeet, RG75, NA.

8. The authorities in Washington did not share Meagher's enthusiasm for his treaty, which was intended to isolate the Blackfeet from white settlements. Believing that neither side would observe the agreement, Secretary Harlan did not submit it to the Senate for approval. Malone and Roeder, *Montana*, 90.

9. Not found.

10. Although Montana did not have enough population to apply for statehood, Meagher's constitutional convention met in Helena on April 9, 1866. Attendance was sparse, and the constitution which was produced was never printed. Ibid., 79–80.

11. Meagher continued as acting governor until October 1866, when Green Clay Smith was appointed. After a few months, when Smith went to Washington on territorial business, Meagher again became acting governor of Montana and was such at his death in mid-1867. Ibid., 80.

12. Nine days later Meagher reported that his "most vicious" enemy, Radical Republican vigilante William F. Sanders, was soon departing for Washington. He lamented that Sanders would "in the most vulgar manner abuse, and defame, and blacken me," and asked the President not to let such "malignity" influence his decision regarding the governorship in Montana. Meagher to Johnson, Jan. 29, 1866, Johnson Papers, LC.

From Robert M. Patton

Montgomery, January 20th 1866

My Dr. Sir

I am informed Lieut Genl. W J Hardee late of Georgia, has become a permanent citizen of this State.[1] The adoption of one so distinguished as is Genl. Hardee, for order, discipline and enterprise is cause of congratulation for the people of Alabama. His valuable services as I am creditably advised are much desired by the stockholders and citizens, to fill the important office of President of a long line of Rail Road extending from Selma in this State, to Meridian in the State of Mississippi.[2] The disabilities growing out of Genl. Hardees late connection with the Confederate Army, greatly impairs his usefulness as a citizen; his special application to you for pardon[3] is now before me. I have no hesitation in saying that he will prove to be a very useful man in carrying into effect your policy of reconstruction. All the facts stated in his application are undoubtedly true, and he will in good faith adhere to the pledges made therein. I would therefore very respectfully urge, and earnestly recommend him as a proper person for executive clemency.[4]

Hoping his application may meet your favourable consideration. . . .

R M Patton   Governor of Alabama

ALS, DNA-RG94, Amnesty Papers (M1003, Roll 5), Ala., William Joseph Hardee.

1. Following his surrender in North Carolina in April 1865, Hardee had managed his wife's two cotton plantations near Demopolis, Ala. Warner, *Gray*; Nathaniel C. Hughes, Jr., *General William J. Hardee: Old Reliable* (Baton Rouge, 1965), 305–7.

2. Hardee assumed the presidency of the company in February 1866 and subsequently moved to Selma. Ibid., 306–7.

3. See Hardee to Johnson, ca. Dec. 8, 1865, Amnesty Papers (M1003, Roll 5), Ala., William Joseph Hardee, RG94, NA.

4. Despite support from prominent men like Governor Patton, Gen. William T. Sherman and others, Hardee's pardon was not granted until some two years later. We have been unable, however, to determine the exact date. Meanwhile, the railroad went into receivership. Hughes, *Old Reliable*, 308–9.

From Benjamin Rush [1]

Mount Airy near Phila.   20. Jany 1866.

Mr. President

I trust I do not transgress the limits of propriety in most respectfully venturing to express an ardent hope, that should the occasion arise, the Constitutional Veto may be applied to avert from our Country the inevitable mischiefs and dangers of the Suffrage Bill just passed by The House.[2]

That power was wisely lodged with the Executive by great and good men to meet just such emergencies as the present, notwithstanding the tempest of hostility which they knew very well its exercise might provoke.

The Country will sustain you Sir in exercising it now, just as the enlarged statesmanship of your beneficent and eminently patriotic reconstruction policy, has already found its way to the hearts as it soon will to the votes, of a large majority of your constituents, The People of The United States, of whom I am one of the least considerable.

That this Bill, if it becomes a Law, will deluge this Land in blood, sooner or later, by a War of Races, I have no more doubt than of my own existence. The People look to you Sir to continue to stand by them, and mistake your character if the event doesnt prove that the spirit of Andrew Jackson still lives and rules.

Benjamin Rush.

ALS, DLC-JP.

1. Rush (1811–1877), an attorney, was a former secretary of the legation and chargé d'affaires at London. *Appletons' Cyclopaedia*.

2. For another protest against the House vote to extend voting rights to blacks in the District of Columbia, see Lewis D. Campbell to Johnson, Jan. 19, 1866.

From Green Clay Smith

Washington D.C.   Jan. 20" 1866.

To the President.

If you will allow me, I will suggest one point upon which I deem it important to touch in your Message to the House transmitting the information requested by Mr. Raymonds resolution.[1] Viz—The qualifications of members of Congress from the seceded states—that is—members elect from the rebellious states must be loyal, *and able to do what we have done who are now in our seats, take the oath*—thus showing that those who would represent the south, & the people of that country are willing to observe the rules prescribed by us, and maintain the Govnmt. In my conversations with a number of gentlemen, we have united in the opinion that you should speak on this subject. We want the doctrine fully enunciated that these states are entitled to representation and if their members are not admitted because of disloyalty—they alone can be to blame, but the true doctrine is maintained and established by the Govt.

I do not propose to argue this point—merely to suggest—nor do I speak authoritatively for any number of gentlemen—but from interviews had I thought it not improper to present the subject.[2]

G. Clay Smith

P.S. I have just had an interview with Laine[3] of Kansas, and he assures me that there are twenty men in the senate perfectly reliable, who will vote against the negro, (House,) Bill—and that their stand will secure votes enough to defeat it. Now what is wanted, is for you to send for these senators and tell them your views and unite them for action. Your friends want you to do this and Mr Laine asked me to see you, but I see no chance this morning, as I am to be in the House on business at 12. Senator Cowan[4] will give you the names of the senators who are sound.

G.C.S.

ALS, DLC-JP.

1. On January 12, Henry J. Raymond of New York had presented a resolution requesting the President to provide the House with copies of all messages and proclamations issued by the provisional governors of former Confederate states, "all acts, ordinances, resolutions, and proceedings of conventions or Legislatures" in those states, and all proclamations issued by Johnson or Lincoln relating thereto. *Congressional Globe*, 39 Cong., 1 Sess., p. 214.

2. Johnson's response has not been found, though the President did eventually comply with similar resolutions of January 5 and February 27, 1866, initiated by the Senate. *Senate Ex. Docs.*, 39 Cong., 1 Sess., No. 26, p. 1 (Ser. 1237).

3. James H. Lane.

4. Edgar Cowan of Pennsylvania. We have not located Cowan's list.

From J. Madison Wells

New Orleans   Jany 20th 1866

A special telegraph from Washington announces the appointment of
A. P. Dostie[1] as Surveyor of the Port of New Orleans. Incredible as the
news is it has startled the community who of all men in the state is the
most odious and who has no qualifications for the position. In the name
of the commercial portion of every class and for the sake of the reputation of your Administration I beg of you that he be not appointed or if
appointed that you withdraw his nomination.[2] I will give further reasons by mail which will convince you that his appointment will disgrace your Administration.[3]

J Madison Welles[*sic*]   Govr.

Tel, DLC-JP.
    1. Anthony P. Dostie.
    2. On January 15, 1866, Johnson had endorsed the nomination of Dostie, which had
been forwarded by McCulloch upon the recommendation of former governor Michael
Hahn. Eleven days after this telegram was sent, the nomination was withdrawn. Mc-
Culloch to Johnson, Jan 12, 1866, Lets. Sent *re* Customs Service Employees (QC Ser.),
Vol. 3, RG56, NA; Ser. 6B, Vol. 4: 202, Johnson Papers, LC.
    3. Not found.

From James W. Schaumburg
(Private and *Confidential*)

Philadelphia (Pa)   January 21st 1866.

Dear Sir:

Some months ago I was made the instrument of communicating to
you, anonymously, an extraordinary narrative[1] of a more extraordinary
Jacobinical congressional conclave met in close secrecy to discuss your
character, personal and political: looking to a possible disagreement
between themselves and yourself and to discuss as what might happen
and what could be done to subordinate you to their schemes.

The conspirators or marplots were various such as Chief Justice
Chase senators, representatives and several members of your cabinet.
They were greatly exorcised to determine what was best to be provided
for as your becoming President was unpalateable to those who had
ruled the roost over poor old Abraham Lincoln and seeing that the new
Executive was a man who did not wear "a nose of wax" and radicalism
was not to go it with a rush as they had programmed out i.e: that the
south should be crushed out—negro equality and amalgamation would
grandly follow the destruction of southern whites except Yankee men
and women propagandists the *Freedmens Bureau* being the machinery
to organize and carry out Yankee notions and plunder.

The narrative of the conspirators conclave on the 6th of March last

(1865) so far told you what they might be called on to do if you did not please them—if you read the narrative you now see that the *disunion* republican party do not intend to show you any quarter and they only wait to openly declare against you—will impeach you if they can find any pretext to do so and will leave no stone unturned to get rid of you. If they cannot impeach you, they will try to make it out that you were not eligible to be elected *Vice* President, this in spite of the fact of your being a Senator from Tennessee until March 1863 & during two years of the rebellion and that the Union National Convention nominated you as an inhabitant of a state within the Union of old states. But what care they for all truth, honor justice and the Constitution when they have their dogmas to carry out and to perpetuate their rule. They oppose your benificent and constitutional plan of reinstating the southern people to their allegiance and obedience to the old Constitution and the laws, because by the return of members of Congress they will not have a continuance of their political powers. They fear you yet would try to terrify you into their vile measures as they often did Mr. Lincoln. They are a cowardly truckling and truculant set of knaves Stanton being their principal Bombastes Furioso and Harlan is no less a bloody tyrant. They have in Congress already by a Resolution assumed to direct how the Army shall be distributed[2] ignoring the fact that the President is *Commander-in-Chief*. They say that there shall be no appeal (in a Bill now before the Senate) from judgements or decisions of Freedmen Bureau Commissioners![3] They say they shall be of the military and have military protection in the "Loyal" States as well as the late rebellious states! They have mounted the high horse of Legislative usurpation by social Resolutions they intend to manage public affairs. They intend to reorganize the army and increase it.[4] The officers some three or four thousand are to be selected by a *Board of Examiners* who will be selected by Stanton who of course only do the bidding of Stanton who will have only radicals to be appointed and promoted. By this cunning arrangement the President would have nothing to do but to sign commissions—of course the President needn't appoint any of his own liking no democrats—no independent union & constitution loving citizen, no anti Jacobin abolition citizen would need apply. Certainly no one from the South will be appointed as all the appointments are to be made from radical regulars (who are but few) and from the volunteers. Yet the south will be called on for taxes to help support an Army and Navy made up of Northerners and Yankees, black and white. There are many union loving citizens of the South who, altho' like yourself, are born there as capable and deserving to be appointed officers in the army as can be found at the North. At all events Congress has no right to dictate to the President who of his fellow citizens he shall appoint to office civil or military. The President is made responsible and therefore has the right to select the persons to be appointed. To exclude one class of *citizens* from benefits all are entitled equally to enjoy is opposed to a democratic or republican government: it is as you say "class legislation" and an attempt to establish an obnoxious Aristocracy.

I feel at liberty to inform you who the member of Congress was who furnished me with the narrative, which I copied from his draft of what transpired or was spoken at the conclave above referred to and sent to you for your information. The gentleman said he could not well, himself personally address you on the momentous subject which you ought to be advised about as being forewarned you would be fore-armed. This gentleman was Mr. Davis⁵ *ex* Member of Congress from Maryland lately deceased. He said the radicals were bent on a course which if not boldly met by you would result in some great trouble if not total destruction of the unity of the federal union. He left it to my judgement whether or not to communicate the matter to your *private* understanding so that you would know how to act advisedly against secret traitors. I copied from his rough draft and minutes and sent it to you anonymously.

Jas. W. Schaumburg
(Philadelphia, Pa)
(272 South 4th St.)

ALS, DLC-JP.

1. Not found.

2. Republican representative Thomas Williams had successfully introduced a resolution asserting that Federal troops should not be withdrawn from the South until Congress "declared their further presence there no longer necessary." *Congressional Globe*, 39 Cong., 1 Sess., p. 137.

3. The bill to continue the Freedmen's Bureau—introduced into the Senate by Lyman Trumbull on January 5, 1866, and subsequently amended and adopted by Congress over Johnson's veto—authorized its agents to assume jurisdiction in cases involving the violation of civil rights for blacks. Trumbull's original proposal contained no specific provisions for appeals but, because both it and the final version delegated presidential authority through the War Department, presumably decisions could be appealed to higher-ranking officials. *Congressional Globe*, 39 Cong., 1 Sess., pp. 129, 210; *U.S. Statutes at Large*, 14: 177.

4. Senator Henry Wilson introduced a bill, approved in July 1866, that increased the peacetime army to almost 60,000 officers and men. Sefton, *Army and Reconstruction*, 65; *U.S. Statutes at Large*, 14: 332–38.

5. Henry Winter Davis.

From Joseph C. Bradley

Huntsville, Alabama, January 22nd 1866.

Genl. P. D. Roddy, formerly of the Rebel Army, will present you his application for Pardon. Genl. Roddy applied to me soon after I returned last summer from Washington, to write you and recommend his petition for Pardon. I declined to write in his behalf for various reasons, and among the number was because you had excepted all military officers from Brigadier Generals up, in your Amnesty Proclamation; and I was fearful from my appreciation of your opinion that you might consider it a little impertinent in me, asking you to pardon Genl. Roddy so soon after you had excepted him from your General Amnesty. There were other reasons why I declined to lend him my little might and getting him relieved.

1st That he had orders and frequently while I was within the Rebel lines, to have me arrested and imprisoned for disloyalty to the Confederate Government.

2nd. That many Union men had been arrested and some executed in his, Genl. Roddy's, department of North Alabama, and I was not then satisfied but what it not only met with his approval but his wishes.

In regard to my first objection, I will say to you frankly that now I am *entirely* satisfied, if it had not been for Genl. Roddy's interposition in my behalf and other Union men of North Alabama, that we would not only have been arrested, but imprisoned until the close of the Rebellion. Genl. Roddy had orders to have myself and others arrested by his superior commanders coming from Richmond, but he declined to execute the orders, and would not allow us to be disturbed.

In reference to the arrest and execution of Union men in his Department, I will state to your Excellincy, that I have made strict and dilligent enquiry to ascertain the facts and truth as regards this then objection to him by me, and after all the care that I have bestowed on this point, I have arrived at the conclusion that Genl. Roddy was a very kind and humane man towards Union men, and never gave his sanction or approval to any acts committed by Rebél and pretended Rebel soldiers on and against Union people; he is innocent of any harshness towards the loyal people of North Alabama; and if there is a Brigadier General of the Rebel Army that ought to receive the clemency of your pardoning power, it should be P. D. Roddy. He was not a secessionist, but he sinned against the Government by taking up arms for her overthrow and the destruction of the best Government on the Globe.

I now believe he accipts of things as they are, and will honestly live up to the terms of the Pardon you may grant him.

I will say to your Excellency, in behalf of Genl. Roddy, that if a war should occur between our Government and *any other* you will find him in the ranks of the Union Army doing battle to uphold and defend with all his valor the Flag of the Free United States of North America.

Genl. Roddy is a self-made man. When I first knew him in Moulton, Alabama, he was following his humble trade, and how he got seduced into the ranks of the enemy of free Government, I could never comprehend. I hope you will extend to him that clemency vested in you as the Executive of the United States, by granting him a pardon for the offences he has committed and let him return home a citizen of the great Republic, and he will not be apt to sin again.[1]

Joseph C Bradley

ALS, DNA-RG94, Amnesty Papers (M1003, Roll 9), Ala., Philip Dale Roddey.
    1. Following the recommendation of General Grant, Philip D. Roddey was pardoned on February 17, 1866. *House Ex. Docs.*, 39 Cong., 2 Sess., No. 31, p. 25 (Ser. 1289); Simon, *Grant Papers*, 16: 52.

From Samuel Galloway[1]
(*Confidential*)

Columbus   Jany 22d 1866

My dear *friend*.

Receive my congratulations on your consistent and patriotic adherence to the leading and characteristic principles and policy of your predecessor. The men who covertly and openly assail you, are the men who denounced the lamented Lincoln for his policy in the Missouri imbroglio, and who so violently protested against his action in the policy in regard to Louisiana. But for the patriotic sentiment of the people they would have thwarted his enlightened Statesmanship. Davis[2] (and with all his faults I loved him) has been summoned to the higher tribunal and I pass his unwise action and that of his coadjutors, Wade, Ashley, Sumner &c in sadness and silence. What was done in all these and kindred topics is well-known—and needs no comment—and my allusion to them is merely prefatory to the statement that, notwithstanding this concentrated opposition of Congress—the unseduced and unpurchased people sustained Lincoln and condemned his opponents. If I am not mistaken, popular sentiment will go equally and signally manifested in the support of your policy—and in opposition to Congressional action.

I am perhaps as well acquainted with the people and opinions of Ohio as any other man—and I am clear and confident in my judgment that the men who sympathise and vote with Stevens, Sumner &c will be terribly rebuked by their constituents. It has been my determination not to be again a candidate for popular suffrage—but if it becomes necessary to secure a Representation in sympathy with the administration—I shall make the necessary personal and pecuniary sacrifice. I have a reasonable conviction that I can at any time, secure the nomination. It is my decided opinion that Mr. Shellabarger[3] has misrepresented and does misrepresent popular sentiment. This utterance is quite consistent with the kindliest feelings towards that gentleman—as I very sincerely regret his mistaken course. A few of us are very earnestly laboring to obtain an expression of our General Assembly in favor of your administration—and I am persuaded this will be done.

Bear with my suggestions. It is quite important to the future of this Nation—that you now secure a cordial and cooperative support on the part of all the members of your cabinet. You need earnest and steadfast counsellors, incapable of duplicity and undoubted in their attachment to your policy. A man who will not subordinate his personal feelings and aspirations to the national welfare and your measures for its advancement, does not deserve the position of a confidential advisory. He must be ready in heart and thought to "sink or swim" with you. Again it is your duty to give your patronage the right direction. My experience during Mr. Lincoln's administration has taught me the importance of having all officials in full sympathy with the *Head*. The (then) collector of this district[4] by his assessor and collector deputees labored industriously during his term of service for the advancement of the "mad ambition" of Gov Chase[5]—and consequently for the overthrow of the good name and governmental measures of Mr. Lincoln. By his activity and official influence he was enabled to neutralise the action of the best men in this District. He was not removed notwithstanding the strongest remonstrances—and well sustained charges against him—until driven by his wickedness to self-slaughter. Mr. Chase consistent in his bad faith sustained him in his perfidy to Mr. Lincoln. Your friends are entitled to the vigorous cooperation of the appointees of the administration in sustaining its vital measures. We are comparatively powerless without it. I am quite impartial in this suggestion—for I have no favors to ask. I cannot enlarge. I wish that I could have an interview of about half an hour so that I could express my thoughts more fully if not more frankly. I labored to obtain a conference at my last visit to Washington but the *pressure crowded* me out—and thus I was grievously disappointed—as the main purpose of my going was to see you. I much regret owing to professional and private engagements, that I have not been able to go south—and report my observations as to the condition of southern loyalty and southern freedmen. It is not improbable that I may go next week to Louisiana & Mississippi. If I do I shall frankly inform you and the public with my views and conclusions.[6] I send this under cover to Honl. Horace Maynard—so that it may certainly reach you.

That you may be largely aided in the present crisis with the sympathising counsel and cooperation of honest men and sound patriots—and that the God of the Fathers of the Republic—and our safe and sufficient Guide through the disasters and tribulations of the Rebellion may lead you to a triumphant accomplishment of your patriotic purposes is the sincere prayer of. . . .

Saml. Galloway

N B Maynard may read this letter if he chooses and you choose.

S G

ALS, DLC-JP.
   1. Former Republican congressman.
   2. Henry Winter Davis.
   3. Samuel Shellabarger (1817–1896), a former Ohio legislator, served as minister to
Portugal after the third of his four terms in Congress (1861–63, 1865–69, 1871–73).
BDAC.
   4. Probably Alfred P. Stone.
   5. Salmon P. Chase.
   6. Galloway allegedly did travel south as Johnson's agent, but no subsequent correspondence with the President on this topic has been found. *NCAB*, 23: 198.

From Lucy E.W. Polk

National Hotel   Monday Jan 22d 66—
Sir.

   I arrived here on yesterday with quite a Party of friends—Ex Gov
Bell & Lady of Texas[1]—Mrs Genl Green[2] of Boston, Mrs Graves[3] of
Vermont all anxious to see the "President." Not an applicant for Office
in this Party. At what hour shall we call to-morrow? If not to-morrow
["]*say when.*" I shall also be happy to make the acquaintance of Mrs
Johnson & Mrs Patterson.[4]

Mrs W. H. Polk

ALS, Nc-Ar, Polk Papers.
   1. Peter H. Bell (1812–1898) and Ella R.E.D. Bell (d. 1897). The former had twice
been elected governor of Texas in the antebellum period. After marriage in 1857 he
moved to his wife's home in North Carolina and subsequently served in the Confederate
army. Sam H. Dixon and Louis W. Kemp, *The Heroes of San Jacinto* (Houston, 1932),
326; Webb et al., *Handbook of Texas*, 1: 141.
   2. Unidentified.
   3. Unidentified.
   4. For earlier communication between the President and Mrs. Polk, see Polk to Johnson, Nov. 27, 1865.

From John Cochrane

New York   Jany 23rd 1866
My Dear Sir

   It is my wish, while availing myself of your kind permission to write
to you, never to intrude upon your attention, but with what may be
serviceable to your interests.

   I have had the opportunity of observing occasionally, since I last saw
you in Washington, what I think it may be useful to communicate. In
any conflict which your covert enemies may precipitate upon you, it is
in my observation, of first consequence that the issue should not permit
even the colour of an inference, that your line of policy is unfriendly to
the negro. Compelling from facts, that concession to public opinion,
and I am confident, that split from your disguised enemies, at whatever
point you may, and *whenever* you will carry with you the vastly prepon-

derating numbers of the North. Till the hour of that split, you will not be surprised to hear that the simulated accord of these enemies with your views, will contribute, as it is contributing, largely to their popular strength. Their notes have currency only on the credit of your name. That with drawn from the partnership and I think that the remaining concern would soon fall into the convulsions of bankruptcy.

I saw Mr Dean Richmond here yesterday. He is awaiting the developments in progress in the capital. His opinion is unchanged upon the formation of future parties. He says that when ever you are in position to accept of the cooperation of him and his friends, that it will not be delayed. Till then he thinks it most proper not to approach you with solicitations, which, as your recognised political friend, he would not hesitate to prefer. He will proceed to Washington in about a weeks time, when doubtless he will see you. Within the circuit of our City politics we find the *November* men, and the *December* men. Our state elections are held annually in November and our charter elections in December. The state elections influence and determine the relation of the state to national politics, while the charter elections, implicate simply questions of Municipal spoils. Hence the *November* men alone are of any practical consequence upon the national stage. Mr. Richmond is a November man and possessed as you know of prodigeous power. I think that his cooperation alone, is necessary to produce an intimate and continuous concert between the temperate Republicans, and the loyal masses of the democratic party. He secured, and the rest may be with safety dismissed. But the mistake should not be permitted of confounding the leaders with their forces. Never within my recollection have men universally so absolved themselves of the obligations of parties. Their former leaders seem to be shorn of their party control, and to be impotent of direction. Their surest guide, as I observe, seems to be your policy. Upon that myriads are in readiness to christalize into an organized & efficient party. They await your signal, nor longer regard with deference the movements of the leaders, whose motives and judgement they have learned to destrust.

Mr Bennett read me the letter of Wright Rives.[1] He was greatly pleased with it. In the course of our conversation I perceived that he felt the want of a knowledge of your intents—stating that his office agent & correspondents did not succeed in compassing them. He remarked that he had directed the Heralds editorial columns exclusively upon his judgment of the exigencies of current events. I answered that I thought that it was precisely because of his uninfluenced judgment, at a point secluded from the central fever in the federal capital, that his advice became of greater value to you. This view was not without its weight upon his judgment. Yet, I think that could you possess Mr Bennett with intimation at suitable intervals of your general policy that your attitude would come to be more satisfactorily visible, and more firm in appearance. I have promised him to visit him at Fort Washington (his home) in a short time, and that previously to my going again to Washington. His desire is that we may then pass together over the general political field. Whenever this occurs I will hope to communicate to you his views & opinions.[2] His general idea is the feasibility and, therefore, the importance of a coalition between the moderate Republicans, and the loyal democrats.

As Mr Blair,[3] I believe is hardly in sympathy with Mr Bennett, I conclude to have this letter placed in the hands of Mr Wright Rives who doubtless will hand it to you.

I suppose that the Suffrage Bill for the District will be modified in the Senate.[4] With deference, I would say that I believe that at that point, is to be found your surest defence against this most artfully contrived and insidiously executed stratagem.

Would the Senate repose Negro suffrage upon any or all of the intelligential tests you have hitherto delineated, such an amendment of the bill would not only devulge the real malignity which directed the House, but exhibit to the world your triumph over it. At some such a day in the political calendar, would the future annalist probably, denote the initiate point of that great and truly democratic party, which in my humble judgment, you are destined to lead forth from the discordant and jarring element of present political confusion and legislative turmoil.

I saw General Steadman[5] here, who promised to confer with you upon the propriety of holding a large meeting here in behalf of your policy and to write me the result.

Whenever you think it seasonable you must be aware that a formidable demonstration can be made.

John Cochrane

ALS, DLC-JP.
1. A copy of this communication, presumably written by Johnson's assistant military secretary to J. Gordon Bennett, has not been found.
2. See Cochrane to Johnson, Feb. 4, 1866, Johnson Papers, LC.
3. Francis P. Blair, Sr.
4. See Lewis D. Campbell to Johnson, Jan. 19, 1866.
5. James B. Steedman.

From Miami Valley Citizens[1]

Hamilton, O.   Jany 23 1866

Excellency!

The undersigned, Citizens of the Miami Valley, do most respectfully request you, to "veto" the "Negro Suffrage Bill," just passed by the House[2] and you will make yourself a subject of our eternal admiration.

Pet, DLC-JP.
1. This missive was signed by 140 persons.
2. See Lewis D. Campbell to Johnson, Jan. 19, 1866.

From Orville S. Dewey[1]

67 Clinton Street Buffalo N.Y.   Jany. 24th. 1866.

Sir:

Early in '64 I was fortunate enough to be of considerable service to the late President. Ever generous he offered me a commission in one of the regular cavalry Regts.

I gladly accepted the *promises*. Within a short time my battery (33rd N.Y.) was ordered to the fields: I never saw Mr Lincoln again. I could hardly [be] remembered amid the great trials which surrounded and oppressed the President. At all events, my case was overlooked or forgotten.

I shall not ask you to commission me because Mr Lincoln forgot to do so, but I do on your own account.

Now I haven't a political friend in the world, all the better for it doubtless. More than that it would not add one vote to either political party if you were to appoint me a full "General."

My claims are no greater than thousands of others. I *did* serve four years however as private and officer during the war. Would have served longer had it been necessary. It wasn't, and I resigned.

Well, I find myself today burning with a restless longing for the service. Not with "Head Quarters" at New York or Boston, but *mounted* and on the *frontier*.

I know you are beseiged by the "thirty millions" whom you represent but be kind enough to tell me Yes, or No. (Hum, but that "No" looks omnious.) Inform me fairly and squarely, whether you *will* or *will not* appoint me to a cavalry regiment, and send me where if the fighting isn't heavy, there is something to *do*.

Orville S. Dewey

P.S. Please dont refer me to any "General Order" or hand my case over to any "Acting Assistant" for consideration, & oblige.[2]

O.S.D.

ALS, DNA-RG94, ACP Branch, File D-39-CB-1866, Orville S. Dewey.

1. Dewey (c1841–1867), a Buffalo resident, served in four New York units before resigning in October 1864. CSR, RG94, NA; Buffalo directories (1857–60); Heitman, *Register*, 1: 371.

2. Dewey repeated his request in April 1866 and M. Chamberlain wrote on his behalf in January 1867. Upon the envelope enclosing the latter missive Johnson wrote: "If there is a vacancy let this young man be appointed Lieutenant." Dewey was appointed 2nd lieutenant, 4th U.S. Cav., January 22, 1867, and five months later died of yellow fever in New Orleans. *Ibid.*; Dewey to Johnson, Apr. 24, 1866; Chamberlain to Johnson, Jan. 31, 1867, ACP Branch, Files D-67-CB-1866 and D-125-CB-1867, RG94, NA.

From Hugh McCulloch

Treasury Department   January 24th 1866
Dear Sir

Referring to the conversation I had with you this morning, I now present to you for nomination to the Senate the name of *Samuel J. Lee*[1] for Assessor, and the name of *Franklin B. Gilbert*[2] for Collector of Internal Revenue for the Territory of Utah.

The present incumbents are Mormons, and I am satisfied that the Government is not receiving anything like the amount of Revenue that ought to be collected in that Teritory.

I am of the opinion that the interests of the public service requires that the proposed changes shall be made.[3]

H. McCulloch   Secretary

LBcopy, DNA-RG56, Lets. Sent *re* Internal Revenue Employees (QD Ser.), Vol. 1.

1. Lees (c1825-fl1874), a native of England, was a Salt Lake City locksmith and merchant. J. R. Kearl et al., comps., *Index to the 1850, 1860, & 1870 Censuses of Utah: Heads of Households* (Baltimore, 1981), 213; Edward L. Sloan, *Gazeteer of Utah, and Salt Lake City Directory* (1874), 242.

2. Gilbert (fl1867) was a Salt Lake City "trader." *Owens' Salt Lake City Directory* (1867), 56.

3. Lees failed to receive an appointment despite the endorsements of several Utah officials, who disparaged incumbent assessor Jessie C. Little as "a fanatical Mormon and a Polygamist." McCulloch later withdrew his nomination of Gilbert, characterizing the candidate as "not a fit and proper person for the appointment." Thomas J. Drake et al. to Johnson, ca. January 1866; Amons Reed et al. to Johnson, ca. January 1866, Appts., Internal Revenue Service, Assessor, Utah, Samuel J. Lees, RG56, NA; McCulloch to Johnson, Apr. 7, 1866, Lets. Sent *re* Internal Revenue Employees (QD Ser.), Vol. 1, RG56, NA.

From Charles J. Jenkins

Milledgeville Georgia   January 25 1866
Sir

I herewith, respectfully forward to your Excellency, certain resolutions of the General Assembly, as requested by them, numbered 1, 2, & 3.[1]

Reluctant, as I really am to intrude upon your attention, and to add to your many annoyances, yet emboldened by your gracious tender of the cooperation of your Government, in perfecting the restoration of my state, I respectfully crave a hearing as to some other matters.

I will not conceal from you the fact, that our People, thoroughly bent on peace, and loyalty, and industry, are kept in a state of anxiety—of hope, not only deferred, but occasionally disappointed.

They have heard it proclaimed by your Excellency's immediate Representative, my Predecessor, that their judicial officers were restored to their functions, yet those officers in the execution of laws, long since passed are often interrupted by the military Authorities of the United States, instances of which appear in enclosed papers, 4 & 5.[2] Our Authorities are denied in some localities, the control and management of even a portion of our own jails, as will appear by paper 6.[3] Planters on the sea-board, though willing and offering to contract with their former slaves, now in possession of their lands, for labor, cannot get restitution of those lands, even after having been pardoned, as I am informed by letters numbered, 7 & 8[4] the writers of which are altogether reliable.

Other greivances, though verbally presented, are *personally* well authenticated. Cotton in the hands of private persons, and even, in one instance, in the hands of the sheriff under execution, is seized by the military authorities, on the ground that the producers had subscribed to the Confederate Cotton loan, when in fact that Government had never perfected its claim either to the Cotton, or its proceeds.[5] If civil authority be invoked, simply to make an issue, and develop, and try the rights, courts are sometimes threatened, & at others the Cotton is removed, regardless of pending legal proceedings.

I called the attention in one case, of Genl. Brannan,[6] now commanding in this Department, to the fact that a subordinate, commander of a Post, had formally notified a Judge of the Superior Court, that he would not permit him to enforce against a *white-man*, (a citizen of the State) a statute, making it penal for a grocer or retailer, or merchant, keeping spirituous liquors for sale, to employ or have, a negro as a clerk or employee, about his store or shop or bar, so that such negro may have access to such liquors. To this he replies, "In regard to Par. 4511 Code of Georgia, that and other paragraphs of the code, enactments of the Legislature of Georgia, based upon the existence of Slavery in the State, distinguishing against the legal rights of the Freedmen, will not be permitted to be carried into effect, to the prejudice of the Freedmen, and that the civil Courts will not be permitted to take cognisance of cases, to which a freedman is a party, when by reason of the existence of such paragraphs in the code, the cases cannot be tried before such courts without prejudice to his rights." Both the letter of the Judge, and the paragraph in question clearly show that neither any penalty, nor any proceeding against a freedmcn, so employed was contemplated, but only against his employer, a white-man. The latter proposition therefore of Gen. Brannan was wholly irrelative to the subject in question. But his first declaration involves the assumption, by the *military* authorities, of the prerogative of expunging from our statute-book, whatever they may consider a discrimination "against the legal rights of the freedmen["]—or in other words the exercise of a veto power upon enactments long since made, visiting penalties upon white-men only. It is nothing less. I would respectfully inquire, whether this be indeed our condition?

Our People do not believe, honored Sir, that you sanction the proceedings herein before detailed. They come to me daily saying "you are interposed between us and the President—he has restored our Courts—he has recognised our Legislature—he has recognised you as our Governor, and has promised you his cooperation, in the restoration of us, to the Union and to prosperity—you know that our thoughts are turned on peace, on fidelity to the Union, and on industrial pursuits. Will you lie still and let these things pass, without report, or remonstrance?" I ask you, Sir who, have, so long, and in so many capacities, served the people, how can I be silent? The legislative proceedings, enclosed, have been, evoked, by no communication, verbal or written, from me. My purpose was to communicate quietly with you, but the Representatives of the People, know the facts recited in their resolutions, and they too have chosen to speak.

Since the Christmas holidays, our Freedmen are doing much better than before—our people are generally both just, and kind to them—good understanding, between the races, is taking place, and if we could but be let deal with the problem of adjustment, my firm conviction is, all would be well.

As parens patria, can you not releive us? Will you not, as far as in you lies, trust and try our People, who confide in you? Will you not at least, with more distinctness define the line to which our civil authorities may go, and within which the military may not intrude?

Charles J. Jenkins

ALS, DNA-RG108, Lets. Recd. *re* Military Discipline.

1. The enclosed resolutions called for, "if not a withdrawal" of occupation troops, at least the restriction of such to federal installations and to the enforcement of federal laws, with a concurrent restoration of habeas corpus; the revocation of the Secretary of War's order for the confiscation of all stock branded "U.S." or "C.S."; and the return to former owners of all Georgia sea island property, "as well as all other property," held by the Freedmen's Bureau. See William T. Weaver to Johnson, Jan. 1, 1866.

2. One set of papers consisted of copies of documents relating to a civil case, tried in Atlanta, during which Gen. John D. Stevenson issued an order suspending further proceedings. The second set of documents concerned the firm of William Battersby & Co. of Savannah. See Jenkins to Johnson, Jan. 29, 1866.

3. Jenkins forwarded a letter from William Doyle, sheriff of Richmond County, who complained about Gen. John H. King's refusal to relinquish possession of the county jail to him.

4. One letter was from William C. Daniell; the other was signed by at least twelve persons. For Daniell's pardon, see James Johnson to Johnson, Nov. 23, 1865.

5. See Jenkins to Johnson, Jan. 1, 1866.

6. John M. Brannan (1819–1892), a career soldier and graduate of West Point, had been brevetted a major general for his services in the artillery during the war. Warner, *Blue*.

To Napoleon III

Washington City   January 25, 1866

Sire

Recent events on the Rio Grande induce me to address your majesty directly upon the relations of your Government and the Government of the United States in that quarter, which have been the subject of much diplomatic correspondence without arriving at any satisfactory result. Information has reached me that collisions have lately taken place between troops of the United States, and troops occupying the west bank of the Rio Grande, in which it is alleged that the United States troops were the aggressors.[1] Your majesty has already been assured that no aggression or departure from strict neutrality has been authorized by me, or in any manner received my countenance or sanction. If the investigation I have ordered, shall show aggression on the part of the United States troops, the offenders, officers and privates, will be dealt with as the circumstances may require for the proper punishment of their offence,[2] and the enforcement of respect for the authority of the government to which the are amenable, and the proper vindication of whatever rights may have been violated. Just compensation shall also be made to parties injured by any such unlawful acts or aggressions.

The painful occurrences to which I allude, impressively call your Majestys attention and my own, to the contingencies arising from the maintenance of your Majestys military force in Mexico; and induce me to submit to your grave and friendly consideration whether the best interests of France require your majesty to continue a military occupation in Mexico, and whether the welfare of France, as well as of the United States, would not be promoted by an early withdrawal of your troops.

The reasons why the presence of such force in Mexico is unsatisfactory to the United States Government, have been set forth so often and so fully in the Diplomatic correspondence referred to, that they cannot fail to be fully comprehended. Removal of that force would be esteemed as a manifestation of your Majestys good will, and of the friendly spirit that has always existed between France and the United States. The period within which such removal might take place is not so material, if it were absolutely fixed not beyond one year, which is longer time than you would probably desire. But the sooner it takes place the hazard of unauthorized acts and aggressions by subordinates on either side would be the more quickly removed, and the public peace secured against the designs of evil disposed persons, and the danger of disturbance by rashness want of discipline, and other perils incident to the presence of troops at remote stations.

This communication I hope will be received by your Majesty in the same frank and friendly spirit that prompts me, and if it should be in accordance with your Majestys views, you and I will have the good fortune by direct and sincere communication with each other, to attain an object that cannot fail to strengthen and confirm the good will and cordial friendship which has so long existed with mutual benefit between two great nations.[3]

Draft, DLC-JP.

1. Philip H. Sheridan, as commander of the U.S. troops along the Mexican border, aggressively supported Benito Juarez against the Maximilian regime installed by France. In January 1866 U.S. infantry assisted in the occupation of Bagdad, Mexico, by the Juaristas. Paul A. Hutton, *Phil Sheridan and His Army* (Lincoln, Neb., 1985), 21; Simon, *Grant Papers*, 16: 28–32.

2. Apparently no action was taken against military personnel, but civilian R. Clay Crawford was arrested on Sheridan's order for his role in the affair at Bagdad. *Ibid.*

3. The President had addressed a similar note to the ruler of France ten days earlier. See Johnson to Napoleon III, Jan. 15, 1866, Johnson Papers, LC.

From Joel Ware[1]
(Copy)

Geneseo. Henry Co. Ills.   Jan. 25. 1866[2]

Dear Sir:

My son, Robert C. Ware,[3] a searjent in Co. E. 1st N.Y. Dragoons was wounded in the battle near Todd's Tavern Va. May 7th 1864—was taken prisoner, and retaken by Federal forces and sent to Douglas Hospital where he died May 18th 1864 and was buried on Arlington Heights. I desire the removal of the body from Arlington Heights that it may be placed beside his mother's kindred in Mass. Oweing to long continued sickness in my family and other causes, my property is gone, and at the age of near three score years, I am left to provide for a feeble wife and sick daughter[4] by days labor, nor have I family or other friends to aid me in accomplishing my wishes. I therefore appeal to you for pecuniary aid to accomplish the removal. I will give one or more reasons why I desire the body to rest in a civil and not a military cemetery, especially the one on Arlington Heights. Your executive acts, together with the policy developed in your message convinces me that Lee—who wielded his sword for the starvation of Federal prisoners, and who, more perhaps than any one else, sent the ball crashing through the right arm and breast of my son, depriving him of the rich boon of life, will be screened from punishment due to his terrible crimes, Arlington Heights returned to him or his heirs—the bones resting there exhumed, and sold perhaps to northern Copperheads for manure. Again the stand you have taken, in your accidental position, against the natural rights of mankind—against natural justice, and the efforts you make to cover up these terrible adjuncts of iniquity by a thin veil of muddled inconsistencies in your theory of States, and the evident desire you exhibit to save to the south the old Oligarchal condition of society in a form, and with an added power to intensify the evils heretofore existing in Southern Society—all—all convince me that another struggle is impending, to be again decided by the Sword, ere freedom can or shall fully triumph over injustice and tyranny. I appeal to your magnanimity to pardon me for the seeming harshness of my remarks, but I could not otherwise convey to your mind the convictions that are forcing themselves upon me, that my poor boy has died in vain, and the consequent desire for the removal of the body from Arlington Hights. Your are a father yourself, and it is with more or less confidence that I appeal to your parental feelings for the sympathy and assistance I stand in need of, hoping too, that by the facts I have presented, you will be at no loss to conceive the feelings of a parent situated as I am, and fondly hoping also, that of your abundance you will spare me enough to effect the desired removal of the body of my son—a debt I will cheerfully repay, if providence permit, and add thereto the gushing thanks of a bereaved heart.[5]

(Signed)   Joel Ware—

You can send a draft on N.Y. for $75. to the Cashier of the first National Bank, Geneseo, to be paid to me on proof of my being the person and in the circumstances represented, if not, to be returned to you. This amount will enable me to reach Washington and the needed balance you can hand me when I reach there.

(S'd)   J. W.

Copy, DNA-RG92, Consolidated Corr. File, 1794–1890.
    1. Ware (c1809-c1896) was a New Hampshire-born farmer who had lived in Allegany County, New York, before moving to Illinois. 1870 Census, Ill., Henry, Geneseo, 7; H. F. Kett & Co., *The History of Henry County, Illinois* . . . (Chicago, 1877), 218; Pension Records, Anna L. Ware, RG15, NA.
    2. March 20 appears under the January date on the copy. This is probably the date on which the original letter was copied.
    3. Ware (c1839–1864) had been an Andover, New York, blacksmith. Ibid.
    4. Lucy (c1814-c1901) and Myra O. Ware (c1843-fl1901) were natives of Massachusetts and New York respectively. After the war the daughter was a hat braider. Ibid.; 1870 Census, Ill., Henry, Geneseo, 7.
    5. This letter was "returned" to the War Department "By Order of the President," and orders were subsequently issued for the removal of Ware's body.

From Granville Moody

Washington City   Jany 26th /66

Sir
    I have the honor to say, that; there is gentleman now in this City who may appear before you, for an office of some kind.
    His name is "*David Cox*"[1]—Son of Judge Cox[2] of Columbus Ohio.

He was "private Secretary" to the Honl. David Tod, whilst he was Governor of Ohio. And the Governor has spoken to me of him in terms of unqualified praise.

I *have known* "David Cox" from his *boyhood*. He is *Honest* and *Capable* and will reflect *credit* on any position he may be entrusted with.

Granville Moody

N B I failed to present him yesterday.

1st P S Allow me to thank you for the *honor* you conferred on me by *your presence* in Foundry Chapel last Sabbath, and for your liberal *contribution* to the cause of the occasion[3]—and for the *great and good influence* your presence had on the *Congregation* and is having throughout the Commonwealth of Methodism (So I see by the notices of the Church and Secular papers) and the Commonwealth of Christianity.

My daily prayer and the prayer of *Millions* is that you may be momentarily guided and guarded by Almighty God in the discharge of your great responsibilities at this great *crisis*!

Granville Moody

2d P.S. The prospect for the passage of an Act of Congress—restoring my Son in Law Lieut. Joseph Fyffe[4] to the Active List of the U S Navy is brightning. He has totally reformed—*Total abstinence*!

Senator Sherman, told me last evening, that he had no doubt that the Senate Naval Committee, will report favorably on the Bill now before them. If so all will be well.

You may recollect you told my daughter "Clifford" now Mrs Joseph Fyffe[5]—that "you would *take care* of her Jo." I hope *all* will come out favorably. In haste to leave for Ohio.

Moody

ALS, DLC-JP.

1. David C. Cox (1831-*fl*1879) served as a clerk for the Ohio legislature and on the staffs of governors David Tod and John Brough before moving to the District of Columbia, where he was an internal revenue supervisor, a pension agent, and Superintendent of Documents. *The Lakeside Annual Directory . . . Chicago* (1879), 304; *The Biographical Encyclopedia of Ohio of the Nineteenth Century* (Cincinnati and Philadelphia, 1876), 371–72.

2. Horatio J. Cox (*c*1803-*fl*1861), a Zanesville paper manufacturer, had been an associate judge of common pleas (1844–52). Ibid.; 1850 Census, Ohio, Muskingum, Zanesville, 1st Ward, 378; Goodspeed's *Biographical and Historical Memoirs of Muskingum County* (Chicago, 1892), 199.

3. On January 21, 1866, Moody preached at the Foundry Methodist Church in Washington. Johnson attended the morning service and subscribed $1,000 to help complete that church's new building. *Washington Chronicle*, Jan. 22, 1866.

4. Joseph P. Fyffe (1832–1896), who commanded several vessels in the North Atlantic Blockading Squadron during the war, eventually retired as a rear admiral. Pension Records, Clifford N. Fyffe, RG15, NA.

5. Clifford N. Moody (1840–1911) had married Fyffe on August 17, 1865. Ibid.; Sylvester Weeks, ed., *A Life's Retrospect: Autobiography of Rev. Granville Moody* (Cincinnati, 1890), 178.

From John A. Bolles [1]

[January 27, 1866] [2]

Acting Ensign *Richard H. Smith* [3] was tried Sept 7. 1863 and found guilty of "Attempt to desert and betray his trust" "Drunkenness" and "Scandalous conduct"—in that, while in command of the Tug Lilly, he hoisted a white flag over that vessel and gave orders to run her through to Vicksburg—that at this time he was drunk—and did curse and challenge certain other officers of the tug who remonstrated with him. [4]

He was sentenced to five years imprisonment, then to be cashiered—and to lose all pay now due or to become due him.

There are considerations that may render it advisable to remit the unexecuted portion of his sentence and dismiss him from the service.

1 He is a volunteer officer, who will never again return to the service nor have any intimate connection with those who remain.

2 He has already been a prisoner over two and a half years.

3 His longer imprisonment—while it will be an expense to the government—will be no advantage.

It is respectfully recommended that so much of his sentence as requires his longer confinement be remitted. [5]

John A. Bolles   Solicitor & Naval Judge Advocate General—

LS, DNA-RG45, Subj. File N, Subsec. NO, Courts-Martial, Box 316, Richard H. Smith.

1. Bolles (1809–1878), a former secretary of state for Massachusetts, served as a staff officer from 1862 to 1865, when he was brevetted brigadier general and appointed naval solicitor. *Appleton's Cyclopaedia*; Powell, *Army List*, 776.

2. This date appears on the envelope containing the papers that pertain to this case.

3. Smith (*fl*1873) piloted several gunboats in engagements along the Mississippi River before receiving a commission as ensign. After the war he worked in St. Louis as a "riverman" as well as steamboat crewman and captain. St. Louis directories (1866–73); Smith to Robert Hughes, Oct. 7, 1865; Smith to John Hogan, May 18, 1866, Subj. File N, Subsec. NO, Courts-Martial, Box 316, Richard H. Smith, RG45, NA.

4. In his petition for release, written while confined at Sing Sing Prison in New York, Smith recalled that he had been arrested on February 23, 1863. He claimed, however, that because he was not present at his court-martial, he did not know upon which charges he had been convicted or when, although he confessed in a later letter that he did plead guilty to "drunkeness and language unbecoming an Officer and a gentleman." The two principal witnesses against him, both of whom were black, he dismissed as men "who bitterly hated me on account of my having punished them." Smith to Hughes, Oct. 7, 1865; Smith to Hogan, May 18, 1866, ibid.

5. This report was issued in response to a request from the Executive Office for a recommendation regarding Smith, whose petition had been forwarded by Charles D. Pennebaker, state agent for Kentucky. After Johnson ordered that "So much of the sentence . . . as relates to Cashiering and confinement" be remitted, Smith was released on February 7, 1866, but his commission was revoked. Hughes to Pennebaker, Jan. 9, 1866; Endorsement of Pennebaker, Jan. 17, 1866; Endorsement of Johnson, Feb. 2, 1866; Smith to Hogan, May 18, 1855, ibid.

From James R. Martin[1]

Kingston Roane County E. Ten   27' Jany 66
His Excellency Andrew Johnson

Please excuse me for troubling you at a time when you are I have no doubt, so pressed with business that you have not a moment, to devote to ordinary matters, neither would I do so, only from the great necesity of myself, and a number of my neighbours, who are in the same situation. In the winter of sixty three & four, owing to the hurried marching and counter marching of the troops in this part of the state, a great portion of the forage for the Army was taken without the posibility of getting regular vouchers for it, and the only prospect for getting anything was by fileing our claims, in a court organised at Knoxville for that purpose, where they have been for two years, without any more prospect, for payment than when first, applied for, and we are really suffering for the want of it. We were stripped of every thing we had by the rebels, and when the federal army came in here we had not a dollar in the world worth anything. The government was compelled to take what we had, and many of us had to pay three dollars per Bushel for corn to make bread, and are still indebt for it, on account of not being able to get what is justly due us. I do think, that we ought to be paid interest as well as the principle, as soon as it is possible to do, it.

There are also a good many Union men who had negroes that enlisted in the army for which they were promised three hundred dollars each which I think ought to be paid, for you know that truer or more reliable Union men than these of East Ten dont live anywhere, and none suffered from the rebellion more than they did. You and I had always differed in politics, until this secession movement got up, and when you made your I believe last speech at this place, I stood by you all the time, and when you had finished, I had a Brother inlaw[2] in the crowd who said to me, can you possibly side with Johnson. I told him I would stand or fall with you and the cause you advocated. He replied I have nothing more to say to you. He went into the rebel army and was captured at Fort Donelson. My Wife[3] was at the speaking considerably advanced in pregnancy. I told her on the way home if she had a boy I would call him Winfield Scott. Sure enough it was a boy, and he is as fine a boy of his age as you ever saw.[4] My life was frequently threatened, and severl times came very near being taken for naming a child Winfield Scott, was not permitted to go to Town for months at a time when there was rebel troops there on account of it and being as they called me a Linconite which gave them perfect liberty to take anything I had with impunity. Genl. Forest took two fine mares from me which I went and offered him five hundred dollars a piece for. He replied I expect you would, you cant get them and I intend to take every horse you have. I told him that had already been done. If I was all that were suffering I should not have troubled you, but it is all E. Ten. and we look to you for to see us provided for, and it cant be done too soon.

Jas. R. Martin

ALS, DLC-JP.
1. Martin (1815–1884) before the war had been a prosperous farmer. Roane County Genealogical Society, *Cemeteries of Roane County Tennessee* (3 vols., Kingston, Tenn., 1988), 1: 20; 1860 Census, Tenn., Roane, 1st Dist., 18.
2. Not identified, but probably a soldier in Co. I, 26th Tenn. Inf., CSA. *TICW*, 1: 228.
3. Emily (c1818-fl1880), formerly Mrs. Metcalf McLester, was Martin's second wife. Emma M. Wells, *The History of Roane County Tennessee 1801–1870* (Chattanooga, 1927), 244; 1880 Census, Tenn., Roane, 221st Enum. Dist., 22.
4. This son (c1861–1896) lived his short life in the Kingston vicinity. *Roane County Cemeteries*, 1: 21.

From Horace Greeley

Confidential

Office of the Tribune, New York, Jan. 28, 1866.

Dear Sir:

The journals generally say that Mr. Stanton has tendered his resignation, and expects soon to leave the War department.[1] Should this be the case, I venture to suggest as his successor Gen. James B. Steedman[2] of Ohio, one of the bravest and truest of our Union Volunteers, and a capable, devoted patriot. Trusting that you are aware of his merits, I remain. . . .

Horace Greeley

ALS, DLC-JP.
1. During the first term of the 39th Congress, demands periodically surfaced for the resignation of Stanton, who considered resigning but was dissuaded by the pleas of his associates. Benjamin P. Thomas and Harold M. Hyman, *Stanton: The Life and Times of Lincoln's Secretary of War* (New York, 1962), 462–63, 469.
2. Former Democratic representative George H. Pendleton of Ohio also wrote to nominate Steedman. Pendleton to Johnson, Jan. 28, 1866, Johnson Papers, LC.

Interview with James Dixon

January 28, 1866

The following is the substance of the conversation, which took place yesterday between the President and a distinguished Senator:

The President said he doubted the propriety at this time of making further amendments to the Constitution. One great amendment had already been made, by which slavery had forever been abolished within the limits of the United States, and a national guarantee thus given that that institution should never again exist in the land. Propositions to amend the Constitution were becoming as numerous as preambles and resolutions at town meetings called to consider the most ordinary questions connected with the administration of local affairs. All this, in his opinion, had a tendency to diminish the dignity and prestige attached to the Constitution of the country, and to lessen the respect and confidence of the people in their great charter of freedom. If, however, amendments are to be made to the Constitution, changing the basis of representation and taxation, (and he did not deem them at all necessary at the present time,) he knew of none better than a simple proposition, embraced in a few lines, making in each State the number of qualified voters the basis of representation, and the value of property the basis of direct taxation. Such a proposition could be embraced in the following terms:

Representatives shall be apportioned among the several States which may be included within this Union, according to the number of qualified voters in each State.

Direct taxes shall be apportioned among the several States which may be included within this Union according to the value of all taxable property in each State.

An amendment of this kind would, in his opinion, place the basis of representation and direct taxation upon correct principles.

The qualified voters were, for the most part, men who were subject to draft and enlistment when it was necessary to repel invasion, suppress rebellion, and quell domestic violence and insurrection. They risk their lives, shed their blood and peril their all to uphold the Government, and give protection, security, and value to property. It seemed but just that property should compensate for the benefits thus conferred, by defraying the expenses incident to its protection and enjoyment.

Such an amendment, the President also suggested, would remove from Congress all issues in reference to the political equality of the races. It would leave the States to determine absolutely the qualifications of their own voters with regard to color; and thus the number of Representatives to which they would be entitled in Congress would depend upon the number upon whom they conferred the right of suffrage.

The President, in this connection, expressed the opinion that the agitation of the negro franchise question in the District of Columbia,[1] at this time, was the mere entering wedge to the agitation of the question throughout the States, and was ill-timed, uncalled for, and calculated to do great harm. He believed that it would engender enmity, contention, and strife between the two races, and lead to a war between them, which would result in great injury to both, and the certain extermination of the negro population. Precedence, he thought, should be given to more important and urgent matters, legislation upon which was essential for the restoration of the Union, the peace of the country, and the prosperity of the people.

Washington Morning Chronicle, Jan. 29, 1866.
   1. See Lewis D. Campbell to Johnson, Jan. 19, 1866.

From Joseph Holt

Washington, D.C., January 29th 1866.

To the President.

The report in the case of *Gurley* called for December 11th, was duly prepared and placed in the hands of the Secretary of War to be submitted to the President.[1] Reference is respectfully had to it, for the views of this Bureau upon the merits of the application for pardon. Nothing is found in the accompanying paper,[2] referred Jan'y 18th, to change the conclusions entertained.

The prisoner is said to have been once exchanged for Federal soldiers who were in "like condition" within the rebel lines.[3]

The Commissary General of Prisoners,[4] in reply to an endorsement of inquiry, states no facts to support the hypothesis intimated by the petitioners, who seem to imply that the persons paroled by the rebels as an equivalent for Gurley and others, occupied a corresponding status. There is nothing from which it can be concluded that those prisoners were, like him, convicted felons, under sentence of death for crime. The contrary, indeed, is fairly inferable, since the report of the Commissary General of Prisoners leads to the belief, that the exchange was a general one, and characterized by no incidents marking it as intended to be a satisfaction of the guilt of the prisoner, or a renunciation by the government of the right and duty to enforce the punishment which had been awarded. In other words, the exchange is supposed to have dealt with him solely in his relations as a prisoner of war, and not as a condemned murderer.

This Bureau is of opinion that neither the parole, nor the subsequent exchange, nor the alleged fact of his being embraced in the surrender of Johnston's army could operate to alter his status in this respect; and this opinion derives strong corroboration from the fact that the government, on learning of the misapprehension whereby he had been released, issued a confidential circular, ordering his re-arrest and execution.

The recommendation that the sentence be carried out is adhered to, and hereby reiterated.[5]

J. Holt. Judge Advocate General.

LS, DNA-RG153, Court-Martial Records, MM-1326.
   1. See Holt to Johnson, Jan. 5, 1866.
   2. Six Nashville area citizens, including several acquaintances of Johnson, had for-

warded a petition reviewing the circumstances of Gurley's exchange and concluding that his case was "one fit and proper for the pardoning power" of the President. Balie Peyton et al. to Johnson, Nov. 30, 1865, Court-Martial Records, MM-1326, RG153, NA.

3. See Joseph C. Bradley to Johnson, Nov. 27, 1865.

4. William Hoffman.

5. After Ulysses S. Grant submitted copies of documents explaining Gurley's exchange and recommended that he "be released as having been duly exchanged," Gurley was freed by order of the President on April 28, 1866. Grant to Johnson, Apr. 10, 1866, ibid.; *Nashville Press and Times*, May 2, 1866.

From Charles J. Jenkins

Milledgeville Ga   Jany 29 1866

Wm. Battersby[1] of Savannah filed a bill stating that Battersby & Co purchased 224 Bales of Cotton in December 1861 as a private investment not for blockade or other purposes hostile to the U.S. and never owned or controlled by the Confederate States, that it had been in a warehouse at Amercus Ga ever since said purchase that W C Bunts[2] who claimed to be a Treasy Agent was about seize and remove it.

Judge Cole[3] of this state granted an injunction but refused to receive from Sheriff[4] the process of the court saying he would receive no paper from any civil officer after injunction but before service Bunts removed the bulk of the cotton in direction of Albany Ga. Please issue order by telegraph that the cotton be stopped[5] and subject to direction of Court. Papers in case sent by mail.[6]

Chas. J Jenkins   Govr

Tel, DLC-JP.

1. Battersby (*c*1814-*fl*1870), an English-born merchant, was the surviving partner of Battersby & Co. 1860 Census, Ga., Chatham, Savannah, 3rd Dist., 224; Savannah directories (1860–70).

2. An assistant special agent for the Treasury Department, Capt. William C. Bunts (*c*1833–1874) soon returned to Cleveland, Ohio, where he served as an assistant U.S. district attorney and city solicitor. Charles T. Clark, *Opdycke Tigers: 125th O.V.I.* (Columbus, Ohio, 1895), 448; *Memorial Record of the County of Cuyahoga and the City of Cleveland, Ohio* (Chicago, 1894), 88; *Macon Telegraph*, Jan. 17, 1866.

3. Carleton B. Cole (*c*1803-*fl*1871), superior court judge for the Macon district, had served as a delegate to the convention in October 1865. 1860 Census, Ga., Bibb, Macon, 120; E. Merton Coulter, *Negro Legislators in Georgia During the Reconstruction Period* (Athens, Ga., 1968), 5; Candler, *Confederate Records of Ga.*, 4: 22, 133.

4. Benjamin L. Cole (b. *c*1815) had also served as sheriff and deputy U.S. marshal before the war. 1860 Census, Ga., Chatham, Savannah, 1st Dist., 84; Savannah directories (1858–60).

5. A few days later Johnson notified Jenkins that McCulloch had ordered Bunts to forward to the Treasury Department "a Statement of all the facts in the case" and that subsequent action would be suspended until further notice. On March 3, 1866, 607 bales belonging to Battersby & Co. were released. Johnson to Jenkins, Feb. 6, 1866, Johnson Papers, LC; *Senate Ex. Docs.*, 40 Cong., 2 Sess., No. 56, p. 21 (Ser. 1317).

6. Copies of Battersby's petition and Judge Cole's injunction had been enclosed in Jenkins to Johnson, Jan. 25, 1866.

From Harvey M. Watterson

Mobile, Ala.   January 29. 1866

Dear Sir.

Here we are—having visited Richmond, Wilmington, Charleston, Savannah, Augusta, Atlanta, Montgomery and Selma. Mr Chandler has kept the Secretary of the Treasury advised of our progress, and the headway we are making towards the fulfillment of our mission.[1] It is enough to say, at this time, that so many parties, official and unofficial, have been engaged in stealing cotton, I fear we can do but little more, in our hurried trip, than to get on their tracks. It is clear to my mind that the Government owes it to its own character to ferret out some of the principal thieves and pursue them to conviction and punishment. A single word on another point: The time has arrived, as I think, when this cotton business should be wound up and the entire lot of cotton agents withdrawn from the South. The subordinates under the principal agents are roving over the country and harrassing the people without any corresponding benefit to the national treasury. In many instances the Government loses in money and loses in character by their operation. Upon all these matters Mr Chandler and I will either report to you verbally or in writing. So far as I know, our views are in perfect harmony.

My own opinion is that Dexter should be left to work out his own salvation, if he can, with the Military.[2]

As this is not intended to be an official letter, I must drop a line in regard to the popular sentiment of the South on public affairs. I find the same feeling of confidence in the President but they fear that he will be overwhelmed by the Radicals. I tell all with whom I come in contact to be of good cheer—there is no danger that radical views will be fastened on the legislation of the country. The South may be kept out of Congress, during the present session, but in the next fall elections the North will speak a voice of terror to all such disunionists as Sumner, Stevens and their coajutors &c &c. &c.

Thanking you most heartily for the evidence you have given of your confidence in my integrity and good sense. . . .

H. M. Watterson

ALS, DLC-JP.

1. On December 29, 1865, Watterson and William E. Chandler were directed by the President to visit the South to investigate "the condition of books and papers of Treasury officers." Johnson to "Military Officers," Dec. 29, 1865, Johnson Papers, LC; *Washington Morning Chronicle*, Jan. 5, 1866.

2. Thomas C.A. Dexter. See James M. Tomeny to Johnson, Nov. 21, 1865.

From J. Madison Wells

New Orleans, Jany 29th 1866

Sir,

I had the honor of telegraphing your Excellency this forenoon,[1] asking whether I should approve or veto a bill, passed by the Legislature now in session, which fixes the 12th of March next, as the day for holding an election for Mayor, Common Council, and other officers of the municipal government of New Orleans.

The reason why I desire information and instruction on this point from the government, is, my recollection, when in Washington, of your intimating a disinclination to have such an election at an early day, observing that New Orleans was a City peculiarly situated in every respect, and that when a return to regular government took place, it would be necessary to have it pass into hands unquestionably loyal to the government and the nation.

I am not without misgivings as to the latter, should an election be held in March, as this bill proposes; and on this and other important grounds, I think it unwise to allow an election before at least the time fixed by the City Charter, the second Monday of June.

I share furthermore, the feeling very general among intelligent persons as to the necessity of having the Charter amended before an election is had; for should the latter precede the amendments, it is justly apprehended that the influence of the newly elected or appointed officers of the corporation would be sufficiently powerful to postpone them indefinitely. Some officers, now elective, such as Police Magistrates, it is almost universally admitted, ought to be appointed, the number reduced, and the salaries increased. At present they receive only two hundred dollars per month; a sum entirely insufficient for their decent support or to secure the services of any but ignorant, unscrupulous and approachable men. And so of others.

Submitting these views to the government in explanation of my telegram. . . .

J Madison Wells   Gov La

ALS, DLC-JP.
1. See Wells to Johnson, Jan. 29, 1866, Johnson Papers, LC.

From William Patton
Strictly Private

Towanda Penna   30 Jany 1866

My old Jacksonian friend.

A card will soon be placed in your hands, in the shape of the negro suffrage Bill for the Dist. of Cola.,[1] which, if played by you, as I have no doubt you will play it, in the shape of a *veto*, will make you the most popular man in the U. States. Your veto wd. probably be sustained by Congress, but, whether or not, you will have the benefit of it before *the people*, and the beauty of it is, that you can veto it without *directly* committing yourself on the negro suffrage question at all: which, I think, it wd. be your policy to avoid for the present; because, if you dont commit yourself on that question, then the radicals wd. have no excuse for not sustaining the veto. Vox populi vox Dei, is a demc. maxim.

The white citizens of the Dist. of Cola. are nearly unanimously opposed to it,[2] and if all the negroes therein, which number only some 20,000, were voters, there wd. still be a very large majority against it.

In all the northern States, except one, where the negro suffrage question has been made a *direct issue*, the popular expression has been against it,[3] notwithstanding their decided majorities in favor of negro emancipation, and it is fairly inferable, from that significant expression, that a majority of the people of the north are opposed to it. I am, myself, now and forever opposed to it, and wd. rather invoke a war of races than see it adopted, or submit to it: because it wd. result in the degradation of the white and eventually in the destruction or extinction of black races: but the reasons for that result, hereafter.

Congress is constitutionally, *ex officio*, the Legislature of the Dist. of Cola.; and, being elected by the *whole people* of the U. States, the voice of the whole people shd. be represented on this question, in which they are as directly interested, as they are in the action of their own state Legislatures; and its passage wd., therefore, be in violation of a cardinal principle of popular govt.; unjust to the southern people; and, in violation of your Presidential obligation to "guaranty to every state, in this union, a Republican form of govt.; which is a govt. of *the people*—the Dist. of Cola. being virtually a state, and you being *ex officio* its Governor.

You have therefore *three* distinct grounds on which it can be veto'd, either of which is tenable, without committing yourself on the abstract merits of the negro suffrage question:

First—a majority of the citizens of the D. of Col. exclusive or inclusive of its negro population, are opposed to it.

Second—as far as the north has expressed itself, in the recent state elections, the people there are opposed to negro suffrage in their own states and, consequently, wd. be opposed to forcing it on the Dist. of Cola.

Third—The present time, when the whole south is unrepresented, is unpropitious for its passage.

To show you that, even some of the radical leaders dare not meet the question, squarely, I will state a fact within my own personal knowledge. David Wilmot the reputed author of the "*Wilmot proviso*," in a speech made by him, in the election campaign, last fall, at Monroeton, four miles from here, sd. that "the negroes of the south, after being in a state of bondage for 200 years, were, in regard to intelligence, but little above the brutes; and, consequently, they were unfit to exercise the right of suffrage at this time."

I presume a large portion of those now in the Dist. of Cola. are of that class, and hence his reasoning applies to that locality.

It is probable that this letter contains nothing new to one of your sagacity and intelligence; but I have been prompted, by my anxiety for your success, to give you my views on this portentous subject; and, if you can glean from them, even one small ray of light to your path, I shall be gratified and fully compensated. As I have no desire for office you will at least appreciate them as being dictated by sincere personal and political friendship.

W. Patton   late Eng. Clerk Senate U.S.

As I cannot expect you to answer letters, personally, may I ask the favor of you, simply, to enclose me your card, that I may know it has been recd. Mr. Van Buren[4] did me the honor to acknowledge the rect. of a commn. of mine in that way & acknowledging its rect. in pencil on the card.

ALS, DLC-JP.

1. See Lewis D. Campbell to Johnson, Jan. 19, 1866.
2. See Henry Addison to Johnson, Jan. 12, 1866.
3. In 1865 there were referenda on this issue only in Minnesota, Wisconsin, and Connecticut, all of which rejected black suffrage. Foner, *Reconstruction*, 223.
4. Presumably Martin Van Buren.

To J. Madison Wells

Washington, D.C., January 30th 1866.

By whom was your city council appointed prior to the rebellion? Is there any good reason why the mayor and other civil officers for the city of New Orleans should not be elected by the loyal qualified voters? The election should be confined to persons who are unquestionably loyal. There may be some facts in connection with this move that I am not aware of. If so please advise.[1]

(Sgd) Andrew Johnson   President U S

Tel, DNA-RG107, Tels. Sent, President, Vol. 3 (1865–68).

1. No direct response from Wells has been found. On February 12 he vetoed the bill providing for municipal elections; but the legislature overrode him, and Johnson ordered the elections to be held. As Wells feared, his candidates were defeated. Johnson to Wells, Mar. 2, 1866, Johnson Papers, LC; Lowrey, "Wells," 1073–75.

From Ann T. Leftwich

January 31, 1866, Hillsville, Va.; ALS, DLC-JP.

A physician's widow, born in Kentucky, asks for "money to get on in this cold uncharitable world." "I Know you are wealthy and you have rich friends that would contribute if you would use your influence." With no living male relatives, she had relied on the support of a black servant "who was a splendid barber" and "dining room servant," as well as "an excellent cook" and a "great musician." He and the other servants and slaves have now left because "I could not get any money to pay them to stay." Moreover, her husband's papers were burned and her bank deposits were taken during a Union cavalry raid on Hillsville. Claiming to be a "lady of high standing" with "a great many friends," she was "much opposed to the Union being dissolved," and has begun "sounding a trumpet for you already with regard to your reelection" to the presidency. Although she "never went by myself a mile in my life," she would borrow funds and travel to Washington for assistance, in which case she asks to stay at the White House "for indeed I do not know a human being" in the capital. [Leftwich added a postscript directing that "The gentleman who opens the Presidents letters will do me a great favor by handing him this." There is no record of a response from Johnson.]

From Hugh McCulloch

Treasury Department   January 31st 1866

Sir

Herewith I hand you an order for, redistricting the State of North Carolina[1] and the names of persons to be nominated to the Senate for Assessors and Collectors in the respective Districts. I beg leave to call your attention to a letter accompanying these papers from the Comr. of Int. Rev.,[2] which will give you some needed explanations and also a letter & Telegram from Govr. Worth.[3] No nominations are to be made for the first District inasmuch as this District is already provided for with competent officers.

I deem it to be my duty in sending you these papers, to say there is apparently some dissatisfaction among the union men in North Carolina, in regard to these nominations of Gov Worth. It is asserted that instead of selecting the officers himself he referred the matter to members of the Legislature, and that some names which have been presented to you do not come up to a very high standard for loyalty.[4]

H. McCulloch   Secretary of the Treasury

LBcopy, DNA-RG56, Lets. Sent *re* Internal Revenue Employees (QD Ser.), Vol. 1.

1. A copy of the order providing for seven internal revenue districts in North Carolina can be found in Internal Revenue, Exec. Orders, 1862–85, RG58, NA.

2. This letter has not been found. Edward A. Rollins (1828–1885), New Hampshire attorney and wartime legislator, served for four years as commissioner of internal revenue following William Orton's resignation in November 1865. *Sketches of Successful New*

Hampshire Men (Manchester, N.H., 1882), 143–47; *New Orleans Picayune*, Nov. 10, 1865; *NUC Manuscript Collections Index* (1967–69), 821.
    3. Not found.
    4. All of the North Carolina internal revenue nominations submitted by the President in March 1866 were confirmed by the Senate. Ser. 6B, Vol. 4: 140, Johnson Papers, LC.

From James Speed

Washington, Jan. 31, 1866

Sir:

   Sundry reports of the facts that go to show that Jefferson Davis, and other rebels, have been guilty of high crimes have been made to you as the Chief Executive officer of the government. Most of the evidence upon which they are based, was obtained Ex parte, without notice to the accused, and whilst they were in close custody as Military prisoners. Their publication might wrong the government, or the accused or both. Whilst I see that much wrong may flow from the publication, I cannot see that any good would come from it.

   In my opinion, their public & private justice alike demands that they should not be made public.[1]

James Speed, Atty. Genl.

LBcopy, DNA-RG60, Office of Atty. Gen., Lets. Sent, Vol. E (M699, Roll 10).
    1. This note, along with another of similar tone from Edwin M. Stanton, was forwarded by Johnson to the House in response to their request for official reports on the continued imprisonment of Davis, Clement C. Clay, Stephen R. Mallory, and David Yulee. *House Ex. Docs.*, 39 Cong., 1 Sess., No. 46, pp. 1–2 (Ser. 1255).

From Alexander H. Stephens

Milledgeville   31 Jany 1866.

   I was elected yesterday to the United States Senate by the Georgia Legislature under Circumstances particularly embarrasing which will be fully explained by mail.[1]

   An effort may be made to impress you with the belief that this was the result of a disposition on the part of the Legislature to oppose the policy of the Administration or the want of a cordial support, & be censured. Such is not the fact—on the contrary my full conviction is that it sprung from an earnest belief whether erroneous or not that it would most effectually aid that policy which it is well known I am faithfully laboring to carry out.[2]

Alexander H. Stephens

Tel, DLC-JP.
    1. We have not found a letter from Stephens in which he explained to Johnson the circumstances of his election. In a letter of early February to the President, Stephens protested that he had no desire for public office but that he could not refuse the "call of

the people to serve them." Stephens furthermore asked Johnson for an enlargement of his parole so that he could confer with the President in Washington and declared that "I do not wish to embarrass you in your policy for the restoration of the Union." By the end of the month he received the requested parole. Avary, *Recollections*, 543–44.

2. On the same day that Stephens telegraphed Johnson, Joseph E. Brown did also. In his dispatch Brown expressed some regret over what had happened but hoped that the election of Stephens and Herschel Johnson "will not be misconstrued." Brown added: "They will both support your policy zealously." Brown to Johnson, Jan. 31, 1866, Johnson Papers, LC.

Appendix I

[Adapted from Robert Sobel, ed., *Biographical Directory of the United States Executive Branch, 1874–1971* (Westport, Conn., 1971).]

Office	Name
Secretary of State, 1865–69	William H. Seward
Secretary of the Treasury, 1865–69	Hugh McCulloch
Secretary of War, 1865–68	Edwin M. Stanton
Secretary of War ad interim, 1867–68	Ulysses S. Grant
Secretary of War, 1868–69	John M. Schofield
Attorney General, 1865–66	James Speed
Attorney General, 1866–68	Henry Stanbery
Attorney General ad interim, 1868*	Orville H. Browning
Attorney General, 1868–69	William M. Evarts
Postmaster General, 1865–66	William Dennison
Postmaster General, 1866–69	Alexander W. Randall
Secretary of the Navy, 1865–69	Gideon Welles
Secretary of the Interior, 1865	John P. Usher
Secretary of the Interior, 1865–66	James Harlan
Secretary of the Interior, 1866–69	Orville H. Browning

*from March 13, 1868, when Stanbery resigned, until July 20, 1868, when Evarts assumed office, Browning discharged the duties of attorney general in addition to his functions as head of the Interior Department.

Appendix II

PROCLAMATIONS AND EXECUTIVE ORDERS (SEPTEMBER 1865–
JANUARY 1866)

[Asterisk indicates item printed in this volume; all are published in
James D. Richardson, comp., *A Compilation of the Messages and Papers
of the Presidents* (10 vols., Washington, D.C., 1896–99), Volume 6.]

Appendix III

PRESIDENTIAL RECONSTRUCTION
UNDER JOHNSON'S PLAN, 1865

Provisional Governor Appointed	Convention Delegates Election	Convention Dates	Governor/ Legislature Election	Legislature Convened	Governor Inaugurated/ Took Office
ALABAMA					
Lewis E. Parsons (June 21)	Aug. 31	Sept. 12–30	Nov. 6	Nov. 20	Robert M. Patton (Dec. 13/20)
FLORIDA					
William Marvin (July 13)	Oct. 10	Oct. 25– Nov. 8	Nov. 29	Dec. 18	David S. Walker (Dec. 20/ Jan. 18, 1866)
GEORGIA					
James Johnson (June 17)	Oct. 4	Oct. 25– Nov. 8	Nov. 15	Dec. 4	Charles J. Jenkins (Dec. 14/19)
MISSISSIPPI					
William L. Sharkey (June 13)	Aug. 7	Aug. 14–24	Oct. 2	Oct. 16	Benjamin G. Humphreys (Oct. 16/ Dec. 25
NORTH CAROLINA					
William W. Holden (May 29)	Sept. 21	Oct. 2–20	Nov. 9	Nov. 27	Jonathan Worth (Dec. 15/28)
SOUTH CAROLINA					
Benjamin F. Perry (June 30)	Sept. 4	Sept. 13–27	Oct. 18	Oct. 25	James L. Orr (Nov. 29/ Dec. 21)
TEXAS					
Andrew J. Hamilton (June 17)	Jan. 8, 1866	Feb. 7– April 2, 1866	June 25, 1866	Aug. 6, 1866	James W. Throckmorton (Aug. 9/13, 1866)

Appendix IV

Date	Provenance	*Advice*
From Carl Schurz		
Sept. 1	New Orleans, La.	117–19
Sept. 2	New Orleans, La.	119
Sept. 3	New Orleans, La.	119–20
Sept. 4	New Orleans, La.	120–33
Sept. 5	New Orleans, La.	133–35
Sept. 15	New Orleans, La.	135–45
Sept. 23	New Orleans, La.	146–49
Sept. 26	Natchez, Miss.	149–50
From Harvey M. Watterson		
Sept. 26	Montgomery, Ala.	157–59
Oct. 3	Mobile, Ala.	159–61
Oct. 7	Jackson, Miss.	161–63
Oct. 14	New Orleans, La.	164–67
Oct. 20	Columbus, Ga.	167–69
Oct. 30	Milledgeville, Ga.	169–73
From Benjamin C. Truman		
Oct. 13	Mobile, Ala.	184–89
Nov. 1	Milledgeville, Ga.	189–92
Nov. 9	Milledgeville, Ga.	192–94
Jan. 5	Memphis, Tenn.	194–96
From Ulysses S. Grant		
Dec. 18	Washington, D.C.	212–15
Johnson's Message to the Senate		
Dec. 18	Washington, D.C.	241–43

Index

Primary identification of a person is indicated by an italic *n* following the page reference. Identifications found in earlier volumes of the *Johnson Papers* are shown by providing volume and page numbers, within parentheses, immediately after the name of the individual. The only footnotes which have been indexed are those that constitute identification notes.

671

674   THE PAPERS OF ANDREW JOHNSON